Semantic Services, Interoperability and Web Applications:

Emerging Concepts

Amit P. Sheth
Wright State University, USA

Senior Editorial Director:	Kristin Klinger
Director of Book Publications:	Julia Mosemann
Editorial Director:	Lindsay Johnston
Acquisitions Editor:	Erika Carter
Development Editor:	Hannah Abelbeck
Production Editor:	Sean Woznicki
Typesetters:	Jennifer Romanchak, Michael Brehm, Natalie Pronio and Keith Glazewski
Print Coordinator:	Jamie Snavely
Cover Design:	Nick Newcomer

Published in the United States of America by
Information Science Reference (an imprint of IGI Global)
701 E. Chocolate Avenue
Hershey PA 17033
Tel: 717-533-8845
Fax: 717-533-8661
E-mail: cust@igi-global.com
Web site: http://www.igi-global.com/reference

Library of Congress Cataloging-in-Publication Data
Semantic services, interoperability, and web applications: emerging concepts
/ Amit P. Sheth, editor.
     p. cm.
 Includes bibliographical references and index.
 Summary: "This book offers suggestions, solutions, and recommendations for
new and emerging research in Semantic Web technology, focusing broadly on
methods and techniques for making the Web more useful and meaningful"--
Provided by publisher.
 ISBN 978-1-60960-593-3 (hardcover) -- ISBN 978-1-60960-594-0 (ebook) 1.
Semantic Web. 2. World Wide Web. I. Sheth, A. (Amit), 1959-
 TK5105.88815.S427 2011
 025.042'7--dc22
                                    2011009952

British Cataloguing in Publication Data
A Cataloguing in Publication record for this book is available from the British Library.

Table of Contents

Detailed Table of Contents

Chapter 1

    Adrian Mocan, SAP Research CEC, Germany
    Federico M. Facca, University of Innsbruck, Austria
    Nikolaos Loutas, University of Macedonia, Greece
    Vassilios Peristeras, National University of Ireland, Ireland
    Sotirios K. Goudos, Aristotle University of Thessaloniki, Greece
    Konstantinos Tarabanis, University of Macedonia, Greece

Interoperability is one of the most challenging problems in modern cross-organizational information systems, which rely on heterogeneous information and process models. Interoperability becomes very important for e-Government information systems that support cross-organizational communication especially in a cross-border setting. The main goal in this context is to seamlessly provide integrated services to the user (citizen). In this paper we focus on Pan European e-Services and issues related with their integration. Our analysis uses basic concepts of the generic public service model of the Governance Enterprise Architecture (GEA) and of the Web Service Modeling Ontology (WSMO), to express the semantic description of the e-services. Based on the above, we present a mediation infrastructure capable of resolving semantic interoperability conflicts at a pan-European level. We provide several examples to illustrate both the need to solve such semantic conflicts and the actual solutions we propose.

Chapter 2

    Myunggwon Hwang, Chosun University, South Korea
    Pankoo Kim, Chosun University, South Korea

This paper deals with research that automatically constructs a lexical dictionary of unknown words as an automatic lexical dictionary expansion. The lexical dictionary has been usefully applied to various fields for semantic information processing. It has limitations in which it only processes terms defined in the dictionary. Under this circumstance, the concept of "Unknown Word (UW)" is defined. UW is considered a word, not defined in WordNet, that is an existing representative lexical dictionary. Here is where a new method to construct UW lexical dictionary through inputting various document collections that are scattered on the WebWeb is proposed. The authors grasp related terms of UW and measure semantic relatedness (similarity) between an UW and a related term(s). The relatedness is obtained by calculating both probabilistic relationship and semantic relationship. This research can extend UW lexical dictionary with an abundant number of UW. It is also possible to prepare a foundation for semantic retrieval by simultaneously using the UW lexical dictionary and WordNet.

Chapter 3

Yan Chen, Georgia State University, USA
Yan-Qing Zhang, Georgia State University, USA

For most Web searching applications, queries are commonly ambiguous because words usually contain several meanings. Traditional Word Sense Disambiguation (WSD) methods use statistic models or ontology-based knowledge models to find the most appropriate sense for the ambiguous word. Since queries are usually short, the contexts of the queries may not always provide enough information for disambiguating queries. Thus, more than one interpretation may be found for one ambiguous query. In this paper, we propose a cluster-based WSD method, which finds out all appropriate interpretations for the query. Because some senses of one ambiguous word usually have very close semantic relations, we group those similar senses together for explaining the ambiguous word in one interpretation. If the cluster-based WSD method generates several contradictory interpretations for one ambiguous query, we extract users' preferences from clickthrough data, and determine suitable concepts or concepts' clusters that meet users' interests for explaining the ambiguous query.

Chapter 4

Christian Bizer, Freie Universität Berlin, Germany
Andreas Schultz, Freie Universität Berlin, Germany

The SPARQL Query Language for RDF and the SPARQL Protocol for RDF are implemented by a growing number of storage systems and are used within enterprise and open Web settings. As SPARQL is taken up by the community, there is a growing need for benchmarks to compare the performance of storage systems that expose SPARQL endpoints via the SPARQL protocol. Such systems include native RDF stores as well as systems that rewrite SPARQL queries to SQL queries against non-RDF relational databases. This article introduces the Berlin SPARQL Benchmark (BSBM) for comparing the performance of native RDF stores with the performance of SPARQL-to-SQL rewriters across architectures. The benchmark is built around an e-commerce use case in which a set of products is offered by different vendors and consumers have posted reviews about products. The benchmark query mix emulates the search and navigation pattern of a consumer looking for a product. The article discusses the design of the BSBM benchmark and presents the results of a benchmark experiment comparing the performance of four popular RDF stores (Sesame, Virtuoso, Jena TDB, and Jena SDB) with the performance of two SPARQL-to-SQL rewriters (D2R Server and Virtuoso RDF Views) as well as the performance of two relational database management systems (MySQL and Virtuoso RDBMS).

Sebastian Hellmann, Universität Leipzig, Germany

Jens Lehmann, Universität Leipzig, Germany

Sören Auer, Universität Leipzig, Germany

The vision of the Semantic Web aims to make use of semantic representations on the largest possible scale - the Web. Large knowledge bases such as DBpedia, OpenCyc, and GovTrack are emerging and freely available as Linked Data and SPARQL endpoints. Exploring and analysing such knowledge bases is a significant hurdle for Semantic Web research and practice. As one possible direction for tackling this problem, the authors present an approach for obtaining complex class expressions from objects in knowledge bases by using Machine Learning techniques. The chapter describes in detail how to leverage existing techniques to achieve scalability on large knowledge bases available as SPARQL endpoints or Linked Data. The algorithms are made available in the open source DL-Learner project and this chapter presents several real-life scenarios in which they can be used by Semantic Web applications.

Aidan Hogan, National University of Ireland – Galway, Ireland

Andreas Harth, Karlsruher Institut für Technologie, Germany

Axel Polleres, National University of Ireland – Galway, Ireland

In this chapter, the authors discuss the challenges of performing reasoning on large scale RDF datasets from the Web. Using ter-Horst's pD* fragment of OWL as a base, the authors compose a rule-based framework for application to Web data: they argue their decisions using observations of undesirable examples taken directly from the Web. The authors further temper their OWL fragment through consideration of "authoritative sources" which counter-acts an observed behaviour which they term "ontology hijacking": new ontologies published on the Web re-defining the semantics of existing entities resident in other ontologies. They then present their system for performing rule-based forward-chaining reasoning which they call SAOR: Scalable Authoritative OWL Reasoner. Based upon observed characteristics of Web data and reasoning in general, they design their system to scale: the system is based upon a separation of terminological data from assertional data and comprises of a lightweight in-memory index, on-disk sorts and file-scans. The authors evaluate their methods on a dataset in the order of a hundred million statements collected from real-world Web sources and present scale-up experiments on a dataset in the order of a billion statements collected from the Web. In this republished version, the authors also present extended discussion reflecting upon recent developments in the area of scalable RDFS/OWL reasoning, some of which has drawn inspiration from the original publication (Hogan, et al., 2009).

With the emergence of high-end smart phones/PDAs there is a growing opportunity to enrich mobile/ pervasive services with semantic reasoning. This paper presents novel strategies for optimising semantic reasoning for realising semantic applications and services on mobile devices. We have developed the mTableaux algorithm which optimises the reasoning process to facilitate service selection. We present comparative experimental results which show that mTableaux improves the performance and scalability of semantic reasoning for mobile devices.

Chapter 8

The term "Linked Data" refers to a set of best practices for publishing and connecting structured data on the Web. These best practices have been adopted by an increasing number of data providers over the last three years, leading to the creation of a global data space containing billions of assertions— the Web of Data. In this article, the authors present the concept and technical principles of Linked Data, and situate these within the broader context of related technological developments. They describe progress to date in publishing Linked Data on the Web, review applications that have been developed to exploit the Web of Data, and map out a research agenda for the Linked Data community as it moves forward.

Chapter 9

User-generated content can help the growth of linked data. However, there are a lack of interfaces enabling ordinary people to author linked data. Secondly, people have multiple perspectives on the same concept and different contexts. Thirdly, there are not enough ontologies to model various data. Therefore, the authors of this chapter propose an approach to enable people to share various data through an easy-to-use social platform. Users define their own concepts and multiple conceptualizations are allowed. These are consolidated using semi-automatic schema alignment techniques supported by the community. Further, concepts are grouped semi-automatically by similarity. As a result of consolidation and grouping, informal lightweight ontologies emerge gradually. The authors have implemented a social software system, called StYLiD, to realize the approach. It can serve as a platform motivating people to bookmark and share different things. It may also drive vertical portals for specific communities with integrated data from multiple sources. Some experimental observations support the validity of the approach.

Chapter 10

The rapid development of the data Web is accompanied by increasing information needs from ordinary Web users for searching objects and their relations. To meet the challenge, this chapter presents Falcons Object Search, a keyword-based search engine for linked objects. To support various user needs expressed via keyword queries, for each object an extensive virtual document is indexed, which consists of not only associated literals but also the textual descriptions of associated links and linked objects. The resulting objects are ranked according to a combination of their relevance to the query and their popularity. For each resulting object, a query-relevant structured snippet is provided to show the associated literals and linked objects matched with the query for reflecting query relevance and even directly answering the question behind the query. To exploit ontological semantics for more precise search results, the type information of objects is leveraged to support class-based query refinement, and Web-scale class-inclusion reasoning is performed to discover implicit type information. Further, a subclass recommendation technique is proposed to allow users navigate class hierarchies for incremental results filtering. A task-based experiment demonstrates the promising features of the system.

Chapter 11

Although tagging is a widely accepted practice on the Social Web, it raises various issues like tags ambiguity and heterogeneity, as well as the lack of organization between tags. We believe that Semantic Web technologies can help solve many of these issues, especially considering the use of formal resources from the Web of Data in support of existing tagging systems and practices. In this article, we present the MOAT—Meaning Of A Tag—ontology and framework, which aims to achieve this goal. We will detail some motivations and benefits of the approach, both in an Enterprise 2.0 ecosystem and on the Web. As we will detail, our proposal is twofold: It helps solve the problems mentioned previously, and weaves user-generated content into the Web of Data, making it more efficiently interoperable and retrievable.

Chapter 12

Exchanging and analyzing ideas across different software tools and repositories is needed to implement the concepts of open innovation and holistic innovation management. However, a precise and formal definition for the concept of an idea is hard to obtain. In this paper, the authors introduce an ontology to represent ideas. This ontology provides a common language to foster interoperability between tools and to support the idea life cycle. Through the use of an ontology, additional benefits like semantic reasoning and automatic analysis become available. Our proposed ontology captures both a core idea concept that covers the 'heart of the idea' and further concepts to support collaborative idea development, including rating, discussing, tagging, and grouping ideas. This modular approach allows the idea ontology to be complemented by additional concepts like customized evaluation methods. The authors present a case study that demonstrates how the ontology can be used to achieve interoperability between innovation tools and to answer questions relevant for innovation managers that demonstrate the advantages of semantic reasoning.

Chapter 13

Nicola Fanizzi, Università degli studi di Bari, Italy
Claudia d'Amato, Università degli studi di Bari, Italy
Floriana Esposito, Università degli studi di Bari, Italy

The tasks of resource classification and retrieval from knowledge bases in the Semantic Web are the basis for a lot of important applications. In order to overcome the limitations of purely deductive approaches to deal with these tasks, inductive (instance-based) methods have been introduced as efficient and noise-tolerant alternatives. In this paper we propose an original method based on a non-parametric learning scheme: the Reduced Coulomb Energy (RCE) Network. The method requires a limited training effort but it turns out to be very effective during the classification phase. Casting retrieval as the problem of assessing the class-membership of individuals w.r.t. the query concepts, we propose an extension of a classification algorithm using RCE networks based on an entropic similarity measure for OWL. Experimentally we show that the performance of the resulting inductive classifier is comparable with the one of a standard reasoner and often more efficient than with other inductive approaches. Moreover, we show that new knowledge (not logically derivable) is induced and the likelihood of the answers may be provided.

Chapter 14

Tuukka Ruotsalo, Aalto University, Finland
Eetu Mäkelä, Aalto University, Finland

In this paper, the authors compare the performance of corpus-based and structural approaches to determine semantic relatedness in ontologies. A large light-weight ontology and a news corpus are used as materials. The results show that structural measures proposed by Wu and Palmer, and Leacock and Chodorow have superior performance when cut-off values are used. The corpus-based method Latent

Semantic Analysis is found more accurate on specific rank levels. In further investigation, the approximation of structural measures and Latent Semantic Analysis show a low level of overlap and the methods are found to approximate different types of relations. The results suggest that a combination of corpus-based methods and structural methods should be used and appropriate cut-off values should be selected according to the intended use case.

Preface

There are clear indications that Semantic Web, if seen as a technology, has passed the early adoption phase of its technology adoption life cycle (Wikipedia Contributors, 2010). The adoption of Semantic Web is fuelled by convergence of a number of factors, including the following:

- accelerating growth of information and resources on the Web, and increasing heterogeneity (both in technological aspects such as representation and media, and in nontechnical aspects such as socio-cultural aspects)
- recognition on the part of not just the researchers but also practitioners and companies that syntactic and statistical solutions near the limit in effectiveness in dealing with scale and heterogeneity, and future gains will come from use of semantics
- good degree of consensus on and adoption of representation languages and core technologies for which W3C's Semantic Web initiative and its recommendations such as RDF, SPARQL, and OWL have played critical role
- availability of technologies, with plenty of open source tools and system exemplified by over 20 RDF stores and query systems, as well as broader ecosystem of available commercial service and product providers
- successful demonstration of its value proposition by a number of early adoption domains as demonstrated by deployed applications (Sheth & Stevens, 2007; Brammer & Terziyan, 2008; Cardoso et al., 2008) in several domains including healthcare (Sheth et al., 2006) and life sciences (Ruttenberg et al., 2009; Baker & Cheung, 2007), pharmaceuticals, financial services (Sheth, 2005), e-government and defense (Mentzas, 2007).

Early commercial use of Semantic Web approach was reported by Taalee (subsequently through acquisiton/merger Voquette, Semagix, Fortent) founded in 1999, the same year in which the term Semantic Web was coined by Tim Berners-Lee. A keynote given in 2000 gives clear examples of the semantic search and other applications that had paying customers (Sheth, 2000). This involves creation of ontologies or background knowledge in variety of domains, automatic semantic annotation of heterogeneous Web content, and applications including semantic search, semantic browsing, semantic personalization, semantic targeting/advertisement, and semantic analysis (Sheth et al., 2001). Those early efforts covered hundreds of websites and semantic processing at the rate of about million documents per hour per server, and was largely limited by the infrastructure available. A number of commercial products and services continued to increase that formed the basis of the innovation and early adoption parts of the technology life cycle.

Now let us see why we are in early majority phase of the lifecycle. A rapidly growing number of companies and organizations are offering products and servicesinvolving Semantic Web technologies or are using them for mission critical applications (Sheth & Stephens, 2007; [³] Herman, 2009). Example companies providing products and services (with example of one key Semantic Web application) include Adobe (internet and desktop application tools), Dow Jones (content delivery), General Electric (energy efficiency), Hakia (search), IBM (content analysis), Nokia (portal tools and services), OpenLink and Oracle (DBMS), WolframAlpha (search), and Reuters (semantic annotation service). A number of companies and organizations are using Semantic Web technologies for mission critical applications, including Office of Management and Budget, Pfizer, Eli Lily, Novartis, and Telefonica. Commercial interest in Semantic Web technology was most vividly demonstrated in the form of acquisitions of several startups and small companies by major Internet and technology companies, best exemplified by Microsoft's acquisition of Powerset (2008), Apple of Siri (April 2010), and Google of Metaweb (June 2010).

While use of Semantic Web technology on a full Web scale is yet to come, what we see is a concrete progress towards using and supporting semantic Web capabilities on the Web scale. The most concrete step taken by these Web scale systems, primarily search and other Web applications, is the creation and/ or reuse of massive amounts of background knowledge, often involving a collection of domains, and each involving (a domain specific) sets of entities (also called objects, concepts, etc). All major search companies—Microsoft's Bing, Google, and Yahoo!—are known to be working towards this capability. Support of disambiguation is a litmus test of a semantic capability (as opposed to keyword/syntax centric approaches), which most of these systems are working hard to support. Equally important is adoption of RDFa and open sharing of metadata (such as Facebook'sOpenGraph).

Arguably, however, the most significant progress in Semantic Web has been that of Linked Data. *International Journal on Semantic Web & Information Systems* is proud to have had its first comprehensive special issue on the topic during 2010.

Let us now review the chapters in this book.

Interoperability is one the most challenging issues for cross-organizational Information Systems. Interoperability becomes very important and relevant for e-government Information Systems, which are capable to support cross-organizational communication in a cross-border setup. In "*Solving Semantic Interoperability Conflicts in Cross-Border E-Government Services,*" Mocan, Loutas, Facca, Peristeras, Goudos, and Tarabanis propose seamless integration of Pan European e-services for citizens to resolve semantic interoperability, and it uses generic public service model of the Governance Enterprise Architecture and Web Service Modeling Ontology. The chapter discusses semantic interoperability conflicts at data-level and schema-level. Data mediation services and solutions are developed in EU funded SemanticGovproject to resolve semantic interoperability conflicts. The solution uses ontology mapping and involves creation of alignments among the domain ontologies at design time and their use at run-time.

Documents containing words not defined in the dictionary like WordNet and such undefined words are called "Unknown Word (UW)." Hwang and Kim in "*A New Similarity Measure for Automatic Construction of the Unknown Word Lexical Dictionary*" propose a new method to construct UW lexical dictionary through inputting various document collections scattered on the Web. To achieve true semantic information processing, the work searches for UWs and terms related to the UW. Bayesian probability is used to assign probabilistic weight and semantic weight based on WordNet is calculated to find the semantic relatedness between an UW and related term(s). The work uses newly designed word sense disambiguation (WSD) method to enable dictionary to have an accurate synset for related terms. Proposed WSD algorithm is designed to automatically construct an UW lexical dictionary with an accuracy of 81% and it demonstrated efficient performance in comparison to SSI algorithm. Results show 15% improvement in performance in comparison to Dice Coefficient method.

Queries for any Web searching applications are likely to be ambiguous as words in queries usually carry several meanings. In *"Extracting Concepts' Relations and Users' Preferences for Personalizing Query Disambiguation,"* Chen and Zhang present a cluster-based Word Sense Disambiguation (WSD) method to find out all appropriate interpretations for the query. Any ambiguous word is likely to have very close semantic relations; the work groups such similar senses together to explain the ambiguous word in one interpretation. In case of several contradictory interpretations for one ambiguous query, users' preferences retrieved from clickthrough data are obtained to determine suitable concepts or cluster of concepts. Experimental result shows better performance of the proposed method compare to case-based WSD and Adapt Lesk algorithms.

Web 2.0 platforms and systems are using RDF and RDFS as basic standards to store, query, update, and exchange the data. Reasoning of RDF data is a critical issue from performance and scalability point of view. There is an urgent need to improve reasoning algorithms to realize the capabilities of Semantic Web. Many researchers are aiming to improve the performance of reasoning algorithm while manipulating large scale RDF/OWL ontologies. SPARQL is used extensively to retrieve data from RDF stores. In *"The Berlin SPARQL Benchmark,"* Bizer and Schultz propose a new benchmark to evaluate efficient performance of SPARQL features like OPTIONAL, ORDER BY, UNION, REGEX, and CONSTRUCT. The work compares the performance of three popular RDF stores to two SPARQL-to-SQL rewriters across architectures and uses e-commerce use case having 100M triple and a single client. The paper discusses design of the Berlin SPARQL Benchmark (BSBM) and compares performance of four popular RDF stores - Sesame, Virtuoso, Jena TDB, and Jena SDB with the performance of two SPARQL-to-SQL rewriters - D2R Server and Virtuoso RDF Views and performance of two RDBMS - MySQL and Virtuoso RDBMS. It employs benchmarking techniques such as executing query mixes, query parameterization, simulation of multiple clients, and system ramp-up. None of the benchmark results was found to be superior for a single client use case for all queries and dataset sizes and it justifies the need to improve the rewriting algorithms. Sophisticated optimization techniques should be developed to make SPARQL optimizers robust.

Hellmann, Lehmann, and Auer apply machine learning techniques to obtain complex class descriptions from objects in a very large knowledge base such as DBpedia, OpenCyc, GovTrack, et cetera. *"Learning of OWL Class Expressions on Very Large Knowledge Bases and its Applications"* aims to increase the scalability of OWL learning algorithms through intelligent pre-processing and develop, implement, and integrate a flexible method in the DL-Learner framework to extract relevant parts of very large knowledge bases for a given learning task.

Reasoning on Web based large scale RDF datasets is a highly challenging task. In *"Scalable Authoritative OWL Reasoning for the Web"* Hogan, Harth, and Polleres propose ter-Horst's pD fragment of OWL to compose a rule-based framework for application, which uses forward-chaining reasoning algorithm called Scalable Authoritative OWL Reasoner (SAOR). Forward-reasoning is used to avoid the runtime complexity of query-rewriting associated with backward-chaining approaches. The proposed system separates terminological data from assertional data, comprises of lightweight in-memory index, on-disk sorting and file-scans. It maintains a separate optimized T-box index to perform reasoning on OWL datasets. To keep the resulting knowledge-base manageable, SAOR algorithm considers only positive fragment of OWL reasoning, analyze the authority of sources to avoid hijacking of ontology and uses pivot identifiers instead of full materialization of equality. Experiments are performed on a database collected from the Web with a billion statements.

To satisfy increase in the demand of services for smart phones/mobile devices, mobile and pervasive services should be capable of semantic reasoning. In "*Enabling Scalable Semantic Reasoning for Mobile Services,*" Steller, Krishnaswamy, and Gaber propose an interesting strategy to optimize semantic reasoning for applications and services targeted for mobile devices. Proposed mTableaux algorithm optimizes description logic reasoning tasks so that large reasoning tasks can be scaled for small resource constrained mobile devices. The work presents comparative analysis of performance of proposed algorithm with semantic reasoners - Pellet, RacerPro and FaCT++ to demonstrate significant improvement in response time. Result accuracy is evaluated using recall and precision values.

Linked Data movement is a set of best practices to publish and connect structured data across the Web and can be considered as one of the pillars of Semantic Web. The number of linked data providers has increased significantly in last three years. In the chapter "*Linked Data: The Story So Far,*" Bizer, Heath, and Berners-Lee publish linked data, and a review of applications based on linked data are described. Efforts related to linked data are classified into three categories: linked data browsers, linked data search engines, and domain specific linked data applications. SWSE and Falcons search engines are keyword based search engines, but compare to existing popular search engines, both exploit the underlying structure of the data, provide summary of the entity selected by the user, and additional structured data crawled from the Web and links to related entities. A number of services are being developed, offering domain-specific functionality by mashing up data from various linked data sources. Revyu, DBpedia Mobile, Talis Aspire, BBC Programmes and Music, DERI Pipes are few such domain specific linked data applications. To use the Web as a single global database, various research challenges: user interfaces and interaction paradigms, application architectures, schema mapping and data fusion, link maintenance, licensing, trust, quality, and relevance - are to be addressed.

In "*Community-Driven Consolidated Linked Data,*" Shakya, Takeda, and Wuwongse propose an approach to enable people to share various data using easy-to-use social platform. The work has implemented social software, called StYLiD. It allows users with multiple perspectives to share various types of structured linked data and derive ontologies to provide online social platform to be used by ordinary people. Users have freedom to define their own concepts. StYLiD consolidates multiple schemas by mapping these schemas semi-automatically with the help of schema alignment techniques. Concepts are grouped semi-automatically based on proposed algorithm to calculate schema similarity. It generates informal ontologies to combine multiple perspectives and unify common elements. StYLiD is built upon Pligg - a Web 2.0 content management system and experiments are performed based on all user-defined schemas definitions or types, retrieved from Freebase.

"*Searching Linked Objects with Falcons: Approach, Implementation and Evaluation*" by Cheng and Qu presents a keyword-based search engine for linked objects called Falcon Object Search. For each object, it constructs comprehensive virtual document consisting of textual descriptions extracted from RDF description of an object. It builds inverted index based on terms in virtual documents. To execute keyword-based query, the system uses inverted index and compares the terms in the query with the virtual documents of objects to generate result set. The objects of result set are ranked by considering their relevance to the query and their popularity. For each resulting object, a query-relevant structured snippet is provided to show the associated literals and linked objects matched with the keyword query. The concept of PD-thread is used as the basic unit, a snippet. The method of ranking PD-threads into a snippet is devised. Type information of objects is expanded by executing class-inclusion reasoning over descriptions of classes to implement class-based query refinement. The system recommends subclasses to allow navigation of class hierarchies to perform incremental result filtering.

In "*A URI is Worth a Thousand Tags: From Tagging to Linked Data with MOAT*," Passant, Laublet, Breslin, and Decker demonstrate how Web 2.0 content and linked data principles could be combined in order to solve issues of free-tagging systems, like ambiguity and heterogeneity of tags. It proposes MOAT ontology, based on quadripartite tagging model, in which each tag can be represented by a quadruple (<User>, <Resource>, <Tag>, <MeaningURI>). It helps to assign tags of choice to a resource while using the huge amount of authoritative URIs from the Web of data to narrow down the intended meaning.

In "*An Idea Ontology for Innovation Management*," Riedl, May, Finzen, Stathel, Kaufman, and Krcmar make an attempt to represent ideas using an ontology. It is difficult to obtain an accurate and formal definition of idea. The ontology is based on OWL, and it provides a common language to support interoperability between innovation tools to support full life cycle of an idea in an open innovation environment. This work defines its own definition of idea, and based on the detailed analysis of innovation management domain, ontology is designed. The ontology is aimed to capture the core concept of idea to support collaborative idea development, rating, discussing, tagging, and grouping of ideas in an open innovation environment.

In "*Inductive Classification of Semantically Annotated Resources through Reduced Coulomb Energy Networks*," Fanizzi, d'Amato, and Esposito propose an interesting method to induce classifiers from ontology to perform concept retrieval. Induced classifier can determine likelihood measure of the induced class-membership assertions to perform approximate query answering and ranking. The work proposes to use instance-based classifier to answer queries based on a non-parametric learning scheme; the Reduced Coulomb Energy (RCE) Network. The work extends classification algorithm using RCE networks based on entropic similarity measure for OWL. Experiments are performed to execute approximate query answering on a number of ontologies from public repositories. Results show induction classification to be competitive with reference to the deductive methods and are able to detect new knowledge assertions, which are not logically derivable.

In "*A Comparison of Corpus-Based and Structural Methods on Approximation of Semantic Relatedness in Ontologies*," Ruotsalo and Mäkelä compare the performance of corpus-based and structural approaches to determine semantic relatedness in light-weight ontologies. The work identifies the strength and weaknesses of the methods in various application scenarios. The experimental results show that neither corpus-based method nor structure-based measures is efficient and competitive. Latent Semantic Analysis (LSA) produces the best performance for the whole dataset. Structural measures produce better performance compare to LSA when cut-off values were applied. The performance of compared methods varies in case of different rank levels. LSA is found to be efficient in filtering out the non-relevant relations, and is able to find relations whereas structural measures fail. The work suggests using a combination of corpus-based methods and structural methods and identification of appropriate cut-off values based on the intended use case(s).

Amit Sheth
Wright State University, USA

REFERENCES

Baker, C. J. O., & Cheung, K.-H. (Eds.). (2007). *Semantic Web: Revolutionizing knowledge discovery in the life sciences*. Springer.

Brammer, M., & Terziyan, V. (Eds.). (2008). *Industrial applications of Semantic Web*. New York, NY: Springer-Verlag.

Cardoso, J., Hepp, M., & Miltiadis, D. (Eds.). (2008). *The Semantic Web, real-world applications from industry*. Springer.

Herman, I. (2009). What is being done today? Presentation given Deutsche Telekom, Darmstadt, Germany, December 14, 2009.

Mentzas, G. (2007). *Knowledge and semantic technologies for agile and adaptive e-government*. 7th Global Forum on Reinventing Government: Building Trust in Government, June 26-29, 2007.

Ruttenberg, A., Rees, J. A., Samwald, M., & Marshall, M. S. (2009). Life sciences on the Semantic Web: The Neurocommons and beyond. *Briefings in Bioinformatics*, *10*(2), 193–204. .doi:10.1093/bib/bbp004

Sheth, A. (2000). *Semantic Web & information brokering: Opportunities, commercialization and challenges*. Keynote talk at the International Workshop on Semantic Web: Models, Architecture and Management, Lisbon, Portugal, September 21, 2000.

Sheth, A. (2005). *Enterprise applications of Semantic Web: The sweet spot of risk and compliance*. IFIP International Conference on Industrial Applications of Semantic Web (IASW2005), Jyvaskyla, Finland, August 25–27, 2005.

Sheth, A., Avant, D., & Bertram, C. (2001). *System and method for creating a Semantic Web and its applications in browsing, searching, profiling, personalization and advertising*. (United States patent Number - 6311194), Taalee, Inc. Oct 30, 2001.

Sheth, A. P., Agrawal, S., Lathem, J., Oldham, N., & Wingate, Y. H.P., & Gallagher, K. (2006). *Active semantic electronic medical record*. 5th International Semantic Web Conference, Athens, GA, November 6–9, 2006.

Sheth, A. P., & Stephens, S. (2007). *Semantic Web: Technologies and applications for the real- world*. 16th World Wide Web Conference (WWW2007), Banff, Canada, May 8-12, 2007

Wikipedia contributors. (2010). *Technology adoption lifecycle*. Retrieved January 6, 2011, from http://en.wikipedia.org/w/index.php?title=Technology_adoption_lifecycle&oldid=386064217

ENDNOTES

[1]   Data from http://www.w3.org/2001/sw/sweo/public/UseCases/accessed in December 2010.

[2]   Data from http://www.w3.org/2005/04/swls/accessed in December 2010.

[3]   Data from http://esw.w3.org/CommercialProducts accessed in December 2010.

Chapter 1
Solving Semantic Interoperability Conflicts in Cross–Border E–Government Services

Adrian Mocan
SAP Research CEC, Germany[1]

Vassilios Peristeras
National University of Ireland, Ireland

Federico M. Facca
University of Innsbruck, Austria

Sotirios K. Goudos
Aristotle University of Thessaloniki, Greece

Nikolaos Loutas
University of Macedonia, Greece

Konstantinos Tarabanis
University of Macedonia, Greece

ABSTRACT

Interoperability is one of the most challenging problems in modern cross-organizational information systems, which rely on heterogeneous information and process models. Interoperability becomes very important for e-Government information systems that support cross-organizational communication especially in a cross-border setting. The main goal in this context is to seamlessly provide integrated services to the user (citizen). In this paper we focus on Pan European e-Services and issues related with their integration. Our analysis uses basic concepts of the generic public service model of the Governance Enterprise Architecture (GEA) and of the Web Service Modeling Ontology (WSMO), to express the semantic description of the e-services. Based on the above, we present a mediation infrastructure capable of resolving semantic interoperability conflicts at a pan-European level. We provide several examples to illustrate both the need to solve such semantic conflicts and the actual solutions we propose.

INTRODUCTION

The Web has been continuously growing in the past decade and its growth conveyed to wide use of information systems based on modern Web technologies (e.g. Web services). The distributed nature of the Web challenged the ability of communication amongst independent information systems based on different technologies and heterogeneous data models. To achieve this com-

DOI: 10.4018/978-1-60960-593-3.ch001

munication, integration efforts are required, which usually trigger various types of problems. These problems are often referred to as interoperability conflicts and significant effort has been spent on finding the silver bullet to solve them. One of the most promising solutions, that opens new opportunities and at the same time new challenges, is the use of semantic technologies (Fensel, D., Lausen, H., Polleres, A., de Bruijn, J., Stollberg, M., Roman, D., & Domingue, J., 2006; Yanosy, J., 2005).

Nowadays, Public Administrations (PA), especially in the European Union context, have to integrate their technological infrastructure and the underlying data models in order to provide high quality national and cross-border services to the European citizens (Tambouris, E., & Tarabanis, K., 2004; Tambouris, E., Manouselis, N., & Costopoulou, C., 2007). The European Union is currently advancing in this direction by supporting the research on solutions for solving interoperability issues among cross-border e-services, through a number of public financed projects. Such projects (e.g. SemanticGov, SEEMP, eGovBus, R4eGov[2]) have been targeting the so called, Pan-European eGovernment Services (PEGS).

This article presents a mediation infrastructure developed in the context of the SemanticGov[3] project. This infrastructure is able to solve PEGS interoperability conflicts based on the conceptual model of the Web Service Modeling Ontology (WSMO) (Fensel, D., et al., 2006) and semantic technologies. The identification of the interoperability conflicts to be addressed is based on a well-known work by Park and Ram (2004). We adopt their framework and instantiate it in the PA domain by using a generic PA service model as proposed by the Governance Enterprise Architecture (GEA).

In particular, we analyze a comprehensive set of semantic interoperability conflicts and we present here the SemanticGov technical solutions to solve them. The technical solutions are based on alignments between heterogeneous data models

and ontologies. Additionally, we give an overview of the infrastructure needed to semi-automatically derive these alignments, such as the human user can interactively create and validate mappings and mapping rules by using a graphical interface. Once such alignments are created, they are ready to be used whenever at run-time heterogeneous data has to be exchanged and mediation is required. The novelty of our work lies on the fact that we propose a comprehensive framework for semantic conflicts analysis and resolution applicable in a Pan-European context, which builds on emerging technologies for semantic-driven data mediation.

The article is organized as follows: Section *Background* gives an overview of the background concepts adopted in this article and in Section *Overview of Semantic Interoperability Conflicts* we briefly review the classification of semantic interoperability conflicts. In Section *Solving Semantic Interoperability Conflicts for Cross-Border e-Government Services* we analyze the semantic interoperability conflicts introduced in the previous section and we propose a set of solutions able to resolve such conflicts. Section *Mediation Services and Solutions: Implementation* re-iterates through these solutions and describes our approach which enables such solutions. These two parts are kept separate since our aim has been to propose a set of technology-independent solutions for solving the semantic interoperability conflicts. These solutions may be implemented in different ways depending on the available technology. The specific technology and software architecture we describe in this article is just one possible choice and serves as a proof of concept to show how these solutions can be actually applied in practice.

Section *Related Work* presents several research efforts related to our work, while Section *Evaluation* analyzes the evaluation results of our tools obtained during three evaluation workshops which were organized for this purpose in three different PA agencies in Greece and Italy. In Section 8 we draw some conclusion and discuss some future research directions.

BACKGROUND

This section gives an overview of the background concepts that form the basis of the work presented in this article. In particular, the classification of the interoperability conflicts (see Section *Overview of Semantic Interoperability Conflicts*) is based on the work of Park and Ram (2004). In order to identify and instantiate these conflicts in the e-Government domain, we need a PA specific vocabulary to provide us with the necessary terms to describe the domain. Therefore, we adopt a PA service model from the Governance Enterprise Architecture framework and we analyze the interoperability conflicts in cross-border e-Government service provision. Our research also relies on the WSMO (Fensel, D., et al., 2006) conceptual framework for describing Semantic Web services, i.e. the examples presented in the next sections are based on this framework and its modeling language (i.e. Web Service Modeling Language – WSML [de Bruijn, J., Lausen, H., Krummenacher, R., Polleres, A., Predoiu, L., Kifer, M., & Fensel, D., 2005]). Data mapping examples rely on WSML and on the Abstract Mapping Language proposed in (Dean, M., & Schreiber, G., 2004). Finally the implementation relies on the components of the SemanticGov architecture as depicted in (Vitvar, T., Mocan, A., Cimpian, E., Nazir, S., Wang, X., Loutas, N., Peristeras, V., Tarabanis, K., Kirgiannakis, E., Winkler, K., Dimitrov, M., Momtchev, V., & Mecella, M., 2006): on the Web Service Execution Environment (WSMX) (Vitvar, T., Mocan, A., Kerrigan, M., Zaremba, M., Zaremba, M., Moran, M., Cimpian, E., Haselwanter, T., & Fensel, D., 2007), which is a semantic middleware infrastructure for run-time support; and on Web Service Modeling Toolkit (WSMT) (Kerrigan, M., Mocan, A., Tanler, M., & Fensel, D., 2007) which is a Semantic Web services design toolkit for WSMO, for the design-time support.

The Governance Enterprise Architecture Object Model for Service Provision

The Governance Enterprise Architecture (GEA) (Peristeras, V., 2006; Peristeras, V., & Tarabanis, K., 2008) is a top-level, generic enterprise architecture for the overall government domain. A key aspect of GEA is that it attempts to be technology-neutral, thus being applicable to different technological environments. GEA currently consists of six models at different levels of analysis. One of these models, namely the GEA object model for service provision (or the PA service model), describes the basic concepts of a PA service. This article is based on this model, as we study interoperability conflicts that are raised during the provision of cross-border e-Government services. The main concepts of this model are briefly described below:

- *Client* is a Societal Entity (i.e. a citizen), a Legal Entity (i.e. a business) or another PA entity, which requests a service from a Service Provider.
- *Service Provider* is a PA agency that is competent for providing a specific service.
- *Preconditions* set the general framework in which the service should be performed and the underlying business rules that should be fulfilled for its successful execution. Preconditions are defined by Laws and can be formally expressed as a set of clauses/rules.
- *Evidence* is the information that the service requires for its execution. Evidences are used to validate the preconditions of the service. As Evidence is pure information, it is stored in Evidence Placeholders.
- *Evidence Placeholder* is the needed input for a service that contains evidences. The most common types of Evidence Placeholders in PA are the administrative documents.

- *Outcome* refers to the different types of results a public service may have. GEA defines three types of Outcome:
- *Output* is the documented and officially registered decision of the Service Provider regarding the service requested by a client. This is currently embedded and reaches the client in the form of an administrative document.
- *Effect* is the change in the state of the real world (e.g. transfer money to an account) that is caused by the execution of a service. In PA, the service Effect is the actual permission, certificate, etc the client is finally entitled. In cases where the provision of a service is refused, there is no Effect.
- *Consequence* is information regarding the executed PA Service that needs to be forwarded to interested third parties, i.e. other PA agencies.

The Web Service Modeling Ontology and Language

In our approach, we use the Web Service Modeling Ontology (WSMO) as a framework for modeling the semantic description of PA services. Additionally, the Web Service Modeling Language (WSML) is adopted as a formal representation language for the WSMO elements. The next two subsections give a brief overview of these technologies.

The Web Service Modeling Ontology

WSMO (Fensel, D., et al., 2006) is a comprehensive framework providing all the necessary means to semantically describe the Semantic Web service aspects. The effort around WSMO includes the WSMO conceptual model itself, the WSML language (de Bruijn, J., et al., 2005), the WSMX execution environment (Vitvar, T., et al., 2006) and the WSMT modeling tool (Kerrigan,

M., Mocan, A., Tanler, M., & Fensel, D., 2007). WSMO comprises of four top level elements:

- *Ontologies* provide the formal semantics and the information models used by all other components. They serve in defining the formal semantics of the information, and in linking machine and human terminologies.
- *Web services* are semantically described from three different points of view: functionality, behavior and non-functional properties. The functionality is captured by a *capability* (e.g., booking of airplane tickets) which include: preconditions (i.e., the required state of the information space before the Web service execution), assumptions (i.e., the state of the world which is assumed before the execution), post-conditions (i.e., the state of the information space reached after the successful execution), and effects (i.e., the state of the world reached after the successful execution). The behavior of a Web service is described by its *interface* from two perspectives: communication (i.e., *choreography*) and collaboration (i.e., *orchestration*). The non-functional properties specify non-functional information about the service such as reliability, robustness, scalability, security, etc.
- *Goals* specify objectives that a client might have when consulting a Web service (e.g. find a public service that gives a monthly allowance to unemployed people). In WSMO, a goal is characterized in a dual way with respect to Web services: goal descriptions include the *requested capability* and the *requested interface*.
- *Mediators* provide interoperability facilities between the WSMO top level elements in order to enable the effective goal-driven Web service interaction. They describe elements that aim to overcome structural, semantic or conceptual mismatches that

Figure 1. Mapping between GEA and WSMO frameworks (Goudos, S.K., et al., 2007)

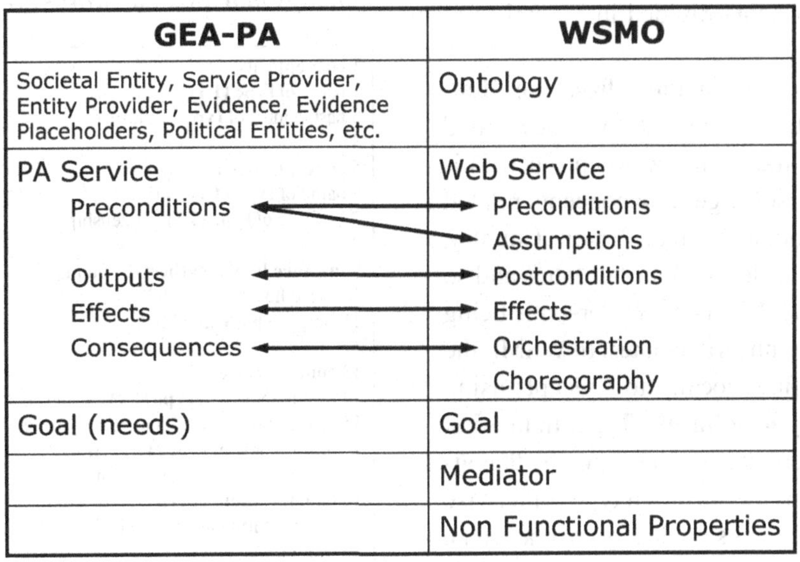

GEA-PA	WSMO
Societal Entity, Service Provider, Entity Provider, Evidence, Evidence Placeholders, Political Entities, etc.	Ontology
PA Service Preconditions Outputs Effects Consequences	Web Service Preconditions Assumptions Postconditions Effects Orchestration Choreography
Goal (needs)	Goal
	Mediator
	Non Functional Properties

appear between the different components. There are four types of mediators: *ooMediators* resolve terminological (data level) mismatches between two ontologies; *wwMediators* connect two different Web services, resolving any data, process and protocol heterogeneity; *ggMediators* connect different goals, enabling goals refinement and by this the reuse of goal definitions; and finally *wgMediators* connect goals and Web services, resolving any data, process and protocol heterogeneity. Since WSMO is a conceptual framework enabling the creation of semantic descriptions, the four types of WSMO mediators are also *description* of mediation functionality. The actual mediation task is performed by a specialized component or service that is being described by a WSMO mediator. The solutions we propose in this article are implemented by such a component and it could be described by an *ooMediator* (however, such a description is out of the scope of this article).

The WSMO and the GEA frameworks share a set of similarities. In order to allow the usage of WSMO as a technological solution for applying the GEA modeling perspective and to express PA specific semantics using WSMO Semantic Web services, a mapping has been created between these two frameworks (Wang, X., Vitvar, T., Mocan, A., Peristeras, V., Goudos, S.K., Tarabanis, K., 2007). Figure 1 presents a high-level overview of the mapping between WSMO and GEA. A WSML representation of the GEA PA service model has been also given in (Goudos, S.K., Loutas, N., Peristeras, V., & Tarabanis, K., 2007).

The Web Service Modeling Language

The Web Service Modeling Language (WSML) (de Bruijn, J., et al., 2005) offers a set of language variants for describing WSMO elements that enable modelers to balance between expressiveness and tractability according to different knowledge representation paradigms.

The conceptual syntax of WSML has a frame-like style (Kifer, M., Lausen, G., & Wu, J., 1995). The information about classes, attributes, relations and their parameters, instances and their attribute values are specified in one large syntactic construct, instead of being divided in a number of atomic chunks.

Listing 1 shows a fragment from the "Italian Citizen" ontology, an ontology developed in the context of the SemanticGov project. This ontology models some generic concepts related to the Italian PA domain: like Person, Country, City, Citizenship, Address, MaritalStatus, and so on. At lines 13 to 22 the concept Person is being defined together with its attributes. In WSML the attributes are defined locally to concepts using the keyword **ofType** or **impliesType**. In the first case it is imposed that the value taken by that attribute has to be of the specified type (otherwise a constraint violation is signaled by the reasoner). When using **impliesType** the reasoner will infer that the attribute value is of the specified type (this is similar with the OWL properties behavior (Dean, M., & Schreiber, G., 2004). Note that concepts can be organized in sub-class hierarchies by using the **subConceptOf** keyword (line 36-37).

Cardinality constraints can be specified as at lines 14 to 22: hasGender has cardinality 1 and hasSecondName has cardinality 0 or more. WSML allows the specification of relations with different arities and the parameters' domains are specified by using **ofType** or **impliesType** (see line 40).

Instances of concepts can be defined as exemplified at lines 9 to 11 and 24 to 27. It is also possible to create instances of relations as well (line 42-43).

A way of using the logical expression syntax in WSML is by the means of axioms (lines 45 to 52). The **italianCitizenRule** axiom states that if a **Person** has as birthplace (hasBirthplace with a given value y), the birthplace is a city situated in a country (hasCountry with value z) and this country is Italy, then the person has the Italian citizenship.

WSML has direct support for different types of concrete data, namely strings, integers, and

Listing 1. A fragment from the "ItalianCitizen" ontology in WSML (keywords are printed in bold)

```
1 concept City
2 name ofType (1 1) _string
3 hasCountry ofType Country
4
5 concept Country
6 name ofType (1 1) _string
7 isoCode ofType (1 1) CitizenshipCode
8
9 instance Italy memberOf Country
10 name hasValue "Italy"
11 isoCode hasValue IT
12
13 concept Person
14 hasFirstName ofType (1 1) _string
15 hasSecondName ofType (0 *) _string
16 hasSurname ofType (1 1) _string
17 hasGender ofType (1 1) Gender
18 hasCitizenship ofType Citizenship
19 hasMaritalStatus ofType (1 1)
20 MaritalStatus
21 hasBirthday ofType (1 1) _dateTime
22 hasBirthplace impliesType (1 1) City
23
24 instance mario memberOf Person
25 hasFirstName hasValue "Mario"
26 hasSurname hasValue "Rossi"
27 hasGender hasValue M
...
28
29 concept Address
30 streetName ofType (1 1) _string
31 streetNumber ofType (1 1) _int
32 city ofType (1 1) City
33 country ofType (1 1) Country
34 zipCode ofType (0 1) _string
35
36 concept ResidenceAddress
37 subConceptOf Address
38
39 relation lives(ofType Person,
40
41 ofType ResidenceAddress)
42 relationInstance
43 lives(mario,
44 marioAddress)
45
46 axiom italianCitizienRule
47 definedBy
48 ?x[hasBirthplace hasValue ?y]
49 memberOf City and
50 ?y[hasCountry hasValue Italy]
51 implies
52 ?x[hasCitizenship hasValue
53 italianCitizenship].
54
```

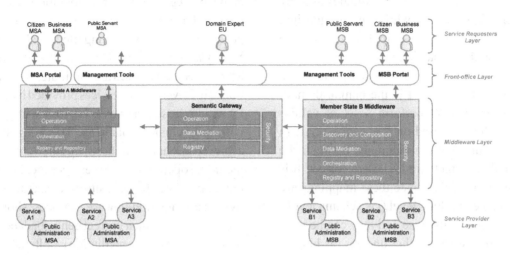

decimals, which correspond to the XML Schema[4]-primitive data types and they can then be used to construct complex data types.

WSML combines different formalisms, most notably Description Logics and Logic Programming. Three main areas can benefit from the use of formal methods in service descriptions: *Ontology description, Declarative functional description of Goals and Web services*, and *Description of dynamics*. WSML defines a syntax and semantics for ontology descriptions. The underlying logic formalisms are used to give a formal meaning to ontology descriptions in WSML, resulting in different variants of the language: WSML-Core, DL, Flight, Rule and Full.

WSML-Core is based on the intersection between the Description Logic SHIQ(**D**) (Horrocks, I., Sattler, U., & Tobies, S., 1999) and Horn Logic and it has the least expressive power of all the WSML variants. WSML-DL captures the Description Logic SHIQ(D), which is a major part of the (DL species of) Web Ontology Language OWL (Dean, M., & Schreiber, G., 2004). WSML-Flight is an extension of WSML-Core, which provides a powerful rule language; it is based on a logic programming variant of F-Logic (Kifer, M., Lausen, G., & Wu, J., 1995) and is semantically equivalent to Datalog with inequality and (locally) stratified

negation. WSML-Rule extends WSML-Flight with further features from Logic Programming while WSML-Full aims to unify WSML-DL and WSML-Rule under a First-Order umbrella.

The SemanticGov Architecture

In this section we give a short description of the global view on the SemanticGov architecture with particular attention to the component called the Semantic Gateway (see Figure 2), which is the component related to the work presented here. The Semantic Gateway's main functionality is to translate the information exchanged between public administrations of Member States without changing its meaning. Therefore, the Semantic Gateway facilitates the integration of member states at the EU level, i.e. integration and interoperation of cross-border PA services (Pan-European e-Government Services - PEGS).

Our solution for data mediation is based on ontologies that semantically describe the data to be mediated and on mapping rules that describe how to mediate between different ontologies. This implies a distinction between the design-time and the run-time phase, where the first represents the support (a prerequisite) for the second. At design-time the mappings between ontologies have to be established (i.e. between the ontologies used by the interacting parties) while during run-time phase these mappings are applied in concrete scenarios on data instances.

In the design-time phase semi-automatic techniques are used, that is the human domain expert is required to perform a set of validations and choices based on tool suggestions, in order to assure that the mappings between the source and the target ontologies are correct. It is important to note that since these mappings are created on the ontology level (i.e. schema level), they are created only once and they can be used multiple times with no other updates (as long as the ontologies do not evolve). The mappings are applied during run-time on concrete data without any human intervention, in an automatic manner. These design-time mappings are applied using the Ontology Mapping Tool which is described in detail in Section *Ontology Mapping Tool*. The run-time Data Mediation component of the Semantic Gateway is called the *Run-time Data Mediator Engine* which is described in detail in Section *Run-time Data Mediator Engine*.

The architecture is composed by different layers: the Service Requestor layer, the Front Office Layer, the Middleware Layer and the Service Provider Layer. A brief description of these layers follows below.

The *Service Requestors Layer* forms the stakeholders of the SemanticGov architecture. The top level group of stakeholders includes (1) *citizens*, (2) *businesses*, and (3) *public servants*.

The *Front-office Layer* provides access to the system for the SemanticGov stakeholders. Citizens and businesses can access the system through member state portals (e.g. portal of the public administration of Italy), while public servants (domain experts and administrators) through management tools e.g. ontology management tools, monitoring tools etc.

The *Middleware Layer* is the core of the SemanticGov architecture. Enhanced with semantic capabilities, it provides the main intelligence to achieve integration and interoperation of services provided by PAs. The Middleware Layer is composed of two major building blocks: (1) *Member State Middleware*, and (2) *Semantic Gateway*. The Member State Middleware facilitates the integration of e-Government services provided by various PA within one state as well as horizontal integration with the Semantic Gateway. The integration is achieved through a number of middleware services including operation, discovery, composition, data mediation, registry/repository, etc. Out of this, two important middleware services should be mentioned, since their correct behavior depends on the correctness of the mediation results: *discovery* and *operation*. The discovery service relies on a specialized engine able to analyze the semantic descriptions of services and to conclude if they match the citizen request (which is formalized as a WSMO goal). As part of the operation service, of most relevance is the invocation engine, which is a component responsible to prepare and to deliver the right data to the appropriate PA service that has to be invoked.

The Middleware Layer could represent the actual information system used by various member states or even by individual PA agencies (depending of the legal landscape of the particular country where the system is deployed). The combined functionality of its components enables the interoperability between the services offered by various agencies. The middleware adopted is based on WSMX (Vitvar, T., et al., 2007) and the core element for the resolution of interoperability conflicts is the Data Mediation component (also referred as the Run-time Data Mediator Engine). Detail description of WSMX architecture and its components forming particular configuration for application layer is described later in this section. Differences in this configuration may occur based on below mentioned aspects of national or communal environments:

- The *Member State Middleware* exists for each member state and takes care of processing the requests (goals) of member states citizens, businesses and civil servants. Based on particular National Interoperability Framework, national interoperability standards should be adopted by all public administrations in the country. Thus we presume that no mediation is necessary in cases when only national services are involved in communication (e.g. services A2 and A3 accessed by Citizen MSA in the Figure 1). On the other hand, national services which are subject to PEGS must be registered in the communal repositories of the communal SWS execution environment allowing their invocation and mediation within the cross-country e-government processes (e.g. services A3 and B1 accessed by Citizen MSA in the Figure 1).

- The *Semantic Gateway* at the EU level. It acts as the Communal Gateway (Overeem, A., & Witters, J., 2004) which facilitates interoperability at (1) the technical level using adapters to adapt different communication protocols and languages, (2) the data/semantic level using data mediators to resolve semantic mismatches of ontologies and (3) final at the process level using process mediators to resolve choreography mismatches of services. In addition, in order to carry out cross-country processes of PEGS, the discovery of PA services in a national environment involves searching for services in the environments own repositories as well as in the communal repositories. Thus, the Semantic Gateway will also provide access to communal services registry of its semantic repository. According to the IDABC specifications, common standards across member states in terms of data and choreography specifications will not always exist, therefore the environment of PEGS will be heterogeneous in nature. The idea is therefore to develop and maintain

domain ontology for PEGS to eliminate the total possible number of n*(n - 1) mappings for n ontologies. This will require the Semantic Gateway to resolve semantic and choreography mismatches and maintain all mappings centrally.

As a consequence, there could be situations when the resolution of the interoperability conflicts can be delegated to a specialized middleware, which role is to behave as a *Semantic Gateway* between the information systems of various member states and PA agencies. However there could be situations when mediation capabilities exist at the Member State Middleware level as well, and they could be use to solve heterogeneity problems between the member states directly, without the help of the Semantic Gateway. The solutions that are described later on in this article are suited both for the deployment at the member state as well as at the Semantic Gateway level (see Section *Applying the Data Mediator* for a discussion on these aspects).

Following is the description of the typical configuration of the WSMX environment based on the standard WSMX specifications (Vitvar, T., et al., 2007). Differences in this configuration may occur based on above mentioned aspects of national or communal environments.

- The *Execution Engine* controls Semantic Web services (SWS) execution processes by calling various WSMX components according to defined execution semantics. Within the SWS execution process, discovery, composition, data and process mediation as well as invocation of services is performed. The typical execution process calls discovery of services on reception of a WSML goal, composition of these services into a process, as well as controlling the invocation of services in the process. Data and process mediation is used to resolve semantic or choreography mismatches respectively.

- *Discovery* finds suitable services that satisfy the requestor's goal by searching semantic repositories. Discovery searches local as well as communal repositories.
- *Composition* returns a definition of a process in which services will be invoked. Typically, a complex goal is satisfied by more services, thus composition ensures the proper sequence of services to be invoked within the execution of the process.
- *Data Mediation* resolves semantic mismatches between two ontologies by using mappings between the concepts in these ontologies. Data mediation is based on ontology mapping and instance transformation principles and consists of a design-time stage when mapping rules are created and a runtime stage when instances are transformed from instances of the source ontology to instances of the target ontology using these mappings. These techniques and their customization for the PA domain represent the scope of this article and they are described in details throughout the rest of this article.
- *Process mediation* performs runtime analysis of two given choreography instances and resolves possible mismatches that may appear, for instance grouping several messages into a single one, changing the order of messages or removing some messages from the communication.
- *Communication* consists of the invoker and receiver components. They implement the WSMX entry points responsible for receiving incoming requests and invoking Web services respectively. The invoker and receiver also handle grounding of services described in WSML to the underlying WSDL descriptions and the SOAP protocol.

- *Semantic Repository* maintains collection of resources for services, predefined goals, mediation rules and ontologies used within the SWS execution process.
- *Management* is a vertical service within WSMX which applies to all components. It includes WSMX management functions (configuration and monitoring of components, deployment of dynamic execution semantics, managing entries in repositories), and WSMX management tools. WSMX management tools include ontology editors such as WSMO Studio and the Web Services Modeling Toolkit (WSMT) (Kerigan, M., et al., 2005) with plugins for ontology management, design-time data mediation mapping creation and WSMX monitoring and management.
- *Security and Privacy* around authentication and authorization of users for accessing services and their resources as well as confidentiality and integrity of exchanged information is an important issue for deploying services. However, security and privacy has not been addressed in the past research within WSMX and thus will be the subject of WSMX near future research.

Finally, the Service Providers Layer contains various PAs in a member state that expose various PA services through their existing back-end applications.

OVERVIEW OF SEMANTIC INTEROPERABILITY CONFLICTS

This section gives an overview of semantic interoperability conflicts that may arise during the communication across European PA agencies. A detailed description can be found in (Peristeras, V., Loutas, N., Goudos, S., & Tarabanis, K., 2008). Identifying and addressing the interoperability problems between European PA agencies is a

Table 1. Data-level and schema-level conflicts in the "change of residence" use case

Data-level	Data Value	The concept of adult is defined differently in the Italian and Belgian ontologies (see Section *Data Value Conflicts*)
	Data Representation	The birthdate attribute of the concept IdentityCard, which exists in both the Italian and the Belgian ontology, is represented differently in each one of them (see Section *Data Representation Conflicts*).
	Data Precision	The Belgian legislation identifies 13 different types of marital statuses, while the Italian one specifies only 4 types for marital status (see Section *Data Precision Conflicts*)
Schema-level	Entity Identifier	All people working in Italy need to have a Fiscal Code, which is the unique identifier of a person according to the Italian law. This identifier is necessary for working legally and paying taxes in Italy, but in Belgium a different type of identifier is used for the same purpose (see Section *Entity Identifier Conflict*).
	Generalization	Differences have been identified between the Italian Birth and Family Certificate, which is needed as input for the "Change of Residence" public service and the corresponding Belgian certificates (see Section *Generalization Conflicts*)

necessary prerequisite for a successful development of cross-border e-Government services. Information systems interoperability is an active research field for decades but has attracted a lot of interest during the past few years, for example, (Tambouris, E., et al., 2005; Vitvar, T., et al., 2006).

For the discussion of the different types of interoperability conflicts that may occur in cross-border e-Government services we refer to the work of Park et al. (2004), who classify semantic interoperability conflicts regardless of the application domain. Furthermore, we use the core GEA concepts (Peristeras, V.) to instantiate the classification of Park and colleagues in the cross-border e-Government services domain (see also Section *Solving Semantic Interoperability Conflicts for Cross-Border e-Government Services* for a detailed discussion on interoperability issues in cross-border e-Government services and their resolution with a semantic gateway). This exercise resulted in a typology of semantic interoperability conflicts that may occur when providing cross-border e-Government services (Peristeras, V., Loutas, N., Goudos, S., & Tarabanis, K., 2008).

In V. Peristeras et al. (2008), we examine how the *data-level* and the *schema-level* can affect different elements in the cross-border e-Government services domain. In particular, according to this analysis, the core service concepts that are usually involved in such conflicts are: evidences,

evidence placeholders, which are either used as service input or produced as service output, service preconditions, service effects and clients.

In the remainder of this section we first introduce the use case that will guide us through the rest of this article and then we provide an overview of the conflicts that appear in this use case.

The use case is based on the "Change of Residence" public service, which is provided by all Italian municipalities. This public service has to be executed every time a citizen is moving to an Italian city. "Change of Residence" is considered to have a cross-border aspect either when the applicant is not an Italian citizen or regardless her/his nationality when his/her former city of residence was not in Italy.

In our use case, a Belgian citizen, currently living in Brussels, needs to move with his family to Turin due to professional reasons. As soon as the Belgian family moves to Turin, they have to register their new residence address. To do so, they have to execute the proper "Change of Residence" public service, which is provided by the municipality of Turin. This use case is also one of the showcases of the SemanticGov project and has been studied there in detail.

During the analysis that took place before designing the showcase, a set of data-level and schema-level conflicts, like the ones provided by the typology of semantic interoperability conflicts proposed in V. Peristeras et al. (2008), were identified. These conflicts are summarized in Table 1 and will be further analyzed and resolved in the rest of this article (Section *Solving Semantic Interoperability Conflicts for Cross-Border e-Government Services* and Section *Resolving the Semantic Interoperability Conflicts*).

Apart from the use case presented in the article, the authors have also studied several other cross-border e-Government services (i.e. the case of a Bulgarian citizen that want to use the Greek naturalization service, the case of a German citizen that want to issue a driving license in Ireland etc.) before defining their approach.

SOLVING SEMANTIC INTEROPERABILITY CONFLICTS FOR CROSS- BORDER E-GOVERNMENT SERVICES

This section shows how semantic interoperability conflicts in cross-boarder e-Government services can be solved by adopting semantic technologies. In a semantic environment all the relevant PA domain notions and the concepts have to be described by ontologies. From our analysis we concluded that in most of the cases the semantic interoperability conflicts are the result of differences in the ontologies modeling the different PAs.

For the mediation between these different models (i.e. different ontologies), our focus is on providing techniques and solutions for seamless transformation of instances expressed in terms of one ontology (source ontology) to terms and instances expressed in another ontology (target ontology). This transformation is necessary since different member states use in an explicit or implicit way different ontologies to model their information space. In the pan-European context, EU Member States (MS) need to cooperate to provide seamless cross-border e-Government services i.e. the Greek PA may implement a cross-border e-Government service for European businesses

that wish to open a new subsidiary in Greece. Consequently information exchange between different MS takes place. It is during these information exchanges that semantic interoperability conflicts are raised.

As already discussed, all the examples are based on WSMO and GEA and they are modeled using WSML (de Bruijn, J., et al., 2005); (Lausen, H., de Bruijn, J., Polleres, A., & Fensel, D., 2005). The ontology mappings are expressed in the Abstract Mapping Language proposed in F. Scharffe and J. de Bruijn, J. (2005) and for which a brief overview is given in the next section.

The Abstract Mapping Language

When different ontologies are used to model identical or overlapping domains, it is often the case that various aspects of these domains are captured in a different or even conflicting manner. Consequently, when later on information has to be exchanged between these domains, heterogeneity problems can rise and hamper the communication.

One of the most common techniques for resolving the heterogeneity problems is to create an *alignment* between these ontologies that formally specifies how they relate. An alignment normally consists of a set of *mappings* where a mapping is either a unidirectional or bidirectional statement that usually captures the semantic relationships existing between the entities that are part of these ontologies (Mocan, A., Cimpian, E., & Kerrigan, M., 2006). Mappings can be expressed either directly in an ontology representation language (e.g. as logical statements) or in specialized mapping language (Euzenat, J., Scharffe, F., Serafini, L., 2006; Scharffe, F., et al., 2005). In the first case the mappings can be directly seen and used as mapping rules (i.e. they can be evaluated in a reasoning engine), while in the second case grounding has to be applied to the mappings in order to obtain rules in a concrete language.

We chose to express the mappings in the Abstract Mapping Language proposed in F. Scharffe et al. (2005) and elaborated in J. Euzenat et al. (2006), because it does not commit to any existing ontology representation language. Later, formal semantics has to be associated with it and the mappings have to be grounded to a concrete language (e.g. WSML or F-Logic [Kifer, J., et al., 2005]). In the current implementation a grounding to a restricted WSML-Rule variant is used, such as no unsafe rules and no recursive function symbols are allowed. As a consequence, the reasoning on the resulting set of WSML rules can be done under the same computational properties as for any Datalog program.

The allowed mapping language statements are briefly described below:

- classMapping specifies mappings between classes in the source and the target ontologies. Such a statement can be restricted by class conditions (attributeValueConditions, attributeTypeConditions, attributeOccurenceConditions)

The attributeValueCondition specifies a constraint over the values of a certain attribute. The relationship between the attribute and values is specified by a comparator as defined in M. Dean et al. (2004). The attributeTypeCondition indicates the type (range) a given attribute should have, while attributeOccurenceCondition only imposes that a given attribute has to be present in the source or the target instance data for that mapping to hold.

- attributeMapping specifies mappings between attributes. Such statements can appear inside with or outside classMapping and can be conditioned by attribute conditions (valueConditions, typeConditions).

The attributeConditions are similar to the classConditions, with the difference that the first are applied on attributes, while the second are applied on classes. They specify the value or the type a certain attribute should have in order for the mapping to hold.

- classAttributeMapping specifies mappings between a class and an attribute (or the other way around).

Since this type of mappings involves classes as well as attributes, both classCondition and attributeCondition are allowed.

- instanceMapping states a mapping between two individuals, one from the source and the other from the target.

In order to increase the expressiveness of the mapping language, classExpr can be used instead of simple classes and attributeExpr instead of attributes in al the above described mappings. That is, the classExpr and attributeExpr can be class identifiers or attribute identifiers, respectively, as well as more complex expressions on these identifiers, e.g. conjunctions, disjunction, negation, etc. The class and attribute identifiers take the form of the identifiers used in the given ontology languages the abstract mapping language is grounded to. For example, if there are WSML ontologies to be mapped, then these identifiers are IRIs (de Bruijn, J., et al., 2005). The logicalExpressions represent extra refinements that can be applied to particular mappings.

The interpretation and the execution of such mappings and mapping rules between the different ontologies takes place in a specialized component of the SemanticGov architecture, which will be further referred to as the *Run-time Data Mediator Engine* or simply the *Data Mediator.* Further details on this component can be found in Section *Data Mediation Solution.*

Data Level Conflicts

Data level conflicts occur when multiple representations and interpretations of similar data

Listing 2. Defining person, human and adult in the source ontology O1 and in the target ontology O_2

Ontology O_1	Ontology O_2
concept person name **ofType** _string age **ofType** _integer **concept** adult **subConceptOf** person **axiom** AdultDefinition **definedBy** ?x **memberOf** Adult:- ?x[age **hasValue** ?y] **memberOf** person and ?y>=17.	**concept** human name **ofType** _string age **ofType** _integer ageCategory **ofType** AgeCategory **concept** AgeCategory **instance** adult **memberOf** AgeCategory **axiom** AdultConstraint **definedBy** !- ?x[ageCategory **hasValue** adult] **memberOf** human and ?x[age **hasValue** ?y] and ?y < 18.

are used in the domain models that need to be mapped. The following types of data conflicts are described in this section: *data value conflicts, data representation conflicts, data unit conflicts,* and *data precision conflicts.*

Data Value Conflicts

Such conflicts appear when identical notions or terms have different meaning in different ontologies.

Listing 2 defines an "adult" in O_1 by subclassing the concept person and defining the new concept adult through an axiom[5]. It also shows how "adult" could be modeled in the ontology O_2 by adding a special attribute to the concept human and by constraining the values of these attribute. The axiom AdultConstraint triggers a constraint violation if an instance of human is created having the attribute age younger than 18 and the value of the attribute ageCategory populated with the instance adult. Both ontologies define the notion of adult but it has different meaning: in O_1 an adult is a person older than 17 while in ontology O_2 adult is an age category that identifies a human older than 18.

The data value conflicts manifest themselves in several ways in the context of PA domain. For each of these cases specialized solutions are required in order to eliminate the conflict. The following subsections discuss both the PA aspect and the required resolution.

Differences in Evidence Domains Caused by the Multiple Representations and Interpretations of Similar Evidence

The example in Listing 2 depicts the situation where similar evidences (i.e. a person or a human is an adult) are differently interpreted from one domain to another. If equivalences have to be established between evidence placeholders referring to the notion of adult mappings have to be created between the semantic models that capture these two definitions of adult (i.e. between the concept of person in ontology O_1 and the concept of human in the ontology O_2).

Listing 3 depicts a set of mappings between the ontologies O_1 and O_2 that are able to capture the differences in the adult definitions in the two ontologies.

From lines 1 to 8 there are three bidirectional mappings that express the semantic relations between person and human: they both have a name and an age. At Lines 10 to 12 we have a unidirectional rule that specifies that a human is a special type of person, an adult, if the age of that human is higher than 17. Because adult is a sub-concept of person, based on the inheritance principles, the previous two mappings assures that the name and the age of an adult are correctly related with those of the human.

The Data Mediator part of the Semantic Gateway (introduced in Section *Background*) has to

Listing 3. Mappings between person and human resolving the adult conflict

```
0.    Mapping(o1o2o1#1
1.      classMapping(two-way o1#person o2#human))
2.    Mapping(o1o2o1#2
3.      attributeMapping(two-way o1#person.name o2#human.name))
4.    Mapping(o1o2o1#3
5.      attributeMapping(two-way o1#person.age o2#human.age))
6.    Mapping(o2o1#1
7.      classMapping(one-way o2#human o1#adult)
8.      attributeValueCondition(o2#human.age >=17))
9.    Mapping(o1o2#1
10.     attributeMapping(one-way o1#person.age o2#human.ageCategory)
11.     attributeValueCondition(o1#person.age >= 18)
12.     attributeValueCondition(o2#human.ageCategory = adult))
```

be able to apply these mappings in order to solve this type of conflicts whenever data is exchanged between different member states.

Differences in Preconditions Domains Caused by the Multiple Representations and Interpretations of Similar Preconditions

Each Goal and Web service is semantically described in terms of the ontology that models that particular domain. Across domains, data value conflicts as the ones described in Table 1 may appear. The preconditions are checked either by the discovery engine to match potential services compatible with the specified Goal or by the invocation engine to actually invoke the service.

As depicted in Figure 3, when a discovery process involving a different MS is triggered (the arrow D1), elements of the source domain used in describing the Goal precondition need to be translated to the corresponding ontological entities in the target domain for enabling the matchmaking between the Goal and Web service. The data mediator has the role to make available the necessary mappings and mapping rules to the discovery engine (which otherwise would fail in finding the right matching services). That is, the precondition of the Goal coming form the source domain, together with the mapping rules from the Data Mediator (arrow D2.a) are loaded into

the Discovery Engine. The preconditions of each candidate Web services from the target domain will be loaded into the Discovery Engine (arrow D2.b), in order to check if the service is a match for the source Goal.

Thanks to the process illustrated above, data value conflicts occurring during service discovery are handled in the same manner as presented in the previous case. Figure 2 also depicts the usage of the Data Mediator for the service invocation task: the Goal holder sends the data to the invocation engine; the data is transformed in terms of the target domain by the mediator and only then sent to the invoked Web service (arrows I1, I2 and I3).

Differences in Effect Domains Caused by the Multiple Representations and Interpretations of Similar Effects

Not only preconditions maybe affected by data conflicts issues but, if a Goal and a Service are represented using two different domain models, their effects can affected as well.

To demonstrate such a case, we use an example from a different SemanticGov use case scenario. Listing 4 shows two different models of a driving license: the Irish driving license (which is divided in two different categories, temporary and permanent) and the German driver license (which

Figure 3. Overview of the process behind the mediated discovery

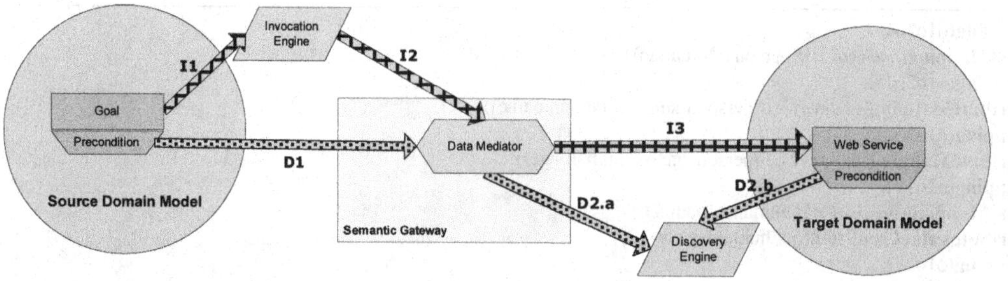

Listing 4. Definition of the Irish and German driving license in the ontology O1 and O2

Ontology O$_1$	Ontology O$_2$
concept IrishDrivingLicense ownerName **ofType** _string type **ofType** IDLType **instance** permanent **memberOf** IDLType **instance** temporary **memberOf** IDLType **concept** person name **ofType** _string age **ofType** _integer hasDrivingLicense **ofType** IrishDrivingLicense **relation** canDrive(**ofType** person, **ofType** _boolean) **axiom** whoCanDrive **definedBy** canDrive(?x, _boolean("true")):- ?x[hasDrivingLicense **hasValue** _#] **memberOf** person.	**concept** human name **ofType** _string age **ofType** _integer ageCategory **ofType** AgeCategory drivingLicense **ofType** GermanDrivingLicense **concept** GermanDrivingLicense ownerName **ofType** _string **relation** canDrive(**ofType** person, **ofType** _boolean) **axiom** whoCanDrive **definedBy** canDrive(?x, _boolean("true")):- ?x[drivingLicense **hasValue** _#] **memberOf** human.

is always permanent and does not distinguish between the previous two categories).

A PA service that issues driving licenses would have as an outcome in both countries the physical driving license card (output) and the permission and ability of the applicant to drive a car (effect). The ability to drive a car is modeled by an instance of the relation canDrive. Instances of this relation are produced either directly as the effect of the invocation of the driving license-issuing service or by an axiom in the form of whoCanDrive axiom, which infers them based on extra knowledge present in the model.

In such a situation a citizen that obtains a temporary driving license in Ireland will have the right to drive in Ireland but he/she is not entitled to drive in Germany. Such a conflict can be resolved by creating mappings stating that a German driving

license corresponds only to the permanent Irish driving license and other way around. Listing 5 depicts such mappings.

Lines 10-11 show a condition specifying that an IrishDrivingLicense is mapped to a German-DrivingLicense only if its type is permanent. Hence if the above condition does not hold, for any human instance in O$_2$ that has to be created (based on instance of person from O$_1$) there is no driving license associated with it. As such, even if an individual obtains a temporary driving license in Ireland it will not be transferred to the German model and he/she will not be allowed to drive in Germany (according to the whoCanDrive axiom).

Listing 5. Mappings between person and human resolving the driving licenses conflicts

```
0. Mapping(o1o2o1#4
1. aa classMapping(two-way o1#person o2#human))
2. Mapping(o1o2o1#5
3. attributeMapping(two-way o1#person.hasDrivingLicense o2#human. drivingLicense))
4. Mapping(o1o2o1#6
5. classMapping(two-way o1#IrishDrivingLicense o2#GermanDrivingLicense)
6. attributeValueCondition(o1#IrishDrivingLicense.type
7. = permanent))
8. Mapping(o1o2o1#7
9. attributeMapping(two-way o1#IrishDrivingLicense.ownerName o2#GermanDrivingLicense.ownerName))
```

Data Representation Conflicts

Data representation conflicts occur when two semantically equivalent data fragments are represented in a different way. For example a date in the extended format in the Italian PA domain can be represented by the following string: "4 Ottobre 1980", while in the short format in any European PA domain it would be 1980-10-04 (according to the standard EN 28601). This kind of conversions requires either the use of specialized data manipulation functions within the reasoning environment or the access to external services that can apply the conversion after the reasoning occurred.

Since the Data Mediator relies on a generic abstract mapping language that is not bounded to any specific runtime reasoning and mediation, the second solution is preferable. In fact, even specific reasoners that could be used after the abstract mapping language is grounded to a concrete language normally support only a limited number of data manipulation functions. The use of external services for the data manipulation after the actual reasoning task offers a higher flexibility and it is independent of the reasoning infrastructure.

The generic support for specifying the call to a service within the grounded mapping rules is obtained by assigning to the target attribute as a value the service call and the appropriate parameters. This is possible thanks to the automatic extension of the supported type of the attribute to be manipulated. The attribute type is extended to support also instances of the ServiceCall concept,

which is a concept used to model calls to data manipulation services. When an instance of this concept is resolved to a concrete service call and the service is eventually invoked, the final value is converted back to initial data type supported by the attribute. For example the instances of ServiceCall can be built as instances without any attribute values but with identifiers constructed out of function symbols of the form serviceId($param_1$, $param_2$, …, $param_n$).

Exactly as the data value conflicts, the data representation conflicts can manifest themselves in different forms in the PA domain, as exemplified in the following subsections.

Differences in Evidence Domain Caused by Multiple Representation of Similar Evidence

This kind of differences can be easily resolved with the technique described above. For example, we can consider the Italian Identity Card, where the date of birth of a person is specified in the extended format (e.g., "4 Ottobre 1980") and this evidence is needed by another European PA, where the standard short date format is used, for example in the form "04/10/1980". Fragments of the two concepts for the two different member states are depicted in Listing 6.

Listing 7 reports an example rule that specifies the mapping between the Italian (ontology O_1) and Belgian PA domain (ontology O_2).

Listing 6. Definition of the Italian and the Belgian Identity Card in the ontology O1 and O2

Ontology O₁	Ontology O₂
concept IdentityCard name **ofType (1 1)** _string … birthdate **ofType (1 1)** _string	concept IdentityCard name **ofType (1 1)** _string … birthdate **ofType (1 1)** _date

Listing 7. Mapping between the source ontology O1 and in the target ontology O2

```
1 Mapping(itbe#1
2 classMapping(one-way it#IdentityCard be#IdentityCard))
3 Mapping(itbe#2
4 attributeMapping(two-way it#IdentityCard.name be#IdentityCard.name))
5 Mapping(itbe#3
6 attributeMapping(one-way
7 it#IdentityCard.birthdate be#IdentityCard.birthdate)
8 attributeValueCondition(be#IdentityCard.birthdate =
9 "http://www.semanticgov.org/services/dateconversion"))
```

Listing 8. Example of fragment from the source ontology O1

```
1   instance MarioIdentityCard memberOf it#IdentityCard
2   name hasValue "Mario"
3   …
4      birthdate hasValue "4 Ottobre 1980"
```

An example of an instance from the original domain is reported in Listing 8.

The resolution of this conflict takes place in two steps: first the Run-time Data Mediator Engine is used as usually to perform the transformation of the source instances in target instances. The only difference appears in the values of the attributes that have to be computed by external services calls (see lines 4-5 in Listing 9).

During the data mediation an instance of ServiceCall is assigned as value to the attribute birthdate. According to the original model, the attribute birthdate expects a *date* as value, so in order to avoid constraints violation[6] the ServiceCall's instance has to be declared of type *date* as well (lines 7-8 in Listing 9). Finally, the data mediation runtime checks the reasoning output to see if any external service invocation is needed to complete the mediation from the source ontology to the target ontology.

Differences in Preconditions Domains Caused By Multiple Representations of Similar Preconditions

In our approach based on WSMO, the requester's needs are formalized as a Goal. Each Goal is defined by a set of elements such as the requested capability (which contains preconditions, postconditions, assumptions and effects) and/or the requested interfaces. This type of conflict appears when the Goal's preconditions are expressed according to the local PA domain model of the requester but they have to be checked against descriptions defined in terms of a different PA domain model. In our approach, this issue is solved by converting evidences from the representation that conforms with the original domain into a representation according to the target domain. As such, the data representation conflicts between the different preconditions are solved by actually

Listing 9. Output of the first step of the data mediation process for the input in Listing 8

```
1 instance MarioIdentityCard memberOf be#IdentityCard
2 name hasValue "Mario"
3 …
4 birthdate hasValue
5 http://www.semanticgov.org/services/dateconversion("4 Ottobre 1980")
6
7 instancehttp://www.semanticgov.org/services/dateconversion("4 Ottobre 1980") memberOf 8 {_date, ServiceCall}
```

Listing 10. Final result of the data mediation process

```
1  instance MarioIdentityCard memberOf be#IdentityCard
2  name hasValue "Mario"
3  …
4     birthdate hasValue _date("1980-10-04")
```

converting the input to the preconditions in the expected data format. The same strategy is also applied to postconditions and effects.

Data Unit Conflicts

Data unit conflicts occur when two different member states adopt different unit of measures. From a technical point of view this conflict is solved exactly as the data representation conflicts (see Section *Data Representation Conflicts*). A *Quantity* concept can be modeled in the ontology as having two attributes *amount* and *unitOfMeasure*. A value transformation service can be used as well to transform the *amount* value to the value corresponding to the target unit of measure.

Data Precision Conflicts

Data precisions conflicts arise often among different members states evidences because of the different legislations. For example, the Belgian law identifies 13 different types of marital statuses, so its registry service provides information according to these types. In the same time, the Italian legislation specifies only 4 types of marital statuses. As a consequence, a conflict occurs when an Italian PA needs to access information about the marital status of a person published by the Belgian registry.

From a technical point of view this issue is solved by creating at design time the mapping rules from the 13 Belgian types to the 4 Italian ones (*m:n mapping*). The created rules are then used by the runtime mediation component to convert any incoming instance of Belgian marital status to the correspondent Italian marital status. The mappings between the two fragments of ontologies in Listing 11 are depicted in Listing 12.

It is important to note that the mapping between instance _40 and _4 is bidirectional while the mapping between _41 and _4 is only from the Belgian domain to the Italian one. This implies that going from the Italian domain to the Belgian one _4 will be always transformed to _40. In general, when dealing with different levels of granularity, the mappings from the course grained model to the finer grained model might require additional knowledge in order to produce the appropriate results. As such, mappings as those presented in Listing 12 might need to be extended to include additional conditions on data from other parts of the target model in order to set up the right semantic relationships between the two domains.

Listing 11. Description of the Belgian and Italian MaritalStatus in ontologies O1 and O2

Ontology O₁	Ontology O₂
concept MaritalStatus hasMaritalStatusCode **ofType** MaritalStatusCode hasMaritalStatusDescription **ofType** MaritalStatusDescription **concept** MaritalStatusCode **instance** _10 **memberOf** MaritalStatusCode **instance** _20 **memberOf** MaritalStatusCode **instance** _25 **memberOf** MaritalStatusCode **instance** _26 **memberOf** MaritalStatusCode **instance** _30 **memberOf** MaritalStatusCode ...	concept MaritalStatus hasMaritalStatusCode **ofType** MaritalStatusCode hasMaritalStatusDescription **ofType** MaritalStatusDescription **concept** MaritalStatusCode **instance** _1 **memberOf** MaritalStatusCode **instance** _2 **memberOf** MaritalStatusCode **instance** _3 **memberOf** MaritalStatusCode **instance** _4 **memberOf** MaritalStatusCode

Listing 12. Mapping between the O1 and O2 ontology

```
 1 Mapping(beit#11
 2 classMapping(two-way be#MaritalStatus it#MaritalStatus))
 3 Mapping(beit#12
 4 attributeMapping(two-way be#MaritalStatus.hasMaritalStatusCode
 5 it#MaritalStatus.hasMaritalStatusCode)
 6 attributeValueCondition(be#MaritalStatus.hasMaritalStatusCode = _10)
 7 attributeValueCondition(it#MaritalStatus.hasMaritalStatusCode = _1))
 8 ...
 9 Mapping(beit#15
10 attributeMapping(two-way be#MaritalStatus.hasMaritalStatusCode
11 it#MaritalStatus.hasMaritalStatusCode)
12 attributeValueCondition(be#MaritalStatus.hasMaritalStatusCode = _40)
13 attributeValueCondition(it#MaritalStatus.hasMaritalStatusCode = _4))
14 Mapping(beit#16
15 attributeMapping(one-way be#MaritalStatus.hasMaritalStatusCode
16 it#MaritalStatus.hasMaritalStatusCode)
17 attributeValueCondition(be#MaritalStatus.hasMaritalStatusCode = _41)
18 attributeValueCondition(it#MaritalStatus.hasMaritalStatusCode = _4))
```

Schema-Level Conflicts

Schema level conflicts involve differences at the structural level in the domain models to be mapped. The schema level conflicts can be divided in several categories: *naming conflicts, entity identifier conflicts, schema-isomorphism conflicts, generalization conflicts* and *aggregation conflicts*.

Naming Conflicts

Naming conflicts arise when similar concepts are labeled in a different way or different concepts are labeled in a similar way (i.e. terms that in different languages, and hence in different member states, have similar spelling but different meaning). In the PA domain, such conflicts can take the following forms:

Naming Conflicts in Service Providers

This issue is hidden by the discovery component, which makes possible to avoid an incorrect naming for a service or its provider to lead to an incorrect discovery or service invocation. This is achieved by matching Goals to services accord-

Listing 13. Description of the person concept in two ontologies without the namespace expansion

Ontology O₁	Ontology O₂
namespace {"http://semantic-gov.org/o1#"} **ontology** Ontology1 **concept** Person hasName **ofType (1 1)** _string hasSurname **ofType (1 1)** _string	**namespace** {"http://semantic-gov.org/o2#"} **ontology** Ontology2 **concept** Person hasName **ofType (1 1)** _string 　hasSurname **ofType (1 1)** _string

Listing 14. Description of the person concept in two ontologies with the namespace expansion

Ontology O₁	Ontology O₂
ontologyhttp://semantic-gov.org/o1#Ontology1 **concept**http://semantic-gov.org/o1#Person http://semantic-gov.org/o1#hasName **ofType** _string http://semantic-gov.org/o1#hasSurname **ofType** _string	**ontology**http://semantic-gov.org/o2#Ontology2 **concept**http://semantic-gov.org/o2#Person http://semantic-gov.org/o2#hasName **ofType** _string 　http://semantic-gov.org/o2#hasSurname**ofType** _string

ing to preconditions and postcondition. Naming conflicts at the level of the conditions on evidences are properly solved by creating mapping rules between the ontologies modeling the different member state domains.

Naming Conflicts in Evidence Placeholders

This issue is solved by creating the correct mapping between concepts representing evidence placeholders in the source and in the target ontology. It is important to clarify that two concepts, or instances having the same label and belonging to two different ontologies, cannot trigger any conflict unless incorrectly mapped. Actually, due to the fact that concepts are not only identified by their labels but also by the namespace of the ontology, they cannot be interpreted to be "similar" by a reasoner, unless differently stated by a mapping rule.

Listing 13 and Listing 14 better clarify the process of naming expansion that occurs within reasoners.

Entity Identifier Conflict

Entity identifier conflicts may appear when in different member states two different identifiers identify similar entities. This kind of conflicts cannot always be solved by simple data mediation or by generating random identifiers due to the fact that such identifier have to be generated by a legal authority (notice that in this context we are not talking about identifiers as, for example, primary keys in a database table).

In many European countries people are identified with a different mechanism, and this can raise many entity identifier conflicts when a person is moving from one country to another. Let us consider the Italian Fiscal Code, which is the unique identifier of a person according to the Italian law. This identifier is created automatically at the birth of every Italian citizen and is used for various purposes (e.g. paying taxes). Hence, to access a tax paying service in Italy everyone (even foreigners working in Italy) has to provide as evidence her Fiscal Code. Foreign people that do not have a Fiscal Code have to apply for it before paying taxes.

Listing 15. Description of the IDCard in two different ontologies

Ontology O₁	Ontology O₂
concept IDcard1 hasName **ofType (1 1)** _string hasSurname **ofType (1 1)** _string hasFatherName **ofType (1 1)** _string hasMotherName **ofType (1 1)** _string hasBirthDate **ofType (1 1)** date	**concept** IDCard2 hasName **ofType (1 1)** _string hasSurname **ofType (1 1)** _string hasFatherName **ofType (1 1)** _string hasMotherName **ofType (1 1)** _string hasBirthDate **ofType (1 1)** date hasAddress **ofType (1 1)** _string hasNationality **ofType (1 1)** _string

These conflicts can be solved by using a service that actually creates a real and valid instance of the missing identifier (such a service would be most probably offered by the Italian Finance Ministry). In our context this issue is solved by exploiting the composition capabilities of the SemanticGov architecture and creating a composed service specific for foreigners. Such service, first invokes a specific service to obtain a Fiscal Code and, once obtained, uses it to invoke the tax payment service. The discovery engine matches the right service to the foreign citizen based on whether the Fiscal Code has been provided as input or not.

However, there are simpler cases that can be solved by creating rules that specifies that two entities are the same if certain conditions holds. Such cases mainly occur when the set of identifiers for a given entity is a discrete set both in the source and in the target domain (e.g. country codes).

Schema-Isomorphism Conflicts

These conflicts occur when different attributes are used to describe semantically equivalent concepts. An example can be seen in Listing 2 and in Listing 4; however this kind of conflicts can take multiple forms. For example, consider the ID card in Italy (ontology O₁) and Belgium (ontology O₂), presented in Listing 15: the information captured by the concept IDCard2 in ontology O₂ is richer than the corresponding concept IDCard1 in ontology O₁ where hasAddress and hasNationality are not present.

An important aspect regarding this conflict is the completeness of the information captured by the source model in respect with the target model and the other way around. As a consequence we can distinguish two cases where interoperability has to be achieved:

a. **The source ontology element covers more information than the target ontology element**. This means that there is information in the source ontology that cannot be "understood" by the target party (i.e., it is useless for the target). As such, interoperability can be achieved by discarding the extra information, simply by not linking this extra information with elements from the target.

b. **The source ontology element covers less information than the target ontology element**. This is one of the interoperability conflicts that hamper the automation degree of the mediation solution. As the source ontology does not capture the extra information required by the target (i.e., the source does not "understand" this information), the source does not have any means to produce that information. There are two approaches to resolve this type of conflict:

1. **Default values generation**. The Semantic Gateway, or the Data Mediator, assumes the responsibility to fill the empty slots with default values. In some situation this task can

Listing 16. Generalization conflict in defining the male and female

Ontology O$_1$	Ontology O$_2$

concept person
  name **ofType** _string
  age **ofType** _integer
  hasGender **ofType** gender
  hasChild **ofType** person
concept gender
  value **ofType** _string
instance male **memberOf** gender
  value **hasValue** "male"
instance female **memberOf** gender
  value **hasValue** "female"
concept birthCertificate
  owner **ofType** person
  birthDate **ofType** _date
  placeOfBirth **ofType** _string
  hasMother **ofType** person
  hasFather **ofType** person
	concept human
	  name **ofType** _string
	  age **ofType** _integer
	
	concept man **subConceptOf** human
	concept woman **subConceptOf** human
	concept birthCertificate
	  owner **ofType** person
	  birthDate **ofType** _date
	  placeOfBirth **ofType** _string
	concept familyCertificate
	  owner **ofType** human
	  hasMother **ofType** woman
	  hasFather **ofType** man

be performed by the target domain as well: e.g., rules in the target ontology allow, when values are not provided for some attributes, to assign them default values. The advantage of this technique is that it can be automatically applied. The disadvantage is that this method fails when the reason for the missing information from the source is not because it is totally meaningless in the source domain but because the model is incomplete or faulty. In this situation, a different value and not the default one should be used.

2. **Additional interactions with the requester.** This method involves the participation of the requester (in the PA domain the citizen) in providing the missing information. Such interactions can be carried on at the portal level and the client can directly fill the required information as specified in the target model. The disadvantage in this case is that the clients needs to understand the information that is required from their side – the portal cannot offer such support since its (source) model

is less expressive that the one of the target (where the conflict originates). The advantage is that the information eventually provided in this way is guaranteed to be correct.

Generalization Conflicts

Generalization conflicts occur when two similar concepts are defined using a different model in two different member states.

Generalization Conflicts in Evidence Placeholders

For example two different member states may model the information for a birth certificate with different aggregation: that is, in the first member the state the birth certificate is only one document (BirthCertificate) while in the second member state the same evidences are captured by more than one documents (BirthCertificate and the FamilyCertificate).

Listing 16 shows another example, the definition of genders in O$_1$ by using a special attribute of the person concept and populating it with one of the two allowed values, male and female, while

Listing 17. Mappings resolving the generalization conflicts in O1 and O2

```
1   Mapping(o1o2o1#1
2   classMapping(two-way o1#person o2#human))
3   Mapping(o1o2o1#7
4   classMapping(two-way o1#person o2#man)
5   attributeValueCondition(o1#person.hasGender = male))
6   Mapping(o1o2o1#7
7   classMapping(two-way o1#person o2#woman)
8   attributeValueCondition(o1#person.hasGender = female))
9   Mapping(o1o2o1#8
10  classMapping(two-way o1#birthCertificate o2#birthCertificate))
11  Mapping(o1o2o1#9
12  attributeMapping(two-way o1#birthCertificate.owner o2#birthCertificate.owner))
13  Mapping(o1o2o1#10
14  attributeMapping(two-way o1#birthCertificate.birthDate o2#birthCertificate.birthDate))
15  Mapping(o1o2o1#11
16  attributeMapping(two-way o1#birthCertificate.placeOfBirth o2#birthCertificate.placeOfBirth))
17  Mapping(o1o2o1#12
18  classMapping(two-way o1#birthCertificate o2#familyCertificate))
19  Mapping(o1o2o1#13
20  attributeMapping(two-way o1#birthCertificate.hasMother o2#familyCertificate.hasMother))
21  Mapping(o1o2o1#14
22  attributeMapping(two-way o1#birthCertificate.hasFather o2#familyCertificate.hasFather))
23
24
25
26
27
```

in ontology O_2, man and woman are subclasses of the human concept.

Listing 17 shows the mappings that assure the right correspondences between the O_1 and O_2 ontologies.

Generalization Conflicts in Service Providers

The description details of service providers are generally considered and modeled as non-functional properties (i.e., exactly who provides the service does not directly influences its capability). The Discovery engine is responsible to analyze not only the non-functional properties of the services (e.g., provider) but also the functional descriptions of the services in order to decide which are the suitable services for a given Goal. In fact, the analyzes of the functional descriptions determines if the service is a match at all for the requester need while the non-functional properties are mostly analyzed to determine the most suited service out of the discovered candidates.

Generalization Conflicts in Clients

Listing 16 depicts an example of this conflict: in O_1 we have one single concept defining a person while in O_2 the human has to sub-classes, man and woman. In Listing 17 the mappings from lines 1 to 16 (together with the inheritance principles) show how this conflict can be resolved.

Aggregation Conflicts

Aggregation conflicts can be of two types: (i) semantically related concepts are aggregated in different hierarchical structures or (ii) a single data value of the source entity corresponds to more data values of the target entity. The first class of aggregation conflicts can be solved by creating the proper mapping rules so as to convert the source hierarchical structure to the target one. Listing 18 depicts an example.

The mapping definitions reported in Listing 19 exemplify how the aforementioned problem can be adressed.

Listing 18. Description of the Person concept in two domains with a different aggregation level

Ontology O$_1$	Ontology O$_2$
concept Person hasName **ofType (1 1)** _string hasSurname **ofType (1 1)** _string hasTelephone **ofType (O *)** _string hasEmail **ofType (O *)** _string	**concept** Person hasName **ofType (1 1)** _string 　hasSurname **ofType (1 1)** _string 　hasContacts **ofType (1 1)** contactDetails 　**concept** contactDetails telephone **ofType (O *)** _string email **ofType (O *)** _string

Listing 19. Mapping between the ontology O1 and O2

```
 1 Mapping(o1o2#1
 2 classMapping(two-way o1#Person o2#Person))
 3 Mapping(o1o2#2
 4 attributeMapping(two-way
 5 o1#Person.hasName o2#Person.hasName))
 6 Mapping(o1o2#3
 7 attributeMapping(two-way
 8 o1#Person.hasSurname o2#Person.hasSurname))
 9 Mapping(o1o2#4
10 classMapping(two-way
11 o1#Person o2#contactDetails))
12 Mapping(o1o2#5
13 classAttributeMapping(one-way
14 o1#Person o2#Person.hasContacts))
15 Mapping(o1o2#6
16 attributeMapping(two-way
17 o1#Person.hasTelephone o2#contactDetails.hasTelephone))
18 Mapping(o1o2#7
19 attributeMapping(two-way
20 o1#Person.hasTelephone o2#contactDetails.hasTelephone))
```

The semantics of the mapping from lines 9 to 11 is that there is information in the concept Person from O$_1$ that is related with information from the contactDetails concept from O$_2$. The mappings from lines 12 to 14 state that the information from o1#Person that is related with the information from o2#contactDetails is referred from the upper level (from o2#Person) by using the attribute hasContacts from o2#Person.

The second class of conflicts requires data manipulation like in the case of data representation conflicts and data unit conflicts. For example, if in a MS an evidence placeholder contains one field for the name and one for the surname, and in another MS the same evidence placeholders contains only the full name as a unique field comprising of the name and surname (see Listing 20), the mediation requires the use of a service able to concatenate strings (in the direction of ontology O$_1$ to ontology O$_2$) and a service able to split strings (in the direction of ontology O$_2$ to ontology O$_1$).

MEDIATION SERVICES AND SOLUTIONS: IMPLEMENTATION EXPERIENCE

This section presents our approach for solving the semantic interoperability conflicts described so far. It gives an overview on the data mediation solution developed in SemanticGov, describing both the design-and run-time support which is provided by the tool. It also presents several con-

Listing 20. Description of the BirthCertficate concept in two domains with data values aggregated in a different way

Ontology O$_1$	Ontology O$_2$
concept BirthCertificate hasName **ofType (1 1)** _string hasSurname **ofType (1 1)** _string	**concept** BirthCertificate hasFullName **ofType (1 1)** _string

crete examples of semantic conflicts resolution from our use case scenario.

Data Mediation Solution

Our solution has two main parts: a) the Ontology Mapping Tool, which is a tool that is used at design-time and b) the Run-time Data Mediator Engine which is a component in the SemanticGov architecture. The following subsections describe these two parts.

Ontology Mapping Tool

To support the design phase we have developed the Ontology Mapping Tool (OMT) as an Eclipse plug-in for the Web Service Modeling Toolkit (WSMT)[7] (Kerrigan, M., Mocan, A., Tanler, M., & Fensel, D., 2007), an integrated environment for ontology creation, visualization and mapping. Currently the only ontological framework supported is WSMO but by providing the appropriate wrappers different ontology languages could be supported as well[8]. It offers different ways of browsing the ontologies using *perspectives* and allows the domain expert to create mappings between two ontologies (source and target) and to store them in a persistent mapping storage. It also supports the specification of external transformation services as described in Section *Data Representation Conflicts*.

Perspectives. The graphical viewpoint adopted to visualize the source and the target ontologies is important to simplify the design of mappings according to their type. These viewpoints are called perspectives and by switching between combina-

tions of these perspectives on the source and the target ontologies, certain types of mappings can be created using only one simple operation, *map*, combined with mechanisms for ontology traversal and contextualized visualization strategies.

A perspective contains a subset of the ontology's entities (e.g. concepts, attributes, relations, and instances) and the relationships between them. Usually the perspective used for browsing the source ontology (source perspective) and the perspective used for browsing the target ontology (target perspective) are of the same type, but there could be cases when different types of perspectives are used. In each of the perspectives there is a predefined number of roles the ontology entities can have. In general, particular roles are fulfilled by different ontology entities in different perspectives and the algorithms (e.g. the decomposition or the suggestions making algorithms) refer to roles rather than to ontology entities.

The roles that can be identified in a perspective are: *Compound Item*, *Primitive Item*, and *Description Item*. A *Compound Item* has at least one description associated with it while a *Primitive Item* does not have any description associated. A *Description Item* offers more information about the Compound Item it describes and usually links it with other Compound or Primitive Items. By this, the *Successor* of a Description Item is defined as the Compound or Primitive Item it links to. More details about perspectives as well as a formal model that governs their main principles can be found in (Mocan, A., et al., 2006).

Not all of the information modeled in the ontology is useful in all stages of the mapping process. As such, a *context* is a subset of a perspective that

Figure 4. Decomposition and context update – abstract view

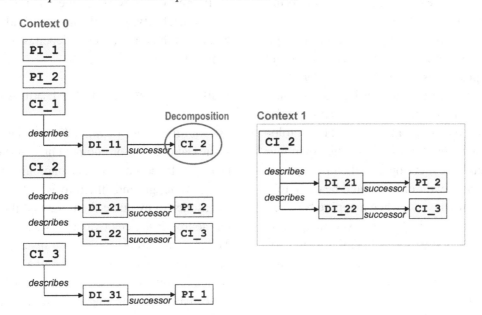

contains only those ontological entities which are relevant to a concrete mapping stage.

A notion tightly related with contexts is the *decomposition*. A context can be created from another context (this operation is called context update) by applying decomposition on an item from a perspective or a context. Decomposition allows navigation between contexts and links consecutive nested levels; the way the contexts are navigated when creating mappings influences the mappings that are created (see Figure 3).

Decomposition algorithm. The decomposition algorithm is used to offer guidance to the domain expert in the mapping process and to compute the structural factor as part of the suggestions algorithms (described later in this section). By decomposing, the descriptions elements of a compound item are exposed and made available to the mapping process. The decomposition algorithm can be applied to description items and returns the description items (if any) for the successors of the initial description items.

Suggestion Algorithms. In order to deliver a truly semi-automatic mapping tool, suggestion

algorithms are a necessity. The suggestion algorithms are used to help the domain expert to make decisions during the mapping process, regarding the possible semantic relationships between the source and the target items in the current mapping context. A combination of two types of such algorithms is used in our Ontology Mapping Tool: the first being a lexical algorithm and the second being the structural algorithms that consider the description items in their computations. Brief descriptions of the functionality that could be provided by such algorithms are provided below.

For each pair of items the suggestion algorithms computes an *eligibility factor* (EF), indicating the degree of similarity between the two items: the smallest value (0) means that the two items are completely different, while the greatest value (1) indicates that the two items may be similar. For dealing with the values between 0 and 1 a threshold value is used: the values lower than this value, indicate different items and values greater than this value indicate similar items. Setting a lower threshold assures a greater number of suggestions, while a higher value for the threshold restricts the number of suggestion to a smaller subset.

The EF is computed as a weighted average between a *structural factor* (SF), referring to the structural properties and a *lexical factor* (LF), referring to the lexical relationships determined for a given pair of items. The weights can be chosen based on the characteristics of the ontologies to be mapped. For example when mapping between ontologies developed in dissimilar spoken languages the weight of LF should be close to 0 in contrast with the case when mapping between ontology developed in the same working groups or institutions as the usage of similar names for related terms is likely to happen. More details about the EF, LF and SF can be found in (Mocan, A., et al., 2006).

Bottom-Up vs Top-Down Approach. Considering the algorithms and methods described above, two possible approaches during the ontology mapping can be followed: *bottom-up* and *top-down* approaches (Mocan, A., et al., 2007).

The *bottom-up approach* is a mapping process that starts with the mappings of the primitive items (if we imagine the ontological model as a tree[9] where the nodes are concepts and the edges attributes, the primitive items are positioned at the leafs level of the model) and then continues with items that reuse primitive items to describe themselves (upper level nodes). According to this, mappings of primitive items act like a minimal basic set of relationships between the two ontologies that can be easily used to gradually derive more complex relationships. This approach is recommended when a complete alignment of the two ontologies is desired.

The *top-down approach* is a mapping process that starts from compound items (non-leaf nodes) and then continues drilling down to primitive items. It is usually adopted when a concrete heterogeneity problem has to be resolved and the domain expert is interested only in resolving a particular item's mismatches and not in fully aligning the ontologies.

In the same way as for the other algorithms, the applicability and advantages/disadvantages of each of these approaches depends on the type of perspective used.

Run-Time Data Mediator Engine

The *Run-time Data Mediator Engine* plays the role of the Data Mediation component in the Semantic Gateway. It uses the abstract mappings created at design-time, grounds them to WSML, and uses a reasoner to evaluate them against the incoming source instances (Mocan, A., et al., 2006). The mapping rules, the source instances and if necessary, source and target schema information are loaded into the reasoning space in what could be seen as a "pseudo-merged" ontology (i.e., the entities from the source and the target and the rules are strictly separated by namespaces). By querying the reasoning space for instances of target concepts, if semantically related source instances exist, the rules fire and produce as results the target instances.

It is important to note that the module for grounding mappings is integrated as part of the run-time component. In this way, the same set of mappings (i.e., the abstract, ontology language-independent mappings) can be grounded to different languages depending on the scenario in which the run-time mediator is used. By grounding, a formal semantics is associated with the mappings, and only at this stage it is unambiguously stated what it means to have two items mapped to each other. This formal semantics can differ from one mediation scenario to another, that is, different grounding need to be applied when using the abstract mappings in instance transformation than when using them in query rewriting. An additional advantage is an easier management of mappings that form the ontology alignment. If ontologies evolve, the mappings should be updated accordingly. It is certainly more efficient to perform these updates free of any language-related peculiarities.

Figure 5.Concept to concept and attribute to attribute mappings

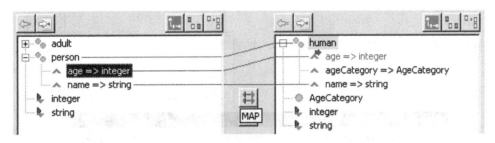

The Run-time Data Mediator Engine has been deployed as a component in the semantic environments (e.g. in the SemanticGov architecture). Moreover, the Engine can become available as a Web service that can be invoked directly via SOAP from specialized tools (one of such invokers is deployed as a plug-in in WSMT) or through a Web interface using a Web browser. Finally, the Run-time Data Mediator Engine can be offered as a standalone application that helps in testing and evaluating the mappings during the mapping process at design-time. The stand-alone version has been already integrated and is delivered together with WSMT as a support tool for ontology mapping.

Resolving the Semantic Interoperability Conflicts

This section presents some representative examples of how our Ontology Mapping Tool solves the semantic conflicts presented earlier in Section *Solving Semantic Interoperability Conflicts for Cross-Border e-Government Services*.

Data Level Conflicts

Using the Ontology Mapping Tool's graphical interface the domain expert can create mappings between various evidence placeholders that need to be aligned. Figure 4 shows how the mapping tool presents the two ontology fragments shown in Listing 2 to the user and how mappings can graphically be created.

Some mappings, as shown in Listing 3, lines 14-18, have conditions associated, meaning that these mappings are applicable to all the cases for which the conditions hold. Such mappings and their associated conditions are transformed into complex logical expressions in the underlying formalism (WSML[10]) but the ontology mapping tool offers the means to isolate the domain expert from the burdensome of the logical language used. Figure 5 illustrates how such conditions can be created: the domain expert can select one comparator for the attribute age of person and set the concrete age the attribute's value will be compared with.

It is important to note that in Figure 6 the *InstanceOf* perspective is used to present the ontologies to the domain expert in contrast to the *PartOf* perspective (Figure 5). The *PartOf* perspective shows the concepts defined in the ontology together with their attributes and attributes' ranges while the *InstanceOf* displays the concepts and the possible attribute values their attributes can take. For the ageCategory attribute the two allowed values adult and minor defined in the ontology are presented as alternatives. In the case of infinite domain data types (e.g. string or integer) it is not possible to show all the possible values for such data type. Instead two placeholders are used, *"?0"* and *"?s"*, to denote a value that can be later manually filled through the *Choose Comparators* dialog. The explicit instances (e.g. adult) appear in this dialog as fixed non-editable values and are directly dependent of selected attribute in their ontology.

Figure 6. Conditions on attributes mapping

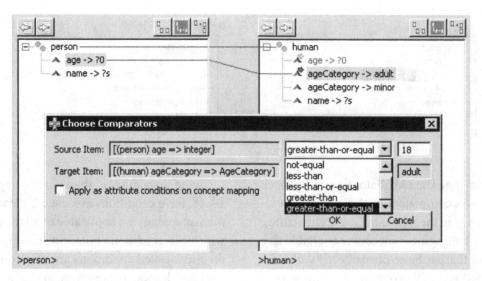

Figure 7. Conditions on concept mappings

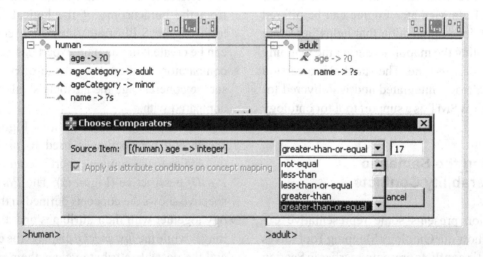

Figure 7 shows that in a similar manner conditions can be associated with a given concept to concept mapping (mapping between human and adult).

In the same fashion, the conflicts generated by differences in effect domains can be solved by having complete descriptions of the contextual knowledge (see Listing 4) complemented by the appropriate mappings between the domains (Listing 5). A special type of mapping (whose creation is shown in Figure 8) is the concept mapping between the IrishDrivingLicense and German-DrivingLicense, with an attribute value condition associated: this mapping does not hold unless the type of the IrishDrivingLicense is permanent. As a consequence even if the attributes hasDrivingLicense and drivingLicense of person and human are mapped (lines 4-5 in Listing 5) no filler for attribute drivingLicense of concept human will be created.

Figure 8. Conditions on concept mappings (solving the differences in the effect domains conflict)

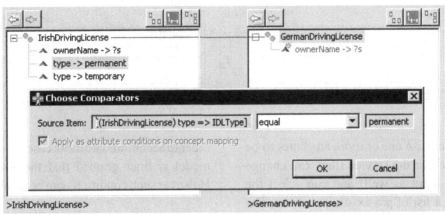

Figure 9. Applying transformation services to solve data representation conflicts

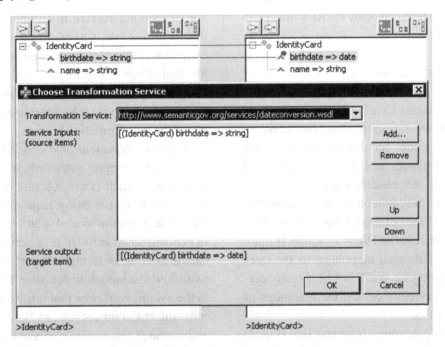

Data Representations Conflicts

In order to solve data representation conflicts external functions have to be applied on the values that need to be transformed from one representation form to another. Our approach uses Web services but it can be easily adjusted to accommodate calls to other (e.g. internal) implementations of these services. The definition of all the details neces-

sary to perform at run-time the service call is not trivial if it has to be done manually as shown in Listing 7. In this way our Ontology Mapping Tool provides graphical support to assist the domain experts in specifying the right service to be used for performing the transformation (see Figure 9).

The domain expert simply selects for the service the source and the target items whose values are to be used as inputs and output. The domain

Figure 10. MaritalStatus concepts displayed in the PartOf perspective

experts may choose one or more attributes to be used as inputs for the service (they can change the order of input as well) and can select the service from a list of pre-existing services. The set of predefined services can be easily extended. If the details of the transformation service are used in creating the mappings, the service must exist in order to be resolved by the Run-time Data Mediator Engine.

Data Precision Conflicts

The Data Precisions Conflicts can be solved by using the *InstanceOf* perspective. As shown in Listing 11 the codes for the marital status are modeled as instances in both the Belgian and Italian ontology. If we use the *PartOf* perspective (which is one of the common views on ontologies used in most of the ontology mapping tools) we see only the concepts and their attributes (Figure 10) such as conditional mappings, as the ones showed in Listing 12, could not be directly created without manually editing the mappings or the mapping rules.

By using the *InstanceOf* perspective (Figure 11), all possible values that can be taken by the hasMaritalStatusCode attributes are revealed and can be used to create the appropriate mappings. The result will consist of a set of attribute mappings with associated conditions on the allowed values for the mapped attreibutes.

At this stage, the mapping tool does not offer support for adding conditions on arbitrary knowledge from the target model. Such conditions would extend the mappings previously presented in

order to accommodate those cases when the target model is finer grained that the source model. However such conditions can be manually added.

Entity Identifier Conflict

This kind of conflicts can be resolved by requesting an external service to compute a value for this identifier that is going to be used in further communications. Such external service can be invoked either from a higher level (i.e. from the architectural level as part of the overall workflow) or from the mapping rules level in a similar manner as the transformation services are invoked in Section *Data Representation Conflicts* (see Figure 12). In our example, since only a piece of data is missing, which is not relevant to the overall functionality that is being requested or offered, we consider that the second solution is preferable. In general, whether to "hide" a service inside the data mediation or to make it part of the overall workflow, is a modeling decision. To be included in the overall workflow that it is executed by the semantic environment (i.e., by the SemanticGov architecture), the service needs to have a WSMO description (including capability/interface descriptions). Additionally, its functionality would need to be exposed and advertised together with the functionality of the service initially requested by the citizen (e.g. the "Change of Residency" service). Such an overload can be justified when the service offers a meaningful functionality from that particular PA scenario perspective.

Figure 11. MaritalStatus concepts displayed in the InstanceOf perspective

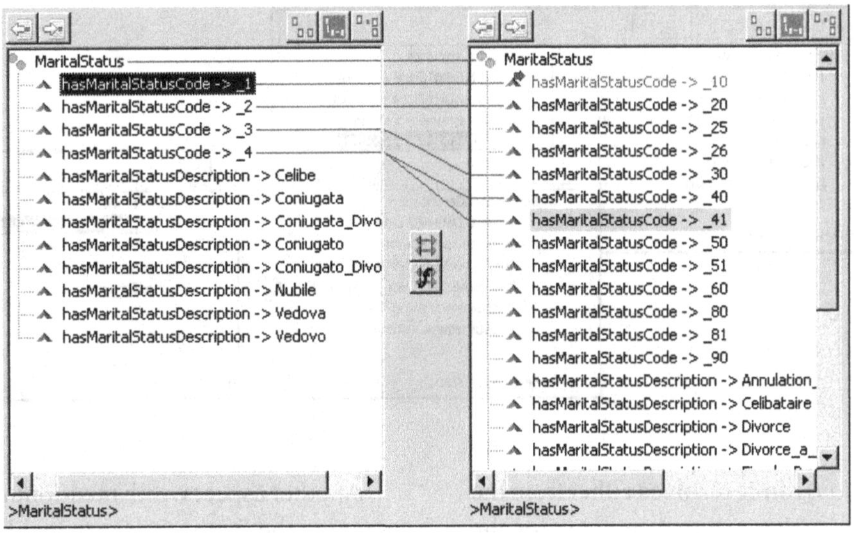

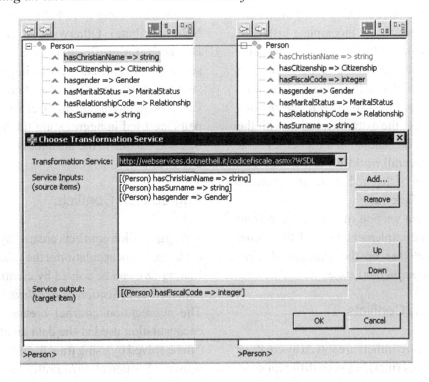

Figure 12. Using an external service to obtain an identifier

Schema-Isomorphism Conflicts

The case when *the source ontology element covers more information than the target ontology* *element* is resolved by not creating mappings for the missing target information. When *the source ontology element covers less information than the target ontology element* the first situation (*Default*

Figure 13. Mapping the BelgianBirthCertificate with the Italian BirthCertificate and FamilyCertificate

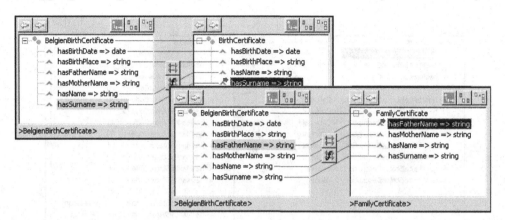

values generation) can be resolved either from the source side (by asking external services for the missing values, in a similar manner as in Section *Entity Identifier Conflict*) or from the target side (by relying on the rules existing in the target ontology that will handle the incomplete instances when they arrive). For the later option the solving of the conflict is out of the scope of the data mediation infrastructure in the Semantic Gateway. For the second situation (*Additional interactions with the requester*) the extra interaction with the requester should be handled at a higher level, at the level of the overall workflow and it is as well out of the control of the mediation infrastructure in the Semantic Gateway.

For the current version of the run-time Data Mediator Engine implementation all the above cases are supported except the "*Additional interactions with the requester*" case.

Generalization Conflicts

The generalization conflicts are solved by creating multiple mappings (n:m) between different conceptualization levels in the source and the target ontologies. The example in Section *Generalization Conflicts* can be solved as shown in Figure 13. It is important to note that for this type of mappings the decomposition and context (see Section *Ontology Mapping Tool*) play an important role in guiding the domain expert.

Another aspect worth mentioning is that when mapping the BirthCertificate and FamilyCertificate to the BelgianBirthCertificate the values of the BirthCertificate's and FamilyCertificate's common attributes need to be identical (e.g. hasName attribute). Otherwise, no instance of the BelgianBirthCertificate is created by the reasoner. This feature can be used implicitly to make sure that from an arbitrary instances set of both BirthCertificate and FamilyCertificate the proper pairs are used in aggregating the information to be encapsulated in the instances of BelgianBirthCertificate.

Aggregation Conflicts

The aggregation conflicts created by using different levels of encapsulation at the schema level (see Listing 18), can be solved by creating mappings as presented in Section *Generalization Conflicts*). The aggregation conflict created by different encapsulation used at the data level (Listing 20) can be solved by using transformation services as shown in Section *Data Representation Conflicts*).

Applying the Data Mediator

The mediation solutions encompass by the Data Mediator in the Semantic Gateway of the SemanticGov architecture can be applied for solving data heterogeneity problems between service

Figure 14. Semantic mediation using a reference ontology

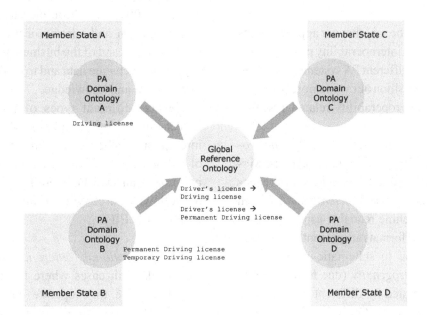

consumers (i.e. citizens) and service providers from and across various member states. We did not make so far any assumption regarding the way these mediation facilities are used. The solution we describe in this article supports both a P2P fashion strategy and a reference ontology-based strategy. In the case of adopting the P2P approach, a set of direct mapping rules between every pair of member states has to be provided (for 27 EU member states, this means over 700 unidirectional sets of mappings); while using an approach based on a reference ontology the number of required mappings are reduced to 2x27 (see Figure 14).

The solutions described here could be used in both approaches. If the semantic conflicts between MS_1 and MS_2 are to be solved via a reference ontology O_G then we need two sets of mappings, between OMS_1 and O_G and between O_G and OMS_2 (and one more pair for the other direction). When these mappings are required for a data mediation task, the reasoning and the derivation of the final mediated instances can be performed in a single invocation of the Data Mediator: based on the OMS_1 instances the first set of rules will trigger

generating the first mediated instances in terms of the O_G ontology which in their turn will trigger the second set of rules that, finally, will generate the corresponding instances in terms of OMS_2.

A third strategy can be adopted as well, when mappings are created between member states in such a way that a full connected directed graph is maintained at all time, where a) the nodes represent the member states, b) the edges the mappings between the two member states and c) where there is always a path between two nodes. The data mediation between two arbitrary member MS_i and MS_j states can be performed by chaining and executing the mappings between OMS_i and OMS_{k1}, OMS_{k1} and OMS_{k2}, …, OMS_{kn} and OMS_2. The chaining of mappings does not require the rewriting of any of the already existing mappings. It is simply achieved through the usage of the Datalog reasoner: once the first set of rules trigger and produce an intermediary set of data the second set of rules will trigger as well and produce the final set of data. This case is a generalization of the case when only an intermediary ontology (reference ontology) is used.

Related Work

In a nutshell, it can be said that our approach aims at solving semantic interoperability problems that may occur among different PA systems. However, it is important to position our work more precisely in the overall interoperability-related research landscape.

In (V. Kashyap, & Sheth, A., 2000) *heterogeneity* is classified in four main classes: *system heterogeneity* (due to technical differences across platforms), *syntactic heterogeneity* (when differences in machine readable aspects of data representation and formats are present), *structural heterogeneity* (due to schematic mismatches) and *semantic heterogeneity* (due to differences in meaning generated by different vocabularies and terminologies used). Our work aims to solve the heterogeneity problems that appear at the structural and semantic levels.

We have selected three major research areas that have significantly contributed to a better understanding and to the solving of the structural and semantic data heterogeneity problems: the semantic interoperability and semantic interoperability conflicts classifications; the ontology mediation, ontology mapping and ontology-based mediation in general; and finally, the relational database integration. In the rest of this section, we analyze and compare our work with some of the most relevant results in these areas.

Semantic Interoperability Conflicts

In literature various definitions for interoperability can be found in *The Governance Enterprise Architecture - GEA - for reengineering public administration*. For example, IEEE defines interoperability as the ability of two or more systems or components to exchange information and to use the information that has been exchanged (Institute of Electrical and Electronics Engineers, 1999). Another definition is given by the "European Interoperability Framework for pan-European

e-Government services" (EIF) (European Commission, 2004), which defines it as the ability of information and communication technology (ICT) systems and of the business processes they support to exchange data and to enable sharing of information and knowledge.

Several different types of interoperability aspects should be considered when discussing interoperability between the information systems of public agencies from different countries at a pan-European level. For identifying these aspects, the following three types of interoperability are identified in EIF:

- *Organizational interoperability*, which deals with cases where the organizations that have to cooperate have differences in their structure and in their business processes.
- *Semantic interoperability* that deals with cases where the information exchanged between organizations is interpreted differently by each side.
- *Technical interoperability*, which deals with the technical issues of linking computer systems and services. Other important issues like open interfaces, interconnection services, data integration and middleware, data presentation and exchange, accessibility and security services are also included here.

While technical incompatibilities are related to and can be solved with technical solutions that are currently more or less available and comparatively easy to be implemented, the other two interoperability aspects are more difficult to be addressed. Although we understand the importance of organizational interoperability, the scope of this work is on the semantic interoperability problems in Pan-European e-Government Services (PEGS) provision.

A more technical and detailed definition was provided by Yanosy (2005). According to this definition semantic interoperability encompasses the capacity for mutually consistent semantic interpretation of intention and shared knowledge within a situational and purposeful context, as a result of a semantic interaction, where intention, context, and knowledge are explicitly represented and expressed in some language of discourse or are implied by convention and use.

In J. Backhouse (2005) a framework has been proposed, which aims at providing a holistic view of interoperability. This framework consists of three layers: the technical, the formal (policy and standards) and the informal. Actually, the technical is the core layer and is contained in the formal one, which in turn is contained in the informal one.

In the "Netcentric Semantic Linking Report: An Approach to Enterprise Semantic" (MITRE, 2004), the experience of exploring the "Network Centric Semantic Linking" as a potential solution for integration across the U.S. Military Enterprise is presented. At a conceptual design level, the approach demonstrates the use of a reference ontology for linking a set of domain ontologies to achieve interoperability across domains, which has been proven to be a powerful solution. This approach obtains particular interest in the e-Government domain, especially, when the focus is on the interoperability problem between different countries administrations.

In J. Witters and A. van Overeem (2004) the authors propose an architecture based on the use of a semantic gateway to overcome semantic interoperability problems. The semantic gateway provides a set of services which aim to harmonize the meaning of the information exchanged between Public Administrations (PA) from different Member States (MS). To fulfill its objective the semantic gateway needs to have access to context data in the MSs, as well as to other kinds of data, including metadata translation tables.

Ontology Mapping Techniques

In the last years many research efforts have concentrated on the definition and creation of frameworks for data mediation: some of them focus on schema matching techniques, others on ontology mapping techniques. A survey of approaches towards schema matching is presented in E. Rahm and P. A. Bernstein (2001). In our approach, we use *schema-only*-based mechanisms to semi-automatically capture the matches between elements of the source and target schema. The tool support we presented in this article also includes a set of basic algorithms for computing mapping suggestions based on structural and lexical similarities. Due to space reasons and to the fact that they do not represent the core of our work, we choose not to elaborate on these algorithms since they just add on top of the main semi-automatic techniques we have proposed. Additionally, if desired, our approach can make use of other approaches for deriving mappings and ontology alignments automatically, as the ones proposed in K. Gomadam, A. Ranabahu, L. Ramaswamy, K. Verma, and A.P.Sheth, 2008 or in J. Euzenat et al. (2007). That is, these automatic methods can generate a set of mappings between the ontologies to be mapped, and the suggestions, instead of being computed in real-time, can be offered out of this set.

The mappings created by using the perspectives presented above are 1:1 element level mappings but by layering support for transformation functions on top of perspectives 1:n and n:1 *element level* can be created as well. Our mappings are represented in the Abstract Mapping Language (see Section *The Abstract Mapping Language* for more details) and they are grounded to a set of rules in an ontology language that can be later on evaluated by a reasoner. Using reasoning and the appropriate queries, the existing rules behave like virtual *structure-level* mappings allowing the creation of data structures expressed in terms of the target ontology based on data expressed in terms of the source ontology. Furthermore, by not explicitly creating mappings between whole structures, enables the reuse of the mapping sets to accommodate any data fragments that can be expressed in terms of the source ontology.

Kalfoglou and Schorlemmer (2003) provide a survey of ontology mapping approaches and classify them in several categories. Three of these approaches are more relevant for our work: Frameworks, Methods and Tools, and Translators. For these categories, several approaches have been identified and analyzed below: MAFRA (Silva, N., & Rocha, J., 2003) and COMA++ (Aumueller, D., et al., 2003)for Frameworks, PROMPT (Noy, N.F., & Munsen, M. A., 2003) for Methods and Tools and Abiteboul and colleagues' approach (Abiteboul, S., Cluet, S., & Milo T., 1997) for Translators.

MAFRA and PROMPT share several similarities with our work: they both adopt a semi-automatic ontology mapping approach. The domain experts are involved in an interactive mapping process where they can choose between a set of available actions to solve existing mismatches between ontologies. COMA++ mainly focuses on automatic techniques for mappings generation and reuse, but it also provides graphical support for the semi-automatic refinement of mappings and alignments. The work presented in S. Abiteboul et al., 1997 tackles integration of heterogeneous data in the database world, but is presented in this section due to its similarity with our approach to instance transformation based on ontology mappings created beforehand.

MAFRA (2003) is a Mapping Framework for Distributed Ontologies, designed to offer support at all stages of the ontology mapping life-cycle. The framework is organized across two dimensions: it contains horizontal and vertical modules. The horizontal modules *(Lift & Normalization, Similarity, Semantic Bridging, Execution, Post-processing)* describe fundamental and distinct phases in the mapping process, while the vertical modules (*Evolution, Domain Constraints & Background Knowledge, Cooperative Consensus Building, Graphical User Interface*) run along the entire mapping process interacting with the

horizontal modules. MAFRA proposes a Semantic Bridge Ontology to represent the mappings. This ontology has as central concept, the so called "Semantic Bridge", which is equivalent to our mapping language statements.

COMA++ (2005) is a generic matching tool focusing more on algorithms and methods for automatic generation and reuse of mappings and alignments between schemas and ontologies, so that it can be considered a complementary approach to our mapping tool. COMA++ also allows domain experts to interact with the overall framework through a user friendly graphical interface. Users can edit mappings and remove false correspondences and can edit, choose or combine already mapped fragments. An interesting similarity with our work is the usage of a fragment-based matching: COMA++ can decompose (either in an automatic mode or in a step-by-step process) large match problems into smaller sub-problems, which can be eventually reduced to an individual match problem. In our approach, by applying decomposition and context updates the domain expert is guided step-by-step to the simple, one-to-one mappings, which in the end represent the building blocks of more complex mapping sets.

QuickMig (Drumm, C., Schmitt, M., Do, H.-H., & Rahm, E., 2007) builds on top of COMA++ by extending it with support for schemas that include instances or with new instance-based matchers that can be combined with the original COMA matchers. QuickMig is a semi-automatic approach for schema mapping where domain experts, besides validation and creation of the mappings that cannot be automatically derived, can define sample instances for the source and target schemas. These instances are exploited later-on by specialized matchers to automatically derive the appropriate schema mappings. Quick-Mig proposes a set of mapping categories and specifies for each of these categories whether the corresponding mappings can be or not automatically derived. Some of the QuickMig mapping categories are: *CreateInstance* (corresponds to the *classMappings* and *attributeClassMappings* in our approach), *KeyMappings* (implicitly covered in our approach by the grounding of the *classAttributeMappings*, *attributeClassMappings* and a subset of *attributeMappings*), *InternalId* and *LookUp* (correspond to mappings extended with conditions on arbitrary knowledge from the spurce/target model, currently not supported by our implementation), *Move* (not applicable in our approach), *ValueMapping* (covered by *attributeMappings* with transformation services), etc.

PROMPT (2003) is an interactive and semi-automatic algorithm for ontology merging. The user is asked to apply a set of given operations to a set of possible matches, based on which the algorithm re-computes the set of suggestions and signals the potential inconsistencies. An interesting aspect is the definition of the term *local context* which perfectly matches our *context* definition: the set of descriptions attached to an item together with the items these descriptions point to. While PROMPT uses the local context in decision-making when computing the suggestions, we also use the context when graphically presenting the ontologies to the domain experts.

Abiteboul et al. (2007) propose a middleware data model as basis for the integration task, and declarative rules to specify the integration. The model is a minimal one and the data structure consists of ordered label trees. The authors claim that "even though a mapping from a richer data model to this model may loose some of the original semantics, the data itself is preserved and the integration with other models is facilitated". Since the main scenario they target is data translation while in our approach we apply our framework to instance transformation, the relation is obvious. The tree model they use, resemble our items model for the perspectives with the difference that our model can be grounded to several "view points" on top of the two ontologies to be mapped. The authors also consider two types of rules: *correspondence rules* used to express relationships between tree nodes and *translation rules*, a decidable sub-case for the actual data translation.

Relational Database Integration

This section positions our work in respect with the work in relational databases on data integration. It does not try to argue on the advantages of using ontologies as a central pivot of the overall SemanticGov architecture, but rather to show how our ontology-based data mediation techniques relate and extend existing work in the area of the data base heterogeneity.

The main mediation problems addressed in the area of database management have been related to *data integration* and *data exchange* (Kolaitis, P.G., 2005). By data integration the aim is to provide a unified, global view on a set of distributed data sources, while by data exchange instance data from a given source has to be transformed into an instance conforming with a given target schema. Even if these two problems have different scope, they both rely on schema mapping, a high level specification of the semantic relationships between a source and a target schema (Kolaitis, P.G., 2005).

Data integration in the context of databases focuses in principal on rewriting queries posed in terms of global views to queries expressed in terms of local schemas and the other way around(Halevy, A.Y., 2001). Consequently, two prominent strategies have been developed for dealing with this aspect: *local-as-view* (LAV) and *global-as-view* (GAV) (Ullman, J.D., 1997). In the LAV approach, the mapping associates to each element of the source schema a query over the global schema, or formally $s \rightarrow q_G$ where s is an element of the source schema S and q_G is a query over the global schema G (Lenzerini, M., 2002). Similarly, in the GAV approach each element in G is associated with a query over the source schemas that is, $g \rightarrow q_S$. Each of these approaches has its own advantages and disadvantages, e.g. LAV allows for easy integration of new sources while the query rewriting is more difficult. In GAV the addition of a new source might imply changes in global view; on the other hand, the mappings explicitly and directly specify how data can be retrieved from the sources.

In our approach, as discussed in Section *Applying the Data Mediator*, we do not make any assumption regarding the nature of the ontologies to be mapped, i.e. if they are global or local. However, we distinguish between a source and a target ontology strictly based on the directionality of the mappings. Using the formalism adopted in (Lenzerini, M., 2002), we can write $t \rightarrow q_S$ where t is an element of the target ontology and q_s is a query over the source ontology S. As a consequence, we can state that in our approach the target ontology behaves as the global ontology in the GAV approach. On the other hand, when it is required to map two ontologies O_1 and O_2 (e.g. used by two member states M_1 and M_2 that want to exchange data) they become alternatively source and target such as two sets of mappings are created: $O_2 \rightarrow q_{O1}$ and $O_1 \rightarrow q_{O2}$. Each of them will be used in materializing a set of instances in one of the ontologies (i.e. the target ontology) based on a set of instances expressed in terms of the second ontology (i.e. source ontology). By this, our approach becomes more related with database data exchange problem.

According to P.G. Kolaitis(2005), the main difference between data integration and data exchange is that while in data integration queries are posed on the global schema and rewritten and posed again on the sources, in data exchange the queries are posed in terms of the target schema and answered based on the materialized target instances. In our approach, the target instances are materialized by a set of rules generated out of the mappings created between the two ontologies, which fire in the presence of the input source instances. Such rules are conceptually the same as the *source-to-target tuple-generating dependencies* introduced in P.G. Kolaitis(2005). In addition, by using the mappings created between

two ontologies, it is possible in our approach to determine the right queries to be posed on the target ontology in order to retrieve the right solution (i.e. mediated instances).

Both data integration and data exchange normally rely on a set of mappings between the databases schemas as the ones introduced by the approach proposed in L. Popa, Y. Velegrakis, R.J. Miller, M.A. Hernandez, and R. Fagin (2002). A set of algorithms are used for determining a collection of *logical mappings* by applying a process called *semantic translation*: based on *inter-schema correspondences* and the *schema semantics* the logical mappings are presented to the human user, which has the role of trimming those mappings that do not conform to the correct semantic relationships existing between the given schemas. The schema mapping tool *Clio* (Yan, L.L., Miller, R.J., Haas, L.M., & Fagin, R., 2001; Miller, R.J., Hernandez, M.A., Haas, L.M., Yan, L., Ho, C. T. H., Fagin, R., & Popa, L., 2001) implements these algorithms and provides to the domain expert the necessary means to complete the mapping process.

There are several differences and similarities between the *Clio* approach and the approach we are proposing. One of the most important differences is that *Clio* exploits specific peculiarities of databases: foreign keys dependencies, nested structures of the schemas, etc. All these database characteristics crucially influence the algorithms used to compute the mappings. The approach in this thesis considers ontology-specific characteristics such as concepts and their attributes, attributes' ranges, instances of concepts, inheritance, etc. Another important difference is the semi-automatic strategy adopted: while this thesis considers an interactive approach (the domain expert creates the mappings one-by-one in an assisted manner) in *Clio* all the possible mappings are automatically generated and the domain expert has the role of refining and correcting them if necessary. Even if *Clio* proposes different types of illustration (e.g. *focused illustration* which allows the user to understand by examples the mappings affecting a selected value), it is likely that this approach and the visualization strategy will not scale for larger schemas (i.e. a high number of attributes per database table) or for a large number of source and target schemas. An interactive approach augmented with the decomposition and context updates can better free the human user from the inherent complexity of the mappings.

Another important aspect that should be taken in consideration when analyzing the mediation efforts carried on in the database community is the classification of mismatches and heterogeneity problems. Such a classification is given in C. Batini, M., Lenzerini, & S.B. Navathe (1986) and it refers two different types of *naming* and *structural* conflicts in a similar manner as in J. Park et al. (1984) (which in their turn have been originally developed for capturing database heterogeneity problems). Section *Solving Semantic Interoperability Conflicts for Cross-Border e-Government Services* describes in details how our approach addresses each of these conflicts. Additionally in C. Batini et al. (1986) a classification of the semantic relationships that can be captured by schema mappings is given. These classification specifies that between two representations in different schemas there could be four types of semantic relationships: *identical*, *equivalent* (which in its turn it can be *behavioral*, *mapping* and *transformational*), *compatible* and *incompatible*. This classification can be seen as the basis of the relationships allowed in a mapping language (e.g. the one described in Section *The Abstract Mapping Language*). In our approach the mappings that are created represent a combination between *equivalent/mapping* and *equivalent/transformational*: two concepts are equivalent if their instances can be put in a one-to-one correspondence and if instances of the target concept can be obtained out of the instances of the source concept through a set of transformation that preserve equivalence.

Evaluation

Our evaluation has been focused on the usefulness and the usability of the Ontology Mapping Tool. For this purpose, three evaluation workshops were organized in different PA agencies, namely in the City of Turin in Italy, the Region of Central Macedonia and the Ministry of Interior in Greece.

A total of 28 public servants participated in the three workshops. All of them come from departments that are involved in service provision, either as direct service provider or as supporting departments. They have been working in PA for an average of 4.8 years. Hence, they are familiar both with the peculiarities and the organizational structure of public administration and with the problems that usually occur in the service provision. 93% of them use the Internet in their work and 44% use other advanced tools and information systems to complete their daily tasks.

The public servants were asked to complete a questionnaire with 11 questions. The questionnaire tried to investigate both the need for a tool that would support the process of addressing semantic interoperability conflicts (i.e., the Data Mediator presented in this article) and the usability and the usefulness of the tool itself.

After processing the responses of the public servants, interesting findings came out. Currently, for example, there are cases when the citizen cannot provide some of the data required as service input due to some semantic interoperability conflict, like the ones presented earlier. 70% of the public servants replied that in such cases extra steps in the process are introduced with the citizens themselves playing the role of the "mediator", while 33% of them replied that other PA agencies are contacted to support the resolution of the conflicts. On the contrary, when the citizen provides more data than necessary, these are usually (70%) discarded.

Moreover, as depicted in the Figure 15, semantic interoperability conflicts often rise (89%) due to different interpretation of personal information of the citizens when they come from different countries/states/regions etc., where different legislative frameworks apply. For example, two different public administrations may have a different interpretation for the age over which a person is considered to be an adult.

Figure 15 shows that there is high likelihood (85%) that differences in the data representation of the evidences, which are provided by citizens as input for a cross-border e-Government service, will lead to semantic interoperability conflicts. It is interesting to mention that, according to the answers of the public servants, there is no chance (never: 0%) that such differences will not cause any semantic interoperability conflicts.

With respect to the evaluation of the Data Mediator, almost 63% of the public servants replied that they find the presentation of the ontologies in the tool and the basic operations for the creation of mappings acceptable, while 22.2% finds them very intuitive. The feedback on the mappings view of the Data Mediator is also quite encouraging, as 29.6% of the respondents found it very intuitive and around 48.2% of them thought it is acceptable (see Table 2).

Finally, more than 70% of the public servants characterised the process of adding value transformation services to the mappings as easy or very easy. It is worth mentioning, that only 11.1% of the respondents found the process difficult and none of them (0%) felt completely lost.

CONCLUSION

Solving the semantic interoperability conflicts between e-Government services at a pan-European level is a challenging exercise that aims to build a distributed infrastructure able to support a new generation of cross-member states interactions. EU citizens and businesses should receive services offered by other EU countries in a transparent way and PA agencies should be able to seamlessly

Figure 15. Changes in the status of citizens coming from different locations due to differences in legislation

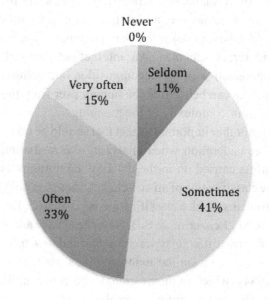

cooperate and interact in solving requests that involve trans-national legal processes.

In this article we have provided an analysis of the technical requirements for solving some of the most relevant types of semantic interoperability conflicts which arise in this demanding environment. We used our implemented system to show how such requirements can be fulfilled and how exactly these conflicts can be solved. The conceptual analysis is based on the GEA PA service model and the well-known interoperability classification framework of information systems proposed in Park et al. (1984). The solution we have adopted is based on ontology mapping and involves the creation of alignments between the domain ontologies at design-time and their use at run-time. The examples we chose to illustrate the interoperability conflicts and the solutions we apply in our approach are based on real case-studies analysed in the context of the EU funded SemanticGov project. An evaluation of our approach based on a statistical survey has also been presented. The survey findings verify

Table 2. Sample from the evaluation of the Data Mediators UI and basic operations

Question	Very Intuitive	Acceptable	Don't know	Not really intuitive	Counter-intuitive
Do you find the presentation of the ontologies and the basic operation for mapping creations intuitive and straightforward?	22.22%	62.96%	7.41%	3.70%	3.70%
Do you find the presentation of mappings in the mapping view as intuitive?	29.63%	48.15%	14.81%	3.70%	3.70%

Figure 16. Differences in data representation formats lead to semantic interoperability conflicts

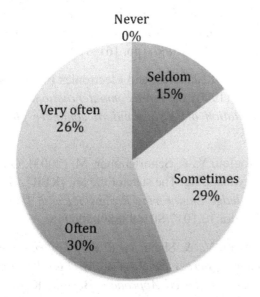

performance evaluation of the run-time execution process and to compare the results when different mediation strategies are used (e.g. global ontology versus P2P or chaining).

ACKNOWLEDGMENT

This article is supported in part by the Semantic-Gov project (FP6-2004-IST-4-027517) and by Science Foundation Ireland (SFI) under Grant No. SFI/02/CE1/I131.

REFERENCES

Abiteboul, S., Cluet, S., & Milo, T. (1997). Correspondence and Translation for Heterogeneous Data. In *Proceedings of the 6th International Conference on Database Theory*, (pp. 351-363).

Aumueller, D., Do, H.-H., Massmann, S., & Rahm, E. (2005). Schema and ontology matching with COMA++. In *Proceedings of the 2005 ACM SIGMOD International Conference on Management of Data*. June 14-16, Baltimore, Maryland.

Backhouse, J. (2005, July). *D4.1: Structured account of approaches on interoperability*. Technical report, FIDIS Deliverable, http://www.fidis.net/fileadmin/fidis/deliverables.

Batini, C., Lenzerini, M., & Navathe, S. B. (1986). A Comparative Analysis of Methodologies for Database Schema Integration. *ACM Computing Surveys, 18*(4), 323–364. doi:10.1145/27633.27634

that resolving semantic interoperability conflicts that rise during the provision of cross-border e-Government services is a real need, which public servants often face on a daily basis. Additionally, there is a high interest among public servants for a tool that would support this task in user friendly manner.

As future work we intend to extend the current approach by providing dynamic support for discovery of value transformation services. That is, instead of having a fixed number of such services we can have an intelligent mechanism in place that would allow the dynamic discovery (e.g. at the mappings creation) of available services registered within given repositories. Also we intend to make de Bruijn, J., Lausen, H., Krummenacher, R., Polleres, A., Predoiu, L., Kifer, M., & Fensel, D. (2005, October). *The Web Service Modeling Language (WSML)*. Technical report, WSML Working Draft, http://www.wsmo.org/TR/d16/d16.1/v0.2/

Dean, M., & Schreiber, G. (2004, February). *OWL Web ontology language reference*. Technical report, World Wide Web Consortium (W3C), http://www.w3.org/TR/owl-ref/.

Drumm, C., Schmitt, M., Do, H.-H., & Rahm, E. (2007, November). QuickMig - Automatic Schema Matching for Data Migration Projects. In *Proceedings of ACM CIKM*, Lisabon.

European Commission (IDABC). (2004). *European Interoperability Framework for Pan-European e-Government Services*. http://ec.europa.eu/idabc/servlets/Doc?id=19528.

Euzenat, J., Scharffe, F., & Serafini, L. (2006, February). *D2.2.6: Specification of the delivery alignment format*. Technical report, Knowledge Web Deliverable. http://www.inrialpes.fr/exmo/cooperation/kWeb/heterogeneity/deli/kWeb-226.pdf.

Euzenat, J., & Shvaiko, P. (2007). *Ontology matching*. Heidelberg, DE: Springer-Verlag.

Fensel, D., Lausen, H., Polleres, A., de Bruijn, J., Stollberg, M., Roman, D., & Domingue, J. (2006). *Enabling Semantic Web Services: The Web Service Modeling Ontology*. Secaucus, NJ, USA: Springer-Verlag New York, Inc.

Gomadam, K., Ranabahu, A., Ramaswamy, L., Verma, K., & Sheth, A. P. (2008, August). Mediatability: Estimating the Degree of Human Involvement in XML Schema Mediation. In *Proceedings of the 2nd IEEE International Conference on Semantic Computing*, Santa Clara, CA.

Goudos, S. K., Loutas, N., Peristeras, V., & Tarabanis, K. (2007). Public Administration Domain Ontology for a Semantic Web Services E-Government Framework. *IEEE International Conference on Services Computing (SCC 2007)*, Salt Lake City, USA, July 9-13.

Halevy, A. Y. (2001). Answering queries using views: A survey. *The VLDB Journal*, *10*(4), 270–294. doi:10.1007/s007780100054

Horrocks, I., Sattler, U., & Tobies, S. (1999). Practical reasoning for expressive description logics. In *Proceeding of the 6th International Conference on Logic for Programming and Automated Reasoning (LPAR99)*, (pp. 161–180).

Institute of Electrical and Electronics Engineers (IEEE) (1990). *Standard computer dictionary - a compilation of IEEE standard computer glossaries*.

Kalfoglou, Y., & Schorlemmer, M. (2003). Ontology mapping: The state of the art. [KER]. *The Knowledge Engineering Review Journal*, *18*(1), 1–31. doi:10.1017/S0269888903000651

Kashyap, V., & Sheth, A. (2000). *Information Brokering across Heterogeneous Digital Data: A Metadata-based Approach*. Boston: Kluwer Academic Publishers.Overeem, A., & Witters, J. (2004). *Architecture for Delivering pan-European e-Government Services*, IDA technical report, Capgemini.

Kerrigan, M., Mocan, A., Tanler, M., & Fensel, D. (2007, June). The Web Service Modeling Toolkit - An Integrated Development Environment for Semantic Web Services. In *Proceedings of the 4th European Semantic Web Conference (ESWC)*, System Description Track, Innsbruck, Austria.

Kifer, M., Lausen, G., & Wu, J. (1995, July). Logical foundations of object-oriented and frame-based languages. *Journal of the ACM*, (42): 741–843. doi:10.1145/210332.210335

Kolaitis, P. G. (2005). Schema mappings, data exchange, and metadata management. In *Proceedings of the twenty-fourth ACM SIGMOD-SIGACT-SIGART symposium on Principles of database systems*, June 13-15, 2005, Baltimore, Maryland

Lausen, H., de Bruijn, J., Polleres, A., & Fensel, D. (2005). WSML - A Language Framework for Semantic Web Services. *W3C Workshop on Rule Languages for Interoperability*.

Lenzerini, M. (2002). Data Integration: A Theoretical Perspective. In *Proceedings of the twenty-first ACM SIGMOD-SIGACT-SIGART symposium on Principles of database systems*, (pp. 233-246).

Miller, R. J., Hernandez, M. A., Haas, L. M., Yan, L., Ho, C. T. H., Fagin, R., & Popa, L. (2001). The Clio Project: Managing Heterogeneity. *SIGMOD Record, 30*(1), 78–83. doi:10.1145/373626.373713

MITRE (2004). Netcentric Semantic Linking Report: *An Approach to Enterprise Semantic*.

Mocan, A., & Cimpian, E. (2007). An ontology-based data mediation framework for semantic environments. [IJSWIS]. *International Journal on Semantic Web and Information Systems, 3*(2), 66–95. doi:10.4018/jswis.2007040104

Mocan, A., Cimpian, E., & Kerrigan, M. (2006, November). Formal Model for Ontology Mapping Creation. In *Proceedings of the 5ᵗʰ International Semantic Web Conference (ISWC 2006)*, Athens, Georgia, USA.

Mocan, A., Kerrigan, M., & Cimpian, E. (2008, June). Applying Reasoning to Instance Transformation. *International Workshop on Ontologies: Reasoning and Modularity (WORM-08)*, Tenerife, Spain

Noy, N. F., & Munsen, M. A. (2003). The PROMPT suite: Interactive tools for ontology merging and mapping. *International Journal of Human-Computer Studies, 6*(59).

Park, J., & Ram, S. (2004). Information systems interoperability: What lies beneath? *ACM Transactions on Information Systems, 22*(4), 595–632. doi:10.1145/1028099.1028103

Peristeras, V. (2006). *The Governance Enterprise Architecture - GEA - for reengineering public administration*. PhD Dissertation, Business Administration, University of Macedonia, Thessaloniki.

Peristeras, V., Loutas, N., Goudos, S., & Tarabanis, K. (2008). A conceptual analysis of semantic conflicts in pan-European e-government services. *Journal of Information Science, 34*(6), 877–891. doi:10.1177/0165551508091012

Peristeras, V., & Tarabanis, K. (2008). The Governance Architecture Framework and Models. In Saha, P. (Ed.), *Advances in Government Enterprise Architecture*. Hershey, PA: IGI Global Information Science Reference.

Popa, L., Velegrakis, Y., Miller, R. J., Hernandez, M. A., & Fagin, R. (2002). Translating Web data. In *Proceedings of the Very Large Data Bases*, (pp. 598-609), Hong Kong SAR, China.

Rahm, E., & Bernstein, P. A. (2001, December). A Survey of Approaches to Automatic Schema Matching. *The International Journal on Very Large Data Bases*, 10(4), 334–350. Scharffe, F., & de Bruijn, J. (2005, December). A language to specify mappings between ontologies. In *IEEE Conference on Internet-Based Systems SITIS6*, Yaounde, Cameroon.

Silva, N., & Rocha, J. (2003). Semantic Web complex ontology mapping. In *Proceedings of the IEEE Web Intelligence (WI2003)*, (p. 82).

Tambouris, E., Manouselis, N., & Costopoulou, C. (2007). Metadata for digital collections of e-government resources. *The Electronic Library, 25*(2), 176–192. doi:10.1108/02640470710741313

Tambouris, E., & Tarabanis, K. (2005, June). E-Government and interoperability. In *European Conference in Electronic Government (ECEG 2005)*, Belgium, (pp. 399–407).

Tambouris, E., & Tarabanis. K. (2004). Overview of DC-based e-Government metadata standards and initiatives. *International Conference on Electronic Government (EGOV 2004)*, Zaragoza, Spain, (pp. 40-47)

Ullman, J. D. (1997). Information integration using logical views. In *Proceedings 6th International Conference on Database Theory (ICDT 97)*, Delphi, Greece.

Vitvar, T., Kerrigan, M., van Overeem, A., Peristeras, V., & Tarabanis, K. (2006, March). Infrastructure for the semantic pan-european e-government services. In *AAAI Spring Symposium on Semantic Web Meets E-Government*, Stanford, CA, USA.

Vitvar, T., Mocan, A., Cimpian, E., Nazir, S., Wang, X., & Loutas, N. (2006). *Devember)*. *D3.1: SemanticGov Architecture (Vol. 1)*. SemanticGov Deliverable.

Vitvar, T., Mocan, A., Kerrigan, M., Zaremba, M., Zaremba, M., Moran, M., Cimpian, E., Haselwanter, T., & Fensel, D. (2007). Semantically-enabled Service Oriented Architecture: Concepts, Technology and Application. *Journal of Service Oriented Computing and Applications*.

Wang, X., Vitvar, T., Mocan, A., Peristeras, V., Goudos, S. K., & Tarabanis, K. (2007, January). WSMO-PA: Formal Specification of Public Administration Service Model on Semantic Web Service Ontology. *Hawaii International Conference on System Sciences (HICSS2007)*, Hawaii

Witters, J., & van Overeem, A. (2004). *PEGS infrastructure architecture v 1.0*. IDABC.

Yan, L. L., Miller, R. J., Haas, L. M., & Fagin, R. (2001). Data-driven understanding and refinement of schema mappings. [ACM Special Interest Group on Management of Data]. *SIGMOD Record*, *30*(2), 485–496. doi:10.1145/376284.375729

Yanosy, J. (2005, August). Semantic interoperability and semantic congruence. In *Collaborative Expedition Workshop*.

ENDNOTES

[1]   Work performed while at Semantic Technology Institute (STI) Innsbruck, University of Innsbruck, Austria

[2]   Please see for more details http://www.semantic-gov.org/, http://www.seemp.org/, http://www.egov-bus.org/ and http://www.r4egov.info/.

[3]   SemanticGov is an EU-funded research and development project that aims at building the infrastructure (software, models, services, etc) necessary for enabling the offering of Semantic Web services by public administration (PA). More details are available at http://www.semantic-gov.org/.

[4]   http://www.w3.org/TR/xmlschema11-2/

[5]   For brevity, we are using the O_1 and the O_2 notation to alternatively denote the ontologies used in our use case by the Belgian PA and by the Italian PA. Exception makes the example in Listing 4.

[6]   Such constraining behaviour can be implemented in the rule-based reasoners and it is similar with the constraints system in the databases. The reasoner used by the Data Mediator in this work has such constraints mechanisms in place.

[7]   Open source project available at http://sourceforge.net/projects/wsmt.

8   In fact WSMT already contains a set of translators able to transform between WSML and OWL and between WSML and RDF/S. By using this translators ontologies expressed in OWL and RDF/S can be loaded and further engineered using the WSMT plug-ins.

9   This is actually an imprecise analogy since the ontology is a directed graph. More precisely, the primitive items (the "leafs") are nodes with no edges leaving from them.

10   See http://www.wsmo.org/wsml

This work was previously published in International Journal on Semantic Web and Information Systems, Volume 5, Issue 1, edited by Amit P. Sheth, pp. 1-47, copyright 2009 by IGI Publishing (an imprint of IGI Global).

Chapter 2
A New Similarity Measure for Automatic Construction of the Unknown Word Lexical Dictionary

Myunggwon Hwang
Chosun University, South Korea

Pankoo Kim
Chosun University, South Korea

ABSTRACT

This paper deals with research that automatically constructs a lexical dictionary of unknown words as an automatic lexical dictionary expansion. The lexical dictionary has been usefully applied to various fields for semantic information processing. It has limitations in which it only processes terms defined in the dictionary. Under this circumstance, the concept of "Unknown Word (UW)" is defined. UW is considered a word, not defined in WordNet, that is an existing representative lexical dictionary. Here is where a new method to construct UW lexical dictionary through inputting various document collections that are scattered on the WebWeb is proposed. The authors grasp related terms of UW and measure semantic relatedness (similarity) between an UW and a related term(s). The relatedness is obtained by calculating both probabilistic relationship and semantic relationship. This research can extend UW lexical dictionary with an abundant number of UW. It is also possible to prepare a foundation for semantic retrieval by simultaneously using the UW lexical dictionary and WordNet.

INTRODUCTION

Extensive research has been carried out on semantic information processing based on a lexical dictionary. Research on semantic document indexing (Hemayati et al., 2007, Kiryakov et al., 2003), on semantic metadata creation (Jovanovic et al., 2006, Handschuh et al., 2004, Alani et al., 2003), on generating semantic Web content using natural language processing (Java et al, 2007), and on detecting document topics (Kong et al., 2006) has been done. In addition, a lexical dictionary

DOI: 10.4018/978-1-60960-593-3.ch002

can become a basis for query expansion (Liu et al., 2004), ontology extension (Navigli et al., 2006, Velardi et al., 2007), information retrieval by semantic similarity (Hliaoutakis et al., 2006), and knowledge integration (Missikoff et al., 2003). While the lexical dictionary is gradually becoming more important and useful for semantic information processing, the most vulnerable aspect of semantic information processing is that it cannot handle concepts that are not defined in the dictionary. This is also true for WordNet, the most representative English lexical dictionary. Even though WordNet has been expanded with manual effort for over ten years, it cannot completely cover all the new words created by changes in real life such as new social phenomena, trends, techniques, product names, and famous persons" name (athletes, entertainers, and politicians). Manually defining such new words requires a lot of time, cost, labor, and controversy (Velardi et al., 2001, Navigli et al., 2003). This hindrance led to many research endeavors to reduce such factors in constructing or expanding knowledge bases using Web documents and data warehouses (Missikoff et al., 2003, Navigli et al., 2004, Navigli et al., 2006, Velardi et al., 2007). These methods have good result but they fail to not deal with relationships and similarity of terms.

WordNet contains semantic relations between concepts. Many research projects have quantified such relations using various methods and have applied the results for semantic information processing. Its limits are apparent since documents frequently contain words not defined in the dictionary. These undefined words are called "Unknown Word (UW)." For true semantic information processing, we search UWs and terms which relate to the UW. The probabilistic weight based on Bayesian probability and the semantic weight based on WordNet will be calculated to ultimately find the semantic relatedness between an UW and a related term(s). In addition since the dictionary handles concepts rather than words, we apply our newly designed word sense dis-

ambiguation (WSD) method, which enables the dictionary to have an accurate synset for related terms. As a result, the dictionary can be compatibly used with WordNet. This research is based on the relation structure of WordNet and uses the synset, therefore it can be regarded as a type of automatic WordNet expansion.

The following paper explains the preprocessing step that covers noun extraction from a document group, UW determination, and the new WSD method. In using these results, terms that relate to the UW are measured for similarity with additional processes. Experimental results are evaluated using various methods in order to validate this approach. Following the conclusion, additional opportunities are suggested for future research.

PREPROCESSING

WordNet[1], which is used as a knowledge base in this research, defines almost all English terms (Miller et al., 1990, Fellbaum et al., 1998). In this section, the methods for extraction of noun and the WSD method will be described.

Extraction of an Unknown Word

In order to extract noun terms from a Web document, pos (part-of-speech) tagging is necessary. We chose pos-tagger version 2006-05-21, developed and provided by The Stanford Natural Language Processing Group[2] (Toutanova et al., 2000, Toutanova et al., 2003). Inserting text into the pos-tagger allows it to assign a POS tag for each word. Among the tags, NN (single noun), NNS (compound noun), NNP (proper noun), and NNPS (compound proper noun) are the types of nouns. Words tagged with NN or NNS are used to create a noun term candidate list (NL_c) and NNP or NNPS are used to create an unknown word candidate list (UL_c).

Let us demonstrate with one sentence. *"Zinedine Yazid Zidane, popularly nicknamed Zizou, is a French former football midfielder,"* NL_c and UL_c can be extracted as:

```
NL_c = {French, football, midfielder}
and
UL_c = {Zinedine, Yazid, Zidane,
Zizou}
```

In NL_c and UL_c, sequential nouns can be factors for compound noun types. Using sequential proper nouns, probable unknown word candidates are created as subsets. From the above sequential case *{Zinedine, Yazid, Zidane}*, three subsets can be created, and unknown compound word candidate list (UCL_c) is consisted of those subsets as:

```
UCL_c = {Zinedine Yazid, Yazid Zidane,
Zinedine Yazid Zidane}
```

If a proper noun represents the name of a person as in the above example, the full name (first name and family name) is presented while only part of the full name is generally used in a document. This is why unknown compound word candidates using subsets are made. In the section for noise removal, unnecessary unknown word candidates will be removed.

Sequential noun words in a text can be factors for compound nouns. Since compound nouns have much more specific meanings than single nouns with most having only one meaning, they can become significant clues in semantic information processing. Sequential noun words are used to create a compound noun candidate list (CNL_c). In the demonstration sentence, the two words "football" and "midfielder" successively appear, therefore "football midfielder" can also be included in a CNL_c.

While the pos-tagger used in this research has a 97.24% tagging accuracy (Toutanova et al., 2000, Toutanova et al., 2003), there is a possibility that it contains errors in analyzing documents. Therefore, a process is necessary to check whether each factor in NL_c, UCL_c, and UL_c was

properly extracted. In addition if the candidate factors in CNL_c are determined to be a compound noun, another process is necessary to remove the candidate factors from NL_c. For those processes, the following three steps must be undertaken in "Extraction of an Unknown Word."

First, each factor (cn_i) in the compound noun candidate list is matched with the noun-index[3], part of WordNet, in order to check whether a compound noun is included in CNL_c. If a synset matches with cn_i, it is regarded as a compound noun, and the noun words which make up cn_i are removed from NL_c. For example if two words ("*football*" and "*player*") successively appear in a document, NL_c will include "*football*" and "*player*" and CNL_c will include "*football player.*" Since "*football player*" is verified to be a compound noun after matching with the noun part, the two factors "*football*" and "*player*" are removed from NL_c. On the other hand, candidates that do not have a matching synset are removed from CNL_c such as "*football midfielder.*" Through this process, CNL_c contains only compound nouns that are actually defined as nouns in WordNet, and NL_c contains pure simple nouns.

The second process checks whether the extraction of each element for NL_c is correct. For each factor (n_i) in NL_c, the noun-index of WordNet must have at least one matching synset. If there is no synset, there is a high probability that n_i is a proper noun or is not a noun at all. In this case if NL_c contains at least one of the same words as n_i or UL_c, then those words (all words identical to n_i that are included in NL_c) are regarded as proper nouns and are sent to UL_c. Otherwise, it is determined to not be a noun and is removed from NL_c.

Lastly, factors included in UCL_c and UL_c are matched with the noun-index of WordNet and the existence of synset(s) is checked. If synset(s) exists, it is judged to be a regular noun, sent to NL_c, and removed from subsets UL_c and UCL_c. For example, there is one sentence *"Carnegie Mellon University is a private research university in Pittsburgh, Pennsylvania, United States."* Tagging yields the following results:

NL$_c$ = {research, university},

UL$_c$ = {Carnegie, Mellon, University, Pittsburgh, Pennsylvania, United, States}, and

UCL$_c$ = {Carnegie Mellon, Mellon University, Carnegie Mellon University}

Through this step, it is verified that *"Carnegie Mellon University"* is a noun. Therefore, *"Carnegie," "Mellon," "University,"* and *"Carnegie Mellon," "Mellon University"* are removed from *UL$_c$* and *UCL$_c$*. In matching WordNet, *"Carnegie," "Mellon,"* and *"University"* are also nouns, however the nouns are considered to be factors for the compound noun *"Carnegie Mellon University."* Moreover, *"Pittsburgh"* and *"Pennsylvania"* are also sent to *NL$_c$*. In another illustration sentence, *"In 1997, Club Car sourced new transaxles which required clockwise input,"* three nouns *{transaxle, clockwise, input}* and three UWs *{Club, Car, Club Car}* are extracted. In the illustration, *"Club Car"* is sent to *NL$_c$* and "Club" and "Car" are removed from *UL$_c$*. The noun *"transaxle"* and *"clockwise"* can be removed or sent to *UL$_c$*.

Through the aforementioned processing, each list (*NL$_c$, CNL$_c$, UCL$_c$,* and *UL$_c$*) is created. For the next process, each compound noun in *CNL$_c$* is integrated with *NL$_c$* and *UCL$_c$* with *UL$_c$* according to the order it appeared in the document and respectively becomes one noun list (*NL*) and one UW list (*UL*). Starting from the next process, the *NL* will be used for the noun list of documents that are extracted in this process and *UL* will be used as the unknown word list.

WSD of Noun List

Each noun of *NL* that was extracted through the previous processes has one or more meaning. This research attempts to build a lexical dictionary that

is a type of expansion of WordNet. Therefore it should contain an accurate synset of noun words. For this, WSD is executed for nouns in *NL*. Many researchers have proposed WSD based on knowledge bases such as WordNet. Recently, R. Navigli et al. (2005) proposed the Structural Semantic Interconnections (SSI) algorithm which utilized a lexical knowledge base (LKB) by combining many kinds of online resources (WordNet 2.0, SemCor[4], FreeNet[5] and so on). This method has an accuracy of more than 10% higher, on average, than existing methods. Because of complications in constructing the same knowledge base, we have proposed and applied a new WSD method based on knowledge base.

The foundation of this new WSD method is that words that appear in the same context can become crucial clues to determine exact meaning. In other words, there is high probability that words in the same context can have a mutual semantic relation. WordNet defines the semantic relation of such words, thus becomes an appropriate knowledge base for execution of WSD. In order to execute WSD using WordNet, two preconditions are defined. WordNet contains various relations (synonym, hyponym, hypernym, meronym, holonym, pertainym, antonym, etc) between concepts by using a variety of symbols (@, ~, #p, #m, ;c, -c, ;r, -r, etc}. The relatedness between concepts should be different depending on each type of relation. For example, there is a "hyponym" relation between *"sedan"* and *"car"* and a "meronym" relation between *"car"* and *"car window"*. There is certainly difference in semantic similarity (relatedness). However, we assume that both values of relatedness are the same. The first precondition is that the relatedness between concepts is same without regard to kinds of relation. Secondly, the distance is inversely proportional to the relatedness, the longer the distance is the smaller the relatedness. Actually, synonyms (Same synset such as *"car"* and *"auto"*) or direct linked terms (*"car"-"sedan"*, *"car"-"car window"*) do not often appear in one document. Instead, longer

Figure 1. The example of relations according to distance

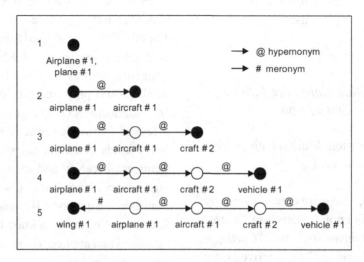

distance relations are generally found. Hence, in this research, we find the relation between two concepts up to 5-distance as shown in Figure 1 and consider distances longer than that to have no relation because almost all methods based on knowledge base use the maximum 5-distance. The SSI algorithm also grasps interconnections up to 5-distance. Figure 1 shows the example expressing the relation between two concepts up to 5-distance.

In order to grasp the relationship between noun words, a synset-list (S_i) is obtained for each noun word (n_i) in *NL*. The following is the synset-list of n_i.

$$S_i = \{s_{ij}, 1 \le j \le k_i\}$$

where, s_{ij} is the jth synset of a n_i contained in *NL* and k_i is a count of synset for n_i. For example:

$$S_{fur} = \{fur\#1, fur\#2, fur\#3\}$$

$$S_{coat} = \{coat\#1, coat\#2, coat\#3\}$$

Between two words ("*fur*" and "*coat*"), many relations can be grasped as shown in Figure 2. The relations are divided into two types; Type-A has relations on different distances between the same

synsets ("*fur#2*"-"*coat#3*"); Type-B has relations on different distances between different synsets ("*fur#3*"-"*coat#1*" and "*fur#3*"-"*coat#2*"). In both cases, we select the relationship with the shortest distance. Even though one synset ("*fur#3*") is related with two synsets ("*coat#1*," and "*coat#2*") like the case of type-B, we select one relationship because what is important is whether "*fur#3*" relates with the word "*coat*" or not. Through this process, the synset of each noun is finally determined through (1), (2), and (3). Equation (1) measures the relatedness (*rd*) based on the distance between synset (s_{ia}) and synset (s_{jb}).

$$rd\left(s_{ia}, s_{jb}\right) = \frac{1}{\min\left(d\left(s_{ia}, s_{jb}\right)\right)}, i \ne j \qquad (1)$$

where, $rd(s_{ia}, s_{jb})$ is the relatedness between s_{ia} and s_{jb}; s_{ia} is the synset a of the ith noun (n_i); d is the distance between two synsets. If there is no relation (or more than 5-distance) between s_{ia} and s_{jb}, $rd(s_{ia}, s_{jb})$ becomes 0. In case of figure 2, $rd(s_{fur\#2}, s_{coat\#3}) = 0.5$ and $rd(s_{fur\#3}, s_{coat\#1}) = 0.25$.

The total relatedness sum defines the context weight (*cw*) of the concept (synset). Equation (2) calculates each context weight. If one concept has the biggest weight, the concept is chosen to

Figure 2. An example of a relation type

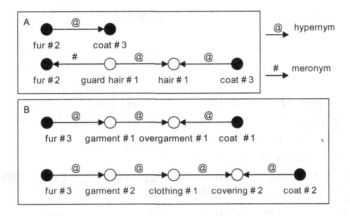

be the most appropriate meaning for that context. Equation (3) determines the concept that has the maximum context weight.

$$cw\left(s_{ia}\right) = \sum_{j=1}^{m} \max_{s_{jb} \in S_j}\left(rd\left(s_{ia}, s_{jb}\right)\right), i \neq j \quad (2)$$

$$wsd\left(s_i\right) = \max_{s_{ia} \in S_i}\left(cw\left(s_{ia}\right)\right) \quad (3)$$

Where cw is the context weight of a synset; j is the word index in context; m is the context size; and s_i is the synset that is finally determined for n_i. If a context (noun list) contains S_{fur}, S_{coat}, and S_{skin}, every context weight is below:

$cw(s_{fur\#2}) = 0.2 + 0.5 = 0.7$

$s_{fur\#2} - s_{coat\#3} - s_{hair\#1} - s_{body\_covering\#1} - s_{skin\#1}$

$s_{fur\#2} - s_{coat\#3}$

$cw(s_{fur\#3}) = 0.25$

$s_{fur\#3} - s_{garment\#1} - s_{overgarment\#1} - s_{coat\#1}$

$cw(s_{coat\#1}) = 0.25$

$s_{coat\#1} - s_{overgarment\#1} - s_{garment\#1} - s_{fur\#3}$

$cw(s_{coat\#2}) = 0.2 + 0.2 = 0.4$

$s_{coat\#2} - s_{covering\#2} - s_{clothing\#1} - s_{garment\#2} - s_{fur\#3}$

$s_{coat\#2} - s_{covering\#2} - s_{artifact\#1} - s_{surfact\#1} - s_{skin\#3}$

$cw(s_{coat\#3}) = 0.5 + 0.25 = 0.75$

$s_{coat\#3} - s_{fur\#2}$

$s_{coat\#3} - s_{hair\#1} - s_{body\_covering\#1} - s_{skin\#4}$

$cw(s_{skin\#1}) = 0.2 + 0.25 = 0.45$

$s_{skin\#1} - s_{body\_covering\#1} - s_{hair\#1} - s_{coat\#3} - s_{fur\#2}$

$s_{skin\#1} - s_{body\_covering\#1} - s_{hair\#1} - s_{coat\#3}$

$cw(s_{skin\#3}) = 0.2$

$s_{skin\#3} - s_{surface\#1} - s_{artifact\#1} - s_{covering\#2} - s_{coat\#2}$

$cw(s_{skin\#4}) = 0.2 + 0.25 = 0.45$

$s_{skin\#4} - s_{body\_covering\#1} - s_{hair\#1} - s_{coat\#3} - s_{fur\#2}$

$s_{skin\#4} - s_{body\_covering\#1} - s_{hair\#1} - s_{coat\#3}$

According to equation (3), $s_{fur\#2}$ and $s_{coat\#3}$ are chosen. The synset for each term in this process will be mapped to *NL* and will be used together for the next process. The following is a set for *NL* that expresses synset together.

$$NL = \left\{ n_i \# s_i, 1 \leq i \leq k \right\}$$

Where, s_i is the absolute synset (ex. fur#01879788) of n_i rather than the relative synset (ex. fur#2). If a word is not determined through this process, its synset is marked with ("-") and deferred without making a decision. From the above example, *NL* = *{coat#01879457, fur#01879788, skin#-}* is created. The experiment contains the estimation of this new WSD method.

In the next step, the related terms for each UW will be found in *NL* and the relatedness will be measured between UW and its related term(s).

MEASURING THE RELATEDNESS

In this section, we will use the unknown word-list (*UL*) and noun-list (*NL*) extracted through the preceding processes. From the lists, a related term-list (*RL*) is created. Then, the relatedness is measured between an UW and its related term(s) using probabilistic weight (The extent to which it is related probabilistically with an UW) and semantic weight (The semantic importance between the terms and the extent to which the terms are semantically related to an UW). In addition, methods to remove noise and to update will finally be handled.

Extraction of Related Terms

In this process, terms related with each unknown word of *UL* are found from *NL*. If an UW and a specific term frequently co-occur in a document, they can have a strong relationship (Hwang et al., 2008, Mandala et al., 1998). According to this, the terms that have appeared together with an UW are used to create an UW-related (co-occurrence)

term list (*RL*). The following shows the related term-list (*RL_i*) of ith unknown word (*uw_i*).

$$RL_i = \left\{ rt_{ij}, 1 \leq j \leq u_i \right\}$$

Where rt_{ij} is the jth term which co-occurs with uw_i and u_i stands for the number of terms that are related to uw_i.

Measurement of Probabilistic Weight

Bayesian probability measures the probabilistic relationship between elements of RL_i and uw_i. Equation (4) measures the probabilistic weight (*pw*) using Bayesian probability.

$$pw\left(rt_{ij}\right) = \frac{P\left(oc\left(uw_i\right) \mid oc\left(rt_{ij}\right)\right) P\left(oc\left(rt_{ij}\right)\right)}{P\left(oc\left(uw_i\right)\right)}$$

(4)

Where, *oc(uw_i) and oc(rt_{ij})* are the occurrence count for uw_i and for rt_{ij} respectively.

Measurement of Semantic Weight

If terms in RL_i have a strong relationship with uw_i, semantic relations can be formed between them in RL_i (Matveeva et al., 2007, Kong et al., 2006). This is similar to the fact that various terms semantically near to the topic of document appear more frequently in the document. Based on this foundation, uw_i is considered to be the topic. In other words, the semantic weight of each element *(rt_{ij})* can be calculated by how much the semantic relationship is among the elements included in RL_i. While this is similar to the WSD method in the previous section, the context to measure the relationship is different. While elements in *NL* are used for WSD, the elements in *RL* related to uw_i are used for semantic weight.

Since the synsets for each element in RL_i are already determined, semantic weight can be measured by the sum of the relatedness between rt_{ij} and each element. Equation (5) measures the semantic weight (*sw*) of each element.

$$sw\left(rt_{ij}\right) = \sum_{k=1}^{u_i} \frac{1}{\min_{rt_{ik} \in RL_i} \left(d\left(rt_{ij}, rt_{ik}\right)\right)}, j \neq k$$

(5)

Measurement of Relatedness

Through previous steps, probabilistic weight and semantic weight were measured by using Bayesian probability and by finding the relationship respectively. Since the two weights do not affect each other, they can be independent and the two can be multiplied to measure the relatedness between an UW and related terms. However, if a term has no relation with any term among factors in RL_i, its semantic weight (*sw*) becomes 0. Since this makes a value of relatedness 0 regardless of the probabilistic weight (*pw*), 1 is added to each semantic weight at the end. Finally, the equation is defined for relatedness (*rd*) between uw_i and rt_{ij} like (6).

$$rd\left(uw_i, rt_{ij}\right) = pw\left(rt_{ij}\right) \times \left(sw\left(rt_{ij}\right) + 1\right)$$

(6)

Through the equation given above, the relatedness between uw_i and rt_{ij} can be measured. In WordNet, the value for the relatedness between two concepts becomes larger if the relation distance is closer. Moreover, the maximum and the minimum value are 1 and 0 respectively. In other words, $rd(uw_i, rt_{ij})$ becomes 1 when the relation between uw_i and rt_{ij} is that of a synonym. In order to make those values (between WordNet and this work) compatible, the range of the relatedness must be adjusted to $0 < rd \leq 1$. Therefore, we find the maximum relatedness in the result of RL_i and each value (relatedness) divided by the maximum value like (7).

$$rd_{\max_i} = \max\left(rd\left(rt_{ij}\right)\right)$$

(7)

$$final\_rd\left(uw_i, rt_{ij}\right) = \frac{rd\left(rt_{ij}\right)}{rd_{\max_i}}$$

Where, $rd_{max i}$ is the maximum relatedness in RL_i.

Noise Removal and Update

Through the preceding process, the relatedness is semantically grasped between an UW and related terms. Subsets are used to create the UW list for the case, a sequence of proper nouns appear in the process to determine an UW in a section for preprocessing, therefore unnecessary UWs could be created. For example if {A B C} is a sequence of proper nouns uw_a, uw_b, uw_c, *then* uw_{ab}, uw_{bc}, and uw_{abc} are created. In such a result, if even one is satisfied among the following two rules, it is determined to be noise and is removed. First, if $RL_{bc} \subset RL_{abc}$, uw_{bc} is judged to be noise and is removed. In other words, if some uw_i is created as a subset of uw_j, and if $RL_i \subset RL_j$, uw_i is judged to be noise. In case of *{Zinedine, Yazid, Zidane, Zinedine Yazid, Yazid Zidane, Zinedine Yazid Zidane}*, the rule grasps *{Zinedine, Yazid, Zinedine Yazid, Yazid Zidane}* as noises because:

$RL_{Zinedine} \subset RL_{Zinedine\ Yazid\ Zidane}$,

$RL_{Yazid} \subset RL_{Zinedine\ Yazid\ Zidane}$,

$RL_{Zinedine\ Yazid} \subset RL_{Zinedine\ Yazid\ Zidane}$, and

$RL_{Yazid\ Zidane} \subset RL_{Zinedine\ Yazid\ Zidane}$.

Second, if uw_{ab} appears only once and $(RL_a \cap RL_b) \supset RL_{ab}$, then it is also considered to be noise. In such a case, uw_i is an UW that consists of a sequence of proper nouns (becomes UW independently) in most cases. For example, if

"Mercedes-Benz" and "S-Class" appear sequentially, "Mercedes-Benz S-Class" is regarded as one UW.

The UW and related terms that remain in such a process are updated to the database. When the UW lexical database is built using various document collections, an identical UW may appear in two documents or more. Almost all identical UW express the same meaning.

However, polysemy (UWs with different meanings) may occur. In such cases, if an identical UW exists when the system updates the UW into the dictionary (database), the system has been setup to manually type the sense number (under development for automatic classification). For example, the first UW is automatically given a synset number 1. If identical UW were extracted from other documents, the system notifies us, and we judge if the meaning is the same. According to the judgment, different synset numbers like #2, #3, ... are assigned. In addition, if a UW has the same meaning, it accumulates as follows.

Assume that a term set $RL_z = \{a, b, c, d\}$ related to uw_z was already accumulated in the dictionary and that another term set $RL_{z''} = \{b'', c'', e, f\}$ related to uw_z has occurred in the new document, where Z and Z'', b and b'', and c and c'' are each an identical term that appears in different documents. In order to appropriately reflect the influence of the existing value and the new value (large influence: the occurrence of uw_z is frequent, the size of RL_z is large, and rd is measured from data in which the value for each pw and sw is large), the values for each pw and sw are added, we obtain rd_{max} again, and rd is measured again. Finally the database is updated through this process as in figure 3.

Demonstration

Using one simple sample, we will explain the entire process of the research. Figure 4 contains the sample that is the first paragraph in a document about "McDonald[6]" in Wikipedia. *NL* and *UL* are the noun term list and unknown word list

Figure 3. Database update method

$$pw(s_{Zb}) = pw(s_{Zb}) + pw(s_{Zb'}), \quad sw(s_{Zb}) = sw(s_{Zb}) + sw(s_{Zb'})$$
$$pw(s_{Zc}) = pw(s_{Zc}) + pw(s_{Zc'}), \quad sw(s_{Zc}) = sw(s_{Zc}) + sw(s_{Zc'})$$
$$rd(uw_Z, s_{Zj}) = pw(s_{Zj}) \times (sw(s_{Zj}) + 1)$$
$$rd_{max_Z} = \max(rd(s_{Zj}))$$
$$final\_rd(uw_Z, s_{Zj}) = \frac{rd(s_{Zj})}{rd_{max_Z}}$$

respectively. They are extracted from the sample in the order of occurrence in the document. Then, the WSD method is applied to the nouns in *NL*, make related term list RL_i using co-occurrence, and measure pw, sw, and rd. Figure 5 represents all of the result for $uw_{MCDONALD}$.

In the process to make $RL_{MCDONALD}$ by using the sample, one sentence (*italic type* in figure 4) does not contain the $uw_{MCDONALD}$. Therefore, $RL_{MCDONALD}$ excludes two noun words (**bold type** in figure 4). Although the input sample consists of a few sentences, the result shows it can extract the related terms relatively well.

Through analyzing experimental results using much longer documents, more specific and meaningful results are extracted. As a result, it is possible to find the semantic relatedness between unknown words and related terms.

EXPERIMENT

Word Sense Disambiguation

In this paper, a new WSD algorithm appropriate for this research was designed in order to automatically construct an UW lexical dictionary.

WSD is one core area in semantic information processing. Even in this research, the performance of the UW lexical dictionary can be changed depending on the WSD algorithm.

The SSI algorithm of Navigli et al. (2005) executes WSD by combining various online resources. It shows at least 10% higher accuracy

Figure 4. A sample

Input Sample	McDonald"s (NYSE: MCD) is the world"s largest chain of fast food restaurants, serving nearly 54 million customers daily. McDonald"s primarily sells hamburgers, cheeseburgers, chicken products, French fries, breakfast items, soft drinks, milkshakes and desserts. *More recently, it also offers salads, wraps and fruit.* Many McDonald"s restaurants have included a playground for children and advertising geared toward children, and some have been redesigned in a more "natural" style, with a particular emphasis on comfort and the absence of hard plastic chairs and tables.
NL	NYSE, world, chain, food, restaurant, customer, hamburger, cheeseburger, chicken, product, fry, breakfast, item, drink, milkshake, dessert, **salad**, **fruit**, restaurant, playground, advertising, style, emphasis, plastic, chair, table
UL	MCDONALD, MCD, MCDONALD, MCDONALD

Figure 5. The result for Figure 4

uw_i	RL_i	synset	pw	sw	rd
MCDONALD	restaurant	04035397	0.667	1.000	1.0000
MCDONALD	drink	07778483	0.334	2.200	0.8000
MCDONALD	breakfast	07471615	0.334	1.600	0.6500
MCDONALD	hamburger	07591635	0.334	1.350	0.5875
MCDONALD	food	00020429	0.334	1.350	0.5875
MCDONALD	world	08066556	0.334	1.000	0.5000
MCDONALD	dessert	07506385	0.334	0.900	0.4750
MCDONALD	milkshake	07815968	0.334	0.900	0.4750
MCDONALD	style	06969739	0.334	0.850	0.4625
MCDONALD	Cheeseburger	07591848	0.334	0.700	0.4250
MCDONALD	chicken	07540264	0.334	0.650	0.4125
MCDONALD	advertising	01086632	0.334	0.600	0.4000
MCDONALD	fry	09771320	0.334	0.600	0.4000
MCDONALD	table	04327412	0.334	0.533	0.3833
MCDONALD	playground	08520200	0.334	0.400	0.3500
MCDONALD	product	03707459	0.334	0.400	0.3500
MCDONALD	chair	02972284	0.334	0.333	0.3333
MCDONALD	plastic	14399008	0.334	0.250	0.3125
MCDONALD	emphasis	07005633	0.334	0.250	0.3125
MCDONALD	item	03548833	0.334	0.200	0.3000
MCDONALD	chain	09107974	0.334	0.200	0.3000
MCDONALD	customer	09836374	0.334	0	0.2500
MCDONALD	NYSE	03780324	0.334	0	0.2500

Figure 6. WSD Result

	Recall (%)	Precision (%)	F_1-measure (%)
SSI	93.087	84.111	88.372
Our Method	94.855	81.017	87.392

compared to existing methods. At this point, we do not think our method can surpass the SSI because it only utilizes WordNet. However, through comparisons with the SSI algorithm, we attempted to confirm how valuable our method is. Navigli et al. (2005) provides the SSI system on the Web[7] and set the context size limit of 10. The condition of our method is adjusted to be same as SSI. The noun list is extracted from the document and input 10 noun words into both the SSI algorithm and our method. If both methods return the same synset of a word, then it is considered to be correct. If it is different, then we catch the exact meaning from the context and find the synset from WordNet. For the experiment, a total of 2,571 noun words were collected from 23 documents about *"s-class," "digital multimedia broadcasting," "Zidane," "Daewoo Nubira," "Lotteria," "Samsung," "Wikipedia," "McDonald"* and so on from Wikipedia[8]. Using the results of both methods, recall, precision, and F_1-measure were calculated in figure 6. Recall is calculated by using (8).

$$recall = \frac{disambiguation\_count}{total\_count} \qquad (8)$$

The recall rate of our WSD method is about 1.8% point higher than that of the SSI algorithm. However the precision is about 3.1% point less than the SSI algorithm. Since the SSI algorithm has shown it has about a 10% higher precision than other existing WSD methods, our method can also be considered valuable and suitable for this research.

Using "Golden Standard" and the Problem

Evaluation of semantic information processing is not an easy task. In the other research, three evaluation methods are mentioned (Missikoff et al., 2003). Of those methods, we tried to evaluate this research using the "golden standard" that enables us to estimate the result in the most objective way. First, we remove one concept (UW) in WordNet, collect a few documents about the concept, and apply this method. The result contains pairs of UW and related term with relatedness. Using the top 30% (it is the best fit for an analysis because one UW has 10 to 20 related terms) of the result, we find the relations between the UW and related term up to 5-distance in WordNet. For example, if *"vehicle #1 (a conveyance that transports people or objects)"* was extracted as related term with *"litter#3 (conveyance consisting of a chair or bed carried on two poles by bearers)"* that we considered being UW, then we searched the relation between *"litter#3"* and *"vehicle#1"* in WordNet as illustrated below:

"litter#3" - "transport#1" - "vehicle#1"

From documents about *"litter#3"*, the related terms were extracted like figure 7. Figure 7 represents the top 30% of the total related terms and semantic relations searched from WordNet while "-" means no relation (more than 5-distance). In order to analyze, 50 concepts are chosen such as *litter#3, fire engine#1, Carnegie Mellon University#1, carriage house#1, donkey jacket#1, electrocardiogram#1, fire hydrant#1, water tank#1,*

Figure 7. Example using Golden Standard

uw$_i$	RL$_i$	Relation Structures
litter#3	**vehicle#1**	litter#3 -> transport#1 -> vehicle#1
litter#3	**pole#1**	-
litter#3	**transport#1**	litter#3 -> transport#1
litter#3	**person#1**	-
litter#3	member#1	-
litter#3	**yoke#6**	litter#3 -> conveyance#3 -> instrumentality#3 -> connection#3 -> york#6
litter#3	**shoulder#1**	-
litter#3	**passenger#1**	litter#3 -> conveyance#3 -> public_transport#1 -> bus#1 -> passenger#1
litter#3	**sedan#2**	litter#3 -> sedan#2
litter#3	tourist#1	-
litter#3	**chair#1**	-
litter#3	**palanquin#1**	litter#3 -> palanquin#1
litter#3	navigator#-	-
litter#3	**curtain#1**	litter#3 -> conveyance#3 -> instrumentality#3 -> furnishing#2 -> curtain#1
litter#3	**door#1**	-
litter#3	load#-	-
litter#3	**bamboo#1**	-

and so on. Then a total of 798 related terms could be extracted from the top 30%. Through analysis, only 258 terms (32.33%) is found to be actually defined in WordNet.

The experimental result seems to be very disappointing using the golden standard. However, we found WordNet is not covering relations even though there are relations in real life. In the case of real world as shown in figure 7, we can say the concept "*litter#3*" is related to {*pole#1, person#1, shoulder#1, chair#1, door#1, bamboo#1*} (**bold type** in figure 7). Generally people express, explain, describe, and illustrate "*litter#3*" using those terms. Furthermore, in the case of "*fire engine#1 (any of various large trucks that carry firemen and equipment to the site of a fire)*," it must relate to "*fireman#4,*" "*fire#1,*" "*flame#1,*" "*blaze#1,*" "*water#1,*" and so forth,; however, WordNet does not actually.

In other words, this research can reflect relationships used in the real world and be a foundation to overcome the semantic gap that is ultimate objective of semantic Web. Therefore, we could not but try to evaluate this research by another method (by domain expert) mentioned from Missikoff et al. (2003).

EVALUATION BY DOMAIN EXPERTS

For the evaluation, we collected 10 experts. There are 4 departments in the college which the author of this paper attends to. The college is attended by more than 2,000 undergraduate and graduate students. Of those, we could collect evaluators who were deeply interested in domains such as *sports, vehicle, food, internet, multimedia*, and so on. The results from this research were conveyed to each domain"s evaluator. They checked whether the extracted term was related to the UW or not. The evaluation result will be shown from various angles in the detailed sections below.

Basic Relevance

The system found 569 UWs for the experiment; 7431 related terms were extracted. The UW (uw_i) and the related term list (RL_i) were shown without regard to the order of the related value (rd). The evaluators were asked to check those that were thought to be related. Relevance was measured using Equation (9).

$$relevance = \frac{related\_term\_count}{total\_term\_count} \times 100 \tag{9}$$

As the result of the measurement, a total of 4182 were checked as having a relation. A relevance of 56.27% was recorded using Equation (9). In the evaluation, since each RL_i shows all terms that co-occur, this result was identical to result that is obtained by not applying the semantic weight (result of the co-occurrence). In order to carry out a more specific and objective evaluation, the evaluation will be carried out in the next section by comparing with result of Dice Coefficient.

Comparison with other Method

Research to construct or extend knowledge bases automatically using Web documents and data warehouses has been carried out (Missikoff et al., 2003, Navigli et al., 2004, Navigli et al., 2006, Velardi et al., 2007). However, it is hard to compare this research with those results because those researches have also been evaluated on human-decision (subjective). Therefore, we developed another application based on probability.

The Dice Coefficient is the existing representative probabilistic method used to find words related with an UW. This method measures the relationship using the independent appearance frequency for an UW and a regular word as well as their co-occurrence frequency (Mandala et al.,

1998, Missikoff et al., 2003). The method uses equation (10).

$$Dice\_Coefficient = \frac{2 \times f_c}{f_{uw} + f_{rt}} \tag{10}$$

Where, f_c is the co-occurrence frequency, f_{uw} is the frequency in which UW appeared independently and f_{rt} is the frequency in which the related term independently appeared.

In order to compare both methods using the same condition, the same processes were carried out such as pos tagging and UW list and noun term list extraction. In addition, co-occurrence was used to give relation uw_i and RL_i. Finally, the relatedness between uw_i and RL_i was measured using Equation (10), and the noise removal technique presented in this paper was applied. Since the pairs of UW and related terms were extracted using the same document set, the total UW count is 569, related term was 7431, and the relevance is also was 56.27(%). It is the same result as ours. Accordingly, it means that an evaluation should be done using pairs of an UW and a related term(s) obtained by limiting relatedness measured through each method (The relatedness of our method and the Dice Coefficient method) to the top 70%, 50%, 40%, 30%, 20%, and 10%. Figure 8 shows the results of the comparison.

While our method is superior to the other method, it is not significantly superior. This is because, most of the UWs that appear once in a document are listed to explain other key terms, as shown in the example in figure 9. The UW list generated from the example in figure 9 is *{Samsung, DRAM, CPT, CDT, SRAM, TFT-LCD, STN-LCD, CDMA, CTV, LCD Driver IC, LDI, PDP, PCB, Frame Retardant ABS, Dimethyl Formamide, DMF}* and the co-occurrence terms are *{product, world, market, share, color, cathode-ray tube, tv, glass, tuner, handset, color television, monitor, flash memory, module, mobile, phone, plate}*. Here, each element of the UW list will get

Figure 8. Result of Comparison with other Method

Method	Rank (%)					
	70	50	40	30	20	10
Our Method	68.25	69.91	71.49	70.23	71.49	78.16
Dice Coefficient	58.74	58.60	60.24	63.89	63.64	65.52

Figure 9. A Paragraph of a Document

Currently, Samsung has sixteen products that have dominated the world"s market share, including: DRAM, color cathode-ray tube TVs (CPT, CDT), SRAM, TFT-LCD glass substrates, TFT-LCD, STN-LCD, tuner, CDMA handset, color television (CTV), monitor, flash memory, LCD Driver IC (LDI), PDP module, PCB for handheld (mobile phone plates), Flame Retardant ABS, and Dimethyl Formamide (DMF).

Figure 10. Comparison based on the UW Occurrence

oc(uw)	Method	Rank (%)					
		70	50	40	30	20	10
>= 2	Our Method	69.92	73.46	75.47	78.44	79.66	85.43
	This Coefficient	63.60	65.79	69.59	73.87	73.03	74.05
>= 3	Our Method	70.41	74.88	77.88	80.13	82.81	87.26
	Dice Coefficient	63.57	66.24	68.98	72.28	72.22	76.65
>= 5	Our Method	71.04	75.31	78.30	81.89	84.72	89.96
	Dice Coefficient	65.33	68.64	70.80	74.71	75.86	77.46
>= 10	Our Method	78.44	80.46	81.94	84.52	89.73	94.27
	Dice Coefficient	63.16	70.90	75.14	77.50	78.67	80.23

all the co-occurrence terms as related terms. As a result, relevance was lowered because only parts of the UWs were related to them while most were not. Such problems also affected the Dice Coefficient result. Hence, another comparison was additionally executed according to the occurrence of UW. The occurrence was limited to those that appeared more than 2, 3, 5, 10 times and pairs of UW and related terms were counted. Figure 10 shows this result. As shown in figure 10, the results of both methods were verified to improve according to the UW occurrence. However, our method is more dramatically influenced because occurrence of UW signifies an expansion of its related

terms which affects the semantic weight between UW and related term.

Relevance Evaluation According to the Relatedness

In the preceding process, this method was compared with the Dice Coefficient. The major goal of this research is to judge how close a related term is to an UW according to the relatedness. Another analysis was carried out by setting the relatedness threshold to 0.9, 0.8, 0.7, 0.5, and 0.3 with relevance results shown in Figure 11.

This research measured a significantly meaningful relatedness. From the experimental evalu-

Figure 11. Relevance rate according to the relatedness

$oc(uw_i)$	Threshold(rd)				
	0.3	0.5	0.7	0.8	0.9
>=1	63.62	64.28	63.56	64.86	70.12
>=2	72.34	75.82	76.41	80.13	86.96
>=3	73.29	76.01	78.34	83.47	87.62
>=5	75.01	77.78	78.47	85.71	89.86
>=10	77.50	80.55	87.26	91.31	95.53

ation, we conclude that better results can be obtained when using more abundant and varied document collection. While our expectation for building the UW lexical dictionary in this research was 100% automation and 100% relevance, both are not yet perfect. However, if the UW occurrence and relatedness (for example, $oc(uw_i)$ >= 10, rd >= 0.7) are restricted simultaneously, it is possible to minimize the time, labor, and additional effort needed for building the dictionary.

CONCLUSION

This research handles the automated construction and expansion UW lexical dictionary. We use the method that extracts UW from document collections and uses co-occurrence to nominate the UWs and related terms. We have proposed the knowledge based WSD method to grasp accurate meaning of the related terms. This WSD method showed close performance to state-of-the-art SSI algorithm. We also calculated probabilistic weight using Bayesian probability and semantic weight based on semantic relation to obtain the semantic relatedness (similarity) between UW and related term(s). Finally, we came across many pairs of UW and related terms, and this research shows about 15% improvement in performance than Dice Coefficient method that was introduced earlier.

We also set the frequency of the occurrence of UWs as a threshold to build an accurate and precise dictionary. The dictionary which is the

final product can be regarded as an expansion of WordNet. It can be applicable in various areas using knowledge base such as:

- Query expansion: There have been researches on query expansion for semantic search. The expansion can be more broadly applied if the UW lexical dictionary is applied.
- WSD: Since UW is almost unique, the relation between UW and regular words are used to simplify execution of WSD and significantly increase accuracy.
- Semantic document processing: A foundation can be prepared for solving the UW that is a large barrier in semantic document indexing, in metadata creation, in topic detection, and so on.
- Inserting new concepts and new instances to an existing ontology, it can also be used for automatic extension of ontology, text mining, and so on.

A certain level of improvement can be expected just by applying this result to the research areas given above. This research can also be applied to relation expansion of existing dictionaries because the UW lexical dictionary includes relations used in the real world unlike current dictionary such as WordNet that only contain conceptual relations. Therefore, it is possible to improve semantic information processing by utilizing both dictionaries together.

Further research is needed to build a more complete dictionary. The lexical dictionary must handle accurate concepts. The WSD method executed in this research shows an accuracy of about 81%. This is a limitation because only the relations that are defined in WordNet are used. In order to improve this, the knowledge base must be expanded or an additional method should be devised. Moreover, it is necessary for methods to detect the noise concept that was determined to be related through this research. Finally, varied and abundant corpora must be utilized for a more complete UW lexical dictionary.

ACKNOWLEDGMENT

"This research was supported by the Ministry of Knowledge Economy, Korea, under the ITRC(Information Technology Research Center) support program supervised by the IITA(Institute of Information Technology Advancement)" (IITA-2008-C1090-0801-0040)

REFERENCES

Alani, H., Kim, S., Millard, D., Weal, M., Hall, W., Lewis, P., & Shadbolt, N. (2003, January). Automatic Ontology-based Knowledge Extraction from Web Documents. *IEEE Intelligent Systems, 18*(1), 14–21. doi:10.1109/MIS.2003.1179189

Amit, P. Sheth, Ramakrishnan, C., & Thomas, C. (2005). Semantics for the Semantic Web: The Implicit, the Formal and the Powerful. *International Journal on Semantic Web and Information Systems, 1*(1), 1–18. doi:10.4018/jswis.2005010101

Fellbaum, C. (1998). *WordNet: An Electronic Lexical Database.* MIT Press.

Handschuh, S., Staab, S., & Ciravegna, F. (2002). S-CREAM - Semi-automatic CREAtion of Metadata. *Knowledge Engineering and Knowledge Management: Ontologies and the Semantic Web, LNCS, 2473,* 165–184.

Hemayati, R., Meng, W., & Yu, C. (2007). Semantic-Based Grouping of Search Engine Results Using WordNet. *Advanced in Data and Web Management, LNCS, 4505,* 678–686. doi:10.1007/978-3-540-72524-4_70

Hliaoutakis, A., Varelas, G., Voutsakis, E., Petrakis, E., & Milios, E. (2006). Information Retrieval by Semantic Similarity. *International Journal on Semantic Web and Information Systems, 2*(3), 55–73. doi:10.4018/jswis.2006070104

Hwang, M., Baek, S., Choi, J., Park, J., & Kim, P. (2008, January). Grasping Related Words of Unknown Word for Automatic Extension of Lexical Dictionary. In *Proceeding of First International Workshop on Knowledge Discovery and Data Mining,* (pp. 31-35).

Java, A., Nirenburg, S., McShane, M., Finin, T., English, J., & Joshi, A. (2007). Using a Natural Language Understanding System to Generate Semantic Web Content. *International Journal on Semantic Web and Information Systems, 3*(4), 50–74. doi:10.4018/jswis.2007100103

Jovanovic, J., Gasevic, D., & Devedzic, V. (2006, April). Ontology-Based Automatic Annotation of Learning Content. *International Journal on Semantic Web and Information Systems, 2*(2), 91–119. doi:10.4018/jswis.2006040103

Kiryakov, A., Popov, B., Terziev, I., Manov, D., & Ognyanoff, D. (2004, December). Semantic annotation, indexing, and retrieval. *Web Semantics: Science. Services and Agents on the World Wide Web, 2*(1), 49–79. doi:10.1016/j.websem.2004.07.005

Kong, H., Hwang, M., Hwang, G., Shim, J., & Kim, P. (2006). Topic Selection of Web Documents Using Specific Domain Ontology. *MICAI 2006: Advances in Artificial Intelligence. LNAI, 4293*, 1047–1056.

Kong, H., Hwang, M., & Kim, P. (2006, August). The Method for the Unknown Word Classification, In *Proceeding of The 2006 Pacific Rim Knowledge Acquisition Workshop, LNCS4303,* (pp. 207-215).

Liu, S., Liu, F., Yu, C., & Meng, W. (2004). An effective approach to document retrieval via utilizing WordNet and recognizing phrases. In *Proceeding of SIGIR 2004*, (pp. 266-272).

Mandala, R., Takenobu, T., & Hozumi, T. (1998). The Use of WordNet in Information Retrieval. In *Proceedings of Use of WordNet in Natural Language Processing Systems*, (pp. 31-37).

Matveeva, I., & Levow, G. (2007, June). Topic Segmentation with Hybrid Document Indexing. In *Proceedings of the 2007 Joint Conference on Empirical Methods in Natural Language Processing and Computational Natural Language Learning*, 351-359.

Miller, G. A., Beckwith, R., Fellbaum, C., Gross, D., & Miller, K. J. (1990). Introduction to wordnet: An on-line lexical database. *Journal of Lexicography*, *3*(4), 235–244. doi:10.1093/ijl/3.4.235

Missikoff, M., Velardi, P., & Fabriani, P. (2003). Text Mining Techniques to Automatically Enrich a Domain Ontology. *Applied Intelligence*, *18*(3), 323–340. doi:10.1023/A:1023254205945

Navigli, R., & Velardi, P. (2004, June). Learning Domain Ontologies from Document Warehouses and Dedicated Web Sites. *Computational Linguistics*, *30*(2), 151–179. doi:10.1162/089120104323093276

Navigli, R., & Velardi, P. (2005). Structural Semantic Interconnections: a knowledge-based approach to word sense disambiguation. *Special Issue-Syntactic and Structural Pattern Recognition. IEEE Transactions on Pattern Analysis and Machine Intelligence*, *27*(7).

Navigli, R., & Velardi, P. (2006). Ontology Enrichment Through Automatic Semantic Annotation of OnLine Glossaries. *EKAW 2006. Managing Knowledge in a World of Networks, LNCS*, *4248*, 125–140.

Navigli, R., Velardi, P., & Gangemi, A. (2003, January/February). Ontology Learning and Its Application to Automated Terminology Translation. *IEEE Intelligent Systems*, *18*(1), 22–31. doi:10.1109/MIS.2003.1179190

Toutanova, K., Klein, D., Manning, C., & Singer, Y. (2003). Feature-Rich Part-of-Speech Tagging with a Cyclic Dependency Network. In *Proceedings of the 2003 Conference of the North American Chapter of the Association for Computational Linguistics on Human Language Technology*, (pp. 173-180).

Toutanova, K., & Manning, C. (2000). Enriching the Knowledge Sources Used in a Maximum Entropy Part-of-Speech Tagger. In *Proceedings of the Joint SIGDAT Conference on Empirical Methods in Natural Language Processing and Very Large Corpora* (EMNLP/VLC-2000), (pp. 63-70).

Velardi, P., Cucchiarelli, A., & Petit, M. (2007, February). A Taxonomy Learning Method and Its Application to Characterize a Scientific Web Community. *IEEE Transactions on Knowledge and Data Engineering*, *19*(2), 180–191. doi:10.1109/TKDE.2007.21

Velardi, P., Fabriani, P., & Missikoff, M. (2001). Using text processing techniques to automatically enrich a domain ontology. In *Proceedings of the international conference on Formal Ontology in Information Systems*, (pp. 270-284).

Velardi, P., Missikoff, M., & Basili, R. (2001). Identification of relevant terms to support the construction of domain ontologies. In *Proceedings of the workshop on Human Language Technology and Knowledge Management*, (pp. 1-8).

ENDNOTES

1. In this research, Wordnet version 2.1 is used. WordNet: http://wordnet.princeton.edu/
2. Stanford Log-linear Part-Of-Speech Tagger of The Stanford Natural Language Processing Group: http://nlp.stanford.edu/software/tagger.shtml
3. WordNet includes 143,847 noun synsets (index.noun) and stores 203,762 relations between synsets in files (data.noun). This is why systems are very slow for semantic processing research based on a lexical dictionary. In order to speed them up, we built a database (Microsoft Access Driver) first in this research.
4. The SemCor corpus: http://multisemcor.itc.it/semcor.php
5. Lexical FreeNet: http://www.lexfn.com
6. McDonald: http://en.wikipedia.org/wiki/McDonald%27s
7. Structural Semantic Interconnections: http://lcl.uniroma1.it/ssi/
8. http://www.wikipedia.org/wiki/main_page

This work was previously published in International Journal on Semantic Web and Information Systems, Volume 5, Issue 1, edited by Amit P. Sheth, pp. 48-64, copyright 2009 by IGI Publishing (an imprint of IGI Global).

Chapter 3
Extracting Concepts' Relations and Users' Preferences for Personalizing Query Disambiguation

Yan Chen
Georgia State University, USA

Yan-Qing Zhang
Georgia State University, USA

ABSTRACT

For most Web searching applications, queries are commonly ambiguous because words usually contain several meanings. Traditional Word Sense Disambiguation (WSD) methods use statistic models or ontology-based knowledge models to find the most appropriate sense for the ambiguous word. Since queries are usually short, the contexts of the queries may not always provide enough information for disambiguating queries. Thus, more than one interpretation may be found for one ambiguous query. In this paper, we propose a cluster-based WSD method, which finds out all appropriate interpretations for the query. Because some senses of one ambiguous word usually have very close semantic relations, we group those similar senses together for explaining the ambiguous word in one interpretation. If the cluster-based WSD method generates several contradictory interpretations for one ambiguous query, we extract users' preferences from clickthrough data, and determine suitable concepts or concepts' clusters that meet users' interests for explaining the ambiguous query.

INTRODUCTION

Nowadays, Web search engines play a key role in retrieving information from the Internet to provide useful Web documents in response to users' queries. The keywords-based search engines, like GOOGLE, YAHOO Search and MSN Live Search, explore documents by matching keywords in queries with words in documents. However, some keywords have more than one meaning, and such words may be related to different concepts in different contexts, so they are potentially

DOI: 10.4018/978-1-60960-593-3.ch003

ambiguous. Since current search engines simply search keywords separately and do not consider the contexts of queries, word sense ambiguity may result in searching errors for Web search applications. For example, if a user searches "drawing tables in a document" by MSN Live Search, five useless results related to the furniture table will be shown in the first result page. Therefore, an exact concept of a query may be determined by the contexts. Moreover, queries are usually short and contexts in queries do not always provide enough information for disambiguating queries. Under these circumstances, users' preferences may be helpful for determining an appropriate concept for an ambiguous word. For an example, if a biologist searches "mouse", we can speculate that the biologist is interested in Web pages related to a rodent "mouse" instead of a computer device "mouse." Thus, both contexts of queries and users' preferences are useful for disambiguating queries in Web search applications.

In fact, query disambiguation (QD) is a special application of Word Sense Disambiguation (WSD) problems. For most WSD problems, the set of possible meanings for a word is known ahead of time and stored in a lexical database. Then, the meaning for an ambiguous word is assigned depending on its contexts (Wilks, Slator, & Guthrie, 1996).

The traditional WSD methods seek one most related concept for an ambiguous word in a given context. However, ambiguous words usually contain some concepts that have very close semantic relations. From the Cambridge Dictionary, "bank" has four senses: (1) an organization where people and businesses can invest or borrow money, change it to foreign money, and so forth; (2) sloping raised land, especially along the sides of a river; (3) a pile or mass of things; or (4) a row of similar things. From above explanations, we may find that sense (3) and (4) have very similar semantics. Commonly, people are not aware of the senses'

small differences and use them interchangeably. Therefore, a cluster of similar senses for an ambiguous word may better describe user's intents.

This paper proposes a cluster-based WSD method. Firstly, this paper presents a new measure to evaluate the concepts similarities, which can better calculate the information content similarities than the Concept Distances proposed in the earlier research (Rada, Mili, Bicknell, & Blettner, 1989). Secondly, based on concept similarities gathered in the first step, this paper presents an agglomerative clustering algorithm to find out all appropriate interpretations (sense clusters) for the query. Also, for a single ambiguous word in the query, more than one similar sense may be grouped to explain the word in one sense cluster, such as sense (3) and sense (4) can be both related to the ambiguous word "bank" in one interpretation. Thirdly, by extracting users' preferences from the clickthrough data, we may provide personalized interpretations that meet users' interests for ambiguous queries.

The main contributions of the paper are listed as follows:

1. Propose a new measure to evaluate the semantic relations between concepts in IS-A semantic tree.
2. Find out all appropriate interpretations for one query.
3. Find out all appropriate senses to explain one ambiguous word in one interpretation of the query.
4. Personalize QD for meeting users' interests.

This article is organized as follows: Firstly, we present a brief overview of the related work. Then, we describe our proposed method, followed by data collection and experiments section. Finally, we address some contributions and future related work.

RELATED WORK

Word Sense Disambiguation (WSD) is a task to determine one appropriate sense of a polysemous word within a specific context. Much research effort has been put on solving the problem using a number of different approaches.

Supervised learning. Supervised machine learning method is one of the most frequently used approaches for WSD, which induce rules for disambiguating words from training data (manually sense-tagged context). Then, those rules can select correct senses of polysemous words in new contexts (Jiang, & Conrath, 1997; Witten, & Frank, 2005). In the training contexts, given polysemous words are manually annotated with senses, like "Java (Island) is the most populated island of Indonesia, situated between Sumatra and Bali." Then, all stop words, the commonly occurring strings that do not have specific linguistic meanings, should be removed from the context, and only meaningful words are reserved for training. Next, the reserved training words are converted into feature vectors, and a supervised learning algorithm such as support vector machines (SVMs) can be used to extract classifiers to disambiguate the target word "java." Finally, classifiers can disambiguate new instances of ambiguous words in contexts.

The limit of such supervised machine learning is that the training data are expensive and sometimes hard to obtain, and the accuracy of WSD is strongly connected to the amount of labeled data available at hand.

Naive Lesk. Based on the assumption that words in a given context will tend to share a common topic, Mike Lesk introduced the Lesk algorithm for WSD problems (Lesk, 1986).The naive Lesk algorithm disambiguates a target word by comparing all glosses of its senses with all glosses of its context words' senses. Then, one sense will be considered as a best explanation

for the target word if the gloss of that sense has the most overlapping or shared words with the glosses of its neighboring words.

PageRank-style WSD. Mihalcea et al. proposes a novel WSD algorithm which applies PageRank algorithms to a WordNet-based concepts graph (Mihalcea, Tarau, & Figa, 2004). Firstly, based on the WordNet concept graph, this algorithm constructs a relation graph by connecting all senses of the target word and its surrounding words. Then, based on the PageRank algorithm, the node (concept) which gets highest rank in the relation graph will be considered as an appropriate sense for the target word.

Statistic-based WSD. Brena and Ramirez proposed an approach for WSD by classifying words into clusters (Brena, & Ramirez, 2006). Through measuring the co-occurrences of words in the large quantities of Web pages on the Internet, collections of keyword clusters can be built. Then, the exact sense for an ambiguous word can be identified by other words in the same cluster. For example, through statistical analysis, the words "beach," "resort," "Florida," and "hotel" usually appear in same Web pages, so they can be in the same cluster. Keyword palm has three meanings: beach, tree, and electrical device. If palm and resort appear in one Web page, then "palm" should be interpreted as a beach, neither a tree nor an electrical device in that page. However, since billions of Web pages exist on the Internet, it is very difficult to select samples for measuring the co-occurrence degrees of words.

In fact, one query may have multiple interpretations, such as "java and cookie" can be interpreted as "programming language and Web file" or "coffee and food." Thus, it is not always reasonable for finding only one interpretation of the query. Compared to previous methods, our method finds out all appropriate interpretations for the query in the contexts. If those interpretations are contradict, we determine suitable concepts or

Figure 1. A IS-A semantic tree

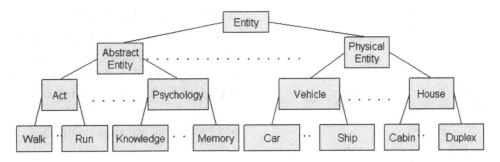

concepts' clusters that meet users' interests for explaining the ambiguous query.

METHOD

In this section, we presents the IS-A semantic trees that can calculate concepts' relations first. Then, the clustered-based QD method is introduced. Finally, we present the personalized QD method that meets users' interests.

IS-A Semantic Trees

The IS-A relation describes the generalization-specialization relationships among concepts. If the concept A is a specialization of the concept B, then A is a sub concept of B and B is the super concept of A. If concepts are organized by IS-A relations among them, a concept hierarchy tree can be established, in which tree nodes represent concepts and links represent generalization-specialization relationships. In the hierarchy tree, every child node only directly links to its parent node and its children nodes, which indicates that a concept only has direct relations with its immediate super concept and immediate sub concepts. The relation between any two nodes in the tree can be explored along with the edges of the tree. Therefore, for one concept, once its super concept and sub concepts are identified, the semantic relations between this concept and any another concept can be simply found in the tree.

Semantic Relations Between Nodes in a IS-A Semantic Tree

In 1989, Rada and Mili defined the concepts' semantic relations by measuring the number of hops between nodes in the IS-A semantic tree (Rada, Mili, Bicknell, & Blettner, 1989). Fewer hops indicate higher semantic relations between concepts. For example, in Figure 1, "car" and "ship" have higher semantic relation than "car" and "cabin" because "car" and "ship" have fewer hops in the IS-A semantic tree. However, the number of hops between concepts may not be a good measure for evaluating concepts relations. For example, WordNet, a semantic dictionary proposed by Miller, defines following IS-A relations: "drink" IS-A "food", "food" IS-A "substance" and "meat" IS-A "food." (1985) Thus, "drink" and "meat" are sub concepts of "food", and "food" is a sub concept of "substance." The numbers of hops between drink-meat and drink-substance are both two, but drink-meat seems more similar than drink-substance. Also, the semantic relations of different level parent-child concept pairs may not be equal. As the previous example, both "food-drink" and "substance-food" are parent-child concept pairs and the level of "food-substance" in the IS-A semantic tree should be higher than the "drink-food", but the "drink-food" concepts pair seems more similar than the "food-substance" pair. Based on above observations, a new measure should be proposed to evaluate the semantic relation between concepts.

Figure 2. The semantic relation of nodes c1 and c2

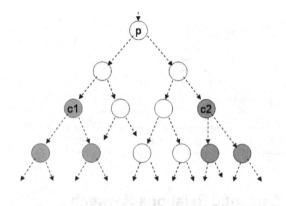

The relations of superclasses and subclasses in the object-oriented programming languages are similar to the generalization-specialization relations in the hierarchy tree. A superclass provides properties to be inherited by the subclasses. The subclasses inherit the properties that superclass has; moreover, the subclasses extend the properties by adding new properties into the superclass. Similarly, if concept B is a child node of concept A, then concept B inherits the information content of concept A; additionally, because it is more specified than the concept A, B extends its information content that concept A does not have. This observation is consistent with the views of information theory: a sub concept has more information content than its super (abstract) concept (Ross, 1976). Based on the standard argumentation of information theory, the information content of a concept C can be quantified as the negative log likelihood, $-\log P(c)$. $P(c)$ is the frequency of encountering an instance of concept c. The frequency of a concept includes the frequency of all its subordinate concepts in the IS-A semantic tree since the count we add to a concept is added to its subsuming concept as well. If the $P(c)$ of the tree root is defined as 1, for any concept node in the tree, its $P(c)$ can be calculated by the formula: N_D/N_A, where N_D represents the number of descendants of that concept node, and N_A represents the number of all nodes in the tree.

Therefore, the information content of a concept is $-\log N_D/N_A$. Then, the relations between any two nodes in the IS-A hierarchy tree can be computed by the overlap of their concepts' contents divided by the union of their concepts' contents. We apply the Jaccard similarity coefficient proposed by Tan, Steinbach, and Kumar to calculate any two nodes' semantic relations,

$$S(c1, c2) = \frac{|-\log \frac{N_P}{N_A}|}{|(-\log \frac{N_{c1}}{N_A}) + (-\log \frac{N_{c2}}{N_A}) - (-\log \frac{N_P}{N_A})|} \tag{1}$$

where N_P is the number of descendants of the lowest common ancestors of $c1$ and $c2$, N_{c1} is the number of descendants of the concept $c1$, N_{c2} is the number of descendants of concept $c2$, and N_A represents the number of all nodes in the tree (2006).

Constructing Senses' Clusters for Queries

For a query "java and bean," both "java" and "bean" are ambiguous words. Based on the WordNet, "java" has three senses {island, coffee, programming language}, and "bean" has five senses {edible seeds, fruit seeds, leguminous plants, software component, human head}. Based on the locations of "java" and "bean" senses shown in the Figure 3, we can apply the formula (1) to calculate the relations between one sense of "java" and one sense of "bean", the relations between any two senses of "bean", and the relations between any two senses of "java". The semantic relations between senses are shown in the Table 1, 2, and 3 respectively.

In the above tables, P.L. means "programming language", S.C. means "software component", and L.P. means "leguminous plants." Based on the semantic relations, we may find that some senses can be grouped as clusters, and each clus-

Figure 3. Senses related to "java" and "bean"

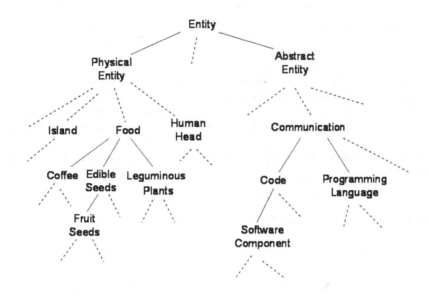

Table 1.

	Island	Coffee	P.L.
Edible Seeds	0.23	0.7	0.06
Fruit Seeds	0.14	0.48	0.04
L.P.	0.16	0.68	0.08
S.C.	0.12	0.03	0.65
Human Head	0.08	0.11	0.1

Table 2.

	Edible Seeds	Fruit Seeds	L.P.	S.C.	Human Head
Edible Seeds	1	0.86	0.8	0.09	0.12
Fruit Seeds		1	0.07	0.04	0.09
L.P.			1	0.06	0.1
S.C.				1	0.1

Table 3.

	Island	Coffee	P.L.
Island	1	0.13	0.08
Coffee		1	0.05
P.L.			1

Algorithm 1. Senses clustering

Input:
The semantic matrixes of senses, which list all semantic relations of senses in words and between words
Output:
Senses' clusters
Step 1: Initialize a sense array by listing all senses of the words in the query.
Step 2: Connect two disjoint nodes A and B, which have the highest weights (semantic relations) in the array. The nodes A and B may be senses, pseudo-senses, or one sense and one pseudo-sense. Then, create a pseudo-sense T to represent the A and B.
Step 3: Update the weights between that pseudo-sense T with all rest senses and pseudo-senses. The updated weight between pseudo-senses T and T' is the highest semantic relation between two senses and one of them comes from T while another of them comes from T'.
Step 4: Repeat the step 2 and 3 until all the weights between any senses or pseudo-senses are smaller than a threshold value δ, or all senses are grouped into one pseudo-sense.

Figure 4. An implementation of senses clustering

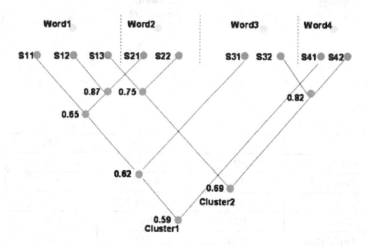

ter represents one interpretation of the query, such as "programming language" and "software component" can be one interpretation for the query "java and bean" while "coffee" and "edible seeds, fruit seeds, and L.P." can be another interpretation of the query.

Then, based on the semantic relations, we propose an agglomerative clustering method to group the senses of ambiguous words into clusters, and each cluster should be one interpretation of the query. Also, because some senses of one ambiguous word usually have very close semantic relations, we may group those similar senses together for explaining the ambiguous word in one interpretation, such as "edible seeds, fruit seeds, and L.P." for explaining "bean" in the previous example.

Before presenting the algorithm, we introduce one term used in our algorithm, "pseudo-sense," which is a node recursively grouped by the senses or pseudo-senses.

Figure 4 give us an example for implementing the algorithm 1. In Figure 4, we have a query contains four words and nine senses in total. The words are represented by the green nodes, senses are represented by blue nodes, and pseudo-concepts are represented by the pink nodes. Then, we always merge the senses that have the highest semantic relations and thus pseudo-concepts are created. Finally, we obtain two sense clusters and their weights.

Based on the algorithm 1, we may obtain many clusters, and some of them can be used as interpretations of the query, but others may not. The first reason is that some clusters have low weights, which may indicate low senses' semantic relations in those clusters. Moreover, some clusters do not cover the senses of most words, so they may not be good candidates for interpreting the query. Thus, we need to evaluate the fitness of clusters based on their coverage and weights. We apply the Harmonic Mean proposed by chou to calculate the fitness of the concept clusters, where coverage is the words covered by the cluster divided by the number of all words, and the weight can be obtained from the algorithm 1, which is the smallest semantic relation between two senses in the cluster (1969).

$$fitness = \frac{2 \times Coverage \times Weight}{Coverage + Weight} \qquad (2)$$

Once the fitness of concept clusters calculated, we propose the following two strategies to determine candidates of clusters for interpreting ambiguous queries.

Strategy 1. One cluster of concepts is considered as one interpretation of one ambiguous query only if the fitness of the cluster is greater than a pre-defined threshold value δ'.

Strategy 2. First, the clusters of concepts will be sorted non-increasingly based on their fitness. Then, one cluster of concepts is considered as one interpretation of the ambiguous query only if the fitness of the cluster is highest in all clusters or it satisfies the following two conditions: its previous cluster is one interpretation of the query; and

$$\frac{fitness(PC) - fitness(CC)}{fitness(PC)} < \delta'', \qquad (3)$$

where *fitness(PC)* represents the fitness of the previous cluster and *fitness(CC)* represents the fitness of the current cluster.

Strategy 1 simply obtains the candidates of clusters by defining a threshold value δ'. Thus, the process of candidates' selection will be much easier than the strategy 2. However, it is difficult to determine the suitable threshold value for gathering adequate candidates of clusters. Small threshold value may result in too many weak candidates while large threshold value may result in no candidates. Therefore, we use strategy 2 to select candidates of clusters, which guarantees at least one good candidate to be selected.

After good concepts' clusters gathered, the membership that one query can be explained by a concepts' cluster is represented by the following formula,

$$\mu_i = \frac{fitness(C_i)}{\sum_{j=1}^{n} fitness(C_j)}, \qquad (4)$$

where *fitness(C_i)* represents the fitness of cluster *i*.

Usually, the correct interpretations of an ambiguous query may be determined by the contexts. However, since queries are usually short, the contexts of the queries may not always provide enough information for disambiguating queries. Thus, based on the concepts' semantic relations and the concepts clustering algorithm, we may be not able to gather even one interpretation for the query because of no context, or gather several unrelated or even contradict interpretations for one ambiguous query. For the above "java and bean" example, we may gather two interpretations ("programming language", "software component"), and ("coffee", edible seeds, fruit seeds, and L.P.). Thus, we have to determine the compatibility of concepts' clusters. If concepts' clusters are unrelated or even contradict, we must select one of concepts' clusters as the interpretation of the ambiguous query.

$$compatibility(C_1, C_2) = \frac{\sum_{i=1,j=1}^{m,n} S(c_{1i},\ c_{2j})}{m \times n} \tag{5}$$

The formula (4) defines the compatibility of two concepts' clusters C_1 and C_2, where c_{1i} is one concept in the C_1 and $S(c_{1i},\ c_{2j})$ represents the semantic relation between concepts c_{1i} and c_{2j}.

In case of not an appropriate interpretation or several contradict interpretations for an ambiguous query, users' preferences may be helpful for determining a suitable concepts' cluster for the query. For the previous query example, the interpretation can be ("programming language", "software component") if one user favors the computer programming topic. Thus, for different users, we may provide personalized interpretation based on their preferences.

Obtaining Users' Preferences

Users' preferences play an important role in personalizing QD applications. We proposed the following two strategies for obtaining users' preferences. The first strategy simply asks users to manually define their interests through an interface of users' preferences. Also, users may specify the degrees of interests through the interface. However, it is not always possible to ask all users to input their interests because of time consuming. Thus, we must propose a strategy for automatically collect users' interests from their click-through data that contain users' queries and corresponding clicked URLs.

The Open Directory Project (ODP) is the largest, most comprehensive and manually edited directory of World Wide Web that has been classified into 787,774 hierarchical categories by 68,983 human editors (Skrenta, & Truel, 2008). Since ODP collects and classifies most popular Web pages, we may assume that most Web pages clicked by users have been collected by the ODP.

Thus, users' interests may be represented by the categories of Web pages clicked by users. Based on this assumption, we proposed our second strategy for obtaining users' preferences.

Since ODP contains hierarchical categories, we selected the second level categories that contain 662 meaningful labels as users' preferences. Once a user clicks a Web page, the category of that page will be recorded as the user's interest. Also, we proposed the following formula to calculate the degree of one interest. In the formula 6, p_i represents the preference i, $w(p_i)$ represents the weight of the p_i, and $click(p_i)$ represents the number of clicked Web pages belonging to p_i.

$$w(p_i) = \frac{click(p_i)}{\sum_{j=1}^{n} click(p_j)} \tag{6}$$

Also, the weights of users' preferences should be dynamically updated based on the users' most recent clickthrough data. For example, if a user clicks on the Web pages belonging to category "food" several times, the weight of category "food" should gradually increases.

Calculating Relations between Concepts' Clusters and Preferences

Once users' preferences are collected from users' clickthrough data, the relations between concepts' clusters and preferences need to be calculated for queries disambiguation.

Since categories of ODP are usually short and clearly defined, we may assume that those categories correspond to some concepts in the IS-A semantic trees. Thus, the formula of concepts' semantic relations can be used for calculating the relations between concepts' clusters and users' preferences.

Based on the formula of concepts' semantic relations, one concept may have relations with several preferences, and several concepts in one

Figure 5. Obtaining users' preferences

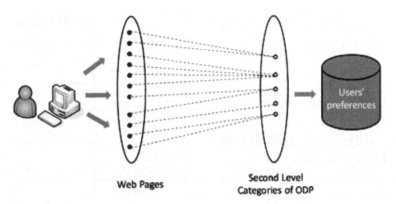

Web Pages   Second Level
Categories of ODP

cluster may have relations with one preference, so there exists a n-n mapping between concepts in one cluster and preferences as shown in the figure 6. For one concept, its relations with preferences are represented by the following set,

$$R(c_i P) = \{S(c_i p_1), S(c_i p_2), ..., S(c_i p_j)\}, \quad (7)$$

where $S(c_i, p_j)$ represents the semantic relation of concept i and preference j. The relations between one concepts' cluster and preferences are defined by the formula (8).

$$R(CP) = \{S(c_1 p_1) \cap S(c_2 p_1) \cap ... \cap S(c_n p_1), ...,$$
$$S(c_1 p_2) \cap S(c_2 p_2) \cap ... \cap S(c_n p_2), ...,$$
$$S(c_1 p_n) \cap S(c_2 p_n) \cap ... \cap S(c_n p_n)\}$$
$$(8)$$

After normalization, the relation between one concepts' cluster and the preference i is defined in formula (9).

$$R(Cp_i) = \frac{S(c_1 p_i) \cap S(c_2 p_i) \cap ... \cap S(c_n p_i)}{\sum_{j=1}^{n} S(c_1 p_j) \cap S(c_2 p_j) \cap ... \cap S(c_n p_j)}$$
$$(9)$$

Figure 6. Relations between concepts' clusters and preferences

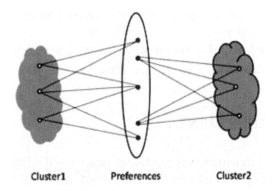

Cluster1   Preferences   Cluster2

Applying Users' Preferences for Queries Disambiguation

After we obtained users' preferences and their weights through the above steps, preferences may be applied for personalizing queries disambiguation. Depending on the weights of preferences and their relations with concepts' clusters, we defined the following formula to updating the membership of a concepts' cluster that can explain one ambiguous query,

$$\mu_i' = \frac{\mu_i(1 + \sum_{k=1}^{m} R(Cp_k) \times w(p_k))}{\sum_{j=1}^{n} \mu_j(1 + \sum_{h=1}^{L} R(Cp_h) \times w(p_h))}, \quad (10)$$

where μ_i represents the original membership, $R(Cp_i)$ the relation between the concepts' cluster and the preference i, and $w(p_i)$ the weight of the preference i. Based on membership function of concepts or concepts' clusters, we may select ones that have high membership as the interpretations of queries.

Based on the formula 6, if a user favors one topic, like "food", the weights of preferences related to "food" should increase. Then, the memberships of concepts' clusters obtained from the algorithm 1, like "coffee, edible seeds, fruit seeds, and L.P.", also increases because they have relations with the preferences containing topic "food."

EXPERIMENTS

We constructed our testing data set based on the TREC queries in the 2004 and 2005 robust track, and 2005 KDDCUP queries. Most TREC robust track queries only have only one interpretation, which is explicitly defined in the topic's description and narrative. The 2005 KDDCUP queries are usually ambiguous and may have more than one interpretation, which may address a number of different topics that search engines should retrieve. We collected 265 queries from the TREC query set, which contain 374 ambiguous terms, and those 265 queries have 289 interpretations in total. Also, we collected 108 queries from the KDDCUP queries, which contain 221 ambiguous terms, and those queries have 174 interpretations in total. Finally, we collected 373 queries for our testing set. Then, we divided our testing set into eight groups. For each group, the number of TREC queries and KDDCUP queries are listed in Table 4.

Table 4.

	# TREC Queries	# KDDCUP Queries
Group 1	44	4
Group 2	42	6
Group 3	38	8
Group 4	34	10
Group 5	30	14
Group 6	29	18
Group 7	26	22
Group 8	22	26

From group 1 to group 8, the number of TREC queries decreases while the number of KDDCUP queries increases. Thus, the number of queries' interpretations in the latter group may be larger than the previous groups.

Evaluating the Cluster-based WSD Method

In order to evaluate our algorithm performance, we used the following two well-known WSD algorithms, Adapt Lesk proposed by Banerjee and Pedersen (2002) and Case-based WSD by Liu, Yu, and Meng (2005), for comparison.

Adapt Lesk: Banerjee and Pedersen proposed an adaptation of the Lesk algorithm that measures words' semantic relatedness by finding overlaps in glosses. One difference between the Adapt Lesk and Naive Lesk is the Adapt Lesk method uses lexical database WordNet rather than a standard dictionary as the source of glosses. Another difference is that the Adapt Lesk method defines an overlap between words to be the longest sequence of consecutive words that occurs in both words' glosses. Each overlap found between two glosses contributes a score equal to the square of the number of words in the overlap. For any two words, if two glosses of them have highest overlap scores, these glosses should be best senses for the words.

Figure 7. The comparison of the algorithms' precisions

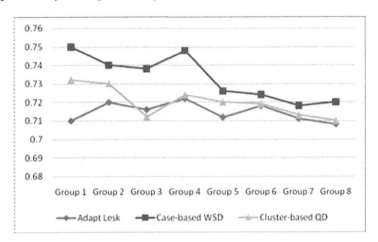

Case-based WSD: Eleven cases are listed for comparing the information of the ambiguous word's synonym set, definitions, and hyponym set with the information of the context words' synonym set, definitions and hyponym set. For each case, based on the information associability between the ambiguous word and its surrounding context words, the correct sense related to the ambiguous word can be determined by the predefined rule.

We propose the following formulas to evaluate the performances of Adapt Lesk, Case-based WSD and our algorithm. Each interpretation of one query is corresponding to one cluster of the senses gathered in the algorithm 1. Let's assume a query has M interpretations, so M clusters of senses can be extracted from this query by the algorithm 1. The precision, recall and F-score of the WSD performance is defined as follows,

$$precision = \frac{1}{M} \sum_{i=1}^{M} \frac{C_{i\_}relevant \cap C_{i\_}retrieved}{C_{i\_}retrieved} \tag{11}$$

$$recall = \frac{1}{M} \sum_{i=1}^{M} \frac{C_{i\_}relevant \cap C_{i\_}retrieved}{C_{i\_}relevant} \tag{12}$$

$$F - score = \frac{2 \times (precision \times recall)}{(precision + recall)}. \tag{13}$$

In above formulas (11) and (12), $C_{i\_}retrieved$ represents the retrieved senses for cluster (interpretation) i, and $C_{i\_}relevant$ represent the relevant senses for cluster (interpretation) i.

Based on Figure 7, case-based WSD method has the highest precision compared to Adapt Lesk and our algorithm. Because Case-based WSD and Adapt Lesk methods always try to find only one most appropriate sense for ambiguous words and our method always try to find all appropriate senses for the words, our method may find more incorrect senses than the previous methods. However, based on the Figure 8 and 9, the recall and F-score of our method is much higher than the case-based WSD and Adapt Lesk methods. Because the previous methods always try to find out the most appropriate interpretation for the query but ignore other possible interpretations, their performance will degrade as the number of KDDCUP queries increases.

Figure 8. The comparison of the algorithms' recalls

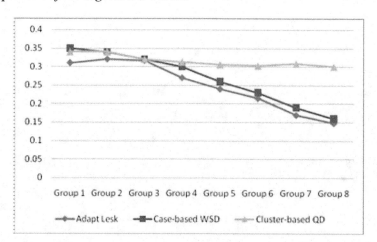

Figure 9. The comparison of the algorithms' F-scores

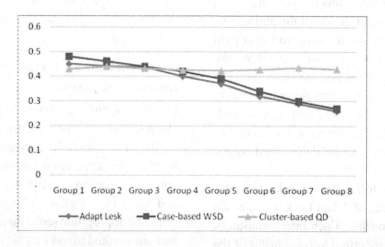

EVALUATING THE PERSONALIZED CLUSTER-BASED QD METHOD

In order to evaluate the personalized cluster-based WSD method, we collected the clickthrough data from the log data of a commercial search engine. The log data consist of more than 20M Web queries from 650k users over three months, from March 1, 2006 to May 31, 2006. The number of clicked URLs for the 20M Web queries is 19,442,629. In order to best speculate users' preferences, we randomly selected thirty two users' IDs who submitted at least twenty ambiguous queries to the search engine and subsequently clicked more than fifty Web search results. For the ambiguous queries in the clickthrough data, although we cannot ask original users their interpretations of the queries, we may analyze the contexts of Web pages that they selected, and manually disambiguated the queries for matching the Web pages' contexts. Then, those users' clickthrough data and the interpretations we speculated are used as test sets for evaluating algorithms' performance.

We implemented the personalized cluster-based QD method, and compare its performance with the previous cluster-based QD method and

Figure 10. The performance of Case-based WSD, Cluster-based QD and Personalized cluster-based QD

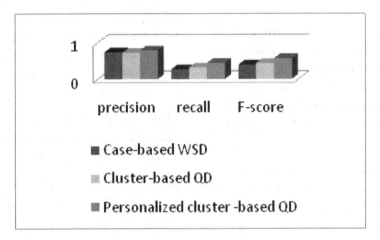

case-based WSD. Their precisions, recalls and F-scores are shown in the Figure 10.

Compared to case-based WSD and cluster-based QD algorithms, the personalized cluster-based QD algorithm obtains slight precision improvement and moderate recall and F-score improvement. Since the cluster-based QD algorithm normally finds all possible interpretations of ambiguous queries but ignores users' interests, it may create unrelated or contradict interpretations, which will decrease the precision of prediction. However, the personalized cluster-based QD algorithm may select interpretations that match users' interests, so it gains precision improvement. Moreover, because of short contexts of queries, the cluster-based QD algorithm may not provide any interpretations if no clusters created. The personalized cluster-based QD algorithm may find concepts closely related to users' interests as interpretations of queries, which will gains recall improvement.

CONCLUSION

Ambiguous queries are a potential source of errors in Web search applications. Much research

effort has been put on solving the problem by a number of different approaches, such as supervised machine learning methods and Naive Lesk. Since queries are usually short and may not provide enough context information for disambiguating queries, more than one appropriate interpretation for ambiguous queries may be found. Compared to previous methods, our method finds out all appropriate interpretations for ambiguous queries. If users input short queries and the context of queries cannot provide enough information for disambiguating queries, our method may finds interpretations that meet users' interests. Based on the experiments, our method's performance is better than the cased-based WSD and Adapt Lesk algorithms.

In future, we will construct a Meta search engine that accepts queries and transfers the queries to traditional search engines. Also, we will deploy our personalized QD agent between the user interface of the Meta search engine and traditional search engines. Thus, the agent can collect users' queries and clicked Web pages, and provide personalized interpretations based on the queries contexts and users' preferences. Based on users' queries and clicked Web pages, we can evaluate the performance of our agent.

REFERENCES

Banerjee, S., & Pedersen, T. (2002). An Adapted Lesk Algorithm for Word Sense Disambiguation Using WordNet. In A. Gelbukh (Ed.), *proceedings of the Third International Conference on Intelligent Text Processing and Computational Linguistics*. (pp. 136-145). London: Springer-Verlag press.

Brena, R. F., & Ramirez, E. Z. (2006). A Soft Semantic Web. *In Proceeding of 1st IEEE Workshop on Hot Topics in Web Systems and Technologies*. (pp. 1-8). Boston: IEEE press.

Chou, Y. (1969). *Statistical Analysis*. New York, NY: Holt International.

Jiang, J., & Conrath, D. (1997). Semantic Similarity based on Corpus Statistics and Lexical Taxonomy. In *Proceeding of International Conference on Research in Computational Linguistics*. Taiwan.

Lesk, M. (1986). Automatic Sense Disambiguation Using Machine Readable Dictionaries: how to tell a pine cone from an ice cream cone. In V. DeBuys (Ed.), *Proceedings of the 5th annual international conference on Systems documentation*. (pp. 24-26). Toronto: ACM press.

Liu, S., Yu, C., & Meng, W. (2005). Word Sense Disambiguation in Queries. *In Proceedings of the 14th ACM international conference on Information and knowledge management*. (pp. 525-532). Bremen: ACM press.

Mihalcea, R., Tarau, P., & Figa, E. (2004). PageRank on Semantic Networks, with application to Word Sense Disambiguation. *In Proceedings of the 20th international conference on Computational Linguistics*. Geneva: Association for Computational Linguistics Press.

Miller, G. (1990). WordNet: An On-line Lexical Database. *International Journal of Lexicography*, *3*, 235–244. doi:10.1093/ijl/3.4.235

Rada, R., Mili, H., Bicknell, E., & Blettner, M. (1989). Development and application of a metric on semantic nets. *IEEE Transactions on Systems, Man, and Cybernetics*, *19*(1), 17–30. doi:10.1109/21.24528

Ross, S. (1976). *A First Course in Probability*. New York, NY: Macmillan.

Skrenta, R., & Truel, B. (2008). Open Directory Project. Retrieved November 6, 2008, from http://www.dmoz.org

Tan, P., Steinbach, M., & Kumar, V. (2006). *Introduction to Data Mining: Concepts and Techniques*. Boston, MA: Pearson Addison Wesley.

Wilks, Y., Slator, B., & Guthrie, L. (1996). *Electric Words: dictionaries, computers and meanings*. Cambridge, MA: MIT Press.

Witten, I., & Frank, E. (2005). *Data Mining: Practical machine learning tools and techniques* (2nd ed.). San Francisco, CA: Morgan Kaufmann.

This work was previously published in International Journal on Semantic Web and Information Systems, Volume 5, Issue 1, edited by Amit P. Sheth, pp. 65-79, copyright 2009 by IGI Publishing (an imprint of IGI Global).

Chapter 4
The Berlin SPARQL Benchmark

Christian Bizer
Freie Universität Berlin, Germany

Andreas Schultz
Freie Universität Berlin, Germany

ABSTRACT

The SPARQL Query Language for RDF and the SPARQL Protocol for RDF are implemented by a growing number of storage systems and are used within enterprise and open Web settings. As SPARQL is taken up by the community, there is a growing need for benchmarks to compare the performance of storage systems that expose SPARQL endpoints via the SPARQL protocol. Such systems include native RDF stores as well as systems that rewrite SPARQL queries to SQL queries against non-RDF relational databases. This article introduces the Berlin SPARQL Benchmark (BSBM) for comparing the performance of native RDF stores with the performance of SPARQL-to-SQL rewriters across architectures. The benchmark is built around an e-commerce use case in which a set of products is offered by different vendors and consumers have posted reviews about products. The benchmark query mix emulates the search and navigation pattern of a consumer looking for a product. The article discusses the design of the BSBM benchmark and presents the results of a benchmark experiment comparing the performance of four popular RDF stores (Sesame, Virtuoso, Jena TDB, and Jena SDB) with the performance of two SPARQL-to-SQL rewriters (D2R Server and Virtuoso RDF Views) as well as the performance of two relational database management systems (MySQL and Virtuoso RDBMS).

1. INTRODUCTION

The SPARQL Query Language for RDF (Prud'hommeaux & Seaborne 2008) and the SPARQL Protocol for RDF (Kendall et al, 2008)

are increasingly used as a standardized query API for providing access to datasets on the public Web[1] and within enterprise settings[2]. Today, most enterprise data is stored in relational databases. In order to prevent synchronization problems, it is preferable in many situations to have direct SPARQL access to this data without having to replicate it

DOI: 10.4018/978-1-60960-593-3.ch004

into RDF. Such direct access can be provided by SPARQL-to-SQL rewriters that translate incoming SPARQL queries on the fly into SQL queries against an application-specific relational schema based on a mapping. The resulting SQL queries are then executed against the legacy database and the query results are transformed into a SPARQL result set. An overview of existing work in this space has been gathered by the W3C RDB2RDF Incubator Group[3] and is presented in (Sahoo et al., 2009).

This article introduces the Berlin SPARQL Benchmark (BSBM) for comparing the SPARQL query performance of native RDF stores with the performance of SPARQL-to-SQL rewriters. The benchmark aims to assist application developers in choosing the right architecture and the right storage system for their requirements. The benchmark might also be useful for the developers of RDF stores and SPARQL-to-SQL rewriters as it reveals the strengths and weaknesses of current systems and might help to improve them in the future.

The Berlin SPARQL Benchmark was designed in accordance with three goals:

1. The benchmark should allow the comparison of storage systems that expose SPARQL endpoints across architectures.
2. The benchmark should simulate an enterprise setting where multiple clients concurrently execute realistic workloads of use case motivated queries against the systems under test.
3. As the SPARQL query language and the SPARQL protocol are often used within scenarios that do not rely on heavyweight reasoning but focus on the integration and visualization of large amounts of data from multiple data sources, the BSBM benchmark should not be designed to require complex reasoning but to measure SPARQL query performance against large amounts of RDF data.

The BSBM benchmark is built around an e-commerce use case, where a set of products is offered by different vendors and consumers have posted reviews about products. The benchmark query mix emulates the search and navigation pattern of a consumer looking for a product.

The implementation of the benchmark consists of a data generator and a test driver. The data generator supports the creation of arbitrarily large datasets using the number of products as scale factor. In order to be able to compare the performance of RDF stores with the performance of SPARQL-to-SQL rewriters, the data generator can output two representations of the benchmark data: An RDF representation and a purely relational representation.

The test driver executes sequences of SPARQL queries over the SPARQL protocol against the system under test (SUT). In order to emulate a realistic workload, the test driver can simulate multiple clients that concurrently execute query mixes against the SUT. The queries are parameterized with random values from the benchmark dataset, in order to make it more difficult for the SUT to apply caching techniques. The test driver executes a series of warm-up query mixes before the actual performance is measured in order to benchmark systems under normal working conditions.

The BSBM benchmark also defines a SQL representation of the query mix, which the test driver can execute via JDBC against relational databases. This allows the comparison of SPARQL results with the performance of traditional RDBMS.

This article makes the following contributions to the field of benchmarking Semantic Web technologies:

1. It complements the field with a use case driven benchmark for comparing the SPARQL query performance of native RDF stores with the performance of SPARQL-to-SQL rewriters.
2. It provides guidance to application developers by applying the benchmark to measure

Figure 1. Overview of the abstract data model

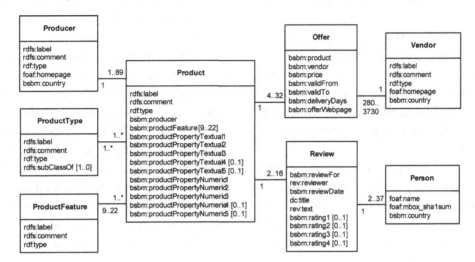

and compare the performance of four popular RDF stores, two SPARQL-to-SQL rewriters and two relational database management systems.

The remainder of the paper is structured as follows: Section 2 gives an overview of the benchmark dataset. Section 3 motivates the benchmark query mix and defines the benchmark queries. Section 4 compares the BSBM benchmark with other benchmarks for Semantic Web technologies. As a proof of concept, Sections 5 and 6 present the results of an experiment that applies the BSBM benchmark to compare the performance of RDF stores and SPARQL-to-SQL rewriters, and sets the results into relation to the performance of RDBMS.

2. THE BENCHMARK DATASET

The BSBM benchmark is settled in an e-commerce use case in which a set of products is offered by different vendors and consumers have posted reviews about these products on various review sites. The benchmark defines an abstract data model for this use case together with data production rules that allow benchmark datasets to

be scaled to arbitrary sizes using the number of products as scale factor. In order to compare RDF stores with SPARQL-to-SQL rewriters, the benchmark defines two concrete representations of the abstract model: An RDF representation and a relational representation.

The data model contains the following classes: *Product, ProductType, ProductFeature, Producer, Vendor, Offer, Review,* and *Person.* Figure 1 gives an overview of the properties of each class, the multiplicity of properties, and the multiplicity ranges into which 99% of the associations between classes fall. In the following we describe the data production rules that are used to generate datasets for a given scale factor n.

The data generator creates n product instances. Products are described by a rdfs:label and a rdfs:comment. Products have between 3 and 5 textual properties. The values of these properties consist of 5 to 15 words which are randomly chosen from a dictionary. Products have 3 to 5 numeric properties with property values ranging from 1 to 2000 with a normal distribution.

Products have a type that is part of a type hierarchy. The depth and width of this subsumption hierarchy depends on the chosen scale factor. The depth of the hierarchy is calculated as $d = round(log10(n))/2 + 1$. The branching factor for the root level of the hierarchy is $bfr = 2*round(log10(n))$. The branching factor for all other levels is 8. Every product has one leaf-level product type. In order to run the benchmark against stores that do not support RDFS inference, the data generator can forward chain the product hierarchy and add all resulting rdf:type statements to the dataset.

Products have a variable number of product features. Two products that share the same product type also share the same set of possible product features. This set is determined as follows: Each product type in the type hierarchy is assigned with a random number of product features. The range of these random numbers is calculated for product types on level i of the hierarchy as $lowerBound = 35 * i / (d * (d+1)/2 - 1)$ and $upperBound = 75 * i / (d * (d+1)/2 - 1)$, with d being the depth of the hierarchy. The set of possible features for a specific product type is the union of the features of this type and all its super-types. For a specific product, each feature from this set is picked with a probability of 25%.

Products are produced by producers. The number of products per producer follows a normal distribution with a mean of $\mu = 50$ and a standard deviation of $\sigma = 16.6$. New producers are created until all products are assigned to a producer.

Products are offered by vendors. Vendors are described by a label, a comment, a homepage URL and a country URI. Countries have the following distribution: US 40%, UK 10%, JP 10%, CN 10%, 5% DE, 5% FR, 5% ES, 5% RU, 5% KR, 5% AT.

There are 20 times n offers. Offers are valid for a specific period and contain a price ($5-$10000) and the number of days it takes to deliver the product (1-21). Offers are distributed over products using a normal distribution with the parameters $\mu = n/2$ and $\sigma = n/4$. The number of offers per vendor follows a normal distribution with the parameters $\mu = 2000$ and $\sigma = 667$. New vendors are created until all offers are assigned to a vendor.

Reviews consist of a title and a review text between 50 and 300 words. Reviews have up to four ratings with a random integer value between 1 and 10. Each rating is missing with a probability of 30%. There are 10 times the scale factor n reviews. The reviews are distributed over products using a normal distribution with the parameters $\mu = n/2$ and $\sigma = n/4$. The number of reviews per reviewer is randomly chosen from a normal distribution with the parameters $\mu = 20$ and $\sigma = 6.6$. New reviewers are generated until each review is assigned. Reviewers are described by their name, mailbox checksum and the country the reviewer lives in. The reviewer countries follow the same distribution as the vendor countries.

Table 1 summarizes the number of instances of each class in BSMB datasets of different sizes.

The BSBM data generator can output an RDF representation and a relational representation of benchmark datasets. As the data production rules are deterministic, it is possible to create RDF and relational representations of exactly the same data.

3. THE QUERY MIX

There are two principle options for the design of benchmark query mixes (Gray, 1993): 1. Design the queries to test specific features of the query language or to test specific data management approaches. 2. Base the query mix on the specific requirements of a real world use case. The second approach leads to sequences of more complex queries that test combinations of different language features. With SP²Bench (Schmidt, et al., 2008a and 2008b), there exists already a benchmark for SPARQL stores that is designed for the comparison of different RDF data management approaches. We therefore decided to follow the second approach and designed the BSBM query mix as a sequence of use case motivated queries that simulate a realistic workload against the SUT.

The query mix emulates the search and navigation pattern of a consumer looking for a product.

Table 1. Number of instances in BSBM datasets of different sizes

Total number of triples	250K	1M	25M	100M
Number of products	666	2,785	70,812	284,826
Number of product features	2,860	4,745	23,833	47,884
Number of product types	55	151	731	2011
Number of producers	14	60	1422	5,618
Number of vendors	8	34	722	2,854
Number of offers	13,320	55,700	1,416,240	5,696,520
Number of reviewers	339	1432	36,249	146,054
Number of reviews	6,660	27,850	708,120	2,848,260
Total number of instances	**23,922**	**92,757**	**2,258,129**	**9,034,027**

In a real world setting, such a query sequence could for instance be executed by a shopping portal which is used by consumers to find products and sales offers.

First, the consumer searches for products that have a specific type and match a generic set of product features. After looking at basic information about some matching products, the consumer gets a better idea of what he actually wants and searches again with a more specific set of features. After going for a second time through the search results, he searches for products matching two alternative sets of features and products that are similar to a product that he likes. After narrowing down the set of potential candidates, the consumer starts to look at offers and recent reviews for the products that fulfill his requirements. In order to check the trustworthiness of the reviews, he retrieves background information about the reviewers. He then decides which product to buy and starts to search for the best price for this product offered by a vendor that is located in his country and is able to deliver within three days. After choosing a specific offer, he retrieves all information about the offer and then transforms the information into another schema in order to save it locally for future reference. Table 2 shows the BSBM query mix resulting from this search and navigation path.

The BSBM benchmark defines two representations of the query mix: A SPARQL representation for benchmarking RDF stores and SPARQL-to-SQL rewriters, and a SQL representation for benchmarking RDBMS.

SPARQL REPRESENTATION

Table 3 contains the SPARQL representation of the benchmark queries. The benchmark queries contain parameters which are enclosed with % chars in the table. During a test run, these parameters are replaced with random values from the benchmark dataset. Queries within two consecutive query mixes differ by the chosen parameters which makes it harder for SUTs to apply query caching. As the test driver uses a deterministic randomizer, the overall query sequence is the same for test runs against different SUTs.

Table 4 gives an overview of the characteristics of the BSBM benchmark queries and highlights specific SPARQL features that are used by the queries. As the queries are motivated by the use case of an e-commerce portal, various queries use LIMIT modifiers in order to restrict the number of query results. Query 3 requires negation. As the SPARQL standard does not directly provide for negation, the query uses a combination of an OPTIONAL pattern and a FILTER clause that

Table 2. The BSBM query mix

1. Query 1: Find products for a given set of generic features.
2. Query 2: Retrieve basic information about a specific product for display purposes.
3. Query 2: Retrieve basic information about a specific product for display purposes.
4. Query 3: Find products having some specific features and not having one feature.
5. Query 2: Retrieve basic information about a specific product for display purposes.
6. Query 2: Retrieve basic information about a specific product for display purposes.
7. Query 4: Find products matching two different sets of features.
8. Query 2: Retrieve basic information about a specific product for display purposes.
9. Query 2: Retrieve basic information about a specific product for display purposes.
10. Query 5: Find products that are similar to a given product.
11. Query 7: Retrieve in-depth information about a product including offers and reviews.
12. Query 7: Retrieve in-depth information about a product including offers and reviews.
13. Query 6: Find products having a label that contains a specific string.
14. Query 7: Retrieve in-depth information about a product including offers and reviews.
15. Query 7: Retrieve in-depth information about a product including offers and reviews.
16. Query 8: Give me recent English language reviews for a specific product.
17. Query 9: Get information about a reviewer.
18. Query 9: Get information about a reviewer.
19. Query 8: Give me recent English language reviews for a specific product.
20. Query 9: Get information about a reviewer.
21. Query 9: Get information about a reviewer.
22. Query 10: Get cheap offers which fulfill the consumer's delivery requirements.
23. Query 10: Get cheap offers which fulfill the consumer's delivery requirements.
24. Query 11: Get all information about an offer.
25. Query 12: Export information about an offer into another schema.

Table 3. SPARQL representation of the BSBM queries

Query 1: Find products for a given set of generic features
| ```
    SELECT DISTINCT ?product ?label
WHERE {
?product rdfs:label ?label .
 ?product rdf:type %ProductType% .
 ?product bsbm:productFeature %ProductFeature1% .
 ?product bsbm:productFeature %ProductFeature2% .
 ?product bsbm:productPropertyNumeric1 ?value1 .
FILTER (?value1 > %x%)}
ORDER BY ?label
LIMIT 10
``` |

Query 2: Retrieve basic information about a specific product for display purposes
| ```
    SELECT ?label ?comment ?producer ?productFeature ?propertyTextual1
?propertyTextual2 ?propertyTextual3 ?propertyNumeric1
?propertyNumeric2 ?propertyTextual4 ?propertyTextual5
?propertyNumeric4
WHERE {
%ProductXYZ% rdfs:label ?label .
%ProductXYZ% rdfs:comment ?comment .
%ProductXYZ% bsbm:producer ?p .
?p rdfs:label ?producer .
%ProductXYZ% dc:publisher ?p .
%ProductXYZ% bsbm:productFeature ?f .
?f rdfs:label ?productFeature .
%ProductXYZ% bsbm:productPropertyTextual1 ?propertyTextual1 .
%ProductXYZ% bsbm:productPropertyTextual2 ?propertyTextual2 .
%ProductXYZ% bsbm:productPropertyTextual3 ?propertyTextual3 .
%ProductXYZ% bsbm:productPropertyNumeric1 ?propertyNumeric1 .
%ProductXYZ% bsbm:productPropertyNumeric2 ?propertyNumeric2 .
OPTIONAL { %ProductXYZ% bsbm:productPropertyTextual4 ?propertyTextual4 }
OPTIONAL { %ProductXYZ% bsbm:productPropertyTextual5 ?propertyTextual5 }
OPTIONAL { %ProductXYZ% bsbm:productPropertyNumeric4 ?propertyNumeric4 }}
``` |

continued on following page

Table 3. continued

Query 3: Find products having some specific features and not having one feature

SELECT ?product ?label
WHERE {
?product rdfs:label ?label .
?product rdf:type %ProductType% .
?product bsbm:productFeature %ProductFeature1% .
?product bsbm:productPropertyNumeric1 ?p1 .
FILTER (?p1 > %x%)
?product bsbm:productPropertyNumeric3 ?p3 .
FILTER (?p3 < %y%)
OPTIONAL {
?product bsbm:productFeature %ProductFeature2% .
?product rdfs:label ?testVar }
FILTER (!bound(?testVar)) }
ORDER BY ?label
LIMIT 10

Query 4: Find products matching two different sets of features

SELECT ?product ?label
WHERE {
{ ?product rdfs:label ?label .
?product rdf:type %ProductType% .
?product bsbm:productFeature %ProductFeature1% .
?product bsbm:productFeature %ProductFeature2% .
?product bsbm:productPropertyNumeric1 ?p1 .
FILTER (?p1 > %x%)
} UNION {
?product rdfs:label ?label .
?product rdf:type %ProductType% .
?product bsbm:productFeature %ProductFeature1% .
?product bsbm:productFeature %ProductFeature3% .
?product bsbm:productPropertyNumeric2 ?p2 .
FILTER (?p2> %y%) }}
ORDER BY ?label
LIMIT 10 OFFSET 10

Query 5: Find products that are similar to a given product
SELECT DISTINCT ?product ?productLabel WHERE { ?product rdfs:label ?productLabel . FILTER (%ProductXYZ% != ?product) %ProductXYZ% bsbm:productFeature ?prodFeature . ?product bsbm:productFeature ?prodFeature . %ProductXYZ% bsbm:productPropertyNumeric1 ?origProperty1 . ?product bsbm:productPropertyNumeric1 ?simProperty1 . FILTER (?simProperty1 < (?origProperty1 + 120) && ?simProperty1 > (?origProperty1 - 120)) %ProductXYZ% bsbm:productPropertyNumeric2 ?origProperty2 . ?product bsbm:productPropertyNumeric2 ?simProperty2 . FILTER (?simProperty2 < (?origProperty2 + 170) && ?simProperty2 > (?origProperty2 - 170)) } ORDER BY ?productLabel LIMIT 5
Query 6: Find products having a label that contains a specific string
SELECT ?product ?label WHERE { ?product rdfs:label ?label . ?product rdf:type bsbm:Product . FILTER regex(?label, "%word1%")}

continued on following page

Table 3. continued

Query 7: Retrieve in-depth information about a product including offers and reviews

SELECT ?productLabel ?offer ?price ?vendor ?vendorTitle ?review ?revTitle ?reviewer ?revName ?rating1 ?rating2
WHERE {
%ProductXYZ% rdfs:label ?productLabel .
 OPTIONAL {
?offer bsbm:product %ProductXYZ% .
 ?offer bsbm:price ?price .
 ?offer bsbm:vendor ?vendor .
 ?vendor rdfs:label ?vendorTitle .
 ?vendor bsbm:country <http://downlode.org/rdf/iso-3166/countries#DE>.
 ?offer dc:publisher ?vendor .
 ?offer bsbm:validTo ?date .
 FILTER (?date > %currentDate%) }
 OPTIONAL {
?review bsbm:reviewFor %ProductXYZ% .
 ?review rev:reviewer ?reviewer .
 ?reviewer foaf:name ?revName .
 ?review dc:title ?revTitle .
 OPTIONAL { ?review bsbm:rating1 ?rating1 . }
 OPTIONAL { ?review bsbm:rating2 ?rating2 . } } }

Query 8: Give me recent English language reviews for a specific product
SELECT ?title ?text ?reviewDate ?reviewer ?reviewerName ?rating1 ?rating2 ?rating3 ?rating4 WHERE { ?review bsbm:reviewFor %ProductXYZ% . ?review dc:title ?title . ?review rev:text ?text . FILTER langMatches(lang(?text), "EN") ?review bsbm:reviewDate ?reviewDate . ?review rev:reviewer ?reviewer . ?reviewer foaf:name ?reviewerName . OPTIONAL { ?review bsbm:rating1 ?rating1 . } OPTIONAL { ?review bsbm:rating2 ?rating2 . } OPTIONAL { ?review bsbm:rating3 ?rating3 . } OPTIONAL { ?review bsbm:rating4 ?rating4 . } } ORDER BY DESC(?reviewDate) LIMIT 20

Query 9: Get information about a reviewer.
DESCRIBE ?x WHERE { %ReviewXYZ% rev:reviewer ?x }

Query 10: Get cheap offers which fulfill the consumer's delivery requirements.
SELECT DISTINCT ?offer ?price WHERE { ?offer bsbm:product %ProductXYZ% . ?offer bsbm:vendor ?vendor . ?offer dc:publisher ?vendor . ?vendor bsbm:country %CountryXYZ% . ?offer bsbm:deliveryDays ?deliveryDays . FILTER (?deliveryDays <= 3) ?offer bsbm:price ?price . ?offer bsbm:validTo ?date . FILTER (?date > %currentDate%) } ORDER BY xsd:double(str(?price)) LIMIT 10

continued on following page

Table 3. continued

Query 11: Get all information about an offer.
SELECT ?property ?hasValue ?isValueOf WHERE { { %OfferXYZ% ?property ?hasValue } UNION { ?isValueOf ?property %OfferXYZ% } }
Query 12: Export information about an offer into another schema.

CONSTRUCT {
%OfferXYZ% bsbm-export:product ?productURI .
%OfferXYZ% bsbm-export:productlabel ?productlabel .
%OfferXYZ% bsbm-export:vendor ?vendorname .
%OfferXYZ% bsbm-export:vendorhomepage ?vendorhomepage .
%OfferXYZ% bsbm-export:offerURL ?offerURL .
%OfferXYZ% bsbm-export:price ?price .
%OfferXYZ% bsbm-export:deliveryDays ?deliveryDays .
%OfferXYZ% bsbm-export:validuntil ?validTo }
WHERE {
%OfferXYZ% bsbm:product ?productURI .
?productURI rdfs:label ?productlabel .
%OfferXYZ% bsbm:vendor ?vendorURI .
?vendorURI rdfs:label ?vendorname .
?vendorURI foaf:homepage ?vendorhomepage .
%OfferXYZ% bsbm:offerWebpage ?offerURL .
%OfferXYZ% bsbm:price ?price .
%OfferXYZ% bsbm:deliveryDays ?deliveryDays .
%OfferXYZ% bsbm:validTo ?validTo }

tests whether the optional variable is unbound to express negation. Query 6 encodes a free text search. As the SPARQL standard does not support free text search and as the BSBM benchmark strictly follows the standard without making use of proprietary extension functions, query 6 uses the SPARQL regex() function. This function is likely to be much slower than proprietary SPARQL extension functions for free text search that are usually backed by a full text index. We hope that negation and free text search will be added to a future version of SPARQL and will then change the queries accordingly.

The benchmark queries do not test all features of the SPARQL query language as various features were not required by the use case. SPARQL and RDF(S) features that are not benchmarked include querying RDF datasets and named graphs, blank nodes, collections and containers, property hierarchies, reified triples, the REDUCED modifier, and the ASK query form.

SQL REPRESENTATION

Table 5 contains the SQL representation of four benchmark queries. The complete SQL representation of the query mix is given in Section 3.4 of the BSBM specification (Bizer & Schultz, 2008a). It is nevertheless important to note that there are no exact counterparts for several SPARQL features in standard SQL. SPARQL features without exact counterparts are: 1. The regex() function in Query 6 which is emulated using the SQL LIKE operator in order to stay in the bounds of standard SQL. 2. The DESCRIBE operator used in Query 9 and emulated in SQL with a SELECT clause that lists attributes that are likely to be returned by a store. Thus, benchmark results obtained using the SQL query mix should only be used for general orientation.

Table 4. Characteristics of the BSBM benchmark queries.

Characteristic	Q1	Q2	Q3	Q4	Q5	Q6	Q7	Q8	Q9	Q10	Q11	Q12
Simple filters	√		√	√			√	√	√	√		
Complex filters					√	√						
More than 9 patterns		√		√			√	√				
Unbound predicates											√	
Negation		√										
OPTIONAL operator		√	√				√	√				
LIMIT modifier	√		√	√	√			√		√		
ORDER BY modifier	√		√	√	√			√		√		
DISTINCT modifier	√				√					√		
REGEX operator						√						
UNION operator				√							√	
DESCRIBE operator									√			
CONSTRUCT operator												√

Table 5. SQL representation of selected BSBM queries

Query 1: Find products for a given set of generic features.
SELECT DISTINCT nr, label FROM product p, producttypeproduct ptp WHERE p.nr = ptp.product AND ptp.productType=@ProductType@ AND propertyNum1 > @x@ AND p.nr IN (SELECT distinct product FROM productfeatureproduct WHERE productFeature=@ProductFeature1@) AND p.nr IN (SELECT distinct product FROM productfeatureproduct WHERE productFeature=@ProductFeature2@) ORDER BY label LIMIT 10;
Query 2: Retrieve basic information about a specific product for display purposes.
SELECT pt.label, pt.comment, pt.producer, productFeature, propertyTex1, propertyTex2, propertyTex3, propertyNum1, propertyNum2, propertyTex4, propertyTex5, propertyNum4 FROM product pt, producer pr, productfeatureproduct pfp WHERE pt.nr=@ProductXYZ@ AND pt.nr=pfp.product AND pt.producer=pr.nr;
Query 6: Find products having a label that contains a specific string.
SELECT nr, label FROM product WHERE label like "%@word1@%";
Query 9: Get information about a reviewer.
SELECT p.nr, p.name, p.mbox_sha1sum, p.country, r2.nr, r2.product, r2.title FROM review r, person p, review r2 WHERE r.nr=@ReviewXYZ@ AND r.person=p.nr AND r2.person=p.nr;

4. PERFORMANCE METRICS

BSBM benchmark experiments should report the following performance metrics:

1. **Query Mixes per Hour (QMpH):** The central performance metric of the BSBM benchmark are query mixes per hour. The metric measures the number of complete BSBM query mixes that are answered by a SUT within one hour. QMpH numbers should always be reported together with the size of the dataset against which the queries were run, and the numbers of clients that concurrently worked against the SUT.

2. **Queries per Second (QpS):** In order to allow a more differentiated analysis, benchmark results should also be reported on a per query type basis. The QpS metric measures the number of queries of a specific type that were answered by the SUT within a second. The metric is calculated by dividing the number of queries of a specific type within a benchmark run by the cumulated execution time of these queries. The metric must be measured by running complete BSBM query mixes against the SUT and may not be measured by running only queries of the specific type. QpS numbers should always be reported together with the size of the dataset against which the queries were run, and the numbers of clients that concurrently worked against the SUT.

3. **Load time (LT):** Cumulative time to load an RDF or relational benchmark dataset from the source file into the SUT. This includes any time spend by the SUT to build initial index structures and generate statistics about the dataset for query optimization. LT numbers should always be reported together with the size of the dataset and the representation type (i.e. Turtle or SQL dump).

5. RELATED WORK

A benchmark is only a good tool for evaluating a system if the benchmark dataset and the workload are similar to the ones expected in the target use case (Gray, 1993; Yuanbo Guo et al, 2007). As Semantic Web technologies are used within a wide range of application scenarios, a variety of different benchmarks for Semantic Web technologies have been developed.

A widely used benchmark for comparing the performance, completeness and soundness of OWL reasoning engines is the Lehigh University Benchmark (LUBM) (Guo et al., 2005). In addition to the experiment in the original paper, (Rohloff et al., 2007) presents the results of benchmarking DAML DB, SwiftOWLIM, BigOWLIM and AllegroGraph using a LUMB(8000) dataset consisting of roughly one billion triples. The LUBM benchmark has been extended in (Ma et al., 2006) to the University Ontology Benchmark (UOBM) by adding axioms that make use of all OWL Lite and OWL DL constructs. As both benchmarks predate the SPARQL query language, they do not support benchmarking specific SPARQL features such as OPTIONAL filters or DESCRIBE and UNION operators. Both benchmarks do not employ benchmarking techniques such as system warm-up, simulating concurrent clients, and executing mixes of parameterized queries in order to test the caching strategy of a SUT.

An early SPARQL-specific performance benchmark is the DBpedia Benchmark (Becker, 2008). The benchmark measures the execution time of 5 queries that are relevant in the context of DBpedia Mobile (Becker & Bizer, 2008) against parts of the DBpedia dataset. Compared to the BSBM benchmark, the DBpedia Benchmark has the drawbacks that its dataset cannot be scaled to different sizes and that the queries only test a relatively narrow set of SPARQL features.

A recent SPARQL benchmark is SP[2]Bench (Schmidt, et al., 2008a and 2008b). SP[2]Bench uses a scalable dataset that reflects the structure of the DBLP Computer Science Bibliography. The benchmark queries are designed for the comparison of different RDF store layouts and RDF data management approaches. The SP[2]Bench benchmark queries are not parameterized and are not ordered within a use case motivated sequence. As the primary interest of the authors is the "basic performance of the approaches (rather than caching or learning strategies of the systems)" (Schmidt, et al., 2008a), they decided for cold runs instead of executing queries against warmed-up systems. Because of these differences, the SP[2]Bench benchmark is likely to be more useful to RDF store developers that want to test "the generality of RDF storage schemes" (Schmidt, et al., 2008a), while the BSBM benchmark aims to support application developers in choosing systems that are suitable for mixed query workloads.

A first benchmark for comparing the performance of relational database to RDF mapping tools with the performance of native RDF stores is presented in (Svihala & Jelinek, 2007). The benchmark focuses on the production of RDF graphs from relational databases and thus only tests SPARQL CONSTRUCT queries. In contrast, the BSBM query mix also contains various SELECT queries.

A benchmarking methodology for measuring the performance of Ontology Management APIs is presented in (García-Castro & Gómez-Pérez, 2005). Like BSBM, this methodology also employs parameterized queries and requires systems to be warmed up before their performance is measured.

Ongoing initiatives in the area of benchmarking Semantic Web technologies are the Ontology Alignment Evaluation Initiative (Caracciolo, et al, 2008) which compares ontology matching systems, and the Billion Triple track of the Semantic Web Challenge[4] which evaluates the ability of Semantic Web applications to process large quantities of RDF data that is represented using different schemata and has partly been crawled from the public Web. Further information about

RDF benchmarks and current benchmark results are found on the ESW *RDF Store Benchmarking* wiki page [5].

5. BENCHMARK EXPERIMENT

As a proof of concept, we ran the Berlin SPARQL Benchmark against four popular RDF stores (Sesame[6], Virtuoso[7], Jena TDB[8], and Jena SDB[9]) and two SPARQL-to-SQL rewriters (D2R Server[10] and Virtuoso RDF Views[11]) for three dataset sizes: One million triples, 25 million triples, and 100 million triples. After describing the setup and the methodology of the experiment, this section presents the benchmark results for a single client as well as for up to 64 clients working concurrently against the SUTs. In order to set the benchmark results into context, we compare them with the performance of two RDBMS (MySQL and Virtuoso RDBMS).

The experiment was conducted on a DELL workstation (processor: Intel Core 2 Quad Q9450 2.66GHz; memory: 8GB DDR2 667; hard disks: 160GB (10,000 rpm) SATA2, 750GB (7,200 rpm) SATA2) running Ubuntu 8.04 64-bit as operating system (kernel version 2.6.24-23). All databases were placed on the 10,000 rpm hard disk. Java version 1.6.0_07 was used and all Java stores were run under the Java HotSpot(TM) 64-Bit Server VM (build 10.0-b23).

SYSTEMS UNDER TEST AND THEIR CONFIGURATION

The systems under test store RDF data either in underlying relational databases or rely on native RDF storage engines. Sesame allows the user to choose between three storage engines (in-memory, native, DBMS-backend). Jena SDB offers three different RDF storage layouts for the underlying RDBMS (layout2, layout2/index und layout2/hash). Virtuoso RDF Views is coupled with the Virtuoso RDBMS, while D2R Server can work on top of MySQL, PostgreSQL, Oracle and other SQL-92 compatible databases. The systems employ cost-based query planning (Erling & Mikhailov, 2007; Owens et al., 2009). The dataset statistics that are used for evaluating the cost of different query execution plans are either generated once after the dataset is loaded (Jena TDB, Jena SDB, D2R Server) or are created on the fly by sampling data (Virtuoso TS). The systems dynamically cache parts of the dataset, indices as well as (intermediate) query results in main memory.

The impact of the storage layout, query plan optimization and caching on the overall query performance highly depends on the concrete configuration of the system as well as on the number and types of queries that contributed to filling the caches. In order to be able to report meaningful benchmark results we therefore optimized the configuration of the systems in cooperation with the developers of the systems and warmed up the caches of the systems by executing query mixes until the average runtime per query mix stabilized (see Methodology of the Experiment below).

In the following, we provide the version numbers of the SUTs and give an overview about their configuration. The exact configuration of each system including all settings that were changed from defaults and all indices that were set is given in (Bizer & Schultz, 2008b).

1. **Sesame** Version 2.2.4 with Tomcat Version 5.5.25.5 as HTTP interface. We used the *native storage* layout, set the *spoc, posc, opsc* indices in the native storage configuration, and increased Java heap size to 6144MB.
2. **Jena TDB** Version 0.7.2 and Joseki Version 3.2 (CVS 2009-02-15) as HTTP interface. The TDB optimizer was configured to use the statistics based optimization strategy.
3. **Jena SDB** Version 1.2.0 and Joseki Version 3.2 (CVS 2009-02-15) as HTTP interface and MySQL Version 5.1.26 as underlying

RDBMS. We configured SDB to use layout2/hash. The MySQL configuration is given below at 7.

4. **Virtuoso Triple Store** Open-Source Edition v5.0.10, abbreviated later in this article as *Virtuoso TS*. We changed the following performance related parameters: NumberOfBuffers = 520000; MaxCheckpointRemap = 1000000; StopCompilerWhenXOverRunTime = 1.
5. **Virtuoso RDF Views** with Virtuoso Open-Source Edition v5.0.10 as underlying RDBMS. Abbreviated later in this article as *Virtuoso RV*. The configuration parameters were the same as for Virtuoso TS. We used a RDBMS-to-RDF mapping provided by the Openlink developers and set 24 indices according to their suggestion. The complete mapping is given in (Bizer & Schultz, 2008b).
6. **D2R Server** Version 0.6 with MySQL Version 5.1.26 as underlying RDBMS. We increased Java heap size to 6144MB and configured MySQL as described within point 7. The complete D2RQ mapping is given in (Bizer & Schultz, 2008b).
7. **MySQL** Version 5.1.26. We set the key_buffer size to 5600M, set indices on every foreign key column as well as on producttypeproduct (productType, product), review(product,person), offer(product, deliveryDays, validTo), and productfeatureproduct(productFeature, product). The *analyze table* command was executed for all tables in the database.
8. **Virtuoso RDBMS** Open-Source Edition v5.0.10, abbreviated later in this article as *Virtuoso SQL*. The configuration was the same as for Virtuoso TS and we set the 24 indices that were proposed by the OpenLink developers.

Methodology of the Experiment

Before we started to measure the performance of the systems, we ran a qualification test against all systems in order to check whether they return correct results for the BSBM queries. Within this test, the one million triple BSBM dataset was loaded into the stores and 15 query mixes (altogether 375 queries, fixed randomizer seed) were run against the stores. The query results returned by the stores were compared with the expected results using the BSBM qualification tool. For the DESCRIBE query (Query 9), the qualification tool only checked whether the result contained any RDF triples as the results of DESCRIBE queries may vary from store to store. All SUTs passed the BSBM qualification test.

We then applied the following test procedure to each store for each dataset size:

1. **Load the benchmark dataset.** The load performance of the systems was measured by loading the Turtle representation of the BSBM datasets into the triple stores and by loading the relational representation in the form of SQL dumps into MySQL and the Virtuoso RDBMS. The loaded datasets were forward chained and contained all *rdf:type* statements for product types. Thus the systems did not have to do any inferencing.

2. **Shutdown store, clear caches, restart store.** After the dataset is loaded and all indices are build, the store and all associated software components were shut down. The operating system caches were freed and the store was restarted.

3. **Execute ramp-up until steady-state is reached.** In order to benchmark the systems under normal working conditions, we warmed them up by executing query mixes until the average runtime per query mix stabilized. We determined this steady-state by using the results of the last 50 query mixes as evaluation window. For this evaluation

window, the average execution time of the first 25 query mixes aqt_{1-25} was calculated. Afterwards, we totaled the positive and negative aberration ta_{26-50} of the execution times of the last 25 query mixes from aqt_{1-25}. We consider a SUT in steady-state when ta_{16-30} deviates less than 3% from aqt_{1-15} and continued to run query mixes until this condition was met.

4. **Execute single-client test run.** The query performance of the systems for a single client was measured by running 500 BSBM query mixes (altogether 12500 queries) against the systems over the SPARQL protocol.

5. **Execute multiple-client test runs.** Afterwards, we executed measurement runs with 2 clients, 4 clients, 8 clients, and 64 clients concurrently working against the SUT. Each run consisted of 500 query mixes.

6. **Execute test run with reduced query mix.** Previous experiments showed that the SUTs spent between 25% and 95% of the overall runtime on only two out of the 25 queries: Query 5 which contains complex filter expressions for identifying similar products and Query 6 which uses a regex() function to emulate free text search. In order to allow the SUTs to optimize their caches for the less resource intensive queries, we excluded Query 5 and 6 from the query mix and repeat steps 2 to 5 with this reduced query mix.

The different test runs use different randomizer seeds to choose query parameters. This ensures that the test driver produces distinctly parameterized queries over all runs and makes it more complicated for the SUTs to apply caching techniques. The test driver and the SUT were running on the same machine in order to reduce the influence of network latency.

In order to make it possible for interested parties to reproduce the results of the experiment, we provide the RDF and the relational representation of the benchmark datasets as well as the qualifica-

Table 6. Load times for different stores and dataset sizes (in [day:]hh:min:sec)

	1M	25M	100M
Sesame	00:02:59	12:17:05	3:06:27:35
Jena TDB	00:00:49	00:16:53	01:34:14
Jena SDB	00:02:09	04:04:38	1:14:53:08
Virtuoso TS	00:00:23	00:39:24	07:56:47
Virtuoso RV	00:00:34	00:17:15	01:03:53
D2R Server	00:00:06	00:02:03	00:11:45
MySQL	00:00:06	00:02:03	00:11:45
Virtuoso SQL	00:00:34	00: 17:15	01:03:53

Table 7. Speed-up factors between the runtime of the second query mix and the average runtime of a query mix in steady-state

	1M	25M	100M
Sesame	15,61	3,98	0,75
Jena TDB	3,03	0,52	0,00
Jena SDB	0,97	2,68	0,64
Virtuoso TS	0,47	26,14	46,65
Virtuoso RV	0,15	1,98	100,09
D2R Server	0,67	0,03	0,04
MySQL	26,30	17,37	8,49
Virtuoso SQL	1,03	13,58	247,20

tion tool and the test driver for download on the BSBM website.

6. RESULTS OF THE EXPERIMENT

In the following we present and discuss the results of the experiment.

Load Times

Table 6 summarizes the time it took to load the Turtle files and the SQL dumps into the different stores. Loading the SQL dump was significantly faster than loading the Turtle representation. Comparing the load performance of the triple stores, it turns out that Virtuoso is fast for small datasets while Jena TDB is fast for large datasets. Sesame Native and Jena SDB altogether showed a poor load performance which culminated in a load time of more than 3 days for loading the 100M dataset into Sesame.

The disk space footprint of the loaded and index datasets varied widely between the triple stores and the RDBMS. The 100M triple dataset consumed 17 GB disk space after being loaded into Sesame, Jena SDB and Virtuoso TS. Loading the dataset into Jena TDB consumed 19 GB disk space. In contrast, the relational representation of the data-

set consumed only 5.6 GB after being loaded into MySQL and 8.4 GB in the Virtuoso RDBMS.

Ramp-Up

The runtime of the first warm-up query mix that was executed against the newly started stores proved to be significantly longer than the runtimes of all other query mixes as the stores were slowed down by connecting to underlying RDBMS or building index structures in memory. In order to give an overview about the effect of system warm-up, Table 7 list the speed-up factors between the runtime of the second warm-up query mix and the average runtime of a query mix in steady-state.

Results for Single Clients

This section presents the results of the single client experiments. The complete run logs of the experiment can be found in (Bizer & Schultz, 2008b).

Overall Performance

Table 8 gives an overview of the overall query performance of the SUTs. The performance was measured by running 500 query mixes against the stores and is reported in query mixes per hour (QMpH). The best performance figure for each

Table 8. Overall performance: Complete query mix (in QMpH)

	1M	25M	100M
Sesame	**18,094**	1,343	254
Jena TDB	4,450	353	81
Jena SDB	10,421	968	211
Virtuoso TS	12,360	4,123	954
Virtuoso RV	17,424	**12,972**	**4,407**
D2R Server	2,828	140	35
MySQL	*235,066*	*18,578*	*4,991*
Virtuoso SQL	*192,013*	*69,585*	*9,102*

Table 9. Overall performance: Reduced query mix without queries 5 and 6 (in QMpH)

	1M	25M	100M
Sesame	**38,727**	**39,059**	3,116
Jena TDB	15,842	1,856	459
Jena SDB	15,692	4,877	584
Virtuoso TS	13,759	10,718	2,166
Virtuoso RV	18,516	17,529	**6,293**
D2R Server	11,520	3,780	1,261
MySQL	*516,271*	*280,993*	*84,797*
Virtuoso SQL	*219,616*	*195,647*	*14,400*

dataset size is set bold in the tables. The results of running the SQL representation of the query mix against MySQL and Virtuoso RDBMS are also included in the tables for comparison but are not considered for determining the best SPARQL performance figure.

Comparing the four triple stores with each other, the Virtuoso triple store shows the best overall performance for the 25M and the 100M datasets. For the 1M dataset, Sesame outperforms Virtuoso TS. In the category of SPARQL-to-SQL rewriters, Virtuoso RV clearly outperforms D2R Server.

The comparison of the fastest triple store with the fastest SPARQL-to-SQL rewriter shows that the performance of both architectures is similar for the 1M triple dataset. For bigger datasets, Virtuoso RV outperforms the triple stores by at least factor 3.

Setting the performance of triple stores and SPARQL-to-SQL rewriter in relation to the result from running the SQL query mix directly against the relational databases reveals an unedifying picture: MySQL outperforms Sesame for the 1M dataset by the factor 13. For the 100M dataset, the Virtuoso triple store is outperformed by Virtuoso SQL by the factor 9.5. In relation to Virtuoso SQL, the fastest SPARQL-to-SQL rewriter (Virtuoso RV) is outperformed by the factor 2.0 (100M dataset).

Examining the times spent on individual queries (see section below), it appears for the 25M and the 100M datasets, that the stores spent up to 95% of the overall runtime on only two out of the 25 queries: Query 5 which contains complex filter expressions for identifying similar products and Query 6 which uses the regex() function to emulate free text search. The time spend on Query 6 also explains the good performance of Virtuoso SQL and Virtuoso RV in relation to MySQL. Virtuoso SQL and Virtuoso RV both recognize that the SPARQL regex() and the SQL LIKE expression in Query 6 are workarounds for expressing free text search and thus use a full text index on the field product.label to evaluate the query. MySQL does not use full text indices to evaluate SQL LIKE expressions and therefore shows a significantly slower overall performance in relation to Virtuoso SQL for the 25M and 100M datasets.

Queries 5 and 6 distort the significance of the overall figures for assessing the performance of the stores on basic tasks such as query pattern matching and simple filtering. We therefore excluded query 5 and 6 from the query mix and rerun the experiment with this reduced mix. The overall performance figures obtained by this second run are given in Table 9.

For the 100M dataset, excluding the two queries leads to a factor 11 speed-up for Sesame, a factor 4.7 speed-up for Jena TDB, factor 1.7 for

Jena SDB, and a factor 1.2 speed-up for Virtuoso TS. For the SPARQL-to-SQL rewriters, excluding the two queries speeds up D2R Server by the factor 35, while Virtuoso RV, which uses a full text index to evaluate query 6, only gains 43%.

Comparing the performance of the three triple stores without queries 5 and 6 Sesame proofs to be the fastest store for all dataset sizes. In the category of SPARQL-to-SQL rewriters, Virtuoso RV again outperforms D2R Server. Comparing the performance of triple stores and SPARQL-to-SQL rewriters across architectures, Sesame outperforms Virtuoso RV for smaller datasets, while Virtuoso RV is twice as fast as Sesame for the 100M dataset. In the RDBMS category, Virtuoso SQL is outperformed by MySQL as it lost the advantage of using the full text index to evaluate Query 6.

Performance by Individual Query

In order to give a more detailed picture of the strengths and weaknesses of the different systems, we present the benchmark results for each individual query in Table 10. The results were measured by running the complete BSBM query mix. For the query-by-query results obtained by running the reduced query mix please refer to (Bizer & Schultz, 2008b). The results in the table are given as queries per second (QpS). The values are calculated based on average runtime of all queries of a specific type within the 500 query mixes. The best performance figure for each dataset size is again set bold.

The picture drawn by the overall runtimes is partly changed when the runtimes of specific queries are analyzed. In the following, we will interpret the results on a query-by-query basis.

Query 1 is very simple and specific and all stores show a good performance on this query. Query 2 consists of 15 triple patterns out of which 3 are optional. For the 1M and 25M datasets, Sesame clearly outperforms all other stores on this query. For the 100M dataset, both SPARQL-to-SQL rewriters show a better performance than the RDF stores. As the query can be evaluated against the relational representation using two simple join, the RDBMS outperform the RDF stores by factors between 15 and 100. Queries 3 and 4 are unproblematic for all stores, with again, Sesame being the fastest store for the 1M dataset and Virtuoso RV and TS performing well for the larger data sets. Jena SDB shows a steep performance slump between the 25M and the 100M dataset for both queries.

Query 5 contains the most demanding FILTER expressions of all queries in the mix. Evaluating this query is time consuming for all RDF stores as well as for the RDBMS. Not taking into account the RDBMS, Virtuoso RV shows the best performance on this query for all dataset sizes and largely outperforms D2R Server which is very slow on this query. The time spent on Query 5 dominates the overall runtime of the complete query mix for several stores: D2R Server spends 90% of the overall runtime on this query, Jena TDB 70%, Jena SDB and Sesame around 20%, the Virtuoso triple store only 6%. The performance on Query 6 is mostly determined by whether a store relies on a full text index or not to answer the query. Stores without text index, like Jena TDB, need up to 11 seconds to evaluate the query against the 100M dataset. Virtuoso RV and Virtuoso SQL recognize that the SPARQL regex() and the SQL LIKE expressions in Query 6 are workarounds for expressing free text search and thus clearly outperform the other stores by using a full text index to answer the query. Query 7 and 8 again contain a large number of triple patters out of which several are optional. They thus proof to be expansive for all stores. For both queries, triple stores (Sesame and Jena TDB) perform best on the 1M dataset, while the SPARQL-to-SQL rewriters show the best performance for the large datasets. The Query 9 uses the DESCRIBE operator. Jena SDB and TDB both have problems with this operator while the other stores show a good performance.

Table 10. Performance by individual query (in QpS)

Query 1: Find products for a given set of generic features.

	1M	**25M**	**100M**
Sesame	**662**	200	15
Jena TDB	494	165	35
Jena SDB	374	198	12
Virtuoso TS	202	192	**132**
Virtuoso RV	199	173	122
D2R Server	328	**236**	79
MySQL	*3,021*	*955*	*476*
Virtuoso SQL	*1,195*	*833*	*470*

Query 2: Retrieve basic information about a specific product for display purposes

	1M	**25M**	**100M**
Sesame	**251**	**168**	32
Jena TDB	61	51	38
Jena SDB	50	47	35
Virtuoso TS	47	46	39
Virtuoso RV	78	75	**64**
D2R Server	41	36	40
MySQL	*4,525*	*3,333*	*3,268*
Virtuoso SQL	*1,592*	*1,456*	*991*

Query 3: Find products having some specific features and not having one feature.

	1M	**25M**	**100M**
Sesame	**505**	140	13
Jena TDB	451	141	28
Jena SDB	283	151	8
Virtuoso TS	176	165	**136**
Virtuoso RV	182	**167**	129
D2R Server	226	115	56
MySQL	*2,833*	*919*	*459*
Virtuoso SQL	*1,079*	*838*	*456*

Query 4: Find products matching two different sets of features.

	1M	**25M**	**100M**
Sesame	**452**	128	10
Jena TDB	429	116	25
Jena SDB	240	132	7
Virtuoso TS	92	86	54
Virtuoso RV	106	96	**84**
D2R Server	224	**167**	72
MySQL	*2,653*	*919*	*428*
Virtuoso SQL	*1,098*	*759*	*443*

Query 5: Find products that are similar to a given product.

	1M	**25M**	**100M**
Sesame	30	1.69	0.52
Jena TDB	1.80	0.13	0.04
Jena SDB	18	1.05	0.46
Virtuoso TS	76	14	5.86
Virtuoso RV	**118**	**30**	**14**
D2R Server	1.08	0.04	0.01
MySQL	*396*	*25*	*8*
Virtuoso SQL	*410*	*43*	*12*

Query 6: Find products having a label that contains specific words.

	1M	**25M**	**100M**
Sesame	14	0.53	0.13
Jena TDB	59	2.40	0.09
Jena SDB	16	0.55	0.12
Virtuoso TS	55	2.12	0.50
Virtuoso RV	**275**	**25**	**6.03**
D2R Server	26	1	0.23
MySQL	*163*	*7*	*1*
Virtuoso SQL	*1,605*	*97*	*21*

continued on following page

Query 10 can be evaluated against the relation representation using a single join between the vendor and the offer tables. The SPARQL-to-SQL rewriters thus clearly outperform the triple stores for larger datasets. For the 1M dataset Sesame and Jena TDB show the best performance. Query 11 contains two triple patterns with unbound predicates. As unbound predicates require SPARQL-to-

SQL rewriters to examine various columns in the relational database, the rewriters are outperformed on this query by the triple stores. Query 12 uses the CONSTRUCT operator. Sesame performs best on this query for the 1M and 25M dataset, while D2R Server shows the best performance for the 100M dataset. The CONSTRUCT operator

Table 10. continued

Query 7: Retrieve in-depth information about a product including offers and reviews

	1M	25M	100M
Sesame	87	57	2
Jena TDB	**189**	28	6
Jena SDB	112	27	2
Virtuoso TS	72	36	5
Virtuoso RV	81	76	**15**
D2R Server	123	**97**	12
MySQL	*1,912*	*1,370*	*407*
Virtuoso SQL	*831*	*733*	*26*

Query 8: Give me recent English language reviews for a specific product.

	1M	25M	100M
Sesame	**297**	90	4
Jena TDB	159	27	8
Jena SDB	134	30	3
Virtuoso TS	116	113	12
Virtuoso RV	132	**129**	**22**
D2R Server	72	62	12
MySQL	*3,497*	*601*	*63*
Virtuoso SQL	*1,715*	*1,603*	*31*

Query 9: Get information about a reviewer.

	1M	25M	100M
Sesame	**924**	128	19
Jena TDB	57	3	1
Jena SDB	129	9	2
Virtuoso TS	541	**533**	53
Virtuoso RV	506	482	**164**
D2R Server	81	73	33
MySQL	*4,255*	*2,849*	*1,370*
Virtuoso SQL	*2,639*	*2,639*	*145*

Query 10: Get cheap offers which fulfill the consumer's delivery requirements.

	1M	25M	100M
Sesame	**429**	93	2
Jena TDB	**429**	62	19
Jena SDB	289	40	2
Virtuoso TS	95	75	8
Virtuoso RV	224	**220**	67
D2R Server	218	200	**77**
MySQL	*4,444*	*3,356*	*1,883*
Virtuoso SQL	*2,004*	*1,587*	*267*

Query 11: Get all information about an offer.

	1M	25M	100M
Sesame	**652**	98	13
Jena TDB	376	45	24
Jena SDB	351	97	23
Virtuoso TS	361	**342**	**44**
Virtuoso RV	102	100	41
D2R Server	33	2	0.4
MySQL	*9,174*	*4,367*	*456*
Virtuoso SQL	*2,494*	*3,195*	*1,248*

Query 12: Export information about an offer into another schema.

	1M	25M	100M
Sesame	**797**	**350**	18
Jena TDB	53	3	1
Jena SDB	119	9	2
Virtuoso TS	133	129	39
Virtuoso RV	151	148	91
D2R Server	203	162	**170**
MySQL	*7,246*	*2,571*	*539*
Virtuoso SQL	*2,801*	*2,985*	*1,524*

is problematic for Jena TDB and SDB which are both very slow for the 25M and 100M datasets.

Results for Multiple Clients

In real-world settings there are often multiple clients working against a SPARQL endpoint. We thus had the test driver simulate up to 64 clients concurrently working against the SUTs. Tables 11 and 12 summarize the results of the multi-client runs against the 1M and 25M datasets. The performance of the systems is measured by the number of query mixes that were answered by the SUT for all clients within one hour. Note that the query mixes per hour values are extrapolated

Table 11. Performance for multiple clients, 1M dataset (in QMpH)

Dataset size 1M	Number of clients				
	1	**2**	**4**	**8**	**64**
Sesame	**18,094**	19,057	16,460	18,295	16,517
Jena TDB	4,450	6,752	9,429	8,453	8,664
Jena SDB	10,421	17,280	23,433	24,959	23,478
Virtuoso TS	12,360	21,356	32,513	29,448	29,483
Virtuoso RV	17,424	**28,985**	**34,836**	**32,668**	**33,339**
D2R Server	2,828	3,861	3,140	2,960	2,938
MySQL	*235,066*	*318,071*	*472,502*	*442,282*	*454,563*
Virtuoso SQL	*192,013*	*199,205*	*274,796*	*357,316*	*306,172*

Table 12. Performance for multiple clients, 25M dataset (in QMpH)

Dataset size 25M	Number of clients				
	1	**2**	**4**	**8**	**64**
Sesame	1,343	1,485	1,204	1,300	**1,271**
Jena TDB	353	513	694	536	**555**
Jena SDB	968	1,346	1,021	883	**927**
Virtuoso TS	4,123	7,610	9,491	5,901	**5,400**
Virtuoso RV	**12,972**	**22,552**	**30,387**	**28,261**	**28,748**
D2R Server	140	187	160	146	**143**
MySQL	*18,578*	*31,093*	*39,647*	*40,599*	*40,470*
Virtuoso SQL	*69,585*	*85,146*	*135,097*	*173,665*	*148,813*

from the time it took the clients to execute 500 query mixes each.

The experiment showed for all systems except Sesame and D2R Server that the number of query mixes per hour doubles on average between the single client and the 4 client runs. Then the performance more or less stabilizes in a 20% variation corridor for the 8 and 64 client runs. For Sesame and D2R Server, the number of query mixes per hour stays mostly constant, which indicates that the systems do not take advantage of the multi-core processor provided by the benchmark machine.

The absolute numbers show that Virtuoso TS outperforms Jena TDB, Jena SDB and Sesame in all multi-client tests. Virtuoso RV also clearly outperforms D2R Server. Virtuoso RV's ability to handle multiple clients combined with the generally good performance of SPARQL-to-SQL rewriting architecture for larger datasets leads to a far-off overall win of Virtuoso RV against all other stores for the 25M dataset: For the 8 client case Virtuoso RV is factor 3.7 faster than Virtuoso TS, factor 20 faster than Sesame, and factor 31 faster than Jena SDB.

7. CONCLUSION

This article introduced the Berlin SPARQL Benchmark for comparing the query performance of native RDF stores with the performance of

SPARQL-to-SQL rewriters across architectures. The benchmark dataset, the benchmark queries as well as the query sequence are grounded within an e-commerce use case. The benchmark focuses on measuring query performance under enterprise conditions. The BSBM benchmark thus employs benchmarking techniques from the database and transaction processing field (Gray, 1993; TPC, 2008), such as executing query mixes, query parameterization, simulation of multiple clients, and system ramp-up.

The BSBM benchmark complements the field of benchmarks for Semantic Web technologies with a benchmark for measuring SPARQL query performance for mixed query workloads as well as for comparing the performance of RDF stores and SPARQL-to-SQL rewriters. The benchmark fills a gap between SP2Bench which is designed for the comparison of different RDF store layouts, LUBM which focuses on reasoning, and the Ontology Alignment Evaluation Initiative which focuses on schema matching and mapping.

As a proof of concept, the article presented the results of a benchmark experiment in which the BSBM benchmark is used to compare the performance of four RDF stores with two SPARQL-to-SQL rewriters and to set the results into relation to the performance of RDBMS. The experiment unveiled several interesting findings:

Within all categories, none of the benchmarked systems was superior within the single client use case for all queries and all dataset sizes. Comparing the RDF stores, Sesame showed a good performance for small datasets while Virtuoso TS was faster for larger datasets. For larger datasets, Jena TDB and SDB could not compete in terms of overall performance. In the category of SPARQL-to-SQL rewriters Virtuoso RV clearly outperformed D2R Server.

Comparing the fastest RDF store with the fastest SPARQL-to-SQL rewriter shows that the rewriting approach outperforms native RDF stor-age with increasing dataset size. This is shown by the overall runtimes as well as by the results for 9 out of 12 individual queries (100M triple, single client).

Setting the results of the RDF stores and the SPARQL-to-SQL rewriters in relation to the performance of classical RDBMS unveiled an unedifying picture. Comparing the overall performance (100M triple, single client, all queries) of the fastest rewriter with the fastest relational database shows an overhead for query rewriting of 106%. This is an indicator that there is still room for improving the rewriting algorithms. Comparing the overall performance (100M triple, single client, all queries) of the fastest RDF store with the fastest RDBMS shows that the RDF store is outperformed by the factor 8.5. There are two potential explanations for this finding: First, as SPARQL is still a very new query language it is likely that the RDF stores have not yet implemented similarly sophisticated optimization techniques as SQL query engines which are under development for decades. Thus, there should be potential for RDF stores to catch up in the future. The second reason is more fundamental and lies in the combination of the RDF data model and the structure of benchmark dataset. The RDF data model has been designed for the open Web use case and thus provides for representing semi-structured data that mixes different schemata. As the BSBM benchmark dataset is relatively homogeneous, the flexibility of the RDF data model turns out to be a disadvantage compared to the relational model which is designed for clearly structured data.

The complete BSBM benchmark specification, current benchmark results, the benchmark datasets, detailed run logs as well as the source code of the data generator and test driver (GPL license) are available from the Berlin SPARQL Benchmark website at http://www4.wiwiss.fu-berlin.de/bizer/BerlinSPARQLBenchmark/

ACKNOWLEDGMENT

We would like to thank Lilly and Company and especially Susie Stephens for making this work possible with a research grant. We also would like to thank Orri Erling (OpenLink Software), Arjohn Kampman (Aduna), Andy Seaborne (Hewlett Packard), Michael Schmidt (Freiburg University), Richard Cyganiak (DERI Galway), Patrick van Kleef (OpenLink Software), and Ivan Mikhailov (OpenLink Software) for their feedback on the benchmark design and their help with configuring the stores for the experiment.

REFERENCES

Becker, C. (2008). *RDF Store Benchmarks with DBpedia comparing Virtuoso, SDB and Sesame*. Retrieved March 2, 2009, http://www4.wiwiss.fu-berlin.de/benchmarks-200801/

Becker, C., & Bizer, C. (2008). DBpedia Mobile: A Location-Enabled Linked Data Browser. *Proceedings of the 1st Workshop about Linked Data on the Web (LDOW2008)*.

Bizer, C., & Schultz, A. (2008a). *Berlin SPARQL Benchmark (BSBM) Specification - V2.0*. Retrieved March 2, 2009, http://www4.wiwiss.fu-berlin.de/bizer/BerlinSPARQLBenchmark/spec/

Bizer, C., & Schultz, A. (2008b). *Berlin SPARQL Benchmark Results*. Retrieved March 2, 2009, http://www4.wiwiss.fu-berlin.de/bizer/BerlinSPARQLBenchmark/results/

Caracciolo, C., et al. (2008). Results of the Ontology Alignment Evaluation Initiative 2008. *Proceedings of the 3rd International Workshop on Ontology Matching (OM-2008), CEUR-WS, 431*.

Erling, O., & Mikhailov, I. (n.d.). RDF Support in the Virtuoso DBMS. *Proceedings of the 1st Conference on Social Semantic Web (CSSW)* (pp. 59-68).

García-Castro, R., & Gómez-Pérez, A. (2005). Guidelines for Benchmarking the Performance of Ontology Management APIs. *The Semantic Web – ISWC 2005. LNCS, 3729*, 277–292.

Gray, J. (1993). *The Benchmark Handbook for Database and Transaction Systems* (2nd ed.). Morgan Kaufmann.

Guo, Y., Pan, Z., & Heflin, J. (2005). LUBM: A Benchmark for OWL Knowledge Base Systems. *Journal of Web Semantics, 3*(2), 158–182. doi:10.1016/j.websem.2005.06.005

Kendall, G. C., Feigenbaum, L., & Torres, E. (2008). *SPARQL Protocol for RDF. W3C Recommendation*. Retrieved March 2, 2009, http://www.w3.org/TR/rdf-sparql-protocol/

Ma, L. (2006). Towards a Complete OWL Ontology Benchmark (UOBM). *The Semantic Web: Research and Applications, LNCS., 4011*, 125–139. doi:10.1007/11762256_12

Owens, A., et al. (2009). *Clustered TDB: A Clustered Triple Store for Jena*. Retrieved March 2, 2009, http://eprints.ecs.soton.ac.uk/16974/

Prud'hommeaux, E., & Seaborne, A. (2008). *SPARQL Query Language for RDF. W3C Recommendation*. Retrieved March 2, 2009, http://www.w3.org/TR/rdf-sparql-query/

Rohloff, K. (2007). An Evaluation of Triple-Store Technologies for Large Data Stores. *On the Move to Meaningful Internet Systems 2007: OTM 2007 Workshops. LNCS, 4806*, 1105–1114.

Sahoo, S., et al. (2009). *A Survey of Current Approaches for Mapping of Relational Databases to RDF*. Retrieved February 25, 2009, http://www.w3.org/2005/Incubator/rdb2rdf/RDB2RDF_SurveyReport.pdf

Schmidt, M., Hornung, T., Küchlin, N., Lausen, G., & Pinkel, C. (2008a). An Experimental Comparison of RDF Data Management Approaches in a SPARQL Benchmark Scenario. *Proceedings of the International Semantic Web Conference (ISWC 2008)*.

Schmidt, M., Hornung, T., Lausen, G., & Pinkel, C. (2008b). *SP2Bench: A SPARQL Performance Benchmark*. Technical Report, arXiv:0806.4627V1 cs.DB.

Svihala, M., & Jelinek, I. (2007). Benchmarking RDF Production Tools. *Proceedings of the 18th International Conference on Database and Expert Systems Applications (DEXA 2007)*.

Transaction Processing Performance Council. (2008). *TPC Benchmark H, Standard Specification Revision 2.7.0*. Retrieved March 2, 2009, http://www.tpc.org/tpch/spec/tpch2.7.0.pdf

Yuanbo, G. (2007). A Requirements Driven Framework for Benchmarking Semantic Web Knowledge Base Systems. *IEEE Transactions on Knowledge and Data Engineering, 19*(2), 297–309. doi:10.1109/TKDE.2007.19

ENDNOTES

[1] http://esw.w3.org/topic/SparqlEndpoints

[2] http://www.w3.org/2001/sw/sweo/public/UseCases/

[3] http://www.w3.org/2005/Incubator/rdb2rdf/

[4] http://challenge.semanticweb.org/

[5] http://esw.w3.org/topic/RdfStoreBenchmarking

[6] http://www.openrdf.org/about.jsp

[7] http://virtuoso.openlinksw.com/dataspace/dav/wiki/Main/

[8] http://jena.hpl.hp.com/wiki/TDB

[9] http://jena.hpl.hp.com/wiki/SDB

[10] http://www4.wiwiss.fu-berlin.de/bizer/d2r-server/

[11] http://virtuoso.openlinksw.com/dataspace/dav/wiki/Main/VOSSQL2RDF

This work was previously published in International Journal on Semantic Web and Information Systems, Volume 5, Issue 2, edited by Amit P. Sheth, pp. 1-24, copyright 2009 by IGI Publishing (an imprint of IGI Global).

Chapter 5
Learning of OWL Class Expressions on Very Large Knowledge Bases and its Applications

Sebastian Hellmann
Universität Leipzig, Germany

Jens Lehmann
Universität Leipzig, Germany

Sören Auer
Universität Leipzig, Germany

ABSTRACT

The vision of the Semantic Web aims to make use of semantic representations on the largest possible scale - the Web. Large knowledge bases such as DBpedia, OpenCyc, and GovTrack are emerging and freely available as Linked Data and SPARQL endpoints. Exploring and analysing such knowledge bases is a significant hurdle for Semantic Web research and practice. As one possible direction for tackling this problem, the authors present an approach for obtaining complex class expressions from objects in knowledge bases by using Machine Learning techniques. The chapter describes in detail how to leverage existing techniques to achieve scalability on large knowledge bases available as SPARQL endpoints or Linked Data. The algorithms are made available in the open source DL-Learner project and this chapter presents several real-life scenarios in which they can be used by Semantic Web applications.

INTRODUCTION

The vision of the Semantic Web aims to make use of semantic representations on the largest possible

DOI: 10.4018/978-1-60960-593-3.ch005

scale - the Web. We currently experience that Semantic Web technologies are gaining momentum and large knowledge bases such as DBpedia (Auer et al., 2007), OpenCyc (Lenat, 1995), GovTrack (Tauberer, 2008) and others are freely available. These knowledge bases are based on semantic knowledge representation standards like RDF and OWL. They contain hundred thousands of properties as well as classes and an even larger number of facts and relationships. These knowledge bases and many more (ESWWiki, 2008) are available as Linked Data (Berners-Lee, 2006; Bizer, Cyganiak, & Heath, 2007) or SPARQL endpoints (Clark, Feigenbaum, & Torres, 2008).

Due to their sheer size, users of these knowledge bases, however, are facing the problem, that they can hardly know which identifiers are used and are available for the construction of queries. Furthermore, domain experts might not be able to express their queries in a structured form at all, but they often have a very precise imagination what kind of results they would like to retrieve. A historian, for example, searching in DBpedia for ancient Greek law philosophers influenced by Plato can easily name some examples and if presented a selection of prospective results he will be able to quickly identify false results. However, he might not be able to efficiently construct a formal query adhering to the large DBpedia knowledge base a priori.

The construction of queries asking for objects of a certain kind contained in an ontology, such as in the previous example, can be understood as a class construction problem: We are searching for a class expression which subsumes exactly those objects adhering to our informal query (e.g. ancient Greek law philosophers influenced by Plato). Recently, several methods have been proposed for constructing ontology classes by means of Machine Learning techniques from positive and negative examples (Lehmann & Hitzler, 2007a, 2007b, 2010). These techniques are tailored for small and medium size knowledge bases, while they cannot be directly applied to large knowledge bases (such as the initially mentioned ones) due to their dependency on reasoning methods. In this paper, we present an approach for leveraging Machine Learning algorithms for learning of ontology class expressions in large knowledge bases, in particular those available as SPARQL (Clark et al.,

2008) endpoints or Linked Data. The scalability of the algorithms is ensured by reasoning only over "interesting parts" of a knowledge base for a given task. As a result users of large knowledge bases are empowered to construct queries by iteratively providing positive and negative examples to be contained in the prospective result set.

Overall, we make the following contributions:

- development of a flexible method for extracting relevant parts of very large and possibly interlinked knowledge bases for a given learning task,
- thorough implementation, integration, and evaluation of these methods in the DL-Learner framework (Lehmann, 2009)
- presentation of several application scenarios and examples employing some of the largest knowledge bases available on the Web.

This article is a revised and extended version. Since the original submission, several applications were created based on the presented method. These include the following tools (presented in the Section "Applications"):

- ORE (Lehmann & Bühmann 2010)
- HANNE (Hellmann et al. 2010)
- The Tiger Corpus Navigator (Hellmann et al. 2010)

In this article, we will first cover preliminaries, namely a quick introduction in Description Logics, OWL, and the learning problem we consider. We then briefly describe the underlying learning algorithm and present in detail how it can be applied on very large knowledge sources. In the next sections, we will mention some possible usage scenarios including some applications, which have been realized. We describe and evaluate our approach in several scenarios in the subsequent sections and, finally, conclude with some related work and an outlook on future work.

OWL, DESCRIPTION LOGICS

Description logics are a family of knowledge representation (KR) formalisms. They emerged from earlier KR formalisms like semantic networks and frames. Their origin lies in the work of Brachmann on structured inheritance networks (Brachman, 1978). Since then, description logics have enjoyed increasing popularity. They can essentially be understood as fragments of first-order predicate logic. They have less expressive power, but usually decidable inference problems and a user-friendly variable free syntax.

Description logics represent knowledge in terms of *objects*, *concepts*, and *roles*. Concepts formally describe notions in an application domain, e.g. we could define the concept of being a father as "a man having a child" (Father ≡ Man ⊓ ∃hasChild.⊤ in DL notation). Objects are members of concepts in the application domain and roles are binary relations between objects. Objects correspond to constants, concepts to unary predicates, and roles to binary predicates in first-order logic.

In description logic systems information is stored in a *knowledge base*. It is divided in two parts: *TBox* and *ABox*. The ABox contains *assertions* about objects. It relates objects to concepts and roles. The TBox describes the *terminology* by relating concepts and roles. (For some expressive description logics this clear separation does not exist.)

As mentioned before, DLs are a family of KR formalisms. We will introduce the ALC description logic as a prototypical example. It should be noted that ALC is a proper fragment of OWL (Horrocks, Patel-Schneider, & Harmelen, 2003) and is considered to be a prototypical description logic for research investigations.

ALC stands for *attributive language with complement*. It allows to construct complex concepts from simpler ones using various language constructs. The next definition shows how such concepts can be built.

Definition 1 (syntax of ALC concepts) Let N_R be a set of *role names* and N_C be a set of concept names ($N_R \cap N_C = \varnothing$). The elements of N_C are also called *atomic concepts*. The set of ALC concepts is inductively defined as follows:

1. Each atomic concept is a concept.
2. If C and D are ALC concepts and $r \in N_R$ a role, then the following are also ALC concepts:
    o ⊤ (top), ⊥ (bottom)
    o - $C \sqcup D$ (disjunction), $C \sqcap D$ (conjunction), $\neg C$ (negation)
    o - $\forall r.C$ (value/universal restriction), $\exists r.C$ (existential restriction)

The semantics of ALC concepts is defined by means of interpretations. See the following definition and Figure 1 listing all ALC concept constructors. The corresponding OWL terminology is also listed (according to Bechofer et al., 2004).

Definition 2 (interpretation) An *interpretation* I consists of a non-empty *interpretation domain* Δ^I and an *interpretation function* $\cdot^I$, which assigns to each $A \in N_C$ a set $A^I \subseteq \Delta^I$ and to each $r \in N_R$ a binary relation $r^I \subseteq \Delta^I \times \Delta^I$.

In the most general case, *terminological axioms* are of the form $C \sqsubseteq D$ or $C \equiv D$, where C and D are concepts. The former axioms are called *inclusions* and the latter *equivalences*. An equivalence whose left hand side is an atomic concept is a *concept definition*. We can define the semantics of terminological axioms in a straightforward way. An interpretation I satisfies an inclusion $C \sqsubseteq D$ if $C^I \subseteq D^I$ and it satisfies the equivalence $C \equiv D$ if $C^I = D^I$.

I satisfies a set of terminological axioms if it satisfies all axioms in the set. An interpretation, which satisfies a (set of) terminological axiom(s) is called a *model* of this (set of) axiom(s). Two (sets of) axioms are *equivalent* if they have the same models. A finite set T of terminological

Figure 1. ALC syntax and semantics along with corresponding OWL constructs

OWL	DL	DL syntax	semantics
named class	atomic concept	A	$A^I \subseteq \Delta^I$
object property	abstract role	r	$r^I \subseteq \Delta^I \times \Delta^I$
Thing	top concept	$\top$	Δ^I
Nothing	bottom concept	$\bot$	$\emptyset$
intersectionOf	conjunction	$C \sqcap D$	$(C \sqcap D)^I = C^I \cap D^I$
unionOf	disjunction	$C \sqcup D$	$(C \sqcup D)^I = C^I \cup D^I$
complementOf	negation	$\neg C$	$(\neg C)^I = \Delta^I \setminus C^I$
someValuesFrom	exists restriction	$\exists r.C$	$(\exists r.C)^I = \{a \mid \exists b.(a,b) \in r^I \text{ and } b \in C^I\}$
allValuesFrom	universal restriction	$\forall r.C$	$(\forall r.C)^I = \{a \mid \forall b.(a,b) \in r^I \text{ implies } b \in C^I\}$

axioms is called a *(general) TBox*. Let N_I be the set of object names (disjoint with N_R and N_C). An *assertion* has the form $C(a)$ *(concept assertion)* or $r(a,b)$ *(role assertion)*, where a, b are object names, C is a concept, and r is a role. An *ABox A* is a finite set of assertions.

Objects are also called individuals. To allow interpreting ABoxes we extend the definition of an interpretation. Additionally to mapping concepts to subsets of our domain and roles to binary relations, an interpretation has to assign to each individual name $a \in N_I$ an element $a^I \in \Delta^I$. An interpretation I is a model of an ABox A (written $I \models A$) if $a^I \in C^I$ for all $C(a) \in A$ and $(a^I, b^I) \in r^I$ for all $r(a,b) \in A$. An interpretation I is a model of a knowledge base $K = (T, A)$ (written $I \models K$) iff it is a model of T and A.

A concept is in *negation normal form* if negation only occurs in front of concept names. The *length* of a concept is defined in a straightforward way, namely as the sum of the numbers of concept names, role names, quantifier, and connective symbols occurring in the concept. The *depth* of a concept is the maximal number of nested concept constructors. The *role depth* of a concept is the maximal number of nested roles. For brevity we sometimes omit brackets. In this case, constructors involving quantifiers have higher priority, e.g. $\exists r.\top \sqcap A$ means $(\exists r.\top) \sqcap A$.

As we have described, a knowledge base can be used to represent the information we have

about an application domain. Besides this *explicit* knowledge, we can also deduce *implicit* knowledge from a knowledge base. It is the aim of *inference algorithms* to extract such implicit knowledge. There are some standard reasoning tasks in description logics, which we will briefly describe.

In *terminological reasoning* we reason about concepts. The standard problems are *satisfiability* and *subsumption*. Intuitively, satisfiability determines if a concept can be satisfied, i.e. it is free of contradictions. Subsumption of two concepts detects whether one of the concepts is more general than the other.

Definition 3 (satisfiability) Let C be a concept and T a TBox. C is *satisfiable* iff there is an interpretation I such that $C^I \neq \varnothing$. C is *satisfiable with respect to* T iff there is a model I of T such that $C^I \neq \varnothing$.

Definition 4 (subsumption, equivalence) Let C, D be concepts and T a TBox. C *is subsumed by* D, denoted by $C \sqsubseteq D$, iff for any interpretation I we have $C^I \subseteq D^I$. C *is subsumed by* D with respect to T, denoted by $C \sqsubseteq_T D$, iff for any model I of T we have $C^I \subseteq D^I$.

C *is equivalent to* D (with respect to T), denoted by $C \equiv D$ ($C \equiv_T D$), iff $C \sqsubseteq D$ ($C \sqsubseteq_T D$) and $D \sqsubseteq C$ ($D \sqsubseteq_T C$).

C *is strictly subsumed by* D (with respect to T), denoted by $C \sqsubset D$ ($C \sqsubset_T D$), iff $C \sqsubseteq D$ ($C \sqsubseteq_T D$) and not $C \equiv D$ ($C \equiv_T D$).

Subsumption allows to build a hierarchy of atomic concepts, commonly called the *subsumption hierarchy*. Analogously, for more expressive description logics *role hierarchies* can be inferred.

In *assertional reasoning* we reason about objects. The *instance check problem* is to find out whether an object is an instance of a concept, i.e. belongs to it. *Retrieval* is the problem of finding all instances of a given concept.

Definition 5 (instance check) Let A be an ABox, T a TBox, $K = (T, A)$ a knowledge base, C a concept, and $a \in N_I$ an object. *a is an instance of C* with respect to A, denoted by $A \models C(a)$, iff in any model I of A we have $a^I \in C^I$. *a is an instance of C* with respect to K, denoted by $K \models C(a)$, iff in any model I of K we have $a^I \in C^I$.

To denote that a is not an instance of C with respect to A (K) we write $A \not\models C(a)$ ($K \models C(a)$).

We use the same notation for sets S of assertions of the form $C(a)$, e.g. $K \models S$ means that every element in S follows from K.

Definition 6 (retrieval) Let A be an ABox, T a TBox, $K = (T, A)$ a knowledge base, C a concept. The *retrieval* $R_A(C)$ of a concept C with respect to A is the set of all instances of C: $R_A(C) = \{a \mid a \in N_I \text{ and } A \models C(a)\}$. Similarly the *retrieval* $R_A(C)$ of a concept C with respect to K is: $R_K(C) = \{a \mid a \in N_I \text{ and } K \models C(a)\}$

CORRESPONDENCE OF OWL AND DESCRIPTION LOGICS

As we move forward in the course of this article, from theoretical foundations and algorithms to practical use cases and real-world applications a shift in terminology is necessary. Decades of research in Description Logics have entered design decisions for OWL, which even results in the fact that a DL knowledge base is "nowadays often called ontology" (as noted by Baader, Ganter,

Figure 2. Generate and test approach used in DL-Learner.

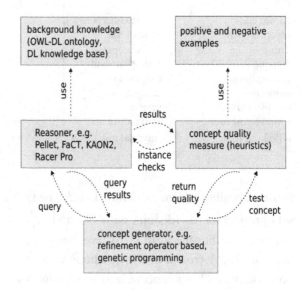

Sertkaya, and Sattler (2007, p. 3)). As we progress, we will use OWL terminology, where appropriate, but keep some notations in Description Logics, especially where the advantages of representation is obvious (e.g. complex class expressions). Cf. Figure 2 for the most commonly used expressions. For a complete mapping from OWL to Description Logics we refer the interested reader to Horrocks and Patel-Schneider (2003). OWL is based on the description language SHOIN and OWL 2 will probably be based on SROIQ (Horrocks, Kutz, & Sattler, 2006).

THE LEARNING PROBLEM IN OWL AND DESCRIPTION LOGICS

In this section, we will briefly describe the learning problem in Description Logics. The process of learning in logics, i.e. finding logical explanations for given data, is also called *inductive reasoning*. In a very general setting this means that we have a logical formulation of background knowledge and some observations. We are then looking for ways to extend the background knowledge such that we can explain the observations, i.e. they can be deduced from the modified knowledge.

For learning in Description Logics we can give a more specific description of the learning problem. The background knowledge is a knowledge base K. The goal is to find a definition for a concept we want to call *Target*. Hence the *examples* are of the form $Target(a)$ where a is an *example instance*. We are then looking for a concept definition of the form $Target \equiv C$ such that we can extend our knowledge base by this definition. Let $K' = K \cup \{Target \equiv C\}$ be this extended knowledge base. Then we want that the positive examples follow from it, i.e. $K' \vDash E^+$, and the negative examples should not to follow, i.e. $K' \nvDash E^-$. Please note that the description language of the background knowledge can be more expressive than the language of the concept C we want to learn.

When we speak about concepts as possible problem solutions it is useful to introduce some shortcuts for the two main criteria: covering all positive examples and not covering negative examples.

Definition 8 (complete, consistent, correct) Let C be a concept, K the background knowledge base, *Target* the target concept, $K' = K \cup \{Target \equiv C\}$ the extended knowledge base, and E^+ and E^- the positive and negative examples.

C is *complete* with respect to E^+ if for any $e \in E^+$ we have $K' \vDash e$. C is *consistent* with respect to E^- if for any $e \in E^-$ we have $K' \nvDash e$. C is *correct* with respect to E^+ and E^- if C is complete with respect to E^+ and consistent with respect to E^-.

Figure 2 gives a brief overview of how the learning problem can be solved by means of a generate and test approach common in Machine Learning. Several concepts are tested during a learning process, each of which is evaluated using an OWL reasoner. The reasoner performs instance checks on the given concept and the examples. Smart algorithms will take the results of those tests into account to suggest further promising concepts. A brief description of the concrete algorithm employed here can be found below.

We implemented the algorithm within the open source framework DL-Learner (Lehmann, 2009), which employs several Machine Learning algorithms for learning complex class expressions from objects. It uses a modular system, which allows to define different types of components: knowledge sources (e.g. OWL files), reasoners (e.g. DIG interface based (Bechhofer, Müller, & Crowther, 2003)), learning problems, and learning algorithms. DL-Learner is easily extensible by defining additional components. The component, which will be presented in this paper, is the SPARQL and Linked Data knowledge source component.

LEARNING ALGORITHM DESCRIPTION

In this section, we will describe the workings of the algorithm for learning complex classes on large knowledge bases.

Before, we referred to Figure 2 for a general overview on how the learning problem in Description Logics can be solved. In Lehmann and Hitzler (2010), we reported about a concrete algorithm solving the task, which is inspired by Inductive Logic Programming techniques (ILP) (Nienhuys-Cheng & Wolf, 1997). We will give a brief overview of the algorithm in this section to give the reader an intuition about class expression learning methods (although the algorithm itself is not a scientific contribution made in this article).

The goal of learning is to find a correct concept with respect to the examples. This can be seen as a search process in the space of concepts. A natural idea is to impose an ordering on this search space and use operators to traverse it. This strategy is well-known in ILP, where refinement operators are widely used to find hypotheses. Intuitively, downward (upward) refinement operators construct specializations (generalizations) of hypotheses.

Definition 8 (refinement operator) A *quasi-ordering* is a reflexive and transitive relation. In a quasi-ordered space $(S, \leq)$ a *downward (upward) refinement operator* ρ is a mapping from S to 2^S, such that for any $C \in S$ we have that $C' \in \rho(C)$ implies $C' \leq C$ ($C \leq C'$). C' is called a *specialization* (*generalization*) of C.

This idea can be used for searching in the space of concepts. As ordering we can use subsumption. (Note that the subsumption relation $\sqsubseteq$ is a quasi-ordering.) If a concept C subsumes a concept D ($D \sqsubseteq C$), then C will cover all examples, which are covered by D. This makes subsumption a suitable order for searching in concepts as it allows to prune parts of the search space without losing possible solutions.

The approach we used is a top-down refinement operator based algorithm. This means that the first concept, which will be tested is the most general concept ($\top$), which is then mapped to a set of more special concepts by means of a downward refinement operator. Naturally, the refinement operator can be applied to the obtained concepts again, thereby spanning up a search tree. The search tree can be pruned when we reach an incomplete concept, i.e. a concept which does not cover all the positive examples. This can be done, because the downward refinement operator guarantees that all refinements of this concept will also not cover all positive examples and therefore cannot be solutions of the learning problem. One example for a path in a search tree spanned up by a downward refinement operator is as follows:

$\top \rightsquigarrow \text{Person} \rightsquigarrow \text{Person} \sqcap \exists \text{participatesIn.Event}$

$\rightsquigarrow \text{Person} \sqcap \exists \text{participatesIn.Conference}$

The heart of such a learning strategy is to define a suitable refinement operator. The refinement operator in the considered algorithm can be found in Lehmann and Hitzler (2007b) and is build on solid theoretical foundations (Lehmann & Hitzler, 2007a). It has been shown to be the best achievable operator with respect to a set of properties (not further described here), which are used to assess the performance of refinement operators. The used refinement operator can reach any OWL class expression, i.e. we are guaranteed to find a solution in finite time if one exists.

While the refinement operator defines the search tree, a heuristic decides on which node to apply the refinement operator. Heuristics can take several criteria into account, e.g. accuracy of class expression on positive and negative examples, accuracy gain compared to parent node, length of class expression, computational resources needed to apply refinement operator. The heuristic we use combines those criteria. Since the focus of this paper is the fragment selection process, we refrain from a formal description. Going back to Figure 2, the refinement operator is used as concept generator, whereas the heuristics is used to evaluate concept quality, which the learning algorithm uses to decide which concept to try next.

SELECTION OF A SUITABLE KNOWLEDGE FRAGMENT

As detailed in the previous section, the used refinement operator is well designed according to the possible properties a refinement operator for DL can have. The used heuristic for traversing the search space is also highly efficient. Nevertheless, both heavily depend on an OWL reasoner for standard reasoning tasks such as subsumption, instance checks and retrieval. The most commonly used reasoners such as Pellet and Fact++ do not, although highly optimized and efficient, have the ability to scale up to large knowledge bases. Thus, it becomes impossible to use the presented learning algorithm as soon as the target knowledge base reaches a certain size and complexity, with two

Figure 3. Process illustration: In a first step, a fragment is selected based on instances from a knowledge source and in a second step the learning process is started on this fragment and the given examples.

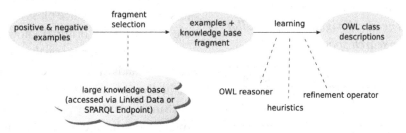

major problems being initialization time (i.e. to load the data into the reasoner) and the time to answer queries involving complex classes (such as retrieval). However, in order to solve the learning problem it is not necessary to consider the complete knowledge base, but only a fragment that holds enough information to produce good results, while at the same time is small enough to allow efficient reasoning.

Desired Fragment We are looking for a sufficiently small fragment F of an ontology O ($F \subset O$), which contains the example instances E and all relevant information to solve a given learning problem LP. If we can successfully apply the learning algorithm on the fragment yielding the concept C, which satisfies the learning problem, then C should also satisfy the learning problem in the large knowledge base O.

The following example shall briefly illustrate, what can be achieved by our fragment selection approach, before we will explain, in the next sections, in detail, how such a fragment is selected and which parameters are used.

Example 1 (Manual Example from Semantic Bible)

Here and also in later experiments, we choose the Semantic Bible ontology (Boisen, 2006), because it is a medium sized ontology, contains rich background knowledge and is still manageable by a reasoner as a whole. This enables us to directly compare the results of learning on the fragment

to results obtained on the whole knowledge base. We manually choose Archelaus and HerodAntipas, two brothers from the New Testament as positive examples, while we choose God, Jesus, Michael and Gabriel (the archangels) as negative examples. The learning algorithm was then executed twice, once in normal mode, where the whole ontology was loaded into the OWL reasoner (Pellet) and once where first a fragment was selected by our extraction method[1], which was then loaded into Pellet (see Figure 3 for an overview). The 20 best learned classes from both runs (like ∃siblingOf. Man or ∃siblingOf.∃spouseOf.Human) are with some exceptions identical and, even more important, all 20 classes learned from the fragment yield 100% accuracy on the whole ontology. Table 1 provides details on the Semantic Bible ontology and solving the learning problem on it as a whole or on a fragment. This example is only meant to illustrate the used methods and algorithms. For a full quantitative evaluation the reader is referred to the later sections of this article.

WHAT PROPERTIES SHOULD THE FRAGMENT HAVE?

In the previous section, we clearly stated what a desired fragment is. It allows fast reasoning and the learned classes achieve (approximately) the same accuracy, when validated versus the original knowledge base. We now take a closer look at what should be included in the fragment for the

Table 1. Manual example to give a first glance at the presented method. Note that not only are reasoner queries faster on average, but also the number of queries needed is significantly smaller (due to the smaller search space.)

Semantic Bible	Normal	Fragment
No. of classes	49	27
No. of instances	724	60
No. of object properties	29	20
No. of data properties	9	0
No. of subclass axioms	51	25
Time needed for extraction	-	4.2s
Reasoner instantiation time	3.6s	1.3s
No. of reasoner queries	1480	313
Avg. time per query	120ms	2ms
Reasoning time	178.0s	0.8s
Learning time without reasoning	0.4s	0.1s
Total time	182.0s	6.4s

learning algorithm to work efficiently while still achieving good results. The first obvious inclusions are the example instances themselves. Secondly, all classes of the example instances and all related instances (via an object property) are necessary. Note that the property between instances will always be included implicitly, when we add related instances to the fragment. Up to now, the fragment consists of the combined Concise Bound Descriptions (CBD (Stickler, 2004)) of the example instances. The information contained is clearly not yet sufficient to learn complex classes. The most complex class definitions derivable when using only CBDs are of the form $C \sqcup R$ or $C \sqcap R$, where C is any conjunction or intersection of classes and R is a conjunction or intersection of unqualified property restrictions of the form $\exists\, property. \top$. While this is of course often not sufficient, it still represents the smallest sensible fragment, where it is possible to learn classes at all with the trade-off scale shifted away from high learning accuracy towards efficient light-weight reasoning. Beyond this point, selec-

tion and extraction of information becomes more complicated. Our aim here is solely to show that it is possible to produce class expressions, which are useful for the original knowledge base. One of the major influences on the validity of learning results stands in direct relation to the possible deductive inferences on the fragment.

Since reasoning in Description Logics is monotonic, the inferences obtained on a fragment of an ontology are also valid for the ontology as a whole (soundness). However, not all possible inferences might be obtainable on the fragment and reasoning thus can be viewed as being "incomplete", e.g. an instance check $C(a)$ answered negatively on the fragment (the reasoner cannot deduce that a is instance of C) might be answered positively on the whole ontology.

As a consequence, the learning problem might be solved incorrectly, because the learning algorithm implicitly assumes that the underlying reasoning methods are complete. So, if for a class expression C the resulting answer set of a retrieval will contain all positive example individuals and none of the negatives, it will present C as a solution. Due to the issues explained above, however, the previously not covered negative example individuals might now be an instance of C when the whole ontology is considered. Thus a correctly learned class definition might turn out to be inconsistent (cf. Definition 3). We tackle this problem by trying to avoid such cases through selection of an ontology fragment containing all relevant information as described in detail below. Furthermore, in most application scenarios the learned class expressions (and/or its implications) are reviewed by a human expert. Because reasoning on large knowledge bases remains impossible, it is hard to give exact measures of the extend to which the negative example coverage problem occurs on very large knowledge bases. However, we will later perform benchmarks on the medium sized Semantic bible ontology and can draw conclusions from those observations.

EXTENSION OF CBDS

In the following, we will give a list containing which information can be additionally extracted to learn more complex classes than with CBDs. We assume that the CBDs of all example individuals are already included in the fragment. On this basis, the following list shows in detail, which information can additionally be included to learn more complex class expressions:

1. *Direct Classes* Retrieving direct classes for all instances in the fragment, that do not yet have any types, will allow to learn qualified property restrictions of the form $\exists$ *property.C* .

2. *Increased Property Depth* A further extension of the CDBs by instances, which are related to an instance, which is again related to an example instance via an object property etc., will enable to learn classes with nested property restrictions of the form $\exists$ *propertyA* . $\exists$ *propertyB*. $\top$. This extension can be continued such that it is possible to learn even deeper nested property restrictions.

3. *Hierarchy* Retrieving all superclasses of all existing classes in the fragment and the corresponding hierarchy, will improve the efficiency of the learning algorithm, because it 1) optimizes the search tree with the help of the subsumption hierarchy and 2) enables the usage of those classes in learned expressions.

4. *Class Definitions and Axioms* Extracting information for all classes in the fragment like definitions via *owl:equivalentClass* or disjointness, etc., will permit the learning algorithm to make use of this valuable background knowledge, e.g. knowing whether classes are disjoint speeds up the reasoning and learning process. Other axioms are of course necessary to draw conclusions. In general, extracting class related axioms re-

duces the above mentioned negative example coverage problem.

The items above directly influence how complex learned classes can be. We continue this list and present in detail, which information influences reasoning on the fragment.

5. *Complex Expressions* All the points in the list mentioned above improve the ability of the reasoner to deduce whether an object is instance of a complex class expression, which directly relates to the ability to learn those class expressions.

6. *Explicit Property Information* Retrieving characteristics of object properties, such as *owl:SymmetricProperty*, domain/range, and the property hierarchy allows more inferences as the fragment is handed to the OWL reasoner.

7. *Inferred Property Information* Because reasoning is normally deactivated in SPARQL endpoints or Linked Data sources, reasoning on the fragment could be improved by also including instances that are related to the example instances via a symmetric, inverse or transitive property. Nevertheless to include such properties, which only become ``visible'' after inference, extensive and costly discovery methods need to be used. Because we follow the general aim to improve performance we accepted this trade-off in favor of a faster extraction procedure.

8. *Complete Class Definitions* There also is the possibility that classes which are contained in the fragment might occur somewhere in the ontology on the right hand side of a class definition (e.g. *SomeClass = AnotherClass* $\sqcup$ *ClassInFragment*). As in the item above, the cost to find such information can become quite large. To completely extract all such information all class axioms would need to be evaluated. As above, such information requires an intensive search, which is why

we refrained from including it, although it might become a parameter in future releases.

Another requirement for the fragment is that it should be in correct OWL-DL, so that it can be processed by OWL Reasoners.

EXTRACTION METHODS

Although the extraction algorithm, we are about to present, was developed to fit the needs of the class learning algorithm, it can basically be applied in any context, where a set of individuals needs to be analyzed with respect to given background knowledge (a circumstance often required in Machine Learning). The size of the fragment can be controlled in a flexible way to regulate the trade-off between complete reasoning and performance. Especially the Linked Data paradigm gives rise to questions concerning reasoning and performance, which cannot merely be answered by optimizing existing reasoning algorithms and using more powerful hardware. Linked Data connects facts across knowledge bases. Due to limited computational resources, we have to decide how far links into other knowledge bases or within the knowledge base itself should be followed and how we retrieve relevant data. In the course of this section, we will describe the extraction algorithm independently from the actual knowledge source, because it is not bound to a certain formalism and works for several variations such as Linked Data or SPARQL endpoints. The actual data provisioning is merely a technical question of implementation. After this section though, we will describe our implementation for SPARQL endpoints, which contains optimizations of the method.

The algorithm traverses the RDF graph of the original knowledge base recursively starting from the example instances. The parameters of the algorithm allow to control the size of the fragment, so that each point in the above mentioned list (information necessary to learn more complex

classes) can be included or excluded. Additionally, filters are used to gain even more flexibility during the extraction of the fragment. The filters are applied to the lowest possible level in the data acquisition and thus we will start with describing the acquisition interface.

Definition 9 (Tuple acquisition interface) A tuple acquisition function of the form $acquire_{KB}$ (resource, predicateFilter, objectFilter, literals) takes as input a resource, a list of unwanted namespaces or URIs for predicates, a list of prohibited namespaces or URIs for objects and a boolean flag *literals*, indicating whether datatype properties should be retrieved. According to its implementation it will retrieve all triples from the knowledge base KB, whose subject is *resource*. The triples (s,p,o) will then be filtered, so that all triples are removed, which contain a namespace or URI from the predicateFilter list as a predicate (same accounts for objectFilter). If *literals* is false, all triples with datatype properties and literals will be removed. It returns a set of tuples of the form (p,o), where (p,o) are the resources (properties and objects) of the remaining triples. We will simply use *acquire*(resource) when the context is clear.

The filters provide the possibility to create a fine-grained selection of the extracted information. They are especially useful for multi-domain knowledge bases such as DBpedia, where retrieving information unfiltered will lead to an unnecessary large fragment. In our case, we avoid retrieving information, that is not important to the learning process. In some cases, we do not want to use datatype properties, so they can be omitted by the literal parameter shown above. The predicate filter removes properties that are not important (e.g. when working with DBpedia we can use this to filter properties pointing to web pages and pictures). The same is true for the object filter, i.e. it filters uninteresting objects in triples.

The configuration of filter criteria is in most cases optional and is clearly content-driven. While

Figure 4. Extraction with three starting example instances. The circles represent different recursion depths. The circles around the starting instances signify recursion depth 0. The larger inner circle represents the fragment with recursion depth 1 and the largest outer circle with recursion depth 2.

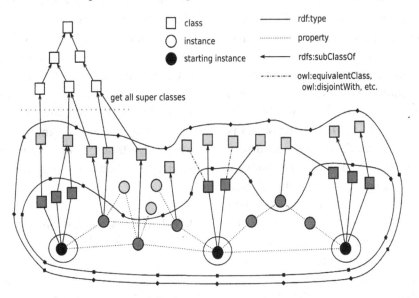

the parameters of the extraction algorithm steer the structural selection of knowledge, filters work at a lower abstraction level. The configuration depends on the particularities of the knowledge source and the intended task and can be optimized for the application. The choice can, on the one hand, add another edge to performance and, on the other hand, allow a content-aware filtering. If the knowledge base makes use of different structural hierarchies such as DBpedia, which uses YAGO classes (Suchanek, Kasneci, & Weikum, 2007) and also the SKOS vocabulary (Miles & Brickley, 2005) combined with its own categories, one of the hierarchies can be selected by excluding the other. Adding the SKOS namespace (http://www.w3.org/2004/02/skos/core) to the predicate and object filter list will guarantee that the fragment will be free of SKOS vocabulary. A Social Semantic Web application for example might be especially interested in FOAF and thus would filter other information. After having defined the filters for the respective knowledge source, a recursive algorithm (see Algorithm 1) extracts relevant knowledge for each of the instances in the example set using *acquire(instance)*. The objects of the retrieved tuples (p,o) are evaluated and manipulated and used to further extract knowledge *(acquire(o))* until a given recursion depth is reached. The process is illustrated in Figure 4.

The algorithm remembers valuable information that is later used to convert the fragment to OWL DL, which we will describe later.

Parameters. In the following, we will relate the influences of the algorithm parameters to the list in the previous section.

The parameter *recursion depth* has the greatest influence on the number of triples extracted and included in the fragment. If set to 0 the fragment will only consist of the example instances. A recursion depth of 1 means, that only the directly related instances and classes are extracted, which results in the combined CBDs of all example instances. A recursion factor of 2 extracts all direct classes of the example instances, their direct super classes and all directly related instances and their direct classes and directly related instances. This will enable the algorithm to learn nested property restrictions (cf. list 2. *Increased Property Depth),* includes some hierarchy information (cf. list 3. *Hierarchy*), allows qualified property restrictions for unnested properties (cf. list 1. *Direct Classes*) and includes definitions of classes directly connected to the starting individuals (cf. list 4. *Class Definitions and Axioms*).

We avoid following cycles, which often occur when encountering inverse properties, *owl:sameAs, owl:equivalentClass* etc., by storing all resources already visited. If the object is a blank node, we will not decrease the recursion counter until no further blank nodes are retrieved.

If we use all existing instances of the original knowledge base as starting seeds with a sufficient recursion depth, the algorithm will extract the whole knowledge base with the exception of unconnected resources, which in most cases barely contain useful information.

To cover other points on the list above, the algorithm retrieves additional information in a post-processing step, which can be switched on and off independently.

Close after recursion For each instance in the fragment that does not yet have any classes assigned to it, classes are retrieved and added to the fragment (cf list 1. *Direct Classes*).

Get all super classes For all classes in the fragment, all super classes are retrieved and the hierarchy is extracted (cf. list 3. *Hierarchy*). Additionally all class definitions are included (cf. list 4. *Class Definitions and Axioms*).

Get all property information For all object properties, types, Domain, Range and the property hierarchy will be retrieved (cf. list 6. *Explicit Property Information*).

Depending on the expected complexity of class expressions (in particular their property depth) and the density of the background knowledge, a recursion depth of 1 or 2 (with all post-processing steps enabled, otherwise 2 or 3) represents a good balance between the amount of useful information and the possibility to reason efficiently.

The retrieved triples can be further manipulated by means of user defined rules. For example, vocabularies that resemble OWL class hierarchies but use different identifiers (such as SKOS) can be mapped to OWL class hierarchies. We also used this technique to embed tags or other structurally important individuals in a class hierarchy in order to enable learning class expressions. Additional information can be easily inserted in this step of the extraction. The function manipulate does not only allow for manipulation, but can also be used to retrieve and include information from other knowledge bases. Even a new extraction can be started based on the current resource.

OWL DL CONVERSION OF THE FRAGMENT

The extracted knowledge has to be altered to adhere to OWL DL for processing, which means explicitly typing classes, properties and instances. Since the knowledge base might not provide (correct) typing information for all individuals, we infer typing information for newly retrieved resources. We follow Bechhofer and Volz (2004), who mention an approach, that is based on the idea that if the type of a triple's subject is known, we can infer the type of the object by analyzing the predicate. Since we always start from instances, we possess additional information and therefore are able to extend the rules mentioned in Bechhofer and Volz (2004, pp. 673-674). Given a triple (s, p, o) we can draw the following conclusions:

- If s is an instance and p is *rdf:type* then o is a class.
- If s is an instance, p is not *rdf:type*, and o not a literal then o is an instance.
- If s is a class then o is a class, unless the knowledge source is in OWL Full, in which case we can configure DL-Learner to either ignore such statements or map *rdf:type* (between classes) to *rdfs:subClassOf*. All

Algorithm 1. Knowledge Extraction Algorithm

```
1     Function: extract
      Input: recursion counter, resource, predicateFilter, objectFilter, literals
      Output: set S of triples
2
3 if recursion counter equals 0 then
4     return ∅;
5 S = empty set of triples;
6 // for acquire see Definition 9
7 resultSet = acquire(resource, predicateFilter, objectFilter, literals);
8 newResultSet = ∅ ;
9 foreach tuple (p,o) from resultSetdo
10     newResultSet = newResultSet ∪ manipulate(typeOfResource,p,o);
11     // the function manipulate allows the alteration
12     // based on the semantic information of the retrieved
13     // URIs and evaluates the type of the newly
14     // retrieved resources
15 create triples of the form (resource,p,o) from the newResultSet ;
16 add triples of the form (resource,p,o) to S;
17 foreach tuple (p,o) from the newResultSetdo
18     if o is a blank node then
19         S = S ∪ extract(recursion counter, o, predicateFilter, objectFilter, literals);
20     else
21         S = S ∪ extract(recursion counter -1, o, predicateFilter, objectFil-
ter, literals);
22 return S
```

properties are then ignored except those in the OWL vocabulary having *owl:Class* as range.

- p is an object property if o is a resource and p is a datatype property if o is a literal.

With the help of these observations, we can type all collected resources iteratively, since we know that the starting resources are instances. Thus, we presented a consistent way to convert the knowledge fragment to OWL DL based on the information collected during the extraction process.

Due to the comparatively small size, deductive reasoning can now be applied efficiently, allowing the application of machine learning techniques.

SPARQL IMPLEMENTATION OF TUPLE ACQUISITION

In this section, we will briefly explain how the tuple acquisition interface is implemented for SPARQL endpoints efficiently. The basic pattern is of the form { < resource > ?p ?o} according to the function *acquire(resource)*, which returns a

Figure 5. In this example we show how we filter out triples using SKOS and DBpedia categories, but leave YAGO classes. Furthermore, links to websites and literals are filtered out.

```
SELECT ?p ?o WHERE {
<http://dbpedia.org/resource/Angela_Merkel> ?p ?o.
FILTER (
    !regex(str(?p),
        'http://dbpedia.org/property/website')
    && !regex(str(?p),
        'http://www.w3.org/2004/02/skos/core')
    && !regex(str(?o),
        'http://dbpedia.org/resource/Category')
    && !isLiteral(?o) ). }
```

tuple (p,o). The remaining parameters are appended using the FILTER keyword as in the example below. To disburden the SPARQL endpoint, caching is used to remember SPARQL query results which were already retrieved. The extraction algorithm's performance for non-local endpoints is mainly determined by the latency for retrieving SPARQL results via HTTP.

Example 2 (Example SPARQL query on DBpedia, see Figure 5)

More optimizations include nested queries according to recursion depth in such a way that it is only necessary to execute one query per example instance. When retrieving the class hierarchy (*Get all superclasses*) already extracted subclass and other class axioms are remembered and not queried a second time. Because blank nodes in SPARQL result sets do often not relate to the internal blank nodes of knowledge bases (they are iteratively numbered for each result set according to the specification), we use a backtracking technique and assign internal blank node ids.

The implementation of other tuple acquisitors is far simpler. Especially Linked Data can be extracted by just a HTTP request, while the filters are applied after the request. The great advantage of the Linked Data tuple acquisitor is that it allows for cross-boundary acquisition of tuples from different knowledge bases without further

configuration and thus enables cross knowledge base accumulation of knowledge.

USAGE SCENARIOS

Instance Data Analysis

The learning algorithm can be used to analyze instance data. With more data on the web, the number of possible applications will increase. We briefly describe two scenarios using GovTrack (Tauberer, 2008) and MusicBrainz (Swartz, 2002).

Last.fm [2] is the worlds largest social music platform. For a given username, we can get information about the last songs a user listened to as RDF[3]. The songs contain ZitGist *owl:sameAs* links, which again refer to MusicBrainz. MusicBrainz is a very large open source music metadata base with plenty of informations about musicians. We want to obtain a description of the last artists a user has listened to. We pick the MusicBrainz URIs of those artists as positive examples and randomly selected artists as negative ones. To improve the learning process, we converted the MusicBrainz tag cloud into a class hierarchy on the fly by adding a property mapping entry, executed in the *manipulate* function (see Algorithm 1). With the positive examples "Genesis", "Children on Stun", "Robbie Williams", and "Dusty Springfield", and as negative ones "Madonna", "Cher", and "Dreadzone" we learned the expression $UK - Artist \sqcup (Rock - Genre \sqcap \exists bioEvent.Death)$. This gives the user feedback (when expressed in natural language) and allows the system to suggest similar songs, e.g. UK-Rock in this case. As there is a variety of existing media players with MusicBrainz support[4], a learning application could be integrated as plugin into those and employ the Semantic Web to provide descriptions of a users favorite artists, songs, etc.

A similar example for instance analysis can be given for GovTrack, a data set about the US congress containing more than 10 million facts. Amongst other uses, we can apply the presented techniques to learn about the interests and working areas of politicians. To do so, we chose a US senator and queried the GovTrack SPARQL endpoint to return all bills, which were sponsored by him or her. We used this as positive examples and applied DL-Learner. As before with the MusicBrainz tags we performed an enrichment step by converting the subject strings of the bills (financial matter, education) to concepts. We queried the Cyc Foundation browser, which uses OpenCyc (Cycorp, 2008) as background knowledge, to find suitable concepts and integrated them in a hierarchy. As a result, we could see which topics a senator is most interested in and who are cosponsors in bills sponsored by a senator. In this case, the advantage of DL-Learner is to reduce the often considerable amount of information about a senator to a concise approximate description.

IMPROVING DATA QUALITY

For large knowledge bases, in particular those developed by an Internet community, it is often difficult to maintain a proper classification scheme. A typical example are the DBpedia classification schemata. There have been various attempts to create a classification hierarchy for DBpedia using e.g. the Wikipedia category system as input. Even with good extraction techniques, human errors cannot be completely eliminated and thus articles are assigned to wrong categories or to superfluously many categories. Class learning can be useful in this scenario to learn a complex class C as a possible definition of an existing class A and then verifying whether the instances of C coincide with those of A. Also class expressions can be used to spot data inconsistencies in instance data and to make suggestions for missing instances. In Example 3 we show how we can successfully apply the algorithm on DBpedia in different ways to either improve the class

schemata, spot inconsistencies in existing Categories or make suggestions to Wikipedia editors. Note that a detailed evaluation of the used methods can be found in the next section. Here we just evaluated the possibilities for future applications.

Example 3 (Re-Learning Wikipedia Categories)

We choose 4 Wikipedia categories (Best Actor Academy Award winners, Prime Ministers of the UK, Fluorescent Dyes, Islands of Tonga), which are included in the DBpedia dataset. These categories as well as the belonging individuals are currently manually maintained by the Wikipedia community, who would benefit greatly from a list of suggestions for missing instances or missing infobox properties. To provide such suggestions a fully automated process is required, when re-learning these categories. While the choice of positive example instances is trivial (all instances assigned to the categories via *skos:subject*), the selection of negative examples is not. If the instances are from a completely different domain or randomly chosen, the correct class expressions are likely to be quite simple. The negative examples were thus obtained by retrieving instances that share the same YAGO classes as the instances in the category. We then randomly selected from this set, such that the number of positive and negative examples were equal. The learning process was then started. The assignment of articles to categories in Wikipedia is done manually by Wikipedia editors and are therefore inconsistent (some categories seem to be confused with tags). The category of British Prime Ministers, for example, also includes instances like *Anthony Eden hat* (a typical hat form worn by Anthony Eden) or *Supermac* (a comic strip about Harold Macmillan). We therefore allowed 20% noise in the accuracy when learning on the fragment. The learned class expressions were used to classify the positive examples in two groups: correctly assigned to the category and incorrectly assigned. We then manually checked these two sets

Table 2. The table shows a probe of the automatic re-learning method for classes. Sets were evaluated manually, falsely classified individuals in brackets

Wikipedia Categories	Prime Min.	Best Actors	Dyes	Tonga
Total number	71	75	56	50
Correctly assigned	53(1)	66(0)	34(0)	50(0)
Incorrectly assigned	18(0)	9(3)	22(7)	0(0)
Accuracy	98%	96%	88%	100%

as a Wikipedia editor would do and compared the classification with the information contained in the Wikipedia article.

The results, which are shown in Table 2, give a first glance at how useful the generated sets can be for Wikipedia authors. A retrieval of learned concepts (see below for explanation) on DBpedia can further find missing instance.

Since the above described process is fully automated (automatic example choice and concept selection), it can be used to conduct data mining automatically. The retrieved lists could support Wikipedia users, when editing lists and make suggestions about missing entries. Also the automatically discovered inconsistencies in DBpedia could contribute to future releases of DBpedia itself.

SPARQL based retrieval. To validate the results in the described scenario above, we assume that we can retrieve all instances of a learned concept. Usually this is a typical reasoner task. However, as mentioned before, it would be too time-consuming to load the complete knowledge base in a reasoner and pose a retrieval query for the learned concept. A way to solve this problem is to use one or more SPARQL queries to obtain an approximation of the retrieval. We can draw on other work in this area here. The open source project SMART (Battista, Villanueva-Rosales, Palenychka, & Dumontier, 2007) implemented a mapping, which they call DL2SPARQL, to query

large knowledge bases. It can be easily tested via their online demonstrator[5]. Other work in the area of efficient approximate inferences for Description Logics is also applicable.

Usage for Navigation

Large knowledge bases are very difficult to navigate and explore for end users, in particular in cases with large TBoxes (schema) *and* large ABoxes (instance data). When users search for interesting knowledge with respect to a certain task, they are often able to find interesting objects by searching, browsing or remembering certain objects. However, users usually will not be able to use the full complexity of a knowledge base for posing sophisticated queries corresponding to their enquiries. In these situations class learning can help to suggest high level concepts, thereby allowing the user to gain new insights and explore other relevant objects, which are otherwise hard to find. As an example we choose the DBpedia SPARQL endpoint again, as it is a multi-domain ontology, which could typically be used for research on a certain topic. A user may browse the knowledge through a user interface, which implicitly or explicitly detects some articles, which are relevant for the current enquiry and others which are not. These can be fed into the DL-Learner system (possibly asynchronously called via AJAX in a web application scenario) as positive and negative examples. An example is given below:

With the help of class navigation we try to relate certain ancient Greek mathematicians to mathematicians throughout history, that have similarities. Interesting articles are: Pythagoras, Philolaus, Archytas (positive examples). Uninteresting articles: Socrates, Plato, Zeno of Elea (negative examples)

In this first run we deduce the class *yago:Mathematician* retrieving more than 2000 instances from DBpedia. Those retrieved instances can further be ranked according to certain keywords or rules. We add one of those instances

(Democritus) to the negative example set and learn the class expression *Theorist* ⊓ (*Mathematician* ⊓ *Physicist*) in the next run, with which we retrieve slightly above 1000 instances from DBpedia. By adding *Aristoxenus* to the negative examples, the algorithm now presents the class expression (among other similar alternatives, which we omitted here) *Believer* ⊓ (*Mathematician* ⊓ *Physicist*). The number of resulting instances from DBpedia shrank to the human manageable size of 159. This list reveals a categorical similarity between the now 8 chosen examples and the instances that belong to the same learned class, containing *Archimedes, Aristotle, Blaise Pascal, Carl Friedrich Gauss, Christian Doppler, Galileo Galilei, Gottfried Leibniz, Isaac Newton, Leonhard Euler, Thales*, just to mention a few famous persons from this list (we might add, that the real value are the not so famous and obvious instances on this list, which are generally harder to identify in a large set of data.).

The obtained class expressions mentioned in the example can be converted into natural language and shown as navigation links to the user. Hence, a user interface can present related objects to a user and also tell why they are related.

Telling the Difference

As we have seen in Auer and Lehmann (2007) DBpedia can provide answers to questions such as 'What Have Innsbruck and Leipzig in Common?'. With the algorithm we can now provide answers to even more sophisticated questions in a minimal use case scenario. We can ask the difference between two instances using them as positive and negative examples for the learning algorithm, thus enabling a user to gain a quick insight without tedious manual searching. The following example shows, how quick and precise answers can be retrieved. Most of the classes are not directly related to the instances and would normally require reasoning methods to be retrieved.

The time for extraction, reasoning and learning was slightly over one second for each example.

Example 5 (Hillary Clinton vs Angela Merkel)

We queried DBpedia and used a filter that only leaves YAGO classes; we switched both instances for each learning problem:

A selection of classes that Angela Merkel belongs to, but Hillary Clinton does not:

CurrentNationalLeaders
Chancellor
ChancellorsOfGermany
Head
HeadOfState
CurrentFemaleHeadsOfGovernment
FemaleHeadsOfGovernment
GermanWomenInPolitics
∃predecessor.⊤
∃president.GermanPoliticians
∃president.PeopleFromLeipzig

A selection of classes that Hillary Clinton belongs to, but Angela Merkel does not:

FirstLadiesOfTheUnitedStates
FirstLady
AmericanWomenInPolitics
NewYorkDemocrats
Democrat
ArkansasLawyers
Lawyer
Professional
∃president.PresidentsOfTheUnitedStates
∃religion.MethodistDenominations

From the above examples we can see how the hierarchy is built up to a certain point in the class tree. Classes such as *Female, WomenInPolitics, Woman, Politician* or ∃*president*.⊤ were not among the learned results. They are also no solutions, as they are shared by both example instances.

APPLICATIONS

In the last years, several applications were created that make use of the described method. In this section we will give a short presentation of these and describe how the fragment approach was implemented and used.

ORE

An interesting use case for the proposed fragment selection approach is the debugging and maintenance of large scale ontologies. The Semantic Web already contains a variety of different ontologies and data adhering to those ontologies. A single knowledge base usually reuses many different external ontologies and vocabularies. Moreover, knowledge bases can be very large (several Million to several Billion facts) and are often interlinked with several other knowledge bases. These properties make it very difficult to apply standard ontology debugging techniques to the Semantic Web at large. These techniques usually involve employing an OWL reasoner, and thus do not scale to larger, interlinked, heterogeneous knowledge bases. In contrast, the fragmentation approach allows to analyze smaller portions of Semantic Web data.

For this reason, the fragmentation approach has been integrated in the ORE (ontology repair and enrichment) tool. ORE (Lehmann & Bühmann, 2010) uses the approach to scale to larger knowledge bases such as DBpedia and OpenCyc. ORE can detect inconsistencies and unsatisfiable classes within large knowledge bases by continuously loading fragments of increasing size. Furthermore, it can also learn new definitions of classes as described in the previous sections. It has been argued in Lehmann and Bühmann (2010) that this allows to spot problems in knowledge bases, which were previously out of reach. Naturally, completeness guarantees, such as the detection of all problems, cannot be made when only fragments are considered. In case, knowledge bases

contain a proportionally large number of problems (i.e. have a *high problem density*), there is a high probability of detecting at least one problem when sufficiently large fragments are analyzed.

To give an example, we present the justification of an inconsistency in DBpedia. Justifications are minimal sets of axioms in a knowledge base, which allow drawing an entailment with inconsistencies being a special kind of entailment. The following justification for an inconsistency was computed in DBpedia using fragment extraction (taken from Lehmann and Bühmann (2010)):

Individual: *dbr:WKWS*, Facts: *geo:longitude* 81.76833343505859, Types: *dbo:Organisation* DataProperty: geo:longitude, Domain: geo:SpatialThing Class: dbo:Organisation, DisjointWith: geo:SpatialThing

In this example, an organization *WKWS* has a property *longitude* with the value of 81.*76833343505859*. As the domain of longitude is *SpatialThing*, a reasoner deducts that *WKWS* is also a *SpatialThing*, which will lead to a contradiction, since an organization itself is not a spatial entity (Disjointness).

The interesting aspect of this example is that information from two knowledge bases is analyzed via fragment extraction by using Linked Data. The additional knowledge base in this case is the W3C Geo vocabulary, which contains the information that the domain of the property *longitude* is *SpatialThing*. Only the combination of both knowledge bases allows to detect this inconsistency.

HANNE

The presented approach speeds up reasoning to an extent that it can be used in an Active Machine Learning Scenario in a Web Application. In Hellmann, Unbehauen and Lehmann (2010), HANNE - a **H**olistic **A**pplication for **N**avigational k**N**owledge **E**ngineering is presented. The methodology of Navigational Knowledge Engineering[6] is much broader and we will focus here on the Active Machine Learning aspect.

HANNE enables users and domain experts to navigate through knowledge bases by selecting examples. From these examples, formal OWL class expressions are learned on the fly by the approach presented in this article. When saved by users, these class expressions form an expressive OWL ontology, which can be exploited in numerous ways: as navigation suggestions for users, as a hierarchy for browsing, and as input for a team of ontology editors.

The tool, available online at http://hanne. aksw.org, addresses the problem of the mostly only shallow semantic representations available on the Web of Data. It lowers the barriers with regard to the elicitation of richer knowledge out of raw data sets: (1) it does not need any deployment and provides a user interface in a familiar environment, the browser, (2) the meaning of the identifiers used in the knowledge source is made explicit by the tool, and, finally, (3) the application uses OWL; the results are thus represented in a readable, portable and sustainable way.

Real Countries in DBpedia

In the following, we will explain step by step, how an OWL class (e.g. *"Real Country that are currently existing"*) can be created with relatively low effort and without precise knowledge of the background data. On the left side of Figure 6, a full text search over the DBpedia data set can be conducted. This represents the entry point, as initial examples have to be chosen to bootstrap the learning process. In our case, a user could start by searching for "Germany" (see 1). From the search result, he picks *Germany* as a positive example and *East Germany, West Germany, Nazi Germany* as negatives. After he has pressed the learn button (see 2) a formal OWL definition (in Manchester OWL Syntax) is presented in the top middle (Learned Concept, see 3) in this case http://www.opengis.net/gml/ *Feature and dbp:sovereigntyType some Thing*. The user now has two options on how to proceed: 1. if he deems the learned concept adequate, he can label (e.g. *"Real Country"*), comment (*"Countries, which are officially accepted and still exist"*) and save the concept in order to export a complete list of adhering instances. 2. Alternatively, he can retrieve instances matching the learned OWL class, which are then displayed on the left side in the Classified Instances box (see 4). These instances can be further evaluated and more positive and negative examples can be chosen to reiterate the process. In our case, a total of 261 instances adhere to the class definition, a quite accurate list (manually checked, including some disputable cases, such as the Azores or the Isle of Man).

Figure 6. Screenshot of the left and middle part of http://hanne.aksw.org:

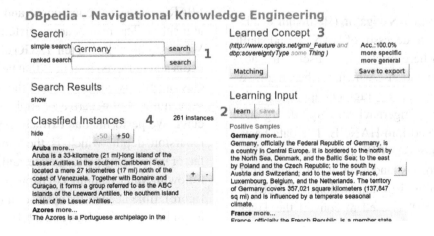

Figure 7. Architecture of the Tiger Corpus Navigator

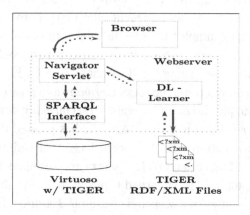

The application realizes a holistic approach to Navigational Knowledge Engineering, as it combines navigational features with knowledge engineering capabilities. It is implemented in Java based on the Google Web Toolkit[7] and is composed out of highly configurable and extensible Spring components, so that it can be customized and tailored for certain data sets. The default implementation of the component interfaces is generic and works with arbitrary SPARQL endpoints offering RDFS reasoning capabilities such as the Virtuoso Universal Server[8] used in the DBpedia demo. The full text search (Figure 4 left side) is realized as a configurable SPARQL template engine.

The Tiger Corpus Navigator

The Tiger Corpus Navigator (Hellmann et al., 2010) was the predecessor of HANNE and shall be mentioned here briefly, as it uses some additional optimizations, which further improve the performance of the fragment approach. It is available at http://tigernavigator.nlp2rdf.org and is now integrated into HANNE. The data basis for the Navigator is an OWL/RDF representation of the Tiger corpus[9] and a set of ontologies that represent its linguistic annotations. NLP2RDF (Hellmann, 2010) is used to convert the Tiger

corpus to RDF and connect it with the OLiA Annotation Model (Chiarcos, 2008).

Figure 7 shows the architecture of the Tiger Corpus Navigator: The Virtuoso triple store contains the whole corpus represented in RDF and allows queries over the complete data for instance retrieval. The Tiger Corpus consists of 50,474 sentences, which can be chosen as positive and negative examples. Instead of constructing the fragment on the fly as presented here, the fragments are constructed once for all sentences and saved in 50,474 OWL files. This *materialized fragment approach* has a high initialization cost, but substantially reduces the time required for each execution of the learning algorithm. Two experiments were conducted with the aim to learn two different kinds of passive sentences. The F-Measure was 86.6% and 53.47% (measured on the test set) and the average learning times were 1.8 sec, 22.6 sec, 31.9 sec and 29.5 sec, and for the second experiment 0.5 sec, 2.2 sec, 5.3 sec, 13.3 sec (both for 10, 20, 30 and 40 examples). It would have been impossible to load all 26.5 million triples into an OWL reasoner and thus no comparison with a solely reasoned based approach could be conducted.

EVALUATION

The evaluation is split into two parts. In the first part, we evaluated the performance of the SPARQL retrieval component and the learning algorithm. The results are depicted in Figure 8. We randomly selected ten YAGO classes in DBpedia and retrieved instances that belonged to the class as positive examples and then selected the same number of negative examples from a super class. We performed an extraction with varying recursion depth, which is the most important factor influencing performance, and recorded the following values: number of triples extracted (left figure), time needed for extraction (right figure, lower line of each color), and total time needed for

Figure 8. Left: extracted triples depending on recursion depth and number of examples. Right: extraction time required depending on recursion depth and number of examples - for each set of lines the lower line is the time required for extraction while the upper line is the total time (including learning).

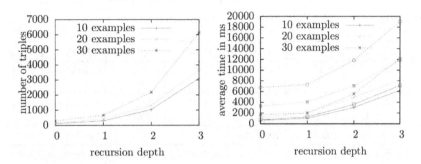

extraction and learning (right figure, upper line of each color). Please note that a recursion depth of e.g. two includes all instances at distance smaller or equal two plus the complete class hierarchy spawned by these instances. The optional parameter *Get all superclasses* and *Close after recursion* were enabled during the post-processing. Each point in the figure is an average over 10 runs and was obtained using a Virtuoso DBpedia mirror on our local network running on a 2.4 GHz dual core machine with 4 GB memory.

We can see that the curves for the time of extraction and learning in the right figure is equally or less steep than the increase in number of extracted triples in the left figure. The time for the learning process increases with more examples used, not only because of the increased time needed for reasoning but also due to the fact that the learned class expressions tend to get more complex for a higher number of examples. Overall, we achieved typical total learning times on a very large and dense (more than 8 properties associated to an instance on average) DBpedia knowledge base of a couple of seconds. Performance could be improved further by merging several SPARQL queries into more complex ones such that the triple store can make use of further internal optimization routines.

In the second part of our evaluation we measured the validity of learned class expressions on the fragment, when compared to the whole ontology. As mentioned before, we choose the Semantic Bible ontology (Boisen, 2006) as target, because it is a medium sized ontology, contains complex background knowledge and is still manageable by a reasoner as a whole. It consists of 49 classes, 724 instances, 29 object properties and 9 data properties (4350 axioms total) and is in OWL-DL (but not OWL-Lite). Also worth mentioning is the large size of object and data property axioms (Domain: 35, Range: 35, Inverse: 17, Symmetric: 6, Subproperty: 12, Functional: 4). To objectively compare the fragment selection approach with the normal approach we randomly selected 100 different sets of learning problems with 10 instances each (5 positive example instances and 5 negative example instances)[10] and conducted the experiments with the same learning algorithm configuration and the same underlying reasoner (Pellet). In the first 4 experiments (S_10s, N_10s, S_100s, N_100s) the learning algorithm was stopped after a fixed time period (10 seconds and 100 seconds) and the best learned concept so far was validated versus the whole ontology. In the remaining 4 experiments (S_1000, N_1000, S_10000, N_10000) the algorithm was stopped after a fixed number of concept test (cf. Figure 1, generate and test approach) independently of time needed. The fragment was extracted with the following parameters: recursion depth 2, close after

Table 3. The table shows the statistics for the fragment selection (S) approach compared to the "normal" (N) usage of the learning algorithm. We tested fixed runtime (10 seconds and 100 seconds) and fixed number of concept tests (1000 and 10000). All values are averaged over the same 100 example sets, standard deviation in brackets. A 2.4 GHz dual core machine with 4 GB memory was used and the fragment was retrieved via SPARQL from a local Joseki endpoint.

Semantic Bible	S_10s	N_10s	S_100s	N_100s	S_1000	N_1000	S_10000	N_10000
acc fragment(%)	67.8 (∓15.5)	61.4 (∓12.0)	73.7 (∓13.7)	67.4 (∓14.6)	65.3 (∓14.7)	62.0 (∓13.0)	67.9 (∓15.5)	69.2 (∓15.0)
acc whole (%)	67.6 (∓15.4)	61.4 (∓12.0)	73.5 (∓13.7)	67.4 (∓14.6)	65.1 (∓14.6)	62.0 (∓13.0)	67.7 (∓15.4)	69.2 (∓15.0)
acc pos (%)	100.0 (∓.0)	100.0 (∓.0)	100.0 (∓.0)	100.0 (∓.0)	100.0 (∓.0)	100.0 (∓.0)	100.0 (∓.0)	100.0 (∓.0)
acc neg (%)	35.2 (∓30.9)	22.8 (∓24.0)	47.0 (∓27.4)	34.8 (∓29.2)	30.2 (∓29.2)	24.0 (∓26.1)	35.4 (∓30.9)	38.4 (∓30.0)
extraction time	1.2s (∓.4s)	.0s (∓.0s)	1.3 (∓.7)	.0s (∓.0s)	1.1s (∓.3s)	.0s (∓.0s)	1.2s (∓.4s)	.0s (∓.0s)
reasoner init time	.1s (∓.1s)	.2s (∓.0s)	.0 (∓.1)	.3s (∓.0s)	.0s (∓.0s)	.3s (∓.2s)	.1s (∓.0s)	.3s (∓.0s)
learning time	10.5s (∓.7s)	27.1s (∓7.1s)	102.3 (∓4.7)	107.0s (∓16.9s)	3.7s (∓2.3s)	52.6s (∓56.9s)	27.9s (∓14.1s)	292.8s (∓92.7s)
axiom number	726 (∓221)	4350	726 (∓221)	4350	726 (∓221)	4350	726 (∓221)	4350
desc. length	3.8 (∓3.0)	2.2 (∓1.6)	5.5 (∓3.8)	3.6 (∓2.7)	3.2 (∓2.5)	2.4 (∓1.8)	3.6 (∓2.9)	4.1 (∓2.8)
desc. depth	2.1 (∓1.1)	1.6 (∓.7)	2.8 (∓1.5)	2.2 (∓1.2)	1.9 (∓1.0)	1.6 (∓.8)	2.2 (∓1.2)	2.3 (∓1.2)

recursion enabled, get all superclasses enabled, get explicit property information, no filters, literals allowed. The result can be viewed in Table 4.

The setup of the experiment is meant to answer two questions. First, we wanted to know how large the actual error is, if the fragmentized approach returns a learned class and analyze if we correctly predicted the type of error that can occur and second, we wanted to compare speed performance (fragment vs. whole).

Because the learning algorithm uses top-down refinement and ignores all class expressions that do not cover all positive examples, the accuracy for positive examples only is always stable at 100%. This is also true for the fragment because of monotonicity of Description Logics. The small error of 0.2% occurred, as predicted, when previously not covered negatives were covered in the whole ontology. We manually checked the data and found that a part of the learned class expression ($Object \sqcup \exists locationOf.\top$) contained an inverse functional property with only an inbound

edge to the example instance, which is not covered on purpose by our extraction method (cf. list 7. Inferred Property Information).

The low overall accuracy of the class expressions (only 60% to 70%) is due to the schematic similarity between random sampled individuals, which made it impossible to induce sensible class expressions. For about 10% of the learning problems all 8 experiments did not return a better class expression than $\top$ with accuracy of (50%). The high expression depth, length and runtime are also a measure that the sampled learning problems were not trivial in general and are difficult to solve.

The speed gain of the fragmentized approach is obvious and can be seen in Figure 9. We would like to note again that we choose the Semantic Bible ontology for evaluation. The real target of the fragment selection approach are even larger knowledge bases, which currently only support minimal reasoning mechanisms, if any. The experiments showed an increase in speed by roughly

Figure 9. Time vs. Accuracy for learning on the Semantic Bible ontology. The two lines are for using only a fragment of the ontology or using the complete ontology.

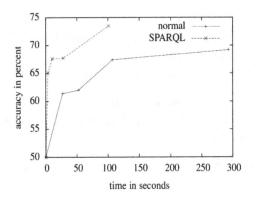

the factor 10 without losing quality. Even more so the highest accuracy (73.5%) in the set time frame was achieved by the reasoning over the fragment. The high expression depth (2.8) and length (5.5) also reveals that it is possible to construct complex class expressions with the information contained in the fragment. Since the extraction method is more syntactical than semantical in nature, it is likely to scale well for larger knowledge bases in terms of extraction time (as also shown in the previous experiment.)

RELATED WORK

Related work can essentially be divided in ABox contraction and summary techniques on the one hand and learning in Description Logics and OWL on the other hand. Regarding the first area Fokoue, Kershenbaum, Ma, Schonberg, and Srinivas (2006) for example present an approach how to compute a possibly much smaller summary of an ABox obeying equivalent reasoning properties. Such approaches are suitable for clean and homogeneous ontologies with small TBoxes and large ABoxes, while our approach is targeted at impure, heterogeneous multi-domain ontologies with both components TBoxes and ABoxes be-

ing large. Another application, that is concerned with reasoning on large ABoxes is instanceStore (Horrocks, Li, Turi, & Bechhofer, 2004), which as of now only works on role-free knowledge bases. A project aiming to enable massive distributed incomplete reasoning is LarKC (Fensel et al., 2008), which has started recently.

Another related approach is described in Seidenberg and Rector (2006), where fragments of the GALEN ontology are extracted to enable efficient reasoning. The major difference compared to our approach is that we focused on providing a fragment extraction algorithm suitable for learning class expressions. We start from instances instead of classes and do not need to extract subclasses of obtained classes. Our approach was implemented with support for SPARQL and Linked Data for querying knowledge bases. Furthermore, we do not require the OWL ontology to be normalized and can handle complex class expressions as fillers of property restrictions. Similarities between both approaches is the idea of a (recursion) depth limit and the extraction of class and property hierarchies.

Regarding learning in Description Logics, the authors of Badea and Nienhuys-Cheng (2000), for example, design a refinement operator for ALER to obtain a top-down learning algorithm for this language. Other approaches to concept learning were presented in Iannone, Palmisano, and Fanizzi (2007), where class expressions are learned based on approximated MSC's (most specific concepts) of the starting instances, which are then merged or refined. A problem of this approach compared to our work is that the proposed algorithm tends to produce very long class expression, which, although they achieve accurate results, can most of the time not be comprehended easily by humans any more, as it is the case in our examples.

CONCLUSION AND FUTURE WORK

The focus of our work was to increase the scalability of OWL learning algorithms. This has been achieved through intelligent pre-processing in the form of a fragment extraction approach, which significantly reduces the burden on the employed OWL reasoner. We successfully showed how machine learning techniques can be applied to very large knowledge bases via fragment extraction. This can help to reduce the burdensome and tedious effort of creating and maintaining schemata for very large knowledge bases.

By shifting the necessity of 'inventing' new class expressions to the simpler process of selecting instances, we open the field of ontology creation to a broader audience, which might add further momentum to the Semantic Web. We presented methods, which can in the future provide semi-automatic tool support for the enrichment of background knowledge and also add a new dimension to navigation and semantic search. The given examples allow a glance at the usefulness of the presented algorithms and what sort of results can be achieved. Building on this, we then presented a set of tools, which already use the fragment extraction approach. For each of those tools, the fragment extraction has significantly increased performance on very large knowledge bases.

During our experiments, we experienced technical and engineering hurdles such as non-standard behaviour, lack of interlinking and semantically rich structures or simply inaccessibility. Hence, working with very large knowledge bases is still challenging from both - engineering and research - perspectives.

REFERENCES

Auer, S., Bizer, C., Kobilarov, G., Lehmann, J., Cyganiak, R., & Ives, Z. G. (2007). *DBpedia: A nucleus for a web of open data. ISWC/ASWC* (pp. 722–735). Springer.

Auer, S., & Lehmann, J. (2007). What have Innsbruck and Leipzig in common? Extracting semantics from wiki content. *Proceedings of the ESWC (2007)* (pp. 503-517). Springer.

Baader, F., Ganter, B., Sertkaya, B., & Sattler, U. (2007). Completing description logic knowledge bases using formal concept analysis. In Veloso, M. M. (Ed.), *IJCAI* (pp. 230–235).

Badea, L., & Nienhuys-Cheng, S.-H. (2000). *A refinement operator for description logics* (pp. 40–58). LNCS.

Battista, A. D. L., Villanueva-Rosales, N., Palenychka, M., & Dumontier, M. (2007). *SMART: A Web-based, ontology-driven, semantic web query answering application.* Semantic web challenge at the ISWC 2007.

Bechhofer, S., Müller, R., & Crowther, P. (2003). The DIG description logic interface. In D. Calvanese, G. D. Giacomo, & E. Franconi (Eds.), *Description logics* (Vol. 81). Retrieved from CEUR-WS.org

Bechhofer, S., van Harmelen, F., Hendler, J., Horrocks, I., McGuinness, D. L., Patel-Schneider, P. F., et al. (2004, Feb). *OWL web ontology language reference.* W3C Recommendation. Retrieved from http://www.w3.org/TR/owl-ref

Bechhofer, S., & Volz, R. (2004). Patching syntax in OWL ontologies. In McIlraith, S. A., Plexousakis, D., & van Harmelen, F. (Eds.), *ISWC* (*Vol. 3298*, pp. 668–682). Springer.

Berners-Lee, T. (2006). *Linked data.* Retrieved August 15, 2008, from http://www.w3.org/DesignIssues/LinkedData.html

Bizer, C., Cyganiak, R., & Heath, T. (2007). *How to publish linked data on the Web.* Retrieved August 15, 2008, from http://sites.wiwiss.fu-berlin.de/suhl/bizer/pub/LinkedDataTutorial/

Boisen, S. (2006). *Semantic bible: New Testament names: A semantic knowledge base.* Retrieved August 15, 2008, from http://www.semanticbible.com/ntn/ntn-overview.html

Brachman, R. J. (1978). *A structural paradigm for representing knowledge (Tech. Rep. No. BBN Report 3605).* Cambridge, MA: Bolt, Beraneck and Newman, Inc.

Chiarcos, C. (2008). An ontology of linguistic annotations. *LDV Forum, 23*(1), 1–16.

Clark, K. G., Feigenbaum, L., & Torres, E. (2008, January 15). *SPARQL Protocol for RDF* (W3C Recommendation). W3C.

ESWWiki. (2008). *Currently alive SPARQL endpoints.* Retrieved August 15, 2008, from http://esw.w3.org/topic/SparqlEndpoints

Fensel, D., van Harmelen, F., Andersson, B., Brennan, P., Cunningham, H., & Valle, E. D. (2008). *Towards LarKC: A platform for Web-scale reasoning.* Los Alamitos, CA: IEEE Computer Society Press.

Fokoue, A., Kershenbaum, A., Ma, L., Schonberg, E., & Srinivas, K. (2006). *The summary ABox: Cutting ontologies down to size* (pp. 343–356). ISWC.

Hellmann, S. (2010). The semantic gap of formalized meaning. In *Proceedings of the European Semantic Web Conference (ESWC)*, Heraklion, Greece.

Hellmann, S., Unbehauen, J., Chiarcos, C., & Ngonga Ngomo, A. (2010). The TIGER Corpus Navigator. In: *Proceedings of the Ninth International Workshop on Treebanks and Linguistic Theories, TLT9.*

Hellmann, S., Unbehauen, J., & Lehmann, J. (2010). HANNE - A Holistic Application for Navigational Knowledge Engineering. In *Posters and Demos of ISWC 2010.*

Horrocks, I., Kutz, O., & Sattler, U. (2006. June 2-5). The even more irresistible SROIQ. In P. Doherty, J. Mylopoulos, & C. A. Welty (Eds.), *Proceedings, tenth International Conference on principles of knowledge representation and reasoning, lake district of the United Kingdom* (pp. 57-67). AAAI Press.

Horrocks, I., Li, L., Turi, D., & Bechhofer, S. (2004). The instance store: DL reasoning with large numbers of individuals. In V. Haarslev & R. Müller (Eds.), *Description logics* (Vol. 104). Retrieved from CEUR-WS.org

Horrocks, I., & Patel-Schneider, P. F. (2003). Reducing OWL entailment to description logic satisfiability. In D. Fensel, K. Sycara, & J. Mylopoulos (Eds.), *Proc. of the 2nd International Semantic Web Conference (ISWC 2003)* (pp. 17-29). Springer.

Horrocks, I., Patel-Schneider, P. F., & van Harmelen, F. (2003). From SHIQ and RDF to OWL: The making of a Web ontology language. *Journal of Web Semantics, 1*(1), 7–26. doi:10.1016/j.websem.2003.07.001

Iannone, L., Palmisano, I., & Fanizzi, N. (2007). An algorithm based on counterfactuals for concept learning in the semantic web. *Applied Intelligence, 26*(2), 139–159. doi:10.1007/s10489-006-0011-5

Lehmann, J. (2007). *DL-Learner project page.* Retrieved from http://dl-learner.org

Lehmann, J. (2009). DL-Learner: Learning concepts in description logic. *Journal of Machine Learning Research.*

Lehmann, J., & Bühmann, L. (2010). ORE - a tool for repairing and enriching knowledge bases. In *Proceedings of the 9th International Semantic Web Conference*, Lecture Notes in Computer Science, Springer.

Lehmann, J., & Hitzler, P. (2007a). Foundations of refinement operators for description logics. In *17th International Conference on Inductive Logic Programming (ILP).*

Lehmann, J., & Hitzler, P. (2007b). A refinement operator based learning algorithm for the ALC description logic. *17th International Conference on Inductive Logic Programming (ILP).*

Lehmann, J., & Hitzler, P. (2010). Concept learning in description logics using refinement operators. *Machine Learning*, *78*, 203–250. doi:10.1007/s10994-009-5146-2

Lenat, D. (1995). CYC: A large-scale investment in knowledge infrastructure. *Communications of the ACM*, *38*(11), 33–38. doi:10.1145/219717.219745

Miles, A., & Brickley, D. (2005, November). *Skos core vocabulary specification*. World Wide Web Consortium. Retrieved August 15, 2008, from http://www.w3.org/TR/2005/WD-swbp-skos-core-spec-20051102/

Nienhuys-Cheng, S.-H., & de Wolf, R. (Eds.). (1997). *Foundations of inductive logic programming*. Springer.

Seidenberg, J., & Rector, A. L. (2006). Web ontology segmentation: Analysis, classification and use. In Carr, L., Roure, D. D., Iyengar, A., Goble, C. A., & Dahlin, M. (Eds.), *WWW* (pp. 13–22). ACM. doi:10.1145/1135777.1135785

Stickler, P. (2004). *CBD - concise bounded description*. Retrieved August 15, 2008, from http://www.w3.org/Submission/CBD/

Suchanek, F. M., Kasneci, G., & Weikum, G. (2007). Yago: A core of semantic knowledge. *WWW '07: Proceedings of the 16th International Conference on World Wide Web* (pp. 697-706). New York, NY: ACM Press.

Swartz, A. (2002). Musicbrainz: A Semantic Web service. *IEEE Intelligent Systems*, *17*(1), 76–77. doi:10.1109/5254.988466

Tauberer, J. (2008). *Govtrack.us - a civic project to track congress*. Retrieved August 15, 2008, from http://www.govtrack.us

ENDNOTES

[1] The ontology was loaded into a local Joseki triple store and queried with SPARQL.

[2] http://www.last.fm/

[3] via http://dbtune.org/last-fm/$username (description at http://dbtune.org/last-fm)

[4] see http://en.wikipedia.org/wiki/Music-Brainz

[5] http://134.117.108.147:8181/smart/query.jsf

[6] http://aksw.org/Projects/NKE

[7] http://code.google.com/webtoolkit

[8] http://virtuoso.openlinksw.com/

[9] http://www.ims.uni-stuttgart.de/projekte/TIGER/TIGERCorpus

[10] Random selection is different from real life problems. However, it is sufficient to gain some insights w.r.t. scalability.

Chapter 6
Scalable Authoritative OWL Reasoning for the Web*

Aidan Hogan
National University of Ireland – Galway, Ireland

Andreas Harth
Karlsruher Institut für Technologie, Germany

Axel Polleres
National University of Ireland – Galway, Ireland

ABSTRACT

In this chapter, the authors discuss the challenges of performing reasoning on large scale RDF datasets from the Web. Using ter-Horst's pD* fragment of OWL as a base, the authors compose a rule-based framework for application to Web data: they argue their decisions using observations of undesirable examples taken directly from the Web. The authors further temper their OWL fragment through consideration of "authoritative sources" which counter-acts an observed behaviour which they term "ontology hijacking": new ontologies published on the Web re-defining the semantics of existing entities resident in other ontologies. They then present their system for performing rule-based forward-chaining reasoning which they call SAOR: Scalable Authoritative OWL Reasoner. Based upon observed characteristics of Web data and reasoning in general, they design their system to scale: the system is based upon a separation of terminological data from assertional data and comprises of a lightweight in-memory index, on-disk sorts and file-scans. The authors evaluate their methods on a dataset in the order of a hundred million statements collected from real-world Web sources and present scale-up experiments on a dataset in the order of a billion statements collected from the Web. In this republished version, the authors also present extended discussion reflecting upon recent developments in the area of scalable RDFS/OWL reasoning, some of which has drawn inspiration from the original publication (Hogan, et al., 2009).

DOI: 10.4018/978-1-60960-593-3.ch006

INTRODUCTION

Information attainable through the Web is unique in terms of scale and diversity. The Semantic Web movement aims to bring order to this information by providing a stack of technologies, the core of which is the Resource Description Framework (RDF) for publishing data in a machine-readable format: there now exists millions of RDF data-sources on the Web contributing billions of statements. The Semantic Web technology stack includes means to supplement instance data being published in RDF with ontologies described in RDF Schema (RDFS) (Brickley & Guha, 2004) and the Web Ontology Language (OWL) (Bechhofer, et al., 2004; Smith, Welty, & McGuinness, 2004), allowing people to formally specify a domain of discourse, and providing machines a more sapient understanding of the data. In particular, the enhancement of assertional data (i.e., instance data) with terminological data (i.e., structural data) published in ontologies allows for deductive reasoning: i.e., inferring implicit knowledge.

In particular, our work on reasoning is motivated by the requirements of the Semantic Web Search Engine (SWSE) project: http://swse.deri.org/, within which we strive to offer search, querying and browsing over data taken from the Semantic Web. Reasoning over aggregated Web data is useful, for example: to infer new assertions using terminological knowledge from ontologies and therefore provide a more complete dataset; to unite fractured knowledge (as is common on the Web in the absence of restrictive formal agreement on identifiers) about individuals collected from disparate sources; and to execute mappings between domain descriptions and thereby provide translations from one conceptual model to another. The ultimate goal here is to provide a "global knowledge-base", indexed by machines, providing querying over both the explicit knowledge published on the Web and the implicit knowledge inferable by machine. However, as we will show,

complete inferencing on the Web is an infeasible goal, due firstly to the complexity of such a task and secondly to noisy Web data; we aim instead to strike a comprise between the above goals for reasoning and what is indeed feasible for the Web.

Current systems have had limited success in exploiting ontology descriptions for reasoning over RDF Web data. While there exists a large body of work in the area of reasoning algorithms and systems that work and scale well in confined environments, the distributed and loosely coordinated creation of a world-wide knowledge-base creates new challenges for reasoning:

- the system has to perform on Web-scale, with implications on the completeness of the reasoning procedure, algorithms and optimisations;
- the method has to perform on collaboratively created knowledge-bases, which has implications on trust and the privileges of data publishers.

With respect to the first requirement, many systems claim to inherit their scalability from the underlying storage — usually some relational database system — with many papers having been dedicated to optimisations on database schemata and access; cf. (Hondjack, Pierra, & Bellatreche, 2007; Pan & Heflin, 2003; Theoharis, Christophides, & Karvounarakis, 2005; Zhou, et al., 2006). With regards the second requirement, there have been numerous papers dedicated to the inter-operability of a small number of usually trustworthy ontologies; cf. (Ghilardi, Lutz, & Wolter, 2006; Jiménez-Ruiz, Grau, Sattler, Schneider, & Llavori, 2008; Lutz, Walther, & Wolter, 2007). We leave further discussion of related work for the end of the chapter, except to state that the combination of Web-scale and Web-tolerant reasoning has received little attention in the literature and that our approach is novel.

Our system, which we call "Scalable Authoritative OWL Reasoner" (SAOR), is designed to accept as input a Web knowledge-base in the form of a body of statements as produced by a Web-crawl and to output a knowledge-base enhanced by forward-chaining reasoning over a given fragment of OWL. In particular, we choose forward-chaining to avoid the runtime complexity of query-rewriting associated with backward-chaining approaches: in the Web search scenario, the requirement for low query response times and resource usage preclude the applicability of query-rewriting for many reasoning tasks.

SAOR adopts a standard rule-based approach to reasoning whereby each rule consists of (i) an 'antecedent': a clause which identifies a graph pattern that, when matched by the data, allows for the rule to be executed and (ii) a 'consequent': the statement(s) that can be inferred given data that match the antecedent. Within SAOR, we view reasoning as a once-off rule-processing task over a given set of statements. Since the rules are all known *a-priori*, and all require simultaneous execution, we can design a task-specific system that offers much greater optimisations over more general rule engines. Firstly, we categorise the known rules according to the composition of their antecedents (e.g., with respect to arity, proportion of terminological and assertional patterns, etc.) and optimise each group according to the observed characteristics. Secondly, we do not use an underlying database or native RDF store and opt for implementation using fundamental data-structures and primitive operations; our system is built from scratch specifically (and only) for the purpose of performing pre-runtime forward-chaining reasoning which gives us greater freedom in implementing appropriate task-specific optimisations.

This paper extends upon earlier work (Hogan, Harth, & Polleres, 2008) in which we presented an initial *modus-operandi* of SAOR; we provided some evaluation of a set of rules which exhibited linear scale and concluded that using dynamic index structures, in SAOR, for more complex rulesets, was not a viable solution for a large-scale reasoner. In this paper, we provide extended discussion of our fragment of OWL reasoning and additional motivation for our deliberate incompleteness in terms of computational complexity and impediments posed by Web data considerations. We also describe an implementation of SAOR which abandons dynamic index structures in favour of batch processing techniques known to scale: namely sorts and file-scans. We present new evaluation of the adapted system over a dataset of 147m triples collected from 665k Web sources and also provide scale-up evaluation of our most optimised ruleset on a dataset of 1.1b statements collected from 6.5m Web sources.

Specifically, we make the following contributions in this paper:

- We discuss and apply a selected rule-based subset of OWL reasoning, i) to be computationally efficient, ii) to avoid an explosion of inferred statements, iii) to be tolerant to noisy Web data and iv) to protect existing specifications from undesirable contributions made in independent locations. That is, our system implements a positive fragment of OWL Full which has roots in ter Horst's pD* (ter Horst, 2005b) entailment rules and our system includes analysis of the authority of sources to counter-act the problem of *ontology hijacking* in Web data.

- We describe a scalable, optimised method for performing rule-based forward-chaining reasoning for our fragment of OWL. In particular, we refine our algorithm to capitalise on the similarities present in different rule antecedent patterns and the low volume of terminological data relative to assertional data. We implement the system using on-disk batch processing operations known to scale: sorts and scans.

- We show experimentally that a forward-chaining materialisation approach is feasible on Web data, showing that, by careful materialisation through our tailored OWL ruleset, we can avoid an explosion of inferred statements. We present evaluation with respect to computation of our most expressive ruleset on a dataset of 147m statements collected from 665k sources and present scale-up measurements by applying our most optimised ruleset on a dataset of 1.1b statements collected from 6.5m sources. We also reveal that the most computationally efficient segment of our reasoning is the most productive with regards inferred output statements.

We wrap up the chapter by discussing related work, concluding, and providing novel discussion on recent developments since the original publication of this chapter.

PRELIMINARIES

Before we continue, we briefly introduce some concepts prevalent throughout the paper. We use notation and nomenclature as is popular in the literature, particularly from Hayes (2004).

RDF Term

Given a set of URI references $\mathcal{U}$, a set of blank nodes $\mathcal{B}$, and a set of literals $\mathcal{L}$, the set of *RDF terms* is denoted by $\mathcal{RDFTerm} = \mathcal{U} \bigcup \mathcal{B} \bigcup \mathcal{L}$. The set of blank nodes $\mathcal{B}$ is a set of existensially quantified variables. The set of literals is given as $\mathcal{L} = \mathcal{L}_p \bigcup \mathcal{L}_t$, where $\mathcal{L}_p$ is the set of *plain literals* and $\mathcal{L}_t$ is the set of *typed literals*. A typed literal is the pair $l = (s, t)$, where s is the lexical form of the literal and $t \in \mathcal{U}$ is a datatype URI. The sets $\mathcal{U}$, $\mathcal{B}$, $\mathcal{L}_p$ and $\mathcal{L}_t$ are pairwise disjoint.

RDF Triple

A triple $t = (s, p, o) \in (\mathcal{U} \bigcup \mathcal{B}) \times \mathcal{U} \times (\mathcal{U} \bigcup \mathcal{B} \bigcup \mathcal{L})$ is called an *RDF triple*. In a triple (s, p, o), s is called subject, p predicate, and o object.

RDF Triple in Context/RDF Quadruple

A pair (t, c) with a triple $t = (s, p, o)$ and $c \in \mathcal{U}$ is called a triple in context c (Guha, McCool, & Fikes, 2004; Harth & Decker, 2005; Prud'hommeaux & Seaborne, 2008). We may also refer to (s, p, o, c) as the RDF quadruple or quad q with context c.

We use the term 'RDF statement' to refer generically to triple or quadruple where differentiation is not pertinent.

RDF Graph/Web Graph

An *RDF graph* $\mathcal{G}$ is a set of RDF triples; that is, a subset of $(\mathcal{U} \bigcup \mathcal{B}) \times \mathcal{U} \times (\mathcal{U} \bigcup \mathcal{B} \bigcup \mathcal{L})$.

We refer to a *Web graph* $\mathcal{W}$ as a graph derived from a given Web location (i.e., a given document). We call the pair $(\mathcal{W}, c)$ a Web-graph $\mathcal{W}$ in context c, where c is the Web-location from which $\mathcal{W}$ is retrieved. Informally, $(\mathcal{W}, c)$ is represented as the set of quadruples (t_w, c) for all $t_w \in \mathcal{W}$.

Generalised Triple

A triple $t = (s, p, o) \in (\mathcal{U} \bigcup \mathcal{B} \bigcup \mathcal{L}) \times (\mathcal{U} \bigcup \mathcal{B} \bigcup \mathcal{L}) \times (\mathcal{U} \bigcup \mathcal{B} \bigcup \mathcal{L})$ is called a *generalised triple*.

The notions of generalised quadruple, generalised statement and generalised graph follow naturally. Our definition of "generalised" is even more liberal than that described in (ter Horst, 2005b) wherein blank nodes are allowed in the predicate position: we also allow literals in the subject and predicate position. Please note that we may refer generically to a "triple", "quadruple", "graph" etc. where a distinction between the "generalised" and "RDF" versions is not pertinent.

Merge

The *merge* $M(\mathcal{S})$ of a set of graphs $\mathcal{S}$ is the union of the set of all graphs $\mathcal{G}'$ for $\mathcal{G} \in \mathcal{S}$ and $\mathcal{G}'$ derived from $\mathcal{G}$ such that $\mathcal{G}'$ contains a unique set of blank nodes for $\mathcal{S}$.

Web Knowledge-Base

Given a set $\mathcal{S}_W$ of RDF Web graphs, our view of a *Web knowledge-base* $\mathbb{KB}$ is taken as a set of pairs $(\mathcal{W}', c)$ for each $\mathcal{W} \in \mathcal{S}_W$, where $\mathcal{W}'$ contains a unique set of blank nodes for $\mathcal{S}_W$ and c denotes the URL location of $\mathcal{W}$.

Informally, $\mathbb{KB}$ is a set of quadruples retrieved from the Web wherein the set of blank nodes are unique for a given document and triples are enhanced by means of context which tracks the Web location from which each triple is retrieved. We use the abbreviated notation $\mathcal{W} \in \mathbb{KB}$ or $\mathcal{W}' \in \mathbb{KB}$ where we mean $\mathcal{W} \in \mathcal{S}_W$ for $\mathcal{S}_W$ from which $\mathbb{KB}$ is derived or $(\mathcal{W}', c) \in \mathbb{KB}$ for some c.

Class

We refer to a *class* as an RDF term which appears in either

- o of a triple t where p is `rdf:type`; or
- s of a triple t where p is `rdf:type` and o is `rdfs:Class` or `:Class`[1].

Property

We refer to a *property* as an RDF term which appears in either

- p of a triple t; or
- s of a triple t where p is `rdf:type` and o is `rdf:Property`.

Membership Assertion

We refer to a triple t as a *membership assertion* of the property mentioned in predicate position p. We refer to a triple t with predicate `rdf:type` as a membership assertion of the class mentioned in the object o. For a class or property v, we denote a membership assertion as $m(v)$.

Meta-Class

A *meta-class* is a class of classes or properties; i.e., the members of a meta-class are either classes or properties. The set of RDF(S) and OWL meta-classes is as follows: { `rdf:Property`, `rdfs:Class`, `rdfs:ContainerMembershipProperty`, `:AnnotationProperty`, `:Class`, `:DatatypeProperty`, `:DeprecatedClass`, `:DeprecatedProperty`, `:FunctionalProperty`, `:InverseFunctionalProperty`, `:ObjectProperty`, `:OntologyProperty`, `:Restriction`, `:SymmetricProperty`, `:TransitiveProperty` }.

Meta-Property

A *meta-property* is one which has a meta-class as it's domain. Meta-properties are used to describe classes and properties. The set of RDFS and OWL meta-properties is as follows: { `rdfs:domain`, `rdfs:range`, `rdfs:subClassOf`, `rdfs:subPropertyOf`, `:allValuesFrom`, `:cardinality`, `:complementOf`, `:disjointWith`, `:equivalentClass`, `:equivalentProperty`, `:hasValue`, `:intersectionOf`, `:inverseOf`, `:maxCardinality`, `:minCardinality`, `:oneOf`, `:onProperty`, `:someValuesFrom`, `:unionOf` }.

Terminological Triple

We define a *terminological triple* as one of the following:

- a membership assertion of a meta-class; or
- a membership assertion of a meta-property; or
- a triple in a non-branching, non-cyclic path $t_0^r, \ldots, t_n^r$ where $t_0^r = (s_0, p_0, o_0)$ for $\in$ { `:intersectionOf`, `:oneOf`, `:unionOf` }; $t_k^r = (o_{k-1}, \text{rdf:rest}, o_k)$

for $1 \leq k \leq n$, $o_{k-1} \in \mathcal{B}$ and $o_n = \texttt{rdf:nil}$; or a triple $t_k^f = (o_k, \texttt{rdf:first}, e_k)$ with o_k for $0 \leq k \leq n$ as before.

We refer to triples $t_1^r, \ldots, t_n^r$ and all triples t_k^f as *terminological collection triples*, whereby RDF collections are used in a union, intersection or enumeration class description.

Triple Pattern, Basic Graph Pattern

A *triple pattern* is defined as a generalised triple where, in all positions, variables from the infinite set $\mathcal{V}$ are allowed; i.e.: $tp = (s_v, p_v, o_v) \in (\mathcal{U} \bigcup \mathcal{B} \bigcup \mathcal{L} \bigcup \mathcal{V}) \times (\mathcal{U} \bigcup \mathcal{B} \bigcup \mathcal{L} \bigcup \mathcal{V}) \times (\mathcal{U} \bigcup \mathcal{B} \bigcup \mathcal{L} \bigcup \mathcal{V})$. A set (to be read as conjunction) of triple patterns $\mathcal{GP}$ is also called a *basic graph pattern*.

We use — following SPARQL notation (Prud'hommeaux & Seaborne, 2008) — alphanumeric strings preceded by '?' to denote variables in this paper: e.g., ?X. Following common notation, such as is used in SPARQL and Turtle [2], we delimit triples in the same basic graph pattern by '.' and we may group triple patterns with the same subject or same subject-predicate using ';' and ',' respectively. Finally, we denote by $\mathcal{V}(tp)$ (or $\mathcal{V}(\mathcal{GP})$, resp.) the set of variables appearing in tp (or in $\mathcal{GP}$, resp.).

Instance

A triple $t = (s, p, o)$ (or, resp., a set of triples, i.e., a graph $\mathcal{G}$) is an *instance* of a triple pattern $tp = (s_v, p_v, o_v)$ (or, resp., of a basic graph pattern $\mathcal{GP}$) if there exists a mapping $\mu: \mathcal{V} \bigcup \mathcal{RDFTerm} \rightarrow \mathcal{RDFTerm}$ which maps every element of $\mathcal{RDF}$. Term to itself, such that $t = \mu(tp) = (\mu(s_v), \mu(p_v), \mu(o_v))$ (or, resp., and slightly simplifying notation, $\mathcal{G} = \mu(\mathcal{GP})$).

Terminological/Assertional Pattern

We refer to a *terminological -triple/-graph pattern* as one whose instance can only be a terminological triple or, resp., a set thereof. We denote a *terminological collection pattern* by ?x p (?e^1, ..., ?e^n). where $p \in \{ \texttt{:intersectionOf}, \texttt{:oneOf}, \texttt{:unionOf} \}$ and ?e^k is mapped by the object of a terminological collection triple $t_k^r = (o_k, \texttt{rdf:first}, e_k)$, as before. An *assertional pattern* is any pattern which is not terminological.

Inference Rule

We define an *inference rule* r as the pair $(\mathcal{Ante}, \mathcal{Con})$, where the *antecedent* $\mathcal{Ante}$ and the *consequent* $\mathcal{Con}$ are basic graph patterns such that $\mathcal{V}(\mathcal{Con})$ and $\mathcal{V}(\mathcal{Ante})$ are non-empty, $\mathcal{V}(\mathcal{Con}) \subseteq \mathcal{V}(\mathcal{Ante})$ and $\mathcal{Con}$ does not contain blank nodes.[3] In this paper, we will typically write inference rules as:

$$\mathcal{Ante} \Rightarrow \mathcal{Con} \qquad (1)$$

Rule Application and Closure

We define a *rule application* in terms of the immediate consequences of a rule r or a set of rules $\mathcal{R}$ on a graph $\mathcal{G}$ (here slightly abusing the notion of the immediate consequence operator in Logic Programming: cf. for example Lloyd (1987)). That is, if r is a rule of the form (1), and $\mathcal{G}$ is a set of RDF triples, then:

$$T_r(\mathcal{G}) = \{\mu(\mathcal{Con}) \mid \exists \mu \text{ such that } \mu(\mathcal{Ante}) \subseteq G\}$$

and accordingly $T_\mathcal{R}(\mathcal{G}) = \bigcup_{r \in \mathcal{R}} T_r(\mathcal{G})$. Also, let $\mathcal{G}_{i+1} = \mathcal{G}_i \bigcup T_\mathcal{R}(\mathcal{G}_i)$ and $\mathcal{G}_0 = \mathcal{G}$; we now define the *exhaustive application* of the $T_\mathcal{R}$ operator on a graph $\mathcal{G}$ as being upto the least fixpoint (the smallest value for n) such that $\mathcal{G}_n = T_\mathcal{R}(\mathcal{G}_n)$. We call $\mathcal{G}_n$ the *closure* of $\mathcal{G}$ with respect to ruleset $\mathcal{R}$, denoted as $Cl_\mathcal{R}(\mathcal{G})$. Note that we may also use the intuitive notation $T_\mathcal{R}(\mathbb{KB})$, $Cl_\mathcal{R}(\mathbb{KB})$ as shorthand for the more cumbersome $T_{\mathcal{R}}(\bigcup_{W' \in \mathbb{KB}} W')$, $Cl_{\mathcal{R}}(\bigcup_{W' \in \mathbb{KB}} W')$ respectively.

Ground Triple/Graph

A *ground triple* or *ground graph* is one without existential variables.

Herbrand Interpretation

Briefly, a *Herbrand interpretation* of a graph G treats URI references, blank nodes, typed literals and plain literals analogously as denoting their own syntactic form. As such, a Herbrand interpretation represents a ground view of an RDF graph where blank nodes are treated as *Skolem names* instead of existential variables; i.e., blank nodes are seen to represent the entities that they assert the existence of, analogously to a URI reference. Henceforth, we view blank nodes as their Skolem equivalents (this also applies to blank nodes as mentioned in the above notation) and only treat the ground case of RDF graphs.

Let us elaborate in brief why this treatment of blank nodes as Skolem constants is sufficient for our purposes. In our scenario, we perform forward-chaining materialisation for query-answering and not "real" entailment checks between RDF graphs. This enables us to treat all blank nodes as Skolem names (Hayes, 2004). It is well known that simple entailment checking of two RDF graphs (Hayes, 2004) – i.e., checking whether an RDF graph G_1 entails G_2 – can be done using the ground "skolemised" version of G_1. That is $G_1 \vDash G_2$ iff $sk(G_1)$ $\vDash G_2$. Likewise, given a set of inference rules $\mathcal{R}$, where we denote entailment with respect to $\mathcal{R}$ as $\vDash_{\mathcal{R}}$, it is again well known that such entailment can be reduced to simple entailment with prior computation of the inference closure with respect to $\mathcal{R}$. That is, $G_1 \vDash_{\mathcal{R}} G_2$ iff $Cl_{\mathcal{R}}(sk(G_1))$ ' G_2; cf. (Gutiérrez, Hurtado, & Mendelzon, 2004; Hayes, 2004). In this paper we focus on the actual computation of $Cl_{\mathcal{R}}(sk(G_1))$ for a tailored ruleset $\mathcal{R}$ in between RDFS and OWL Full.

PRAGMATIC INFERENCING FOR THE WEB

In this section we discuss the inference rules which we use to approximate OWL semantics and are designed for forward-chaining reasoning over Web data. We justify our selection of inferences to support in terms of observed characteristics and examples taken from the Web. We optimise by restricting our fragment of reasoning according to three imperatives: *computational feasibility (CF)* for scalability, *reduced output* statements *(RO)* to ease the burden on consumer applications and, finally, *Web-tolerance (WT)* for avoiding undesirable inferences given noisy data and protecting publishers from unwanted, independent third-party contributions. In particular, we adhere to the following high-level restrictions:

- we are incomplete (CF, RO, WT);
- we deliberately ignore the explosive behaviour of classical inconsistency (CF, RO, WT);
- we follow a rule-based, finite, forward-chaining approach to OWL inference (CF);
- we do not invent new blank nodes (CF, RO, WT);
- we avoid inference of extended-axiomatic triples (RO);
- we focus on inference of non-terminological statements (CF);
- we do not consider :sameAs statements as applying to terminological data (CF, WT);
- we separate and store terminological data in-memory (CF);
- we support limited reasoning for non-standard use of the RDF(S) and OWL vocabularies (CF, RO, WT);
- we ignore non-authoritative (third-party) terminological statements from our reasoning procedure to counter an explosion of inferred statements caused by hijacking ontology terms (RO, WT).

Infeasibility of Complete Web Reasoning

Reasoning over RDF data is enabled by the description of RDF terms using the RDFS and OWL standards; these standards have defined entailments determined by their semantics. The semantics of these standards differs in that RDFS entailment is defined in terms of "if" conditions (intensional semantics), and has a defined set of complete standard entailment rules (Hayes, 2004). OWL semantics uses "iff" conditions (extensional semantics) without a complete set of standard entailment rules. RDFS entailment has been shown to be decidable and in P for the ground case (ter Horst, 2005b), whilst OWL Full entailment is known to be undecidable (Horrocks & Patel-Schneider, 2004). Thus, the OWL standard includes two restricted fragments of OWL whose entailment is known to be decidable from work in description logics: (i) OWL DL whose worst-case entailment is in NEXPTIME (ii) OWL Lite whose worst-case entailment is in EXPTIME (Horrocks & Patel-Schneider, 2004).

Although entailment for both fragments is known to be decidable, and even aside from their complexity, most OWL ontologies crawlable on the Web are in any case OWL Full: idealised assumptions made in OWL DL are violated by even very commonly used ontologies. For example, the popular Friend Of A Friend (FOAF) vocabulary (Brickley & Miller, 2007) deliberately falls into OWL Full since (i) in the FOAF RDF vocabulary[4], `foaf:name` is defined as a sub-property of the core RDFS property `rdfs:label` and (ii) `foaf:mbox_sha1sum` is defined as both an `:InverseFunctionalProperty` and a `:DatatypeProperty`: both are disallowed by OWL DL (and, of course, OWL Lite). In (Bechhofer & Volz, 2004), the authors identified and categorised OWL DL restrictions violated by a sample group of 201 OWL ontologies (all of which were found to be in OWL Full); these include incorrect or missing typing of classes

and properties, complex object-properties (e.g., functional properties) declared to be transitive, inverse-functional datatype properties, etc. In (Wang, Parsia, & Hendler, 2006), a more extensive survey with nearly 1,300 ontologies was conducted: 924 were identified as being in OWL Full. Taking into account that most Web ontologies are in OWL Full, and also the undecidability/computational-infeasiblity of OWL Full, one could conclude that complete reasoning on the Web is impractical. However, again for most Web documents only categorisable as OWL Full, infringements are mainly syntactic and are rather innocuous with no real effect on decidability ((Wang, et al., 2006) showed that the majority of Web documents surveyed were in the base expressivity for Description Logics after patching infringements). The main justification for the infeasibility of complete reasoning on the Web is inconsistency.

Consistency cannot be expected on the Web; for instance, a past Web-crawl of ours revealed the following:

```
>   #timbl a foaf:Person;
    foaf:homepage <http://w3.org/> .
>   #w3c a foaf:Organization;
    foaf:homepage <http://w3.org/> .
>   foaf:homepage
    a:InverseFunctionalProperty .
>   foaf:Organization:disjointWith
    foaf:Person .
```

These triples together infer that Tim Berners-Lee is the same as the W3C and thus cause an inconsistency.[5] Aside from such examples which arise from misunderstanding of the FOAF vocabulary, there might be cases where different parties deliberately make contradictive statements; resolution of such contradictions could involve "choosing sides". In any case, the explosive nature of contradiction in classical logics suggests that it is not desirable within our Web reasoning scenario.

Rule-Based Web Reasoning

As previously alluded to, there does not exist a standard entailment for OWL suitable to our Web reasoning scenario. However, incomplete (wrt. OWL Full) rule-based inference (i.e., reasoning as performed by logic progamming or deductive database engines) may be considered to have greater potential for scale, following the arguments made in (Fensel & van Harmelen, 2007) and may be considered to be more robust with respect to preventing explosive inferencing through inconsistencies. Several rule expressible non-standard OWL fragments; namely OWL-DLP (Grosof, Horrocks, Volz, & Decker, 2004), OWL– (de Bruijn, 2008) (which is a slight extension of OWL-DLP), OWLPrime (Wu, et al., 2008), pD* (ter Horst, 2005a, 2005b), and Intensional OWL (de Bruijn, 2008); have been defined in the literature and enable incomplete but sound RDFS and OWL Full inferences.

In (ter Horst, 2005b), pD* was introduced as a combination of RDFS entailment, datatype reasoning and a distilled version of OWL with rule-expressible intensional semantics: pD* entailment maintains the computational complexity of RDFS entailment, which is in NP in general and P for the ground case. Such improvement in complexity has obvious advantages in our Web reasoning scenario; thus SAOR's approach to reasoning is inspired by the pD* fragment to cover large parts of OWL by positive inference rules which can be implemented in a forward-chaining engine.

Table 1 summarises the pD* ruleset. The rules are divided into D*-entailment rules and P-entailment rules. D*-entailment is essentially RDFS entailment (Hayes, 2004) combined with some datatype reasoning. P-entailment is introduced in (ter Horst, 2005b) as a set of rules which applies to a property-related subset of OWL.

Given pD*, we make some amendments so as to align the ruleset with our requirements. Table 2 provides a full listing of our own modified ruleset, which we compare against pD* in this section. Note that this table highlights characteristics of the rules which we will discuss in later sections; for the moment we point out that **rule′** is used to indicate an amendment to the respective pD* rule. Please also note that we use the notation **rulex*** to refer to all rules with the prefix **rulex**.

pD* Rules Directly Supported

From the set of pD* rules, we directly support rules **rdfs2**, **rdfs9**, **rdfp2**, **rdfp4**, **rdfp7**, and **rdfp17**.

pD* Omissions: Extended-Axiomatic Statements

We avoid pD* rules which specifically produce what we term *extended-axiomatic* statements mandated by RDFS and OWL semantics. Firstly, we do not infer the set of pD* axiomatic triples, which are listed in (ter Horst, 2005b) for RDF(S) and OWL respectively; according to pD*, these are inferred for the empty graph. Secondly, we do not materialise membership assertions for `rdfs:Resource` which would hold for every URI and blank node in a graph. Thirdly, we do not materialise reflexive `:sameAs` membership assertions, which again hold for every URI and blank node in a graph. We see such statements as inflationary and orthogonal to our aim of reduced output.

pD* Amendments::sameAs Inferencing

From the previous set of omissions, we do not infer reflexive `:sameAs` statements. However, such reflexive statements are required by pD* rule **rdfp11**. We thus fragment the rule into **rdfp11′** and **rdfp11″** which allows for the same inferencing without such reflexive statements. (see Table 1)

In a related issue, we wittingly do not allow `:sameAs` inferencing to interfere with terminological data: for example, we do not allow `:sameAs` inferencing to affect properties in the predicate position of a triple or classes in the object

Table 1. ter-Horst rules from (ter Horst, 2005b) in Turtle-like syntax

pD*	rule	where
	D*-entailment rules	
lg	?x ?P ?l . ⇒ ?v ?P _:bl .	?l∈ $\mathcal{L}^a$
gl	?x ?P _:bl . ⇒ ?x ?P ?l .	?l∈ $\mathcal{L}$
rdf1	?x ?P ?y . ⇒ ?P a rdf:Property .	
rdf2-D	?x ?P ?l . ⇒ _:bl ?type ?t .	?l= $(s,t) \in \mathcal{L}_t$
rdfs1	?x ?P ?l . ⇒ _:bl a Literal .	?l∈ $\mathcal{L}_p$
rdfs2	?P rdfs:domain ?C . ?x ?P ?y . ⇒ ?x a ?C .	
rdfs3	?P rdfs:range ?C . ?x ?P ?y . ⇒ ?y a ?C .	?y ∈ $\mathcal{U} \cup \mathcal{B}$
rdfs4a	?x ?P ?y . ⇒ ?x a rdfs:Resource .	
rdfs4b	?x ?P ?y . ⇒ ?y a rdfs:Resource .	?y∈ $\mathcal{U} \cup \mathcal{B}$
rdfs5	?P rdfs:subProperty ?Q . ?Q rdfs:subProperty ?R . ⇒ ?P rdfs:subProperty ?R .	
rdfs6	?P a rdf:Property . ⇒ ?P rdfs:subProperty ?P .	
rdfs7	?P rdfs:subProperty ?Q . ?x ?P ?y . ⇒ ?x ?Q ?y .	?Q∈ $\mathcal{U} \cup \mathcal{B}$
rdfs8	?C a rdfs:Class . ⇒ ?C rdfs:subClassOf rdfs:Resource .	
rdfs9	?C rdfs:subClassOf ?D . ?x a ?C . ⇒ ?x a ?D .	
rdfs10	?C a rdfs:Class . ⇒ ?C rdfs:subClassOf ?C .	
rdfs11	?C rdfs:subClassOf ?D . ?D rdfs:subClassOf ?E . ⇒ ?C rdfs:subClassOf ?E .	
rdfs12	?P a rdfs:ContainerMembershipProperty . ⇒ ?P rdfs:subPropertyOf rdfs:member .	
rdfs13	?D a rdfs:Datatype . ⇒ ?D rdfs:subClassOf rdfs:Literal .	
	P-entailment rules	
rdfp1	?P a :FunctionalProperty . ?x ?P ?y , ?z . ⇒ ?y :sameAs ?z .	?y ∈ $\mathcal{U} \cup \mathcal{B}$
rdfp2	?P a :InverseFunctionalProperty . ?x ?P ?y . ?z ?P ?z . ⇒ ?x :sameAs ?y .	
rdfp3	?P a :SymmetricProperty . ?x ?P ?y . ⇒ ?y ?P ?x .	?y ∈ $\mathcal{U} \cup \mathcal{B}$
rdfp4	?P a :TransitiveProperty . ?x ?P ?y . ?y ?P ?z . ⇒ ?x ?P ?z .	
rdfp5a	?x ?P ?y . ⇒ ?x :sameAs ?x .	
rdfp5b	?x ?P ?y . ⇒ ?y :sameAs ?y .	?y∈ $\mathcal{U} \cup \mathcal{B}$
rdfp6	?x :sameAs ?y . ⇒ ?y :sameAs ?x .	?y∈ $\mathcal{U} \cup \mathcal{B}$
rdfp7	?x :sameAs ?y . ?y :sameAs ?z . ⇒ ?x :sameAs ?z .	
rdfp8a	?P :inverseOf ?Q . ?x ?P ?y . ⇒ ?y ?Q ?x .	?y,?Q∈ $\mathcal{U} \cup \mathcal{B}$
rdfp8b	?P :inverseOf ?Q . ?x ?Q ?y . ⇒ ?y ?P ?x .	?y ∈ $\mathcal{U} \cup \mathcal{B}$
rdfp9	?C a :Class ; :sameAs ?D . ⇒ ?C rdfs:subClassOf ?D .	
rdfp10	?P a :Property ; :sameAs ?Q . ⇒ ?P rdfs:subPropertyOf ?Q .	
rdfp11	?x :sameAs ?_x . ?y :sameAs ?_y . ?x ?P ?y . ⇒ ?_x ?P ?_y .	?_x ∈ $\mathcal{U} \cup \mathcal{B}$
rdfp12a	?C :equivalentClass ?D . ⇒ ?C rdfs:subClassOf ?D .	
rdfp12b	?C :equivalentClass ?D . ⇒ ?D rdfs:subClassOf ?C .	?D∈ $\mathcal{U} \cup \mathcal{B}$
rdfp12c	?C rdfs:subClassOf ?D . ?D rdfs:subClassOf ?C . ⇒ ?C :equivalentClass ?D .	
rdfp13a	?P :equivalentProperty ?Q . ⇒ ?P rdfs:subPropertyOf ?Q .	
rdfp13b	?P :equivalentProperty ?Q . ⇒ ?Q rdfs:subPropertyOf ?P .	?Q∈ $\mathcal{U} \cup \mathcal{B}$
rdfp13c	?P rdfs:subPropertyOf ?Q . ?Q rdfs:subPropertyOf ?P . ⇒ ?P :equivalentProperty ?Q .	
rdfp14a	?C :hasValue ?y ; :onProperty ?P . ?x ?P ?y . ⇒ ?x a ?C .	
rdfp14b	?C :hasValue ?y ; :onProperty ?P . ?x a ?C . ⇒ ?x ?P ?y .	?P∈ $\mathcal{U} \cup \mathcal{B}$
rdfp15	?C :someValuesFrom ?D ; :onProperty ?P . ?x ?P ?y . ?y a ?D . ⇒ ?x a ?C .	
rdfp16	?C :allValuesFrom ?D ; :onProperty ?P . ?x a ?C; ?P ?y . ⇒ ?y a ?D .	?y∈ $\mathcal{U} \cup \mathcal{B}$

[a]_:bl is a surrogate blank node given by an injective function on the literal ?l

position of an rdf:type triple. In Hogan, Harth, and Decker (2007) we showed that :sameAs inferencing through :InverseFunctional-Property reasoning caused fallacious equalities to be asserted due to noisy Web data. This is the primary motivation for us also omitting rules **rdfp9**, **rdfp10** and the reason why we place the restriction on ?p for our rule **rdfp11″**; we do not want noisy equality inferences to be reflected in the terminological segment of our knowledge-base, nor to affect the class and property positions of membership assertions.

pD* Omissions: Terminological Inferences

From pD*, we also omit rules which infer only terminological statements: namely **rdf1**, **rdfs5**, **rdfs6**, **rdfs8**, **rdfs10**, **rdfs11**, **rdfs12**, **rdfs13**, **rdfp9**, **rdfp10**, **rdfp12*** and **rdfp13***. As such, our use-case is query-answering over assertional data; we therefore focus in this paper on materialising assertional data.

We have already motivated omission of inference through :sameAs rules **rdfp9** and **rdfp10**. Rules **rdf1**, **rdfs8**, **rdfs12** and **rdfs13**

Table 2. Supported rules in Turtle-style syntax. Terminological patterns are underlined whereas assertional patterns are not; further, rules are grouped according to arity of terminological/assertional patterns in the antecedent. The source of a terminological pattern instance must speak authoritatively for at least one boldface variable binding for the rule to fire.

SAOR	rule	where
	$\mathcal{R}0$: only terminological patterns in antecedent	
rdfc0	?C :oneOf (?x$_1$ ... ?x$_n$) . $\Rightarrow$?x$_1$ ... ?x$_n$ a ?C .	?C $\in \mathcal{B}$
	$\mathcal{R}1$: at least one terminological/only one assertional pattern in antecedent	
rdfs2	**?P** rdfs:domain ?C . ?x ?P ?y . $\Rightarrow$?x a ?C .	
rdfs3'	**?P** rdfs:range ?C . ?x ?P ?y . $\Rightarrow$?y a ?C .	
rdfs7'	**?P** rdfs:subPropertyOf ?Q . ?x ?P ?y . $\Rightarrow$?x ?Q ?y .	
rdfs9	**?C** rdfs:subClassOf ?D . ?x a ?C . $\Rightarrow$?x a ?D .	
rdfp3'	**?P** a :SymmetricProperty . ?x ?P ?y . $\Rightarrow$?y ?P ?x .	
rdfp8a'	**?P** :inverseOf ?Q . ?x ?P ?y . $\Rightarrow$?y ?Q ?x .	
rdfp8b'	?P :inverseOf **?Q** . ?x ?Q ?y . $\Rightarrow$?y ?P ?x .	
rdfp12a'	**?C** :equivalentClass ?D . ?x a ?C . $\Rightarrow$?x a ?D .	
rdfp12b'	?C :equivalentClass **?D** . ?x a ?D . $\Rightarrow$?x a ?C .	
rdfp13a'	**?P** :equivalentProperty ?Q . ?x ?P ?y . $\Rightarrow$?y ?Q ?x .	
rdfp13b'	?P :equivalentProperty **?Q** . ?x ?Q ?y . $\Rightarrow$?y ?P ?x .	
rdfp14a'	?C :hasValue ?y ; :onProperty **?P** . ?x ?P ?y . $\Rightarrow$?x a ?C .	?C $\in \mathcal{B}$
rdfp14b'	**?C** :hasValue ?y ; :onProperty ?P . ?x a ?C . $\Rightarrow$?x ?P ?y .	?C $\in \mathcal{B}$
rdfc1	?C :unionOf (?C$_1$...**?C$_i$**...?C$_n$) . ?x a ?C$_i$^{a} . $\Rightarrow$?x a ?C .	?C $\in \mathcal{B}$
rdfc2	?C :minCardinality 1 ; :onProperty **?P** . ?x ?P ?y . $\Rightarrow$?x a ?C .	?C $\in \mathcal{B}$
rdfc3a	**?C** :intersectionOf (?C$_1$ ... ?C$_n$) . ?x a ?C . $\Rightarrow$?x a ?C$_1$, ..., ?C$_n$.	?C $\in \mathcal{B}$
rdfc3b	?C :intersectionOf (**?C$_1$**) . ?x a ?C$_1$. $\Rightarrow$?x a ?C . ^{b}	?C $\in \mathcal{B}$
	$\mathcal{R}2$: at least one terminological/multiple assertional patterns in antecedent	
rdfp1'	**?P** a :FunctionalProperty . ?x ?P ?y , ?z . $\Rightarrow$?y :sameAs ?z .	
rdfp2	**?P** a :InverseFunctionalProperty . ?x ?P ?z . ?y ?P ?z . $\Rightarrow$?x :sameAs ?y .	
rdfp4	**?P** a :TransitiveProperty . ?x ?P ?y . ?y ?P ?z . $\Rightarrow$?x ?P ?z .	
rdfp15'	?C :someValuesFrom **?D** ; :onProperty **?P** . ?x ?P ?y . ?y a ?D . $\Rightarrow$?x a ?C .	?C $\in \mathcal{B}$
rdfp16'	**?C** :allValuesFrom ?D ; :onProperty ?P . ?x a ?C ; ?P ?y . $\Rightarrow$?y a ?D .	?C $\in \mathcal{B}$
rdfc3c	?C :intersectionOf (**?C$_1$ ... ?C$_n$**) . ?x a ?C$_1$, ..., ?C$_n$. $\Rightarrow$?x a ?C .	?C $\in \mathcal{B}$
rdfc4a	?C :cardinality 1 ; :onProperty **?P** . ?x a ?C ; ?P ?y , ?z . $\Rightarrow$?y :sameAs ?z .	?C $\in \mathcal{B}$
rdfc4b	?C :maxCardinality 1 ; :onProperty **?P** . ?x a ?C ; ?P ?y , ?z . $\Rightarrow$?y :sameAs ?z .	?C $\in \mathcal{B}$
	$\mathcal{R}3$: only assertional patterns in antecedent	
rdfp6'	?x :sameAs ?y . $\Rightarrow$?y :sameAs ?x .	
rdfp7	?x :sameAs ?y . ?y :sameas ?z . $\Rightarrow$?x :sameAs ?z .	
rdfp11'	?x :sameAs ?_x ; ?P ?y . $\Rightarrow$?_x ?P ?y . ^{c}	
rdfp11''	?y :sameAs ?_y . ?x ?P ?y . $\Rightarrow$?x ?P ?_y . ^{c}	

^{a}?C$_i \in \{$?C$_1, ...,$?C$_n\}$
^{b}**rdfs3b** is a special case of **rdfs3c** with one A-Box pattern and thus falls under $\mathcal{R}1$.
^{c}Only where **?p** is not an RDFS/OWL property used in any of our rules (see $\mathcal{P}_{SAOR}$, Section 3.3)

infer memberships of, or subclass/subproperty relations to, RDF(S) classes and properties; we are not interested in these primarily syntactic statements which are not directly used in our inference rules. Rules **rdfs6** and **rdfs10** infer reflexive memberships of `rdfs:subPropertyOf` and `rdfs:subClassOf` meta-properties which are used in our inference rules; clearly however, these reflexive statements will not lead to unique assertional inferences through related rules **rdfs7'** or **rdfs9** respectively. Rules **rdfs5** and **rdfs11** infer transitive memberships again of `rdfs:subPropertyOf` and `rdfs:subClassOf`; again however, exhaustive application of rules **rdfs7′** or **rdfs9** respectively ensures that all possible assertional inferences are materialised without the need for the transitive rules. Rules **rdfp12c** and **rdfp13c** infer additional `:equivalentClass`/`:equivalentProperty` statements from `rdfs:subClassOf`/`rdfs:subPropertyOf` statements where assertional inferences can instead be conducted through two applications each of rules **rdfs9** and **rdfs7′** respectively. (see Table 2)

pD* Amendments: Direct Assertional Inferences

The observant reader may have noticed that we did not dismiss inferencing for rules **rdfp12a**, **rdfp12b**/**rdfp13a**, **rdfp13b** which translate `:equivalentClass`/`:equivalentProperty` to `rdfs:subClassOf`/`rdfs:subPropertyOf`. In pD*, these rules are required to support indirect assertional inferences through rules **rdfs9** and **rdfs7** respectively; we instead support assertional inferences directly from the `:equivalentProperty`/`:equivalentClass` statements using symmetric rules **rdfp12a′**, **rdfp12b′**/**rdfp13a′**, **rdfp13b′**.

pD* Omissions: Existential Variables in Consequent

We avoid rules with existential variables in the consequent; such rules would require adaptation of the T_r operator so as to "invent" new blank nodes for each rule application, with undesireable effects for forward-chaining reasoning regarding termination. For example, like pD*, we only support inferences in one direction for `:someValuesFrom` and avoid a rule such as:

```
>   ?C:someValuesFrom ?D ;:onProperty ?P
    . ?x a ?C Ð ?x ?P _:b . _:b a ?D .
```

Exhaustive application of the rule to, for example, the following data (more generally where `?D` is a subclass of `?C`):

```
>   ex:Person rdfs:subClassOf [:som-
    eValuesFrom ex:Person ;:onProp-
    erty ex:mother .]
>   _:Tim a ex:Person .
```

would infer infinite triples of the type:

```
>   _:Tim ex:mother _:b0 .
>   _:b0 a ex:Person ; ex:mother _:b1 .
>   _:b1 a ex:Person ; ex:mother _:b2 .
>   ...
```

In fact, this rule is listed in (ter Horst, 2005b) as **rdf-svx** which forms an extension of pD* entailment called *pD*sv*. This rule is omitted from pD* and from SAOR due to obvious side-effects on termination and complexity.

Unlike pD*, we also avoid inventing so called "surrogate" blank nodes for the purposes of representing a literal in intermediary inferencing steps (Rules **lg**, **gl**, **rdf2-D**, **rdfs1** in RDFS/D* entailment). Thus, we also do not support datatype reasoning (Rule **rdf2-D**) which involves the creation of surrogate blank nodes. Although surrogate blank nodes are created according to a direct mapping from a finite set of literals (and thus, do not prevent termination), we view "surrogate statements" as inflationary.

pD* Amendments: Relaxing Literal Restrictions

Since we do not support surrogate blank nodes as representing literals, we instead relax restrictions placed on pD* rules. In pD*, blank nodes are allowed in the predicate position of triples; however, the restriction on literals in the subject and predicate position still applies: literals are restricted from travelling to the subject or predicate position of a consequent (see *where* column, Table

1). Thus, surrogate blank nodes are required in pD* to represent literals in positions where they would otherwise not be allowed.

We take a different approach whereby we allow literals directly in the subject and predicate position for intermediate inferences. Following from this, we remove pD* literal restrictions on rules **rdfs3**, **rdfs7**, **rdfp1**, **rdfp3**, **rdfp6**, **rdfp8***, **rdfp14b**, **rdfp16** for intermediate inferences and omit any inferred non-RDF statements from being written to the final output.

Additions to pD*

In addition to pD*, we also include some "class based entailment" from OWL, which we call C-entailment. We name such rules using the **rdfc*** stem, following the convention from P-entailment. We provide limited support for enumerated classes (**rdfc0**), union class descriptions (**rdfc1**), intersection class descriptions (**rdfc3***),[6] as well as limited cardinality constraints (**rdfc2**, **rdfc4***).

pD* Amendments: Enforcing OWL Abstract Syntax Restrictions

Finally, unlike pD*, we enforce blank nodes as mandated by the OWL Abstract Syntax (Patel-Schneider & Horrocks, 2004), wherein certain abstract syntax constructs (most importantly in our case: *unionOf(description$_1$... description$_n$)*, *intersectionOf(description$_1$... description$_n$)*, *oneOf(iID$_1$...iID$_n$)*, *restriction(ID allValuesFrom(range))*, *restriction(ID someValuesFrom(required))*, *restriction(ID value(value))*, *restriction(ID maxCardinality(max))*, *restriction(ID minCardinality(min))*, *restriction(ID cardinality(card))* and *SEQ item$_1$...item$_n$)* are strictly mapped to RDF triples with blank nodes enforced for certain positions: such mapping is necessitated by the idiosyncrasies of representing OWL in RDF. Although the use of URIs in such circumstances is allowed by RDF, we enforce the

use of blank nodes for terminological patterns in our ruleset; to justify, let us look at the following problematic example of OWL triples taken from two sources:

```
>   SOURCE <ex:>
>   ex:Person:onProperty ex:parents
    ;:someValuesFrom ex:Person .
>   SOURCE <ex2:>
>   ex:Person:allValuesFrom ex2:Human .
```

According to the abstract syntax mapping, neither of the restrictions should be identified by a URI (if blank nodes were used instead of ex:Person as mandated by the abstract syntax, such a problem could not occur as each Web-graph is given a unique set of blank nodes). If we consider the RDF-merge of the two graphs, we will be unable to distinguish which restriction the :onProperty value applies to. As above, allowing URIs in these positions would enable "syntactic interference" between data sources. Thus, in our ruleset, we always enforce blank-nodes as mandated by the OWL abstract syntax; this specifically applies to pD* rules **rdfp14***, **rdfp15'** and **rdfp16'** and to all of our C-entailment rules **rdfc***. We denote the restrictions in the **where** column of Table 2. Indeed, in our treatment of terminological collection statements, we enforced blank nodes in the subject position of rdf:first/rdf:rest membership assertions, as well as blank nodes in the object position of non-terminating rdf:rest statements; these are analogously part of the OWL abstract syntax restrictions.

Separation of T-Box from A-Box

Aside from the differences already introduced, our primary divergence from the pD* fragment and traditional rule-based approaches is that we separate terminological data from assertional data according to their use of the RDF(S) and OWL vocabulary; these are commonly known as the "T-Box" and "A-Box" respectively (loosely borrowing Description Logics terminology). In particular, we require a separation of T-Box data as part of a core optimisation of our approach; we wish to perform a once-off load of T-Box data from our input knowledge-base into main memory.

Let $\mathcal{P}_{SAOR}$ and $\mathcal{C}_{SAOR}$ and be, resp., the exact set of RDF(S)/OWL meta-properties and -classes used in our inference rules; viz. $\mathcal{P}_{SAOR}$ = { `rdfs:domain`, `rdfs:range`, `rdfs:subClassOf`, `rdfs:subPropertyOf`, `:allValues-From`, `:cardinality`, `:equivalent-Class`, `:equivalentProperty`, `:has-Value`, `:intersectionOf`, `:inverseOf`, `:maxCardinality`, `:minCardinality`, `:oneOf`, `:onProperty`, `:sameAs`, `:som-eValuesFrom`, `:unionOf` } & $\mathcal{C}_{SAOR}$ = { `:FunctionalProperty`, `:InverseFunc-tionalProperty`, `:SymmetricProp-erty`, `:TransitiveProperty` }; our T-Box is a set of terminological triples restricted to only include membership assertions for $\mathcal{P}_{SAOR}$ and $\mathcal{C}_{SAOR}$ and the set of terminological collection statements. Table 2 identifies T-Box patterns by underlining. Statements from the input knowledge-base that match these patterns are all of the T-Box statements we consider in our reasoning process: inferred statements or statements that do not match one of these patterns are not considered being part of the T-Box, but are treated purely as assertional. We now define our T-Box:

Definition 1 (T-Box) Let $\mathcal{T}_{\mathcal{G}}$ be the union of all graph pattern instances from a graph $\mathcal{G}$ for a terminological (underlined) graph pattern in Table 2; i.e., $\mathcal{T}_{\mathcal{G}}$ is itself a graph. We call $\mathcal{T}_{\mathcal{G}}$ the T-Box of $\mathcal{G}$.

Also, let $\mathcal{P}_{SAOR}^{domP}$ = { `rdfs:domain`, `rdfs:range`, `rdfs:subPropertyOf`, `:equivalentProperty`, `:inverseOf` } and $\mathcal{P}_{SAOR}^{ranP}$ = { `rdfs:subPropertyOf`, `:equivalentProperty`, `:inverseOf`, `:onProperty` }, We call ϕ a property in T-Box $\mathcal{T}$ if there exists a triple $t \in \mathcal{T}$ where

- $s = \phi$ and $p \in \mathcal{P}_{SAOR}^{domP}$
- $p \in \mathcal{P}_{SAOR}^{ranP}$ and $o = \phi$
- $s = \phi$, $p =$ `rdf:type` and $o \in \mathcal{C}_{SAOR}$

Similarly, let $\mathcal{P}_{SAOR}^{domC}$ = { `rdfs:subClassOf`, `:allValuesFrom`, `:cardinality`, `:equivalentClass`, `:hasValue`, `:in-tersectionOf`, `:maxCardinality`, `:minCardinality`, `:oneOf`, `:onProp-erty`, `:someValuesFrom`, `:unionOf` } and $\mathcal{P}_{SAOR}^{ranC}$ = { `rdfs:domain`, `rdfs:range`, `rdfs:subClassOf`, `rdf:first`, `:all-ValuesFrom`, `:equivalentClass`, `:some-ValuesFrom` }. We call $\mathcal{X}$ a *class in T-Box* $\mathcal{T}$ if there exists a triple $t \in \mathcal{T}$ where

- $p \in \mathcal{P}_{SAOR}^{domC}$ and $s = \mathcal{X}$
- $p \in \mathcal{P}_{SAOR}^{ranC}$ and $o = \mathcal{X}$

We define the signature of a T-Box $\mathcal{T}$ to be the set of all properties and classes in $\mathcal{T}$ as above, which we denote by $sig(\mathcal{T})$.

For our knowledge-base $\mathbb{KB}$, we define our T-Box $\mathbb{T}$ as the set of all pairs $(\mathcal{T}_{\mathcal{W}'}, c)$ where $(\mathcal{W}', c) \in \mathbb{KB}$, and $\mathcal{T}_{\mathcal{W}'} \neq \emptyset$. Again, we may use the intuitive notation $\mathcal{T}_{\mathcal{W}'} \in \mathbb{T}$. We define our A-Box $\mathbb{A}$ as containing all of the statements in $\mathbb{KB}$, including $\mathbb{T}$ and the set of class and property membership assertions possibly using identifiers in $\mathcal{P}_{SAOR} \bigcup \mathcal{C}_{SAOR}$; i.e., unlike description logics, our $\mathbb{A}$ is synonymous with our $\mathbb{KB}$. We use the term A-Box to distinguish data that are stored on-disk (which includes T-Box data also stored in memory).

We now define our notion of a *T-split inference rule*, whereby part of the antecedent is a basic graph pattern strictly instantiated by a static T-Box $\mathcal{T}$.

Definition 2 (T-split inference rule) We define a $\mathcal{T}$-split inference rule r as the triple $(Ante_{\mathcal{T}}, Ante_{\mathcal{G}}, Con)$, where $Ante_{\mathcal{T}}$ is a basic graph pattern matched by a static T-Box $\mathcal{T}$ and $Ante_{\mathcal{G}}$ is matched by data in the graph G, C*on* does not contain blank nodes, $\mathcal{V}(Con) \neq \emptyset$, $\mathcal{V}(Con) \subseteq \mathcal{V}(Ante_T) \bigcup \mathcal{V}(Ante_G)$; also, if both $Ante_T$ and $Ante_G$ are non-empty, then $\mathcal{V}(Ante_T) \bigcap \mathcal{V}(Ante_G) \neq \emptyset$.

We generally write $(Ante_T, Ante_G, Con)$ as $Ante_T, Ante_G \Rightarrow Con$. We call $Ante_T$ the terminological or T-Box antecedent pattern and $Ante_G$ the assertional or A-Box pattern.

Definition 3 (Rule-sets $\mathcal{R}_T$, $\mathcal{R}_{TG}$, $\mathcal{R}_G$) We define $\mathcal{R}_T$ as the set of T-split rules for which $Ante_T \neq \emptyset$ and $Ante_G = \emptyset$. We define $\mathcal{R}_{TG}$ as the set of T-split rules for which $Ante_T \neq \emptyset$ and $Ante_G \neq \emptyset$. We define $\mathcal{R}_G$ as the set of T-split rules for which $Ante_T = \emptyset$ and $Ante_G \neq \emptyset$.

In Table 2, we categorise the T-split rules into four rulesets: $\mathcal{R}0 \subset \mathcal{R}_T$; $\mathcal{R}1 \subset \mathcal{R}_{TG}$ where $|Ante_G| = 1$; $\mathcal{R}2 \subset \mathcal{R}_{TG}$ where $|Ante_G| > 1$ and $\mathcal{R}0 \subset \mathcal{R}_G$.

We now introduce the notion of a $\mathcal{T}$-split inference rule application for a graph $\mathcal{G}$ w.r.t. a T-Box $\mathcal{T}$:

Definition 4 ($\mathcal{T}$-split inference rule application) We define a $\mathcal{T}$-split rule application to be $T_r(\mathcal{T}, \mathcal{G})$ for $r = (Ante_T, Ante_G, Con)$ as follows:

$$T_r(\mathcal{T}, \mathcal{G}) = \{\mu(Con) \mid \exists \mu \text{ such that } \mu(Ante_T) \subseteq \mathcal{T} \text{ and } \mu(Ante_G) \subseteq \mathcal{G}\}$$

Again, $T_{\mathcal{R}}(\mathcal{T}, \mathcal{G}) = \bigcup_{r \in \mathcal{R}} T_r(\mathcal{T}, \mathcal{G})$; also, given $\mathcal{T}$ as static, the exhaustive application of the $T_{\mathcal{R}}(\mathcal{T}, \mathcal{G})$ up to the least fixpoint is called the $\mathcal{T}$-*split closure* of $\mathcal{G}$, denoted as $Cl_{\mathcal{R}}(\mathcal{T}, \mathcal{G})$. Again we use abbreviations such as $T_{\mathcal{R}}(\mathbb{T}, \mathbb{KB})$ and $Cl_{\mathcal{R}}(\mathbb{T}, \mathbb{KB})$, where $\mathbb{KB}$ should be interpreted as $\bigcup_{\mathcal{W}' \in \mathbb{KB}} \mathcal{W}'$ and $\mathbb{T}$ as $\bigcup_{\mathcal{T}_{\mathcal{W}'} \in \mathbb{T}} \mathcal{T}_{\mathcal{W}'}$.

Please note that since we enforce blank nodes in all positions mandated by the OWL abstract syntax for our rules, each instance of a given graph pattern $Ante_T$ can only contain triples from one Web-graph $\mathcal{W}'$ where $\mathcal{T}_{\mathcal{W}'} \in \mathbb{T}$. Let $\mathcal{V}_B(\mathcal{GP})$ be the set of all variables in a graph pattern $\mathcal{GP}$ which

we restrict to only be instantiated by a blank node according to the abstract syntax. For all $Ante_T$ in our rules where $|Ante_T| > 1$ let $Ante_T'$ be any proper non-empty subset of $Ante_T$; we can then say that $\mathcal{V}_B(Ante_T') \bigcap \mathcal{V}_B(Ante_T \setminus Ante_T') = \emptyset$. In other words, since for every rule either (i) $Ante_T = \emptyset$; or (ii) $Ante_T$ consists of a single triple pattern; or (iii) no sub-pattern of any $Ante_T$ in our rules contains a unique set of blank-node enforced variables; then a given instance of $Ante_T$ can only contain triples from one Web-graph with unique blank nodes as is enforced by our knowledge-base. For our ruleset, we can then say that $T_R(\mathbb{T}, \mathbb{KB}) = T_R(\bigcup_{\mathcal{T}_{\mathcal{W}'} \in \mathbb{T}} \mathcal{T}_{\mathcal{W}'}, \mathbb{KB}) = \bigcup_{\mathcal{T}_{\mathcal{W}'} \in \mathbb{T}} T_R(\mathcal{T}_{\mathcal{W}'}, \mathbb{KB})$. In other words, one Web-graph cannot re-use structural statements in another Web-graph to instantiate a T-Box pattern in our rule; this has bearing on our notion of authoritative reasoning as we will discuss later.

Further, a separate static T-Box within which inferences are not reflected has implications upon the completeness of reasoning w.r.t. the presented ruleset. Although we do not infer terminological statements and thus can support most inferences directly from our static T-Box, SAOR still does not fully support meta-modelling (Motik, 2007): by separating the T-Box segment of the knowledge-base, we do not support all possible entailments from the simultaneous description of both a class (or property) and an individual. In other words, we do not fully support inferencing for meta-classes or meta-properties defined outside of the RDF(S)/OWL specification.

However, we do provide limited reasoning support for meta-modelling in the spirit of "punning" by conceptually separating the individual-, class- or property-meanings of a resource; cf. (Grau, Horrocks, Parsia, Patel-Schneider, & Sattler, 2006). More precisely, during reasoning we not only store the T-Box data in memory, but also store the data on-disk in the A-Box. Thus, we perform punning in one direction: viewing class and property descriptions which form our

T-Box also as individuals in our A-Box. Interestingly, although we do not support terminological reasoning directly, we can through our limited punning perform reasoning for terminological data based on the RDFS descriptions provided for the RDFS and OWL specifications. For example, we would infer the following by storing the three input statements in both the T-Box and the A-Box:

```
>  rdfs:subClassOf rdfs:domain
   rdfs:Class; rdfs:range rdfs:Class .
>  ex:Class1 rdfs:subClassOf
   ex:Class2 . ⇒
>  ex:Class1 a rdfs:Class . ex:Class2
   a rdfs:Class .
```

However, again our support for meta-modelling is limited; SAOR does not fully support so-called "non-standard usage" of RDF(S) and OWL: the use of properties and classes which make up the RDF(S) and OWL vocabularies in locations where they have not been intended, cf. (de Bruijn & Heymans, 2007; Muñoz, Pérez, & Gutiérrez, 2007). We adapt and refine the definition of non-standard vocabulary use for our purposes according to the parts of the RDF(S) and OWL vocabularies relevant for our inference ruleset:

Definition 5 (Non-standard Vocabulary Usage)
An RDF triple t has non-standard vocabulary usage for our ruleset if one of the following conditions holds:

- a property in $\mathcal{P}_{SAOR}$ appears in a position different from the predicate position; or
- a class in $\mathcal{C}_{SAOR}$ appears in a position different from the object position of an rdf:type triple.

Continuing, we now introduce the following example wherein the first input statement is a case of non-standard usage with rdfs:subClassOf $\in \mathcal{P}_{SAOR}$ in the object position:[7]

```
>  ex:subClassOf rdfs:subPropertyOf
   rdfs:subClassOf .
>  ex:Class1 ex:subClassOf ex:Class2 . ⇒
>  ex:Class1 rdfs:subClassOf ex:Class2 .
```

We can see that SAOR provides inference through rdfs:subPropertyOf as per usual; however, the inferred triple will not be reflected in the T-Box, thus we are incomplete and will not translate members of ex:Class1 into ex:Class2. As such, non-standard usage may result in T-Box statements being produced which, according to our limited form of punning, will not be reflected in the T-Box and will lead to incomplete inference.

Indeed, there may be good reason for not fully supporting non-standard usage of the ontology vocabulary: non-standard use could have unpredictable results even under our simple rule-based entailment if we were to fully support meta-modelling. One may consider a finite combination of only four non-standard triples that, upon naive reasoning, would explode all Web resources R by inferring $|R|^3$ triples, namely:

```
>  rdfs:subClassOf rdfs:subPropertyOf
   rdfs:Resource.
>  rdfs:subClassOf rdfs:subPropertyOf
   rdfs:subPropertyOf.
>  rdf:type rdfs:subPropertyOf
   rdfs:subClassOf.
>  rdfs:subClassOf
   rdf:type:SymmetricProperty.
```

The exhaustive application of standard RDFS inference rules plus inference rules for property symmetry together with the inference for class membership in rdfs:Resource for all collected resources in typical rulesets such as pD* lead to inference of any possible triple (r_1, r_2, r_3) for arbitrary $r_1, r_2, r_3 \in R$. Thus, although by maintaining a separate static T-Box we are incomplete w.r.t non-standard usage, we show that complete support of such usage of the RDFS/OWL vocabularies is undesirable for the Web.[8]

Authoritative Reasoning against Ontology Hijacking

During initial evaluation of a system which implements reasoning upon the above ruleset, we encountered a behaviour which we term "ontology hijacking", symptomised by a perplexing explosion of materialised statements. For example, we noticed that for a single `foaf:Person` membership assertion, SAOR inferred in the order of hundreds of materialised statements as opposed to the expected six. Such an explosion of statements is orthogonal to the aim of reduced materialised statements we have outlined for SAOR; thus, SAOR is designed to annul the diagnosed problem of ontology hijacking through anaylsis of the authority of Web sources for T-Box data. Before formally defining ontology hijacking and our proposed solution, let us give some preliminary definitions:

Definition 6 (Authoritative Source) A Web-graph $\mathcal{W}$ from source (context) c speaks authoritatively about an RDF term n iff:

- $n \in \mathcal{B}$; or
- $n \in \mathcal{U}$ and c coincides with, or is redirected to by, the namespace[9] of n.

Firstly, all graphs are authoritative for blank nodes defined in that graph (remember that according to the definition of our knowledge-base, all blank nodes are unique to a given graph). Secondly, we support namespace redirects so as to conform to best practices as currently adopted by Web ontology publishers.[10]

For example, as taken from the Web:

- Source `http://usefulinc.com/ns/doap` is authoritative for all classes and properties which are within the

`http://usefulinc.com/ns/doap` namespace; e.g., `http://usefulinc.com/ns/doap#Project`.

- Source `http://xmlns.com/foaf/spec/` is authoritative for all classes and properties which are within the `http://xmlns.com/foaf/0.1/` namespace; e.g., `http://xmlns.com/foaf/0.1/knows`; since the property `http://xmlns.com/foaf/0.1/knows` redirects to `http://xmlns.com/foaf/spec/`.

We consider the authority of sources speaking about classes and properties in our T-Box to counter-act ontology hijacking; ontology hijacking is the assertion of a set of non-authoritative T-Box statements such that could satisfy the terminological pattern of a rule in $\mathcal{R}_{\mathcal{TG}}$ (i.e., those rules with at least one terminological and at least one assertional triple pattern in the antecedent). Such third-party sources can then cause arbitrary inferences over membership assertions of classes or properties (contained in the A-Box) for which they speak non-authoritatively. We can say that only rules in $\mathcal{R}_{\mathcal{TG}}$ are relevant to ontology hijacking since: (i) inferencing on $\mathcal{R}_{\mathcal{G}}$, which does not contain any T-Box patterns, cannot be affected by non-authoritative T-Box statements; and (ii) the $\mathcal{R}_{\mathcal{T}}$ ruleset does not contain any assertional antecedent patterns and therefore, cannot hijack assertional data (i.e., in our scenario, the `:oneOf` construct can be viewed as directly asserting memberships, and is unable, according to our limited support, to redefine sets of individuals). We now define ontology hijacking:

Definition 7 (Ontology Hijacking) Let $\mathcal{T}_{\mathcal{W}}$ be the T-Box extracted from a Web-graph $\mathcal{W}$ and let $\widehat{sig}(\mathcal{W})$ be the set of classes and properties for which $\mathcal{W}$ speaks authoritatively; then if $Cl_{\mathcal{R}_{\mathcal{TG}}}(\mathcal{T}_{\mathcal{W}}, \mathcal{G}) \neq \mathcal{G}$ for any $\mathcal{G}$ not mentioning any element of $\widehat{sig}(\mathcal{W})$, we say that Web-graph $\mathcal{W}$ is performing ontology hijacking.

In other words, ontology hijacking is the contribution of statements about classes or properties in a non-authoritative source such that reasoning on members of those classes or properties is affected. One particular method of ontology hijacking is defining new super-classes or properties of third-party classes or properties. As a concrete example, if one were to publish today a description of a property in an ontology (in a location non-authoritative for `foaf:` but authoritative for `my:`), `my:name`, within which the following was stated: `foaf:name rdfs:subPropertyOf my:name .`, that person would be hijacking the `foaf:name` property and effecting the translation of all `foaf:name` statements in the Web knowledge-base into `my:name` statements as well. However, if the statement were instead `my:name rdfs:subPropertyOf foaf:name .`, this would not constitute a case of ontology hijacking but would be a valid example of translating from a local authoritative property into an external non-authoritative property.

Ontology hijacking is problematic in that it vastly increases the amount of statements that are materialised and can potentially harm inferencing on data contributed by other parties. With respect to materialisation, the former issue becomes prominent: members of classes/properties from popular/core ontologies get translated into a plethora of conceptual models described in obscure ontologies (we quantify the problem in the evaluation section). However, taking precautions against harmful ontology hijacking is growing more and more important as the Semantic Web features more and more attention; motivation for spamming and other malicious activity propagates amongst certain parties with ontology hijacking being a prospective avenue. With this in mind, we assign sole responsibility for classes and properties

and reasoning upon their members to those who maintain the authoritative specification.

Related to the idea of ontology hijacking is the idea of "non-conservative extension" described in the Description Logics literature: cf. (Ghilardi, et al., 2006; Jiménez-Ruiz, et al., 2008; Lutz, et al., 2007). However, the notion of a "conservative extension" was defined with a slightly different objective in mind: according to the notion of deductively conservative extensions, a graph $\mathcal{G}_a$ is only considered malicious towards $\mathcal{G}_b$ if it causes additional inferences with respect to the intersection of the signature of the original $\mathcal{G}_b$ with the newly inferred statements. Returning to the former `my:name` example from above, defining a super-property of `foaf:name` would still constitute a conservative extension: the closure without the non-authoritative `foaf:name rdfs:subPropertyOf my:name .` statement is the same as the closure with the statement after all of the `my:name` membership assertions are removed. However, further stating that `my:name a:InverseFunctionalProperty.` would not satisfy a model conservative extension since members of `my:name` might then cause equalities in other remote ontologies as side-effects, independent from the newly defined signature. Summarising, we can state that every non-conservative extension (with respect to our notion of deductive closure) constitutes a case of ontology hijacking, but not vice versa; non-conservative extension can be considered "harmful" hijacking whereas the remainder of ontology hijacking cases can be considered "inflationary".

To negate ontology hijacking, we only allow inferences through *authoritative rule applications*, which we now define:

Definition 8 (Authoritative Rule Application)

Again let $\widehat{sig}(\mathcal{W})$ be the set of classes and properties for which $\mathcal{W}$ speaks authoritatively and let $\mathcal{T}_\mathcal{W}$ be the T-Box of $\mathcal{W}$. We define an authoritative rule application for a graph $\mathcal{G}$ w.r.t. the T-Box $\mathcal{T}_\mathcal{W}$

to be a T-split rule application $T_r(\mathcal{T_W}, \mathcal{G})$ where additionally, if both $Ante_T$ and $Ante_\mathcal{G}$ are non-empty ($r \in \mathcal{R}_{T\mathcal{G}}$), then for the mapping μ of $T_r(\mathcal{T_W}, \mathcal{G})$ there must exist a variable $v \in (\mathcal{V}(Ante_T) \bigcap \mathcal{V}(Ante_\mathcal{G}))$ such that $\mu(v) \in \widehat{sig}(\mathcal{W})$. We denote an authoritative rule application by $T_{\hat{r}}(\mathcal{T_W}, \mathcal{G})$.

In other words, an authoritative rule application will only occur if the rule consists of only assertional patterns ($\mathcal{R}_\mathcal{G}$); or the rules consists of only terminological patterns ($\mathcal{R}_T$); or if in application of the rule, the terminological pattern instance is from a Web-graph authoritative for at least one class or property in the assertional pattern instance. The $T_{\hat{\mathcal{R}}}$ operator follows naturally as before for a set of authoritative rules $\hat{\mathcal{R}}$, as does the notion of authoritative closure which we denote by $Cl_{\hat{\mathcal{R}}}(\mathcal{T}, \mathcal{W})$. We may also refer to, e.g., $T_{\hat{\mathcal{R}}}(\mathbb{T}, \mathbb{KB})$ and $Cl_{\hat{\mathcal{R}}}(\mathbb{T}, \mathbb{KB})$ as before for a $\mathcal{T}$-split rule application.

Table 2 identifies the authoritative restrictions we place on our rules wherein the underlined T-Box pattern is matched by a set of triples from a Web-graph $\mathcal{W}$ iff $\mathcal{W}$ speaks authoritatively for at least one element matching a boldface variable in Table 2; i.e., again, for each rule, at least one of the classes or properties matched by the A-Box pattern of the antecedent must be authoritatively spoken for by an instance of the T-Box pattern. These restrictions only apply to $\mathcal{R}1$ and $\mathcal{R}2$ (which are both a subset of $\mathcal{R}_{T\mathcal{G}}$). Please note that, for example in rule **rdfp14b'** where there are no boldface variables, the variables enforced to be instantied by blank nodes will always be authoritatively spoken for: a Web-graph is always authoritative for its blank nodes.

We now make the following proposition relating to the prevention of ontology-hijacking through authoritative rule application:

Proposition 1 Given a T-Box $\mathcal{T_W}$ extracted from a Web-graph $\mathcal{W}$ and any graph $\mathcal{G}$ not mentioning any element of $\widehat{sig}(\mathcal{W})$, then $Cl_{\widehat{\mathcal{R}_{T\mathcal{G}}}}(\mathcal{T_W}, \mathcal{G}) = \mathcal{G}$.

Proof: Informally, our proposition is that the authoritative closure of a graph $\mathcal{G}$ w.r.t. some T-Box $\mathcal{T_W}$ will not contain any inferences which constitute ontology hijacking, defined in terms of ruleset $\mathcal{R}_{T\mathcal{G}}$. Firstly, from Definition 3, for each rule $r \in \mathcal{R}_{T\mathcal{G}}$, $Ante_T = \emptyset$ and $Ante_\mathcal{G} = \emptyset$. Therefore, from Definitions 4 & 8, for an authoritative rule application to occur for any such r, there must exist both (i) a mapping μ such that $\mu(Ante_T) \subseteq \mathcal{T_W}$ and $\mu(Ante_\mathcal{G}) \subseteq \mathcal{G}$; and (ii) a variable $v \in (\mathcal{V}(Ante_T) \bigcap \mathcal{V}(Ante_\mathcal{G}))$ such that $\mu(v) \in \widehat{sig}(\mathcal{W})$. However, since $\mathcal{G}$ does not mention any element of $\widehat{sig}(\mathcal{W})$, then there is no such mapping μ where $\mu(v) \in \widehat{sig}(\mathcal{W})$ for $v \in \mathcal{V}(Ante_\mathcal{G})$, and $\mu(Ante_\mathcal{G}) \subseteq \mathcal{G}$. Hence, for $r \in \mathcal{R}_{T\mathcal{G}}$, no such application $T_{\hat{r}}(\mathcal{T_W}, \mathcal{G})$ will occur; it then follows that $T_{\widehat{\mathcal{R}_{T\mathcal{G}}}}(\mathcal{T_W}, \mathcal{G}) = \emptyset$ and $Cl_{\widehat{\mathcal{R}_{T\mathcal{G}}}}(\mathcal{T_W}, \mathcal{G}) = \mathcal{G}$. □

The above proposition and proof holds for a given Web-graph $\mathcal{W}$; however, given a set of Web-graphs where an instance of $Ante_T$ can consist of triples from more that one graph, it is possible for ontology hijacking to occur whereby some triples in the instance come from a non-authoritative graph and some from an authoritative graph. To illustrate we refer to the following example, wherein (and without enforcing abstract syntax blank nodes) the second source could cause ontology hijacking by interfering with the authoritative definition of the class restriction in the first source as follows:

```
>  RULE (adapted so that ?C need not
   be a blank node)
>  ?C:allValuesFrom ?D ;:onProperty
   ?P . ?x a ?C ; ?P ?y . Ð ?y a ?D .
>  SOURCE <ex:>
>  ex:Person:onProperty ex:parent .
>  SOURCE <ex2:>
>  ex:Person:allValuesFrom ex2:Human .
>  ASSERTIONAL
>  _:Jim a ex:Person ; ex:parent
   _:Jill .
```

```
>  ⇒
>  _:Jill a ex2:Human .
```

Here, the above inference is authoritative according to our definition since the instance of $Ante_T$ (specifically the first statement from source `<ex:>`) speaks authoritatively for a class/property in the assertional data; however, the statement from the `<ex2:>` source is causing inferences on assertional data not containing a class or property for which `<ex2:>` is authoritative.

As previously discussed, for our ruleset, we enforce the OWL abstract syntax and thus we enforce that $\mu(Ante_T) \subseteq \mathcal{T}_{w}$, where $\mathcal{T}_{w} \in \mathbb{T}$. However, where this condition does not hold (i.e., an instance of $Ante_T$ can comprise of data from more than one graph), then an authoritative rule application should only occur if each Web-graph contributing to an instance of $Ante_T$ speaks authoritatively for at least one class/property in the $Ante_g$ instance.

REASONING ALGORITHM

In the following we first present observations on Web data that influenced the design of the SAOR algorithm, then give an overview of the algorithm, and next discuss details of how we handle T-Box information, perform statement-wise reasoning, and deal with equality for individuals.

Characteristics of Web Data

Our algorithm is intended to operate over a Web knowledge-base as retrieved by means of a Web crawl; therefore, the design of our algorithm is motivated by observations on our Web dataset:

1. Reasoning accesses a large slice of data in the index: we found that approximately 61% of statements in the 147m dataset and 90% in the 1.1b dataset produced inferred statements through authoritative reasoning.

2. Relative to assertional data, the volume of terminological data on the Web is small: < 0.9% of the statements in the 1.1b dataset and < 1.7% of statements in the 147m dataset were classifiable as SAOR T-Box statements.[11]

3. The T-Box is the most frequently accessed segment of the knowledge-base for reasoning: although relatively small, all but the rules in $\mathcal{R}3$ require access to T-Box information.

Following from the first observation, we employ a file-scan batch-processing approach so as to enable sequential access over the data and avoid disk-lookups and dynamic data structures which would not perform well given high disk latency; also we avoid probing the same statements repeatedly for different rules at the low cost of scanning a given percentage of statements not useful for reasoning.

Following from the second and third observations, we optimise by placing T-Box data in a separate data structure accessible by the reasoning engine. Currently, we hold all T-Box data in-memory, but the algorithm can be generalised to provide for a caching on-disk structure or a distributed in-memory structure as needs require.[12]

To be able to scale, we try to minimise the amount of main memory needed, given that main memory is relatively expensive and that disk-based algorithms are thus more economical (Kunkle & Cooperman, 2008). Given high disk latency, we avoid using random-access on-disk data structures. In our previous work a disk-based updateable random-access data structure (a B+-Tree) proved to be the bottleneck for the reasoning due to a high volume of inserts, leading to frequent index reorganisations and hence inadequate performance. As a result, our algorithms are now build upon two disk-based primitives known to scale: file scanning and sorting.

Figure 1. High-level architecture

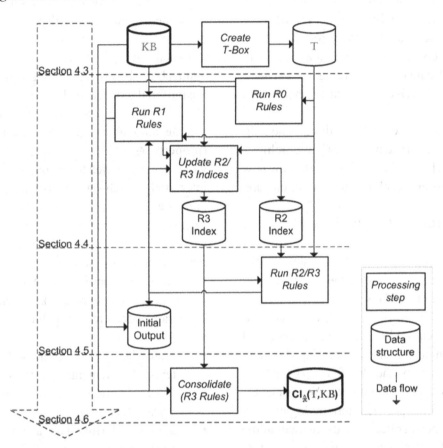

Algorithm Overview

The SAOR algorithm performs a fixpoint computation by iteratively applying the rules in Table 2. Figure 1 outlines the architecture. The reasoning process can be roughly divided into the following steps:

1. Separate $\mathbb{T}$ from $\mathbb{KB}$, build in-memory representation $\mathbb{T}$, and apply ruleset $\mathcal{R}0$.
2. Perform reasoning over $\mathbb{KB}$ in a statement-wise manner:
    2.1. Execute rules with only a single A-Box triple pattern in the antecedent ($\mathcal{R}1$): join A-Box pattern with in-memory T-Box; recursively execute steps over inferred statements; write inferred RDF statements to output file.
    2.2. Write on-disk files for computation of rules with multiple A-Box triple patterns in the antecedent ($\mathcal{R}2$); when a statement matches one of the A-Box triple patterns for these rules and the necessary T-Box join exists, the statement is written to the on-disk file for later rule computation.
    2.3. Write on-disk equality file for rules which involve equality reasoning ($\mathcal{R}3$); :sameAs statements found during the scan are written to an on-disk file for later computation.
3. Execute ruleset $\mathcal{R}2 \bigcup \mathcal{R}3$: on-disk files containing partial A-Box instances for rules in $\mathcal{R}2$ and $\mathcal{R}3$ are sequentially analysed producing further inferred statements. Newly inferred statements are again subject to step

2 above; fresh statements can still be written to on-disk files and so the process is iterative until no new statements are found.

4. Finally, consolidate source data along with inferred statements according to : sameAs computation ($\mathcal{R}3$) and write to final output.

In the following sections, we discuss the individual components and processes in the architecture as highlighted, whereafter we will show how these elements are combined to achieve closure.

Handling Terminological Data

In the following, we describe how to separate the T-Box data and how to create the data structures for representing the T-Box.

T-Box data from RDFS and OWL specifications can be acquired either from conventional crawling techniques, or by accessing the locations pointed to by the dereferenced URIs of classes and properties in the data. We assume for brevity that all the pertinent terminological data have already been collected and exist within the input data. If T-Box data are sourced separately via different means we can build an in-memory representation directly, without requiring the first scan of all input data.

We apply the following algorithm to create the T-Box in-memory representation, which we will analyse in the following sections:

- *FULL SCAN 1*: separate T-Box information as described in Definition 1.
- *TBOX SCAN 1 & 2*: reduce irrelevant RDF collection statements.
- *TBOX SCAN 3:* perform authoritative analysis of the T-Box data and load in-memory representation.

Separating and Reducing T-Box Data

Firstly, we wish to separate all possible T-Box statements from the main bulk of data. $\mathcal{P}_{SAOR}$ and

$\mathcal{C}_{SAOR}$ are stored in memory and then the data dump is scanned. Quadruples with property $\in \mathcal{P}_{SAOR} \bigcup$ { rdf:first, rdf:rest } or rdf:type statements with object $\in \mathcal{C}_{SAOR}$ (which, where applicable, abide by the OWL abstract syntax) are buffered to a T-Box data file.

However, the T-Box data file still contains a large amount of RDF collection statements (property $\in$ { rdf:first, rdf:rest }) which are not related to reasoning. SAOR is only interested in such statements wherein they form part of a : unionOf, : intersectionOf or : oneOf class description. Later when the T-Box is being loaded, these collection fragments are reconstructed in-memory and irrelevant collection fragments are discarded; to reduce the amount of memory required we can quickly discard irrelevant collection statements through two T-Box scans:

- scan the T-Box data and store contexts of statements where the property $\in$ { :unionOf, :intersectionOf, :oneOf }.
- scan the T-Box data again and remove statements for which both hold:
  - property $\in$ { rdf:first, rdf:rest }
  - the context does not appear in those stored from the previous scan.

These scans quickly remove irrelevant collection fragments where a : unionOf, : intersectionOf, : oneOf statement does not appear in the same source as the fragment (i.e., collections which cannot contribute to the T-Box pattern of one of our rules).

Authoritative Analysis

We next apply authoritative analysis to the T-Box and load the results into our in-memory representation; in other words, we build an *authoritative T-Box* which pre-computes authority of T-Box

Table 3. T-Box patterns and associated links kept between classes and properties in the in-memory T-Box

$\mathcal{R}0$		
rdfc0	?C :oneOf (?x$_1$ ... ?x$_n$) .	(?x$_1$ ... ?x$_n$) $\overset{\mathbf{rdfc0}}{\to}$?C

$\mathcal{R}1$		
rdfs2	?P rdfs:domain ?C .	?P $\overset{\mathbf{rdfs2}}{\to}$?C
rdfs3'	?P rdfs:range ?C .	?P $\overset{\mathbf{rdfs3'}}{\to}$?C
rdfs7'	?P rdfs:subPropertyOf ?Q .	?P $\overset{\mathbf{rdfs7'}}{\to}$?Q
rdfs9	?C rdfs:subClassOf ?D .	?C $\overset{\mathbf{rdfs9}}{\to}$?D
rdfp3'	?P a :SymmetricProperty .	?P $\overset{\mathbf{rdfp3'}}{\to}$ TRUE
rdfp8a'	?P :inverseOf ?Q .	?P $\overset{\mathbf{rdfp8a'}}{\to}$?Q
rdfp8b'	?P :inverseOf **?Q** .	?Q $\overset{\mathbf{rdfp8b'}}{\to}$?P
rdfp12a'	?C :equivalentClass ?D .	?C $\overset{\mathbf{rdfp12a'}}{\to}$?D
rdfp12b'	?C :equivalentClass **?D** .	?D $\overset{\mathbf{rdfp12b'}}{\to}$?C
rdfp13a'	?P :equivalentProperty ?Q .	?P $\overset{\mathbf{rdfp13a'}}{\to}$?Q
rdfs13b'	?P :equivalentProperty **?Q** .	?Q $\overset{\mathbf{rdfs13b'}}{\to}$?P
rdfp14a'	?C :hasValue ?y ; :onProperty **?P** .	?P $\overset{\mathbf{rdfp14a'}}{\to}$ { ?C, ?y }
rdfp14b'	?C :hasValue ?y ; :onProperty ?P .	?C $\overset{\mathbf{rdfp14b'}}{\to}$ { ?P, ?y }
rdfc1	?C :unionOf (?C$_1$...**?C**$_i$...?C$_n$) .	?C$_i$ $\overset{\mathbf{rdfc1}}{\to}$?C
rdfc2	?C :minCardinality 1 ; :onProperty ?P .	?P $\overset{\mathbf{rdfc2}}{\to}$?C
rdfc3a	?C :intersectionOf (?C$_1$ ... ?C$_n$) .	?C $\overset{\mathbf{rdfc3a}}{\to}$ { ?C$_1$, ..., ?C$_n$ }
rdfc3b	?C :intersectionOf (**?C**$_1$) .	?C$_1$ $\overset{\mathbf{rdfc3b}}{\to}$?C

$\mathcal{R}2$		
rdfp1'	?P a :FunctionalProperty .	?P $\overset{\mathbf{rdfp1'}}{\to}$ TRUE
rdfp2	?P a :InverseFunctionalProperty .	?P $\overset{\mathbf{rdfp2}}{\to}$ TRUE
rdfp4	?P a :TransitiveProperty .	?P $\overset{\mathbf{rdfp4}}{\to}$ TRUE
rdfp15'	?C :someValuesFrom **?D** ; :onProperty **?P** .	?P $\overset{\mathbf{rdfp15'}}{\leftrightarrow}$?D $\overset{\mathbf{rdfp15'}}{\to}$?C
rdfp16'	?C :allValuesFrom ?D ; :onProperty **?P** .	?P $\overset{\mathbf{rdfp16'}}{\leftrightarrow}$?C $\overset{\mathbf{rdfp16'}}{\to}$?D
rdfc3c	?C :intersectionOf (**?C**$_1$ ... **?C**$_n$) .	{ ?C$_1$, ..., ?C$_n$ } $\overset{\mathbf{rdfc3c}}{\to}$?C
rdfc4a	?C :cardinality 1 ; :onProperty ?P .	?C $\overset{\mathbf{rdfc4a}}{\leftrightarrow}$?P
rdfc4b	?C :maxCardinality 1 ; :onProperty ?P .	?C $\overset{\mathbf{rdfc4b}}{\leftrightarrow}$?P

data. We denote our authoritative T-Box by $\hat{\mathbb{T}}$, whereby $Cl_{\hat{\mathcal{R}}}(\mathbb{T}, \mathbb{KB}) = Cl_{\mathcal{R}}(\hat{\mathbb{T}}, \mathbb{KB})$; for each rule, $\hat{\mathbb{T}}$ only contains T-Box pattern instances for $Ante_{\mathcal{T}}$ which can lead to an authoritative rule application.

Each statement read is initially matched without authoritative analysis against the patterns enumerated in Table 3. If a pattern is initially matched, the positions required to be authoritative, as identified in boldface, are checked. If one such authoritative check is satified, the pattern is loaded into the T-Box. Indeed the same statement may be matched by more than one T-Box pattern for different rules with different authoritative restrictions; for example the statement foaf:name :equivalentProperty my:name . retrieved from my: namespace matches the T-Box pattern of rules **rdfp13a'** & **rdfp13b'**, but only conforms to the authoritative restriction for rule **rdfp13b'**. Therefore, we only store the statement in such a fashion as to apply to rule **rdfp13b'**; that is, the authoritative T-Box stores T-Box pattern instances separately for each rule, according to the authoritative restrictions for that rule.

Checking the authority of a source for a given namespace URI, as presented in Definition 6, may require a HTTP connection to the namespace URI

Figure 2. In-memory T-Box structure

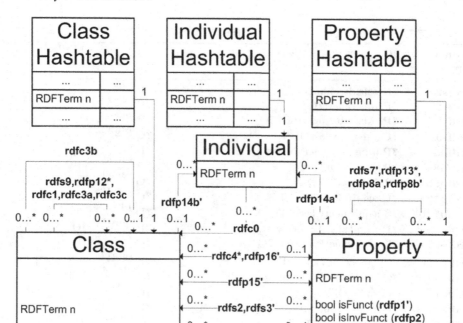

so as to determine whether a redirect exists to the authoritative document (HTTP Response Code 303). Results of accessing URIs are cached once in-memory so as to avoid establishing repetitive connections. If the pattern is authoritatively matched, the statement is reflected in the in-memory T-Box. Alternatively, where available, a crawler can provide a set of redirect pairs which can be loaded into the system to avoid duplicating HTTP lookups; we presume for generality that such information is not provided.

In-Memory T-Box

Before we proceed, we quickly discuss the storage of :oneOf constructs in the T-Box for rule **rdfc0**. Individuals ($?x_1$ ... $?x_n$) are stored with pointers to the one-of class **?C**. Before input data are read, these individuals are asserted to be of the rdf:type of their encompassing one-of class.

Besides the one-of support, for the in-memory T-Box we employ two separate hashtables, one for classes and another for properties, with RDF terms as key and a Java representation of the class or property as value. The representative Java objects contain labelled links to related objects as defined in Table 3 and Figure 2. The property and class objects are designed to contain all of the information required for reasoning on a membership assertion of that property or class: that is, classes/properties satisfying the A-Box antecedent pattern of a rule are linked to the classes/properties appearing in the consequent of that rule, with the link labelled according to that rule. During reasoning, the class/property identifier used in the membership assertion is sent to the corresponding hashtable and the returned internal object used for reasoning on that assertion. The objects contain the following:

- Property objects contain the property URI and references to objects representing domain classes (**rdfs2**), range classes (**rdfs3'**), super properties (**rdfs7'**), inverse properties (**rdfs8***) and equivalent properties (**rdfp13***). References are kept to restrictions where the property in question is the object of an `:onProperty` statement (**rdfp14a'**, **rdfp16'**, **rdfc2**, **rdfc4***). Where applicable, if the property is part of a some-values-from restriction, a pointer is kept to the some-values-from class (**rdfp15'**). Boolean values are stored to indicate whether the property is functional (**rdfp1'**), inverse-functional (**rdfp2**), symmetric (**rdfp3'**) and/or transitive (**rdfp4**).

- Class objects contain the class URI and references to objects representing super classes (**rdfs9**), equivalent classes (**rdfp12***) and classes for which this class is a component of a union (**rdfc1**) or intersection (**rdfc3b/c**). On top of these core elements, different references are maintained for different types of class description:

  - intersection classes store references to their constituent class objects (**rdfc3a**)

  - restriction classes store a reference to the property the restriction applies to (**rdfp14b'**, **rdfp15'**, **rdfc2**, **rdfc4***) and also, if applicable to the type of restriction:

    - the values which the restriction property must have (**rdfp14b'**)
    - the class for which this class is a some-values-from restriction value (**rdfp15'**)

The algorithm must also performs in-memory joining of collection segments according to `rdf:first` and `rdf:rest` statements found during the scan for the purposes of building union, intersection and enumeration class descriptions. Again, any remaining collections not relevant to the T-Box segment of the knowledge-base (i.e., not terminological collection statements) are discarded at the end of loading the input data; we also discard cyclic and branching lists as well

as any lists not found to end with the `rdf:nil` construct.

We have now loaded the final T-Box for reasoning into memory; this T-Box will remain fixed throughout the whole reasoning process.

4.4 Initial Input Scan

Having loaded the terminological data, SAOR is now prepared for reasoning by statement-wise scan of the assertional data. We provide the high-level flow for reasoning over an input statement in Function 1. The reasoning scan process can be described as recursive depth-first reasoning whereby each unique statement produced is again input immediately for reasoning. Statements produced thus far for the original input statement are kept in a set to provide uniqueness testing and avoid cycles; a uniquing function is maintained for a common subject group in the data, ensuring that statements are only produced once for that statement group. Once all of the statements produced by a rule have been themselves recursively analysed, the reasoner moves on to analysing the proceeding rule and loops until no unique statements are inferred.

Function 1: ReasonStatement(s)

Input: statement s
Global: $\mathbb{T}$, index, output
foreach *rule* r ∈ $\mathcal{R}1$ **do**
  fire rule r w.r.t s and $\mathbb{T}$;
  foreach *inferred statement:* i **do**
    if i *is unique* **then**
      if i *is valid RDF* **then**
        write to output;
      ReasonStatement (i) ;

foreach *rule* r ∈ $\mathcal{R}2 \cup \mathcal{R}3$ **do**
  if s *relevant for* r *w.r.t.* $\mathbb{T}$ **then**
    write s to index$_r$;

There are three disjoint categories of statements which require different handling: namely (i) `rdf:type` statements, (ii) `:sameAs` statements, (iii) all other statements. We assume disjointness between the statement categories: we

Table 4. Table enumerating the A-Box joins to be computed using the on-disk files with key join variables in boldface font and sorting order required for statements to compute join

R2		
rdfp1′	?x ?P ?y , ?z .	SPOC
rdfp2	?x ?P ?z . ?y ?P ?z .	OPSC
rdfp4	?x ?P ?y . ?y ?P ?z .	SPOC & OPSC
rdfp15′	?x ?P ?y . ?y a ?D .	SPOC / OPSC
rdfp16′	?x a ?C ; ?P ?y .	SPOC
rdfc3c	?x a ?C₁, ..., ?Cₙ .	SPOC
rdfc4a	?x a ?C ; ?P ?y , ?z .	SPOC
rdfc4b	?x a ?C ; ?P ?y , ?z .	SPOC

R3		
rdfp7	?x :sameAs ?y . ?y :sameas ?z .	SPOC & OPSC
rdfp11′	?x :sameAs ?_x ; ?P ?y .	SPOC
rdfp11″	?y :sameAs ?_y . ?x ?P ?y .	SPOC / OPSC

do not allow any external extension of the core `rdf:type`/`:sameAs` semantics (non-standard use/non-authoritative extension). Further, the assertions about rdf:type in the RDFS specification define the rdfs:domain and rdfs:range of rdf:type as being rdfs:Resource and rdfs:Class; since we are not interested in inferring membership of such RDFS classes we do not subject rdf:type statements to property-based entailments. The only assertions about :sameAs from the OWL specification define domain and range as :Thing which we ignore by the same justification.

The `rdf:type` statements are subject to class-based entailment reasoning and require joins with class descriptions in the T-Box. The `:sameAs` statements are handled by ruleset $R3$, which will be discussed in detail later. All other statements are subject to property-based entailments and thus requires joins with T-Box property descriptions.

Ruleset $R2 \bigcup R3$ cannot be computed solely on a statement-wise basis. Instead, for each rule, we assign an on-disk file (blocked and compressed to save disk space). Each file contains statements which may contribute to satisfying the antecedent of its pertinent rule. During the scan, if an A-Box statement satisfies the necessary T-Box join for a rule, it is written to the index for that rule. For example, when the statement

```
>  ex:me foaf:isPrimaryTopicOf
   ex:myHomepage .
```

is processed, the property object for `foaf:isPrimaryTopicOf` is retrieved from the T-Box property hashtable. The object states that this property is of type `:Inverse-FunctionalProperty`. The rule cannot yet be fired as this statement alone does not satisfy the A-Box segment of the antecedent of rdfp2 and the method is privy to only one A-Box statement at a time. When, later, the statement:

```
>  ex:me2 foaf:isPrimaryTopicOf
    ex:myHomepage .
```

is found, it also is written to the same file – the file now contains sufficient data to (although it cannot yet) fire the rule and infer:

```
>  ex:me:sameAs ex:me2 .
```

During the initial scan and inferencing, all files for ruleset $R2 \bigcup R3$ are filled with pertinent statements analogously to the example above. After the initial input statements have been exhausted, these files are analysed to infer, for example, the `:sameAs` statement above.

On-Disk A-Box Join Analysis

In this section, we discuss handling of the on-disk files containing A-Box statements for ruleset $\mathcal{R}2 \bigcup \mathcal{R}3$. We firstly give a general overview of the execution for each rule using an on-disk file and then look at the execution of each rule.

Table 4 presents the joins to be executed via the on-disk files for each rule: the key join variables, used for computing the join, are shown in boldface. In this table we refer to *SPOC and OPSC sorting order*: these can be intuitively interpreted as quads sorted according to subject, predicate, object, context (natural sorting order) and object, predicate, subject, context (inverse sorting order) respectively. For the internal index files, we use context to encode the sorting order of a statement and the iteration in which it was added; only joins with at least one new statement from the last iteration will infer novel output.

Again, an on-disk file is dedicated for each rule/join required. The joins to be computed are a simple "star shaped" join pattern or "one-hop" join pattern (which we reduce to a simple star shaped join computation by inverting one one or more patterns to inverse order). The statements in each file are initially sorted according to the key join variable. Thus, common bindings for the key join variable are grouped together and joins can be executed by means of sequential scan for common key join variable binding groups.

We now continue with a more detailed description of the process for each rule beginning with the more straightforward rules.

Functional Property
Reasoning - Rule rdfp1'

From the initial input scan, we have a file containing only statements with functional properties in the predicate position. As can be seen from Table 4, the key join variable is in the subject position for all A-Box statements in the pattern. Thus, we can sort the file according to SPOC (natural)

order. The result is a file where all statements are grouped according to a common subject, then predicate, then object. We can now scan this file, storing objects with a common subject-predicate. We can then fire the rule stating equivalence between these objects.

Inverse Functional
Reasoning - Rule rdfp2

Reasoning on statements containing inverse functional properties is conducted analogously to functional property reasoning. However, the key join variable is now in the object position for all A-Box statements in the pattern. Thus, we instead sort the file according to OPSC (inverse) order and scan the file inferring equivalence between the subjects for a common object-predicate group.

Intersection Class Reasoning
- Rule rdfc3c

The key join variable for rule **rdfc3c** is in the subject position for all A-Box triple patterns. Thus we can sort the file for the rule (filled with memberships assertions for classes which are part of some intersection) according to SPOC order. We can scan common subject-predicate (in any case, the predicates all have value `rdf:type`) groups storing the objects (all types for the subject resource which are part of an intersection). The containing intersection for each type can then be retrieved and the intersection checked to see if all of it's constituent types have been satisfied. If so, membership of the intersection is inferred.

All-Values-From Reasoning
- Rule rdfp16'

Again, the key join variable for rule **rdfp16'** is in the subject position for all A-Box triple patterns and again we can sort the file according to SPOC order. For a common subject group, we store `rdf:type` values and also all predicate/object edges for the given subject. For every membership assertion of an all-values-from restriction class (as is given by all of the `rdf:type` statements in the file), we wish to infer that objects of the `:onProperty` value (as is given by all the non-`rdf:type` statements) are of the all-values-from class. Therefore, for each restriction membership assertion, the objects of the corresponding `:onProperty`-value membership-assertions are inferred to be members of the all-values-from object class (?D).

Some-Values-From Reasoning - Rule rdfp15'

For some-values-from reasoning, the key join variable is in the subject position for `rdf:type` statements (all membership assertions of a some-values-from object class) but in the object position for the `:onProperty` membership assertions. Thus, we order class membership assertions in the file according to natural SPOC order and property membership assertions according to inverse OPSC order. In doing so, we can scan common ?y binding groups in the file, storing `rdf:type` values and also all predicate/subject edges. For every member of a some-values-from object class (as is given by all of the `rdf:type` statements in the file according to the join with the T-Box on the ?D position), we infer that subjects of the `:onProperty`-value statements (as is given by all the non-`rdf:type` statements according to the T-Box join with ?P) are members of the restriction class (?C).

Transitive Reasoning (Non-Symmetric) - Rule rdfp4

Transitive reasoning is perhaps the most challenging to compute: the output of rule **rdfp4** can again recursively act as input to the rule. For closure, recursive application of the rule must be conducted in order to traverse arbitrarily long transitive paths in the data.

Firstly, we will examine sorting order. The key join variable is in the subject position for one pattern and in the object position for the second pattern. However, both patterns are identical: a statement which matches one pattern will obviously match the second. Thus, every statement in the transitive reasoning file is duplicated with one version sorted in natural SPOC order, and another in inverse OPSC.

Take for example the following triples where `ex:comesBefore` is asserted as being of type `:TransitiveProperty` in the T-Box:

```
> INPUT:
> ex:a ex:comesBefore ex:b .
> ex:b ex:comesBefore ex:c .
> ex:c ex:comesBefore ex:d .
```

In order to compute the join, we must write the statements in both orders, using the context to mark which triples are in inverse order, and sort them accordingly (for this internal index, we temporarily relax the requirement that context is a URI).

```
> SORTED FILE - ITERATION 1:13
> ex:a ex:comesBefore ex:b _:spoc1 .
> ex:b ex:comesBefore ex:a _:opsc1 .
> ex:b ex:comesBefore ex:c _:spoc1 .
> ex:c ex:comesBefore ex:b _:opsc1 .
> ex:c ex:comesBefore ex:d _:spoc1 .
> ex:d ex:comesBefore ex:c _:opsc1 .
```

The data, as above, can then be scanned and for each common join-binding/predicate group (e.g., `ex:b ex:comesBefore`), the subjects of statements in inverse order (e.g., `ex:a`) can be linked to the object of naturally ordered statements (e.g., `ex:c`) by the transitive property. However, such a scan will only compute a single one-hop join. From above, we only produce:

```
> OUTPUT - ITERATION 1 / INPUT -
> ITERATION 2:
```

```
>  ex:a ex:comesBefore ex:c .
>  ex:b ex:comesBefore ex:d .
```

We still not have not computed the valid statement ex:a ex:comesBefore ex:d. which requires a two hop join. Thus we must iteratively feedback the results from one scan as input for the next scan. The output from the first iteration, as above, is also reordered and sorted as before and merge-sorted into the main **SORTED FILE**.

```
>  SORTED FILE - ITERATION 2:
>  ex:a ex:comesBefore ex:b _:spoc1 .
>  ex:a ex:comesBefore ex:c _:spoc2 .
>  ex:b ex:comesBefore ex:a _:opsc1 .
>  ex:b ex:comesBefore ex:c _:spoc1 .
>  ex:b ex:comesBefore ex:d _:spoc2 .
>  ex:c ex:comesBefore ex:a _:opsc2 .
>  ex:c ex:comesBefore ex:b _:opsc1 .
>  ex:c ex:comesBefore ex:d _:spoc1 .
>  ex:d ex:comesBefore ex:b _:opsc2 .
>  ex:d ex:comesBefore ex:c _:opsc1 .
```

The observant reader may already have noticed from above that we also mark the context with the iteration for which the statement was added. In every iteration, we only compute inferences which involve the delta from the last iteration; thus the process is comparable to semi-naïve evaluation. Only joins containing at least one newly added statement are used to infer new statements for output. Thus, from above, we avoid repeat inferences from **ITERATION 1** and instead infer:

```
>  OUTPUT - ITERATION 2:
>  ex:a ex:comesBefore ex:d .
```

A fixpoint is reached when no new statements are inferred. Thus we would require another iteration for the above example to ensure that no new statements are inferable. The number of iterations required is in $\circ(\log n)$ according to the longest unclosed transitive path in the input data. Since the algorithm requires scanning of not only the delta but all data, performance using on-disk file scans alone would be sub-optimal. For example, if one considers that most of the statements constitute paths of, say ≤ 8 vertices, one path containing 128 vertices would require four more scans after the bulk of the paths have been closed.

With this in mind, we accelerate transitive closure by means of an in-memory transitivity index. For each transitive property found, we store sets of linked lists which represent the graph extracted for that property. From the example **INPUT** from above, we would store.

```
>  ex:comesBefore | ex:a -> ex:b ->
>  ex:c -> ex:d
```

From this in-memory linked list, we would then collapse all paths of length ≥ 2 (all paths of length 1 are input statements) and infer closure at once:

```
>  OUTPUT - ITERATION 1 / INPUT -
>  ITERATION 2:
>  ex:a ex:comesBefore ex:c .
>  ex:a ex:comesBefore ex:d .
>  ex:b ex:comesBefore ex:d .
```

Obviously, for scalability requirements, we do not expect the entire transitive body of statements to fit in-memory. Thus, before each iteration we calculate the in-memory capacity and only store a pre-determined number of properties and vertices. Once the in-memory transitive index is full, we infer the appropriate statements and continue by file-scan. The in-memory index is only used to store the delta for a given iteration (everything for the first iteration). Thus, we avoid excess iterations to compute closure of a small percentage of statements which form a long chain and greatly accelerate the fixpoint calculation.

Transitive Reasoning (Symmetric) - Rules rdfp3'/rdfp4

We use a separate on-disk file for membership assertions of properties which are both transitive *and* symmetric. A graph of symmetric properties is direction-less, thus the notion of direction as evident above though use of inverted ordered statements is unnecessary. Instead, all statements and their inverses (computed from symmetric rule **rdfp3'**) are written in natural SPOC order and direct paths are inferred between all objects in a common subject/predicate group. The in-memory index is again similar to above; however, we instead use a direction-less doubly-linked list.

Equality Reasoning - Ruleset $\mathcal{R}3$

Thus far, we have not considered :sameAs entailment, which is supported in SAOR through rules in $\mathcal{R}3$. Prior to executing rules **rdfp11'** & **rdfp11''**, we must first perform symmetric transitive closure on the list of all :sameAs statements (rules **rdfp6'** & **rdfp7**). Thus, we use an on-disk file analogous to that described for symmetric transitive reasoning.

However, for rules **rdfp6'** & **rdfp7**, we do not wish to experience an explosion of inferencing through long equivalence chains (lists of equivalent individuals where there exists a :sameAs path from each individual to every other individual). The closure of a symmetric transitive chain of n vertices results in $n(n-1)$ edges or statements (ignoring reflexive statements). For example, in Hogan et al. (2007) we found a chain of 85,803 equivalent individuals inferable from a Web dataset.[14] Naïvely applying symmetric transitive reasoning as previously discussed would result in a closure of 7.362b :sameAs statements for this chain alone.

Similarly, :sameAs entailment, as according to rules **rdfp11'** & **rdfp11''**, duplicates data for all equivalent individuals which could result in a massive amount of duplicate data (particularly when considering uniqueness on a quad level: i.e., including duplicate triples from different sources). For example, if each of the 85,803 equivalent individuals had attached an average of 8 unique statements, then this could equate to 8*85,803*85,803 = 59b inferred statements.

Obviously, we must avoid the above scenarios, so we break from complete inference with respect to the rules in $\mathcal{R}3$. Instead, for each set of equivalent individuals, we chose a pivot identifier to use in rewriting the data.[15] The pivot identifier is used to keep a consistent identifier for the set of equivalent individuals: the alphabetically highest pivot is chosen for convenience of computation. For alternative choices of pivot identifiers on Web data see Hogan et al. (2007). We use the pivot identifier to consolidate data by rewriting all occurrences of equivalent identifiers to the pivot identifier effectively merging the equivalent set into one individual.

Thus, we do not derive the entire closure of :sameAs statements as indicated in rules **rdfp6'** & **rdfp7** but instead only derive an equivalence list which points from equivalent identifiers to their pivots. As highlighted, use of a pivot identifier is necessary to reduce the amount of output statements, effectively compressing equivalent resource descriptions: we hint here that a fully expanded view of the descriptions could instead be supported through backward-chaining over the semi-materialised data.

To achieve the pivot compressed inferences we use an on-disk file containing :sameAs statements. Take for example the following statements:

```
>   INPUT:
>   ex:a:sameAs ex:b .
>   ex:b:sameAs ex:c .
>   ex:c:sameAs ex:d .
```

We only wish to infer the following output for the pivot identifier ex:a:

```
> OUTPUT PIVOT EQUIVALENCES:
> ex:b:sameAs ex:a .
> ex:c:sameAs ex:a .
> ex:d:sameAs ex:a .
```

The process is the same as that for symmetric transitive reasoning as described before: however, we only close transitive paths to nodes with the highest alphabetical order. So, for example, if we have already materialised a path from `ex:d` to `ex:a` we ignore inferring a path from `ex:d` to `ex:b` as `ex:b > ex:a`.

To execute rules **rdfp11'** & **rdfp11''** and perform "consolidation" (rewriting of equivalent identifiers to their pivotal form), we perform a zig-zag join: we sequentially scan the `:sameAs` inference output as above and an appropriately sorted file of data, rewriting the latter data according to the `:sameAs` statements. For example, take the following statements to be consolidated:

```
> UNCONSOLIDATED DATA:
> ex:a foaf:mbox <mail@example.org> .
> ...
> ex:b foaf:mbox <mail@example.org> .
> ex:b foaf:name "Joe Bloggs" .
> ...
> ex:d:sameAs ex:b .
> ...
> ex:e foaf:knows ex:d .
```

The above statements are scanned sequentially with the closed `:sameAs` pivot output from above. For example, when the statement `ex:b foaf:mbox <mailto:mail@example.org> .` is first read from the unconsolidated data, the `:sameAs` index is scanned until `ex:b:sameAs ex:a .` is found (if `ex:b` is not found in the `:sameAs` file, the scan is paused when an element above the sorting order of `ex:b` is found). Then, `ex:b` is rewritten to `ex:a`.

```
> PARTIALLY CONSOLIDATED DATA:
> ex:a foaf:mbox <mail@example.org> .
> ...
> ex:a foaf:mbox <mail@example.org> .
> ex:a foaf:name "Joe Bloggs" .
> ...
> ex:a:sameAs ex:b .
> ...
> ex:e foaf:knows ex:d .
```

We have now executed rule **rdfp11'** and have the data partially consolidated as shown. However, the observant reader will notice that we have not consolidated the object of the last two statements. We must sort the data again according to inverse OPSC order and again sequentially scan both the partially consolidated data and the `:sameAs` pivot equivalences, this time rewriting `ex:b` and `ex:d` in the object position to `ex:a` and producing the final consolidated data. This equates to executing rule **rdfp11''**.

For the purposes of the on-disk files for computing rules requiring A-Box joins, we must consolidate the key join variable bindings according to the `:sameAs` statements found during reasoning. For example consider the following statements in the functional reasoning file:

```
> ex:a ex:mother ex:m1 .
> ex:b ex:mother ex:m2 .
```

Evidently, rewriting the key join position according to our example pivot file will lead to inference of:

```
> ex:m1:sameAs ex:m2
```

The final step in the SAOR reasoning process is to finalise consolidation of the initial input data and the newly inferred output statements produced by all rules from scanning and on-disk file analysis. Although we have provided exhaustive application of all inferencing rules, and we have the complete set of `:sameAs` statements, elements in the input and output files may not be in their equivalent pivotal form. Therefore, in order to ensure proper consolidation of all of the data according to the final set of :sameAs statements, we must firstly sort both input and inferred sets of data in SPOC order, consolidate subjects according to the pivot file as above; sort according to OPSC order and consolidate objects.

However, one may notice that :sameAs statements in the data become consolidated into reflexive statements: i.e., from the above example ex:a:sameAs ex:a. Thus, for the final output, we remove any :sameAs statements in the data and instead merge the statements contained in our final pivot :sameAs equivalence index, and their inverses, with the consolidated data. These statements retain the list of all possible identifiers for a consolidated entity in the final output.

Achieving Closure

We conclude this section by summarising the approach, detailing the overall fixpoint calculations (as such, putting the jigsaw together) and detailing how closure is achieved using the individual components. Along these lines, in Algorithm 2, we provide a summary of the steps seen so far and, in particular, show the fixpoint calculations involved for exhaustive application of ruleset $R2 \cup R3$; we compute one main fixpoint over all of the operations required, within which we also compute two local fixpoints.

Firstly, since all rules in $R2$ are dependant on :sameAs equality, we perform :sameAs inferences first. Thus, we begin closure on $R2 \cup R3$ with a local equality fixpoint which (i) executes all rules which produce :sameAs inferences (**rdfp1'**, **rdfp2, rdfc4***); (ii) performs symmetric-transitive closure using pivots on all :sameAs inferences; (iii) rewrites **rdfp1'**, **rdfp2** and **rdfc4*** indexes according to :sameAs pivot equivalences and (iv) repeats until no new :sameAs statements are produced.

```
Algorithm 2: SAOR reasoning algorithm
Input: KB
Output: Cl_R(T,KB)
for scan KB (Section 4.3.1) do
  └ obtain candidate statements for T.
reduce T, derive T̂ (Sect. 4.3.2) ;
load T̂ in-memory (Sect. 4.3.3) ;
run R0 rules ;
for inferred statement i do
  if i is valid RDF then
    └ write to output;
  └ ReasonStatement (i) (Funct. 1) ;
for s ∈ KB (Sect. 4.4) do
  └ ReasonStatement (s) (Funct. 1) ;
// output contains R0 ∪ R1 inferences for initial input
// index contains initial statements relevant for R2
// sameas contains initial statements relevant for R3
repeat
  repeat
    for rule r : {rdfp1',rdfp2,rdfc4*} (Sect. 4.5) do
      if new, is set then
        └ rewrite index, w.r.t. sameas/ unset new,;
      if index, has changed or was rewritten then
        run r on index, ;
        └ write to sameas;
    if sameas has changed then
      run rules rdfp6' and rdfp7 on sameas (Sect. 4.6) ;
      └ write sameas/ set all new;
  until fixpoint reached (no changes in previous iteration) ;
  if new_rdfp4 is set then
    └ rewrite index_rdfp4 w.r.t. sameas/ unset new_rdfp4;
  repeat
    run rule rdfp4 on index_rdfp4 (Sect. 4.5.6 and 4.5.7) ;
    for inferred statement i do
      write to index_rdfp4 ;
      if i is RDF then
        └ write to output;
    └ ReasonStatement (i) (Funct. 1) ;
  until fixpoint reached (no changes in previous iteration) ;
  for rule r ∈ {rdfp15',rdfp16',rdfc3c} (Sect. 4.5) do
    if new, is set then
      └ rewrite index, w.r.t. sameas/ unset new,;
    if index, has changed or was rewritten then
      run r on index,;
      for inferred statement i do
        if i is RDF then
          └ write to output;
      └ ReasonStatement (i) (Funct. 1) ;
until fixpoint reached (no changes in previous iteration) ;
// output contains all inferences in non-pivotal form
for subject and object (Sect. 4.6) do
  for scan KB and output do
    rewrite according to sameas;
    └ write to Cl_R(T,KB);
  └ write sameas and sameas⁻ to Cl_R(T,KB);
```

Next, we have a local transitive fixpoint for recursively computing transitive property reasoning: (i) the transitive index is rewritten according to the equivalences found through the above local fixpoint; (ii) a transitive closure iteration is run, output inferences are recursively fed back as input; (iii) ruleset $R1$ is also recursively applied over output from previous step whereby the output from ruleset $\mathcal{R}1$ may also write new statements to any $\mathcal{R}2$ index. The local fixpoint is reached when no new transitive inferences are computed.

Finally, we conclude the main fixpoint by running the remaining rules: **rdfp15'**, **rdfp16'** and **rdfc3c**. For each rule, we rewrite the corresponding index according to the equivalences found from the first local fixpoint, run the inferencing over the index and send output for reasoning through ruleset $\mathcal{R}1$. Statements inferred directly from the rule index, or through subsequent application of ruleset $\mathcal{R}1$, may write new statements for $\mathcal{R}2$ indexes. This concludes one iteration of the main fixpoint, which is run until no new statements are inferred.

For each ruleset $\mathcal{R}0 - 3$, we now justify our algorithm in terms of our definition of closure with respect to our static T-Box. Firstly, closure is achieved immediately upon ruleset $\mathcal{R}0$, which requires only T-Box knowledge, from our static T-Box. Secondly, with respect to the given T-Box, every input statement is subject to reasoning according to ruleset $\mathcal{R}1$, as is every statement inferred from ruleset $\mathcal{R}0$, those recursively inferred from ruleset $\mathcal{R}1$ itself, and those recursively inferred from on-disk analysis for ruleset $\mathcal{R}1 \bigcup \mathcal{R}2$. Next, every input statement is subject to reasoning according to ruleset $\mathcal{R}2$ with respect to our T-Box; these again include all inferences from $\mathcal{R}0$, all statements inferred through $\mathcal{R}1$ alone, and all inferences from recursive application of ruleset $\mathcal{R}1 \bigcup \mathcal{R}2$.

Therefore, we can see that our algorithm applies exhaustive application of ruleset $\mathcal{R}0 \bigcup \mathcal{R}1 \bigcup \mathcal{R}2$ with respect to our T-Box, leaving only consideration of equality reasoning in ruleset $\mathcal{R}3$. Indeed, our algorithm is not complete with respect to ruleset $\mathcal{R}3$ since we choose pivot identifiers for representing equivalent individuals. However, we still provide a form of "pivotal closure" whereby backward-chaining support of rules **rdfp11'** and **rdfp11"** over the output of our algorithm would provide a view of closure as defined; i.e., our output contains all of the possible inferences according

to our notion of closure, but with equivalent individuals compressed in pivotal form.

Firstly, for rules **rdfp6'** and **rdfp7**, all statements where $p = $: sameAs from the original input or as produced by $\mathcal{R}0 \bigcup \mathcal{R}1 \bigcup \mathcal{R}2$ undergo on-disk symmetric-transitive closure in pivotal form. Since both rules only produce more : sameAs statements, and according to the standard usage restriction of our closure, they are not applicable to reasoning under $\mathcal{R}0 \bigcup \mathcal{R}1 \bigcup \mathcal{R}2$. Secondly, we loosely apply rules **rdfp11'** and **rdfp11"** such as to provide closure with respect to joins in ruleset $\mathcal{R}2$; i.e., all possible joins are computed with respect to the given : sameAs statements. Equivalence is clearly not important to $\mathcal{R}0$ since we strictly do not allow : sameAs statements to affect our T-Box; $\mathcal{R}1$ inferences do not require joins and, although the statements produced will not be in pivotal form, they will be output and rewritten later; inferences from $\mathcal{R}2$ will be produced as discussed, also possibly in non-pivotal form. In the final consolidation step, we then rewrite all statements to their pivotal form and provide incoming and outgoing : sameAs relations between pivot identifiers and their non-pivot equivalent identifiers. This constitutes our output, which we call *pivotal authoritative closure*.

EVALUATION AND DISCUSSION

We now provide evaluation of the SAOR methodology firstly with quantitative analysis of the importance of authoritative reasoning, and secondly we provide performance measurements and discussion along with insights into the fecundity of each rule w.r.t. reasoning over Web data. All experiments are run on one machine with a single Opteron 2.2 GHz CPU and 4 GB of main memory. We provide evaluation on two datasets: we provide complete evaluation for a dataset of 147m statements collected from 665k sources and scale-up experiments running scan-reasoning (rules in $\mathcal{R}0 \bigcup \mathcal{R}1$) on a dataset of 1.1b statements collected

Table 5. Comparison of authoritative and non-authoritative reasoning for the number of unique inferred RDF statements produced (w.r.t. ruleset $\mathcal{R}1$ over the five most frequently occurring classes and properties in both input datasets. '*' indicates a datatype property where the object of m(P) is a literal. The amount of statements produced for authoritative reasoning for a single membership assertion of the class or property is denoted by $|Cl_{\mathcal{R}1}(\hat{\mathbb{T}}, \{m(C)\})|$ and $|Cl_{\mathcal{R}1}(\hat{\mathbb{T}}, \{m(P)\})|$ respectively. Non-authoritative counts are given by $|Cl_{\mathcal{R}1}(\mathbb{T}, \{m(C)\})|$ and $|Cl_{\mathcal{R}1}(\mathbb{T}, \{m(P)\})|$. n is the number of membership assertions for the class C or property P in the given dataset.

147m Dataset					
C	$|Cl_{\mathcal{R}1}(\hat{\mathbb{T}}, \{m(C)\})|$	$|Cl_{\mathcal{R}1}(\mathbb{T}, \{m(C)\})|$	n	$n|Cl_{\mathcal{R}1}(\hat{\mathbb{T}}, \{m(C)\})|$	$n|Cl_{\mathcal{R}1}(\mathbb{T}, \{m(C)\})|$
rss:item	0	356	3,558,055	0	1,266,667,580
foaf:Person	6	388	3,252,404	19,514,424	1,261,932,752
rdf:Seq	2	243	1,934,852	3,869,704	470,169,036
foaf:Document	1	354	1,750,365	1,750,365	619,629,210
wordnet:Person	0	236	1,475,378	0	348,189,208
TOTAL	9	1,577	11,971,054	25,134,493	3,966,587,786
P	$|Cl_{\mathcal{R}1}(\{\hat{\mathbb{T}}, m(P)\})|$	$|Cl_{\mathcal{R}1}(\mathbb{T}, \{m(P)\})|$	n	$n|Cl_{\mathcal{R}1}(\{\hat{\mathbb{T}}, m(P)\})|$	$n|Cl_{\mathcal{R}1}(\mathbb{T}, \{m(P)\})|$
dc:title*	0	14	5,503,170	0	77,044,380
dc:date*	0	377	5,172,458	0	1,950,016,666
foaf:name*	3	418	4,631,614	13,894,842	1,936,014,652
foaf:nick*	0	390	4,416,760	0	1,722,536,400
rss:link*	1	377	4,073,739	4,073,739	1,535,799,603
TOTAL	4	1,576	23,797,741	17,968,581	7,221,411,701
1.1b Dataset					
C	$|Cl_{\mathcal{R}1}(\hat{\mathbb{T}}, \{m(C)\})|$	$|Cl_{\mathcal{R}1}(\mathbb{T}, \{m(C)\})|$	n	$n|Cl_{\mathcal{R}1}(\hat{\mathbb{T}}, \{m(C)\})|$	$n|Cl_{\mathcal{R}1}(\mathbb{T}, \{m(C)\})|$
foaf:Person	6	4,631	63,271,689	379,630,134	293,011,191,759
foaf:Document	1	4,523	6,092,322	6,092,322	27,555,572,406
rss:item	0	4,528	5,745,216	0	26,014,338,048
oboInOwl:DbXref	0	0	2,911,976	0	0
rdf:Seq	2	4,285	2,781,994	5,563,988	11,920,844,290
TOTAL	9	17,967	80,803,197	391,286,444	358,501,946,503
P	$|Cl_{\mathcal{R}1}(\hat{\mathbb{T}}, \{m(P)\})|$	$|Cl_{\mathcal{R}1}(\mathbb{T}, \{m(P)\})|$	n	$n|Cl_{\mathcal{R}1}(\hat{\mathbb{T}}, \{m(P)\})|$	$n|Cl_{\mathcal{R}1}(\mathbb{T}, \{m(P)\})|$
rdfs:seeAlso	2	8,647	113,760,738	227,521,476	983,689,101,486
foaf:knows	14	9,709	77,335,237	1,082,693,318	716,820,311,753
dc:title*	0	4,621	71,321,437	0	329,576,360,377
foaf:nick*	0	4,635	65,855,264	0	305,239,148,640
foaf:weblog	7	9,286	55,079,875	385,559,125	511,471,719,250
TOTAL	23	36,458	383,352,551	1,695,773,919	2,846,796,641,506

from 6.5m sources; both datasets are from Web-crawls using MultiCrawler (Harth, Umbrich, & Decker, 2006). We create a unique set of blank nodes for each graph $\mathcal{W}' \in M(\mathcal{S}_W)$ using a function on c and the original blank node label which ensures a one-to-one mapping from the original blank node labels and uniqueness of the blank nodes for a given context c.

To show the effects of ontology hijacking we constructed two T-Boxes with and without authoritative analysis for each dataset. We then ran reasoning on single membership assertions for the top five classes and properties found natively in each dataset. Table 5 summarises the results. Taking `foaf:Person` as an example, with an authoritative T-Box, six statements are output for every input `rdf:type foaf:Person` statement in both datasets. With the non-authoritative T-Box, 388 and 4,631 statements are output for every such input statement for the smaller and larger datasets respectively. Considering that there are 3.25m and 63.33m such statements in the respective datasets, overall output for `rdf:type foaf:Person` input statements alone approach 1.26b and 293b statements for non-authoritative reasoning respectively. With authoritative reasoning we only produce 19.5m and 379.6m statements, a respective saving of 65x and 772x on output statement size.[16]

Table 6. Authoritative analysis of T-Box statements in 1.1b dataset for each primitive where dropped statements are highlighted in bold

Property	AuthSub	AuthObj	AuthBoth	AuthNone	Total	Drop
rdfs:subClassOf	25,076	**583,399**	1,595,850	**1,762,414**	3,966,739	2,345,813
:onProperty	1,041,873	-	97,921	-	1,139,843	-
:intersectionOf	-	-	216,035	-	216,035	-
:someValuesFrom	681,968	-	217,478	-	899,446	-
:equivalentClass	574	189,912	162,886	**3,198**	356,570	3,198
rdfs:domain	5,693	**7,788**	66,338	**79,748**	159,567	87,536
rdfs:range	32,338	**4,340**	37,529	**75,338**	149,545	79,678
rdf:first	273,805	-	392,707	-	666,512	-
rdf:rest	249,541	-	416,946	-	666,487	-
:hasValue	9,903	0	82,853	0	92,756	-
:allValuesFrom	51,988	-	22,145	-	74,133	-
rdfs:subPropertyOf	3,365	**147**	22,481	**26,742**	52,734	26,888
:maxCardinality	26,963	-	-	-	26,963	-
:cardinality	20,006	-	-	-	20,006	-
:inverseOf	75	52	6,397	**18,363**	24,887	18,363
:unionOf	-	-	21,671	-	21,671	-
:minCardinality	15,187	-	-	-	15,187	-
:oneOf	-	-	6,171	-	6,171	-
:equivalentProperty	105	24	187	**696**	1,012	696
Class						
:FunctionalProperty	9,616	-	-	**18,111**	27,727	18,111
:InverseFunctionalProperty	872	-	-	**3,080**	3,952	3,080
:TransitiveProperty	807	-	-	**1,994**	2,801	1,994
:SymmetricProperty	265	-	-	**351**	616	351
OVERALL	2,450,020	785,661	3,365,595	1,990,035	8,591,311	2,585,708

It should be noted that reasoning on a membership assertion of the top level class (:Thing/ rdfs:Resource) is very large for both the 147m (234 inferences) and the 1.1b dataset (4251 inferences). For example, in both datasets, there are many :unionOf class descriptions with :Thing as a member;[17] for the 1.1b dataset, many inferences on the top level class stem from, for example, the OWL W3C Test Repository[18]. Of course we do not see such documents as being malicious in any way, but clearly they would cause inflationary inferences when naïvely considered as part of Web knowledge-base.

Next, we present some metrics regarding the first step of reasoning: the separation and in-memory construction of the T-Box. For the 1.1b dataset, the initial scan of all data found 9,683,009 T-Box statements (0.9%). Reducing the T-Box by removing collection statements dropped a further 1,091,698 (11% of total) collection statements leaving 733,734 such statements in the T-Box (67% collection statements dropped) and 8,591,311 (89%) total. Table 6 shows, for membership assertions of each class and property in C_{SAOR} and P_{SAOR}, the result of applying authoritative analysis. Of the 33,157 unique namespaces probed, 769 (2.3%) had a redirect, 4068 (12.3%) connected but had no redirect and 28,320 (85.4%) did not connect at all. In total, 14,227,116 authority checks were performed. Of these, 6,690,704 (47%) were negative and 7,536,412 (53%) were positive. Of the positive, 4,236,393 (56%) were blank-nodes, 2,327,945 (31%) were a direct match between namespace and source and 972,074 (13%) had a redirect from the namespace to the source. In total, 2,585,708 (30%) statements were dropped as they could not contribute to a valid authoritative inference. The entire process of separating, analysing and loading the T-Box into memory took 6.47 hours: the most costly operation here

Figure 3. Performance of applying entire ruleset on the 147m statements dataset (without final consolidation step)

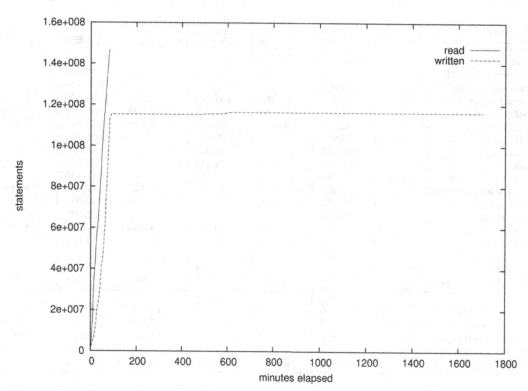

is the large amount of HTTP lookups required for authoritative analysis, with many connections unsuccessful after our five second timeout. The process required ~3.5G of Java heap-space and ~10M of stack space.

For the 147m dataset, 2,649,532 (1.7%) T-Box statements were separated from the data, which was reduced to 1,609,958 (61%) after reducing the amount of irrelevant collection statements; a further 536,564 (33%) statements were dropped as they could not contribute to a valid authoritative inference leaving 1,073,394 T-Box statements (41% of original). Loading the T-Box into memory for the 147m dataset took 1.04 hours.

We proceed by evaluating the application of all rules on the 147m dataset. Figure 3 shows performance for reaching an overall fixpoint for application of all rules. Clearly, the performance plateaus after 79 mins. At this point the input

statements have been exhausted, with rules in $\mathcal{R}0$ and $\mathcal{R}1$ having been applied to the input data and statements written to the on-disk files for $\mathcal{R}2$ and $\mathcal{R}3$. SAOR now switches over to calculating a fixpoint over the on-disk computed $\mathcal{R}2$ and $\mathcal{R}3$ rules, the results of which become the new input for $\mathcal{R}0$ and $\mathcal{R}1$ and further recursive input to the $\mathcal{R}2$ and $\mathcal{R}3$ files.

Figure 4 shows performance specifically for achieving closure on the on-disk $\mathcal{R}2$ and $\mathcal{R}3$ rules. There are three pronounced steps in the output of statements. The first one shown at (a) is due to inferencing of :sameAs statements from rule **rdfp2** (:InverseFunctionalProperty - 2.1m inferences). Also part of the first step are :sameAs inferences from rules **rdfp1'** (:FunctionalProperty - 31k inferences) and rules **rdfc4*** (:cardinality/:maxCardinality - 449 inferences). For the first plateau shown at

Figure 4. Performance of inferencing over $\mathcal{R}2$ and $\mathcal{R}3$ on-disk indexes for the 147m statements dataset (without final consolidation)

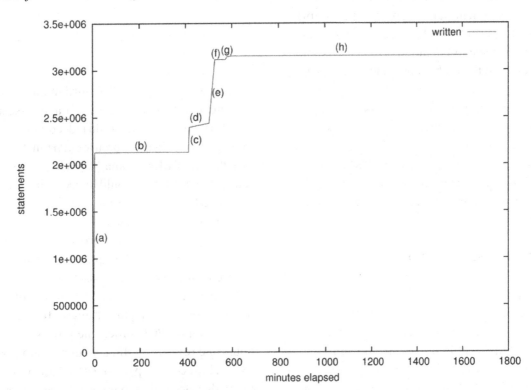

(b), the :sameAs equality file is closed for the first time and a local fixpoint is being calculated to derive the initial :sameAs statements for future rules; also during the plateau at (b), the second iteration for the :sameAs fixpoint (which, for the first time, consolidates the key join variables in files for rules **rdfp2, rdfp1', rdfc4a, rdfc4b** according to all :sameAs statements produced thus far) produces 1,018 new such statements, with subsequent iterations producing 145, 2, and 0 new statements respectively.

The second pronounced step at (c) is attributable to 265k transitive inferences, followed by 1.7k symmetric-transitive inferences. The proceeding slope at (d) is caused by inferences on **rdfc3c** (:intersectionOf - 265 inferences) and **rdfp15'** (:someValuesFrom - 36k inferences) with rule **rdfp16'** (:allValuesFrom - 678k inferences) producing the final significant

step at (e). The first complete iteration of the overall fixpoint calculation is now complete.

Since the first local :sameAs fixpoint, 22k mostly rdf:type statements have been written back to the cardinality rule files, 4 statements to the :InverseFunctionalProperty file and 14 to the :FunctionalProperty file. Thus, the :sameAs fixpoint is re-executed at (f), with no new statements found. The final, minor, staggered step at (g) occurs after the second :sameAs fixpoint when, most notably, rule **rdfp4** (:TransitiveProperty) produces 24k inferences, rule **rdfc3c** (:intersectionOf) produces 6.7k inferences, and rule **rdfp16'** (:allValuesFrom) produces 7.3k new statements.

The final, extended plateau at (h) is caused by rules which produce/consume rdf:type statements. In particular, the fixpoint encounters :allValuesFrom inferencing producing a minor contribution of statements (≤ 2) which lead to an update and re-execution of `:allValues-From` inferencing and `:intersectionOf` reasoning. In particular, `:allValuesFrom` required 66 recursive iterations to reach a fixpoint. We identified the problematic data as follows:

```
> @prefix veml: <http://www.icsi.
  berkeley.edu/snarayan/VEML.owl#>
> @prefix verl: <http://www.icsi.
  berkeley.edu/snarayan/VERL.owl#>
> @prefix data: <http://www.icsi.
  berkeley.edu/snarayan/meeting01.
  owl#>
> ...
> FROM veml: (T-BOX):
> veml:sceneEvents rdfs:range
  veml:EventList .
> veml:EventList rdfs:subClassOf
  _:r1 ; rdfs:subClassOf _:r2 .
> _:r1:allValuesFrom verl:Event
  ;:onProperty rdf:first .
> _:r2:allValuesFrom veml:EventList
  ;:onProperty rdf:rest .
> FROM data: (A-BOX):
> data:scene veml:sceneEvents
  (data:1, ..., data:65) .
> EXAMPLE COLLECTION SNIPPET:
> _:cN rdf:first data:N ; rdf:rest
  _:cN+1 .
```

From the above data, each iteration of :all-ValuesFrom reasoning and subsequent subclass reasoning produced:

```
> IN ALL-VALUES-FROM, ITER 0:
> FROM INPUT:
> (_:c1 ... _:c65) rdf:first (data:1
  ... data:65) .
> FROM RANGE:
> _:c1 a veml:EventList .
> OUTPUT ALL-VALUES-FROM, ITER N:
> _:dataN a verl:Event .
> _:cN+1 a veml:EventList .
```

```
> FROM SUBCLASS ON ABOVE
> ADDED TO ALL-VALUES-FROM, ITER
  N+1:
> _:cN+1 rdf:type _:r1 ; rdf:type
  _:r2 .
```

In particular, a small contribution of input statements requires a merge-sort and re-scan of the file in question. This could indeed be solved by implementing binary-search lookup functionality over the sorted files for small input from a previous round; however, this would break with our initial aim of performing reasoning using only the primitives of file-scanning and multi-way merge-sort.

Finally in the reasoning process, we must perform consolidation of the input data and the output inferred statements according to the `:sameAs` index produced in the previous step. The first step involves sorting the input and inferred data according to natural SPOC order; the process took 6.4 hours and rewrote 35.4m statements into pivotal form. The second step involves subsequent sorting of the data according to inverse OPSC order; the process took 8.2 hours and rewrote 8.5m statements. The expense of these steps is primarily attributable to applying multi-way merge-sorting over all data in both sorting orders.

Although the degradation of performance related to the on-disk fixpoint computation of ruleset $\mathcal{R}2 \bigcup \mathcal{R}3$ is significant, if one is prepared to trade completeness (as we define it) for computational efficiency, the fixpoint calculation can be restrained to only perform a small, known amount of iterations (e.g., inferencing of the majority of statements in Figure 4 takes place over approx. 3 hours). Only minute amounts of inferred statements are produced in latter iterations of the fixpoint.

Further still, most inferences are produced after the initial scan which takes approx. 79 minutes. Thus, even after application of only $\mathcal{R}0$ and $\mathcal{R}1$ rules, the majority of inferencing has been conducted. This simpler more practical reasoning subset exhibits linear scale, as is visible for the

Figure 5. Performance of applying ruleset $\mathcal{R}0 \bigcup \mathcal{R}1$ on the 1.1b dataset

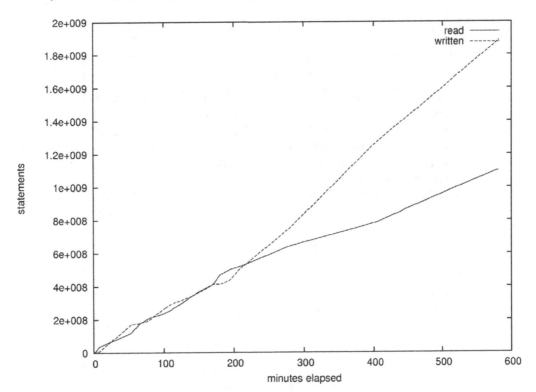

first stage of Figure 3 prior to the on-disk computations. Along these lines, we present in Figure 5 the performance of applying rules $\mathcal{R}0$ and $\mathcal{R}1$ to the 1.1b statement dataset, in one scan, with respect to the T-Box derived from that dataset as described above. In particular, we refer to the linear trend present; upon inspection, one can see that minor slow-down in the rate of statements read is attributable to an increased throughput in terms of output statements (disk write operations).

Finally, Table 7 lists the number of times each rule was fired for reasoning on the 1.1b dataset, reasoning using only $\mathcal{R}0 \bigcup \mathcal{R}1$ on the 147m dataset and also of applying all rules to the 147m dataset. Again, from both Figure 3 and Table 7 we can deduce that the bulk of current Web reasoning is covered by those rules ($\mathcal{R}0 \bigcup \mathcal{R}1$) which exhibit linear scale.

RELATED WORK

OWL reasoning, specifically query answering over OWL Full, is not tackled by typical DL Reasoners; such as FaCT++ (Haarslev & Möller, 2003; Tsarkov & Horrocks, 2006), RACER (Haarslev & Möller, 2003) or Pellet (Sirin, Parsia, Grau, Kalyanpur, & Katz, 2007); which focus on complex reasoning tasks such as subsumption checking and provable completeness of reasoning. Likewise, KAON2 (Motik, 2006), which reports better results on query answering, is limited to OWL-DL expressivity due to completeness requirements. Despite being able to deal with complex ontologies in a complete manner, these systems are not tailored for the particular challenges of processing large amounts of RDF data and particularly large A-Boxes.

Systems such as TRIPLE (Sintek & Decker, 2002), JESS[19], or Jena[20] support rule represent-

Table 7. Count of number of statements inferred for applying the given ruleset on the given dataset.

Rule	1.1b - $\mathcal{R}0 - 1$	147M - $\mathcal{R}0 - 1$	147M - $\mathcal{R}0 - 3$
$\mathcal{R}0$			
rdfc0	35,157	6,084	6,084
$\mathcal{R}1$			
rdfs2	591,304,476	30,203,111	30,462,570
rdfs3'	596,661,696	31,789,905	32,048,477
rdfs7'	156,744,587	27,723,256	27,882,492
rdfs9	1,164,619,890	64,869,593	65,455,001
rdfp3'	562,426	483,204	483,204
rdfp8a'	231,661,554	9,404,319	9,556,544
rdfp8b'	231,658,162	9,404,111	9,556,336
rdfp12a'	8,153,304	23,869	38,060
rdfp12b'	57,116	17,769	25,362
rdfp13a'	5,667,464	11,478	11,478
rdfp13b'	6,642	4,350	4,350
rdfp14a'	98,601	39,422	39,902
rdfp14b'	104,780	43,886	44,390
rdfc1	15,198,615	1,492,395	1,595,293
rdfc2	584,913	337,141	337,279
rdfc3a	115,416	3,075	17,224
rdfc3b	54	8	8
$\mathcal{R}2$			
rdfp1'	-	-	31,174
rdfp2	-	-	2,097,007
rdfp4	-	-	291,048
rdfp15'	-	-	42,098
rdfp16'	-	-	685,738
rdfc3c	-	-	6,976
rdfc4a	-	-	211
rdfc4b	-	-	246

able RDFS or OWL fragments as we do, but only work in-memory whereas our framework is focused on conducting scalable reasoning using persistent storage.

The OWLIM (Kiryakov, Ognyanov, & Manov, 2005) family of systems allows reasoning over a version of pD* using the TRREE: Triple Reasoning and Rule Entailment Engine. Besides the in-memory version SwiftOWLIM, which uses TRREE, there is also a version offering query-processing over a persistent image of the repository, BigOWLIM, which comes closest technically to our approach. In evaluation on 2 x

Dual-Core 2GHz machines with 16GB of RAM, BigOWLIM is claimed to index over 1 bn triples from the LUBM benchmark (Guo, Pan, & Heflin, 2005) in just under 70 hours ("BigOWLIM Sys. Doc.", "BigOWLIM: System Documentation," 2006); however, this figure includes indexing of the data for query-answering, and is not directly comparable with our results, and in any case, our reasoning approach strictly focuses on sensible reasoning for Web data.

Some existing systems already implement a separation of T-Box and A-Box for scalable reasoning, where in particular, assertional statements are stored in some RDBMS; e.g. DLDB (Pan & Heflin, 2003), Minerva (Zhou, et al., 2006) and OntoDB (Hondjack, et al., 2007). Similar to our approach of reasoning over Web data, (Pan, Qasem, Kanitkar, Prabhakar, & Heflin, 2007) demonstrates reasoning over 166m triples using the DLDB system. Also like us, (and as we had previously introduced in Hogan et al. (2007)) they internally choose pivot identifiers to represent equivalent sets of individuals. However, they use the notion of perspectives to support inferencing based on T-Box data; in their experiment they manually selected nine T-Box perspectives, unlike our approach that deals with arbitrary T-Box data from the Web. Their evaluation was performed on a workstation with dual 64-bit CPUs and 10GB main memory on which they loaded 760k documents / 166m triples (14% larger than our 147m statement dataset) in about 350 hrs; however, unlike our evaluation, the total time taken includes indexing for query-answering.

In a similar approach to our authoritative analysis, Cheng, Ge, Wu, and Qu (2008) introduced restrictions for accepting sub-class and equivalent-class statements from third-party sources; they follow similar arguments to that made in this paper. However, their notion of what we call authoritativeness is based on hostnames and does not consider redirects; we argue that in both cases, e.g., use of PURL services[21] is not properly supported: (i) all documents using the same service (and having the same namespace hostname) would be 'authoritative' for each other, (ii) the document cannot be served directly by the namespace location, but only through a redirect. Indeed, further work presented in Cheng and Qu (2008) introduced the notion of an *authoritative description* which is very similar to ours. In any case, we provide much more extensive treatment of the issue, supporting a much more varied range of RDF(S)/OWL constructs.

One promising alternative to authoritative reasoning for the Web is the notion of "context-dependant" or "quarantined reasoning" introduced

in Delbru, Polleres, Tummarello, and Decker (2008), whereby inference results are only considered valid within the given context of a document. As opposed to our approach whereby we construct one authoritative model for all Web data, their approach uses a unique model for each document, based on implicit and explicit imports of the document; thus, they would infer statements within the local context which we would consider to be non-authoritative. However, they would miss inferences which can only be conducted by considering a merge of documents, such as transitive closure or equality inferences based on inverse-functional properties over multiple documents. Their evaluation was completed on three machines with quad-core 2.33GHz and 8GB main memory; they claimed to be able to load, on average, 40 documents per second.

CONCLUSION

We have presented SAOR: a system for performing reasoning over Web data based on primitives known to scale: file-scan and sorting. We maintain a separate optimised T-Box index for our reasoning procedure. To keep the resulting knowledge-base manageable, both in size and quality, we made the following modifications to traditional reasoning procedures:

- only consider a positive fragment of OWL reasoning;
- analyse the authority of sources to counter ontology hijacking;
- use pivot identifiers instead of full materialisation of equality.

We show in our evaluation that naïve inferencing over Web data leads to an explosion of materialised statements and show how to prevent this explosion through analysis the authority of data sources. We also present metrics relating to the most productive rules with regards inferencing on the Web.

Although SAOR is currently not optimised for reaching full closure, we show that our system is suitable for optimised computation of the approximate closure of a Web knowledge-base w.r.t. the most commonly used RDF(S) and OWL constructs. In our evaluation, we showed that the bulk of inferencing on Web data can be completed with two scans of an unsorted Web-crawl.

RECENT DEVELOPMENTS

Since the original publication of this work (Hogan, et al., 2009), there have been significant developments relating to the work presented in this paper; herein, we provide a chronological discussion of this new literature.

Urbani et al. (2009) and Weaver & Hendler (2009) identified that the RDFS fragment is composed entirely of rules which do not require A-Box joins: they subsequently use a separation of RDFS T-Box information to enable efficient and near-complete RDFS reasoning in a manner familiar from this work. Both works also identified the potential distributability of the approach over a cluster of commodity hardware in a shared-nothing configuration; this can be achieved by replicating the (presumably small) T-Box on all machines in the cluster, and reasoning over the local A-Box. Assuming that the rules under execution do not require A-Box joins, each machine can perform reasoning independently on its local segment of the A-Box (although duplicates may possibly be introduced). Weaver & Hendler (2009) apply RDFS over 346 million triples of synthetic data, and using 128 machines produce 307 million inferences in under five minutes. Urbani et al. (2009) apply RDFS over a heterogeneous Web crawl of 865 million triples, and using 64 machines produce 30 billion inferences in under an hour.

Of particular interest was the following result reported by Urbani et al. (2009): "On a real-world dataset (Falcon, 35M triples) we stopped OWL Horst inference after 12 hours, at which point more than 130 MapReduce jobs had been launched, and some 3.8B triples had been derived." Here, OWL Horst is synonymous with pD* discussed herein; they report that naïve reasoning with respect to this fragment over real-world data caused an explosion of materialised inferences.

In (Hogan & Decker, 2009), we discussed the new OWL 2 RL/RDF ruleset which had then recently been standardised by the W3C. OWL 2 RL/RDF includes an expressive set of reasoning primitives which (i) almost entirely subsumes RDFS and pD* reasoning discussed herein; (ii) includes support for new OWL 2 constructs; and (iii) includes much more expressive reasoning on a terminological level. We discussed the new ruleset in light of the results presented herein, categorising the new OWL 2 RL/RDF ruleset based on the arity of terminological and assertional patterns in the rule antecedents. We additionally demonstrated some potential use-cases for novel OWL 2 primitives within popular Web vocabularies.

Kiryakov et al. (2009) have also described an approach for reasoning over RDF Web data – titled LDSR – but manually select large data exports from a small number of publishers (as opposed to our arbitrarily crawled corpus). They apply reasoning over 426 million explicit statements and use some similar optimisations to those presented herein, including canonicalisation of equivalent identifiers.

Extending upon their previous work, Urbani et al. (2010) provided detailed discussion on optimisations for a more mature MapReduce-based implementation of the pD* ruleset: these included some techniques presented herein, including, for example, canonicalisation of equivalent identifiers; they provide scale-up experiments detailing reasoning over 100 billion synthetic triples using 64 machines. However, we believe that scalable and exhaustive reasoning involving A-Box join rules over arbitrary RDF Web data is still an open research question, and is perhaps not suited to full materialisation given the potentially massive number of inferences involved.

Very recently, Kolovski et al. (2010) have demonstrated an optimised OWL 2 RL/RDF engine integrated into an Oracle database engine. These optimisations again include a form of canonicalisation for equality reasoning, and methods for distributing reasoning. Also, they identify highly-selective patterns for each rule (as such, a generalisation of our T-Box) and "simplify" rules by only considering parallel execution of low-selectivity patterns at scale. They provide extensive evaluation and discussion of optimisation techniques tailored to their Oracle setting. Again, however, scale-up experiments are over synthetic and closed-domain datasets.

Finally, in Hogan, Pan, Polleres, and Decker (2010), we have presented our latest results on SAOR. We demonstrated some formal properties of the "partial-indexing" approach –separating terminological data from assertional data as presented herein – demonstrating that this approach is sound with respect to standard rule application (e.g., as implementable by means of semi-naïve evaluation) and is thereby complete if a rule requiring assertional knowledge does not produce novel terminological data (usually the result of non-standard use of the core RDF(S)/OWL vocabulary). We then described rule-agnostic optimisations based on a-priori binding of terminological antecedent patterns, proposing a rule-index and other optimisations to speed up access to terminological data without need for a hard-coded T-Box structure. Following related works in the field, we extended our approach to be applicable over a cluster of commodity hardware. Again employing authoritative reasoning as presented herein, we demonstrated the feasibility and efficiency of our approach over an arbitrary crawl of 3.95 million RDF/XML documents crawled from the Web, comprising of 1.12 billion quadruples.

As such, we are delighted to see scalable OWL reasoning becoming a more mature field, with a number of research groups tackling the problem from a number of different perspectives. We believe this to be an important step towards realising the ever elusive Semantic Web, making reasoning feasible for a host of new applications operating over large RDF corpora.

REFERENCES

Bechhofer, S., van Harmelen, F., Hendler, J., Horrocks, I., McGuinness, D. L., Patel-Schneider, P. F., et al. (2004, February). *OWL Web ontology language reference.*

Bechhofer, S., & Volz, R. (2004). *Patching syntax in OWL ontologies.* International Semantic Web Conference (Vol. 3298, pp. 668-682). Hiroshima, Japan: Springer.

BigOWLIM. (2006). *System documentation.*

Brickley, D., & Guha, R. V. (2004). *RDF vocabulary description language 1.0: RDF schema.*

Brickley, D., & Miller, L. (2007). *FOAF vocabulary specification 0.91.*

Cheng, G., Ge, W., Wu, H., & Qu, Y. (2008). Searching Semantic Web objects based on class hierarchies. *Proceedings of Linked Data on the Web Workshop.*

Cheng, G., & Qu, Y. (2008). *Term dependence on the Semantic Web.* International Semantic Web Conference (pp. 665-680). Karlsruhe, Germany.

de Bruijn, J. (2008). *Semantic Web language layering with ontologies, rules, and meta-modeling.* University of Innsbruck.

de Bruijn, J., & Heymans, S. (2007). *Logical foundations of (e)RDF(S): Complexity and reasoning.* 6th International Semantic Web Conference (pp. 86-99). Busan, Korea.

Delbru, R., Polleres, A., Tummarello, G., & Decker, S. (2008). Context dependent reasoning for semantic documents in Sindice. *Proceedings of the 4th International Workshop on Scalable Semantic Web Knowledge Base Systems (SSWS 2008)*. Karlsruhe, Germany.

Fensel, D., & van Harmelen, F. (2007). Unifying reasoning and search to Web scale. *IEEE Internet Computing, 11*(2), 96, 94-95.

Ghilardi, S., Lutz, C., & Wolter, F. (2006). Did I damage my ontology? A case for conservative extensions in description logics. *Proceedings of the Tenth International Conference on Principles of Knowledge Representation and Reasoning* (pp. 187-197). Lake District of the United Kingdom.

Grau, B. C., Horrocks, I., Parsia, B., Patel-Schneider, P., & Sattler, U. (2006). *Next steps for OWL*. OWL: Experiences and Directions Workshop. Athens, Georgia, USA.

Grosof, B., Horrocks, I., Volz, R., & Decker, S. (2004). *Description logic programs: Combining logic programs with description logic*. 13th International Conference on World Wide Web.

Guha, R. V., McCool, R., & Fikes, R. (2004). *Contexts for the Semantic Web*. 3rd International Semantic Web Conference, Hiroshima.

Guo, Y., Pan, Z., & Heflin, J. (2005). LUBM: A benchmark for OWL knowledge base systems. *Journal of Web Semantics, 3*(2-3), 158–182. doi:10.1016/j.websem.2005.06.005

Gutiérrez, C., Hurtado, C., & Mendelzon, A. O. (2004). *Foundations of Semantic Web databases.* 23rd ACM SIGACT-SIGMOD-SIGART Symposium on Principles of Database Systems, Paris.

Haarslev, V., & Möller, R. (2003). *Racer: A core inference engine for the Semantic Web*. International Workshop on Evaluation of Ontology-based Tools.

Harth, A., & Decker, S. (2005). *Optimized index structures for querying RDF from the Web*. 3rd Latin American Web Congress (pp. 71-80). Buenos Aires, Argentina: IEEE Press.

Harth, A., Umbrich, J., & Decker, S. (2006). *MultiCrawler: A pipelined architecture for crawling and indexing Semantic Web data*. International Semantic Web Conference (pp. 258-271).

Hayes, P. (2004, February). *RDF semantics*.

Hogan, A., & Decker, S. (2009). *On the ostensibly silent 'W' in OWL 2 RL*. Paper presented at the Web Reasoning and Rule Systems, Third International Conference (RR), Chantilly, VA, USA.

Hogan, A., Harth, A., & Decker, S. (2007). *Performing object consolidation on the Semantic Web data graph*. 1st I3 Workshop: Identity, Identifiers, Identification Workshop.

Hogan, A., Harth, A., & Polleres, A. (2008). SAOR: Authoritative reasoning for the Web. *Proceedings of the 3rd Asian Semantic Web Conference (ASWC 2008)*. Bankok, Thailand.

Hogan, A., Harth, A., & Polleres, A. (2009). Scalable authoritative OWL reasoning for the Web. *International Journal on Semantic Web and Information Systems, 5*(2), 45–90. doi:10.4018/IJSWIS.2009040103

Hogan, A., Pan, J. Z., Polleres, A., & Decker, S. (2010). *SAOR: Template rule optimisations for distributed reasoning over 1 billion linked data triples*. Paper presented at the 9th International Semantic Web Conference (ISWC), Shanghai, China.

Hondjack, D., Pierra, G., & Bellatreche, L. (2007). OntoDB: An ontology-based database for data intensive applications. *Proceedings of the 12th International Conference on Database Systems for Advanced Applications* (pp. 497-508). Bangkok, Thailand.

Horrocks, I., & Patel-Schneider, P. F. (2004). Reducing OWL entailment to description logic satisfiability. *Journal of Web Semantics*, *1*(4), 345–357. doi:10.1016/j.websem.2004.06.003

Jiménez-Ruiz, E., Grau, B. C., Sattler, U., Schneider, T., & Llavori, R. B. (2008). Safe and economic re-use of ontologies: A logic-based methodology and tool support. *Proceedings of the 21st International Workshop on Description Logics (DL2008)*. Dresden, Germany.

Kiryakov, A., Ognyanoff, D., Velkov, R., Tashev, Z., & Peikov, I. (2009). *LDSR: Materialized reasonable view to the Web of linked data*. Paper presented at the OWL: Experiences and Directions Workshop (OWLED), Chantilly, VA, USA.

Kiryakov, A., Ognyanov, D., & Manov, D. (2005). *OWLIM - a pragmatic semantic repository for OWL* (pp. 182–192). New York, USA: Web Information Systems Engineering Workshops.

Kolovski, V., Wu, Z., & Eadon, G. (2010). *Optimizing enterprise-scale OWL 2 RL reasoning in a relational database system*. Paper presented at the 9th International Semantic Web Conference (ISWC), Shanghai, China.

Kunkle, D., & Cooperman, G. (2008). Solving Rubik's cube: Disk is the new RAM. *Communications of the ACM*, *51*(4), 31–33. doi:10.1145/1330311.1330319

Lloyd, J. W. (1987). *Foundations of logic programming* (2nd ed.). Springer-Verlag.

Lutz, C., Walther, D., & Wolter, F. (2007). Conservative extensions in expressive description logics. *IJCAI 2007, Proceedings of the 20th International Joint Conference on Artificial Intelligence* (pp. 453-458). Hyderabad, India.

Motik, B. (2006). *Reasoning in description logics using resolution and deductive databases*. Karlsruhe, Germany: Forschungszentrum Informatik.

Motik, B. (2007). On the properties of metamodeling in OWL. *Journal of Logic and Computation*, *17*(4), 617–637. doi:10.1093/logcom/exm027

Muñoz, S., Pérez, J., & Gutiérrez, C. (2007). *Minimal deductive systems for RDF* (pp. 53–67). ESWC.

Pan, Z., & Heflin, J. (2003). DLDB: Extending relational databases to support Semantic Web queries. *PSSS1 - Practical and Scalable Semantic Systems, Proceedings of the First International Workshop on Practical and Scalable Semantic Systems*. Sanibel Island, Florida, USA.

Pan, Z., Qasem, A., Kanitkar, S., Prabhakar, F., & Heflin, J. (2007). *Hawkeye: A practical large scale demonstration of Semantic Web integration*. *Proceedings of On the Move to Meaningful Internet Systems Workshops* (pp. 1115–1124). OTM-II.

Patel-Schneider, P. F., & Horrocks, I. (2004, February). *OWL Web ontology language semantics and abstract syntax section 4. Mapping to RDF graphs*.

Prud'hommeaux, E., & Seaborne, A. (2008, January). *SPARQL query language for RDF*.

Sintek, M., & Decker, S. (2002). *TRIPLE - a query, inference, and transformation language for the Semantic Web*. 1st International Semantic Web Conference (pp. 364-378).

Sirin, E., Parsia, B., Grau, B. C., Kalyanpur, A., & Katz, Y. (2007). Pellet: A practical OWL-DL reasoner. *Journal of Web Semantics*, *5*(2), 51–53. doi:10.1016/j.websem.2007.03.004

Smith, M. K., Welty, C., & McGuinness, D. L. (2004, February). *OWL Web ontology language guide*.

ter Horst, H. J. (2005a). *Combining RDF and part of OWL with rules: Semantics, decidability, complexity*. 4th International Semantic Web Conference (pp. 668-684).

ter Horst, H. J. (2005b). Completeness, decidability and complexity of entailment for RDF schema and a semantic extension involving the OWL vocabulary. *Journal of Web Semantics, 3,* 79–115. doi:10.1016/j.websem.2005.06.001

Theoharis, Y., Christophides, V., & Karvounarakis, G. (2005). Benchmarking database representations of RDF/S stores. *Proceedings of the Fourth International Semantic Web Conference* (pp. 685-701). Galway, Ireland.

Tsarkov, D., & Horrocks, I. (2006). *FaCT++ description logic reasoner: System description.* International Joint Conf. on Automated Reasoning (pp. 292-297).

Urbani, J., Kotoulas, S., Maassen, J., van Harmelen, F., & Bal, H. E. (2010). *OWL reasoning with WebPIE: Calculating the closure of 100 billion triples.* Paper presented at the 7th Extended Semantic Web Conference (ESWC), Heraklion, Crete, Greece.

Urbani, J., Kotoulas, S., Oren, E., & van Harmelen, F. (2009). *Scalable distributed reasoning using MapReduce.* Paper presented at the 8th International Semantic Web Conference (ISWC), Chantilly, VA, USA.

Wang, T. D., Parsia, B., & Hendler, J. A. (2006). A survey of the Web ontology landscape. *Proceedings of the 5th International Semantic Web Conference (ISWC 2006)* (pp. 682-694). Athens, GA, USA.

Weaver, J., & Hendler, J. A. (2009). *Parallel materialization of the finite RDFS closure for hundreds of millions of triples.* Paper presented at the 8th International Semantic Web Conference, ISWC, Chantilly, VA, USA.

Wu, Z., Eadon, G., Das, S., Chong, E. I., Kolovski, V., Annamalai, M., et al. (2008). *Implementing an inference engine for RDFS/OWL constructs and user-defined rules in Oracle.* 24th International Conference on Data Engineering. IEEE.

Zhou, J., Ma, L., Liu, Q., Zhang, L., Yu, Y., & Pan, Y. (2006). Minerva: A scalable OWL ontology storage and inference system. *Proceedings of The First Asian Semantic Web Conference (ASWC)* (pp. 429-443). Beijing, China.

ENDNOTES

* This is an invited republication of an article originally published as (Hogan, Harth, & Polleres, 2009). Herein, we add some minor improvements and provide an updated discussion on developments in the area since the original publication. *This work has been supported by Science Foundation Ireland project Lion (SFI/02/CE1/I131), European FP6 project inContext (IST-034718), COST Action ``Agreement Technologies''(IC0801) and an IRCSET Postgraduate Research Scholarship.*

[1] Throughout this paper, we assume that http://www.w3.org/2002/07/owl#is the default namespace with prefix ":", i.e. we write e.g. just ":Class", ":disjointWith", etc. instead of using the commonly used owl: prefix. Other prefixes such as rdf:, rdfs:, foaf: are used as in other common documents. Moreover, we often use the common abbreviation 'a' as a convenient shortcut for rdf:type.

[2] http://www.dajobe.org/2004/01/turtle/

[3] Unlike some other rule systems for RDF, the most prominent of which being CONSTRUCT statements in SPARQL, we forbid blank nodes; i.e., we forbid existential variables in rule consequents which would require the "invention" of blank nodes.

[4] http://xmlns.com/foaf/spec/index.rdf

[5] Tim (now the same entity as the W3C) is asserted to be a member of the two disjoint classes: foaf:Person and foaf:Organization.

[6] In (ter Horst 2005), rules using RDF collection constructs were not included (such

as our rules **rdfc0,rdfc1,rdfc3***) as they have variable antecedent-body length and, thus, can affect complexity considerations. It was informally stated that:intersectionOf and:unionOf could be supported under pD* through reduction into subclass relations; however no rules were explicitly defined and our rule **rdfc3b** could not be supported in this fashion. We support such rules here since we are not so concerned for the moment with theoretical worst-case complexity, but are more concerned with the practicalities of web-reasoning.

[7]   A similar example from the Web can be found at http://thesauri.cs.vu.nl/wordnet/rdfs/wordnet2b.owl.

[8]   In any case, as we will see in Section 3.4, our application of authoritative analysis would not allow such arbitrary third-party re-definition of core RDF(S)/OWL constructs.

[9]   Here, slightly abusing XML terminology by "namespace" of a URI we mean the prefix of the URI obtained from stripping off the final NCname

[10]   See Appendix A&B of http://www.w3.org/TR/swbp-vocab-pub/

[11]   Includes some RDF collection fragments which may not be part of a class description

[12]   We expect that a caching on-disk index would work well considering the distribu-

tion of membership assertions for classes and properties in web data; there would be a high hit-rate for the cache.

[13]   In N-Quads format: cf. http://sw.deri.org/2008/07/n-quads/

[14]   This is from incorrect use of the FOAF ontology by prominent exporters. We refer the interested reader to (Hogan, et al., 2007).

[15]   We would like to acknowledge Harold Boley for originally suggesting to us the use of pivot elements as a common-sense approach for handling large sets of equivalent identifiers.

[16]   For example, the document retrievable from http://pike.kw.nl/files/documents/pietzwart/RDF/PietZwart200602.owl defines super-classes/-properties for all of the FOAF vocabulary.

[17]   Thirty-four such:unionOf class descriptions can be found in http://colab.cim3.net/file/work/SICoP/ontac/reference/ProtegeOntologies/COSMO-Versions/TopLevel06.owl; fifty-five can be found in http://lsdis.cs.uga.edu/oldham/ontology/wsag/wsag.owl

[18]   http://www.w3.org/2002/03owlt/

[19]   http://herzberg.ca.sandia.gov/

[20]   http://jena.sourceforge.net/

[21]   http://purl.org/

Chapter 7
Enabling Scalable Semantic Reasoning for Mobile Services

Luke Albert Steller
Monash University, Australia

Shonali Krishnaswamy
Monash University, Australia

Mohamed Methat Gaber
Monash University, Australia

ABSTRACT

With the emergence of high-end smart phones/PDAs there is a growing opportunity to enrich mobile/ pervasive services with semantic reasoning. This paper presents novel strategies for optimising semantic reasoning for realising semantic applications and services on mobile devices. We have developed the mTableaux algorithm which optimises the reasoning process to facilitate service selection. We present comparative experimental results which show that mTableaux improves the performance and scalability of semantic reasoning for mobile devices.

1 INTRODUCTION

The semantic web offers new opportunities to represent knowledge based on meaning rather than syntax. Semantically described knowledge can be used to infer new knowledge by reasoners in an automated fashion. Reasoners can be utilised in a broad range of semantic applications, for instance matching user requirements with specific information in search engines, matching match client needs with functional system components such as

DOI: 10.4018/978-1-60960-593-3.ch007

services for automated discovery and orchestration or even providing diagnosis of medical conditions. A significant drawback which prevents the large uptake and deployment of semantically described knowledge is the resource intensive nature of reasoning. Currently available semantic reasoners are suitable for deployment on high-end desktop or service based infrastructure. However, with the emergence of high-end smart phones / PDAs the mobile environment is increasingly information rich. For instance, information on devices may include sensor data, traffic conditions, user preferences or habits or capability descriptions of remotely invokable web services hosted on these devices. This information is can be highly useful to other users in the environment. Thus, there is a need to describe this knowledge semantically and to support scalable reasoning for mobile semantic applications, especially in highly dynamic environments where high-end infrastructure is unsuitable or not available. Computing power is limited to that available on resource constrained devices and as shown in figure 1, there is insufficient memory on these devices to complete reasoning tasks which require significant time and memory to complete.

Since mobile users are often on the move and in a highly dynamic situation, they generally require information quickly. Studies such as (Roto & Oulasvirta, 2005) have established that mobile users typically have a tolerance threshold of about 5 to 15 seconds in terms of response time, before their attention shifts elsewhere, depending on their environment. Therefore, there is a need for mobile

Figure 1. Error showing that there was not enough memory to perform reasoning when attempting to run Pellet on a PDA (the reasoning task was the Printer inference check given in section 6.1).

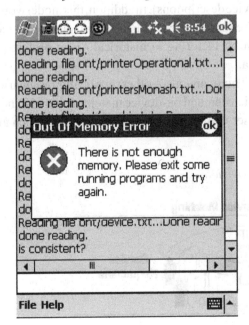

reasoners which can meet the twin constraints of time and memory.

For example, consider the following mobile application scenario. A mobile user has just arrived in Sydney airport and wishes to search for food and other products. Sydney airport provides touch screen kiosk terminals which allow the user to search for stores (and other airport facilities) by category. The location of the store and facility is then displayed on a map as well as the location of the user (which is the fixed location of the kiosk), as illustrated in figure 2. These kiosks are not very convenient as they are only located at fixed point locations, are limited in their search options and user request complexity and do not take user context into account. Additionally, they do not scale, as kiosks can only be used by one user at a time.

Alternatively, the increasing abundance of mobile devices such as PDAs and mobile phones as well as their increasing computational and communication capabilities provide new opportunities for on-board service discovery. Consider the case where the information kiosk is a directory/repository of services available in the airport which mobile users can connect to from their phone or PDA. The user can then access, search and use this information using their respective phones at their convenience.

There are two modes of service matching:

- centralised service matching which occurs on a server on behalf of the user and
- partially or completely decentralised approaches where matching occurs on the resource constrained device itself.

Under a centralised approach (see figure 3) the kiosk (or a connected machine) is a high-end server which handles all service discovery requests on the mobile user's behalf. However, there are two major drawbacks with this approach. Firstly, although purchase of a server is relatively cheap, there are significant costs involved for this kind

Figure 2. Sydney airport store finder kiosk. The store search screen is shown on the left, while the search result for an Internet café is on the right. The location of the Internet café is indicated by the computer icon in the bottom right side of the screen.

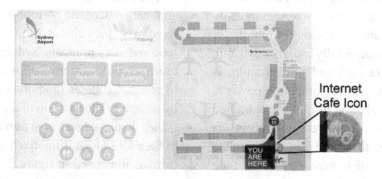

of service provision, including scalability to handle potentially thousands of requests, wireless network provision, maintenance costs, security considerations and quality of service issues. The significant costs would outweigh the limited benefit to a central authority such as the Sydney airport. In environments where there is no such central authority this infrastructure may not even be possible (eg a city center or decentralised precinct). Secondly, if users are faced with the choice of paying for wireless access to a service matcher or utilising existing kiosks such as those already at Sydney airport, they are likely to choose the kiosk since it is free (albeit limited in its service provision capability).

For this environment we advocate a partially decentralised approach (see figure 4a) in which the kiosk is merely a directory or repository, to which users can sync with, to download service

advertisements for the airport, using short range WiFi or Bluetooth. The ontology file provider could also be a provider accessed via the Internet or even shared using secondary storage such as an SD card downloaded previously at home or by another person. Service matching can then occur independently as needed, on the user's device itself. This solution would be inexpensive to deploy and to use as there are no overheads for the service providing authority and there are no connectivity overheads for the user (eg they may simply use Bluetooth for once-off access to the service descriptions). In addition, this model would be better suited to provision of personalised selection by factoring in historical / user preference data.

There are also other application scenarios which demand on-device matching. For instance, a user may wish to discovery services which are

Figure 3. Example: Centralised server-based matching provision.

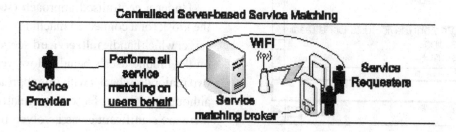

Figure 4. Three example configurations of on-device matching: (a) partial decentralisation where files are served centrally (by a WiFi/Bluetooth connected server or Internet provider) but matching occurs on-board the device, (b) on-device matching of remote services hosted on other mobile devices in a mobile ad-hoc network (c) on-device matching of services on the same device (local services only).

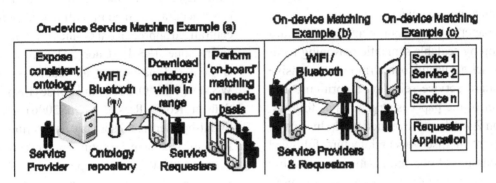

hosted remotely by devices in a temporary mobile ad-hoc network (see figure 4b) such scenarios include: students sharing data on a field trip (Chatti, Srirama, Kensche & Cao, 2006), emergency situations, traffic information sharing, etc. Alternatively, services may be installed or removed from a user's own device on a needs basis. Determining which services should be installed or removed requires comparing current or prospective services to the user's current needs on the device itself (see figure 4c), for example Google[1] and Yahoo[2] already offer many mobile applications such as blogging, news, finance, sports, etc.

We have provided three examples demonstrating a growing number of situations where there is a clear need for approaches to enable mobile reasoning on resource constrained devices. The next question remains as to how the user will access these services from the mobile device and perform service discovery on the device. There are two main challenges here:

1. the mechanism to perform semantically-driven service selection on a mobile device in an efficient way;
2. the interface challenges of presenting this information to the user.

In order to facilitate the matching of user needs, context and requests with a set of potential services such as those outlined in the scenarios above, our focus is on the first key issue of enabling scalable service discovery mechanisms to operate on a mobile device. This approach requires new strategies to enable mobile reasoning on resource constrained devices, to perform matching of request to services. The Tableaux algorithm is well known and used by reasoners such as Pellet, RacerPro and FaCT++. Therefore this paper aims to enable these reasoners to perform mobile semantic reasoning. The key challenge is to enable semantic reasoning to function in a computationally cost-efficient and resource-aware manner on a mobile device.

In this paper we present our mTableaux algorithm, which implements strategies to optimise description logic (DL) reasoning tasks so that relatively large reasoning tasks of several hundred individuals and classes can be scaled to small resource constrained devices. We present comparative evaluations of the performance of Pellet, RacerPro and FaCT++ semantic reasoners which demonstrate the significant improvement to response time achieved by our mTableaux algorithm. In order to gain efficiency, some strategies reduce completeness, in a controlled manner, so we also evaluate result accuracy using recall and precision. Finally, in our evaluation we present experimental evaluations that demonstrate the feasibility of the semantic service discovery to operate on a mobile device.

This paper takes an important step forward in developing scalable semantic reasoning techniques which are useful for both mobile / pervasive and standard service selection algorithms. The remainder of the paper is structured as follows. In section 2 we describe related work. In section 3 we present our discovery architecture, followed by a discussion of our optimisation and ranking strategies in section 4. In section 5 we formally define our strategies. Section 6 we provide an implementation and performance evaluations and in section 7 we conclude the paper.

2 RELATED WORK IN PERVASIVE SERMANTIC SERVICE REASONING

The limitations of syntactic, string-based matching for web service discovery coupled with the emergence of the semantic web implies that next generation web services will be matched based on semantically equivalent meaning, even when they are described differently (Broens, 2004) and will include support for partial matching in the absence of an exact match. While current service discovery architectures such as Jini (Arnold, O'Sullivan, Scheifler, Waldo & Woolrath, 1999), UPnP (UPnP, 2007), Konark (Lee, Helal, Desai, Verma & Arslan, 2003), SLP (Guttman, 1999), Salutation (Miller & Pascoe, 2000) and SSDM (Issarny & Sailhan, 2005), UDDI (UDDI, 2009) and LDAP (Howes & Smith, 1995) use either interface or string based syntactic matching, there is a growing emergence of DAML-S/OWL-S semantic matchmakers. DReggie (Chakraborty, Perich, Avancha & Joshi, 2001) and CMU Matchmaker (Srinivasan, Paolucci & Sycara, 2005) are examples of such matchmakers which support approximate matching but they require a

centralised high-end node to perform reasoning using Prolog and Racer, respectively. Similarly, LARKS (Sycara, Widoff, Klusch & Lu, 2002) which is designed to manage the trade-off between result accuracy and computation time, employs a centralised approach but defines its own language and reasoner. IRS-III (Cabral, Domingue, Galizia, Gugliotta, Tanasescu et al., 2006) is based on WSMX (WSMO, 2009) and utilises Lisp. DIANE (Küster, König-Ries & Klein, 2006) is designed for ad-hoc service discovery and defines its own semantic language. It captures request preferences as fuzzy sets defining acceptable ranges. DIANE also supports dynamic attributes, which are realised at runtime. Anamika (Chakraborty, Joshi, Yesha & Finin, 2004) is an ad-hoc architecture which utilises an ontological approach for routing and discovery based on service type but does not perform complex reasoning or support context.

There are in addition, architectures developed specifically for the pervasive service discovery domain which are driven by context, such as MobiShare (Doulkeridis, Loutas & Vazirgiannis, 2005) which utilised RDF subclass relations for service type, with no reasoning, COSS (Broens, 2004) which utilises semi-OWL for service type, inputs and outputs with lattice structures for ranking Boolean context attributes, and CASE (Sycara et al., 2002) and Omnipresent (Almeida, Bapista, Silva, Campelo, Figueiredo et al., 2006) which utilise OWL with Jena (Jena, 2009) rules. However all of these architectures too, require the existence of a high-end central node.

This reliance on a high-end, centralised node for performing semantically driven pervasive service discovery can clearly be attributed to the fact that semantic reasoners used by these architectures (including Prolog, Lisp and Jess, as well as more newly available OWL reasoners such as FaCT++ (2008), RacerPro (2008) and KAON2 (2008)) are all resource intensive. These reasoners cannot be deployed onto small resource constrained devices in their current form, due to the twin constraints of memory and processing time.

Kleeman et. al. (Kleemann, 2006) have developed KRHyper, a novel first order logic (FOL) reasoner for deployment on resource constrained devices. In order to use DL with KRHyper it must be transformed into a set of disjunctive first order logic clauses. It implements the common DL optimisations of backjumping, semantic branching, Boolean constraint propagation, lazy unfolding and absorption as described in (Horrocks & Patel-Schneider, 1999). These optimisations are also implemented by widely used reasoners such as FaCT++ and Pellet. A performance evaluation shows that it performs first order reasoning quickly, solving 35% of satisfiable horn clauses, 29% of unsatisfiable clauses, 54%, non-horn satisfiable problems, 39% of non-horn unsatisfiable problems in 10 seconds. It does not utilise caching schemes which incur additional overhead and memory consumption for smaller tasks, but optimise larger tasks. Performance comparisons with RacerPro show that it performs better for small tasks and not as well for larger tasks. This FOL reasoner meets the goal of providing competitive performance results with a DL reasoner. However, it still exhausts all memory when the reasoning task becomes too large for a small device to handle and fails to provide any result.

Therefore, there is a need for an optimised semantic reasoner which performs better than currently available reasoners. This reasoner must also support adaptation to the environment, to reduce memory consumption of the processing required (which may reduce result accuracy) according to resource or time constraints. In the next section we outline our novel architecture to meet this need.

3 RESOURCE-AWARE AND COST-EFFICIENT PERVASIVE SERVICE DISCOVERY

Our pervasive service discovery architecture is illustrated in figure 5. The modules in this diagram all reside on the user's device. The database of ontologies includes those collected from service repositories or kiosks or other sources, as described in section 1.

In this model, the mobile user submits a request to his or her device and discovery manager utilises the semantic reasoner to match the request with services from the database of collected ontologies. The discovery manager takes available resources such as available memory, CPU usage, remaining battery life or remaining time (provided by the context manager), into consideration. It may load the entire ontology into memory in the beginning, or if memory is low it will load portions of ontology on demand. The adaptive discovery manager also may stop matching a particular request with a service after the service failed to match a particular request attribute or it may instruct the mTableaux reasoner to reduce the accuracy of its result when resources become low (eg low memory) or when the result is taking too long to process. The semantic reasoner module contains our mTableaux algorithm, which incorporates our optimised reasoning strategies. It also includes strategies to reduce result accuracy to meet resource constraints.

In summary, our architecture addresses two main goals. Firstly, it addresses the need for scalable reasoning on a mobile device by provid-

Figure 5. Pervasive Service Discovery Architecture

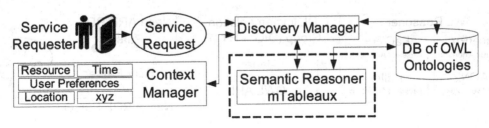

ing strategies to optimise the reasoning process. Secondly, when there are not enough resources or time remaining to complete a request, our architecture provides strategies to reduce the result's accuracy in order to utilise less resources and time. This paper concentrates on providing a semantic reasoner that is able to operate in on a mobile device (mTableaux module) and discuss this in more detail in the next section. As a simple extension to this reasoner we also discuss adaptive accuracy reduction to reduce resource or time consumption where there are insufficient resources to complete a task in full.

4 MTABLEAUX – REASONING FOR PERVASIVE SERVICE DISCOVERY

In this section we discuss current Tableaux semantic reasoners and present mTableaux, our algorithm for enabling Tableaux reasoning on mobile devices.

4.1 Semantic Reasoners

The effective employment of semantic languages requires the use of semantic reasoners such as Pellet (2003), FaCT++ (2008), RacerPro (2008) and KAON2 (2008). Most of these reasoners employ the widely used Tableaux (Horrocks & Sattler, 2005) algorithm. These reasoners are shown in Figure 6, which is a detailed version of the semantic reasoner and ontology database components from figure 5 and illustrates the component parts required for OWL reasoning. Reasoners can be

deployed on servers and interacted with via DL Implementation Group (DIG) interface specification which uses XML over HTTP. Alternatively, interaction may be facilitated directly using native APIs, which requires RDF/XML parsing functionality to load OWL files into the reasoner. Pellet utilises either Jena or OWL-API for interaction and RDF parsing.

Semantic OWL Reasoners contain a knowledge base K which encompasses terminological knowledge *TBox* and assertional knowledge *ABox,* such that $K = TBox$ABox. *TBox* encompasses class definitions and expressions while *ABox* encompasses individual and literal assertions of class membership and relations. The knowledge base is stored as a set of triples $<C, R, O>$, where C is the set of classes, R is a set of roles and O is the set of object assertions. The object assertions are organised into a graph structure of the form $<O_1, R, O_2>$ where O_1 is an object connected to O_2 by role R. DL Tableaux reasoners such as Pellet, reduce all reasoning tasks to a consistency check.

Tableaux is a branching algorithm, in which disjunctions form combinations of branches in the tree. Inferred membership for an individual I to class type RQ implies $I \in RQ$, where $RQ \in$ TBox and $I \in$ ABox. $I \in RQ$ is checked by adding $\neg RQ$ as a type for I, in an otherwise consistent ontology. If the assertion of $I: \neg RQ$ results in a clash for all branches dependant on $\neg RQ$ for I, then class membership $I \in RQ$ is proven.

Figure 7 presents an example containing individuals $d, e, f, g, h, i, j, k, n, m, o$ which are connected by roles Q, R, S, P and some individu-

Figure 6. Semantic reasoner components

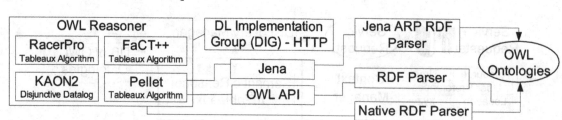

als are asserted to be members of class types A, B, C, T. For instance, individual d is connected to f by role R and f is a member of class A. Assume we want to find the truth of $d \in RQ$ where $RQ = \exists P.(\geq 1P) \wedge \exists R.(A \wedge \exists R.(B \wedge C))$, using the Tableaux algorithm, $\neg RQ$ is first added asserted as a type label to individual d, where $\neg RQ = \forall P.(\leq 0P) \vee \forall R.(\neg A \vee \forall R.(\neg B \vee \neg C))$. Tableaux applies the first element of the disjunction, a universal quantifier: $\forall P.(\leq 0P)$, which asserts the max cardinality rule $\leq 0P$ to node e, because e is a P-neighbour to individual h. h violates the max cardinality of 0 for P and creates a clash, because e has a P-neighbour h. All remaining disjunction elements and sub-elements also clash thereby proving $d \in$ RQ as true.

The shaded nodes in figure 7 indicate those which contribute to a clash. Application of any expansion rules to other nodes results in unnecessary processing. The full Tableaux extract for the standard Tableaux method is listed below:

Assert d:
$\forall P.(\leq 0P) \vee \forall R.(\neg A \vee \forall R.(\neg B \vee \neg C))$
Apply Unfolding Rule k: $\neg X \vee \forall Q.(\neg Y \vee \neg Z)$
Apply Universal Quantifier o: $\neg Y \vee \neg Z$.
Apply Branch 1, Element (1/2) o: $\neg Y$, no clash.
Apply Branch 2, Element (1/2) n:U, no clash.
Apply Branch 3, Element (1/2) i: $\forall P.(\leq 0P)$
Apply Universal Quantifier j: $\leq 0P$ **Apply Max Rule** j: $\leq 0P$, CLASH.
Apply Branch 3, Element (2/2) i: $\forall R.(\neg A \vee \forall R.(\neg B \vee \neg C))$.

Apply Universal Quantifier g: $\neg A \vee \forall R.(\neg B \vee \neg C)$.
Apply Branch 4 Element (1/2) g: $\neg$ A, CLASH.
Apply Branch 4 Element (2/2) g: $\forall R.(\neg B \vee \neg C)$.
Apply Universal Quantifier l,j: $\neg B \vee \neg C$.
Apply Branch 6 Element (1/2) i: $\neg$ B, CLASH.
Apply Branch 6 Element (2/2) i: $\neg$ C, no clash.
Apply Branch 7 Element (1/2) j: $\neg$ B, CLASH.
Apply Branch 7 Element (2/2) j: $\neg$ C, CLASH.

All elements of the negated request generate a clash, so $d \in RQ$ is proven to be true. Those disjunction branches and expansion rules which contributed to clashes proving $d \in RQ$ are bolded. The processing involved in applying all other rules did not contribute to the proof of $d \in RQ$.

4.2 mTableaux Strategies

The work in this paper concentrates on optimisations for the Tableaux algorithm. As observed in section 4.1 (see figure 7), Tableaux reasoners leave scope for optimisation by dropping rules which do not contribute to an inference check, or applying first the rules which are more likely to create a clash. In addition, since inference proofs relate only to a subset of the ontology, it is not necessary to load the entire ontology into memory. Minimising the processing time and memory consumption are the twin goals of our reasoning approach as this enables scalable deployment of reasoners to small/resource constrained devices.

Figure 7: Example Clash

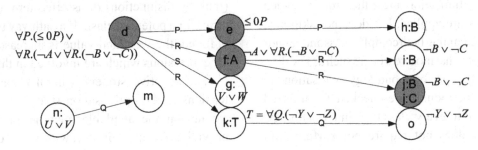

We provide an overview of our optimisations as follows.

Semantic reasoners initially check ontologies for overall consistency. Since this check need only occur once for each ontology, we assume this has already been performed on the kiosk (i.e., the location from which the ontology is downloaded) or by the service advertiser before the ontology is released for download. Alternatively, there may be a service that is able to provide consistent versions of ontologies. Our mTableaux algorithm provides strategies to for reducing processing time and memory consumption for inference checks of the form: $I \in RQ$ by providing strategies for:

- optimisation - by dropping and reordering tableaux expansion rules and
- adaption - to reduce result accuracy when resources become low and only load ontology subsets which are relevant to the inference task.

The optimisation strategies include: 1. selective application of consistency rules, 2. skipping disjunctions, 3. associate weights with disjunctions and other expansion rules (such as existential quantifiers and cardinality restrictions) and increasing the weight of those which are likely to lead to clashes if applied in order to apply these first, by 3a. searching for potential clashes from specific disjunctions and 3b. searching from a specific term. The first two strategies drop expansion rules (disjunctions, existential quantifiers and maximum cardinality restrictions), therefore completeness cannot be guaranteed (soundness is in tact) because some clashes may not be found. The third optimisation alters the order in which expressions are applied, but does not skip any, thereby maintaining both completeness and soundness. We note, that most reasoners such as FaCT++ and RacerPro perform ontology realisation, in which all individuals are checked for inferred membership to every class type in the ontology. mTableaux does not require nor perform full ontology realisation, rather only specific individual I to class type RQ membership $I \in RQ$ is performed, where RQ is a user request and I denotes a set of potential service individuals to be checked.

In the first strategy (selective consistency), application of consistency rules to a subset of individuals only, reduces the reasoning task. This subset can be established using the universal quantifier construct of the form $\forall R.C = \{ \forall b.(a, b) \in R \rightarrow b \in C\}$ (Baader, Calvanese, McGuinness, Nardi & Patel-Schneider, 2003), where R denotes a relation and C denotes a class concept. The quantifier implies that all object fillers of relation R, are of type C. Application of this rule adds role filler type C to all objects for the given role R, which can give rise to an inconsistency. Therefore, we define the subset as being limited to the original individual being checked for membership to a class, and all those individuals which branch from this individual as objects of roles specified in universal quantifiers.

The second optimisation (disjunction skipping), applies or skips disjunctions, according to whether they relate to the request type. A disjunction may be applied when one of its elements contains a type which can be derived from the request type. Derived types include elements of conjunctions/disjunctions and role fillers of universal quantifiers and their unfolded types.

For the third strategy, expressions are ordered by weight using a weighted queue. To establish weights for expansion rules (disjunctions, existential quantifiers and maximum cardinality restrictions) these expressions are ranked by recursively checking each element in a particular disjunction (rank by disjunction) or asserted term (rank by term) for a potential clash. If a pathway to a clash is found, the weighted value is increased for of all expressions which are involved in this path.

The adaptive strategies involve simple extensions to the optimisation strategies to avoid exhausting the available memory or time by providing a result to the user with a level of uncertainty, when resources become low. We describe our optimisation strategies in detail, in the next section, which the adaptive extensions are briefly discussed in future work (section 7).

5 MTABLEAUX ALGORITHM - OPTIMISATION AND RANKING STRATEGIES

In this section we formally describe the optimisation strategies listed in the previous section.

5.1 Selective Consistency

In the selective consistency strategy, Tableaux completion rules are only applied to a subset of individuals, rather than all those individuals in the ontology, let SC denote this set. Completion rules which are added as types to individual A are only applied if $A \in SC$.

For the membership inference check $I \in RQ$, before reasoning begins, SC is initially populated using the function $popuInds(IS)$, such that $SC = popuInds(\{I\})$. $popuInds(IS)$ is a function which recursively calls $getInds(e, AV)$ to select universally quantified r-neighbour individuals of e, and those neighbour's universally quantified r-neighbours, etc. $popuInds(IS)$ is given by equation 1, where $e.AV$ denotes the set of universal quantifiers of the form $\forall R.C$ which have been added as type labels to an individual e.

$$popuInds(IS) = \bigcup_{e \in IS} popInds(getInds(e, e.AV)) \tag{1}$$

$getInds(e, AV)$ is the function which returns the set of r-neighbours for the individual e, where the relation r is restricted by a universal quantifier of the form $\forall r.c$, which has been added as a type to the individual e. The function is given by equation 2, where OS is the set of objects in the triple $<e, r, OS>$ that contains e and r, and av must be

a universal construct. A universal quantifier can be added to e by the unfolding of a concept already added to e or by application of another expansion rule.

$$getInds(e, AV) = \bigcup_{av \in AV} OS, < e, r, OS >, av \rightarrow \{\forall r.c\} \tag{2}$$

After reasoning has begun, new universal quantifiers may be added to an individual a which is in the set SC. If the new quantifier restricts role R which is not yet restricted by another quantifier added to a, and a has R-neighbours, these neighbours need to be added to SC. Therefore, whenever a universal quantifier av_{new} is added an individual a in SC, R-neighbours are added to SC by a call to $getInds(e, AV)$ such that $\{a.AV = a.AV + av_{new}\} \wedge \{SC = SC + addInds(a, \{av_{new}\})\}$ where $A \in SC$.

For example, for the inference check in section 4.1, $d \in RQ$, a call to $popuInds(\{d\})$ returns only $\{d\}$ because d does not yet contain any universal quantifies. Application of the first element of the disjunction RQ asserts d: $\forall P.(\le 0P)$. A call to $getInds(d, d.AV)$ returns $\{e\}$, because e is a P-neighbour of d and P was restricted in $\forall P.(\le 0P)$, thus $SC = \{d, e\}$ therefore expansion rules for e can now be applied. Application of the second element in RQ asserts d: $\forall R.(\neg A \vee \forall R.(\neg B \vee \neg C))$ and a call to $getInds(d, d.AV_{new})$ returns $\{f\}$ because f is an R-neighbour of d and R was restricted in $\forall R.(\neg A \vee \forall R.(\neg B \vee \neg C))$. Figure 8 illustrates that SC = $\{d, e, f, i, j, k, o\}$, therefore any expansion rules relating to all other individuals n, m, g or h were not applied (shown as crossed out in figure 8).

5.2 Disjunction Skipping

When a disjunction is encountered during the reasoning process, the disjunction skipping strategy determines whether this disjunction is applied to create a new branch or skipped. Let D denote a disjunction, of the form $D = \{d_1 d_2 \dots d_m\}$, where d_i is a disjunction element. Let $nn(e)$ denote e in non-negated form. Non-negated form implies that a negated term is made positive such that $nn(e) = x$ if $e = x$, or $nn(e) = x$ if $e = x$, where x is a class type name or logical expression. D is applied if at least one of its non-negated elements $nn(d_i)$ is contained within the set DS, such that $\exists_{d_i \in D} nn(d_i) \in DS$. Let DS denote a set of class type names and logical expressions defined in the ontology.

For the membership inference check IRQ, DS is populated using the $popu(E)$ function such that $DS = popu(RQ)$, where RQ is the negated request type definition. We assume RQ was a conjunction, RQ is a disjunction D. $popu(E)$, given in expression 3, recursively collects terms which can be derived from elements in the set E of class terms or expressions.

$$popu(E) = \bigcup_{e \in E} nn(e) + pop(decomp(e)) \quad (3)$$

E may be a conjunction of the form $E = \{e_1 \dots e_m\}$, a disjunction of the form $E = \{e_1 \dots e_m\}$, or generic set $E = \{e_1, \dots, e_m\}$. Let $decomp(e)$ denote the function which returns a empty or non-empty set, of terms and expressions which can be derived from e. $decomp(e)$ is given in expression 4. Derived implies that where e is a universal or existential quantifier then $decomp(e)$ returns a

set containing the role filler for e or where e is a unary atomic term an empty or non-empty set is returned containing its expanded expressions, retrieved, using the $unfold(e)$ function.

$$decomp(e) \begin{cases} \{C\} & if \quad e = \forall R.C \vee e = \exists R.C, \\ unfold(e) & if \quad e^1 \end{cases} \quad (4)$$

For example for the type check in section 4.1, $d \in RQ$, $\neg RQ$ unfolds to

$$\forall P.(\leq 0P) \vee \forall R.(\neg A \vee \forall R.(\neg B \vee \neg C)).$$

Therefore, $DS = popu(\neg RQ) = \{RQ, \forall P.(\leq 0P) \vee \forall R.(\neg A \vee \forall R.(\neg B \vee \neg C))$, $\forall P.(\leq 0P)$, $\forall R.(\neg A \vee \forall R.(\neg B \vee \neg C))$, $\neg A \vee \forall R.(\neg B \vee \neg C))$, A, $\forall R.(\neg B \vee \neg C)$, $\neg B \vee \neg C$, $B\}$. As a result, the disjunctions $\{UY\}$ and $\{\neg Y \ \neg Z\}$ are skipped because none of their non-negated elements are contained in DS, while all other disjunctions are applied, as illustrated in figure 9.

5.3 Weighted Disjunctions and Terms

This strategy seeks to manage the order in which completion rules for disjunctions, existential quantifiers and maximum cardinality in the knowledge base are applied, such that the expressions which are most likely to contribute to a clash, are ap-

Figure 8. Selective Consistency

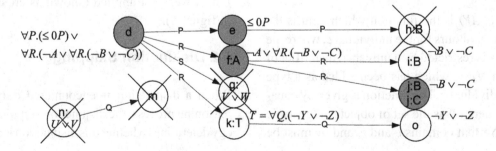

plied first. The order of application for all other expressions remains arbitrary. This strategy does not compromise completeness.

A weighted queue Q is used in two instances. A weighted disjunction queue Q^{disj} maintains the order in which disjunctions will be applied for a particular individual A. The order of existential quantifier and maximum cardinality rule application is maintained by the role restriction queue Q^{rest}. A queue Q contains pairs $<object(x), weight(x)>$ such that $object(x)$ is an object and $weight(x)$ is a positive integer representing the weight of $object(x)$ and multiple $object(x)$ can have the same weight(x). $nweight(x)$ is a double value representing a normalised weight for $object(x)$ *such that* $0 \leq normalised(x) \leq 1$. Normalised values are calculated by dividing the current weight by the highest weight in the queue, given by

$$nweight(x) = weight(x)\Big/\max_{x \in Q^{ind}}(weight(x))$$

Queue objects $object(x)$ are given by the queue iterator in descending $nweight(x)$ order [1..0].

This strategy employs two different approaches: disjunction weighting and term weighting. Both approaches utilise the *ClashDetect(C, I, CP)* function which attempts to find a pathway from term C (asserted to individual I) to a potential clash and returns a set CP containing terms (disjunctions, existential quantifiers and maximum cardinality expressions) if a clash pathway was found, or an empty set if no clash was found. All weight values $weight(x)$ of expressions x in the clash pathway are incremented, such that $increment_{x \in ClashDetect(C,I,CP)}(weight(x))$ and $increment(v) = v++$. Note, if a term forms a clash path, but is not yet asserted to the individual, its weight is maintained by the queue and used in the event that it is added as a type for the individual.

ClashDetect(I, C, CP) calls the function which handles each kind of expression passed to it. For instance, if C is a maximum cardinality restriction it calls *CheckMaxRestriction(I, mx, CP)*. *ClashDetect(I, C, CP)* pseudo code is given below. Each of the functions referred to in the above pseudo code, are described in Appendix A.

```
ClashDetect:
Inputs: Let I be an individual, Let C
be a type, Let CP be a set of indi-
viduals and logic expressions in-
volved in a clash.
Outputs: CP
Switch(C)
Case C is primitive, negation, nomi-
nal or literal value:
Return CheckPrimitive(I, C, CP).
Case C is a disjunction:
Return CheckDisjunction(I, C, CP).
Case C is a conjunction:
Return CheckConjunction(I, C, CP).
Case C is a universal quantifier
logic expression:
Return CheckUniversalQuantifier(I, C,
CP).
```

Figure 9. Selective Consistency

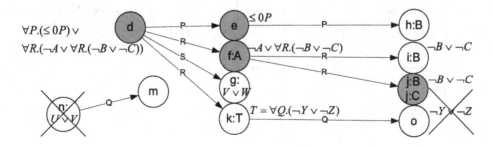

```
Case C is an existential quantifier
logic expression:
Return CheckExistentialQuantifier(I,
C, CP).
Case C is a maximum role restriction
logic expression:
Return CheckMaxRestriction(I, C, CP).
```

For example for the type check in section 4.1, $d \in RQ$, $\neg RQ$ unfolds to $\forall P.(\leq 0P) \lor \forall R.(\neg A \lor \forall R.(\neg B \lor \neg C))$. A clash pathway exists which includes: $\{$d:$\neg$RQ, e: $\leq 0P$, f: $\neg A \lor \forall R.(\neg B \lor \neg C)$, j: $\neg B \lor \neg C$ $\}$. Therefore all the disjunctions and expressions involved in this path are incremented. The individuals involved are shaded in figure 7, section 4.1. The queues are illustrated in figure 10.

Now that we have detailed our optimisation strategies, we discuss our work in implementing the strategies in the next section. We also provide a performance evaluation comprising a comparison with current reasoners and performance on a resource-constrained device.

6 IMPLEMENTATION AND PERFORMANCE EVALUATION

In this section we provide two case studies in order to evaluate our mTableaux algorithm to answer the following two main questions:

1. How does mTableaux perform when compared to other reasoners?
   a. Since mTableaux does not guarantee completeness for all strategies, how much does mTableaux impact on result accuracy reduced, as measured using recall and precision?
2. How does mTableaux scale in terms of meeting the twin constraints of processing time and memory usage on a mobile device?
   a. Does mTableaux enable successful completion of a reasoning task such that a result can be obtained on a resource constrained device (i. e., available memory was not exceeded)?
   b. Does mTableaux significantly improve performance compared to normal execution of Tableaux with no optimisation strategies enabled?
   c. Which mTableaux strategies or combination of strategies work best?
   d. Do different strategies work better for different scenarios / reasoning tasks?
   e. Do the optimisation strategies improve performance for positive as well as negative type checks?

We do this using two case studies as well as the Galen[3] ontology. Our two case studies are detailed in the next two subsections.

Figure 10. Example disjunction and role restriction queue

Q_{disj} *object(x)*	Q_{disj} *nweight(x)*
d: $\neg A \lor \forall R.(\neg B \lor \neg C)$.	1.0
j: $\neg B \lor \neg C$	1.0
i: $\neg B \lor \neg C$.	0
n: $U \lor V$.	0
o: $\neg Y \lor \neg Z$.	0

Q_{rest} *object(x)*	Q_{rest} *nweight(x)*
e: $\leq 0P$.	1.0

6.1 Case Study 1: Searching for a Printer

Bob is walking around at his university campus and wishes to locate laser printer-fax machine (to print some documents and send a fax). He issues a service request from his PDA for a listing of black and white, laser printers which support a wireless network protocol such as Bluetooth, WiFi or IrDA, a fax protocol and which have a dialup modem with a phone number. Equations 5-8 show Bob's request in Description Logic (DL) (Baader et al., 2003) form, while equation 9 presents a possible printer.

$$\text{PrinterRequest} \equiv \text{PhModem} \wedge \text{hasColour.}\{\text{Black}\} \wedge \text{hasComm.}\{\text{Fax}\} \wedge \text{LaserPrinterOperationalWNet} \quad (5)$$

$$\text{PhModem} \equiv \text{hasComm.}(\text{Modem} \wedge \geq 1 \text{ phNumber}) \quad (6)$$

$$\text{LaserPrinterOperational} \equiv \text{Printer} \wedge \text{hasCartridge.}\{\text{Toner}\} \wedge \geq 1 \text{ hasOperationalContext} \quad (7)$$

$$\text{WNet} \equiv \text{hasComm.}\{\text{BT}\} \wedge \text{hasComm.}\{\text{WiFi}\} \wedge \text{hasComm.}\{\text{IrDA}\} \quad (8)$$

Printer(LaserPrinter1),hasColour(LaserPrinter1, Black), hasCartridge(LaserPrinter1, Toner), hasComm(LaserPrinter1, BT), hasComm(LaserPrinter1, Fax), hasOperationalContext(LaserPrinter1, Ready), Modem(Modem1), hasComm(LaserPrinter1, Modem1), phNumber (Modem1, "9903 9999") $\quad (9)$

Note, these equations are simplified for illustrative purposes, the actual ontology used for this case study comprises 141 classes, 337 individuals and 126 roles. Equation 5 defines five attributes in the request, the first is unfolded into equation 6, specifying the printer must have a modem which has a phone number. The second attribute specifies

a black and white requirement. The third attribute requires support for the fax protocol, and the fourth unfolds into equation 7, specifying a printer which has a toner cartridge and at least one operational context. The fifth unfolds into equation 8, which specified that one of the wireless protocols (Bluetooth, WiFi or IrDA) are supported. Equation 9 shows a DL fragment defining the LaserPrinter1 individual as meeting the service request. We also define an individual LaserPrinter2 as the same as equation 9, but without a phone number.

6.2 Case Study 2: Searching for a Movie Cinema

Bob is in a foreign city centre and has walked past several shops, short range ontology download points, and other people carrying devices with accumulated ontologies of their own. As such Bob collects a range of ontologically described service advertisements. He sits down in a park out of network range, and decides to find a movie cinema with a café attached which has a public phone and WiFi public Internet. He issues a request for a retail outlet which has at least 5 cinemas that each screen movies, has a section which sells coffee and tea, sells an Internet service which supports access using the WiFi protocol and sells a fixed phone service. We specify that an individual VillageCinemas matches the service request and GreaterUnionCinemas is the same as VillageCinemas except it provides Bluetooth Internet access rather than by WiFi, and therefore fails to match the request. The request specifies universal and existential quantifier and cardinality restrictions. The ontologies for this scenario contain 204 classes, 241 individuals and 93 roles.

6.3 Implementation

Our mTableaux strategies have been implemented as an extension to the Pellet 1.5 reasoner which supports OWL-DL with SHOIN expressivity. That is, mTableaux is implemented into the Pellet source tree. (Sirin, Parsia, Grau, Kalyanpur & Katz, 2007) discusses the implementation and design of Pellet. We chose Pellet because it is open source, allowing us to provide a proof of concept and compare performance with and without the strategies enabled. We selected Pellet over FaCT++ because it is written in Java, making it easily portable to small devices such as PDAs and mobile phones, while FaCT++ is written in C++. An addition, we are using Jena as the ontology repository used by Pellet to read the ontology. We implemented the optimisation strategies: selective consistency, skip disjunctions, and rank by disjunctions and terms, and we evaluate the impact these have on performance in the next sections. We intend to make the source code for the system available for download on completion of the project.

6.4 Comparison of mTableaux with Other Reasoners

In order to show how mTableaux compares to other widely used OWL semantic reasoners, we provide a performance comparison with FaCT++ 1.1.11, RacerPro 1.9.2 beta and Pellet 1.5 without our optimisations. As stated in section 4.2, these reasoners perform an ontology "realisation" in which consistency checks are used to determine all the inferred class types for every individual in the ontology, $I_{[1, 2,..,n]} \in RQ_{[1, 2,..,m]}$, where n denotes the number of individuals in the ontology and m denotes the number of classes, resulting in $n.m$ possible individual and class combinations. Subsequent queries to the reasoner then draw from this pre-inferred data. Since an ontology realisation is unnecessary for service discovery in which specific service candidates are compared against single request class types, mTableaux does not perform an ontology realisation. Therefore, our performance evaluation presents two results for mTableaux one with full realisation and one where a subset of individuals are compared against a single user request class type such that $I_{[1, 2,..,n]} \in$

RQ. The individuals represent discoverable services.

The evaluation was conducted on a Pentium Centrino 1.82GHz computer with 2GB memory with Java 1.5 (J2SE) allocated maximum of 500MB for each experiment. All times are presented are computed as the average of 10 independent runs. We performed our evaluation using both of the case studies described in section 6.1 and 6.2, as well as several publically available ontologies, including: Galen[iii], Tambis[4], Koala[5] and Teams[6]. Galen is a large ontology of medical terms with 2748 classes and 844 roles. Tambis, Koala and Teams ontologies have 183, 20 and 9 classes respectively. For each of our Printer and Product ontologies we checked 20 service candidates against the request printer and product user request, respectively. The Galen, Tambis, Koala and Teams ontologies did not contain individuals so we created a matching (positive) and non-matching (negative) individual for request each class type that we checked. The expected results for each ontology are illustrated in table 1.

Figure 11 presents the total time required to perform the 8 inference checks for the Galen ontology and figures 12 and 13 present the total time to check all 20 service individuals against the user request class for the product and printer case studies, respectively. The 4 inference checks for each of the Tambis, Koala and Teams ontologies are not graphed because they completed in under 1 second.

As illustrated in figure 11, mTableaux significantly outperformed the other reasoners for the Galen ontology, requiring only 0.67 seconds to perform the 8 inference checks. mTableaux with realisation almost performed as well as FaCT++ and outperforms RacerPro. Pellet with no optimisations performed poorly, requiring more than 40 seconds to complete. Figure 12 and 13 show that RacerPro performed worst, followed by Pellet, for the Product and Printer ontologies. mTableaux is slower when a full realisation is performed, because this compares irrelevant in-

Table 1. Expected Results for each Ontology

Ontology	Request Class	Positive	Negative	Total
Printer	PrinterRequest	3	17	20
Product	ProductRequest	3	17	20
Galen	BacterialGramPositiveStainResult	1	1	2
	FailureOfCellUptakeOfBloodGlu-coseDueToCellInsulinResistance	1	1	2
	AcutePulmonaryHeartDisease	1	1	2
	LocalAnaesthetic	1	1	2
Tambis	small-nuclear-rna	1	1	2
	peptidase	1	1	2
Koala	MaleStudentWith3Daughters	1	1	2
	KoalaWithPhD	1	1	2
Teams	MarriedPerson	1	1	2
	MixedTeam	1	1	2
Total		16	44	60

Figure 11. Reasoner comparison using Galen ontology

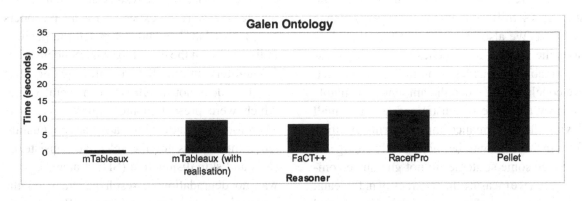

Figure 12. Product Ontology Reasoner Comparison

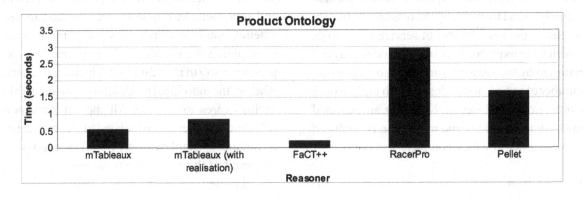

Figure 13. Printer Ontology Reasoner Comparison

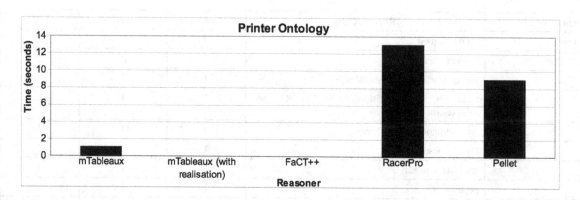

dividuals against the user request. FaCT++ performed slightly better than mTableaux for the Product ontology, which we attribute to its implementation in C++. We note that mTableaux with realisation and FaCT++ could not complete the printer ontology and did not provide a result.

These results show, that our optimisation strategies significantly improve the performance of Pellet. We also observed that for all evaluations the number of branches applied when using mTableaux was less than half that of Pellet. We conclude that when the amount of available memory available is constrained as on a small device, the performance improvements resulting from mTableaux will be significantly enlarged.

Since some strategies to not guarantee completeness, we measure the accuracy of mTableaux compared to other reasoners using recall and precision metrics, as illustrated in equations 10 and 11, where x denotes the number of service individuals which were expected to match but also actually found to match by the reasoner to match, n denotes the total number of service individuals which were expected to match (including any not returned by the reasoner) and N denotes the total number of service individuals which the reasoner claims do indeed match. Note that an expected match implies that a true match can be deduced by a reasoner in which completeness holds.

$$Recall = x \, / \, n. \tag{10}$$

$$Precision = x \, / \, N. \tag{11}$$

The recall and precision results obtained by completing the matching detailed in table 1, are provided in table 2. For instance mTableaux returned all 16 of the service individuals which were expected to match. The results show that the actual results were as expected for all reasoners except that FaCT++ did not match the positive individual with the class type MaleStudentWith-3Daughters in the Koala ontology, because FaCT++ does not match Boolean literal values which were present in the request class type. Therefore, although mTableaux does not guarantee completeness for the selective consistency (SC) and skip disjunction (SD) strategies, there was no degradation in result accuracy on the ontologies tests in our evaluation. We conclude in data sets representing realistic scenarios such as the ones we used, mTableaux does not compromise result completeness as measured by recall and precision. In our tests, we checked to see whether ontology consistency was compromised by applying the negation of a specific class expression $\neg RQ$ to an individual I, in order to check whether the individual holds inferred membership to this expression $I \in RQ$. All applied expansion rules and disjunctions which led to clashes (causing an inconsistent ontology for all models) were the result of the negated expression $\neg RQ$ having been asserted. Since CS and SD strategies include or exclude individuals and disjunctions based on universal quantifies and expressions which result from the individual I and expression $\neg RQ$, respectively, there was no breach of completeness. Completeness may be compromised when the application of disjunctions, or expressions resulting from these disjunctions, do not relate to the expression RQ, which would result in a failure of mTableaux to prove a positive inference. In models of the knowledge base, parts of the ontology which do not relate to the class type RQ involved in the inference check may interact with each other to create clashes. It is in these cases where completeness is not guaranteed.

Since mTableaux outperformed all reasoners except for FaCT++ in some case while preserving completeness in our case studies, we now provide a performance evaluation to show how mTableaux performs on a small resource constrained device, in the next section. We also show which strategies work best together and the level of overhead incurred by using each optimisation.

6.5 mTableaux Performance on a Mobile Device

We performed an evaluation on a HP iPAQ hx2700 PDA, with Intel PXA270 624Mhz processor, 64MB RAM, running Windows Mobile 5.0 with Mysaifu Java J2SE Virtual Machine (JVM) (Mysaifu, 2009), allocated 15MB of memory. We executed the four type check combinations shown in table 1, to evaluate both case study requests against a matching/positive and non-matching/negative service individual, defined as individual A and B, respectively. We executed each of the 4 consistency checks outlined in table 3 with every combination of the 4 optimisation strategies enabled (16 times). Table 4 indicates which strategies were enabled for each of the 16 tests (organised in bitwise order). Pellet with SHOIN expressivity was used for all tests. Test 16 represents normal execution of the Tableaux algorithm, with none of our optimisations strategies enabled. Successfully executed tests returned the expected result shown in table 3.

Figure 14 shows two graphs, which each show the consistency time to perform a type check for individual A and B against the request for the tests in table 3, using Pellet with SHOIN expressivity. The left and right graph present results for the printer and product case studies, respectively. Tests which did not complete due to insufficient available memory or which required more than 800 seconds to execute, omitted from the graph. In addition to consistency checking, an additional 35-40 seconds was required load the ontology into the reasoner (not shown on graph).

Test a, with no optimisations (standard Tableaux algorithm) failed to complete due to insufficient memory. The same occurred for many of the tests which are not shown on the graph. This demonstrates that our strategies reduce memory consumption, making reasoning feasible on resource constrained devices. We note that in all tests, the Java virtual machine (JVM) used all of the memory allocated to it. Since the graphs in figure 14 are difficult to interpret, we re-ordered (see table 5) the tests in an attempt to arrange the fastest processing times at the front of the graph.

Table 2. Total Actual Results for each Reasoner

Reasoner	Actual Positive	Actual Negative	Recall	Precision
mTableaux	16	44	16/16 = 1.0	16/16 = 1.0
Pellet	16	44	16/16 = 1.0	16/16 = 1.0
RacerPro	16	44	16/16 = 1.0	16/16 = 1.0
FaCT++	15	45	15/16 = 0.937	15/15 = 1.0

Table 3. Type membership checks.

Case Study	Request		Individual	Expected Result
Case Study 1	Fax Laser Printer	A	#LaserPrinter1 (with phone number)	Match
		B	#LaserPrinter2 (no phone number)	No Match
Case Study 2	Movie Cinema	A	#MovieCinema2 (WiFi Internet)	Match
		B	#MovieCinema2(Bluetooth Internet)	No Match

Table 4. Optimisation tests.

Test	a	b	c	d	e	f	g	h	i	j	k	l	m	n	o	p
Selective Consistency		×		×		×		×		×		×		×		×
Skip Disjunctions			×	×			×	×			×	×			×	×
Rank by Disjunction					×	×	×	×					×	×	×	×
Rank by Term									×	×	×	×	×	×	×	×

Figure 14. processing time required to perform each test, for Selective Consistency (SC), Skip Disjunction (SD), Rank by Disjunction (RD) and Rank by Term (RT) strategies, showing total consistency time to perform an inferred membership check for matching individual A and non-matching individual B, for the Printer ontology (left) and Product ontology (right).

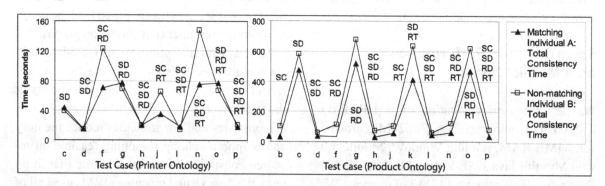

We show the re-ordered results in the graph in figure 15.

With optimisations enabled the best result for case study 1 and 2 was 18 and 35-70 seconds, respectively. This illustrates significant performance improvements in both scenarios.

When used in isolation, the selective consistency strategy proved to be the most effective in case study 2, while skip disjunctions was more effective in case study 1. Utilising both of these strategies together provided even better results,

which suggests there is no advantage in selecting different strategies for different scenarios.

We found that the weighted strategies (rank by disjunctions and terms) did reduce the number of disjunction branches applied, by up to half in some cases, but this failed to significantly reduce the number of consistency rules applied overall. In addition, the ranking strategies did not improve performance when used in combination with the selective consistency and skip disjunction strategies. However, we observed that tests 13, 14, and

Table 5. Re-ordered Optimisation tests.

Test #	1	2	3	4	5	6	7	8	9	10	11	12	13	14	15	16
Selective Consistency	×	×	×	×	×	×		×	×							
Skip Disjunctions	×	×	×	×			×			×	×	×				
Rank by Disjunction			×	×				×	×	×	×		×	×		
Rank by Term		×	×			×			×	×		×	×		×	

Figure 15. Re-ordered processing time required to perform each test, for Selective Consistency (SC), Skip Disjunction (SD), Rank by Disjunction (RD) and Rank by Term (RT) strategies, showing total consistency time to perform an inferred membership check for matching individual A and non-matching individual, for the Printer ontology (left) and Product ontology (right).

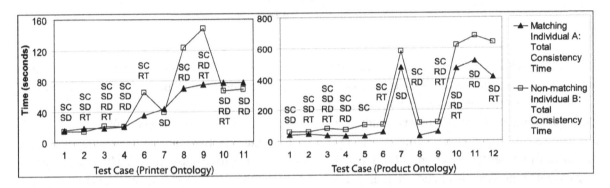

15, when matching individual A, in case study two, completed in 972, 982 and 983 seconds (not shown on graph), respectively, compared to 2139 seconds in test 16. This suggests that the rank disjunction and individual strategies improve performance but are far less effective than selective consistency or skip disjunction strategies. These ranking algorithms need to be improved in future work.

Due to the fact that our selective consistency and disjunction skipping strategies reduce the number of potential rules and disjunctions to be applied, they improve performance in all cases. However, the results also showed that the optimisations can be less effective in improving performance for non-matching individuals B than with matching individuals A, as shown in every test in case study 2 and some in case study 1. This is because the Tableaux algorithm continues applying branches and consistency rules until a clash is found. This will inherently result in more rules to apply for non-matching individuals which do not clash for all branches. This finding also motivates the need for a resource-aware strategy, in which branches below a certain threshold are not applied, where resources are low, to assume no-match with some uncertainty rating.

Figure 16 illustrates the overhead cost incurred in executing the optimisation strategies for each test in from table 5, and shows the level to which each strategy contributes to the total overhead for the test. Each test is completed twice, for both matching individual A and non-matching individual B. We observed that skip disjunctions resulted in little to no overhead in all cases. Overhead costs for selective consistency was similar for both case studies, usually remaining under 5 seconds and peaking to 18 in tests 8B and 9B (test 8 and 9 for individual B) in case study 1, indicating a greater number of individuals to

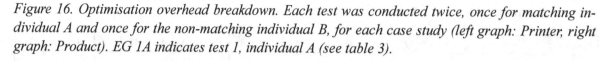

Figure 16. Optimisation overhead breakdown. Each test was conducted twice, once for matching individual A and once for the non-matching individual B, for each case study (left graph: Printer, right graph: Product). EG 1A indicates test 1, individual A (see table 3).

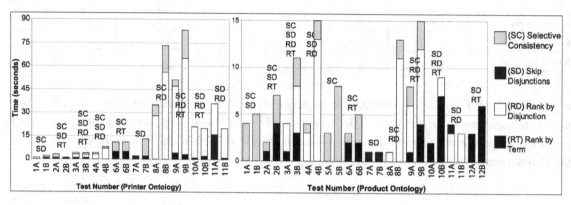

add to the weighted queue. Case study 1 recorded higher rank disjunction overhead than case study 2, suggesting there were fewer disjunctions and clash paths in the ontologies of case study 2, to evaluate. Rank disjunction overhead was also significantly higher for tests 8 and 9 for both case studies due to the skip disjunction strategy being disabled. It was also higher when type checking individual B compared to A, due to the reasoner exhaustively branching on disjunctions where a clash is never found.

In summary, we have demonstrated that:

1. mTableaux outperforms reasoners such as RacerPro and Pellet, performs comparatively with FaCT++ when full realisation is performed and faster than FaCT++ when it is not,

2. mTableaux does not compromise completeness as measured by recall and precision when all clashes are the direct consequence of the inference check rather than other unrelated concepts in the ontology as in realistic data sets such as those in our evaluation,

3. mTableaux minimises memory consumption such that successful completion of reasoning tasks on resource limited devices is possible,

4. mTableaux significantly reduces processing time compared with normal Tableaux with no optimisations,

5. selective consistency and skip disjunction strategies work best together while rank by disjunction and term strategies provided no added performance benefit,

6. the selective consistency strategy was more effective in case study 2 while skip disjunctions was more effective in case study 1, and provided the best results for both scenarios when used together, and

7. mTableaux strategies improved performance for both positive and negative type checks, however overall performance for negative type checks in case study 2 was poorer, leaving scope for resource-aware reasoning in future work.

7 CONCLUSION AND FUTURE WORK

We have presented a novel strategy for improving the scalability of the Tableaux algorithm for mobile semantic reasoning. mTableaux was shown to significantly reduce processing time and minimize memory consumption of pervasive discovery reasoning tasks in two case studies, so that they can be completed on small resource constrained devices. It was also shown to outperform RacerPro and Pellet without reducing the quality of results returned in realistic datasets such as in our scenarios. It also performed comparatively with FaCT++ when a full realisation was undertaken and outperformed FaCT++ when a realisation was not. The mTableaux strategies achieve this by limiting the number of branches and expansion rules applied and by applying the most important branches first to avoid the need for full branch saturation.

However, despite these significant optimisations, it is still possible that large ontologies may still exhaust all available memory before completing the task or require excessive amounts of time. In order to cater for time and memory constraints in situations where ontology or request size is too large even with the optimisation strategies enabled we are implementing the adaptive strategies briefly mentioned in section 4.2 which take available memory and time into consideration:

- The adaptive request condition matching strategy has the goal of matching first, the most important conditions in the request as deemed by the user, at the request level. The user is asked to specify weights of importance to each request condition. The most important conditions are matched first. In the event that important conditions do not match the reasoner will not continue to attempt to match less important conditions, if a threshold is exceeded. The threshold is determined based on the amount of time and memory available, under the assumption that limited processing power is better spent attempting to match another potential service.

- Our adaptive expansion rule application strategy utilises the weighted expansion rules from the weighted disjunctions and terms strategy in section 5.3. Similar to the strategy above, its goal is to stop the application of expansion rules which have a weight that falls below a certain threshold, except this occurs at the reasoner level.

The threshold is increased when remaining time or memory becomes low.

- On-demand ontology loading has a goal of only loading of portions of the total ontology into the reasoner's memory. Reasoners such as Pellet, currently utilise an ontology parser and loader such as Jena (Jena, 2009) or OWL-API (WonderWeb, 2008) to load ontology files into memory. This data is then supplied in its entirety to the reasoner which creates classes, roles and individuals to represent all of this information as objects. Loading all of these parsed triples into the reasoner incurs significant initialisation costs and requires more processing time for lookup and retrieval during reasoning. In addition, if there is insufficient memory available to complete the reasoning task, the task fails even if most of the ontology data was irrelevant to the inference check. Unfder this on-demand loading strategy, rather than iterating all triples in the ontology to create objects in the reasoner, the reasoner instead queries the triples in order to create only the specific classes, roles or individuals which it requires during the reasoning process. That is if a URI of an individual is encountered by the Tableaux algorithm and no individual object is found within the reasoner to match the URI, it asks that the individual and the data associated with it is, be loaded into its knowledge base.

Our current work focuses on implementation and evaluation of these adaptive strategies to enhance the operation of mTableaux.

REFERENCES

Almeida, D. R. d., Bapista, C. S., Silva, E. R. d., Campelo, C. E. C., Figueiredo, H. F. d., & Lacerda, Y. A. (2006). A Context-Aware System Based on Service-Oriented Architecture. In *20th International Conference on Advanced Information Networking and Applications (AINA '06)* (pp. 205-210). IEEE Computer Society.

Arnold, K., O'Sullivan, B., Scheifler, R. W., Waldo, J., & Woolrath, A. (1999). *The Jini Specification*. Addison-Wesley.

Baader, F., Calvanese, D., McGuinness, D. L., Nardi, D., & Patel-Schneider, P. F. (2003). *The Description Logic Handbook: Theory, Implementation, and Applications*. Cambridge University Press.

Broens, T. (2004). *Context-aware, Ontology based, Semantic Service Discovery*. Enschede, The Netherlands, University of Twente: 87.

Cabral, L., Domingue, J., Galizia, S., Gugliotta, A., Tanasescu, V., Pedrinaci, C., et al. (2006). IRS-III: A Broker for Semantic Web Services based Applications. In *5th International Semantic Web Conference (ISWC 2006)*, Athens, GA, USA.

Chakraborty, D., Joshi, A., Yesha, Y., & Finin, T. (2004). Towards Distributed Service Discovery in Pervasive Computing Environments. *IEEE Transactions on Mobile Computing*.

Chakraborty, D., Perich, F., Avancha, S., & Joshi, A. (2001). DReggie: Semantic Service Discovery for M-Commerce Applications. In *Workshop on Reliable and Secure Applications in Mobile Environment, In Conjunction with 20th Symposium on Reliable Distributed Systems (SRDS)*.

Chatti, M. A., Srirama, S., Kensche, D., & Cao, Y. (2006). Mobile Web Services for Collaborative Learning. In *4th International Workshop on Wireless, Mobile and Ubiquitous Technology in Education* (pp. 129-133). IEEE.

Doulkeridis, C., Loutas, N., & Vazirgiannis, M. (2005). A *System Architecture for Context-Aware Service Discovery*.

FaCT++. (2008). Retrieved May 1, 2007, from http://owl.man.ac.uk/factplusplus/.

Guttman, E. (1999). Service Location Protocol: Automatic Discovery of IP Network Services. *IEEE Internet Computing, 3*(4), 71–80. doi:10.1109/4236.780963

Horrocks, I., & Patel-Schneider, P. F. (1999). Optimising Description Logic Subsumption. *Journal of Logic and Computation, 9*(3), 267–293. doi:10.1093/logcom/9.3.267

Horrocks, I., & Sattler, U. (2005). A Tableaux Decision Procedure for SHOIQ. *19th International Conference on Artificial Intelligence (IJCAI 2005)*.

Howes, T. A., & Smith, M. C. (1995). *A Scalable, Deployable Directory Service Framework for the Internet. Technical report.* Center for Information Technology Integration, Univerity of Michigan.

Issarny, V., & Sailhan, F. (2005). Scalable Service Discovery for MANET. *Third IEEE International Conference on Pervasive Computing and Communications (PerCom)*, Kauai Island, Hawaii.

Jena - HP Semantic Framework. (2009). from http://www.hpl.hp.com/semweb/.

KAON2. (2008). Retrieved June 21, 2007, from http://kaon2.semanticweb.org.

Kleemann, T. (2006). Towards Mobile Reasoning. *International Workshop on Description Logics (DL2006)*, Windermere, Lake District, UK.

Küster, U., König-Ries, B., & Klein, M. (2006). Discovery and Mediation using DIANE Service Descriptions. *Second Semantic Web Service Challenge 2006 Workshop*, Budva, Montenegro.

Lee, C., Helal, A., Desai, N., Verma, V., & Arslan, B. (2003). Konark: A System and Protocols for Device Independent, Peer-to-Peer Discovery and Delivery of Mobile Services. *IEEE Transactions on Systems, Man, and Cybernetics, 33*(6).

Miller, B. A., & Pascoe, R. A. (2000). Salutation Service Discovery in Pervasive Computing Environments. *IBM Pervasive Computing White Paper*.

Mysaifu, J. V. M. (2009). Retrieved from http://www2s.biglobe.ne.jp/~dat/java/project/jvm/index_en.html.

OWL-API. (2008). Retrieved from http://owlapi.sourceforge.net/.

Pellet. (2003). Retrieved from http://www.mindswap.org/2003/pellet/.

RacerPro. (2008). Retrieved May 23, 2007, from http://www.racer-systems.com.

Roto, V., & Oulasvirta, A. (2005). Need for Non-Visual Feedback with Long Response Times in Mobile HCI. *International World Wide Web Conference Committee (IW3C2)*, Chiba, Japan.

Sirin, E., Parsia, B., Grau, B. C., Kalyanpur, A., & Katz, Y. (2007). Pellet: A Practical OWL-DL Reasoner. *Web Semantics: Science, Services and Agents on the World Wide Web, 5*(2).

Srinivasan, N., Paolucci, M., & Sycara, K. (2005). Semantic Web Service Discovery in the OWL-S IDE. *39th Hawaii International Conference on System Sciences*, Hawaii.

Sycara, K., Widoff, S., Klusch, M., & Lu, J. (2002). LARKS: Dynamic Matchmaking Among Heterogeneous Software Agents in Cyberspace. *Autonomous Agents and Multi-Agent Systems, 5*, 173–203. doi:10.1023/A:1014897210525

Universal Description Discovery and Integration (UDDI). (2009). Retrieved from http://uddi.xml.org/.

Universal Plug and Play (UPnP). (2007). Retrieved March 12, 2007, from http://www.upnp.org.

Web Service Modelling Ontology (WSMO) Working Group. (2009). Retrieved from http://www.wsmo.org/.

ENDNOTES

1   http://www.google.com/mobile
2   http://www.yahoo.com/mobile
3   http://www.cs.man.ac.uk/~horrocks/OWL/Ontologies/galen.owl
4   http://www.mindswap.org/ontologies/debugging/miniTambis.owl
5   http://protege.stanford.edu/plugins/owl/owl-library/koala.owl
6   http://www.mindswap.org/ontologies/team.owl

APPENDIX A

This section provides pseudo code detailing the functions referred to in section 5.3. Note that hasType(I, C) returns true if individual I has been assigned the class type C, and unfold(C) returns a set of all logic expressions and type names which type C is the equivalent of.

CheckPrimitive

```
Inputs: I, C, CP. Outputs: CP.
Let I denote an individual.
Let C denote a primitive class name or a literal value.
Let CP denote a set (clash path).
Let S denote a set S = {}.
If hasType(I, ¬ C):
CP ← I + CP.
Return CP.
Else:
S ← unfold(C).
Foreach y_i in S:
CP ← ClashDetect(I, y_i, CP).
If CP ≠ null: Return CP.
Return null.
CheckDisjunction
Inputs: I, D, CP. Outputs: CP.
Let I denote an individual.
Let D denote a disjunction.
Let CP denote a set (clash path).
Let S denote a set S = {}.
Let e denote a disjunct element in D where D = {e_1 ∨ e_2 ∨...∨e_n }.
For each e_i in D:
S ← ClashDetect(I, e_i, CP).
If S = null: Return null.
Else: CP ← S + CP.
Return CP.
CheckConjunction
Inputs: I, C, CP. Outputs: CP.
Let I denote an individual.
Let C denote a conjunction.
Let CP denote a set (clash path).
Let S denote a set S = {}.
Let e denote a conjunct element in C where C = {e_1 ∧ e_2 ∧ ... ∧ e_n }.
For each e_i in C:
S ← ClashDetect(I, e_i, CP).
If S ≠ null:
CP ← S + CP.
Return CP.
Return null.
```

CheckUniversalQuantifier

Inputs: I, av, CP.
Outputs: CP.
Let I denote an individual.
Let CP denote a set (clash path).
Let av denote a universal restriction expression, let avR denote the role to which av applies to, let avC denote the role filler type defined in av for avR, such that av=$\forall avR.avC$.
Let o_i denote an avR-neighbour to I.
Let O = {o_1, o_2, o_n}.
Let denote a set S = {}.
For each o_i in O:
S ← ClashDetect(O_i, avC, CS).
If $S \neq$ null:
CP ← S + CP.
Return CP.
Return null.

CheckExistentialQuantifier

Inputs: I, sv, CP. Outputs: CP.
Let I denote an individual.
Let CP denote a set (clash path).
Let sv denote an existential quantifier restriction, let svR denote the role to which sv applies to and let svC denote the role filler type for svR defined in sv such that sv = $\exists svR.svC$.
Let mx denote a maximum cardinality role restriction, let mxN denote the cardinality value defined in mx and let mxR denote the role to which mx applies to, such that mx=($\leq$ mxR mxN).
Let o_i denote an svR-neighbour to I.
Let O = {o_1, o_2, o_n}, where $o_i \neq o_{i+1..n}$.
Let mx_i^{SVR} denote an mx which applies to the role svR.
Let MX = {mx_1^{SVR}, mx_2^{SVR}, mx_m^{SVR}}.
For each o_i in O:
If (svR is a functional role) AND ($n \geq 1$ AND hasType(o_i, $\neg SVC$)):
Return $CP + I + SV$.
Else:
For each mx_i^{SVR} in MX:
If $mxN_i \leq n + 1$ AND hasType(o_i, $\neg SVC$):
Return $CP + I + SV + MX$.

CheckMaxRestriction

Inputs: I, mx, CP. Outputs: CP.
Let I denote an individual.
Let CP denote a set (clash path).
Let mx denote a maximum cardinality role restriction, let mxN denote the cardinality value defined in mx and let mxR denote the role to which mx applies to, such that mx=($\leq$ mxR mxN)
Let o_i denote an mxR-neighbour to I.
Let $O = \{o_1, o_2, o_n\}$, where $o_i \neq o_{i+1..n}$.
If $mxN < n$:
Return $CP + I + mx$.

This work was previously published in International Journal on Semantic Web and Information Systems, Volume 5, Issue 2, edited by Amit P. Sheth, pp. 91-116, copyright 2009 by IGI Publishing (an imprint of IGI Global).

Chapter 8
Linked Data:
The Story So Far

Christian Bizer
Freie Universität Berlin, Germany

Tom Heath
Talis Information Ltd, UK

Tim Berners-Lee
Massachusetts Institute of Technology, USA

ABSTRACT

The term "Linked Data" refers to a set of best practices for publishing and connecting structured data on the Web. These best practices have been adopted by an increasing number of data providers over the last three years, leading to the creation of a global data space containing billions of assertions— the Web of Data. In this article, the authors present the concept and technical principles of Linked Data, and situate these within the broader context of related technological developments. They describe progress to date in publishing Linked Data on the Web, review applications that have been developed to exploit the Web of Data, and map out a research agenda for the Linked Data community as it moves forward.

INTRODUCTION

The World Wide Web has radically altered the way we share knowledge by lowering the barrier to publishing and accessing documents as part of a global information space. Hypertext links allow users to traverse this information space using Web browsers, while search engines index the documents and analyse the structure of links between them to infer potential relevance to users' search queries (Brin & Page, 1998). This functionality has been enabled by the generic, open and extensible nature of the Web (Jacobs & Walsh, 2004), which is also seen as a key feature in the Web's unconstrained growth.

Despite the inarguable benefits the Web provides, until recently the same principles that enabled the Web of documents to flourish have not been applied to data. Traditionally, data published on the Web has been made available as raw dumps in formats such as CSV or XML, or marked up as HTML tables, sacrificing much of its structure

DOI: 10.4018/978-1-60960-593-3.ch008

and semantics. In the conventional hypertext Web, the nature of the relationship between two linked documents is implicit, as HTML is not sufficiently expressive to enable individual entities described in a particular document to be connected by typed links to related entities.

However, in recent years the Web has evolved from a global information space of linked documents to one where both documents and data are linked. Underpinning this evolution is a set of best practices for publishing and connecting structured data on the Web known as Linked Data. The adoption of the Linked Data best practices has lead to the extension of the Web with a global data space connecting data from diverse domains such as people, companies, books, scientific publications, films, music, television and radio programmes, genes, proteins, drugs and clinical trials, online communities, statistical and scientific data, and reviews. This Web of Data enables new types of applications. There are generic Linked Data browsers which allow users to start browsing in one data source and then navigate along links into related data sources. There are Linked Data search engines that crawl the Web of Data by following links between data sources and provide expressive query capabilities over aggregated data, similar to how a local database is queried today. The Web of Data also opens up new possibilities for domain-specific applications. Unlike Web 2.0 mashups which work against a fixed set of data sources, Linked Data applications operate on top of an unbound, global data space. This enables them to deliver more complete answers as new data sources appear on the Web.

The remainder of this article is structured as follows. In Section 2 we provide an overview of the key features of Linked Data. Section 3 describes the activities and outputs of the Linking Open Data project, a community effort to apply the Linked Data principles to data published under open licenses. The state of the art in publishing Linked Data is reviewed in Section 4, while Section 5 gives an overview of Linked Data ap-

plications. Section 6 compares Linked Data to other technologies for publishing structured data on the Web, before we discuss ongoing research challenges in Section 7.

What is Linked Data?

In summary, Linked Data is simply about using the Web to create typed links between data from different sources. These may be as diverse as databases maintained by two organisations in different geographical locations, or simply heterogeneous systems within one organisation that, historically, have not easily interoperated at the data level. Technically, Linked Data refers to data published on the Web in such a way that it is machine-readable, its meaning is explicitly defined, it is linked to other external data sets, and can in turn be linked to from external data sets.

While the primary units of the hypertext Web are HTML (HyperText Markup Language) documents connected by untyped hyperlinks, Linked Data relies on documents containing data in RDF (Resource Description Framework) format (Klyne and Carroll, 2004). However, rather than simply connecting these documents, Linked Data uses RDF to make typed statements that link arbitrary things in the world. The result, which we will refer to as the Web of Data, may more accurately be described as a web of things in the world, described by data on the Web.

Berners-Lee (2006) outlined a set of 'rules' for publishing data on the Web in a way that all published data becomes part of a single global data space:

1. Use URIs as names for things
2. Use HTTP URIs so that people can look up those names
3. When someone looks up a URI, provide useful information, using the standards (RDF, SPARQL)
4. Include links to other URIs, so that they can discover more things

These have become known as the 'Linked Data principles', and provide a basic recipe for publishing and connecting data using the infrastructure of the Web while adhering to its architecture and standards.

The Linked Data Technology Stack

Linked Data relies on two technologies that are fundamental to the Web: Uniform Resource Identifiers (URIs) (Berners-Lee et al., 2005) and the HyperText Transfer Protocol (HTTP) (Fielding et al., 1999). While Uniform Resource Locators (URLs) have become familiar as addresses for documents and other entities that can be located on the Web, Uniform Resource Identifiers provide a more generic means to identify any entity that exists in the world.

Where entities are identified by URIs that use the *http://* scheme, these entities can be looked up simply by dereferencing the URI over the HTTP protocol. In this way, the HTTP protocol provides a simple yet universal mechanism for retrieving resources that can be serialised as a stream of bytes (such as a photograph of a dog), or retrieving descriptions of entities that cannot themselves be sent across the network in this way (such as the dog itself).

URIs and HTTP are supplemented by a technology that is critical to the Web of Data – RDF, introduced above. Whilst HTML provides a means to structure and link documents on the Web, RDF provides a generic, graph-based data model with which to structure and link data that describes things in the world.

The RDF model encodes data in the form of *subject, predicate, object* triples. The subject and object of a triple are both URIs that each identify a resource, or a URI and a string literal respectively. The predicate specifies how the subject and object are related, and is also represented by a URI.

For example, an RDF triple can state that two people, *A* and *B*, each identified by a URI, are related by the fact that *A* knows *B*. Similarly an RDF triple may relate a person *C* to a scientific article *D* in a bibliographic database by stating that *C* is the author of *D*. Two resources linked in this fashion can be drawn from different data sets on the Web, allowing data in one data source to be linked to that in another, thereby creating a Web of Data. Consequently it is possible to think of RDF triples that link items in different data sets as analogous to the hypertext links that tie together the Web of documents.

RDF links (Bizer, Cyganiak, & Heath, 2007) take the form of RDF triples, where the subject of the triple is a URI reference in the namespace of one data set, while the object of the triple is a URI reference in the other. Figure 1 shows two example RDF links. The first link states that a resource identified by the URI http://www.w3.org/People/Berners-Lee/card#i is member of another resource called http://dig.csail.mit.edu/data#DIG. When the subject URI is dereferenced over the HTTP protocol, the *dig.csail.mit.edu* server answers with a RDF description of the identified resource, in this case the MIT Decentralized Information Group. When the object URI is dereferenced the W3C server provides an RDF graph describing Tim Berners-Lee. Dereferencing the predicate URI http://xmlns.com/foaf/0.1/member yields a definition of the link type *member*, described in RDF using the RDF Vocabulary Definition Language (RDFS), introduced below. The second RDF link connects the description of the film Pulp Fiction in the Linked Movie Database with the description of the film provided by DBpedia, by stating that the URI http://data.linkedmdb.org/resource/film/77 and the URI http://dbpedia.org/resource/Pulp_Fiction_%28film%29 refer to the same real-world entity - the film Pulp Fiction.

RDF Vocabulary Definition Language (RDFS) (Brickley & Guha, 2004) and the Web Ontology Language (OWL) (McGuinness & van Harmelen, 2004) provide a basis for creating vocabularies that can be used to describe entities in the world and how they are related. Vocabularies are collections of classes and properties. Vocabularies

Figure 1. Example RDF links.

```
Subject: ://dig.csail.mit.edu/data#DIG
Predicate: ://xmlns.com/foaf/0.1/member
Object: ://www.w3.org/People/Berners-Lee/card#i

Subject: http://data.linkedmdb.org/resource/film/77
Predicate: http://www.w3.org/2002/07/owl#sameAs
Object: http://dbpedia.org/resource/Pulp_Fiction_%28film%29
```

are themselves expressed in RDF, using terms from RDFS and OWL, which provide varying degrees of expressivity in modelling domains of interest. Anyone is free to publish vocabularies to the Web of Data (Berrueta & Phipps, 2008), which in turn can be connected by RDF triples that link classes and properties in one vocabulary to those in another, thereby defining mappings between related vocabularies.

By employing HTTP URIs to identify resources, the HTTP protocol as retrieval mechanism, and the RDF data model to represent resource descriptions, Linked Data directly builds on the general architecture of the Web (Jacobs & Walsh, 2004). The Web of Data can therefore be seen as an additional layer that is tightly interwoven with the classic document Web and has many of the same properties:

- The Web of Data is generic and can contain any type of data.
- Anyone can publish data to the Web of Data.
- Data publishers are not constrained in choice of vocabularies with which to represent data.
- Entities are connected by RDF links, creating a global data graph that spans data sources and enables the discovery of new data sources.

From an application development perspective the Web of Data has the following characteristics:

- Data is strictly separated from formatting and presentational aspects.
- Data is self-describing. If an application consuming Linked Data encounters data described with an unfamiliar vocabulary, the application can dereference the URIs that identify vocabulary terms in order to find their definition.
- The use of HTTP as a standardized data access mechanism and RDF as a standardized data model simplifies data access compared to Web APIs, which rely on heterogeneous data models and access interfaces.
- The Web of Data is open, meaning that applications do not have to be implemented against a fixed set of data sources, but can discover new data sources at run-time by following RDF links.

The Linking Open Data Project

The most visible example of adoption and application of the Linked Data principles has been the Linking Open Data project[1], a grassroots community effort founded in January 2007 and supported by the W3C Semantic Web Education and Outreach Group[2]. The original and ongoing aim of the project is to bootstrap the Web of Data by identifying existing data sets that are available under open licenses, converting these to RDF according to the Linked Data principles, and publishing them on the Web.

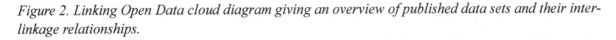

Figure 2. Linking Open Data cloud diagram giving an overview of published data sets and their inter-linkage relationships.

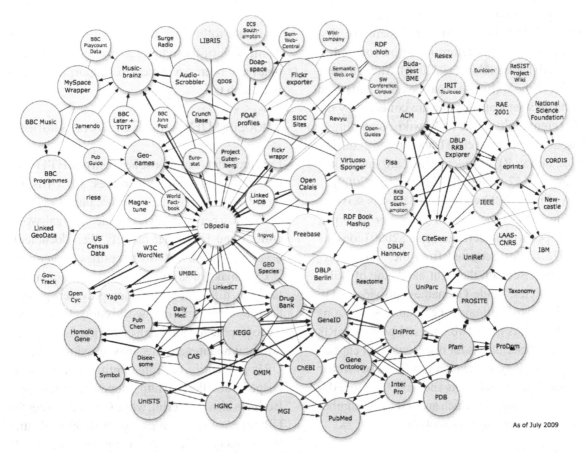

Participants in the early stages of the project were primarily researchers and developers in university research labs and small companies. Since that time the project has grown considerably, to include significant involvement from large organisations such as the BBC, Thomson Reuters and the Library of Congress. This growth is enabled by the open nature of the project, where anyone can participate simply by publishing a data set according to the Linked Data principles and interlinking it with existing data sets. An indication of the range and scale of the Web of Data originating from the Linking Open Data project is provided in Figure 2. Each node in this cloud diagram represents a distinct data set published as Linked Data, as of July 2009.

The arcs in Figure 2 indicate that links exist between items in the two connected data sets. Heavier arcs roughly correspond to a greater number of links between two data sets, while bidirectional arcs indicate the outward links to the other exist in each data set.

The content of the cloud is diverse in nature, comprising data about geographic locations, people, companies, books (Bizer, Cyganiak, & Gauss, 2007), scientific publications (Van de Sompel et al., 2009), films (Hassanzadeh & Consens, 2009), music, television and radio programmes (Kobilarov et al, 2009), genes, proteins, drugs and clinical trials (Belleau et al., 2008; Jentzsch et al., 2009), online communities, statistical data, census results, and reviews (Heath & Motta, 2008).

Calculating the exact size of the Web of Data is challenging due to the fact that much of the data is being generated by wrappers around existing relational databases or APIs and therefore first need to be crawled before it can be counted or analyzed (Hausenblas et al., 2008). Alternatively, the size of the Web of Data can be estimated based on the data set statistics that are collected by the LOD community in the ESW wiki. According to these statistics, the Web of Data currently consists of 6.7 billion RDF triples, which are interlinked by around 142 million RDF links (July 2009)[3].

As Figure 2 shows, certain data sets serve as linking hubs in the Web of Data. For example, the DBpedia data set (Bizer, et al., 2009) consists of RDF triples extracted from the "infoboxes" commonly seen on the right hand side of Wikipedia articles, while Geonames[4] provides RDF descriptions of millions of geographical locations worldwide. As these two data sets provide URIs and RDF descriptions for many common entities or concepts, they are frequently referenced in other more specialised data sets and have therefore developed into hubs to which an increasing number of other data sets are connected.

Publishing Linked Data on the Web

By publishing data on the Web according to the Linked Data principles, data providers add their data to a global data space, which allows data to be discovered and used by various applications. Publishing a data set as Linked Data on the Web involves the following three basic steps:

1. Assign URIs to the entities described by the data set and provide for dereferencing these URIs over the HTTP protocol into RDF representations.
2. Set RDF links to other data sources on the Web, so that clients can navigate the Web of Data as a whole by following RDF links.
3. Provide metadata about published data, so that clients can assess the quality of published

data and choose between different means of access.

In the following, we will give an overview about each of these tasks as well as about tools that have been developed to support publishers with each task.

Choosing URIs and RDF Vocabularies

Data providers can choose between two HTTP URI usage patterns to identify entities: 303 URIs and hash URIs. Both patterns ensure that clients can distinguish between URIs that identify real-world entities and URIs that identify Web documents describing these real-world entities (Sauermann & Cyganiak, 2008). In an open environment like the Web, different information providers publish data about the same real-world entity, for instance a geographic location or a celebrity. As they may not know about each other, they introduce different URIs to identify the same entitiy. For instance, DBpedia uses the URI http://dbpedia.org/resource/Berlin to identify Berlin, while Geonames uses the URI http://sws.geonames.org/2950159/ to identify Berlin. As both URIs refer to the same real-world entity, they are called URI aliases. URI aliases are common on the Web of Data, as it can not realistically be expected that all information providers agree on the same URIs to identify an entity. URI aliases also provide an important social function to the Web of Data as they are dereferenced to different descriptions of the same real-world entity and thus allow different views and opinions to be expressed on the Web. In order to still be able to track that different information providers speak about the same entity, it is common practice that information providers set *owl:sameAs* links to URI aliases they know about.

Different communities have specific preferences on the vocabularies they prefer to use for publishing data on the Web. The Web of Data is therefore open to arbitrary vocabularies being used in parallel. Despite this general openness, it is considered good practice to reuse terms from well-known RDF vocabularies such as FOAF, SIOC, SKOS, DOAP, vCard, Dublin Core, OAI-ORE or GoodRelations wherever possible in order to make it easier for client applications to process Linked Data. Only if these vocabularies do not provide the required terms should data publishers define new, data source-specific terminology (Bizer, Cyganiak, & Heath, 2007). If new terminology is defined, it should be made self-describing by making the URIs that identify terms Web dereferencable (Berrueta & Phipps, 2008). This allows clients to retrieve RDF Schema or OWL definitions of the terms as well as term mappings to other vocabularies. The Web of Data thus relies on a pay as you go data integration approach (Das Sarma & Dong & Halevy, 2008) based on a mixture of using common vocabularies together with data source-specific terms that are connected by mappings as deemed necessary.

A common serialization format for Linked Data is RDF/XML (Beckett, 2004). In situations where human inspection of RDF data is required, Notation3 (Berners-Lee, 1998), and its subset Turtle (Beckett & Berners-Lee, 2008), are often provided as alternative, inter-convertible serializations, due to the greater perceived readability of these formats. Alternatively, Linked Data can also be serialized as RDFa (Adida et al., 2008) which provides for embedding RDF triples into HTML. In the second case, data publishers should use the RDFa *about* URIs to entities in order to allow other data providers to set RDF links to them.

Link Generation

RDF links allow client applications to navigate between data sources and to discover additional data. In order to be part of the Web of Data, data sources should set RDF links to related entities in other data sources. As data sources often provide information about large numbers of entities, it is common practice to use automated or semi-automated approaches to generate RDF links.

In various domains, there are generally accepted naming schemata. For instance, in the publication domain there are ISBN and ISSN numbers, in the financial domain there are ISIN identifiers, EAN and EPC codes are widely used to identify products, in life science various accepted identification schemata exist for genes, molecules, and chemical substances. If the link source and the link target data sets already both support one of these identification schema, the implicit relationship between entities in both data sets can easily be made explicit as RDF links. This approach has been used to generate links between various data sources in the LOD cloud.

If no shared naming schema exist, RDF links are often generated based on the similarity of entities within both data sets. Such similarity computations can build on a large body of related work on record linkage (Winkler, 2006) and duplicate detection (Elmagarmid et al., 2007) within the database community as well as on ontology matching (Euzenat & Shvaiko, 2007) in the knowledge representation community. An example of a similarity based interlinking algorithm is presented in (Raimond et al., 2008). In order to set RDF links between artists in the Jamendo and Musicbrainz data sets, the authors use a similarity metric that compares the names of artists as well as the titles of their albums and songs.

There are several RDF link generation frameworks available, that provide declarative languages for specifying which types of RDF links should be created, which combination of similarity metrics should be used to compare entities and how similarity scores for specific properties are aggregated into an overall score. The Silk framework (Volz et al., 2009) works against local and remote SPARQL endpoints and is designed to be employed in distributed environments without having to replicate data sets locally. The LinQL framework (Hassanzadeh et al., 2009) works over relational databases and is designed to be used together with database to RDF mapping tools such as D2R Server or Virtuoso.

Metadata

Linked Data should be published alongside several types of metadata, in order to increase its utility for data consumers. In order to enable clients to assess the quality of published data and to determine whether they want to trust data, data should be accompanied with meta-information about its creator, its creation date as well as the creation method (Hartig, 2009). Basic provenance meta-information can be provided using Dublin Core terms or the Semantic Web Publishing vocabulary (Carroll et al., 2005). The Open Provenance Model (Moreau et al., 2008) provides terms for describing data transformation workflows. In Zhao et al. (2008), the authors propose a method for providing evidence for RDF links and for tracing how the RDF links change over time

In order to support clients in choosing the most efficient way to access Web data for the specific task they have to perform, data publishers can provide additional technical metadata about their data set and its interlinkage relationships with other data sets: The Semantic Web Crawling sitemap extension (Cyganiak et al., 2008) allows data publishers to state which alternative means of access (SPARQL endpoint, RDF dumps) are provided besides dereferenceable URIs. The Vocabulary Of Interlinked Datasets (Alexander et al., 2009) defines terms and best practices to categorize and provide statistical meta-information about data sets as well as the linksets connecting them.

Publishing Tools

A variety of Linked Data publishing tools has been developed. The tools either serve the content of RDF stores as Linked Data on the Web or provide Linked Data views over non-RDF legacy data sources. The tools shield publishers from dealing with technical details such as content negotiation and ensure that data is published according to the Linked Data community best practices (Sauermann & Cyganiak, 2008; Berrueta & Phipps,

2008; Bizer & Cyganiak & Heath, 2007). All tools support dereferencing URIs into RDF descriptions. In addition, some of the tools also provide SPARQL query access to the served data sets and support the publication of RDF dumps.

- **D2R Server:** D2R Server (Bizer & Cyganiak, 2006) is a tool for publishing non-RDF relational databases as Linked Data on the Web. Using a declarative mapping language, the data publisher defines a mapping between the relational schema of the database and the target RDF vocabulary. Based on the mapping, D2R server publishes a Linked Data view over the database and allows clients to query the database via the SPARQL protocol.

- **Virtuoso Universal Server:** The OpenLink Virtuoso server[5] provides for serving RDF data via a Linked Data interface and a SPARQL endpoint. RDF data can either be stored directly in Virtuoso or can be created on the fly from non-RDF relational databases based on a mapping.

- **Talis Platform:** The Talis Platform[6] is delivered as Software as a Service accessed over HTTP, and provides native storage for RDF/Linked Data. Access rights permitting, the contents of each Talis Platform store are accessible via a SPARQL endpoint and a series of REST APIs that adhere to the Linked Data principles.

- **Pubby:** The Pubby server (Cyganiak & Bizer, 2008) can be used as an extension to any RDF store that supports SPARQL. Pubby rewrites URI requests into SPARQL DESCRIBE queries against the underlying RDF store. Besides RDF, Pubby also provides a simple HTML view over the data store and takes care of handling 303 redirects and content negotiation between the two representations.

- **Triplify:** The Triplify toolkit (Auer et al, 2009) supports developers in extending existing Web applications with Linked Data front-ends. Based on SQL query templates, Triplify serves a Linked Data and a JSON view over the application's database.

- **SparqPlug:** SparqPlug (Coetzee, Heath and Motta, 2008) is a service that enables the extraction of Linked Data from legacy HTML documents on the Web that do not contain RDF data. The service operates by serialising the HTML DOM as RDF and allowing users to define SPARQL queries that transform elements of this into an RDF graph of their choice.
- **OAI2LOD Server:** The OAI2LOD (Haslhofer & Schandl, 2008) is a Linked Data wrapper for document servers that support the Open Archives OAI-RMH protocol.
- **SIOC Exporters:** The SIOC project has developed Linked Data wrappers for several popular blogging engines, content management systems and discussion forums such as WordPress, Drupal, and phpBB[7].

A service that helps publishers to debug their Linked Data site is the Vapour validation service[8]. Vapour verifies that published data complies with the Linked Data principles and community best practices.

Linked Data Applications

With significant volumes of Linked Data being published on the Web, numerous efforts are underway to research and build applications that exploit this Web of Data. At present these efforts can be broadly classified into three categories: Linked Data browsers, Linked Data search engines, and domain-specific Linked Data applications. In the following section we will examine each of these categories.

Linked Data Browsers

Just as traditional Web browsers allow users to navigate between HTML pages by following hypertext links, Linked Data browsers allow users to navigate between data sources by following links expressed as RDF triples. For example, a user may view DBpedia's RDF description of the city of Birmingham (UK), follow a 'birthplace' link to the description of the comedian Tony Hancock (who was born in the city), and from there onward into RDF data from the BBC describing broadcasts in which Hancock starred. The result is that a user may begin navigation in one data source and progressively traverse the Web by following RDF rather than HTML links. The Disco hyperdata browser[9] follows this approach and can be seen as a direct application of the hypertext navigation paradigm to the Web of Data.

Data, however, provides human interface opportunities and challenges beyond those of the hypertext Web. People need to be able to explore the Web of links between items, but also to powerfully analyze data in bulk. The Tabulator (Berners-Lee et al, 2006; Berners-Lee et al, 2008), for example, allows the user traverse the Web of Data, and expose pieces of it in a controlled way, in "outline mode"; to discover and highlight a pattern of interest; and then query for any other similar patterns in the data Web. The results of the query form a table that can then be analyzed with various conventional data presentation methods, such as faceted browsers, maps, timelines, and so on.

Tabulator and Marbles (Becker & Bizer, 2008) (see Figure 3) are among the data browsers which track the provenance of data, while merging data about the same thing from different sources. While authors such as (Karger & Schraefel, 2006) have questioned the use of graph-oriented views over RDF data, as seen in browsers such as FOAF-Naut[10], (Hastrup, Cyganiak, & Bojars, 2008) argue that such interfaces fill an important niche, and describe their Fenfire browser that follows this display paradigm.

Figure 3. The Marbles Linked Data browser displaying data about Tim Berners-Lee. The colored dots indicate the data sources from which data was merged.

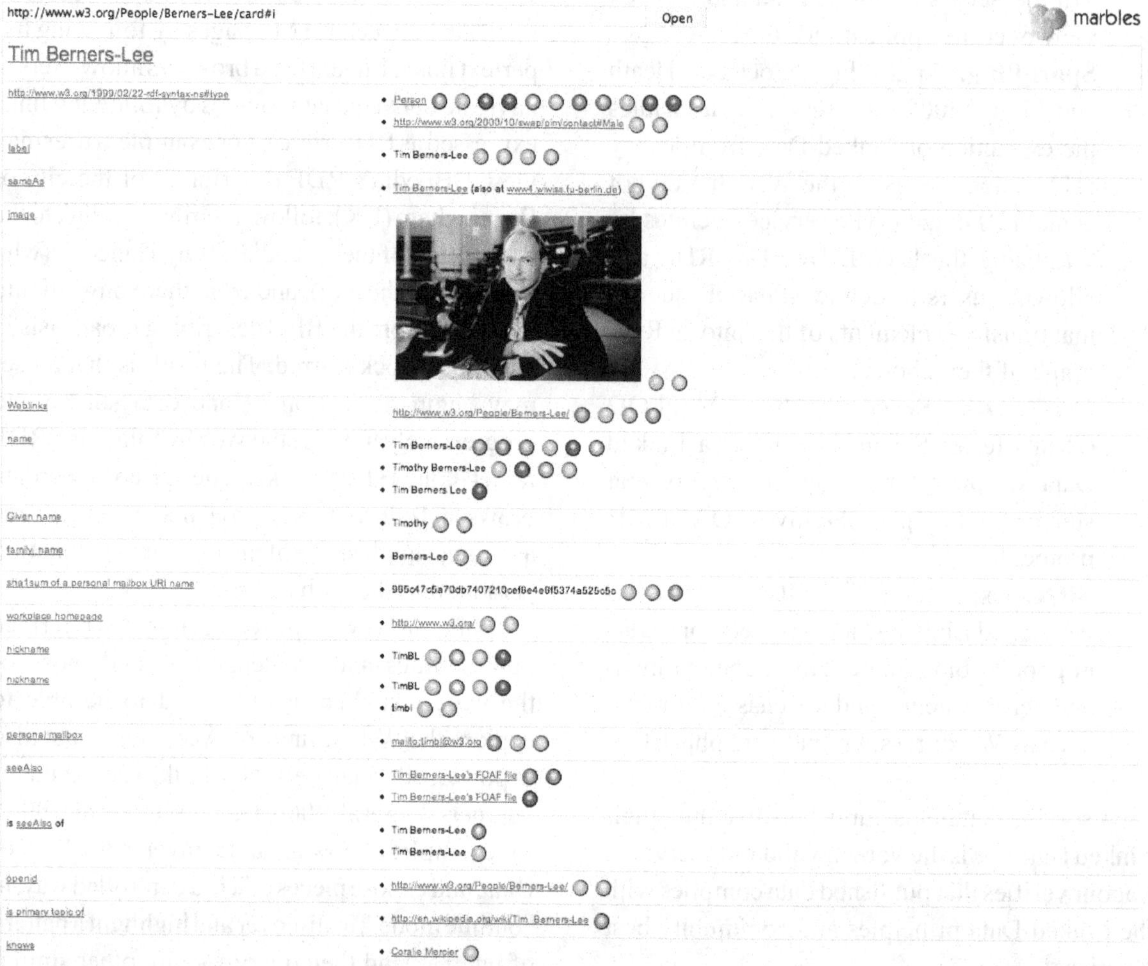

Linked Data Search Engines and Indexes

In the traditional hypertext Web, browsing and searching are often seen as the two dominant modes of interaction (Olston & Chi, 2003). While browsers provide the mechanisms for navigating the information space, search engines are often the place at which that navigation process begins. A number of search engines have been developed that crawl Linked Data from the Web by following RDF links, and provide query capabilities over aggregated data. Broadly speaking, these services can be divided into two categories: human-oriented search engines, and application-oriented indexes.

Human-Oriented Search Engines

Search engines such as Falcons (Cheng & Qu, this issue) and SWSE (Hogan et al., 2007) provide keyword-based search services oriented towards human users, and follow a similar interaction paradigm to existing market leaders such as Google and Yahoo. The user is presented with a search box into which they can enter keywords related to the item or topic in which they are interested, and the application returns a list of results that may be

Figure 4. Falcons object search results for the keyword 'Berlin'

relevant to the query. However, rather than simply providing links from search results through to the source documents in which the queried keywords are mentioned, both SWSE and Falcons provide a more detailed interface to the user that exploits the underlying structure of the data. Both provide a summary of the entity the user selects from the results list, alongside additional structured data crawled from the Web and links to related entities.

Falcons provides users with the option of searching for objects, concepts and documents, each of which leads to slightly different presentation of results. While the object search (Figure 4) is suited to searching for people, places and other more concrete items, the concept search is oriented to locating classes and properties in ontologies published on the Web. The document

search feature provides a more traditional search engine experience, where results point to RDF documents that contain the specified search terms.

It is worth noting that, while they may be referred to as distinct entities, the document Web and the data Web form one connected, navigable information space. For example, a user may perform a search in the existing document Web, follow a link from an HTML document into the Web of Data, navigate this space for some time, and then follow a link to a different HTML document, and so on.

It is interesting to note that while both SWSE and Falcons operate over corpuses of structured data crawled from the Web, they choose to provide very simple query capabilities that mimic the query interfaces of conventional Web search engines.

While one may intuitively expect the additional structure in the data to be exploited to provide sophisticated query capabilities for advanced users at least, this has not proved to be the case to date, with the exception of Tabulator's style of query-by-example and faceted browsing interfaces for query refinement. SWSE does provide access to its underlying data store via the SPARQL query language, however this is suitable primarily for application developers with a knowledge of the language rather than regular users wishing to ask very specific questions through a usable human interface.

Application-Oriented Indexes

While SWSE and Falcons provide search capabilities oriented towards humans, another breed of services have been developed to serve the needs of applications built on top of distributed Linked Data. These application-oriented indexes, such as Swoogle (Ding et al, 2005), Sindice (Oren et al, 2008) and Watson (d'Aquin et al, 2008) provide APIs through which Linked Data applications can discover RDF documents on the Web that reference a certain URI or contain certain keywords. The rationale for such services is that each new Linked Data application should not need to implement its own infrastructure for crawling and indexing all parts of the Web of Data of which it might wish to make use. Instead, applications can query these indexes to receive pointers to potentially relevant documents which can then be retrieved and processed by the application itself. Despite this common theme, these services have slightly different emphases. Sindice is oriented more to providing access to documents containing instance data, while in contrast the emphasis of Swoogle and Watson is on finding ontologies that provide coverage of certain concepts relevant to a query.

Domain-Specific Applications

While the Linked Data browsers and search engines described above provide largely ge-neric functionality, a number of services have been developed that offer more domain-specific functionality by 'mashing up' data from various Linked Data sources.

Revyu

Revyu (Heath & Motta, 2008) is a generic review-ing and rating site based on Linked Data principles and the Semantic Web technology stack. In addition to publishing Linked Data, Revyu consumes Linked Data from the Web to enhance the experience of site users. For example, when films are reviewed on Revyu, the site attempts to match these with the corresponding entry in DBpedia. Where a match is made, additional information about the film (such as the director's name and the film poster) is retrieved from DBpedia and shown in the human-oriented (HTML) pages of the site. In addition, links are made at the RDF level to the corresponding item, ensuring that while human users see a richer view of the item through the mashing up of data from various sources, Linked Data-aware applications are provided with references to URIs from which related data may be retrieved. Similar principles are followed to link items such as books and pubs to corresponding entries in external data sets, and to enhance user profiles with FOAF data.

DBpedia Mobile

DBpedia Mobile (Becker & Bizer, 2008) is a location-aware Linked Data browser designed to be run on an iPhone or other mobile device. DBpe-dia Mobile is oriented to the use case of a tourist exploring a city. Based on the current GPS position of the mobile device, the application provides a location-centric mashup of nearby locations from DBpedia, associated reviews from Revyu, and related photos via a Linked Data wrapper around the Flickr photo-sharing API. Figure 5 shows DBpedia Mobile displaying data from DBpedia and Revyu about the Brandenburg Gate in Berlin. Besides accessing Web data, DBpedia Mobile also enables users to publish their current location, pictures and reviews to the Web as Linked Data, so that they can be used by other applications. Instead of simply being tagged with geographical coordinates, published content is interlinked with a nearby DBpedia resource and thus contributes to the overall richness of the Web of Data.

Talis Aspire

Talis Aspire (Clarke, 2009) is a Web-based Resource List Management application deployed to university lecturers and students. As users create lists through a conventional Web interface, the application produces RDF triples which are persisted to an underlying Linked Data-compatible store. The use of Linked Data principles enables items present on one list to be transparently linked to the corresponding items featured on lists at other institutions, thereby building a Web of scholarly data through the actions of non-specialist users.

BBC Programmes and Music

The British Broadcasting Corporation (BBC) uses Linked Data internally as a lightweight data integration technology. The BBC runs numerous radio stations and television channels. Traditionally, these stations and channels use separate content management systems. The BBC has thus started to use Linked Data technologies together with DBpedia and MusicBrainz as controlled vocabularies to connect content about the same topic residing in different repositories and to augment content with additional data from the Linking Open Data cloud. Based on these connections, BBC Programmes and BBC Music build Linked Data sites for all of its music and programmes related brands (Kobilarov et al., 2009).

DERI Pipes

Modelled on Yahoo Pipes, DERI Pipes (Le Phuoc et al., 2009) provides a data level mashup

Figure 5. DBpedia Mobile displaying information about Berlin

platform that enables data sources to be plugged together to form new feeds of data. The resulting aggregation workflows may contain sophisticated operations such as identifier consolidation, schema mapping, RDFS or OWL reasoning, with data transformations being expressed using SPARQL CONSTRUCT operations or XSLT templates. Figure 6 shows the assembly of a workflow to integrate data about Tim Berners-Lee within the DERI pipes development environment.

Related Developments (in Research and Practice)

There are several other developments related to Linked Data happening on the Web or being pursued by related research communities. In the following sections, we will compare these developments with Linked Data.

Microformats

Similar to Linked Data, Microformats[11] aim at extending the Web with structured data. Microformats define a set of simple data formats that are embedded into HTML via class attributes. Two major differences between Microformats and Linked Data in its RDFa serialization are: Linked Data is not limited in the vocabularies that can be used to represent data, and the vocabulary development process itself is completely open, while Microformats are restricted to a small set of vocabularies developed through a process closely managed by a specific community. Data items that are included in HTML pages via Microformats

Figure 6. DERI pipes workflow integrating data about Tim Berners-Lee from three data sources

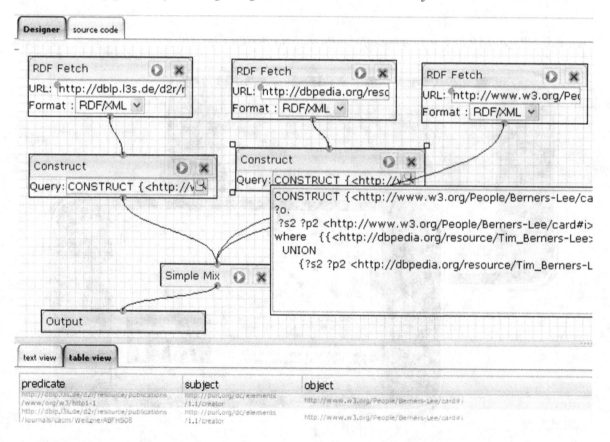

do not have their own identifier. This prevents the assertion, across documents and Web sites, of relationships between data items. By using URIs as global identifiers and RDF to represent relationships, Linked Data does not have these limitations.

Web APIs

Many major Web data sources such as Amazon, eBay, Yahoo!, and Google provide access to their data via Web APIs. The website ProgrammableWeb.com currently lists 1309 Web APIs as well as 3966 mashups based on these APIs. Web APIs are accessed using a wide range of different mechanisms, and data retrieved from these APIs is represented using various content formats. In contrast, Linked Data commits itself to a small set of standardized technologies: URIs and HTTP as identification and access mechanism, RDF as content format. Using a single set of technologies instead of relying on diverse interfaces and result formats allows data sources to be more easily crawled by search engines and accessed using generic data browsers. Beside these technical details, there is also a major conceptual difference between Web APIs and Linked Data: most Web APIs do not assign globally unique identifiers to data items. Therefore it is not possible to set links between items in different data sources in order to connect data into a global data space. Mashups based on these APIs are therefore always implemented against a fixed set of data sources. In contrast, Linked Data applications can work on top of an unbounded, global data space. They can discover new data sources by following RDF links and take advantage of new data sources as they appear on the Web without needing to change the application code. Therefore, Linked Data technologies can contribute to connecting the different data silos that currently exist on the Web back into the single global information space.

Dataspaces

A recent concept within the databases community that is very similar to Linked Data is dataspaces (Franklin et al., 2005). Dataspaces provide a target system architecture around which ongoing research on reference reconciliation, schema matching and mapping, data lineage, data quality and information extraction are unified (Halevy et al., 2006). In contrast with other information-integration systems, dataspaces systems offer best-effort answers before complete semantic mappings are provided to the system. A key idea of dataspaces is that the semantic cohesion of a dataspace is increased over time by different parties providing mappings; the same pay as you go data integration approach that currently emerges on the Web of Data. The Web of Data can therefore be seen as a realization of the dataspaces concept on global scale, relying on a specific set of Web standards in order to be closely aligned with the overall architecture of the Web. It is therefore likely that the Web of Data will benefit considerably from research into dataspaces that is ongoing in the database community.

Semantic Web

The desire to extend the capabilities of the Web to publishing of structured data is not new, and can be traced back to the earliest proposal for the World Wide Web[12] and subsequent papers on the topic (Berners-Lee et al., 1994). Trends foreseen at these early stages of the Web's existence included "Evolution of objects from being principally human-readable documents to contain more machine-oriented semantic information" (Berners-Lee et al., 1994), which can be seen as the seeds of an idea that became known as the Semantic Web.

The vision of a Semantic Web has been interpreted in many different ways (e.g., Berners-Lee, Hendler, & Lassila, 2001; Marshall & Shipman, 2003). However, despite this diversity in interpretation, the original goal of building a global Web of machine-readable data remains constant across the original literature on the subject. According to (Berners-Lee, 2000, p.191), "The first step is putting data on the Web in a form that machines can naturally understand, or converting it to that form. This creates what I call a Semantic Web – a web of data that can be processed directly or indirectly by machines." Therefore, while the Semantic Web, or Web of Data, is the goal or the end result of this process, Linked Data provides the means to reach that goal.

By publishing Linked Data, numerous individuals and groups have contributed to the building of a Web of Data, which can lower the barrier to reuse, integration and application of data from multiple, distributed and heterogeneous sources. Over time, with Linked Data as a foundation, some of the more sophisticated proposals associated with the Semantic Web vision, such as intelligent agents, may become a reality.

Research Challenges

By publishing and interlinking various data sources on the Web, the Linking Open Data community has created an crystallization point for the Web of Data and a challenging test bed for Linked Data technologies. However, to address the ultimate goal of being able to use the Web like a single global database, various remaining research challenges must be overcome.

User Interfaces and Interaction Paradigms

Arguably the key benefit of Linked Data from the user perspective is the provision of integrated access to data from a wide range of distributed and heterogeneous data sources. By definition, this may involve integration of data from sources not explicitly selected by users, as to do so would likely incur an unacceptable cognitive overhead. While the browsers described in Section 5 dem-

onstrate promising trends in how applications may be developed that exploit Linked Data, numerous challenges remain in understanding appropriate user interaction paradigms for applications built on data assembled dynamically in this fashion (Heath, 2008b). For example, while hypertext browsers provide mechanisms for navigation forwards and backwards in a document-centric information space, similar navigation controls in a Linked Data browser should enable the user to move forwards and backwards between entities, thereby changing the focal point of the application. Linked Data browsers will also need to provide intuitive and effective mechanisms for adding and removing data sources from an integrated, entity-centric view. Sigma (Catasta, Cyganiak, & Tummarello, 2009), a search engine based on the Sindice service, gives an indication of how such functionality could be delivered. However understanding how such an interface can be realised when data sources number in the thousands or millions is a captivating research challenge.

Application Architectures

In principle, Linked Data may be accessed through advance crawling and caching, or on-the-fly at application runtime through link traversal or federated querying. Search engines such as SWSE, Sindice, Falcons, and Watson crawl the Web of Data and provide applications with access to crawled data through APIs. Federated query architectures for Linked Data include DARQ (Quilitz & Leser, 2008) and SemaPlorer (Schenk et al., 2008). The Semantic Web Client Library (Hartig, Bizer, & Freytag, 2009) has demonstrated that expressive queries can be answered against the Web of Data by relying on runtime link traversal. The appropriate mixture of these methods will always depend on the specific needs of a Linked Data application. However, due to the likelihood of scalability problems with on-the-fly link traversal and federated querying, it may transpire that widespread crawling and caching will become the norm in making data available to applications in a timely fashion, while being able to take advantage of the openness of the Web of Data by discovering new data sources through link traversal.

Schema Mapping and Data Fusion

Once data has been retrieved from distributed sources, it must be integrated in a meaningful way before it is displayed to the user or is further processed. Today, most Linked Data applications display data from different sources alongside each other but do little to integrate it further. To do so does require mapping of terms from different vocabularies to the applications target schema, as well as fusing data about the same entity from different sources, by resolving data conflicts.

Linked Data sources either use their own schemata or use a mixture of terms from existing, well-known vocabularies together with self-defined terms specific to the particular data source. In order to support clients in transforming data between different schemata, data sources can publish correspondences between their local terminology and the terminology of related data sources on the Web of Data. Current W3C recommendations such as RDF Schema (Brickley & Guha, 2004) and OWL (McGuinness & van Harmelen, 2004) define basic terminology like *owl:equivalentClass*, *owl:equivalentProperty*, *rdfs:subClassOf*, *rdfs:subPropertyOf* that can be used to publish basic correspondences. In many situations, these correspondences are too coarse-grained to properly transform data between schemata. Problems include for instance structural heterogeneity as well as value transformations. An open research issue is therefore the development of languages to publish more fine grained schema mappings on the Web. Ideally, such languages would support transitive mappings and provide for combining partial mappings in order to cover cases where data sources mix terminology from different vocabularies. Candidate technologies for this include the alignment languages presented in (Haslhofer, 2008) and (Euzenat, Scharffe, & Zim-

mermann, 2007) as well as the rules interchange format (RIF)[13].

In addition to enhanced support for schema mapping, further research is needed in the area of data fusion for Linked Data applications. Data fusion is the process of integrating multiple data items representing the same real-world object into a single, consistent, and clean representation. The main challenge in data fusion is the resolution of data conflicts, i.e. choosing a value in situations where multiple sources provide different values for the same property of an object. There is a large body of work on data fusion in the database community (Bleiholder & Naumann, 2008) and an increasing body of work on identity reconciliation in the Web community (Halpin & Thomson, 2008). Specific requirements that distinguish the Web of Data from other data fusion scenarios arise from the autonomy of data sources and the scarceness and uncertainty of quality-related meta-information that is required to assess data quality in order to resolve inconsistencies. Prototypical systems for fusing Linked Data from multiple sources include DERI Pipes (Le Phuoc et al., 2009) and the KnoFuss architecture (Nikolov et al., 2008).

Link Maintenance

The content of Linked Data sources changes: data about new entities is added, outdated data is changed or removed. Today, RDF links between data sources are updated only sporadically which leads to dead links pointing at URIs that are no longer maintained and to potential links not being set as new data is published. Web architecture is in principle tolerant to dead links, but having too many of them leads to a large number of unnecessary HTTP requests by client applications. A current research topic within the Linked Data community is therefore link maintenance. Proposed approaches to this problem range from recalculating links at regular intervals using frameworks such as Silk (Volz et al., 2009) or LinQL (Hassanzadeh et al., 2009), through data sources publishing update feeds (Auer et al.,

2009) or informing link sources about changes via subscription models (Volz et al., 2009) to central registries such as Ping the Semantic Web[14] that keep track of new or changed data items.

Licensing

Applications that consume data from the Web must be able to access explicit specifications of the terms under which data can be reused and republished. Availability of appropriate frameworks for publishing such specifications is an essential requirement in encouraging data owners to participate in the Web of Data, and in providing assurances to data consumers that they are not infringing the rights of others by using data in a certain way. Initiatives such as the Creative Commons[15] have provided a framework for open licensing of creative works, underpinned by the notion of copyright. However, as (Miller et al., 2008) discuss, copyright law is not applicable to data, which from a legal perspective is also treated differently across jurisdictions. Therefore frameworks such as the Open Data Commons Public Domain Dedication and License[16] should be adopted by the community to provide clarity in this area. In situations where attribution is a condition of data reuse, further research may also be required to explore how this can be achieved in user interfaces that combine data from large numbers of sources.

Trust, Quality and Relevance

A significant consideration for Linked Data applications is how to ensure the data most relevant or appropriate to the user's needs is identified and made available. For example, in scenarios where data quality and trustworthiness are paramount, how can this be determined heuristically, particularly where the data set may not have been encountered previously?

An overview of different content-, context-, and rating-based techniques that can be used to heuristically assess the relevance, quality and trustworthiness of data is given in (Bizer &

Cyganiak, 2009; Heath, 2008a). Equivalents to the PageRank algorithm will likely be important in determining coarse-grained measures of the popularity or significance of a particular data source, as a proxy for relevance or quality of the data, however such algorithms will need to be adapted to the linkage patterns that emerge on the Web of Data.

From an interface perspective, the question of how to represent the provenance and trustworthiness of data drawn from many sources into an integrated view is a significant research challenge. (Berners-Lee, 1997) proposed that browser interfaces should be enhanced with an "Oh, yeah?" button to support the user in assessing the reliability of information encountered on the Web. Whenever a user encounteres a piece of information that they would like to verify, pressing such a button would produce an explanation of the trustworthiness of the displayed information. This goal has yet to be realised, however existing developments such as WIQA (Bizer & Cyganiak, 2009) and InferenceWeb (McGuinness & da Silva, 2003) can contribute to work in this area by providing explanations about information quality as well as inference processes that are used to derive query results.

Privacy

The ultimate goal of Linked Data is to be able to use the Web like a single global database. The realization of this vision would provide benefits in many areas but will also aggravate dangers in others. One problematic area are the opportunities to violate privacy that arise from integrating data from distinct sources. Protecting privacy in the Linked Data context is likely to require a combination of technical and legal means together with a higher awareness of the users about what data to provide in which context. Interesting research initiatives in this domain are Weitzner's work on the privacy paradox (Weitzner, 2007) and the recent work by the TAMI project on information accountability (Weitzner et al., 2008).

CONCLUSION

Linked Data principles and practices have been adopted by an increasing number of data providers, resulting in the creation of a global data space on the Web containing billions of RDF triples. Just as the Web has brought about a revolution in the publication and consumption of documents, Linked Data has the potential to enable a revolution in how data is accessed and utilised. The success of Web APIs has shown the power of applications that can be created by mashing up content from different Web data sources. However, mashup developers face the challenge of scaling their development approach beyond fixed, predefined data silos, to encompass large numbers of data sets with heterogeneous data models and access methods. In contrast, Linked Data realizes the vision of evolving the Web into a global data commons, allowing applications to operate on top of an unbounded set of data sources, via standardised access mechanisms. If the research challenges highlighted above can be adequately addressed, we expect that Linked Data will enable a significant evolutionary step in leading the Web to its full potential.

REFERENCES

Adida, B., et al. (2008). *RDFa in XHTML: Syntax and Processing - W3C Recommendation.* Retrieved June 14, 2009, http://www.w3.org/TR/rdfa-syntax/

Alexander, K., Cyganiak, R., Hausenblas, M., & Zhao, J. (2009). Describing Linked Datasets. In *Proceedings of the 2nd Workshop on Linked Data on the Web (LDOW2009).*

Auer, S., et al. (2009). Triplify – Light-Weight Linked Data Publication from Relational Databases. In *Proceedings of the 18th World Wide Web Conference (WWW2009).*

Becker, C., & Bizer, C. (2008). DBpedia Mobile - A Location-Aware Semantic Web Client. In *Proceedings of the Semantic Web Challenge at ISWC 2008.*

Beckett, D. (2004). *RDF/XML Syntax Specification (Revised) - W3C Recommendation.* Retrieved June 14, 2009, http://www.w3.org/TR/rdf-syntax-grammar/

Beckett, D., & Berners-Lee, T. (2008). *Turtle - Terse RDF Triple Language - W3C Team Submission.* Retrieved July 23, 2009, http://www.w3.org/TeamSubmission/turtle/

Belleau, F., Nolin, M., Tourigny, N., Rigault, P., & Morissette, J. (2008). Bio2RDF: Towards a mashup to build bioinformatics knowledge systems. *Journal of Biomedical Informatics, 41*(5), 706–716. doi:10.1016/j.jbi.2008.03.004

Berners-Lee, T. (1997). *Cleaning up the User Interface, Section - The "Oh, yeah?"-Button.* Retrieved June 14, 2009, http://www.w3.org/DesignIssues/UI.html

Berners-Lee, T. (1998). *Notation3 (N3) A readable RDF syntax.* Retrieved July 23, 2009, http://www.w3.org/DesignIssues/Notation3.html

Berners-Lee, T. (2000). *Weaving the Web: The Past, Present and Future of the World Wide Web by its Inventor.* London, Texere.

Berners-Lee, T. (2006). *Linked Data - Design Issues.* Retrieved July 23, http://www.w3.org/DesignIssues/LinkedData.html

Berners-Lee, T. (1994). The World-Wide Web. *Communications of the ACM, 37*(8), 76–82. doi:10.1145/179606.179671

Berners-Lee, T., et al. (2005). *Uniform Resource Identifier (URI): Generic Syntax. Request for Comments: 3986.* Retrieved June 14, 2009, http://tools.ietf.org/html/rfc3986

Berners-Lee, T., et al. (2006), Tabulator: Exploring and Analyzing Linked Data on the Semantic Web. In *Procedings of the 3rd International Semantic Web User Interaction Workshop (SWUI06)*.

Berners-Lee, T., et al. (2008). Tabulator Redux: Browsing and Writing Linked Data. In *Proceedings of the 1st Workshop on Linked Data on the Web (LDOW2008)*.

Berners-Lee, T., Hendler, J., & Lassila, O. (2001). The Semantic Web. *Scientific American, 284*(5), 34–43.

Berrueta, D., & Phipps, J. (2008). *Best Practice Recipes for Publishing RDF Vocabularies - W3C Working Group Note*. Retrieved June 14, 2009, http://www.w3.org/TR/swbp-vocab-pub/

Bizer, C., & Cyganiak, R. (2006). D2R Server - Publishing Relational Databases on the Semantic Web. *Poster at the 5th International Semantic Web Conference (ISWC2006)*.

Bizer, C., & Cyganiak, R. (2009). Quality-driven Information Filtering using the WIQA Policy Framework. *Journal of Web Semantics, 7*(1), 1–10. doi:10.1016/j.websem.2008.02.005

Bizer, C., Cyganiak, R., & Gauß, T. (2007). The RDF Book Mashup: From Web APIs to a Web of Data. In *Proceedings of the 3rd Workshop on Scripting for the Semantic Web (SFSW2007)*.

Bizer, C., Cyganiak, R., & Heath, T. (2007). *How to publish Linked Data on the Web*. Retrieved June 14, 2009, http://www4.wiwiss.fu-berlin.de/bizer/pub/LinkedDataTutorial/

Bizer, C., Lehmann, J., Kobilarov, G., Auer, S., Becker, C., Cyganiak, R., & Hellmann, S. (2009). (in press). DBpedia - A Crystallization Point for the Web of Data. Journal of Web Semantics. *Special Issue on the Web of Data.*

Bleiholder, J., & Naumann, F. (2008). Data Fusion. *ACM Computing Surveys, 41*(1), 1–41. doi:10.1145/1456650.1456651

Brickley, D., & Guha, R. (2004). *RDF Vocabulary Description Language 1.0: RDF Schema - W3C Recommendation*. Retrieved June 14, 2009, http://www.w3.org/TR/rdf-schema/

Brin, S., & Page, L. (1998). The Anatomy of a Large-Scale Hypertextual Web Search Engine. *Computer Networks and ISDN Systems, 30*(1-7), 107-117.

Carroll, J., Bizer, C., Hayes, P., & Stickler, P. (2005). Named graphs. *Journal of Web Semantics, 3*(4), 247–267. doi:10.1016/j.websem.2005.09.001

Catasta, M., Cyganiak, R., & Tummarello, G. (2009). Towards ECSSE: live Web of Data search and integration. In *Proceedings of the Semantic Search 2009 Workshop at WWW2009.*

Cheng, G., & Qu, Y. (2009). Searching Linked Objects with Falcons: Approach, Implementation and Evaluation. *International Journal on Semantic Web and Information Systems, Special Issue on Linked Data.*

Clarke, C. (2009). A Resource List Management Tool for Undergraduate Students based on Linked Open Data Principles. In *Proceedings of the 6th European Semantic Web Conference (ESWC2009).*

Coetzee, P., Heath, T., & Motta, E. (2008). SparqPlug. *In Proceedings of the 1st Workshop on Linked Data on the Web (LDOW2008).*

Cyganiak, R., & Bizer, C. (2008). *Pubby - A Linked Data Frontend for SPARQL Endpoints*. Retrieved June 14, 2009, http://www4.wiwiss.fu-berlin.de/pubby/

Cyganiak, R., Delbru, R., Stenzhorn, H., Tummarello, G., & Decker, S. (2008). Semantic Sitemaps: Efficient and Flexible Access to Datasets on the Semantic Web. In *Proceedings of the 5th European Semantic Web Conference (ESWC2008).*

d'Aquin, M. (2008). Toward a New Generation of Semantic Web Applications. *IEEE Intelligent Systems, 23*(3), 20–28. doi:10.1109/MIS.2008.54

Das Sarma, A., Dong, X., & Halevy, A. (2008). Bootstrapping pay-as-you-go data integration systems. In *Proceedings of the Conference on Management of Data (SIGMOD2008)*.

Ding, L., et al. (2005, November). Finding and Ranking Knowledge on the Semantic Web. In *Proceedings of the 4th International Semantic Web Conference*.

Elmagarmid, A., Ipeirotis, P., & Verykios, V. (2007). Duplicate Record Detection: A survey. *IEEE Transactions on Knowledge and Data Engineering, 19*(1), 1–16. doi:10.1109/TKDE.2007.250581

Euzenat, J., Scharffe, F., & Zimmermann, A. (2007). Expressive alignment language and implementation. *Knowledge Web project report, KWEB/2004/D2.2.10/1.0.*

Euzenat, J., & Shvaiko, P. (2007). *Ontology Matching.* Heidelberg: Springer.

Fielding, R., et al. (1999). *Hypertext Transfer Protocol -- HTTP/1.1.* Request for Comments: 2616. Retrieved June 14, 2009, http://www.w3.org/Protocols/rfc2616/rfc2616.html

Franklin, M., Halevy, A., & Maier, D. (2005). From databases to dataspaces: a new abstraction for information management. *SIGMOD Record, 34*(4), 27–33. doi:10.1145/1107499.1107502

Halevy, A., Franklin, M., & Maier, D. (2006). Principles of dataspace systems. In *Proceedings of the Symposium on Principles of database systems (PODS2006)*.

Halpin, H., & Thomson, H. (2008). Special Issue on Identiy, Reference and the Web. *International Journal on Semantic Web and Information Systems, 4*(2), 1–72.

Hartig, O. (2009). Provenance Information in the Web of Data. In *Proceedings of the 2nd Workshop on Linked Data on the Web (LDOW2009)*.

Hartig, O., Bizer, C., & Freytag, J.-C. (2009). Executing SPARQL Queries over the Web of Linked Data. In *Proceedings of the 8th International Semantic Web Conference (ISWC2009)*.

Haslhofer, B. (2008). *A Web-based Mapping Technique for Establishing Metadata Interoperability.* PhD thesis, Universität Wien.

Haslhofer, B., & Schandl, B. (2008). The OAI2LOD Server: Exposing OAI-PMH Metadata as Linked Data. In *Proceedings of the 1st Workshop about Linked Data on the Web (LDOW2008)*.

Hassanzadeh, O., et al. (2009). A Declarative Framework for Semantic Link Discovery over Relational Data. *Poster at 18th World Wide Web Conference (WWW2009)*.

Hassanzadeh, O., & Consens, M. (2009). Linked Movie Data Base. In *Proceedings of the 2nd Workshop on Linked Data on the Web (LDOW2009)*.

Hastrup, T., Cyganiak, R., & Bojars, U. (2008). Browsing Linked Data with Fenfire. In *Proceedings of the 1st Workshop about Linked Data on the Web (LDOW2008)*.

Hausenblas, M., Halb, W., Raimond, Y., & Heath, T. (2008). What is the Size of the Semantic Web? In *Proceedings of the International Conference on Semantic Systems (I-Semantics2008)*.

Heath, T. (2008a). *Information-seeking on the Web with Trusted Social Networks – from Theory to Systems.* PhD Thesis, The Open University.

Heath, T. (2008b). How Will We Interact with the Web of Data? *IEEE Internet Computing, 12*(5), 88–91. doi:10.1109/MIC.2008.101

Heath, T., & Motta, E. (2008). Revyu: Linking reviews and ratings into the Web of Data. *Journal of Web Semantics, 6*(4), 266–273. doi:10.1016/j.websem.2008.09.003

Hogan, A., Harth, A., Umrich, J., & Decker, S. (2007). Towards a scalable search and query engine for the web. In *Proceedings of the 16th Conference on World Wide Web (WWW2007)*.

Jacobs, I., & Walsh, N. (2004). *Architecture of the World Wide Web, Volume One - W3C Recommendation*. Retrieved June 14, 2009, http://www.w3.org/TR/webarch/

Jentzsch, A., Hassanzadeh, O., Bizer, C., Andersson, B., & Stephens, S. (2009). Enabling Tailored Therapeutics with Linked Data. In *Proceedings of the 2nd Workshop on Linked Data on the Web (LDOW2009)*.

Karger, D., & Schraefel, M. C. (2006). Pathetic Fallacy of RDF. In *Proceedings of 3rd Semantic Web User Interaction Workshop (SWUI2006)*.

Klyne, G., & Carroll, J. (2004). *Resource Description Framework (RDF): Concepts and Abstract Syntax - W3C Recommendation*. Retrieved June 14, 2009, http://www.w3.org/TR/rdf-concepts/

Kobilarov, G., et al. (2009). Media Meets Semantic Web - How the BBC Uses DBpedia and Linked Data to Make Conections. In *Proceedings of the 6th European Semantic Web Conference (ESWC2009)*.

Le Phuoc, D., Polleres, A., Morbidoni, C., Hauswirth, M., & Tummarello, G. (2009). Rapid semantic web mashup development through semantic web pipes. In *Proceedings of the 18th World Wide Web Conference (WWW2009)*.

Marshall, C., & Shipman, F. (2003). Which semantic web? In *Proceedings of the 14th ACM Conference on Hypertext and Hypermedia (HT2003)*.

McGuinness, D., & da Silva, P. (2003). Infrastructure for Web Explanations. In *Proceedings of the 2nd International Semantic Web Conference (ISWC2003)*.

McGuinness, D., & van Harmelen, F. (2004). *OWL Web Ontology Language - W3C Recommendation*. Retrieved June 14, 2009, http://www.w3.org/TR/owl-features/

Miller, P., Styles, R., & Heath, T. (2008). Open Data Commons, a License for Open Data. In *Proceedings of the 1st Workshop about Linked Data on the Web (LDOW2008)*.

Moreau, L., et al. (2008). *The Open Provenance Model*. Technical report, Electronics and Computer Science, University of Southampton.

Nikolov, A., et al. (2008). Integration of Semantically Annotated Data by the KnoFuss Architecture. In *Proceedings of the 16th International Conference on Knowledge Engineering and Knowledge Management*.

Olston, C., & Chi, E. (2003). ScentTrails: Integrating Browsing and Searching on the Web. *ACM Transactions on Computer-Human Interaction, 10*(3), 177–197. doi:10.1145/937549.937550

Oren, E. (2008). Sindice.com: A document-oriented lookup index for open linked data. *Journal of Metadata. Semantics and Ontologies, 3*(1), 37–52. doi:10.1504/IJMSO.2008.021204

Quilitz, B., & Leser, U. (2008). Querying distributed RDF data sources with SPARQL. In *Proceedings of the 5th European Semantic Web Conference (ESWC2008)*.

Raimond, Y., Sutton, C., & Sandler, M. (2008). Automatic Interlinking of Music Datasets on the Semantic Web. In *Proceedings of the 1st Workshop about Linked Data on the Web (LDOW2008)*.

Sauermann, L., & Cyganiak, R. (2008). *Cool URIs for the Semantic Web. W3C Interest Group Note*. Retrieved June 14, 2009, http://www.w3.org/TR/cooluris/

Schenk, S., et al. (2008). SemaPlorer—Interactive Semantic Exploration of Data and Media based on a Federated Cloud Infrastructure. In *Proceedings of the Semantic Web Challenge at ISWC 2008.*

Van de Sompel, H., Lagoze, C., Nelson, M., Warner, S., Sanderson, R., & Johnston, P. (2009). Adding eScience Assets to the Data Web. In *Proceedings of the 2nd Workshop on Linked Data on the Web (LDOW2009).*

Volz, J., Bizer, C., Gaedke, M., & Kobilarov, G. (2009). Discovering and Maintaining Links on the Web of Data. In *Proceedings of the 8th International Semantic Web Conference (ISWC2009).*

Weitzner, D. (2007). Beyond Secrecy: New Privacy Protection Strategies for Open Information Spaces. *IEEE Internet Computing, 11*(5), 94–96. doi:10.1109/MIC.2007.101

Weitzner, D. (2008). Information Accountability. *Communications of the ACM, 51*(6), 82–87. doi:10.1145/1349026.1349043

Winkler, W. (2006). *Overview of Record Linkage and Current Research Directions.* US Bureau of the Census, Technical Report.

Zhao, J., Klyne, G., & Shotton, D. (2008). Provenance and Linked Data in Biological Data Webs. In *Proceedings of the 1st Workshop about Linked Data on the Web (LDOW2008).*

ENDNOTES

1. http://esw.w3.org/topic/SweoIG/TaskForces/CommunityProjects/LinkingOpenData/
2. http://www.w3.org/2001/sw/sweo/
3. http://esw.w3.org/topic/TaskForces/CommunityProjects/LinkingOpenData/DataSets/LinkStatistics and http://esw.w3.org/topic/TaskForces/CommunityProjects/LinkingOpenData/DataSets/Statistics
4. http://www.geonames.org/ontology/
5. http://www.openlinksw.com/dataspace/dav/wiki/Main/VOSRDF
6. http://www.talis.com/platform/
7. http://sioc-project.org/exporters
8. http://vapour.sourceforge.net/
9. http://www4.wiwiss.fu-berlin.de/bizer/ng4j/disco/
10. http://www.jibbering.com/foaf/
11. http://microformats.org/
12. http://www.w3.org/History/1989/proposal.html
13. http://www.w3.org/2005/rules/wiki/RIF_Working_Group
14. http://pingthesemanticweb.com/
15. http://creativecommons.org/
16. http://www.opendatacommons.org/licenses/pddl/1.0/

This work was previously published in International Journal on Semantic Web and Information Systems, Volume 5, Issue 3, edited by Amit P. Sheth, pp. 1-22, copyright 2009 by IGI Publishing (an imprint of IGI Global).

Chapter 9
Community–Driven Consolidated Linked Data

Aman Shakya
Tribhuvan University, Nepal

Hideaki Takeda
National Institute of Informatics, Japan

Vilas Wuwongse
Asian Institute of Technology, Thailand

ABSTRACT

User-generated content can help the growth of linked data. However, there are a lack of interfaces enabling ordinary people to author linked data. Secondly, people have multiple perspectives on the same concept and different contexts. Thirdly, there are not enough ontologies to model various data. Therefore, the authors of this chapter propose an approach to enable people to share various data through an easy-to-use social platform. Users define their own concepts and multiple conceptualizations are allowed. These are consolidated using semi-automatic schema alignment techniques supported by the community. Further, concepts are grouped semi-automatically by similarity. As a result of consolidation and grouping, informal lightweight ontologies emerge gradually. The authors have implemented a social software system, called StYLiD, to realize the approach. It can serve as a platform motivating people to bookmark and share different things. It may also drive vertical portals for specific communities with integrated data from multiple sources. Some experimental observations support the validity of the approach.

INTRODUCTION

Linked data is a method of exposing, sharing and connecting data on the Semantic Web. It provides the mechanisms for publishing and interlinking structured data into a Web of Data. This forms a data commons where people and organizations can post and consume data about anything. Due to the network effect, usefulness of data increases the more it is linked with other data. Organizations benefit by being in this global data network, accessible to both people and machines. Linked data can be fully realized with existing technologies maintaining compatibility with legacy applica-

DOI: 10.4018/978-1-60960-593-3.ch009

tions while exposing data from them. Thus, linked data is a significant practical movement towards the vision of the Semantic Web (Berners-Lee, 2006; Bizer, Cyganiak, & Heath, 2007).

However, some issues still remain which need to be addressed for wider adoption of linked data. Firstly, it is not obvious how ordinary people, without any technical expertise, can publish and share linked data directly. Linked data research can benefit from the combination of Semantic Web and social web techniques. A lot of data on the web comes from the people. However, there is a lack of human interfaces to publish linked data explicitly. So people still share unstructured data and it is hard to derive semantic structure and links from such contents.

Secondly, the fact that there may be multiple perspectives on the same concept, different aspects or contexts to be considered, is often ignored. In the distributed web, different parties may have different schemas or conceptualizations for the same type of data because of different requirements or preferences. So organizations usually need to integrate their data at the schema level. However, today data is mainly being linked at the instance level only (Jhingran, 2008) though knowledge of schema is very important for information exchange and integration between systems and for querying data sources. Therefore, we should also link data at the schema level to explicitly encode the knowledge of relations among multiple conceptualizations. Currently, it is not obvious how to link or relate such multiple concept schemas in the linked data web.

Lastly, the state of the art lacks structures that can represent and organize the wide range of concepts needed by the community. There are still not enough ontologies or vocabularies for describing linked data about various things (Siorpaes & Hepp, 2007a; Van Damme, Hepp, & Siorpaes, 2007). There is a long tail of information domains for which people have information to share (Huynh, Karger, & Miller, 2007). Developing individual solutions for the long tail is infeasible because data

modeling is difficult. Also it is not always practical for different parties to commit to a single data model or common vocabulary. It may be possible to achieve some level of consensus but the process of collaborative interaction with common understanding is itself difficult and time-consuming.

Considering the above issues, we propose the following contributions.

Social linked data authoring. We attempt to enable ordinary users to publish structured linked data directly through simple authoring interfaces. We have implemented a linked data authoring social software for sharing a wide variety of data in the community.

Multiple conceptualizations. Users may freely define their own concept schemas and share different types of structured linked data. We propose allowing different people to have multiple conceptualizations.

Concept consolidation. At the same time, these multiple concept schemas are consolidated by mapping and linking them at the schema level. This is done semi-automatically, supported by the community, using data integration principles with schema alignment techniques. We propose concept consolidation as a new way of building up conceptualizations from the community. This is a loose collaborative approach requiring minimum understanding and allowing different parties to maintain individual requirements.

Emergence of lightweight ontologies. Besides community-based formation of conceptualizations by consolidation, concepts can evolve and gradually emerge out by popularity. Further, similar concept schemas can be grouped and organized semi-automatically. Together these processes enable emergence of informal lightweight ontologies.

The rest of the article is structured as follows. We will start with an overview of our approach and the architecture in the next section. Next, we will discuss about user motivation and some possible application scenarios. Then, we will describe about social linked data authoring fol-

Figure 1. Proposed architecture

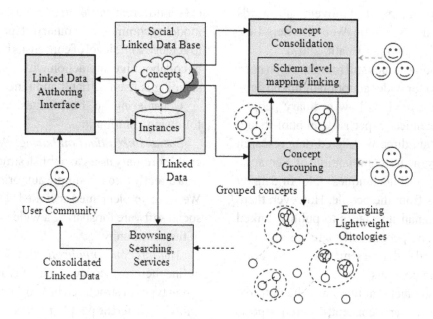

lowed by a section on usability experiment. Next, we will describe about consolidated linked data along with an experiment on conceptualization. Then, we will discuss about the emergence of lightweight ontologies. Following this, we will show some experimental observations on an existing collection of community-created concepts. Then, we will discuss related works. Finally we will conclude in the last section along with some future directions.

OVERVIEW

The basic motivation of this work is to enable communities of ordinary people with multiple heterogeneous perspectives to share various types of structured linked data and, in the process, to derive ontologies for structuring different things. Our approach for achieving this consists of providing an online social platform intended to be easy for ordinary people to share data about various things. We give users the freedom to define their own concepts thereby allowing multiple concep-

tualizations. We propose consolidation of these multiple conceptual schemas. This can be done by mapping the schemas semi-automatically with the help of schema alignment techniques and the community. Further, we organize the concepts semi-automatically by grouping them based on similarity. As a result of this consolidation and grouping of concepts, informal ontologies can emerge that combine multiple perspectives and unify common elements.

Architecture

The major parts of our architecture, as illustrated in Figure 1, are as follows.

Linked data authoring interface. We propose a social platform for linked data authoring to enable the ordinary user community to publish linked data directly. The users contribute concept schemas for the data they want to share. They may also directly use or adapt existing concepts defined by the community. The users post data instances though the authoring interface, with the help of the schemas. All the concepts and linked data instances are maintained in the social linked data base.

Concept consolidation. Multiple versions of the same concept or similar concepts can be consolidated. This process includes mapping the schemas and linking them. Concept consolidation is a semi-automatic process supported by the user community. This produces consolidated concepts combining the features of the constituents.

Concept grouping. Similar concepts are considered as related and are grouped together. Groups with multiple versions of the same or similar concepts that may be consolidated are forwarded to the concept consolidation process. Moreover, grouping similar concepts helps in organizing the concepts, both individual and consolidated, so that relations among them become more apparent. Concept grouping is also a semi-automatic process supported by the community. The groups of concepts may further be linked up, if related. Hence, emerging lightweight ontologies can form gradually in a bottom-up fashion. Popularity in the community also helps in the emergence of widely acceptable definitions from the cloud of concepts.

Services for using linked data. The consolidation, grouping and organization of concepts can also transform the way of viewing the associated linked data instances. The instances can be viewed as consolidated linked data, an integrated collection from multiple sources using the consolidated vocabulary. We can provide user interfaces for browsing and searching the different types of structured linked data. The organization of concepts by similarity makes browsing and locating information easy. Other useful services may also be provided to exploit the structured linked data.

We have implemented the entire architecture as a social web application called StYLiD (an acronym for Structure Your own Linked Data). It is available online at http://www.stylid.org/ open for all to share any type of data.

Technologies Used

StYLiD has been built upon Pligg (http://www.pligg.com/), a popular Web 2.0 content management system. It is open source social software with a long list of useful features and a strong community support. Pligg has an extensible plug-in architecture which allows us to extend it for structured data and semantic capabilities. Further, it also supports extra fields besides the bookmarked URL. It uses PHP and MySQL. The structured concepts and data are stored as RDF triples in a MySQL database. We have used the RDF API for PHP (RAP) as the Semantic Web framework.

Besides serving RDF when URIs are dereferenced, the system also embeds machine understandable data in the HTML posts using RDFa. RDFa is a set of extensions that enable us to express RDF inside XHTML elements. Many useful RDFa tools and plug-ins are available (http://esw.w3.org/topic/RDFa) and we may expect more in the future. Users with programming knowledge may even code small scripts with the Operator browser extension (http://www.kaply.com/weblog/operator/) to create useful operations for different types of data. Operator is an extension for Firefox that adds the ability to interact with semantic data embedded in web pages.

MOTIVATION AND APPLICATION SCENARIOS

One of the major bottlenecks for collaborative creation of structured data and ontologies is how to motivate the users (Hepp, 2007). Social software has been successful in motivating users by providing visible personal benefits. There is active ongoing research on incentives for the Semantic Web. Siorpaes and Hepp (2007b) have tried to provide incentives as enjoyable experience through online games. Hasen and Jameson (2008) have pointed out some factors that can affect user motivation including algorithms, user interface, user input, affordances of situations and use of external resources. Often, a favorable combination of these factors achieves good results. Following are some aspects that may motivate the users of our proposed system.

Data Bookmarking. Using the system, users may bookmark a wide variety of things they are interested in and care about. They need not be limited to bookmarking only web URLs, one at a time. While social bookmarking helps us to remember data sources, data bookmarking would help us remember the data as well. We would not need to go through all the documents again to find the important or useful facts, saving us from a lot of effort in the future. The system can act as a personal knowledge management system to organize one's own data collection.

Social Information Sharing. As an online social platform the system inherits some motivating features of social software in general. Users may freely share interesting and useful things in the community modeled in their own formats. The system can also be an effective way of collecting data from the community in desired formats.

Information Utilization. The users' data get organized under different concepts and can be retrieved by desired criteria. Useful operations like sorting, filtering, exporting, etc and other automatic operations are possible. Moreover, data from different sources can be viewed and processed homogenously at one place.

Ease of use and freedom. It is easy to get started with the system without requiring any special knowledge or training. It serves as a single platform for publishing different types of data. Users are free to create their own concepts to suit their own needs. Most of the users can simply post their data using concepts created by others or modify and reuse existing concepts with little effort. A relaxed interface allows the user to type in any data freely.

Targeting Specific Users. It has been observed for online social systems that most of the con-

tents are contributed by a very small percentage of users (Nielsen, 2006) and others are usually passive consumers. It is enough to motivate this small percentage of contributors to sustain the system. A different approach for ensuring user participation is to provide solutions for targeted users who have specific requirements that can be met by the system. Then they would be self-motivated. Further, as mentioned earlier, the fact that the value of one's data increases when it is combined with others' in the network can motivate optimistic stakeholders.

Application Scenarios

Considering these motivating aspects, various application scenarios may be conceived with the proposed platform for collaborative modeling and sharing of different types of structured linked data. Two important scenarios are discussed below.

Information Sharing Social Platform

StYLiD can be used as or may be adapted to create a social website for structured information sharing as illustrated in Figure 2. It provides a CMS (Content Management System) where users can freely contribute their own concept schemas and share structured instance data. It is a step towards a social Linked Data CMS (It has been used to create a dynamic website for a musical community (http://www.odaibacampur.com/) in the Tokyo International Exchange Center, Odaiba, Tokyo). Data integration is done by concept consolidation using semi-automatic schema alignment techniques supported by the community. Concepts are also grouped and organized by the community. The structured data can further be annotated with external resources like Wikipedia.

The system can be used to bookmark and share things of personal interest and invite data from the community in desired schematic formats. Linked data produced in such a way may be called collaborative or social linked data. With linked

Figure 2. Information sharing social platform scenario

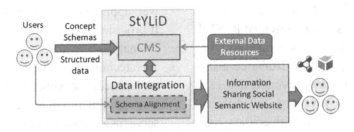

Figure 3. Integrated semantic portal scenario

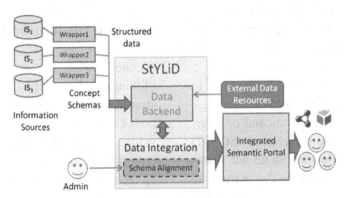

data and Semantic Web formats, users can enjoy various semantic capabilities while sharing data they are interested in.

Integrated Semantic Portal

Another application scenario for StYLiD may be as an integrated semantic portal as illustrated in Figure 3. In this scenario, the concept schemas and structured data may come from different information sources, websites or online systems, besides the users. Wrappers may be needed to export data from the systems into StYLiD acting as a data backend (In fact, we have built some wrappers using the Dapper online service (http://www.dapper.net/) to scrap some data from the website of NII, Japan and others). The different information sources can maintain their own conceptual schemas and continue to serve their consumers. At the same time, these are also integrated in StYLiD by concept consolidation with schema

alignment which can be handled by the system administrators. The data may further be enriched by linking to external data resources. The system can act as a semantic portal providing integrated linked data and semantic capabilities to the user community or drive such vertical portals. In this scenario, StYLiD can comfortably be used with legacy systems. It would be easier to convince data providers when they can still maintain their own local systems while enjoying exposure to the linked data web through vertical portals.

StYLiD is being used in a project to integrate research staff directories from various Japanese universities (Kurakawa, Shakya, & Takeda, 2009). Most Japanese universities maintain their own staff directories on the web. However, these cannot be accessed in an integrated way. StYLiD can be used to map the conceptual schemas of the universities and provide a consolidated view over them. Currently, data from the Osaka University and Nagoya University of Japan have been imported into the system. The websites of the universities were crawled and the structured data was scraped from the pages and represented in XML format. The XML data was then imported into StYLiD by custom scripting. The database consists of 1106 records from Osaka University and 1888 records from Nagoya University. The different schemas for the staff in the universities were aligned by creating a consolidated concept. The system automatically suggested total 10 alignments which were all correct (Most of the attribute labels were in Japanese). These alignments were verified by human and 9 other missing alignments were added resulting into total 19 mappings.

Besides these, StYLiD may also be used in other scenarios, both in public and closed settings. It may be used for inter-departmental or inter-organizational information exchange (StYLiD has also been used to develop an ad hoc document management system in the Asian Institute of Technology, Thailand) and integration over separately maintained information systems. It may also be adapted as a structured blogging platform for personal or corporate use. It can be used for simple collaborative designing of conceptual schemas and serve as a simple inexpensive tool for rapid prototyping.

SOCIAL LINKED DATA AUTHORING

People want to share a wide variety of data. Today, social software has enabled ordinary people to publish documents on the web easily. In the web of documents, people mostly publish unstructured documents and interlink those using hyperlinks. Linked data shifts the paradigm from document publishing to *data publishing* and from hyperlinking to *data-linking*. This paradigm shift has to come in the publishing interface too that people use to share data. We need to enable ordinary people to publish *data* on the web instead of unstructured documents and *data-links* instead of hyperlinks.

We implemented StYLiD basically as a social web application to share structured linked data. It provides a linked data authoring interface for ordinary users without any knowledge of Semantic Web technologies. It allows users to define their own concept schemas freely and share different types of structured data they are interested in. It serves as a content management system to produce linked data directly. A screenshot of the system is shown in Figure 4.

Defining Structured Concepts

A concept is a representation of a category/class of things (Murphy, 2004). A concept schema is a structured representation for showing the properties of an instance of the concept as attributes and values of these attributes for the instance. The notions have been treated formally in (Shakya, Takeda, & Wuwongse, 2008). The users may define their own concept schemas by specifying the concept name along with a set of attributes. Each attribute has a name and some description as shown in Figure 5. This description is not necessarily the independent definition of the attribute. It is usually for clarifying the role of the attribute in the context. Trying to give abstract dictionary definitions to common labels would rather confuse the ordinary users. However, when the labels are not obvious more explanatory descriptions would be desired. Further, the user may select a set of concepts as the suggested value range. Some possible values may also be enumerated which would appear as a drop-down list to help in data input.

Users do not need to define concepts from scratch. They may modify an existing concept into a new version (The system keeps a link to the source concept). Schema attributes from an existing concept can also be imported to define a new concept with similar structure. Users may update definitions incrementally as and when needed. Users may even define multiple versions of the same concept. Thus, concepts can evolve incrementally along with different versions.

Figure 4. StYLiD screenshot

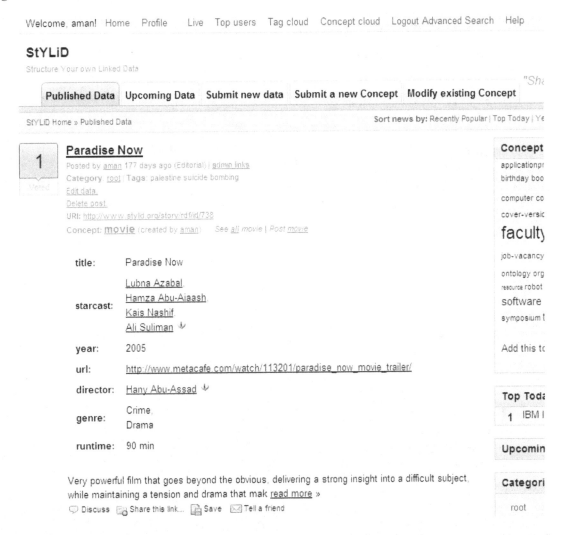

A schema is helpful in guiding people to input structured data. Although a schema-less environment offers full flexibility, users may not know what to input. So it would be better to maintain flexible and extensible schemas. However, schemas defined by others may be difficult to understand or may not fit individual requirements well. Therefore, StYLiD allows people to define their own concept schemas on the fly according to their own perspectives. The system also offers a personal "Concept Collection". Concepts created or adopted by the user are automatically added to this collection while any other useful concept may also be added.

Sharing Structured Linked Data

Any user may enter instance data using system generated online forms for each concept schema, as shown in Figure 6. Data instances can be linked to each other by directly entering resource URIs as *data-links* for attribute values. The system helps the user to pick up suitable values by suggesting range of values for the attributes. For the user, the data appears as usual hyperlinked entries (see

Figure 5. Interface to create a new concept

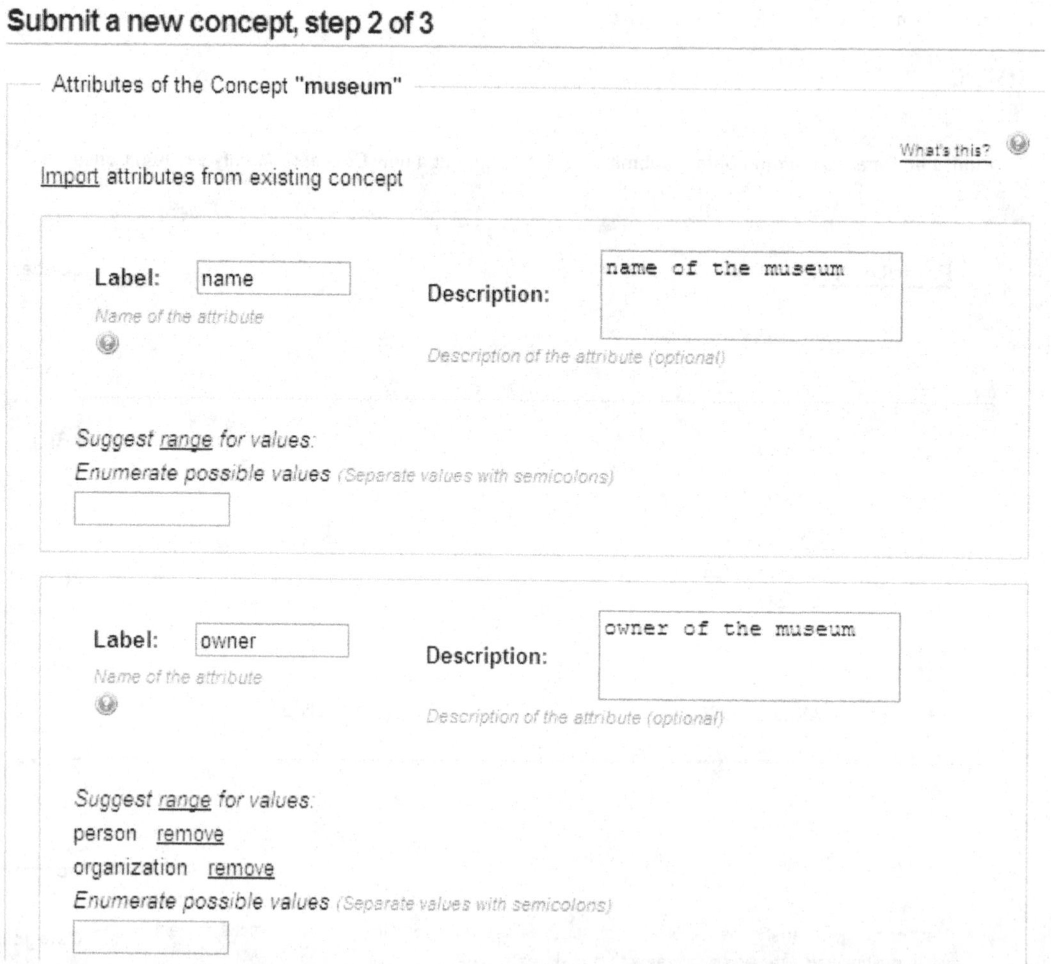

Submit a new concept, step 2 of 3

Attributes of the Concept **"museum"**

What's this?

Import attributes from existing concept

Label: name
Name of the attribute

Description: name of the museum
Description of the attribute (optional)

Suggest range for values:
Enumerate possible values (Separate values with semicolons)

Label: owner
Name of the attribute

Description: owner of the museum
Description of the attribute (optional)

Suggest range for values:
person remove
organization remove
Enumerate possible values (Separate values with semicolons)

Figure 4). However, the *data-links* behind can be crawled by machines to feed powerful linked data applications.

The system generates unique dereferenceable URIs for each concept, attribute and instance. The URI dereferencing is based on the guidelines provided by Bizer et al. (2007) for publishing linked data. Concepts and attributes are represented by hash URIs. An instance URI dereferences to its RDF description by an HTTP 303 redirect. For both types of URIs, content negotiation is used to return the RDF description in case of "application/rdf+xml" request and HTML otherwise. The description also contains backlinks

from other instances that link to the instance. For the users, the backlinks are shown under the instance as an "Appears in" list, similar to trackbacks.

Linking to Wikipedia and External Resources

The user may directly enter any external URI for an attribute value. The system currently provides some support to link to Wikipedia contents. The familiar Wikipedia icon appears next to the URI field (see Figure 6). When the user clicks on the icon it searches for the Wikipedia page about the text attribute value typed by the user. The user may

Figure 6. Interface to enter instance data

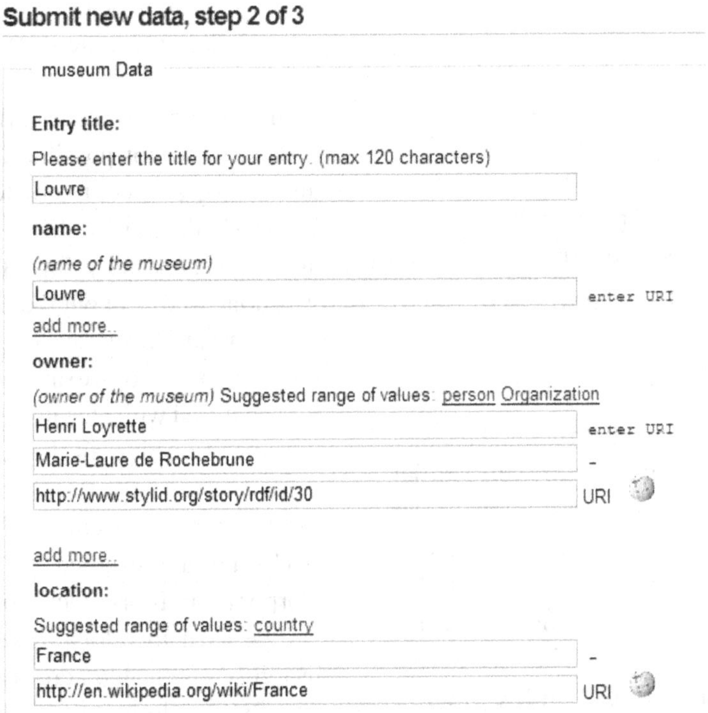

Submit new data, step 2 of 3

museum Data

Entry title:

Please enter the title for your entry. (max 120 characters)

Louvre

name:

(name of the museum)

Louvre   enter URI

add more..

owner:

(owner of the museum) Suggested range of values: person Organization

Henri Loyrette   enter URI

Marie-Laure de Rochebrune   -

http://www.stylid.org/story/rdf/id/30   URI

add more..

location:

Suggested range of values: country

France   -

http://en.wikipedia.org/wiki/France   URI

copy the Wikipedia page URL as the URI. Transparent to the user, the system converts it into the corresponding DBpedia (Auer et al., 2007) URI. Unlike DBpedia, Wikipedia is well understood by general people. The users would be motivated to link to Wikipedia pages to make their data more informative, interesting and useful. Some short description and depiction from Wikipedia (through DBpedia) is pulled dynamically and shown as an annotation balloon as shown in Figure 7.

Flexible Definitions and Relaxed Data Entry

It is difficult to think of all attributes and all possible value ranges. While defining a concept A, if an attribute takes a resource of type B, we would need to ensure that concept B has already been defined. If concept B has an attribute which takes values of type C, then concept C must be defined first, and so on. Moreover, we may not always

have perfect data at the time of data entry. The system tries to avoid these difficulties by allowing flexible and relaxed definitions. The range of values defined for attributes, as seen in Figures 5 and 6, is only suggestive and does not impose strict constraints. Rather the system assists the user to pick instances from the suggested range. The system accepts both literal values and resource URIs, single or multiple values for any attribute.

EXPERIMENT ON USABILITY

An experiment was conducted to study the usability of the system and to observe how users use the system. Specific user tasks were designed to cover various capabilities of the system. They were asked to perform the same tasks using the Freebase system too, as a baseline for comparison. Freebase (Bollacker, Tufts, Pierce, & Cook, 2007) is a community-driven open database of world's

Figure 7. Annotation with Wikipedia contents using DBpedia linked data

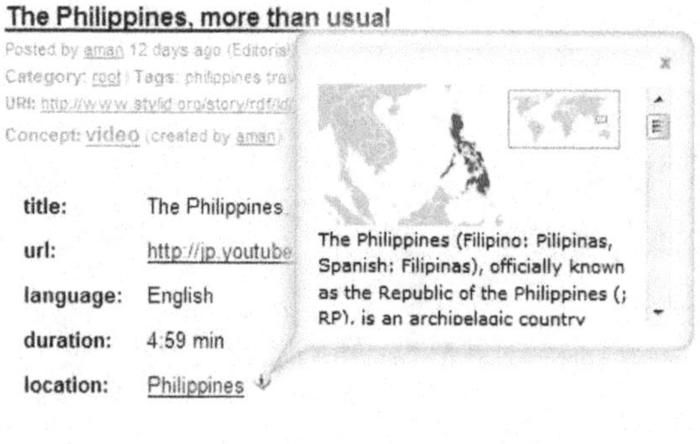

information (http://www.freebase.com/). Freebase was chosen because it is functionally very similar to StYLiD. It also allows users to define their own schemas and input structured data instances.

There were total 15 participants from 10 different countries, 8 male and 7 female. The age range was from 22 to 43 years. They were from various fields, including 6 from completely non-IT backgrounds. The following tasks were assigned to the user, provided with the data to enter.

1.   *Structured data authoring*: Input the given data about "The Beatles" as an instance of the "band" concept in the system.
2.   *Structured concept creation*: Input the given "concert" concept schema into the system.
3.   *Modifying and reusing an existing concept*: Enter the given "singer" concept. The concept already existed in the system but the users were not informed. This was to see whether the users reuse the existing concept or create a new version form scratch.
4.   *Updating one's own concept*: Modify the "singer" concept just defined to add new attributes.
5.   *Structured concepts and instances authoring*: Input the given structured data instance of an "album". The "album" concept did not exist, so the user would have to create the concept first.

6.   *Searching*: Find all the movies directed by "Martin Scorsese" which had "Leonardo DiCaprio" in the starcast.

Tasks 3 and 4 were performed on StYLiD only, because it is not possible in Freebase to reuse an existing concept to create a new version. For each task, the order of StYLiD and Freebase was switched alternately for each participant. This was done to cancel out the effect that learning to perform a task in one system may affect the use of the next system for the same task. The screen video was captured while the user performed each task.

After finishing all the tasks, the participants were asked to fill the System Usability Scale (SUS), for both systems. The SUS (Brooke, 1996) is a likert scale designed by the Digital Equipment Corporation. It provides a broad measure which can be used for global assessments of systems usability applicable across a range of contexts. The SUS scale has also been used by Pfisterer, Nitsche, Jameson, and Barbu (2008) to evaluate the Semantic Mediawiki.

The average SUS score obtained for StYLiD was 69.67% and that for Freebase was 39.33%. Thus, the participants clearly ranked StYLiD as more usable than Freebase for the given tasks. However, it should be stressed that this should not be taken as an evaluation of Freebase. Freebase has many other attractive features not covered by the experimental tasks. The comparison is only valid for the given tasks of interest.

After each task, the participants were also asked to fill a short questionnaire to rate their confidence level and ease of use in a scale of 0 to 4, 0 for the worst case and 4 for the best. For each task, the number of errors made by user and the time taken to perform the task were also noted from the captured video. Table 1 shows the aggregated results from tasks applicable to both the systems.

The results show that users felt more confident with StYLiD, found it easier to use, required lesser time to perform each of the given tasks and required less assistance compared to Freebase.

Table 1. Aggregated results from the tasks

Task no.	Confidence		Ease		Time (in mins)		Errors		Assistance	
	S	F	S	F	S	F	S	F	S	F
1	2.8	1.87	3.07	1.73	10.23	12.07	0.93	0.47	1.53	3.93
2	2.93	2.27	3.13	2.33	7.43	11.4	1.13	0.4	1.13	2.33
5	3.2	2.33	3.4	2.07	5.87	10.4	0.87	1	0.53	2
6	2.8	1.53	2.4	1.47	4.93	7.07	0	0	2	2.4
Average/ Total	2.93	2	3	1.9	28.47	40.93	2.93	1.87	5.2	10.67

Note: S stands for StYLiD and F stands for Freebase

However, StYLiD allowed some more errors probably due to its relaxed interface for data entry.

Discussion

Some observations made from the experiment are discussed below. It should be noted that the users were not acquainted with the systems beforehand. Thus, this indicates that users are, in fact, able to use StYLiD without any training or with minimal guidance.

However, the notion of concept and instances was not obvious for many users. It was observed that people try to enter data directly in one step, without creating the concept first. Some tried to enter the instance data in the interface to create the concept schema itself. Therefore, it would be better to have a combined interface to define the concept and input instance data at the same time.

From task 3, it was observed that most people modify and reuse an existing concept rather than starting from scratch. This is explicitly possible in StYLiD unlike Freebase.

It was observed that people mostly tend to type in data freely, instead of bothering to link to existing instances. The participants even suggested that the system should have an auto-complete mechanism, like in Freebase, to link instances. Though the auto-complete in Freebase was handy, some users found it difficult to choose when there were multiple things with the same name.

In Freebase, it was difficult to create schema for most users because of the strict constraints to be specified. A user is not allowed to save a property without specifying the data type but choosing proper data types and formats was not so easy. Imperfect type definitions later posed problems while entering instance data and the users had to revise the schema definitions again. StYLiD does not impose such strict constraints. Nevertheless, specifying the value range for attributes was not obvious for many, in both systems. They did not understand that concepts can be selected as range, and so, typed in the range simply as descriptions. Hence, though the users were fairly able to use the system there are still several usability issues to be considered.

CONSOLIDATED LINKED DATA

Multiple heterogeneous or overlapping conceptualizations always exist due to different requirements, perspectives or contexts (Ankolekar, Krötzsch, Tran, & Vrandečić, 2007). Thus, multiple definitions for the same concept should be allowed. As illustrated in Figure 8, the same "Hotel" concept may be defined by 3 users in different ways. Even the same user may have multiple versions for the concept in different contexts. These can be grouped together and consolidated into a single virtual "Hotel" concept combining all the features of the individual definitions. The

Figure 8. Concept consolidation

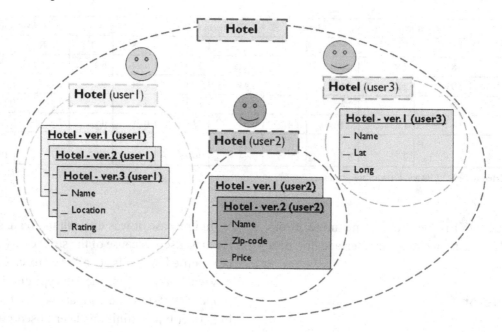

user may need to retrieve all instances of a concept regardless of the concept version.

Our approach for consolidation is based on the Global-as-View (GaV) approach for a data integration system where a global schema is defined in terms of the source schemas (Lenzerini, 2002).

We define a concept consolidation C as a triple $<\bar{C}, S, A>$ where

- $\bar{C}$ is called the *consolidated concept*
- S is the set of *constituent concepts* $\{C_1, C_2, \ldots C_n\}$, n is the number of constituent concepts
- A is the *alignment* between $\bar{C}$ and S.

The alignment A consists of a set of mappings between the schema attributes of each concept in S and $\bar{C}$. Details of the formalization have been published in (Shakya et al., 2008). The consolidated concept $\bar{C}$ acts as a new virtual concept with *consolidated attributes* aligned to the attributes of each of the constituent concepts.

The main advantage of a GaV based approach over other approaches for data integration is that queries on the global schema can simply be unfolded to the source schemas by substituting the terms (Lenzerini, 2002). In our case, queries on the consolidated concept $\bar{C}$ can be unfolded to queries on the constituent concepts using the attribute alignments in A. The union of individual results produces the total result. Using the alignment in the concept consolidation, translation of structured data instances from one conceptualization into another is also possible. This can be done by first converting the data instance of one concept into the consolidated concept form and then converting this consolidated concept instance into the target concept form, using the alignment mapping. Similarly, we can also translate queries over one concept schema into queries over another. The details have been explained formally in (Shakya et.al, 2008).

The system provides a structured search interface, as shown in Figure 9, to searched linked data instances of a concept by specifying attribute, value pairs as criteria. When the search is done over a consolidated concept, all the constituent concept instances are also searched. The query terms are unfolded from the consolidated concept attributes to the aligned attributes of the constituent concepts. The system also provides a SPARQL query interface for open external access.

Schema Mapping and Linking

Multiple concept schemas in a consolidated group can be aligned semi-automatically to relate them and to integrate them into a unified view. When the user explicitly aligns a set of concepts or tries to view instances of a consolidated group of concepts as a single table, the system automatically suggests alignments between the attributes, as shown in Figure 10.

Matching attributes are automatically selected in the form-based interface. Each set of aligned attributes forms a consolidated attribute. The Alignment API (Euzenat, 2004) implementation (http://alignapi.gforge.inria.fr/) with its WordNet extension has been used for the purpose. It utilizes a WordNet based similarity measure between attribute labels to find alignments. This may be replaced by more sophisticated alignment methods in the future. However, more sophisticated user interfaces may be required and it may be

Figure 9. Structured search interface

difficult to maintain usability keeping ordinary users in mind.

No matter how sophisticated techniques we use, it is not possible to make the alignment fully automatic and accurate. So it is necessary to have the user in loop to complete the process by adding or modifying mappings not suggested by the system correctly. Any user, who wants to retrieve or search over all data from different sources in a unified form, can make the alignment, assisted by the automatic suggestions. Completing the alignment can be done collaboratively. An individual may perform the alignment up to his needs and

Figure 10. Aligning the attributes of multiple concepts

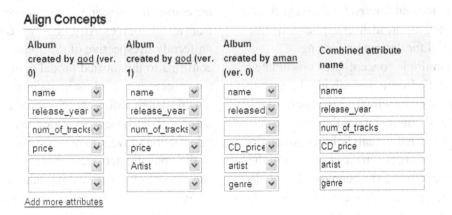

understanding. The mappings are saved by the system. Other users may successively add the missing parts and refine the alignment. Conflicts may be resolved in a wiki manner. Once a proper alignment is in place, rest of the users can directly access the unified data. Hence, the action of one or few can benefit all in the community. The alignment can be updated incrementally as more concepts are added to the group or the existing ones updated.

The alignment API represents the schema level linking in an expressive alignment specification language capable of representing complex alignments (Euzenat, 2004). Although the system currently does not determine complex alignments, this allows for more sophisticated mappings in the future. The alignments are also represented using the alignment ontology (Hughes & Ashpole, 2004) (http://www.atl.lmco.com/projects/ontology/) and saved by the system. The API also has provisions to export the alignment in other formats like C-OWL, SWRL, OWL axioms, XSLT, SEKT-ML and SKOS. The alignments are published as schema level linked data which allows machines to understand the relations among the data sources. This, in turn, can help in linking data instances by providing a basis to compare them.

A unified schema is formed by consolidating the multiple concept schemas. The user can customize this unified view according to his needs, and view integrated data from heterogeneous sources as a uniform table. The table of structured data can be sorted and filtered by different fields or even exported to spreadsheet applications like Microsoft Excel for desired processing.

Although multiple concepts are consolidated into a single unified view, the individual concepts are also retained along with their own definitions and descriptions. This maintains the multiple perspectives different individuals hold. Commonalities and differences between the intensions of the concepts can be identified by people with the help of individual descriptions of the concepts. The consolidation process only abstracts the compatible and complementary attributes from the individual concepts into a virtual unified concept. We do not attempt to produce a consolidated description for the concepts at this stage.

Consolidated Linked Data Instances

If we consider the concept instances, consolidation results in two levels of linked data – *consolidated/global* linked data and *local/contextual* linked data.

The data originating from an individual source fully confirms to the conceptualizations within the context of the source though it may not be consistent in a different context for a different source. So this data can be treated as *local/contextual* with respect to the source. It includes all and only the original data instances from the source. The local/contextual linked data mainly serves the local requirements that need to be fulfilled for the application and context associated with the source, irrespective of other sources. These are the requirements of the direct users of the information source who share the same local context and perspectives. With the local linked data, it is easy to maintain compatibility with existing legacy systems and useful semantic applications may be provided at the local level.

On the other hand, the data source is also exposed for integration with other sources. The *consolidated/global* linked data is the result of integration of several local linked data at the schema level. It provides an integrated view of the complete collection of data instances derived from all the sources. All global data can be treated uniformly irrespective of the source of origin. It confirms to the unified model compatible to all the sources involved. Schema elements that are not consistent with a source would not appear in the consolidated view. So some context-dependent information and requirements may not be retained in the consolidated view. Therefore, both local and global linked data are maintained and shared.

While combining partial schemas from multiple sources a consolidated vocabulary to structure data instances gradually emerges. Hence, while the Semantic Web is usually considered for data integration at the record level, data integration, in the first place, can produce rich linked data and emerging vocabulary for the Semantic Web. The consolidation also serves information exchange among the different local linked data sources. The schema level mappings relate these two levels of linked data and allow information translation to suit different needs.

The consolidated/global linked data may be materialized or simply used as immaterialized views depending upon the situation and implementation choice. If the local sources have stabilized, i.e., further updates or additions to the local database would rarely be done, and integrated data is more significant, it would be better to materialize the consolidated/global linked data. When the local sources update rapidly and the local view is more important, the consolidated linked data may be computed only when needed without materializing the instances. Otherwise it would be difficult to keep the consolidated linked data up-to-date.

EXPERIMENT ON CONCEPTUALIZATION

An experiment was conducted to study conceptualizations done by different people on the same thing. This was done with the following questions in mind.

- Can people express their conceptualization in terms of a schema with attributes and values?
- How different people conceptualize and model the same thing?
- Can we consolidate independent conceptualizations to form richer consolidated conceptualizations?

The participants were given short text passages to read and asked to list down facts about the thing

each text was about. By showing some examples, they were asked to list down important facts in the form of attributes and values. They were provided with blank tables to fill such attribute-value pairs. All the participants were given the same 6 short text passages, in the domain of travel in Japan. These included 2 passages about hotels, 2 about temples and 2 about museums in Japan. The participants were from 5 different countries and all were fluent in English. They were graduate students from different fields.

The participants required about 57 minutes in average (from 45 to 80 minutes) to complete this experiment (for total 6 passages of text, or about 10 minutes per passage). This includes the time to read, conceptualize and to write down all the attribute and values on the provided sheet. Thus, this indicates that people are able to conceptualize and express things in a structured way in terms of attributes and values, within reasonable time.

The attributes defined by the different participants for each text instance were then consolidated manually. Corresponding attributes were aligned and unified as consolidated or global attributes. 47 such consolidated attributes were formed in total. It was observed that none of the participants have the same conceptualization over the same given texts. Each person has at least some unique aspects to add. Only when all these conceptualizations were consolidated, the full consolidated schema was formed.

Most of these conceptualizations overlapped significantly in spite of the fact that the individual conceptualizations were done independently. Almost all attributes overlapped with at least some attribute in someone else's conceptualization. Hence, we can say that it is possible to combine conceptualizations of the same thing by different people and form a richer consolidated conceptualization. The different types of alignment relations found in the consolidated attributes are shown in Table 2.

It shows that most of the overlapping parts can be aligned and mostly by equivalence relations.

Table 2. Different types of alignments found

Alignment relation	Number
Equivalent	16
almost equivalent	8
Composite	3
Similar	3
mixed (unifiable)	9
mixed (complex)	7
Unary	1
Sum	47

16 were equivalent and 8 were almost equivalent with slight differences in coverage. Some relations may be more complex but still can be mapped or unified. For the 3 composite alignment relations, two or more attributes combined could be aligned to a single attribute in another schema. 3 alignments were similar with similar intension for the values. 9 alignments were unifiable - the attribute sets in multiple schemas were all about one thing when unified. 7 other consolidated attributes had more complex mixed relations that could not be mapped directly. There was only a single unary alignment relation, i.e., an attribute which did not have any other corresponding attribute. Hence, most of the attributes could be aligned into a consolidated schema.

If we consider the labels of aligned attributes, only 9 consolidated attributes had same labels in all the constituent attributes, 16 had similar attribute labels mapped, 21 consolidated attributes consisted of mixed labels including similar, different and related labels. Thus, attribute labels need not necessarily be the same or similar to be aligned with other attributes.

EMERGENCE OF LIGHTWEIGHT ONTOLOGIES

Enabling people to contribute concepts freely would result in a huge cloud of concepts. However, there are several ways by which prominent, stable and converging knowledge structures can emerge from the user contributions. Firstly, provision for collaborative maintenance and reuse helps in evolution and refinement of existing concepts. Secondly, consolidation of the user-defined schemas, which may be partial definitions from different perspectives, results into more complete definitions satisfying wider requirements. Thirdly, popularity in the community can bring out good contributions to prominence. The popularity may be decided by various indicators like usage, ratings, etc. Finally, we can organize the concepts systematically by grouping or clustering similar concepts. This can be done semi-automatically with computations and community effort while organizing contents for themselves. These mechanisms facilitate the emergence of ontological structures embodying the knowledge and consensus of the community. Such ontologies fall on the lightweight side of the spectrum of expressiveness defined by Corcho, Fernández-López and Gómez-Pérez (as cited in Schaffert, Gruber and Westenthaler, 2005, p. 7) as emerging informal vocabularies of concepts and relations for structured information sharing.

Ontology emergence in our approach is similar to that in the business semantics management approach (De Leenheer, Christiaens, & Meersman, 2010) based on the DOGMA approach. We describe more details about it in the related work section. In the approach, a common shared ontology base is formed by the consolidation of multiple perspectives of the stakeholders in the community. Our approach also fits quite well into the model of ontology maturing described by Braun, Schmidt, Walter, Nagypal and Zacharias (2007). In the first phase, emergence of ideas, the community freely contributes structured concept schemas. In the second phase, consolidation in communities, people use each others' concepts as common vocabulary to share structured data, concepts evolve with refinements along with appropriate versions and these are explicitly consolidated by aligning corresponding features.

Figure 11. Concept Cloud in StYLiD

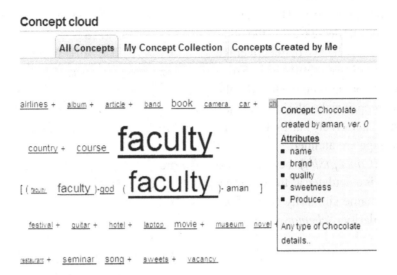

The third phase, formalization, is partly covered by grouping and organizing similar or related concepts to form lightweight ontologies. However, the organization is quite informal and we do not proceed towards the final phase of axiomatization for making heavyweight ontologies.

Consolidated Concept Cloud

All concepts are visualized in a *Concept Cloud* as shown in Figure 11. As the community collaboratively contributes and updates concept definitions, these evolve to satisfy more people. Popular concepts having more data instances appear bigger in the cloud and, in turn, gain more attention for use. In this way, prominent definitions gradually emerge out from the cloud as concepts evolve incrementally and more data instances are contributed.

A consolidated concept can be expanded into a *sub-cloud* showing all the versions defined by different users, labeled with the creator name and version number. In the sub-cloud, multiple versions defined by the same user are subgrouped together. In Figure 11, the "faculty" concept has been expanded to show two versions by the user

"god" and one version by "aman". The sizes of all versions in the sub-cloud add up to form the size of the consolidated concept. Clicking on the consolidated concept retrieves all instances of all its versions. We can also list instances of the versions defined by a single user by clicking on the user name. Hence, the concept cloud helps in browsing concept instances at different levels of granularity.

Grouping Similar Concepts

Similar concepts are automatically grouped by the system. This can serve two purposes. Firstly, it becomes easy to find out same or similar concepts that can be consolidated. For simplicity, concepts with the same name are grouped together first. Then, groups of other similar concepts are also suggested by clustering them under some similarity threshold. However, the user is free to consolidate any concepts if he/she considers them the same or similar. Secondly, grouping similar concepts helps in organizing the concepts so that browsing and locating information becomes easy and relations among concepts become more apparent.

A higher threshold will result in tight concept groups with higher similarity. However, the coverage of concepts will decrease. On the other hand, a lower threshold will have better coverage at the cost of allowing lower similarities. Some experimental observations are demonstrated in the next section. An appropriate threshold value may be reached by testing iteratively until satisfactory accuracy and coverage are attained.

The similarity (*ConceptSim*) between two concepts, C_1 and C_2, is calculated as the weighted sum of the concept name similarity (*NameSim*) and the schema similarity (*SchemaSim*).

$$ConceptSim(C_1,C_2) = w_1*NameSim(N_1, N_2) + w_2*SchemaSim(S_1, S_2) \qquad (1)$$

where N_1 and N_2 are the names of the concepts, S_1 and S_2 are the associated schemas respectively and w_1 and w_2 are the percentage weights ($w_1 + w_2 = 1.0$).

Appropriate values for the weights are also determined by iterative testing with a fixed threshold. As described in the next section, it has been observed that w_1, the name similarity, is much more significant than w_2, the schema similarity, and has to be assigned a higher weight accordingly.

Schema Similarity. The algorithm used to calculate the schema similarity *SchemaSim*(S_1, S_2) is shown in following pseudocode.

```
Function SchemaSim (S_1, S_2)
Begin
A_1 = {attributes (S_1)}, A_2 = {attri-
butes (S_2)}, n_1 = | A_1 |, n_2 = | A_2 |
For  i = 1 to n_1
Begin
For  j = 1 to n_2
Begin
    SimilarityMatrix [ i ] [ j ] =
NameSim (A_1 [ i ], A_2 [ j ])
End
```

```
End
BestMatchingPairs = HungarianAlgo-
rithm (SimilarityMatrix)
Sum = 0,  m = | BestMatchingPairs |
For  k = 1 to m
    Begin
(p, q) = BestMatchingPairs [ k ]
Sum = Sum + SimilarityMatrix [ p ] [
q ]
End
Return  2.0 * Sum / (n_1 +  n_2)
End
```

The algorithm calculates the name similarities (*NameSim*) between all possible pairs of attributes to create an $n_1 * n_2$ matrix. *NameSim* is described next. The Hungarian algorithm (Kuhn, 1955), described below, is applied over this matrix to determine the best matching pairs of attributes. Finally, *SchemaSim*(S_1, S_2) is calculated as the matching average of these sets of attribute similarities.

matching average = $2*\sum$ name similarity of matching attribute pairs/($|A_1|+|A_2|$) (2)

where A_1 and A_2 are the attribute sets of S_1 and S_2 respectively.

Hungarian algorithm. The Hungarian algorithm is a combinatorial optimization method for solving the assignment problem - given a weighted complete bipartite graph $G = (X \cup Y, X \times Y)$ where edge xy has weight w(xy), find a matching M from X to Y with maximum weight.

Simpson and Dao (2005) used the Hungarian algorithm to find the semantic similarity between two sentences. We have adapted their technique to find the similarity between two schemas. The time complexity of the Hungarian algorithm is $O(n^3)$. There are more sophisticated approaches for calculating the schema similarity (Castano, De Antonellis, Fugini, & Pernici, 1998; Rahm & Bernstein, 2001) depending on the complexity of the schema and accuracy needed. We do not have complex hierarchical schemas and strict data types and we do not expect perfection in informal user-defined schemas. So we rather used a simple and fast method with acceptable results.

Name Similarity. The name similarity *NameSim* between the concept labels, or attribute labels, is calculated using the Lin's algorithm for WordNet-based similarity (Lin, 1998) (WordNet 2.1 has been used). However, if a word is not found in WordNet, the Levenshtein distance is used to calculate the edit distance similarity. The Levenshtein distance measures the difference between two strings by the minimum number of operations needed to transform one into the other.

For all possible pairs of concepts C_1, C_2 *ConceptSim* is calculated using equation 1. Pairs of concepts with *ConceptSim* above the threshold are considered to be related. Finally, all related concepts are collected into groups.

Browsing Concept Groups. Browsing different types of concepts and data becomes more convenient and intuitive when related concepts are grouped together. Clusters of similar concepts can be effectively visualized using tools like Cytoscape (http://www.cytoscape.org/) which is an open source platform for visualizing graphs with large number of nodes and relations. A screenshot of Cytoscape is shown in Figure 12.

Concepts are the nodes and relation edges may be drawn between similar concepts weighted by the similarity value (*ConceptSim*). Visualization techniques are available to show more similar nodes close to each other than less similar nodes. This provides a clearer and meaningful visualization of the groups of similar concepts. These groups of concepts may further be connected up into a single network with the help of relations in WordNet or other semantic networks like the ConceptNet (Liu & Singh, 2004) or an upper ontology like OpenCyC (http://www.opencyc. org/).

Multiple Concept Generalizations

Similar or related concepts may also be consolidated to form a more generic concept. For example, 'hotel' and 'apartment' concepts can be consolidated to form an 'accommodation' concept. Then all hotels and apartments can be searched together conveniently as 'accommodation'. Different users may group and consolidate the same concepts in different ways depending upon their requirements or perspectives. For example, another user may group 'hotel' with 'restaurant' to create an 'eating place' concept. Hence, the same set of concepts may be organized in bottom-up fashion in multiple ways by different people.

In this way, concepts can be grouped and organized collaboratively by the community along with some automatic assistance. This results in an informal organization of the user-defined concepts which evolves according to the needs of the community.

Effective Usage of the System

As discussed in the application scenarios the system may be used for general purpose or within specific domains and communities. The basic workflow consists of user actions like defining new concepts, posting data instances, grouping related concepts and consolidating similar concepts by aligning their schemas. Although help manuals and some initial training may be useful, we want that zero or minimal training should be required. Users are also assisted automatically by the system to some extent. The usage of the system also depends upon domain specific requirements and nature of the user community.

The system gives freedom to the users in order to accommodate personal requirements and perspectives. It can be self-regulated though some moderation may be needed for control. As existing social applications have demonstrated, we can expect reasonable contributions from users and meaningful knowledge structures to

Figure 12. Visualization of similar concept groupings using Cytoscape

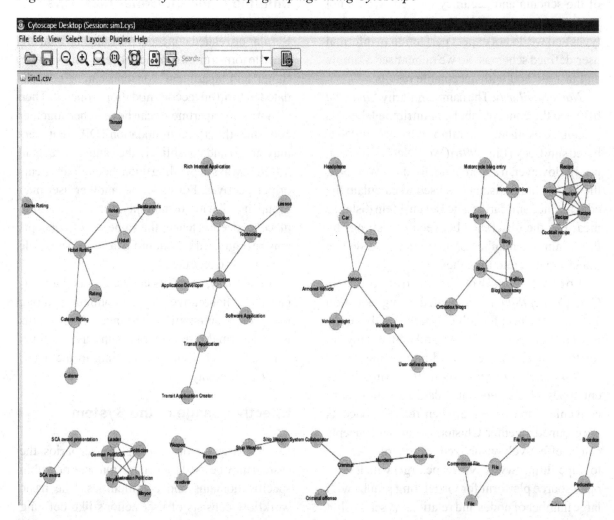

emerge. Online social applications like wikis and tagging collect huge amounts of good data in spite of having totally relaxed interface and complete freedom. Popularity also helps in filtering out noise from mass contributions and further these can be monitored collaboratively.

EXPERIMENTS WITH EXISTING DATA

We did some experiments using data from Freebase. Freebase has a large collection of user-defined types and data which is freely available and also provides a convenient API.

These experiments are mainly intended to make some observations about the user-defined concepts, verify our views about multiple conceptualizations and to validate the techniques we used for concept consolidation and grouping. The experiments are not meant to be a full evaluation of the proposed approach. However, this can be considered as a partial indirect evaluation as we validate the methods used in the important steps. We can say that if our assumptions and arguments are valid and the methods work correctly then the output should also be as expected. It is not straightforward to evaluate the outputs, including the user-generated concepts, structured linked data, consolidated concepts and the informal lightweight ontologies. Ontology evaluation is a very difficult, indirect and imperfect area (Brank, Grobelnik, & Mladenić, 2005). Moreover, the ontologies, in our case, emerge as informal vocabulary for information sharing, providing lesser basis to evaluate. As users are an integral part of the approach, we should involve them directly in future evaluation.

Freebase User-Defined Types

We retrieved all user-defined schema definitions, or types, from the system (as on May 20, 2008) by querying it directly using the provided API. We only considered user-defined types, contained in the user's domain, and not standard freebase types, as we are interested in how different people model their data. Firstly, many unwanted user-defined types had to be filtered out including types created by the users for test purposes, spam, etc. (though Freebase provides a sandbox for test purpose). This resulted in 1,852 types. We further filtered out types with no instance leaving us with total 1,412 types. There were total 500 users who defined at least one concept. This considerable number of types defined by many users, from a system in its initial stages, indicates that there is, in fact, a wide variety of data types different users are interested in and that users are willing to define their own concept schemas. We also observed that most people define very few concepts (only 1 to 5) but altogether it amounts to so many concepts. This makes up the long tail of information types that small groups of people are interested in.

Concept Consolidation

We tested our method of concept consolidation by automatically consolidating user-defined Freebase types with the same name, slight morphological variants or synonyms (using WordNet-based similarity as 1.0) assuming that they represent the same concept. From the 1,412 concepts, 57 such groups were found. There may also be other sets

of same concepts but differently named. Anyway this supports our view that different people define the same concept in their own ways. Even up to 6 versions of the same concept were found. There were also a few cases where the same user defined multiple versions of a concept. There were 2 to 6 constituent concepts in each group to be consolidated.

Then we tested our schema alignment mechanism on the Freebase user-defined schemas. A similarity threshold of 0.6 was used in the alignment API implementation for determining attribute alignments. The threshold has been chosen by trial to achieve a good coverage with satisfactory precision. 44 sets of aligned attributes (forming the consolidated attributes) with total 51 alignment relations were found from the consolidated concepts.

Most of the alignments were found to be reasonable along with about 6 wrong alignment relations (i.e., 45 right relations or a precision of 88.24%). A PhD student with informatics background helped in the evaluation judgments. The sets of aligned attributes were made into a list. The judge was asked to mark the attributes in each set that do not seem to match with the other attributes in the set, if any. The attributes in each set were considered to be connected by similarity relations. Then, we tried to list out all the correct alignment relations manually, though it is difficult to point out all and some may be subjective. We found total 67 alignment relations. Hence, the recall is about 67.16%. So we see that even with simple methods for schema alignment, the precision can be quite good with a satisfactory recall. Certainly, more alignments with better accuracy can be found with more sophisticated techniques and human involvement.

Grouping Similar Concepts

Using the process described earlier, clusters of similar user-defined concepts were determined (as seen in Figure 12). Concept groupings were

Table 3. Evaluation of similar concept grouping

Threshold	Groups found	Nodes covered	Relations found	Correct nodes (%)	Correct relations (%)
0.5	177	639 (45.25%)	608	87.95	79.44
0.8	108	275(19.48%)	194	95.64	94.33

formed using different values for the concept similarity threshold. Concepts were considered to be related if the similarity was above the threshold. Each of these groups of concepts was shown to the same human judge. He was asked to mark if any concept does not seem to belong to the group. The similarity relations were listed as concept pairs and the judge was asked if each pair was similar or not. The total number of nodes and relations in each cluster, total number of incorrect nodes and total number of incorrect relations were noted. Observations are summarized in Table 3 below (for $w_1 = 0.7$ and $w_2 = 0.3$ in Equation 1).

The different values for the threshold were used to observe its effect in finding relations and groupings. The shown values may not be the optimal ones but these help in observing the trend. Also, the results are not meant to be perfect due to the subjective nature of the decisions. However, it gives us a general idea and, moreover, relative observations helps us to analyze the effect of changing the parameters. Appropriate values for the threshold and the weights may be determined iteratively.

The observed results show that groups of similar concepts can be formed with good precision. Further, it suggests that with tighter threshold more precise groups can be formed but the coverage of nodes and relations decreases, forming

lesser number of groups. With a lower threshold, the coverage can increase significantly while the precision still remains quite good. Thus, the threshold can be tuned to produce appropriate level of groupings.

We also experimented by varying the weights for *NameSim* and *SchemaSim* (w_1 and w_2 respectively) in Equation 1. Table 4 shows the effect of varying the weights keeping a constant threshold of 0.8. Grouping with schema similarity alone (w1 = 0, w2 = 1), ignoring concept name similarity, produced poor results. Only 42.65% nodes were grouped correctly. The coverage was also low (9.63%). This is because even dissimilar concepts may sometimes have similar schemas. On the other hand, using the concept name similarity alone (w1 = 1, w2 = 0), ignoring the schema similarity, already produces much better results. Hence, the concept name similarity plays a much more significant role than the schema similarity in calculating overall schema similarity.

However, weighted combination of both the similarity measures produced best results. For w1 = 0.7 and w2 = 0.3, the number of groups found, total nodes and relations covered, percentage of correct nodes and relations were all higher than the other two cases. The optimal weight parameters may be determined by testing iteratively.

Table 4. Concept grouping results by varying weight parameters (threshold = 0.8)

Parameters Threshold = 0.8	Groups found	Nodes covered	Relations found	Correct nodes (%)	Correct relations (%)
$w_1 = 0$, $w_2 = 1$	60	136 (9.63%)	98	42.65	32.65
$w_1 = 1$, $w_2 = 0$	101	233 (16.5%)	175	78.97	83.43
$w_1 = 0.7$, $w_2 = 0.3$	108	275(19.48%)	194	95.64	94.33

RELATED WORK

There are several related works if we consider various aspects of the proposed approach. However, none of the works cover all these aspects together.

The combination of social software with Semantic Web technologies has been gaining significant attention recently (Ankolekar et al., 2007; Gruber, 2008; Schaffert, 2006b) and there are several works that try to enable ordinary users to produce Semantic Web contents by using social software. There had been a lot of work on semantic blogging (Cayzer, 2004; Karger & Quan, 2005; Möller, Bojars, & Breslin, 2006) which exploits the easy publishing paradigm of blogs and enhance them with semantic structure. However, only limited types of instance data are produced and the schemas do not evolve. Revyu (Heath & Motta, 2007) allows sharing a wide variety of data by reviewing and rating anything. Things are interlinked using URIs to produce linked data. However, most concepts are modeled simply as things without modeling the detailed structure of the information.

Freebase (Bollacker et al., 2007), similar to Google Base (http://base.google.com/), allows users to define their own schemas to model different types of data. StYLiD also follows the same way. However, in these systems, the structured types defined by different users are kept separate in their own spaces and not consolidated or related in any way. Though some instance level reconciliation ("dataserver/reconciliation," 2008) is done in Freebase, schema level consolidation is not done. So it is difficult to fully utilize the structured schemas defined by the mass. Further, it is difficult for casual users to create their own types because of strict constraint requirements and the elaborate interface. It is difficult to enter instance data because of the strict type constraints. It is also difficult to link to external resources from within Freebase.

Exhibit (Huynh et al., 2007) is a lightweight framework which enables casual users to publish web pages with different types of structured data based on their own schema. However, authoring such structured data pages seems to be cumbersome to the users. DataPress (Benson, Marcus, Howahl, & Karger, 2010) is a blogging platform extension which enables structured data sharing. It also allows user-defined schema, defined personally or collaboratively. However, it does not publish data directly in linked data format.

There are many other works on collaborative knowledge base creation. Semantic wikis facilitate collaborative creation of resources by defining properties as wiki links with well-defined semantics. Many semantic wikis support the building of ontologies too. Buffa, Gandon, Ereteo, Sander and Faron (2008) have reported on the state-of-art of semantic wikis. The Semantic MediaWiki (Krötzsch, Vrandečić, & Völkel, 2006) and IkeWiki (Schaffert, 2006a) are among the most popular ones. The myOntology project (Siorpaes & Hepp, 2007a) also uses wikis for community-driven horizontal lightweight ontology building by enabling general users to contribute. But when the direct goal is ontology construction, it may be difficult to motivate people. Moreover, though these collaborative platforms are semantically powerful and consistent, they seem to have considerable learning curve for ordinary people and usability issues to be addressed by interface enhancements (Pfisterer et al., 2008). There are also other community-driven lightweight ontology construction applications like ImageNotion and SOBOLEO (Braun et al., 2007), where users collaboratively build a SKOS taxonomy from tags while using them to annotate resources. In most of the collaborative systems, mainly wiki-based systems like semantic wikis, Freebase, myOntology, etc., each concept or resource has a single prominent model which everyone is assumed to settle with. However, in practice, multiple conceptualizations may exist. Moreover, collaborative interaction for consensus is itself a difficult and time-consuming process. Therefore, we allow multiple conceptualizations without mandating direct collaboration and consensus.

The necessity for representing and relating multiple conceptualizations has also been pointed out by others. Takeda, Iino and Nishida (1995) modeled heterogeneous system of ontologies using aspects. Afsharchi and Behrouz (2006) have proposed an approach for automated ontology evolution in a multi-agent system in which individual agents maintain their own ontologies rather than committing to a common global ontology. The approaches presented by Bailin and Truszkowski (2002), Wiesman and Roos (2004) also consist of agents having different domain models of the same domain, and enable the agents to mutually augment their ontologies.

Distributed Description Logics (DDLs) (Borgida & Serafini, 2003) is a formalism for loosely combining different DL knowledge bases preserving the identity and independence of each local ontology. C-OWL (Bouquet, Giunchiglia, Van Harmelen, Serafini, & Stuckenschmidt, 2004) is an extension to OWL using DDL for contextual ontologies. ε-connections (Kutz, Lutz, Wolter, & Zakharyaschev, 2004) is also a method for combining logical formalisms. Grau, Parsia and Sirin (2004) had proposed extensions to OWL based on ε-connections.

Our approach is in line with the DOGMA approach (Meersman, 1999; Jarrar & Meersman, 2002; Jarrar & Meersman, 2008) for formal ontology engineering which distinguishes between domain and application-specific axiomatizations or conceptualizations as stated in the "ontology double articulation principle". There may be multiple application-specific perspectives sharing the same domain conceptualization. The domain conceptualization is maintained as an ontology base consisting of context-specific binary fact-types called *lexons*. Contexts can accommodate different, even inconsistent, conceptualizations in the same ontology base. De Leenheer et al. (2010) have proposed an approach for business semantics

management (BSM) based on the foundations of DOGMA and DOGMA-MESS (De Leenheer & Debruyne, 2008). BSM enables collaboration among business stakeholders and the reconciliation of heterogeneous business metadata in different organizations. In a phase of community-based semantic reconciliation business semantics are modeled by extracting, refining, articulating and consolidating fact-types from existing sources. The consolidation is based on semantic equivalence and removal of redundancies resulting into consolidated semantic patterns stored in the community-shared semantic pattern base.

There is a large body of research about data integration (Lenzerini, 2002), schema matching (Rahm & Bernstein, 2001) and ontology alignment (Euzenat et al., 2004) and we do not intend to develop new methods for these. Rather we propose the utilization of data integration principles and alignment techniques to create new consolidated concept definitions from user-defined schemas and produce integrated linked data. Zhdanova and Shvaiko (2006) have introduced the notion of community-driven ontology matching. Potluck (Huynh, Miller, & Karger, 2007) is a user-friendly interface enabling casual users to align structured data schemas. We also propose community-driven schema alignment, but assisted with some automation. The mapping is among small user-defined schemas, which would be easier for ordinary users, unlike mapping entire ontologies. Further, we propose exposing the alignments as schema level linked data. Jain, Hitzler, Sheth, Verma, and Yeh (2010) have also highlighted the need for schema-level linking among Linked Open Datasets by proposing an ontology alignment system.

Tijerino, Embley, Lonsdale, Ding and Nagy (2005) have proposed an approach to generate ontologies from tables semi-automatically. Tables are reverse engineered to create mini-ontologies. These are mapped and merged to form a growing global ontology. In our approach, concepts are created by social participation, not by automatic generation. Mapping and merging is also supported by the community. Concept consolidation creates richer concept definitions rather than directly adding up to a monolithic ontology. The consolidated concepts can later be grouped to form emerging ontologies.

There are many works on deriving emergent knowledge structures from social data. Lightweight ontologies may be derived from folksonomies (Specia & Motta, 2007; Van Damme et al., 2007) applying basic ideas like grouping similar tags, forming emergent concepts from them, making the semantics more explicit and utilizing external knowledge resources to find semantic relations. Mika (2007) had proposed a unified model of social networks and tagged resources serving emergence of informal lightweight ontologies. Tang, Leung, Luo, Chen and Gong (2009) propose an ontology learning approach to construct hierarchical structure from folksonomies. Similar techniques are also applicable in our case over the concept schemas defined by the community. Folksonomies serve collaborative organization of objects using tags. However, the actual data objects are still left unstructured and cannot be processed by machines.

The HyperTag conceptual model (García-Castro, Hepp, & García, 2009) allows tags to be used to consolidate related tags. Relations between the tags are established by the community, similar to the community-supported alignment in our approach. The TagSorting approach (García-Castro, Hepp, & García, 2010), which is built upon the HyperTag model, is a collaborative ontology building process conducted iteratively by a group of participants. A consolidation is automatically generated taking into account all participants' taggings and votes. Then, the manager does a final review to approve the ontology. The approach eventually expects to achieve consolidation and interlinking of knowledge in social tagging systems and deriving lightweight ontologies.

CONCLUSION

In this article, we suggested enabling ordinary users to author linked data with the help of simple human interfaces. This is significant for the paradigm shift from document publishing and hyperlinking to data publishing and data-linking on the linked data web. We have implemented a simple linked data authoring system, StYLiD, a social software which enables ordinary people to share a wide variety of structured data. We can facilitate free data contribution by allowing users to define their own concept schemas and providing a flexible input interface. The system combines various aspects of social software and Semantic Web technologies into a synergetic whole. The usability experiment showed people are able to use StYLiD even without any training, although the usability still needs to be improved.

We proposed allowing multiple conceptualizations and, at the same time, consolidating them into a unified model. This is possible with data integration principles and semi-automatic schema alignment methods. Data sources are linked at the schema level and integrated linked data can be produced which is richer than the individual sources. We proposed consolidation of multiple user-defined concepts as a new approach for community-driven creation of conceptualizations. Such loose collaboration requires minimal interaction and consensus unlike the usual form of collaboration based on common understanding over a single model. Experimental observations also suggested that different people conceptualize in multiple ways and such conceptualizations can practically be consolidated by aligning the schemas.

Concepts defined by the community can evolve incrementally and emerge by popularity while users share structured data. These can be grouped and organized semi-automatically. Hence, informal lightweight ontologies can gradually emerge as a by-product of structured information sharing which is the primary objective of the community, and not ontology construction.

Experiments on Freebase user-defined schemas supported our view that different people are interested in a wide range of things and maintain multiple conceptualizations. The experiments also validated the methods we used for concept consolidation and grouping similar concepts.

Future Directions

Many directions are open for the future. We may work on computing hierarchical and non-hierarchical relations between structured concepts besides just similarity relations. We may employ sophisticated alignment techniques and enable more complex alignments. Consolidation of data instances is still an open problem though some dataset-specific automated linking algorithms have been demonstrated (Bizer et al., 2007). This work focuses on the creation of new concept definitions by the community. However, we should also devise ways to reuse existing vocabularies and ontologies or map concept definitions to them without requiring ordinary users to understand the ontologies. The posts containing the structured data objects may also be weaved into the social linked data web using SIOC (Bojārs, Passant, Cyganiak, & Breslin, 2008). We can introduce plugins and mash-ups, which may be contributed by the community itself, to exploit different types of structured data. We may also enable users to share scrapers for collecting data from existing websites easily.

REFERENCES

Afsharchi, M., & Behrouz, H. F. (2006). Automated ontology evolution in a multi-agent system. In *Proceedings of the 1st international conference on Scalable information systems (InfoScale '06)*, Hong Kong. ACM Press.

Ankolekar, A., Krötzsch, M., Tran, T., & Vrandečić, D. (2007). The two cultures: Mashing up Web 2.0 and the Semantic Web. In *Proceedings of the 16th International World Wide Web Conference (WWW2007)* (pp. 825–834). New York, NY: ACM Press.

Auer, S., Bizer, C., Lehmann, J., Kobilarov, G., Cyganiak, R., & Ives, Z. (2007). DBpedia: A nucleus for a web of open data. In K. Aberer, K. S. Choi, N. Noy, D. Allemang, K. I. Lee, L. J. B. Nixon, … P. Cudré-Mauroux (Eds.), *Proceedings of the 6th International Semantic Web Conference and 2nd Asian Semantic Web Conference (ISWC/ASWC2007)*. (LNCS 4825) (pp. 715–728). Heidelberg, Germany: Springer.

Bailin, S., & Truszkowski, W. (2002). Ontology negotiation between intelligent information agents. *The Knowledge Engineering Review*, *17*(1), 7–19. doi:10.1017/S0269888902000292

Benson, E., Marcus, A., Howahl, F., & Karger, D. (2010). Talking about data: Sharing richly structured information through blogs and wikis. In *Proceedings of the 9th International Semantic Web Conference (ISWC2010)*, Shanghai, China.

Berners-Lee, T. (2006). *Design issues: Linked data*. Retrieved December 24, 2008, from http://www.w3.org/DesignIssues/LinkedData.html

Bizer, C., Cyganiak, R., & Heath, T. (2007). *How to publish linked data on the Web*. Retrieved December 25, 2008, from http://www4.wiwiss.fu-berlin.de/bizer/pub/LinkedDataTutorial/

Bojārs, U., Passant, A., Cyganiak, R., & Breslin, J. (2008). Weaving SIOC into the web of linked data. In *Proceedings of the Workshop on Linked Data on the Web (LDOW2008)*.

Bollacker, K., Tufts, P., Pierce, T., & Cook, R. (2007). *A platform for scalable, collaborative, structured information integration*. In AAAI-07, Sixth International Workshop on Information Integration on the Web.

Borgida, A., & Serafini, L. (2003). Distributed description logics: Assimilating information from peer sources. *Journal of Data Semantics, 1*, 153–184. doi:10.1007/978-3-540-39733-5_7

Bouquet, P., Giunchiglia, F., Van Harmelen, F., Serafini, L., & Stuckenschmidt, H. (2004). Contextualizing ontologies. *Web Semantics: Science* [Elsevier.]. *Services and Agents on the World Wide Web, 1*(4), 325–343. doi:10.1016/j.websem.2004.07.001

Brank, J., Grobelnik, M., & Mladenić, D. (2005). A survey of ontology evaluation techniques. In *Proceedings of the Conference on Data Mining and Data Warehouses (SiKDD 2005)*.

Braun, S., Schmidt, A., Walter, A., Nagypal, G., & Zacharias, V. (2007). Ontology maturing: A collaborative Web 2.0 approach to ontology engineering. In *Proceedings of the Workshop on Social and Collaborative Construction of Structured Knowledge at the 16th International World Wide Web Conference (WWW 07)* (pp. 8-12).

Brooke, J. (1996). SUS: A quick and dirty usability scale. *Usability Evaluation in Industry*, 189-194.

Buffa, M., Gandon, F., Ereteo, G., Sander, P., & Faron, C. (2008). SweetWiki: A semantic wiki. *Journal of Web Semantics, 6*(1), 84–97. doi:10.1016/j.websem.2007.11.003

Castano, S., De Antonellis, V., Fugini, M. G., & Pernici, B. (1998). Conceptual schema analysis: Techniques and applications. [New York, NY: ACM.]. *ACM Transactions on Database Systems, 23*(3), 286–333. doi:10.1145/293910.293150

Cayzer, S. (2004). Semantic blogging and decentralized knowledge management. *Communications of the ACM, 47*(12), 48–52. doi:10.1145/1035134.1035164

Dataserver/reconciliation. (2008). *Freebase.* Retrieved December 25, 2008, from http://www.freebase.com/view/guid/9202a8c04000641f8000000007beed56

De Leenheer, P., Christiaens, S., & Meersman, R. (2010). Business semantics management: A case study for competency-centric HRM. *Journal of Computers in Industry: Special Issue about Semantic Web* [Elsevier.]. *Computers in Industry, 61*(8), 760–775. doi:10.1016/j.compind.2010.05.005

De Leenheer, P., & Debruyne, C. (2008). DOGMA-MESS: A tool for fact-oriented collaborative ontology evolution. In Meersman, R., Tari, Z., & Herrero, P. (Eds.), *OTM 2008 Workshops, (LNCS 5333)* (pp. 797–806). Berlin/ Heidelberg, Germany: Springer-Verlag.

Euzenat, J. (2004). An API for ontology alignment. In S.A. McIlraith, D. Plexousakis, & F. Van Harmelen (Eds.), *International Semantic Web Conference.* (LNCS 3298) (pp. 698–712). Springer.

Euzenat, J., Le Bach, T., Barrasa, J., Bouquet, P., De Bo, J., Dieng-Kuntz, et al. (2004). *State of the art on ontology alignment.* Knowledge Web Deliverable D2.2.3.

García-Castro, L. J., Hepp, M., & García, A. (2009). Tags4Tags: Using tagging to consolidate tags. In S. Bhowmick, J. Küng, & R. Wagner (Eds.), *Database and expert systems applications* (LNCS 5690, pp. 619-628).

García-Castro, L. J., Hepp, M., & García, A. (2010). TagSorting: A tagging environment for collaboratively building ontologies. In *Proceedings of the 17th International Conference on Knowledge Engineering and Knowledge Management (EKAW2010)*, Lisbon, Portugal (LNCS 6317).

Grau, B. C., Parsia, B., & Sirin, E. (2004). Working with multiple ontologies on the Semantic Web. In *The Semantic Web – ISWC 2004, (LNCS 3298)* (pp. 620–634). Berlin / Heidelberg, Germany: Springer. doi:10.1007/978-3-540-30475-3_43

Gruber, T. (2008). Collective knowledge systems: Where the social Web meets the Semantic Web. *Journal of Web Semantics, 6*(1), 4–13.

Hasan, T., & Jameson, A. (2008). Bridging the motivation gap for individual annotators: What can we learn from photo annotation systems? In *Proceedings of the 1st Workshop on Incentives for the Semantic Web (INSEMTIVE 2008), Karlsruhe, Germany.*

Heath, T., & Motta, E. (2007). Revyu.com: A reviewing and rating site for the web of data. In K. Aberer, K. S. Choi, N. F. Noy, D. Allemang, K. I. Lee, L. J. B. Nixon, … P. Cudré-Mauroux (Eds.), *ISWC/ASWC 2007,* (LNCS 4825), (pp. 895–902). Springer.

Hepp, M. (2007). Possible ontologies: How reality constrains the development of relevant ontologies. *IEEE Internet Computing, 11*(1), 90–96. doi:10.1109/MIC.2007.20

Hughes, T. C., & Ashpole, B. C. (2004). The semantics of ontology alignment. In *Proceedings of Information Interpretation and Integration Conference (I3CON), Performance Metrics for Intelligent Systems, PerMIS '04.*

Huynh, D., Karger, D., & Miller, R. (2007). Exhibit: Lightweight structured data publishing. In *Proceedings of the 16th international conference on World Wide Web* (pp. 737–746). New York, NY: ACM Press.

Huynh, D. F., Miller, R. C., & Karger, D. R. (2007). Potluck: Data mash-up tool for casual users. In K. Aberer, K. S. Choi, N. Noy, D. Allemang, K. I. Lee, L. J. B. Nixon, … P. Cudré-Mauroux (Eds.), *ISWC/ASWC 2007.* (LNCS 4825), (pp. 239–252). Springer.

Jain, P., Hitzler, P., Sheth, A. P., Verma, K., & Yeh, P. Z. (2010). Ontology alignment for linked open data. In *Proceedings of the 9th International Semantic Web Conference (ISWC2010)*, Shanghai, China.

Jarrar, M., & Meersman, R. (2002). Formal ontology engineering in the DOGMA approach. In R. Meersman, & Z. Tari (Eds.), *Proceedings of DOA/CoopIS/ODBASE 2002,* (LNCS 2519), (pp. 1238-1254). Berlin/Heidelberg, Germany: Springer-Verlag.

Jarrar, M., & Meersman, R. (2008). Ontology engineering - the DOGMA approach. In *Advances in Web semantics I. (LNCS 4891)*. Springer.

Jhingran, A. (2008). *Web 2.0, enterprise 2.0 and information management. Keynote speech at the Linked Data Planet conference & expo, spring 2008.* New York City.

Karger, D. R., & Quan, D. (2005). What would it mean to blog on the Semantic Web? *Journal of Web Semantics, 3*(2), 147–157. doi:10.1016/j.websem.2005.06.002

Krötzsch, M., Vrandečić, D., & Völkel, M. (2006). Semantic MediaWiki. In *Proceedings of the 5th International Semantic Web Conference (ISWC06)* (pp. 935–942). Springer.

Kuhn, H. W. (1955). The Hungarian method for the assignment problem. *Naval Research Logistics Quarterly, 2*, 83–97. doi:10.1002/nav.3800020109

Kurakawa, K., Shakya, A., & Takeda, H. (2009). A trial on extracting and integrating concepts of university staff directories for federated search. In *Proceedings of the 23rd Annual Conference of the Japanese Society for Artificial Intelligence.*

Kutz, O., Lutz, C., Wolter, F., & Zakharyaschev, M. (2004). ε-connections of abstract description systems. *Artificial Intelligence, 156*(1), 1–73. doi:10.1016/j.artint.2004.02.002

Lenzerini, M. (2002). Data integration: A theoretical perspective. In *Proceedings of the twenty-first ACM SIGMOD-SIGACT-SIGART symposium on Principles of database systems* (pp. 233–246).

Lin, D. (1998). An information-theoretic definition of similarity. In *Proceedings of the 15th International Conference on Machine Learning*.

Liu, H., & Singh, P. (2004). ConceptNet – a practical commonsense reasoning tool-kit. [Springer.]. *BT Technology Journal, 22*(4), 211–226. doi:10.1023/B:BTTJ.0000047600.45421.6d

Meersman, R. (1999). The use of lexicons and other computer-linguistic tools in semantics, design and cooperation of database systems. In *Proceedings of the Conference on Cooperative Database Systems (CODAS99)*, (pp. 1-14). Springer.

Mika, P. (2007). Ontologies are us: A unified model of social networks and semantics. *Web Semantics: Science* [Springer.]. *Services and Agents on the World Wide Web, 5*(1), 5–15. doi:10.1016/j.websem.2006.11.002

Möller, K., Bojārs, U. U., & Breslin, J. G. (2006). Using semantics to enhance the blogging experience. In *The Semantic Web: Research and Applications. (LNCS 4011)* (pp. 679–696). Heidelberg, Germany: Springer. doi:10.1007/11762256_49

Murphy, G. L. (2004). *The big book of concepts.* MIT press.

Nielsen, J. (2006). Participation inequality: Encouraging more users to contribute. *Alertbox: Current Issues in Web Usability.* Retrieved April 16, 2009, from http://www.useit.com/alertbox/participation_inequality.html

Pfisterer, F., Nitsche, M., Jameson, A., & Barbu, C. (2008). *User-centered design and evaluation of interface enhancements to the semantic mediawiki.* In Workshop on Semantic Web User Interaction at CHI 2008.

Rahm, E., & Bernstein, P. (2001). A survey of approaches to automatic schema matching. *The International Journal on Very Large Data Bases, 10*(4), 334–350. doi:10.1007/s007780100057

Schaffert, S. (2006a). IkeWiki: A semantic wiki for collaborative knowledge management. In *Proceedings of the 15th IEEE International Workshops on Enabling Technologies: Infrastructure for Collaborative Enterprises* (pp. 388–396). Washington, DC: IEEE Computer Society.

Schaffert, S. (2006b). Semantic social software: Semantically enabled social software or socially enabled Semantic Web? In *Proceedings of the Semantics 2006 Conference* (pp. 99–112).

Schaffert, S., Gruber, A., & Westenthaler, R. (2005). A semantic wiki for collaborative knowledge formation. In *Proceedings of SEMANTICS 2005 Conference, Vienna, Austria.*

Shakya, A., Takeda, H., & Wuwongse, V. (2008). Consolidating user-defined concepts with StYLiD. In J. Domingue, & C. Anutariya (Eds.), *Proceedings of the 3rd Asian Semantic Web Conference,* (LNCS 5367), (pp. 287-301). Berlin/Heidelberg, Germany: Springer.

Simpson, T., & Dao, T. (2005). *WordNet-based semantic similarity measurement.* Retrieved December 25, 2008, from http://www.codeproject.com/KB/string/semanticsimilaritywordnet.aspx

Siorpaes, K., & Hepp, M. (2007a). myOntology: The marriage of ontology engineering and collective intelligence. In *Bridging the Gap between Semantic Web and Web 2.0 (SemNet 2007)* (pp. 127–138).

Siorpaes, K., & Hepp, M. (2007b). OntoGame: Towards overcoming the incentive bottleneck in ontology building. In *Proceedings of the 3rd International IFIP Workshop on Semantic Web and Web Semantics (SWWS'07), Vilamoura, Portugal.*

Specia, L., & Motta, E. 2007. Integrating folksonomies with the Semantic Web. In E. Franconi, M. Kifer, & W. May (Eds.), *Proceedings of the European Semantic Web Conference (ESWC2007),* (LNCS 4519), (pp. 624–639). Heidelberg, Germany: Springer.

Takeda, H., Iino, K., & Nishida, T. (1995). Agent organization and communication with multiple ontologies. *International Journal of Cooperative Information Systems, 4*(4), 321–337. doi:10.1142/S0218843095000147

Tang, J., Leung, H., Luo, Q., Chen, D., & Gong, J. (2009). Towards ontology learning from folksonomies. In *Proceedings of the International Joint Conference on Artificial Intelligence,* Pasadena, CA, USA.

Tijerino, Y. A., Embley, D. W., Lonsdale, D. W., Ding, Y., & Nagy, G. (2005). Towards ontology generation from tables. *World Wide Web: Internet and Web Information Systems, 8*(3), 261–285. Netherlands: Springer.

Van Damme, C., Hepp, M., & Siorpaes, K. (2007). An integrated approach for turning folksonomies into ontologies. In *Bridging the Gap between Semantic Web and Web 2.0 (SemNet 2007)* (pp. 57–70). FolksOntology.

Wiesman, F., & Roos, N. (2004). Domain independent learning of ontology mappings. In *Proceedings of the 3rd International Joint Conference on Autonomous Agents and Multiagent Systems,* New York, USA (pp. 846–853).

Zhdanova, A. V., & Shvaiko, P. (2006). Community-driven ontology matching. In *The Semantic Web: Research and Applications,* (LNCS: Vol. 4011), (pp. 34-49). Berlin/Heidelberg, Germany: Springer.

Chapter 10

Searching Linked Objects with Falcons:
Approach, Implementation and Evaluation

Gong Cheng
Nanjing University, China

Yuzhong Qu
Nanjing University, China

ABSTRACT

The rapid development of the data Web is accompanied by increasing information needs from ordinary Web users for searching objects and their relations. To meet the challenge, this chapter presents Falcons Object Search, a keyword-based search engine for linked objects. To support various user needs expressed via keyword queries, for each object an extensive virtual document is indexed, which consists of not only associated literals but also the textual descriptions of associated links and linked objects. The resulting objects are ranked according to a combination of their relevance to the query and their popularity. For each resulting object, a query-relevant structured snippet is provided to show the associated literals and linked objects matched with the query for reflecting query relevance and even directly answering the question behind the query. To exploit ontological semantics for more precise search results, the type information of objects is leveraged to support class-based query refinement, and Web-scale class-inclusion reasoning is performed to discover implicit type information. Further, a subclass recommendation technique is proposed to allow users navigate class hierarchies for incremental results filtering. A task-based experiment demonstrates the promising features of the system.

DOI: 10.4018/978-1-60960-593-3.ch010

SEARCHING LINKED OBJECTS WITH FALCONS

Approach, Implementation and Evaluation

The Web is developing toward the era of data Web, or the Semantic Web. In recent years, substantial RDF data describing objects and their relations in various domains has been published as linked data on the Web. More importantly, these data sets have been interlinked, leading to a Web of data, grounded on which a lot of interesting applications have been developed.

Meanwhile, as before, search is one of the most common activities in daily life. People use text-based Web search engines at all times. Thus naturally, a key feature of the emerging data Web that would benefit ordinary Web users is to assist them in finding more accurate information on the Web in a shorter time. Recall that on the hypertext Web, people who seek information have to firstly retrieve Web documents, and then look through the texts for the desired knowledge by themselves. By contrast, on the data Web, knowledge has been represented in a structured manner so that it is possible to answer the question behind a query more efficiently. For example, previously in order to find relations between two people, we usually combine their names into a single keyword query and submit it to a text-based Web search engine. Then, we manually locate the two names in the text of each resulting webpage, read their contexts, and finally conclude potential relations from texts. Evidently, the entire process is rather time-consuming. Differently, linked data exactly describes the attributes of and the relations between objects. Thereby, a search engine that utilizes such data having well-defined meanings may automatically find and present accurately defined relations between two people.

Many novel search engines have been developed for the data Web. Most of these systems focus on RDF document search (d'Aquin, Baldassarre,

Gridinoc, Sabou, Angeletou, & Motta, 2007; Oren, Delbru, Catasta, Cyganiak, Stenzhorn, & Tummarello, 2008) or ontology search (Ding, Pan, Finin, Joshi, Peng, & Kolari, 2005). Recall that an RDF document serializes an RDF graph; an ontology, as a schema on the data Web, defines classes and properties for describing objects. Although both RDF document search and ontology search are essential for application developers, they can hardly serve ordinary Web users directly. Instead, object-level search is in demand and dominates all other Web queries (Pound, Mika, & Zaragoza, 2010).

To meet the challenge, we present our solution called Falcons Object Search (http://ws.nju.edu.cn/falcons/objectsearch/), which firstly is a keyword-based object search engine. For each discovered object, the system constructs an extensive virtual document consisting of textual descriptions extracted from its concise RDF description. Then an inverted index is built from terms in virtual documents to objects for supporting basic keyword-based search. That is, when a keyword query arrives, based on the inverted index, the system matches the terms in the query with the virtual documents of objects to generate a result set. The resulting objects are ranked in terms of both their relevance to the query and their popularity. For each resulting object, the system computes a query-relevant structured snippet to show the associated literals and linked objects matched with the query. Thereby, the extensiveness of virtual documents and the structural nature of snippets make the system go beyond searching for a particular object. For example, users can search for objects having a certain property, or can submit keyword queries describing two or more objects to seek their relations. Besides, the type information of objects, expanded by class-inclusion reasoning, is used to provide class-based query refinement. A technique of recommending subclasses is implemented to allow navigating class hierarchies for incremental results filtering.

These form a means to exploit ontological semantics for achieving more accurate search results.

RELATED WORK

Swoogle (Ding et al., 2005), as one of the most popular search engines for Semantic Web data, mainly serves class/property search and ontology search based on a PageRank-like ranking framework. It provides rich statistical metadata for the results. Watson (d'Aquin et al., 2007) organizes the results by RDF documents, and for each resulting document it presents those described classes/properties/objects matched with the keyword query. It enables to specify the scope that the terms in a keyword query should be matched with, such as label or comment. Sindice (Oren et al., 2008) allows property-value pair look-up to find RDF documents knowing a property of an object, and also allows keyword-based RDF document and Microformats search. All these systems mainly focus on searching for an RDF document or an ontology but not objects.

TAP (Guha, McCool, & Miller, 2003) is one of the earliest keyword-based object search engines. It matches the terms in a keyword query with the label of every object, and then selects and returns a matched object as well as its surrounding subgraph. The selection is based on popularity, user profile, and search context. SWSE (Harth, Hogan, Delbru, Umbrich, O'Riain, & Decker, 2007), another keyword-based object search engine, enables to filter the resulting objects by specifying a class, based on explicit type information presented in the data. For ranking the results, it adapts the PageRank algorithm by combining ranks from the RDF graph with ranks from the data source graph (Hogan, Harth, & Decker, 2006). Recent researches have started to address faceted search (Hildebrand, van Ossenbruggen, & Hardman, 2006; Oren, Delbru, & Decker, 2006; Harth, 2009). The basic idea is to derive a collection of property restrictions from the structured descriptions of

the resulting objects as refinement candidates for users to perform results filtering.

Different from the above IR-based search engines, semantic search (Tran, Cimiano, Rudolph, & Studer, 2007; Zhou, Wang, Xiong, Wang, & Yu, 2007; Wang, Zhang, Liu, Tran, & Yu, 2008; Tran, Wang, Rudolph, & Cimiano, 2009) promises to provide more accurate results. It translates keyword queries into formal queries such as SPARQL queries. After that, user interaction is needed to select a formal query (usually graph-structured) from automatically computed candidates. Nevertheless, such paradigm often meets scalability issues.

Scenarios

Firstly we illustrate the functions of our system by two scenarios, showing how it could help users quickly find linked objects. For example, users can submit keyword queries describing an object and a relation to find linked objects, or describing two or more objects to search for their relations.

Scenario A

In our system, keyword queries not only can describe object names, but also can describe relations between objects. Thereby, users could submit keyword queries to seek objects linked to a specified object via a specified kind of relation.

For example, a user wants to know the demo chair of ISWC2008. She submits a keyword query "ISWC2008" AND "demo chair" to the system, and obtains a resulting object as shown in Figure 1. The first line gives the name and types of the object. The user can click on the name to browse its detailed descriptions. Below that, a structured snippet, consisting of part of the RDF descriptions of the object in which query keywords are boldfaced, is presented to explain why this object is returned to answer the query. The snippet can help the user quickly determine its relevance or even directly obtain knowledge. The last line gives

Figure 1. A results page for the keyword query "ISWC2008" AND "demo chair"

the full URI of the object, and clicking on it will call the browser to directly dereference the URI. In this case, the user immediately finds in the snippet that Anupam Joshi and Chris Bizer are the demo chairs of ISWC2008, without performing any further actions.

Or taking another example, the user wants to seek people that know Tom Heath. She submits a keyword query "knows" AND "Tom Heath" to the system, and obtains a results page as shown in Figure 2. The user immediately finds that people such as Richard Cyganiak and Nigel Shadbolt know Tom Heath.

Scenario B

Now suppose that the user wants to find relations between two people, say Chris Bizer and Tom Heath. She submits a keyword query "Chris Bizer" AND "Tom Heath" to the system, and obtains a

Figure 2. A results page for the keyword query "knows" AND "Tom Heath"

Figure 3. A results page for the keyword query "Chris Bizer" AND "Tom Heath"

page as shown in Figure 3. In this case, the first result tells that Tom Heath knows Chris Bizer, and the fourth result tells that they are both known by Richard Cyganiak. The second result shows they are co-authors of a system demonstration. The third result shows they are both chairs of a workshop, and so on. Consequently, the user immediately obtains plenty of relations between the two people, including both direct and indirect relations, revealed by the linked objects in the snippets.

Besides, the left part of this page is a type panel that presents several types in the form of tags. If, for example, the user is interested in only those documents related to the two people, she can click on the "Document" tag to filter the resulting objects to include only those instances of some "Document" class, as shown in Figure 4. Meanwhile, the type panel is updated to include only the subclasses of "Document", such as "System Demonstration". The user can select these new tags to further filter the results, or she can go back by using the tree structure of the type panel. It means actually the user can filter the resulting objects by navigating a class hierarchy.

Figure 4. A results page for the keyword query "Chris Bizer" AND "Tom Heath" after the tag "Document" is selected

To conclude, each result returned by our system is an object. Users can submit keyword queries describing any properties of the desired objects, including both property names (links) and property values (literals or linked objects). Users can also filter the results by navigating class hierarchies. Query-relevant structured snippets help users quickly determine the relevance of the resulting objects to the query. In many cases, the resulting objects and their snippets can directly answer the question behind the query, and users do not need to spend time in reading possibly lengthy detailed descriptions.

System Architecture

This section presents the architecture of our system, introduces how data flows between components, and briefly explains how each component

works. Details of these components will be given in the next sections. Figure 5 depicts the system architecture.

All the crawled RDF documents are parsed by Jena (jena.sourceforge.net). The URIs newly discovered in these documents are submitted to the *URI repository* for further crawling (cf. Sect. Data Crawling). Each RDF triple in an RDF document and the document URI form a quadruple and is stored in the *quadruple store*, which is implemented based on a MySQL database. The *meta-analysis* component periodically performs an overall analysis to compute several kinds of global information and updates them to the *metadata* module, for example, determining the types of objects by analyzing their descriptions and provenances, extracting class inclusion/equivalence axioms from authoritative descriptions of ontologies, and performing reasoning to discover implicit types of objects (cf. Sect. Discovering Implicit Type Information by Class-inclusion Reasoning).

Then also periodically, the *indexer* updates a *combined inverted index*, which serves keyword-based search with filters. The combined inverted index is designed to support the described interaction mode, and consists of two inverted indexes. Firstly, for each object, a virtual document is constructed, which consists of terms extracted from RDF descriptions of the object (cf. Sect. Keyword-based Object Search). An inverted in-

Figure 5. System architecture

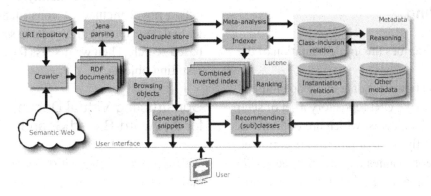

dex, which is a classic information retrieval data structure, is built from terms in virtual documents to objects, to serve keyword-based object search. Secondly, an inverted index is built from classes to their instances, to support class-based results filtering (cf. Sect. Filtering the Resulting Objects with Class Restrictions). Thereby, for a keyword query with class restrictions, the results are obtained by performing the intersection operation on the two result sets separately returned by these inverted indexes. The combined inverted index is implemented based on Apache Lucene (lucene. apache.org).

The *ranking* process is also implemented heavily based on Lucene (cf. Sect. Ranking Objects). A popularity score is calculated and assigned to each object at indexing time. At ranking time, Lucene ranks objects based on both their pre-computed popularity scores and the term-based similarity between their virtual documents and the keyword query.

For each resulting object, a query-relevant structured snippet is generated online (cf. Sect. Generating Query-relevant Structured Snippets for Resulting Objects). Meanwhile, several (sub) classes are recommended to the user as class restriction candidates for further query refinement (cf. Sect. Recommending Subclasses for Incremental Refinement).

Besides, for each object on demand, its detailed RDF descriptions are loaded from the quadruple store by the *browsing objects* component, and then are organized and presented to the user.

Data Crawling

This section describes the implementation of the crawler.

The construction of the data set is bootstrapped by submitting to the URI repository a set of seed URIs of RDF documents, which are obtained in three ways. Firstly, a list of phrases are extracted from the category names at the top three levels of the Open Directory Project (dmoz.org), ran-

domly combined as keyword queries, and sent to the Swoogle search engine and Google search engine (for "filetype:rdf" and "filetype:owl") to retrieve URIs of potential RDF documents. Secondly, the URIs of RDF documents from several online repositories are added to the URI repository, including pingthesemanticweb.com, schemaweb.info, etc. Thirdly, several sample URIs and entry-point URIs of the data sets published in the Linking Open Data project are manually added to the URI repository.

A multithreading crawler is then implemented to dereference URIs with content negotiation and download RDF documents. For simplicity, the "Accept" field in the header of HTTP requests is always set to "application/rdf+xml", and only well-formed RDF/XML documents will be successfully parsed by Jena and included in the data set. After parsing, the URIs newly discovered in these documents are submitted to the URI repository for further crawling.

The crawler downloads about 300 thousand documents per day on average. Until September 2009, more than 21 million well-formed RDF/XML documents had been indexed, containing 2.9 billion quadruples, from which 2.8 million classes, 264 thousand properties, and 171 million objects had been identified.

Keyword-Based Object Search

As shown in the scenarios, various kinds of keyword queries are enabled to describe linked objects. To provide such ability, this section presents a novel method of constructing extensive textual descriptions of objects to serve keyword-based search. Then we discuss the ranking of the resulting objects.

Constructing Virtual Documents for Keyword-Based Search

Web users are familiar with keyword-based search mainly due to its simplicity. Besides, the high efficiency of keyword-based search has been proved by traditional Web search engines such as Google. To implement keyword-based search for webpages, an inverted index from terms to webpage URIs is usually built. However, for the data Web, an object identified by a URI has no such content except for the URI itself. Therefore, for each object, we need to construct its virtual document (Watters, 1999) that includes its textual descriptions so that an inverted index from terms in virtual documents to objects can be built to serve keyword-based search.

We firstly review traditional methods of constructing virtual documents, and then present a new solution.

Existing Methods. If we treat the entire data Web as a universal RDF graph, for an object as a node in this graph, there are no hard boundaries to indicate from which parts terms should be extracted to form its virtual document. Nevertheless, similar solutions have been used by existing search engines (d'Aquin et al., 2007; Ding et al., 2005; Harth et al., 2007). Generally, they construct the virtual document of an object by extracting terms from either or both of the following places:

1. Local name of the object URI. The local name of an object URI is a unique string in its namespace. In many cases, the local name is a human-readable string, for example, "Chris_Bizer" and "ISWC2008". But in some cases, local names are just numbers used as unique identifiers, which are less useful in keyword-based search.
2. Literals associated with the object. The values of rdfs:label and rdfs:comment of an object are usually included in its virtual document, which give its human-readable names and descriptions, respectively, as defined in the RDFS specification. Literal values of other properties may also be included.

Basically, existing methods assume that the terms in a keyword query are mainly matched with literals associated with objects. However, to describe an object in RDF, we not only can associate it with literals by using literal-valued properties, but also can connect it to other objects by using object-valued properties. For example, to describe that Chris Bizer is a demo chair of ISWC2008, three different ways may be used, as shown in Figure 6. We can connect the ISWC2008 object to a URI identifying Chris Bizer, to a blank node identifying Chris Bizer, or to a literal with the lexical form "Chris Bizer". Therefore, it is inadequate to extract terms from only literal-valued properties.

Besides, keyword queries may also include terms that indicate property names rather than only property values. For example, in order to find the demo chairs of ISWC2008, users may submit keyword queries like "ISWC2008" AND "demo chair". Evidently, existing methods fail to support such expressive queries.

RDF Sentence. We leverage the notion of RDF sentence (Zhang, Cheng, & Qu, 2007) to formalize our solution. Two RDF triples are *b-connected* if they contain common blank nodes. The b-connected relation is defined as transitive. Then in an RDF graph, an *RDF sentence* is a maximum subset of b-connected RDF triples. Formally

Figure 6. Three ways to describe that Chris Bizer is a demo chair of ISWC2008: (a) by connecting to a URI identifying Chris Bizer, (b) by connecting to a blank node identifying Chris Bizer, or (c) by associating with a literal

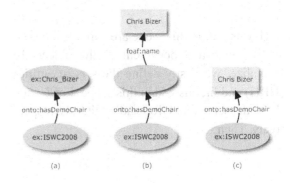

speaking, in an RDF graph g as a set of RDF triples, an RDF sentence $\tilde{s} \subseteq g$ satisfies the following conditions:

$\forall t_i, t_j \in \tilde{s}$, t_i, t_j are b-connected;

$\forall t_i \in \tilde{s}, t_j \in g \setminus \tilde{s}$, t_i, t_j are not b-connected.

Furthermore, we define:

$$\mathrm{Subj}(\tilde{s}) = \{s \mid \exists \langle s, p, o \rangle \in \tilde{s}\}, \qquad (1)$$

$$\mathrm{Pred}(\tilde{s}) = \{p \mid \exists \langle s, p, o \rangle \in \tilde{s}\}, \qquad (2)$$

$$\mathrm{Obj}(\tilde{s}) = \{o \mid \exists \langle s, p, o \rangle \in \tilde{s}\}. \qquad (3)$$

Besides, Tummarello, Morbidoni, Bachmann-Gmür, and Erling (2007) have proposed a notion of *minimal self-contained graph*, which is an equivalent definition of RDF sentence. They have proved that an RDF graph g can be decomposed into a unique set of RDF sentences, denoted by $\mathrm{Sent}(g)$. α

Constructing Virtual Documents with RDF Sentences. Let G be the universal RDF graph combined from all the RDF documents in the data set. For an object o, all the RDF sentences decomposed from G that describe o form its *concise RDF description*:

$$\mathrm{RDFDesc}(o) = \{\tilde{s} \mid \tilde{s} \in \mathrm{Sent}(G) \wedge o \in \mathrm{Subj}(\tilde{s})\}. \qquad (4)$$

Terms within this scope are extracted to construct the virtual document of the object. To formalize, we firstly define the sets of entities (URIs) and literals within this scope. Let U and L be the sets of all URIs and all literals, respectively. Then,

$$\mathrm{DescEnt}(o) =$$
$$\{u \in U \mid \exists \tilde{s}(\tilde{s} \in \mathrm{RDFDesc}(o) \wedge u \in (\mathrm{Pred}(\tilde{s}) \cup \mathrm{Obj}(\tilde{s})))\}, \qquad (5)$$

and

$$\mathrm{DescLit}(o) = \{l \in L \mid \exists \tilde{s}(\tilde{s} \in \mathrm{RDFDesc}(o) \wedge l \in \mathrm{Obj}(\tilde{s}))\}. \qquad (6)$$

For a clear presentation, we use the vector space model to represent text, that is, text is represented as a term vector where each component corresponds to the weight, for example, the number of occurrences, of a particular term in the text. $\forall u \in U$, let $\mathrm{LN}(u)$ be the term vector representing its local name, and let $\mathrm{Lbl}(u)$ be the term vector representing its labels encoded in its dereference document (that is, the RDF document obtained by dereferencing its URI). $\forall l \in L$, let $\mathrm{LexForm}(l)$ be the term vector representing its lexical form.

Finally, the virtual document of an object o is constructed as follows:

$$\mathrm{VDoc}(o) = \alpha \cdot \mathrm{LN}(o) + \beta \cdot \mathrm{Lbl}(o)$$
$$+ \gamma \cdot \sum_{u \in \mathrm{DescEnt}(o)} (\mathrm{LN}(u) + \mathrm{Lbl}(u))$$
$$+ \delta \cdot \sum_{l \in \mathrm{DescLit}(o)} \mathrm{LexForm}(l), \qquad (7)$$

where β, γ, and δ are weighting coefficients, and in the system they are set to 10, 10, 1, and 1, respectively, based on our previous experience of using virtual documents in ontology matching (Qu, Hu, & Cheng, 2006) as well as user feedback during a running period of one year of the system. It means, we assume that the terms in a keyword query mostly indicate the name of the desired object directly, but we still allow the user to describe all the properties of the object in the keyword query.

In addition, it is worth noting that, with regard to the object in question, only forward links in RDF graph are considered in its concise RDF description and thus in its virtual document. However, the direction of a property in RDF is somewhat arbitrary so that backward links should also be considered. Although it is not difficult to also include backward links, only forward links are considered here because they could be easily presented in the search results page in a user-friendly way, as shown in Sect. Scenarios, whereas we lack a satisfying way to present backward links. Therefore, backward links are not considered in the system at the time of writing, but they may be addressed in future work.

Implementation

After constructing a virtual document for each object, the implementation of keyword-based object search is transformed into the more general problem of information retrieval, that is, document search. We use Lucene to build an inverted index from terms in virtual documents to objects. With Lucene, the system can support multi-term keyword queries, Boolean queries, etc. By default, terms in a keyword query are considered to be in conjunction so that inputting more terms will obtain fewer but probably more precise results. Terms with different weights according to (7) are indexed in different *Lucene fields*, and are assigned different weights when queries arrive.

Ranking Objects

In our system, the resulting objects are ranked based on two factors. Firstly, objects relevant to the keyword query are ranked higher. Secondly, popular objects are ranked higher. In the following, we will describe how these two factors are separately calculated and then integrated to rank objects.

Query Relevance. On the one hand, a virtual document is constructed for each object. On the other hand, a keyword query could be treated as a short document. Then, the problem of calculating

similarity between an object and a keyword query is transformed into the problem of calculating similarity between two documents, which has been extensively studied in information retrieval.

For an object o, let $\mathrm{VDoc}(o)$ be the term vector representing its virtual document, calculated according to (7), which is further refined by inverse document frequency (IDF) factors (Jones, 1972), that is, a higher weight is assigned to a term in a virtual document if the term occurs in fewer documents. For a keyword query q, let $\mathrm{Vector}(q)$ be its term vector form. The similarity between o and q is calculated based on the cosine similarity measure:

$$\mathrm{TextSim}(o, q) = \frac{\mathrm{VDoc}(o) \cdot \mathrm{Vector}(q)}{|\mathrm{VDoc}(o)| \cdot |\mathrm{Vector}(q)|},$$

(8)

where the numerator is the dot product of the two vectors, and the denominator is the product of their magnitudes.

Compared with previous methods, a virtual document of an object in our system contains far more terms, which is possible to reduce the "precision" of the search results. To deal with this issue, according to (7), higher weights are assigned to the terms from local names and labels of objects. When calculating query-relevance, the objects whose local names or labels rather than other properties exactly or partially match the terms in the keyword query will be ranked higher. In this way, the top-ranking results are expected to be still with a high precision for name-oriented object search.

Popularity. Another factor being considered in ranking is popularity. When several retrieved objects happen to share the same name, we argue that the user is more likely looking for the most popular one.

We measure the popularity of an object by looking at the data publisher side. Specifically, for an object o, let $\mathrm{Docs}(o)$ be the set of RDF documents where o occurs. The popularity score of o is calculated as follows:

$$\text{Popularity}(o) = \log(|\text{Docs}(o)|+1). \qquad (9)$$

Integration and Implementation. The final ranking score of a resulting object o w.r.t a keyword query q is defined as:

$$\text{ObjectScore}(o,q) = \text{TextSim}(o,q) \cdot \text{Popularity}(o). \qquad (10)$$

With Lucene, the implementation of the ranking process is not difficult. Each object together with its virtual document are treated as a *Lucene document*. The popularity score of an object is set as the *boost factor* of the corresponding *Lucene document*, which is used by Lucene at ranking time. Finally, Lucene automatically performs ranking based on the above equations when queries arrive.

Generating Query-Relevant Structured Snippets for Resulting Objects

For each resulting object, a query-relevant structured snippet is provided to explain why this object is returned to answer the keyword query. It helps the user quickly determine the relevance of the object to the query by presenting part of its descriptions that are matched with the terms in the query. More importantly, we have illustrated that snippets could directly present linked objects to the user, which may immediately satisfy the information need behind the query.

This section proposes to take RDF sentence as the unit of a snippet, and then introduces a method of ranking RDF sentences and selecting the top-ranking ones into a snippet.

RDF Sentence: The Basic Unit of a Snippet

In traditional Web search engines, a snippet of a webpage is usually a piece of text extracted from the webpage as the contexts of those terms in the webpage that are matched with the terms in the keyword query. Text in a webpage can be treated as a character sequence so that it is flexible to control the size of a snippet.

In RDF, an object is a node in RDF graph, and its snippet should be some subgraph extracted from its RDF descriptions. Particularly, a snippet is expected to contain the terms in the keyword query. As described, the terms in a keyword query are matched with the terms in the virtual document of each object, which are constructed by extracting terms from the concise RDF description of the object.

We believe that an RDF triple is not suitable for being the basic unit of a snippet. It is because when blank nodes are involved, a single RDF triple is less informational. For example, as shown in Figure 6(b), a single RDF triple ⟨ ex:ISWC2008, onto:hasDemoChair, _:b1 ⟩ (here _:b1 indicates the blank node) gives unclear information because of the involved blank node.

Instead, recall that the concise RDF description of an object is a set of RDF sentences. It is naturally to select a subset of RDF sentences that are matched with the terms in the keyword query as a snippet. In consideration of space, at most five RDF sentences will be selected to form a snippet in the system. Therefore, the problem of generating snippets is transformed into a new problem: ranking RDF sentences according to a given keyword query.

Besides, an RDF sentence could be of various topologies. Instead of presenting the entire graph structure in some cases, which might be too complex to be quickly inspected, we choose to present its DFS (depth-first search) tree starting from the present object, as illustrated by Figure 2, because tree structures widely exist in desktop file systems and thus are believed to be more user-friendly. Actually, in most cases, the topology of an RDF sentence is exactly its DFS tree.

Ranking RDF Sentences

Inspired by text summarization (Gong & Liu, 2001), the overall ranking algorithm is designed as follows:

1. Set up a set of RDF sentence candidates.
2. Calculate and assign a ranking score to each candidate.
3. Move the best-scoring candidate into the snippet.
4. If the desired number of RDF sentences, five here, has not been reached, go back to Step 2.

The algorithm actually selects one RDF sentence per round. The ranking score of an RDF sentence is concerned with its relevance to the keyword query. Because an RDF sentence is essentially an RDF graph, in order to calculate the relevance between an RDF sentence and a keyword query, a virtual document is constructed, which (a) for each URI that occurs in the RDF sentence (including both cases of being as a node and being as an arc), includes its local name and labels encoded in its dereference document, and (b) for each literal that occurs in the RDF sentence, includes its lexical form. All the terms involved are not further weighted.

For an RDF sentence $\tilde{s}$, let $\mathrm{VDoc}(\tilde{s})$ be the term vector representing its virtual document. For a keyword query q, let $\mathrm{Vector}(q)$ be its term vector form. The ranking score of an RDF sentence $\tilde{s}$ w.r.t. a keyword query q is defined as the cosine value of $\mathrm{VDoc}(\tilde{s})$ and $\mathrm{Vector}(q)$, which is calculated similar to (8).

However, for a multi-term keyword query, the cosine measure may fail to create a snippet that covers as more terms in the query as it could, and lead to a sort of redundancy. For example, for a keyword query with two terms, all of the selected RDF sentences in a snippet may match only the same term but none of them matches the other one.

To solve this, the weights of the terms in the keyword query are adjusted dynamically (Nenkova, Vanderwende, & McKeown, 2006). For a multi-term keyword query q and its term vector form $\mathrm{Vector}(q)$, after an RDF sentence is selected into the snippet, the components of $\mathrm{Vector}(q)$ corresponding to the terms occurring in the virtual document of this RDF sentence will be set to a very small number, 0.001 in the system. Then in the next rounds, other unmatched terms in q will dominate the scoring of RDF sentence candidates, and the generated snippet is more likely to cover more terms in the keyword query.

Query Refinement with Class Hierarchies

The Semantic Web brings structured data with well-defined semantics, which cannot be satisfactorily utilized by a purely keyword-based search engine to serve object search. Cognitive science has shown that people are predisposed to use type information rather than other property information to perform human reasoning (Yamauchi, 2007), whereas type information (rdf:type) is also widely considered by data producers. Therefore, it is practical and also feasible to exploit type information in the system for improving object search, for example, enabling to filter the resulting objects by specifying the type of objects being sought for.

This section describes the implementation of class-based query refinement for keyword queries, and discusses class-inclusion reasoning in order to discover implicit type information. Then we give a way to recommend subclasses to let users navigate class hierarchies for incremental refinement.

Filtering the Resulting Objects with Class Restrictions

As introduced, a combined inverted index, including two separated inverted indexes, is constructed to support keyword-based object search with class restrictions. We have described how to design the first index. To design the second one, a key problem is to determine the types of every object.

Everyone can say anything on the Web, for example, someone can describe in RDF that an object is an instance of some class (but actually may be not) and publish it on the Web. A Web-scale search engine should be able to deal with insufficient or inconsistent information of different qualities. Evidently, the most reliable description of an object comes from its dereference document. But currently a lot of URIs are not dereferenceable, or their servers do not provide RDF descriptions. It is also possible that, limited by the capability of the crawler, some URIs may have never been dereferenced at a particular time.

In our system, all the RDF documents describing an object are classified into three categories: its dereference document, all of its same-host documents, and all the other documents. An RDF document is called a *same-host document* of an object iff the object URI and the URI of the document have the same host part, that is, they are expected to have the same owner. The types of an object are determined by looking up its description in the three categories of document in the above order. Once any type information has been found in a category, the next categories will not be considered.

Discovering Implicit Type Information by Class-Inclusion Reasoning

Using only explicitly defined type information is insufficient. As is often the case, data producers may only describe that an object is an instance of some class, but search engine users may select its superclass when refining queries. Assume that only explicitly described type information is indexed, for example, the object ex:ISWC2008 is an instance of some "conference" class. Then, if the user selects some "academic event" class to filter the resulting objects including ex:ISWC2008, this object will be filtered out undesirably, although we know that "conference" is a subclass of "academic event" and a semantic-aware search engine is expected to perform such basic reasoning.

Before performing such class-inclusion reasoning, it is required to recognize reliable axioms from various descriptions available on the Web. Or else, someone can easily mess up the system by, for example, publishing that rdfs:Resource is a subclass of foaf:Person. To solve this, inspired by Grau, Horrocks, Kazakov, and Sattler (2007), we consider that only the dereference document of a class is allowed to constrain its meaning. For example, the above axiom will be accepted by the system iff it occurs in the dereference document of rdfs:Resource. In particular, if the dereference document of a class c_1 describes that c_1 is equivalent to some class c_2, the system accepts only that c_1 is a subclass of c_2. A similar idea is described by Hogan, Harth, and Polleres (2008).

Accepted class inclusion axioms are stored in a two-column table of a relational database. Then, transitive closure computation is performed to discover implicit class inclusion axioms, and these inferred axioms are also stored in that table. Computing all the superclasses of a class is to, in the digraph view, find all its reachable nodes. Based on this, a parallel program is implemented, where each thread starts with a class, recursively looks up the table to obtain all its superclasses, and stores those newly discovered class inclusion axioms in the table. Details of the implementation and experiments are referred to Cheng and Qu (2008).

In order to obtain a quick response to queries, when constructing the inverted index from classes to objects, both explicit and inferred type information are physically indexed. To be specific, for each object, its explicitly specified classes and their superclasses obtained by looking up the class inclusion closure are both indexed. In this way, when the user selects "academic event" to filter the results, ex:ISWC2008 will not be filtered out because the system has indexed from the "academic event" class to ex:ISWC2008 attributed to the previous offline reasoning.

Recommending Subclasses for Incremental Refinement

As shown in the scenarios, users can filter the resulting objects by navigating class hierarchies to submit class restrictions. To support such mode of interaction, a key step in the implementation is to recommend several subclasses as incremental restriction candidates to be selected after some class has been specified.

Note that the system does not directly show classes such as foaf:Person to users, but recommend some tags such as "Person". It is because ordinary Web users are not familiar with ontologies, and also they do not need to. Consequently, one tag may correspond to more than one classes with the same name so that a class restriction given by the user is actually a set of classes rather than a single one.

Besides, initially no class restrictions are given by the user. In such case, rdfs:Resource is treated as the default class restriction since it is a superclass of all other classes.

Now we are ready to formalize the problem: the input of the problem includes a set of classes C_q as the current restrictions, a set of objects O_q that are instances of at least one class in C_q and whose virtual documents are matched with the keyword query, and a number k indicating up to how many subclasses should be recommended; the output is a new set of classes as restriction candidates for further query refinement.

To solve the problem, we devise a method composed of the following steps.

Firstly, for all the objects in O_q, we collect their types (including both explicitly specified and inferred) as the set of class candidates for recommendation, denoted by C. However, in some cases, the cardinality of O_q is very large so that this step may take too much time online. To make a trade-off between coverage and efficiency, according to their ranking scores, at most the first 1,000 objects in O_q will be considered in the system.

Secondly, all the classes in C are ranked and sorted according to their ranking scores in descending order. The ranking score of a class in C is defined as the number of its instances in O_q. It is based on the assumption that: if more instances of a class is in the current result set O_q, this class is more likely to capture the user's intention behind the query.

Next, all the sorted classes in C are checked one by one to determine whether they will be recommended, until the number of desired classes k or the end of the sorted list has been reached. Let C_k be the set of classes to be recommended finally, which is empty initially. A class $c \in C$ will be selected into C_k only if two conditions are satisfied. Firstly, there exists $c' \in C_q$ such that c is a proper subclass of c'. This condition indicates that the system always recommends subclasses but not superclasses or equivalent classes. Secondly, there does not exists $c' \in C_k$ such that c is a subclass of c' or vice versa, that is, the class inclusion relation never holds between any pair of classes to be recommended. This is for increasing the variety of the recommended classes. For example, an "academic event" class and its subclass "conference" will never be recommended together.

Finally, all the classes in C_k are mapped to user-friendly tags, which currently in the system are just their normalized local names. All the tags are sorted in alphabetical order in the type panel.

Figure 7. A class hierarchy where a ranking score is attached to each class

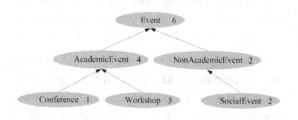

We illustrate the entire method by an example. Figure 7 depicts a class hierarchy in which a ranking score is attached to each class. Suppose that the user has selected Event, that is, $C_q = \{\text{Event}\}$. According to the ranking scores, the sorted list C is: Event, AcademicEvent, Workshop, NonAcademicEvent, SocialEvent, and Conference. And let $k = 2$.

Firstly, Event will not be selected because it is not a proper subclass of itself. Next, its proper subclass AcademicEvent is selected into C_k, but then Workshop will not be selected because it is a subclass of AcademicEvent, which has been selected into C_k.

Similarly, NonAcademicEvent should be selected but SocialEvent should not. However, another heuristic is applied here: if two classes are with equal ranking scores and the class inclusion relation holds between them, the more specific one of them will be selected. So here SocialEvent instead of NonAcademicEvent is selected. It is mainly because in this case these two classes, as restrictions, will function in exactly the same way, but the more specific one usually carries more information to the user, as its name indicates.

Finally, two classes AcademicEvent and SocialEvent have been selected into C_k, and the recommended tags are "Academic Event" and "Social Event".

Table 1. Tasks for evaluation

T1	Give a brief description of Tim Berners-Lee.
T2	Find out the homepage and phone number of the person with email chris@bizer.de.
T3	Find out three people that know or are known by the person in T2.
T4	Find out three kinds of relation between the two people in T1 and T2.
T5	Find out three conferences on Artificial Intelligence as well as their homepages.
T6	Find out five popular buildings in Berlin.
T7	What is Lehman Brothers? What happened to it in 2008 and why?
T8	Find out a song titled Forget-me-nots and its singer, genre, and year. Also describe a kind of plant called forget-me-nots.

Experiments

Different from traditional information retrieval, we lack a gold standard to evaluate an object search engine. Therefore, to compare our system with other search engines, we have designed a task-based experiment. Task-based evaluation is for users determining fitness of systems for particular purposes. It does not directly evaluate a single method such as ranking or snippet generation, but instead, it gives an overall evaluation of the entire system involving many of its components.

Evaluation

We set eight simple tasks in the experiment, as shown in Table 1. Considering that different search engines have different data sets, we have tried several keywords related to each task on all the search engines to be evaluated and have verified that at least something related could be found on each system. It is worth noting that this experiment shows only how well these systems perform in these eight tasks, but should not be regarded as a comprehensive evaluation of these systems.

Three systems, including one traditional Web search engine (Google or Yahoo!) and two Semantic Web search engines (Sindice, Swoogle, SWSE, Watson, or Falcons Object Search), are assigned at random to each of the twenty-six participants, all of whom are postgraduates and know almost nothing about the Semantic Web, that is, they are not experts in the Semantic Web but are just ordinary Web users. The participants are never instructed to use any of these systems, although it is very likely that they are familiar with traditional Web search engines. For each task, the participants are asked to give an answer by using only each assigned system. The quality of each answer, ranging from 0 (the worst) to 1 (the best), are blindly reviewed by two human experts who set these tasks. We also record the number of clicks paid during the searching process. We do not measure the completion time spent on each task, because due to the slow Internet connection available for the experiments, the transmission time of the Internet is a significant part of the total completion time for some of the evaluated systems.

Figure 8 summarizes the evaluation results of each task.

T1 is a typical subject-oriented knowledge seeking task. Our system Falcons performs closely to traditional Web search engines, although it costs much more clicks, maybe because the participants are not familiar with novel search engines at the very beginning of the experiment, whereas they use Google or Yahoo! almost every day.

T2 asks for knowledge of an object specified by an inverse functional property, in which Falcons and traditional Web search engines show no difference.

In T3 and T4, the participants are asked to find relations between objects. They obtain slightly better results on traditional Web search engines than they perform on Falcons, but they pay more clicks. It is because RDF data exactly describes links between objects, and the structured snippets provided by Falcons help users quickly find such relations.

T5 and T6 are typical resource seeking tasks, in which Falcons and traditional Web search engines differ not much.

However, traditional Web search engines dominate news seeking, illustrated by T7. It is because traditional Web search engines crawl data from the entire Web, including a lot of popular websites publishing news. But there were only a few websites that provide RDF data at the time of experiments, not to mention news.

T8 requires finding two distinct objects with exactly the same name. Clearly, the participants obtain similar results but have paid fewer clicks on Falcons than on Google, mostly due to the function of class-based query refinement. But it is interesting that Yahoo! dominates all the other systems in this task.

The results also show that in most tasks the participants do not obtain better results on other Semantic Web search engines than on Falcons. It is because some systems like Sindice are mainly designed to serve applications, and some others like Swoogle and Watson mainly serve researchers or developers but not ordinary Web users. Falcons is also the only system that provides query-relevant structured snippets, which seem quite useful to users.

We have also collected the participants' comments. We find that, out of the 26 participants: 16 thought that traditional Web search engines are easy to use and are likely to have indexed far more data; 16 complained about the response time of Semantic Web search engines; 11 felt that Falcons is good at seeking relations; and 3 were impressed by the high precision of Falcons.

Lessons Learned

The evaluation has demonstrated that the capability of object search provided by Falcons is promising and has opened a door for Web users to perform high-precision retrieval tasks on the Web

Figure 8. Evaluation results

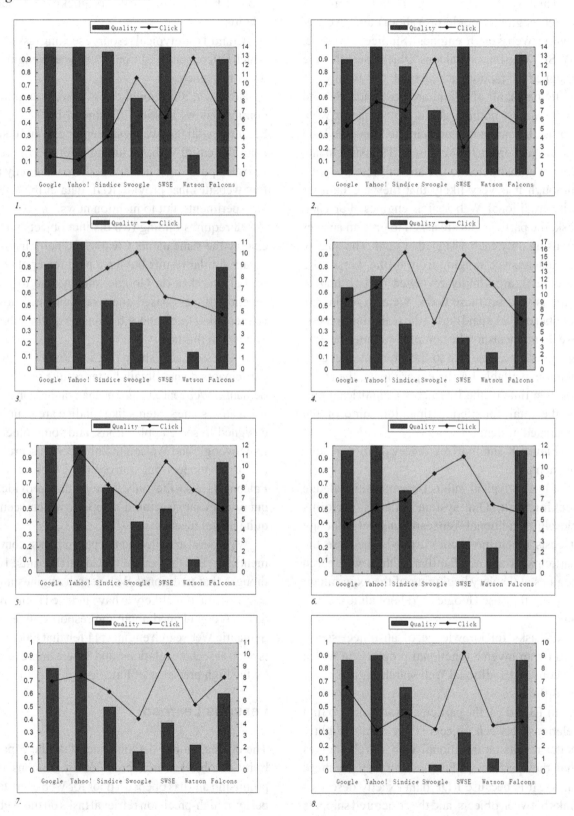

of data. In particular, Falcons is strong in relation finding. However, existing Semantic Web search engines still cannot replace traditional Web search engines. Firstly, Web users are more familiar with the interfaces and features of traditional Web search engines. Falcons and many other Semantic Web search engines have introduced several new features, such as class-based query refinement, which also confuse many users. Some users consider these new features as advanced functions and do not like or do not understand how to use them. Secondly, most Semantic Web data sources are transformed from existing databases or webpages, and lack updating, causing that a lot of data is not up-to-date enough. If competing with traditional Web search engines is a goal to be pursued, more up-to-date Semantic Web data is greatly in demand. Thirdly, semantic heterogeneity is a big problem. For example, some participants have reported that they find "Conference" and "Conference Event" being recommended together by Falcons. These two tags correspond to two different classes (but actually should be semantically equivalent) defined in two different ontologies. However, it is a great challenge for a Web-scale search engine to integrate thousands of such ontologies.

CONCLUSION

In this chapter, we have presented the design of Falcons Object Search, a system that has the capability of searching linked objects on the data Web. By exploiting the nature of linked data and taking full advantage of traditional IR techniques, the system has already demonstrated its ability to provide Web users with a more accurate object search service, which is also easy-to-use and efficient.

Firstly, a novel method of constructing extensive textual descriptions of objects is designed for building inverted index and serving keyword-based search. This method allows more expressive keyword queries to describe linked objects. The ranking of the resulting objects considers not only the similarity between the textual descriptions of objects and the keyword query but also the popularity of objects. Secondly, for each resulting object, a query-relevant structured snippet is provided to show the associated literals and linked objects matched with the keyword query. RDF sentence is taken as the basic unit of a snippet, and a method of ranking RDF sentences is devised for selecting a subset of RDF sentences into a snippet. Thirdly, type information of objects, which is expanded by performing class-inclusion reasoning over authoritative descriptions of classes, is utilized to implement class-based query refinement. Furthermore, a way of recommending subclasses is designed to allow navigating class hierarchies for incremental results filtering.

A task-based evaluation together with user feedback during a running period of three years of the system have demonstrated the feasibility of the proposed approach and the utility value of the system. The semantic nature of linked data has displayed its promising ability to let people find accurate results easily and quickly. However, issues like semantic heterogeneity have also emerged in practice and await practical solutions.

One direction of future work is interpreting keyword queries. It is attractive to find a better trade-off between traditional IR approaches and structured queries. We will also try to improve the reasoning ability of the system. Before that, it is necessary to match ontologies and fuse the schema-level of linked data. Both automatic approaches (Euzenat & Shvaiko, 2007) and social approaches will be considered.

ACKNOWLEDGMENT

The work is supported by the NSFC under Grant 60973024. We would like to thank Dr. Honghan Wu for his valuable suggestions during the development of the system, and thank Dr. Xiang Zhang and Weiyi Ge for designing the experiment. We are also grateful to the anonymous reviewers for their insightful comments and suggestions that considerably improved the journal version of this chapter.

REFERENCES

Cheng, G., & Qu, Y. (2008). Integrating lightweight reasoning into class-based query refinement for object search. In J. Domingue & C. Anutariya (Eds.), *The Semantic Web: Proceedings of the 3rd Asian Semantic Web Conference,* Bangkok, Thailand (LNCS 5367, pp. 449-463).

d'Aquin, M., Baldassarre, C., Gridinoc, L., Sabou, M., Angeletou, S., & Motta, E. (2007, October 5-8). Watson: Supporting next generation Semantic Web applications. In P. Isaías, M. B. Nunes, & J. Barroso (Eds.), *Proceedings of the IADIS International Conference WWW/Internet 2007,* Vila Real, Portugal (pp. 363-371). IADIS Press.

Ding, L., Pan, R., Finin, T., Joshi, A., Peng, Y., & Kolari, P. (2005). Finding and ranking knowledge on the Semantic Web. In Y. Gil, E. Motta, V. R. Benjamins, & M. Musen (Eds.), *The Semantic Web: ISWC 2005: Proceedings of the 4th International Semantic Web Conference,* Galway, Ireland (LNCS 3729, pp. 156-170).

Euzenat, J., & Shvaiko, P. (2007). *Ontology matching.* Berlin/Heidelberg, Germany: Springer.

Gong, Y., & Liu, X. (2001). Generic text summarization using relevance measure and latent semantic analysis. In D. H. Kraft, W. B. Croft, D. J. Harper, & J. Zobel (Eds.), *Proceedings of the 24th Annual International ACM SIGIR Conference on Research and Development in Informational Retrieval,* New Orleans, LA (pp. 19-25). New York, NY: ACM.

Grau, B. C., Horrocks, I., Kazakov, Y., & Sattler, U. (2007). A logical framework for modularity of ontologies. In M. M. Veloso (Eds.), *Proceedings of the 20th International Joint Conference on Artificial Intelligence,* Hyderabad, India (pp. 298-303).

Guha, R., McCool, R., & Miller, E. (2003, May 20-24). Semantic search. In G. Hencsey, B. White, Y.-F. R. Chen, L. Kovács, & S. Lawrence (Eds.), *Proceedings of the 12th International World Wide Web Conference,* Budapest, Hungary (pp. 700-709). New York, NY: ACM.

Harth, A. (2009). VisiNav: Visual Web data search and navigation. In S. S. Bhowmick, J. Küng, & R. Wagner (Eds.), *Proceedings of the 20th International Conference on Database and Expert Systems Applications,* Linz, Austria (LNCS 5690, pp. 214-228).

Harth, A., Hogan, A., Delbru, R., Umbrich, J., O'Riain, S., & Decker, S. (2007). SWSE: Answers before links! In J. Golbeck & P. Mika (Eds.), *Proceedings of the Semantic Web Challenge 2007,* Busan, Korea (Vol. 295). Retrieved from CEUR-WS.org

Hildebrand, M., van Ossenbruggen, J., & Hardman, L. (2006). /facet: A browser for heterogeneous Semantic Web repositories. In I. Cruz, S. Decker, D. Allemang, C. Preist, D. Schwabe, P. Mika, M. Uschold, & L. Aroyo (Eds.), *The Semantic Web: ISWC 2006: Proceedings of the 5th International Semantic Web Conference,* Athens, GA (LNCS 4273, pp. 272-285).

Hogan, A., Harth, A., & Decker, S. (2006, Novmber). *ReConRank: A scalable ranking method for Semantic Web data with context.* Paper presented at the 2nd International Workshop on Scalable Semantic Web Knowledge Base Systems, Athens, GA.

Hogan, A., Harth, A., & Polleres, A. (2008). SAOR: Authoritative reasoning for the Web. In J. Domingue & C. Anutariya (Eds.), *The Semantic Web: Proceedings of the 3rd Asian Semantic Web Conference,* Bangkok, Thailand (LNCS 5367, pp. 76-90).

Jones, K. S. (1972). A statistical interpretation of term specificity and its application in retrieval. *The Journal of Documentation, 28*(1), 11–21. doi:10.1108/eb026526

Nenkova, A., Vanderwende, L., & McKeown, K. (2006). A compositional context sensitive multi-document summarizer: Exploring the factors that influence summarization. In E. N. Efthimiadis, S. Dumais, D. Hawking, & K. Järvelin (Eds.), *Proceedings of the 29th Annual International ACM SIGIR Conference on Research and Development in Information Retrieval,* Seattle, WA (pp. 573-580). New York, NY: ACM.

Oren, E., Delbru, R., Catasta, M., Cyganiak, R., Stenzhorn, H., & Tummarello, G. (2008). Sindice. com: A document-oriented lookup index for open linked data. *International Journal of Metadata. Semantics and Ontologies, 3*(1), 37–52. doi:10.1504/IJMSO.2008.021204

Oren, E., Delbru, R., & Decker, S. (2006). Extending faceted navigation for RDF data. In I. Cruz, S. Decker, D. Allemang, C. Preist, D. Schwabe, P. Mika, M. Uschold, & L. Aroyo (Eds.), *The Semantic Web: ISWC 2006: Proceedings of the 5th International Semantic Web Conference,* Athens, GA (LNCS 4273, pp. 559-572).

Pound, J., Mika, P., & Zaragoza, H. (2010). Ad-hoc object retrieval in the Web of data. In M. Rappa, P. Jones, J. Freire, & S. Chakrabarti (Eds.), *Proceedings of the 19th Intertional World Wide Web Conference,* Raleigh, NC (pp. 771-780). New York, NY: ACM.

Qu, Y., Hu, W., & Cheng, G. (2006, May 23-26). Constructing virtual documents for ontology matching. In L. Carr, D. D. Roure, A. Iyengar, C. Goble, & M. Dahlin (Eds.), *Proceedings of the 15th International Conference on World Wide Web,* Edinburgh, Scotland (pp. 23-31). New York, NY: ACM.

Tran, T., Cimiano, P., Rudolph, S., & Studer, R. (2007). Ontology-based interpretation of keywords for semantic search. In K. Aberer, K-S. Choi, N. Noy, D. Allemang, K-I. Lee, L. Nixon, et al. (Eds.), *The Semantic Web: Proceedings of the 6th International Semantic Web Conference and the 2nd Asian Semantic Web Conference,* Busan, Korea (LNCS 4825, pp. 523-536).

Tran, T., Wang, H., Rudolph, S., & Cimiano, P. (2009). Top-k exploration of query candidates for efficient keyword search on graph-shaped (RDF) data. In *Proceedings of the 25th International Conference on Data Engineering,* Shanghai, China (pp. 405-416). Washington, DC: IEEE Computer Society.

Tummarello, G., Morbidoni, C., Bachmann-Gmür, R., & Erling, O. (2007). RDFSync: Efficient remote synchronization of RDF models. In K. Aberer, K.-S. Choi, N. Noy, D. Allemang, K.-I. Lee, L. Nixon, et al. (Eds.), *The Semantic Web: Proceedings of the 6th International Semantic Web Conference and the 2nd Asian Semantic Web Conference,* Busan, Korea (LNCS 4825, pp. 537-551).

Wang, H., Zhang, K., Liu, Q., Tran, T., & Yu, Y. (2008, June 1-5). Q2Semantic: A lightweight keyword interface to semantic search. In S. Bechhofer, M. Hauswirth, J. Hoffmann, & M. Koubarakis (Eds.), *The Semantic Web: Research and Applications: Proceedings of the 5th European Semantic Web Conference,* Canary Islands, Spain (LNCS 5021, pp. 584-598).

Watters, C. (1999). Information retrieval and the virtual document. *Journal of the American Society for Information Science American Society for Information Science, 50*(11), 1028–1029. doi:10.1002/(SICI)1097-4571(1999)50:11<1028::AID-ASI8>3.0.CO;2-0

Yamauchi, T. (2007). The Semantic Web and human inference: A lesson from cognitive science. In K. Aberer, K.-S. Choi, N. Noy, D. Allemang, K.-I. Lee, L. Nixon, et al. (Eds.), *The Semantic Web: Proceedings of the 6th International Semantic Web Conference and the 2nd Asian Semantic Web Conference,* Busan, Korea (LNCS 4825, pp. 609-622).

Zhang, X., Cheng, G., & Qu, Y. (2007, May 8-12). Ontology summarization based on RDF sentence graph. In C. Williamson, M. E. Zurko, P. Patel-Schneider, & P. Shenoy (Eds.), *Proceedings of the 16th International Conference on World Wide Web,* Banff, Alberta, Canada (pp. 707-716). New York, NY: ACM.

Zhou, Q., Wang, C., Xiong, M., Wang, H., & Yu, Y. (2007). SPARK: Adapting keyword query to semantic search. In K. Aberer, K.-S. Choi, N. Noy, D. Allemang, K.-I. Lee, L. Nixon, et al. (Eds.), *The Semantic Web: Proceedings of the 6th International Semantic Web Conference and the 2nd Asian Semantic Web Conference,* Busan, Korea (LNCS 4825, pp. 694-707).

Chapter 11
A URI is Worth a Thousand Tags:
From Tagging to Linked Data with MOAT

Alexandre Passant
National University of Ireland, Ireland

Philippe Laublet
Université Paris-Sorbonne, France

John G. Breslin
National University of Ireland, Ireland

Stefan Decker
National University of Ireland, Ireland

ABSTRACT

Although tagging is a widely accepted practice on the Social Web, it raises various issues like tags ambiguity and heterogeneity, as well as the lack of organization between tags. We believe that Semantic Web technologies can help solve many of these issues, especially considering the use of formal resources from the Web of Data in support of existing tagging systems and practices. In this article, we present the MOAT—Meaning Of A Tag—ontology and framework, which aims to achieve this goal. We will detail some motivations and benefits of the approach, both in an Enterprise 2.0 ecosystem and on the Web. As we will detail, our proposal is twofold: It helps solve the problems mentioned previously, and weaves user-generated content into the Web of Data, making it more efficiently interoperable and retrievable.

INTRODUCTION

The Social Web, or Web 2.0 (O'Reilly, 2005), has become an important trend during the last few years. While end-users of the Web were previously considered as being only consumers of content, the paradigms that the Social Web introduced has led them to become producers as well. For instance, blogs allow anyone to publish and share

DOI: 10.4018/978-1-60960-593-3.ch011

their thoughts on the Web whereas wikis are used to collaboratively build consensual information within a community. In the meantime, social network services have allowed people to define acquaintance networks and to keep in touch with each other on the Web. Moreover, apart from providing a means to create discussions and to define or manage social networks, an important feature of social Web sites is the ability to share content with one's peers. On many social Web sites, this data can be shared either with whoever is subscribed to (or just browsing) the Web site or else it can be shared within a restricted community. Also, not only textual content can be shared, but various types of media or other content objects: pictures (Flickr), videos (YouTube), slides (Slideshare), trips (Dopplr), and so forth. To make this content more easily discoverable, most of these websites allow users to add free-form keywords, or tags, that act like subjects or categories for anything they wish to share. For example, this article could be tagged with "semanticweb" and "socialweb" on a scientific bibliography management system such as Bibsonomy or Connotea.

Although tags can be generally considered as a type of metadata, since they provide additional information about a tagged item, it is important to keep in mind that they are user-driven. Indeed, while a blog engine may automatically assign a creation date to any blog post or a photo sharing service could use embedded EXIF information to display the aperture of a camera, tags are added voluntarily by users themselves. To that extent, they clearly reflect the needs and the will of the user who assigns the tags. In this way, tags focus on what a user considers as important regarding the way he or she wants to share and present information. The main advantage of tagging for end users is that one can use the keywords that fit exactly with his or her needs and they do not have to learn a pre-defined vocabulary scheme (such as a taxonomy). Tags and tagging actions lead to what is generally called a folksonomy (VanderWal, 2007), an open and user-driven clas-

sification scheme that evolves during time thanks to the tagging actions of the community itself, contrary to pre-defined and authoritative classification directories, which are generally fixed.

Yet, in spite of its advantages when annotating content items, tagging leads to various issues regarding information retrieval, which makes the task of retrieving tagged content sometimes quite costly. Mathes (2004) estimates that a "folksonomy represents simultaneously some of the best and worst in the organization of information." Indeed, even if dedicated algorithms like FolkRank (Hotho, Jäschke, Schmitz, & Stumme, 2006) and clustering techniques can be used to improve retrieval of tagged-content—in spite of the shortcomings we will discuss later—tag-dedicated search engines are generally simply based on plain-text strings, that is, a user types a tag and gets only the content that has been tagged with that particular keyword. Therefore, this can lead to various issues, since such an engine only considers a set of characters that it cannot interpret which consequently introduces some noise and silence issues.

In the Semantic Web domain, the Web of Data is considered a more pragmatic vision of the Semantic Web, focused mainly on exposing data in RDF and interlinking it, that is, providing Linked Data on the Web, rather than on using formal ontologies and inference principles that form the complete Semantic Web vision. Interlinking user-generated content with URIs of well-known and unambiguous resources from the Semantic Web would help to solve the aforementioned issues, as user-generated content would be then interlinked with well-defined and unambiguous identifiers. Moreover, it offers a way to weave such content into the Semantic Web, hence considering Web 2.0 and the Web of Data not as disjoint domains but as being beneficial to each other.

In this article, we describe the MOAT framework that aims to provide an intuitive and lightweight way to bridge this gap between free-tagging and Linked Data, in what we consider a twofold approach with strong benefits for both the

Social Web and the Semantic Web communities. The article is organized as follows. In the first section, we describe some of the main issues of free-tagging systems regarding data querying and information retrieval. We also emphasize, based on a corporate-blogging use-case, why current tag-based clustering algorithms may not be enough to solve these issues. Then, we introduce our proposal, MOAT, beginning with its theoretical background in which we extend the usual tripartite model of tagging to a quadripartite one, taking into account the meaning of tags. We then describe the related OWL ontology and continue by reviewing the MOAT framework architecture, combining the "architecture of participation" principles of Web 2.0 together with Semantic Web technologies and RDF(S)/OWL data representation principles to let people intuitively bridge this gap between tagging and Linked Data. We then detail two use-cases for the approach. The first relates to the corporate blogging platform that initially motivated the MOAT approach. The second describes LODr, an application based on MOAT dedicated to weaving existing user-generated content from well-known services like Flickr or Delicious into the Web of Data. The analysis of these two use-cases helps evaluate the approach, both in terms of how it can be used to solve tagging issues and how it weaves user-generated content into the Semantic Web in a twofold approach. We then present an overview of related work and detail our position in relation to it, before concluding the article.

Common Issues with Free-Tagging Systems

In this section, we give an overview of current issues in free-tagging systems, based on some observations and an analysis both of the Web and of corporate blogging systems. Interestingly, the issues below have parallels in the world of libraries and are one reason why librarians use classification schemes like thesauri or taxonomies, such as the Dewey Decimal Classification or the ACM

Taxonomy. Therefore, we may consider how to find a smoother transition between the openness of tagging systems and the rigidity of such classification schemes, and we will later describe how our proposal aims to solve this.

Tag Ambiguity

Since tags are text-strings only, without any semantics or obvious interpretation (rather than a set of characters) for a software program that reads these tags, ambiguity is an important issue. Although a person knows that the tag "apple" means something different when it is used to tag a blog post about a laptop, a picture of a bag of fruit, or a review of a Beatles record, a tag-based information system cannot distinguish between them. Indeed, the only thing it understands is that the content is tagged with a text string composed of the characters "a-p-p-l-e" in this particular order. Hence, a tag-based query engine will retrieve various items for a search on "apple" even if the user had the computer brand in mind: items about fruits will be mixed up with iPod-related ones. Consequently, users must sort out themselves what is relevant or not regarding their expectations. Depending on the context and the number of retrieved items, it can be a costly task.

For example, the following figure shows the result of a search for the most relevant items tagged "apple" on Flickr, mixing pictures of fruits and Apple devices. Similar issues can be observed on Delicious, for example with the "swig" tag, since the acronym identifies both the "Semantic Web Interest Group" and "Simplified Wrapper and Interface Generator." Both are unrelated, but unfortunately a user subscribed to the related RSS feed have to face a noise and information overload issue, as they will be delivered unrelated content.

Tag Heterogeneity

Tag ambiguity refers to when the same tag it used to refer to different things, but a parallel issue is

Figure 1. Tag ambiguity on a Flickr search for pictures tagged "apple"

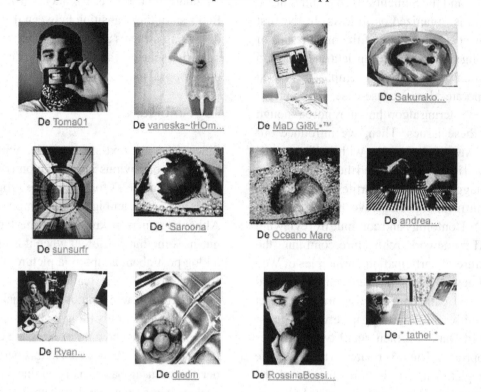

that different tags can also be used to refer to the same thing. Such heterogeneity is mainly caused by the multilingual nature of tags (e.g., "semantic-web" in English and "websemantique" in French), but also due to the fact that people use acronyms or shortened versions ("sw" and "semweb"), as well as linguistic and morpho-syntactic variations (synonyms, plurals, case variations, etc.). As an example, the following table lists some of the various tags used on Delicious to identify the concept of "Semantic Web," not taking into account related tags like RDFa, SPARQL, and so forth, as we will describe later. In this case, one must use various queries to get Semantic Web related content and, most importantly, one must know that each tag exists, which sometimes requires serendipitous discovery.

Lack of Organization and Relationships between Tags

Since a folksonomy is essentially a flat bundle of tags, the lack of relationship between them makes difficult to find information if one is not directly looking at the right tag, in addition to the previously-mentioned issues. This is clearly a problem in the practice of tagging, especially if people use different tags depending on their level on expertise or if they search for broader or narrower tags, as noted by (Golder & Huberman, 2006) when analysing Delicious. Indeed, although we mentioned the tags "semanticweb" or "social-web" regarding this article, an expert on Semantic Web technologies may not use those terms (as they will be too broad for him) but instead would prefer tags like "moat," "linkeddata," or "sparql" to better classify the article. Then, someone simply looking at items tagged "semanticweb" will not be

Table 1. Example of tag heterogeneity for the "Semantic Web" concept on Delicious

Tag	URL of related content
Semanticweb	http://delicious.com/tag/semanticweb
semantic-web	http://delicious.com/tag/semantic-web
Semaweb	http://delicious.com/tag/semaweb
Semweb	http://delicious.com/tag/semweb
Websemantic	http://delicious.com/tag/websemantic
web-semantic	http://delicious.com/tag/web-semantic
Websemantique	http://delicious.com/tag/websemantique
Websemantica	http://delicious.com/tag/websemantica
web-semantica	http://delicious.com/tag/web-semantica
Websemantico	http://delicious.com/tag/websemantico
web-semantico	http://delicious.com/tag/web-semantico
Websem	http://delicious.com/tag/websem

able to retrieve this article even though there is a clear relationship between these tags in terms of the technological domain. This relates, as Golder and Huberman (2006) noted, to a more generic issue regarding how different people consider different things as being the "basic level" for a knowledge domain, depending on their cognitive background and expertise in a field (Tanaka & Taylor, 1991). To that extent, the "semanticweb" tag might be considered to be a basic-level term for someone not involved in the domain, whereas it will be too broad for an expert or researcher, which may consider "sparql" or "linkeddata" as basic-level terms, depending on their research field. Since tags are unrelated, neither hierarchically nor by other means, bridging these basic levels between people and communities is hence an v issue of such systems.

Why is Clustering not Enough?

To overcome the issues we described, tag-based clustering algorithms have been proposed to identify similar and related tags (Begelman, Keller, & Smadja, 2006). However, their success depends on the tagging distribution, that is, if there is a

strong co-occurrence between tags or not, which may not be the case in some folksonomies, even for tags that identify related concepts. In relation to this, an analysis of a corporate blogging system at Electricité de France R&D (http://retd.edf.fr), part of a general Enterprise 2.0 ecosystem in the company, raised some interesting issues. Enterprise 2.0 (McAfee, 2006) defines a corporate information system in which Web 2.0 tools and paradigms are used as a means to engage discussions and carry out knowledge sharing internally in an organisation. Firstly, we noticed that most of the tags used in this platform were used only a few times. In a total of 12,257 tags used on 21,614 blog posts, more than 68% were used twice or less, while only 10% were used more than ten times (Figure 2). As Hayes and Avesani (2007) reported, tag-based clustering may not be adapted for this kind of distribution, unless it is combined with other techniques such as reusing background information extracted from the tagged content itself.

Moreover, another interesting lesson that came out of from our analysis is that knowledge workers tag differently depending on their level of expertise, as we have already mentioned. The observations of Golder and Huberman (2006) regarding Delicious were confirmed by our study of corporate tagging. For example, experts in solar energies used tags like "TF" (an acronym for Thin Film, a particular kind of solar cell), whereas non-experts used generic ones like "solaire" (English for solar). Furthermore, experts often did not use any broader terms. Only 1% of the 194 items tagged with "TF" were tagged together with "solaire," while less than 0.5% of the 704 items tagged with "solaire" tagged with "TF." Therefore, tag-based clustering algorithms cannot be used to find related tags since they are too weakly related, as discussed in (Begelman et al., 2006). Consequently, non-experts cannot retrieve blog posts written by experts, even if there is a clear link between the different concepts. In such corporate contexts, that issue is clearly a problem:

Figure 2. Tag distribution in a corporate blogging platform

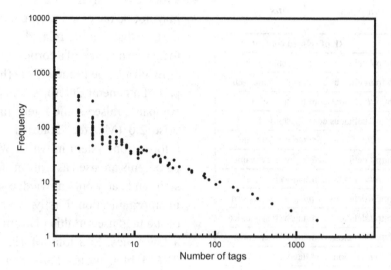

experts will write knowledgeable blog posts that non-experts will not be able to retrieve since they cannot be connected to broader concepts. These posts lie in the "long tail" where they generally contain high-value information. This gap regarding expertise and tagging behaviours is hence an important limitation for knowledge management in organizations that use such tagging systems.

INTRODUCING MOAT

Tagging as a Quadripartite Model

Various theoretical definitions have been proposed to model tagging activities (Marlow, Naaman, Boyd, & Davis, 2006; Mika 2005). A widely agreed way is to represent a tagging action as a tripartite model between a User, a Resource, and a Tag and is defined as follows:

Tagging(User, Resource, Tag)

Hence, the following figure represents three different tagging actions (T1, T2, T3) made by two different users (U1, U2) on a particular photo. It also emphasizes on the social aspect of tagging existing in many applications, that is, different users tagging the same item, using the same tags or not.

The three tagging actions on this figure can then be represented as:

```
T1(U1, photo, apple)
T2(U2, photo, apple)
T3(U2, photo, laptop)
```

Yet, in our opinion, an important aspect of tagging is missing here, that is, the representation of the meaning of the tag used. As we explained, tags do not have any machine-readable semantic information, being simple text strings. However, there is generally a clear and unambiguous meaning associated with a tag by a user in a particular tagging action. Considering the previous example, it is clear that both users have in mind the computer brand when using the keyword "apple" to tag the picture. Hence, our first proposal is to extend the usual tripartite model of tagging to a quadripartite one as follows:

```
Tagging(User, Resource, Tag, Meaning)
```

Figure 3. Representing different tagging actions related to the same content

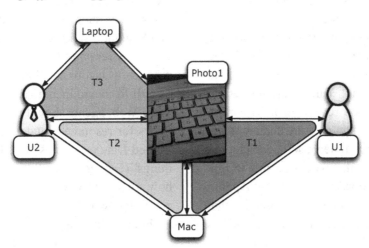

The previous tagging actions can then be represented as:

```
T1(U1, photo, apple, Apple computers)
T2(U2, photo, apple, Apple computers)
T3(U2, photo, laptop, a particular
kind of computer)
```

While a picture about fruits will be tagged as

```
T4(U3, photo, apple, a fruit)
```

Defining the meaning of tags using a simple text string leads to the same issues as before, since one user can describe apple as "Apple computers" and another user as "Apple Inc." Hence, our proposal is to consider each meaning being represented not by a text string but by a URI that defines it. Thanks to efforts conducted via the Linking Open Data (LOD) community project (Bizer, Heath, Ayers, & Raimond, 2007), millions of URIs for representing items as varied as places, brands, companies, people, and so forth, are now available on the Web from sources, such as DBpedia (Auer, Bizer, Lehmann, Kobilarov, Cyganiak, & Ives, 2007), Geonames, DBTune (Raimond & Sandler, 2008), and so forth, and can be efficiently used as identifiers as shown by

(Hepp, Siorpaes, & Bachlechner, 2007). Adding this URI as a fourth element and not forcing users to directly use a URI when tagging content, permits them to keep their existing free-tagging habits, for example, using acronyms or multilingual tags, and selecting the exact tag they want, keeping intact their "desire lines" as Merholz(2004) called them. Hence, one can rely on those URIs to represent the meaning of each tag in tagging actions in a non-ambiguous and machine-readable way, as in the following extension to our example and using URIs provided by DBpedia.

```
T1(U1, photo, apple, <http://dbpedia.
org/resource/Apple_Inc.>)
T2(U2, photo, apple, <http://dbpedia.
org/resource/Apple_Inc.>)
T3(U2, photo, laptop, <http://dbpe-
dia.org/resource/Laptop>)
T4(U2, photo, apple, <http://dbpedia.
org/resource/Apple>)
```

This proposal solves both the ambiguity and heterogeneity issues with tagging. Regarding ambiguity, a user can now tag a fruits picture using "apple" with the meaning being defined differently to a laptop photo with the same tag? This can be done using a URI representing the apple as a fruit, for example, <http://dbpedia.org/resource/Apple>, as identified in T4 above. Considering the heterogeneity issue, another tag (e.g., "apple_computers") can be used and linked to the same meaningful URI (i.e., <http://dbpedia.org/resource/Apple_Inc.>) in a tagging action, solving the issue when retrieving information. Multi-lingual issues of tagging are taken into account in a similar way. Indeed, someone tagging a picture with "manzana" would be able to link it to the same <http://dpedia.org/resource/Apple> URI. To that extent, it is important to mention that the meanings of tags are defined thanks to URIs of entities, and not URLs of documents (as these would be as ambiguous as free-tags), conforming to the vision of an (ongoing) Web of Data in addition to the (current) Web of Documents.

In some cases, different URIs can be used for the same meaning, for example, <http://dbpedia.org/resource/Paris> and <http://sws.geonames.org/2988507/> for the city of Paris. Here, systems should take into consideration any owl:sameAs links that may exist between such resources (such as the two previous URIs) to identify that, in spite of different URIs, they represent the same entity. Such links may not yet exist and hence must be introduced separately. It is important to consider issues related to the use of owl:sameAs, which has a strong semantic meaning regarding identity, and other techniques could be considered to identify relatedness between entities (Jaffri, Glaser, & Millard, 2008). In addition, it may happen that an entity is being considered from a different point of view with different meanings, for example a city as a populated place and as an administrative division, their meaning being different. In that case, different URIs must be employed in the tagging action, for example <http://sws.geonames.org/2988507/>, for the city of Paris and <http://sws.geonames.org/6455259/> for Paris as an administrative division, both being defined in Geonames.

Moreover, in some cases, there may be no URI to represent the desired concept, for example, in the case where it is a very specific topic. In these cases, users should rely on external applications like Semantic Wikis to create a new URI for the concept. Creating such URIs is, in general, a good practice, as Jacobs and Walsh (2004) suggest, "To benefit from and increase the value of the World Wide Web, agents should provide URIs as identifiers for resources" and as emphasized by the Linked Data principles "Use URIs as names for things" (Berners-Lee, 2006). We will also see later how some MOAT clients can ease the process of creating new URIs when tagging content.

Finally, one important thing to consider is that these URIs are not isolated, but linked together to build a single Giant Global Graph (Berners-Lee, 2007) of structured knowledge. Hence, a system can infer that a blog post tagged (via MOAT) with the URI <http://dbpedia.org/resource/Apple_Inc.> is somehow related to a picture tagged with <http://dbpedia.org/resource/iPhone> as both are related thanks to DBpedia, following the Linked Data principles, by including links to related URIs as well as to other relevant information. We will later on give some more example of how such interlinks can be used in real-world applications and for querying purposes, but we will first focus on how we represent this quadripartite model in a formal way, that is, using a dedicated OWL ontology.

THE MOAT ONTOLOGY

To model our proposal in a formal way, allowing software agents to represent and to query tagged items taking into account their links to entities from the Web of Data, we designed the MOAT project—Meaning Of A Tag (Passant & Laublet, 2008) (http://moat-project.org)—consisting of (1) a lightweight ontology and (2) a related collaborative framework. The ontology is based on prior work on tagging ontologies and reuses the Tag Ontology (http://www.holygoat.co.uk/projects/tags).

First, the MOAT ontology introduces a Tag class (as a subclass of the Tag one defined in the Tag Ontology) to define the concept of Tag, allowing each tag to get a proper URI, being linked to the tag (as a keyword) with a name property. This class addresses one of the problems of the Tag Ontology, since in this model, an instance of Tag can be assigned different labels without any restriction. This can lead to tags labelled with both "RDF" and "Ireland," which does not make any sense from a user point of view, but no software can detect this inconsistency since it is not defined in the model. Hence, MOAT introduces an OWL cardinality constraint so that an instance of Tag can have a single name. In addition, MOAT reuses the RestrictedTagging class defined in the Tag Ontology to model the tripartite action of tagging and simply introduces a tagMeaning property in order to link to the URI of the tag meaning in a tagging action. The following snippet of code and the related figure (Figure 4) hence represent how to model that, in a particular tagging context, the tag "apple" means <http://dbpedia.org/resource/Apple_Inc./>, that is, the computer brand. As one can see, in addition to MOAT and the Tagging Ontology, we use FOAF to represent the agent that realised the tagging action, SIOC (Breslin, Harth, Bojārs, & Decker, 2005) and DublinCore to represent the tagged item, whereas DBpedia is used to define the meaning of the tag in that example.

```
@prefix moat: <http://moat-project.
org/ns#>.
@prefix foaf: <http://xmlns.com/
foaf/0.1/>.
@prefix sioc: <http://rdfs.org/sioc/
ns#>.
@prefix dct: <http://purl.org/dc/
terms/>.
<http://example.org/post/1> a
sioc:Post ;
foaf:maker <http://apassant.net/alex>
;
```

```
dct:title "Browsing Linked on iPhone"
;
moat:taggedWith <http://dbpedia.org/
resource/Apple_Inc.>.
<http://example.org/tagging/1> a
tags:RestrictedTagging ;
tag:associatedTag <http://example.
org/tag/apple> ;
tag:taggedBy <http://apassant.net/
alex> ;
tag:taggedResource <http://example.
org/post/1> ;
moat:tagMeaning <http://dbpedia.org/
resource/Apple_Inc.>.
```

As we can also see in this figure, the vocabulary uses a taggedWith property to model a direct link between the tagged item and the meaning URI. This can be used when the tripartite relationship is not needed, providing a shorter path for querying data. Although properties like dc:subject from DublinCore or skos:subject from SKOS (while recently deprecated) could have been used here, their semantics specifically indicate that the related object is a subject of the annotated item, which may not be the case. Tags can indeed be seen not only as descriptive metadata but also as structural or administrative metadata, considering the digital libraries terminology regarding metadata (Taylor, 1999). Hence, there is a need to model that a URI is linked to an item via a tagging action, but is not a subject, for example <http://dbpedia/GNU_Free_Documentation_License> could be used to identify that the annotated work is licensed under GNU FDL but is not about GNU FDL, and this is the goal of the taggedWith property.

In this quadripartite model representing tagging actions, we consider the meaning of tag to be local, that is, depending on the tagging action itself, and we call it the *local meaning* of a tag. However, taken out of context, the same tag can have multiple meanings, that is, the tag apple can refer to various things. This is a particular feature of tags that that we also want to model in MOAT

Figure 4. Modelling the meaning of a tag in a particular tagging action with MOAT

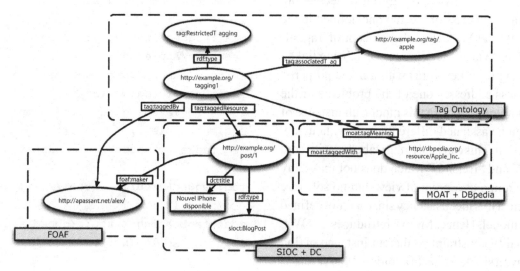

and that we named the *global meanings* of a tag. To model it, we defined by the following theoretical model, in which {User} represents the set of users that assign a particular meaning to this tag.

Meaning(Tag) = {(Meaning, {User})}

Based on this model, the following snippet of code and the related figure (Figure 5) show how to represent two different global meanings for the apple tag in a given folksonomy, respectively

<http://dbpedia.org/resource/Apple_Inc.> by one user and <http://dbpedia.org/resource/Apple> by two of them. To represent these global meanings with MOAT, we introduced a particular Meaning class and hasMeaning and meaningURI properties, allowing us to reifying these relationships, that is, taking into account the different users that assign a particular meaning to a tag.

```
@prefix moat: <http://moat-project.
org/ns#>.
```

Figure 5. Representing two different meanings for the tag "apple"

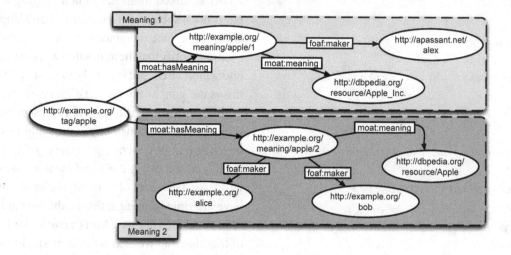

```
@prefix foaf: <http://xmlns.com/
foaf/0.1/>.
<http://example.org/tag/apple> a
moat:Tag ;
moat:hasMeaning <http://example.org/
meaning/apple/1> ;
moat:hasMeaning <http://example.org/
meaning/apple/2>.
<http://example.org/meaning/apple/1>
a moat:Meaning ;
moat:meaningURI <http://dbpedia.org/
resource/Apple_Inc.> ;
foaf:maker <http://apassant.net/
alex/>
<http://example.org/meaning/apple/2>
a moat:Meaning ;
moat:meaningURI <http://dbpedia.org/
resource/Apple> ;
foaf:maker <http://example.org/alice>
;
foaf:maker <http://example.org/bob>.
```

Then, an overview of local and global meanings of tags defined in MOAT can then be represented as follows (Figure 6), with the complete ontology being available at http://moat-project.org/ns.

THE MOAT FRAMEWORK

To the apply these principles of semantically enhanced tagging and to allow people to assign meaning to their tags, we designed a complete framework associated with the MOAT ontology that consists of: a MOAT server, which people can be subscribed to—as they can do with Annotea (http://www.w3.org/2001/Annotea/) (Kahan & Koivunen, 2001)—and that stores global meanings of tags for a given community of users;

MOAT clients that interact with servers to identify global meanings when users tag content to let them choose a local meaning for their tags. If needed, new URIs can be added by the user through the client. Clients also generate the related RDF data once the content has been semantically tagged.

The MOAT framework and its related workflow are depicted in the following picture (Figure 7), and it is worth mentioning that the client and server simply interact by exchanging RDF graphs via HTTP.

Since the community can add new meanings, this framework combines the architecture of participation principles of Web 2.0 (i.e., sharing

Figure 6. The MOAT Ontology

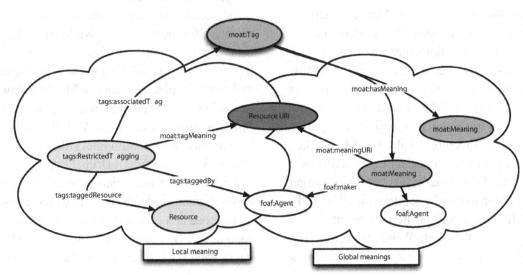

Figure 7. Workflow associated with the MOAT framework

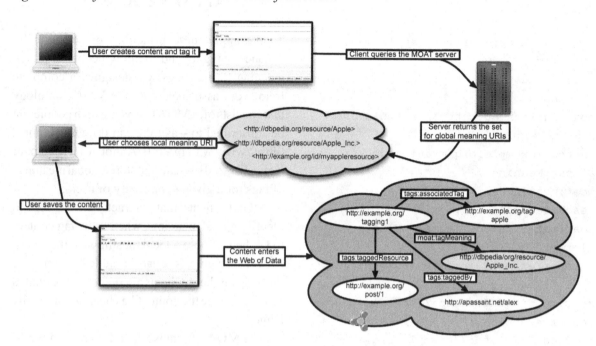

and adding meanings within a community) and the knowledge representation paradigms from the Semantic Web (i.e., providing RDF data for tagging actions). To model users within this architecture, we rely on FOAF (as previously mentioned) to ensure the uniqueness of one's identity and in a distributed manner if required (Bojārs, Passant, Breslin, & Decker, 2008). The use of FOAF can also be combined with authentication schemes like OpenID or FOAF+TSL (Story, Harbulot, Jacobi, & Jones, 2009) in the future.

The previous architecture has been implemented as open-source framework, available at http://moat-project.org. A MOAT server is available in PHP and can be used in combination with various triple stores, to ease its integration in existing architectures. It also provides Linked Data for any tag URI. For example, one can browse the tag <http://tags.moat-project.org/paris> to get the list of global meanings, retrieving RDF/XML or HTML depending on the user agent. It can also deliver JSON to help Web 2.0 developers to build MOAT-based applications without learning

Semantic Web principles. A Drupal module has been designed to interact with such servers. To let users add new URIs when nothing relevant is retrieved from the server, we rely on the Sindice (Tumarrello et al., 2007) search widget. The following picture (Figure 8) displays the use of the MOAT client for three different tags: at the bottom, for the tag "sparql" a single URI has been suggested by the server and selected by the user; in the middle, three URIs were suggested (and one selected) for the tag "paris" while on the top, the Sindice widget is used to find a new URI for the tag "barcamp." In addition to these public client and server implementations, a MOAT client and server has been integrated in the OpenLink Data Space platform, a complete Web 2.0 suite built on Semantic Web technologies (Idehen & Erling, 2008). While the current Drupal implementation displays URIs, a user-friendly way would be to expose human-readable labels, as we have recently carried out in a corporate environment and will soon detail. On the Web, a solution would be to query each URI to retrieve its label, or one can

Figure 8. Using the Drupal MOAT client

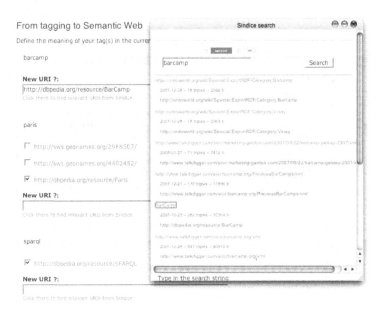

use the recent SPARCool service (http://sparcool. net) that has a more elaborate interface to make such queries easier.

USING MOAT IN ENTERPRISE 2.0

Background Context and Related Use-Case

As we mentioned earlier, one of our first motivations for MOAT originated in the use and analysis of a corporate blogging platform at Electricité De France R&D, in the context of a project in which we studied how Semantic Web technologies could improve Enterprise 2.0 ecosystems (Passant, 2008). In this context, and while not directly related to MOAT, we reused data from Geonames in a Semantic Wiki to build runtime semantic mash-ups combining internal and external data sources (see Figure 9). We believe that these mash-ups can be the future of Enterprise 2.0 applications: similar to how RSS allows companies to benefit from public information, reusing publicly avail-

able Linked Data allows us to take advantage of large-scale knowledge about different topics for relatively minor cost. Hence, we believe that Linked Data—particularly data available using open licences—has an important role to play in business information systems and could be a key feature for the Web of Data and related technologies in corporate contexts, as also demonstrated recently by the BBC (Kobilarov et al., 2009).

To embed MOAT in our architecture (since we did not want end users to be faced with URIs in order to define the meaning of their tags), we updated the generic Drupal client to display not URIs, but rather human-readable labels (based on the rdfs:label property) of resources from our internal knowledge base (populated mainly via our Semantic Wiki). To add global meanings to tags, our client allows users to simply browse our internal knowledge base and choose the right resource to assign the tag, or create a new one, without having to face any RDF(S)/OWL data and using a simple Flash interface (Figure 10). This interface also allows us to see which tags are related to any resource.

Figure 9. A semantic mashup with Exhibit, combining internal and external RDF data from the LOD-cloud

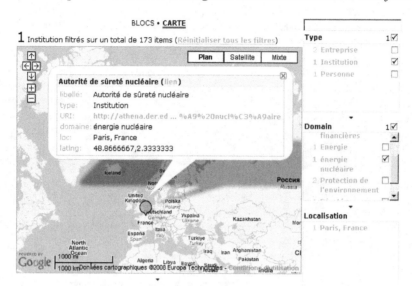

BENEFITS OF MOAT IN ENTERPRISE 2.0

In order to derive benefit from the semantic tagging process, we integrated MOAT in a semantic search engine that we built internally, aggregating RDF data from various internal sources (Passant,

Laublet, Breslin, & Decker, 2009). The engine uses MOAT to:

- suggest relevant and appropriate resources based on a searched term. Hence, a user searching for the term "france" will be asked if he or she wants to retrieve in-

Figure 10. Browsing the internal knowledge base to create a new resource from a given tag

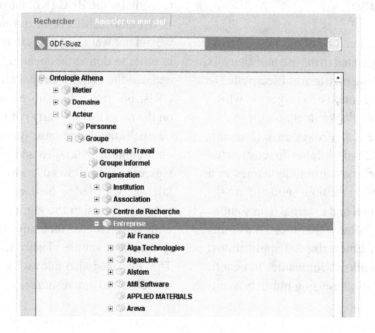

formation about the resource "France," "Electricité de France," or "Gaz de France," using the links between tags and related URIs;

- once the relevant resource has been identified, the system retrieves all content linked to that URI, also identifying its source (i.e., Wiki or blogging platform). As the search is based on URIs and not on keywords anymore, it solves both ambiguity and heterogeneity issues.

Although the engine relies completely on RDF(S)/OWL data and SPARQL queries, these are hidden from users as the goal (Figure 11) is to showcase the benefits of Linked Data technologies without any complex interfaces.

We previously mentioned an important issue related to differing expertise levels and its effect on tagging behaviour, leading to some content that is difficult to find for some users. Hence, our search engine also suggests concepts related to the one a user is currently searching for, by analysing the underlying knowledge base and displaying related concepts based on some rules (e.g.,

using the skos:broader relationship which links to a broader concept).

EVALUATING THE APPROACH

From a total of 12,257 tags used in our platform, 1176 of them were related to 715 different URIs, both from our internal knowledge base and from GeoNames. Analysing these relationships showed that while only one tag was subject to ambiguity issues, heterogeneity was important. As the following table shows, a total of 205 resources (i.e., URIs) were subject to heterogeneity with more than one tag assigned to each URI. Specifically, 39 were assigned at least five or more tags. For example, "Supercapacitor" (a component used in electrical engineering) was related to the five following tags: "supercapacité," "supercondensateur," "ultracapacité," "ultracapacitor," and "ultracondensateur." As expected, it emphasises the usual heterogeneity issues of tagging systems, such as synonymy ("supercondensateur," "ultracondensateur," etc.) and multi-lingual issues ("ultracapacité," "ultracapacitor").

Figure 11. Semantic Search engine taking advantage of MOAT

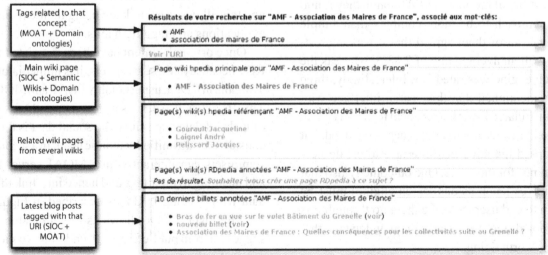

Table 2. Statistics of tag heterogeneity

Number of tag(s)	Related URI
1	510
2	96
3	70
4 or more	39

Using MOAT and URIs instead of simple tags helped to solve this heterogeneity issue since our engine retrieves information because of these URIs. Then, a single query is needed to retrieve information about "Supercapacitor," instead of the five related tag-based queries that it originally implied.

In addition, we noticed that even for a single user, different tags were used for the same concept. For example, only three users were involved in the previous example, with one of them using three different tags. More generally, we particularly noticed that "personal heterogeneity" issues regarding tags referring to people (i.e., tags used for the full name versus last name only) and locations (e.g., "USA" and "Etats-Unis"), as well as some technologies (multilingual issues and acronyms), displaying some interesting behaviour regarding personal tagging habits.

We also interviewed six users and asked them to rate both their interest in the system and the complexity of the approach. Although they found this approach to be more complex than simple tagging, all of them agreed that it was interesting, with an average rate of 2.83/5, whereas the search engine was rated 3.5. Interestingly, three users mentioned that this search interface with links to related items helped them to discover new content. In addition, four also acknowledged that they used the advanced interface to create new meanings for their tags. One outcome is also that incentives (such as our search engine) must be given to end users to make them go through this additional step and to make them understand that this is worth doing.

LODr: WEAVING HETEROGENEOUS USER-GENERATED CONTENT INTO THE WEB OF DATA

Goals and Principles

To apply MOAT principles on the Web, we implemented LODr (http://lodr.info), a personal application that allows one to re-tag their existing Web 2.0 content and to weave it into the Web of Data thanks to the aforementioned principles. Its main objective is to provide a simple way to create RDF and interlinked content from existing Web 2.0 tools, so that queries like "list all SlideShare items tagged with a topic related to the Semantic Web" can be answered. LODr is an open-source application written in PHP5 using an object-oriented model, and although it is completely RDF-based, it simply uses a generic LAMP setup thanks to ARC2 (http://arc.semsol.org). LODr is based on a set of wrappers translating user-generated content from various services into RDF, featuring wrappers for major Web 2.0 services (Twitter, SlideShare, Flickr, Delicious, Bibsonomy) while new wrappers can be easily written. One motivation for writing a standalone application is that we did not want to create another tagging service but rather produce a system offering users with a way to enrich existing data to avoid social network fatigue (Fitzpatrick & Recordon, 2007), and this allows users to keep using their existing applications and tagging habits.

Once original content have been translated to RDF because of these wrappers, it is immediately available in RDFa, using notably FOAF and SIOC. This first step also allows us to get over the issue of isolated data silos since the social data is then considered via a unified semantic layer. In a second step, users can interact with a MOAT server to add meaning to their tags and hence interlink this data with existing URIs, as described in Figure 12. Moreover, LODr allows us to get meanings suggested from public SPARQL endpoints, which can make the process easier in some cases as a

Figure 12. The LODr architecture

MOAT server
Aggregating
Producing
LODr client
LINKINGOPENDATA
Semantic Web
Distributed W eb 2.0 tagged content
Semantically-enhanced Linked Data

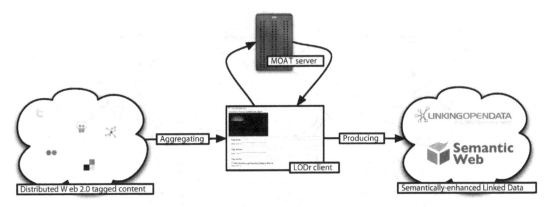

user can choose an endpoint corresponding to his or her particular interests.

BENEFITS OF THE APPROACH

LODr provides advanced interfaces to browse semantically tagged data, as Figure 13 depicts. By analysing RDF data corresponding to the chosen meaning (in that case via the SPARQL URI on DBpedia), it displays additional information about it as well as suggesting relevant URIs based on direct and indirect relationships. For example. GRDDL is suggested when browsing SPARQL as both share a similar value for the skos:subject property, that is, dbpedia:Category:World_Wide_Web_Consortium_standards.

More generally, by being interlinked to other data sources, this user-generated content becomes more valuable than the original, since it is no longer (1) locked in proprietary data silos, and (2) is not just related to simple meaningless free-text tags. As Metcalfe's law defines, the value of a network is proportional to the number of nodes

Figure 13. Browsing items related to a particular URI with LODr

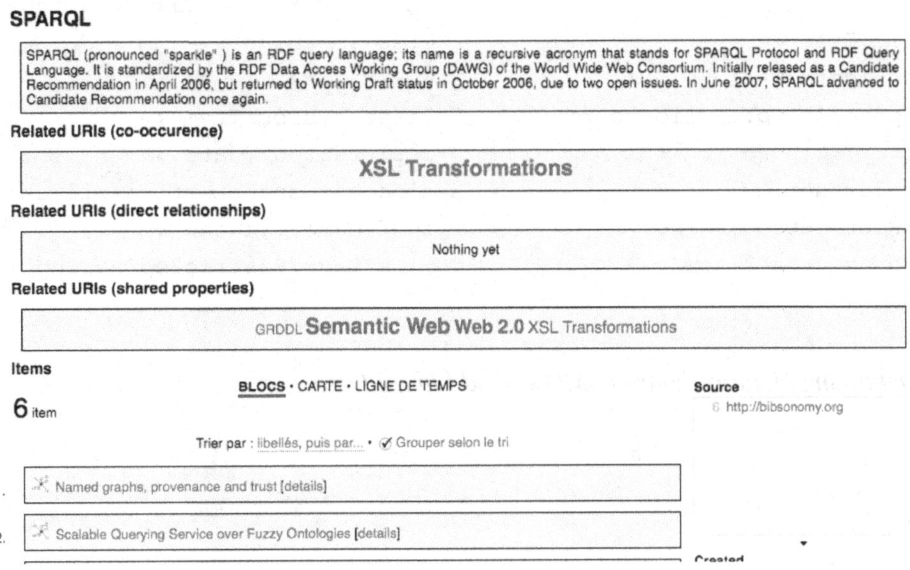

SPARQL
SPARQL (pronounced "sparkle") is an RDF query language; its name is a recursive acronym that stands for SPARQL Protocol and RDF Query Language. It is standardized by the RDF Data Access Working Group (DAWG) of the World Wide Web Consortium. Initially released as a Candidate Recommendation in April 2006, but returned to Working Draft status in October 2006, due to two open issues. In June 2007, SPARQL advanced to Candidate Recommendation once again.
Related URIs (co-occurence)
XSL Transformations
Related URIs (direct relationships)
Nothing yet
Related URIs (shared properties)
GRDDL Semantic Web Web 2.0 XSL Transformations
Items
6 item
BLOCS · CARTE · LIGNE DE TEMPS
Source
http://bibsonomy.org
Trier par : libellés, puis par... · Grouper selon le tri
Named graphs, provenance and trust [details]
Scalable Querying Service over Fuzzy Ontologies [details]

Figure 14. Interlinking user-generated content through various paths thanks to MOAT

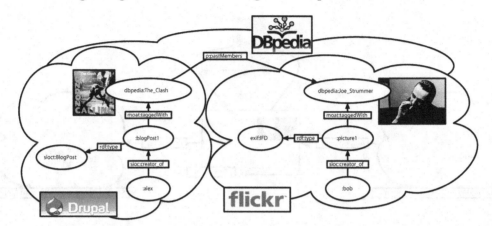

in the network. Hence, by providing new links, we augment the network effect and hence the value of this user-generated data. For example, content tagged on Flickr and re-published using MOAT can be interlinked to Drupal content thanks to DBpedia as seen in Figure 14.

Furthermore, advanced queries can be answered once these links have been provided. For example, the following query (with prefixes omitted) identifies the last five SlideShare items related to Semantic Web technologies.

```
SELECT DISTINCT ?item ?author ?date
?tag ?meaning
WHERE {
?item a sioc:Item ;
dct:created ?date ;
sioc:has_space <http://slideshare.
net> ;
foaf:maker ?author.
[] a tags:RestrictedTagging ;
tags:taggedResource ?item ;
```

```
tags:taggedWithTag [
tags:name ?tag.
] ;
moat:tagMeaning ?meaning.
?meaning ?p <http://dbpedia.org/re-
source/Category:Semantic_Web>.
}
ORDER BY DESC(?date) LIMIT 5
```

The next SPARQL query provides a similar use case that retrieves pictures related to a particular place, identified by its GeoNames URI, with results being displayed in Figure 15.

```
SELECT DISTINCT ?item ?author ?date
?tag ?meaning
WHERE {
?item a sioc:Item ;
dct:created ?date ;
sioc:has_space <http://flickr.com> ;
foaf:maker ?author.
[] a tags:RestrictedTagging ;
```

Figure 15. Identifying pictures thanks to MOAT and Linked Data

item	author	date	tag	meaning
http://www.flickr.com/photos /terraces/2924436932/	http://apassant.net/alex	2008-10-08T14:26:06+01:00	eswc2008	http://data.semanticweb.org /conference/eswc/2008

Figure 16. Ubiquity command to retrieve user-generated content within the Linked Data Web

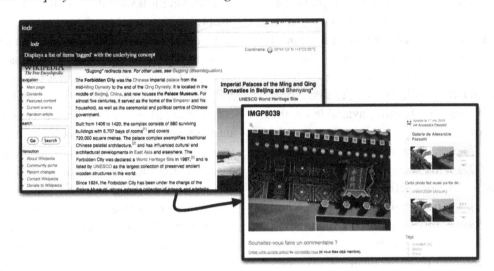

```
tags:taggedResource ?item ;
tags:taggedWithTag [
tags:name ?tag.
] ;
moat:tagMeaning ?meaning.
?meaning foaf:based_near <http://sws.
geonames.org/2522437/>.
}
ORDER BY DESC(?date) LIMIT 5
```

What is of particular interest in this query is how Linked Data can be leveraged to enhance information discovery. The original picture does not contain any geolocation-related tag. However, it has been linked to the <http://data.semanticweb.org/conference/eswc/2008> URI using LODr. This URI represents the ESWC 2008 conference and delivers lots of associated information including its location (identified as <http://sws.geonames.org/2522437/>), which allows us to answer the previous query.

As these SPARQL queries are geared toward advanced users, we also deployed a Mozilla Ubiquity command to allow everyone benefit from this method. This command retrieves tagged-data linked to the concept behind a browseable page. The following picture describes a related use-case:

someone browsing the German Wikipedia page about the Forbidden City calls the command that will get, via DBpedia, the related URI and then, via LODr, the related tagged item. Then, the user can browse the original pictures in Flickr (Figure 16).

Thanks to this service as well as the previous SPARQL query, one can see the benefits of linking Web 2.0 content to URIs with MOAT rather than using simple free-text tags alone. By following the Linked Data principles, these various links enable increased integration between data originally locked into independent and proprietary silos, which become better connected thanks to common representation models and the interlinks between them. Such services also provide incentives for people to do enrich existing data with semantics.

Related Works

We mainly consider related works in terms of (1) ontologies used to represent tagged data, (2) mining ontologies from folksonomies to solve tagging issues and (3) providing users with means to organise their tags, MOAT being at the frontier of these three approaches.

Firstly, since MOAT defines a particular ontology dedicated to tagging activities, it is worth mentioning that various models have been already defined to achieve this goal. The Tag Ontology (Newman, Ayers, & Russell, 2005), on which MOAT is built, is then the first ontology of this kind that became available on the Web, is provided in OWL-Full, and is used in various applications such as Revyu.com (Heath & Motta 2007). This vocabulary is based on the theoretical foundations defined by Gruber (2007) and provides a representation of both tags and tagging actions. It relies on FOAF for modelling taggers as well as using SKOS to model tags and to allow people to organise them. SCOT—Semantic Cloud Of Tags (Kim, Yang, Breslin, & Kim, 2007)—provides a comprehensive model dedicated to model tag clouds and related objects such as tags co-occurrences, aiming to provide interoperability and portability between tagging applications. Other models that can be used to represent tags include the Nepomuk Annotation Ontology (NAO), SIOC, and the Annotea annotation and bookmark schemas. Both NAO and SIOC define a new Tag class, the latter one subclassing skos:Concept. SIOC also defines a topic property to link a resource to some of its topics. Although not explicitly using the "tag" word in its definition, the Annotea bookmark model provides a Topic class and a hasTopic property to link an item to some related keywords, and provides the ability to model a hierarchy of topics thanks to subTopicOf relationships. However, these vocabularies do not consider the tripartite tagging model of tagging (but simply the relationship between an item and its tags) and consequently cannot capture the complete essence of folksonomies. Although each of the previous ontologies focuses on a particular aspect of tagging, none of them takes the meaning of tags into account. Combined together, SCOT, SIOC, MOAT, and the Tag Ontology provide a complete framework for tagged data.

Other approaches have been considered to help solve the issues with free tagging, especially by analysing folksonomies to create taxonomies or ontologies from them, based on the ideas that emergent semantics appear. Among others, Halpin, Robu, and Shepard (2006) used an approach based on related co-occurrences of tags to extract hierarchical relationships between concepts. (Mika, 2005) defined a socially aware approach for automatically building ontologies by combining social network analysis and clustering algorithms based on folksonomies. Schmitz (2006) describes how to create hierarchical models from Flickr tags while FolksOntology (Van Damme, Hepp, & Siorpaes, 2007) provides another method to bridge the gap between folksonomies and ontologies. More recently, the FoLksonomy Ontology enRichment (FLOR) technique has provided a completely automated approach to semantically enrich tag spaces by mapping tags to Semantic Web entities (Angeletou, 2008). By enriching tag spaces with semantic information about the meaning of each tag, some issues of tagging in relation to information retrieval (such as tag ambiguity as mentioned earlier) can be solved.

It is worth noticing that these two domains are not disjoint and can be combined together. For example, MOAT can be used as a background model in support of automated approaches like FLOR. (Abel, 2008) uses the MOAT ontology in combination with an automated method to enrich existing tagging spaces in the GroupMe application. Such improvements may be considered in the future to make the MOAT process simpler for end-users.

Finally, we must also consider other manual approaches and tools used to solve the issues of tags. For example, tools like Gnizr or Bibsonomy allow users to define manually hierarchical relationships between tags and then provide some personal tagging organisation schemes. Although the MOAT approach does not take into account this personal contextualisation aspect as it relies on shared knowledge bases for tag meanings (such as DBpedia), we believe it can be more beneficial, especially as we have noticed that most of the relationships defined in these tools are widely known relationships, such as "france" defined as a subtag of "europe," and so forth. Moreover, this way of manually organising hierarchies of tags does not solve the ambiguity issue. In addition, machine tags, as introduced by Flickr, can also be considered. Due to their "prefix:property=value" approach, these are mainly dedicated to advanced users or automated-tagging systems, such as applications for GPS-enabled camera phones. Finally, Faviki uses a similar approach that relies only on DBpedia URIs and does not consider the free-tagging aspect; that is, it asks users to directly use DBpedia URIs and does not consider that users will have their own ways to tag content.

CONCLUSION

In this article, we demonstrated how Web 2.0 content and Linked Data principles could be combined in order to solve usual tagging issues. We showed how that integration allows to envisioning a better convergence between those two visions of the Web, leading to a Web of structured, interoperable and user-driven data, also known as the Social Semantic Web (Breslin & Decker, 2007).

We described some common issues with free-tagging systems, including tag heterogeneity and ambiguity, and a lack of relationships amongst tags. We introduced the MOAT ontology, which is based on a quadripartite tagging model, and demonstrated its general usefulness through two use cases in a corporate intranet and on the public Web.

The methods described here will help machines and humans to work more closely, by having people voluntary publishing large sets of tagged user-generated content as RDF so that it can be more efficiently reused for information discovery and navigation through attractive mash-ups and query interfaces. However, we must also keep in mind that while technology and especially the Linked Data principles may help to achieve this goal, a key component to its success is the social aspects and people themselves.

ACKNOWLEDGMENT

The work presented in this article has been funded in part by Science Foundation Ireland under Grant No. SFI/08/CE/I1380 (Lion-2).

REFERENCES

Abel, F. (2008). The benefit of additional semantics in folksonomy systems, In *Conference on Information and Knowledge Management: Proceedings of the 2nd PhD Workshop on Information and Knowledge Management*, Napa Valley, CA (pp. 49-56). New York: ACM Publishers.

Angeletou, S. (2008, October 26-30). Semantic enrichment of folksonomy tagspaces. In A. Sheth, S. Staab, M. Dean, M. Paolucci, D. Maynard, T. Finin, et al. (Eds.), *The Semantic Web-ISWC 2008*, Karlsruhe, Germany (LNCS 5318, pp. 889-894).

Auer, S., Bizer, C., Lehmann, J., Kobilarov, G., Cyganiak, R., & Ives, Z. (2007, November 11-15). DBpedia: A nucleus for a web of open data. In K. Aberer, K. S. Choi, N. Noy, D. Allemang, K. I. Lee, L. J. B. Nixon, et al. (Eds.), *The Semantic Web: Proceedings of the 6th International Semantic Web Conference and 2nd Asian Semantic Web Conference (ISWC/ASWC2007)*, Busan, Korea (LNCS 4825, pp. 715-728).

Begelman, G., Keller, P., & Smadja, F. (2006, May 22-26) *Automated tag clustering: Improving search and exploration in the tag space*. Paper presented at the Collaborative Web Tagging Workshop, 15th International World Wide Web Conference (WWW 2006), Edinburgh, Scotland.

Berners-Lee, T. (2007, November 21). Giant global graph. Retrieved May 8, 2009, from http://dig. csail.mit.edu/breadcrumbs/node/215

Berners-Lee, T. (2006, June 27). *Linked data-design issues*. Retreived May 8, 2009, from http://www.w3.org/DesignIssues/LinkedData.html

Bizer, C., Heath, T., Ayers, D., & Raimond, Y. (2007). *Interlinking open data on the Web*. Poster session presented at the 4th European Semantic Web Conference (ESWC 2007), Innsbruck, Austria.

Bojārs, U., Passant, A., Breslin, J. G., & Decker, S. (2008, May 6) *Social network and data portability using Semantic Web technologies*. Paper presented at the 2nd Workshop on Social Aspects of the Web (SAW 2008), Innsbruck, Austria.

Breslin, J. G., & Decker, S. (2007). The future of social networks on the Internet: The need for semantics. *IEEE Internet Computing, 11*, 86–90. doi:10.1109/MIC.2007.138

Breslin, J. G., Harth, A., Bojārs, U., & Decker, S. (2005, May 29-June 1). Towards semantically-interlinked online communities. In A. Gómez-Pérez & J. Euzenat (Eds.), *The Semantic Web: Research and Applications: Proceedings of the 2nd European Semantic Web Conference (ESWC 2005)*, Heraklion, Crete (LNCS 3532, pp. 500-514).

Fitzpatrick, B., & Recordon, D. (2007, August 17). *Thoughts on the social graph*. Retrieved May 8, 2009, from http://bradfitz.com/social-graph-problem/

Golder, S., & Huberman, B. A. (2006). The structure of collaborative tagging systems. *Journal of Information Science, 32*(2), 198–208. doi:10.1177/0165551506062337

Gruber, T. (2007). Ontology of folksonomy: A mash-up of apples and oranges. *International Journal on Semantic Web and Information Systems, 3*(1), 1–11.

Halpin, H., Robu, V., & Shepard, H. (2006, November 6). The dynamics and semantics of collaborative tagging. In *Proceedings of the 1st Semantic Authoring and Annotation Workshop (SAAW 2006), 5th International Semantic Web Conference (ISWC 2006)*, Athens, GA (Vol. 209) CEUR Workshop Proceedings.

Hayes, C., & Avesani, P. (2007, March) *Using blog tags to identify topic authorities*. Paper presented at the 1st International Conference on Weblogs and Social Media (ICWSM 2007), Boulder, Colorado.

Heath, T., & Motta, E. (2007, November 11-15). Revyu.com: A reviewing and rating site for the Web of Data. In K. Aberer, K. S. Choi, N. Noy, D. Allemang, K. I. Lee, L. J. B. Nixon, et al. (Eds.), *The Semantic Web: Proceedings of the 6th International Semantic Web Conference and 2nd Asian Semantic Web Conference (ISWC/ASWC2007)*, Busan, Korea (LNCS 4825, pp. 895-902).

Hepp, M., Siorpaes, K., & Bachlechner, D. (2007). Harvesting Wiki consensus: Using Wikipedia entries as vocabulary for knowledge management. *IEEE Internet Computing, 11*(5), 54–65. doi:10.1109/MIC.2007.110

Hotho, A., Jäschke, R., Schmitz, C., & Stumme, G. (2006, June 11-14). Information retrieval in folksonomies: Search and ranking. In Y. Sure & J. Domingue (Eds.), *The Semantic Web: Research and Applications: 3rd European Semantic Web Conference (ESWC 2006)*, Budva, Montenegro (LNCS 4011, pp. 411-426).

Idehen, K., & Erling, O. (2008, April 22). Linked data spaces & data portability. In *Proceedings of the Linked Data on the Web Workshop (LDOW 2008)*, Beijing, China (Vol. 369). CEUR Workshop Publishers.

Jacobs, I., & Walsh, N. (2004, December 15). *Architecture of the World Wide Web, volume one*. Retrieved May 8, 2009, from W3C Recommendation's Web site: http://www.w3.org/TR/webarch/

Jaffri, A., Glaser, H., & Millard, I. (2008, June 2). *Managing URI synonymity to enable consistent reference on the Semantic Web*. Paper presented at the Workshop on Identity and Reference on the Semantic Web (IRSW 2008) at the 5th European Semantic Web Conference (ESWC 2008), Tenerife, Spain.

Kahan, J., & Koivunen, M.-R. (2001, May 1-5). Annotea: An open rdf infrastructure for shared Web annotations. In *Proceedings of the 10th international conference on World Wide Web (WWW 2001)*, Hong Kong, China (pp. 623-632). New York: ACM Publishers.

Kim, H. L., Yang, S. K., Breslin, J. G., & Kim, H. G. (2007, November 2-5). Simple algorithms for representing tag frequencies in the SCOT exporter. In *Proceedings of the IEEE/WIC/ACM International Conference on Intelligent Agent Technology*, Silicon Valley, CA (pp. 536-539). IEEE Computer Society.

Kobilarov, G., Scott, T., Raimond, Y., Oliver, S., Sizemore, C., Smethurst, M., et al. (2009, May 31-June 9). *Media meets Semantic Web-how the BBC uses DBpedia and linked data to make connections*. Paper presented at the 6th Annual European Semantic Web Conference (ESWC 2009), Heraklion, Greece.

Marlow, C., Naaman, M., Boyd, D., & Davis, M. (2006, August 23-25). *HT06, tagging paper, taxonomy, Flickr, academic article, to read*. Paper presented at the 17th Conference on Hypertext and Hypermedia, Odense, Denmark.

Mathes, A. (2004). *Folksonomies: Cooperative classification and communication through shared metadata* (Computer Mediated Communication, LIS590CMC). [Graduate School of Library and Information Science, University of Illinois Urbana-Champaign.]. *Urbana (Caracas, Venezuela)*, IL.

McAfee, A. (2006). Enterprise 2.0: The dawn of emergent collaboration. *MIT Sloan Management Review, 47*(3), 21–28.

Merholz, P. (2004, October 19). Metadata for the masses. Retrieved May 8, 2009, http://www.adaptivepath.com/ideas/essays/archives/000361.php

Mika, P. (2005, November 6-10). Ontologies are us: A unified model of social networks and semantics. In Y. Gil, E. Motta, V. R. Benjamins, & M. A. Musen (Eds.), *The Semantic Web: ISWC 2005: 4th International Semantic Web Conference*, Galway, Ireland (LNCS 3729, pp. 522-536).

Newman, R., Ayers, D., & Russell, S. (2005). *Tag ontology*. Retrieved May 8, 2009, from http://www.holygoat.co.uk/owl/redwood/0.1/tags/

O'Reilly, T. (2005, September 30). *What is Web 2.0: Design patterns and business models for the next generation of software*. Retrieved May 8, 2009, from http://www.oreillynet.com/lpt/a/6228

Passant, A. (2008, June). Case study: Enhancement and integration of corporate social software using the Semantic Web. *Semantic Web use cases and case studies*. Retrieved May 8, 2009, from the W3C Semantic Web Education and Outreach Interest Group's Web site: http://www.w3.org/2001/sw/sweo/public/UseCases/EDF

Passant, A., & Laublet, P. (2008, April 22). Meaning Of A Tag: A collaborative approach to bridge the gap between tagging and linked data. In *Proceedings of the Linked Data on the Web Workshop (LDOW 2008)*, Beijing, China (Vol. 369). CEUR Workshop Publishers.

Passant, A., Laublet, P., Breslin, J. G., & Decker, S. (2009, April 21). Semantic search for Enterprise 2.0. Paper presented at the Workshop on Semantic Search (SemSearch 2009) at the 18th International World Wide Web Conference (WWW 2009), Madrid, Spain.

Raimond, Y., & Sandler, M. (2008, September 14-18). *A web of musical information*. Paper presented at the Ninth International Conference on Music Information Retrieval (ISMIR 2008), Philadelphia.

Schmitz, P. (2006, May). *Inducing ontology from Flickr tags*. Paper presented at the Workshop on Collaborative Web Tagging at the 15ᵗʰ International World Wide Web Conference (WWW 2006), Edinburgh, Scotland.

Story, H., Harbulot, B., Jacobi, I., & Jones, M. (2009, June 1). FOAF+TLS: RESTful authentication for the social Web. In *Proceedings of the First Workshop on Trust and Privacy on the Social and Semantic Web (SPOT 2009)*, Heraklion, Greece (Vol. 447). CEUR Workshop Proceedings.

Tanaka, J., & Taylor, M. (1991). Object categories and expertise: Is the basic level in the eye of the beholder. *Cognitive Psychology, 23*(3), 457–482. doi:10.1016/0010-0285(91)90016-H

Taylor, A. G. (1999). *The organization of information*. Santa Barbara, CA: Libraries Unlimited.

Van Damme, C., Hepp, M., & Siorpaes, K. (2007). FolksOntology: An integrated approach for turning folksonomies into ontologies. In *Proceedings of the Workshop on Bridging the Gap between Semantic Web and Web 2.0 (SemNet 2007)*, Innsbruck, Austria (pp. 55-70). University of Kassel.

VanderWal, T. (2007, February 2). *Folksonomy coinage and definition*. Retrieved May 8, 2009, from http://www.vanderwal.net/folksonomy.html

This work was previously published in International Journal on Semantic Web and Information Systems, Volume 5, Issue 3, edited by Amit P. Sheth, pp. 71-94, copyright 2009 by IGI Publishing (an imprint of IGI Global).

Chapter 12
An Idea Ontology for Innovation Management

Christoph Riedl
Technische Universität München, Germany

Stephan Stathel
FZI, Germany

Norman May
SAP CEC Karlsruhe, Germany

Viktor Kaufman
SAP CEC Karlsruhe, Germany

Jan Finzen
Fraunhofer IAO, Germany

Helmut Krcmar
Technische Universität München, Germany

ABSTRACT

Exchanging and analyzing ideas across different software tools and repositories is needed to implement the concepts of open innovation and holistic innovation management. However, a precise and formal definition for the concept of an idea is hard to obtain. In this paper, the authors introduce an ontology to represent ideas. This ontology provides a common language to foster interoperability between tools and to support the idea life cycle. Through the use of an ontology, additional benefits like semantic reasoning and automatic analysis become available. Our proposed ontology captures both a core idea concept that covers the 'heart of the idea' and further concepts to support collaborative idea development, including rating, discussing, tagging, and grouping ideas. This modular approach allows the idea ontology to be complemented by additional concepts like customized evaluation methods. The authors present a case study that demonstrates how the ontology can be used to achieve interoperability between innovation tools and to answer questions relevant for innovation managers that demonstrate the advantages of semantic reasoning.

INTRODUCTION

What is an idea? How does it relate to an innovation? While people may have an intuitive understanding of what these terms mean, there is

no accepted precise and formal definition for the concept of an idea. As holistic innovation management and, in particular, the concept of open innovation gains traction, it becomes increasingly important to close this gap: a commonly agreed concept of an idea would support exchanging and analyzing ideas across different idea platforms and

DOI: 10.4018/978-1-60960-593-3.ch012

innovation tools, and hence be the basis to realize the vision of open innovation (Chesbrough, 2006; Gassmann & Enkel, 2004; Ogawa & Piller, 2006; Riedl, Böhmann, Leimeister, & Krcmar, 2009).

In this paper, we provide our own definition of the concept of an "idea" and introduce an ontology to represent ideas. Our research was motivated by the observation that various innovation management systems implement the concept of an idea based on similar core concepts but also distinct features. The goal is to capture the common core of different approaches to facilitate reuse and better integration. We also want to allow modular extensions required for the needs of specific innovation tools. Hence, we present a core idea concept that is enriched by concepts required to deal with ideas, e.g., rating, collaboration, tagging, or grouping of ideas. Thereby, we also illustrate how the Idea Ontology can be complemented by further concepts like customized evaluation methods.

The remainder of this paper is structured as follows: first, we study the challenges that arise as a result of recent trends in innovation management. We suggest meeting these challenges by following an ontology approach and analyzing related work. Then we describe our idea ontology in detail followed by an evaluation section. Using a case study, we demonstrate how technical integration between innovation tools has been achieved and how the ontology can be used to answer questions relevant for innovation managers in order to demonstrate the advantages of semantic reasoning. Finally, we discuss the results of the case application and identify opportunities for future work.

Innovation Management

The Oxford English Dictionary defines an *idea* as: "1 a thought or suggestion about a possible course of action. 2 a mental impression. 3 a belief." An *innovation* is defined as: "1 the action or process of innovating. 2 a new method, idea, product, etc." Rogers defines an innovation as "an idea, practice

or object that is perceived as new by an individual or other unit of adoption" (Rogers, 2003). This definition indicates that an innovation is more than an idea. To become an innovation, an idea has to be adopted. This concept is further developed by linking an idea or invention not only to adoption but to the concept of commercialization. Thus, Porter defines innovation as "a new way of doing things (termed invention by some authors) that is *commercialized*" (Porter, 1990). A precise definition of the meaning of the term "innovation" has been contentious and problematical and terms are often used loosely and interchangeably (Storey, 2000). However, there seems to be agreement on a general distinction between "invention" and "innovation" (Storey, 2000). Bullinger (2008) defines an innovative idea as "the more or less vague perception of a combination of purpose and means, qualitatively different from existing forms." She thus claims it to mark the starting point of an innovation activity. As innovative ideas form the basis of innovation, idea collection and development is considered one of the first steps in most innovation process models (e.g., Cooper, 1990; Tidd, Bessant, & Pavitt, 2005; Wheelwright & Clark, 1992).

In the context of providing a tool to support the management of innovation processes, these definitions are not adequate because they do not specify (1) what information should be conveyed in an idea and (2) which methods or operations are applied to ideas. Hence, for the purpose of developing a semantic representation of the concept of an idea in innovation management applications, we informally define an *idea* as:

An explicit description of an invention or problem solution with the intention of implementation as a new or improved product, service, or process within an organization.

This central concept of an idea which we term *Core Idea* can be supplemented with various concepts that relate to feasibility and marketability,

Table 1. Analysis of a sample of publicly available idea portals

Name	Comments	Rating	Classes	Tags	Status Model
Crowdspirit (FR)[2]	Yes	Thumb Up/Down	Single	Yes	Incubator (Ongoing, Evaluated, Rejected), Elevator, Idea in Market
Dell (US)[2]	Yes	Thumb Up/Down	Multiple	No	Already Offered, Implemented, In Progress, Partially Implemented, Reviewed, Under Review
ErfinderProfi (DE)[2]	Yes	Scale 1 to 10	Single	Yes	n/a
Incuby (US)[2]	Yes	5-Star	Single	Yes	With patent (Pending, Provisional, Full, Pat.-No.), Without Patent, Concept or Idea
Starbucks (US)[2]	Yes	Thumb up/Down	Single	No	New, Under Review, Reviewed, Coming soon, Launched
Atizo (CH)[2]	Yes	Thumb up	n/a	Yes	Open, In Evaluation
IdeaJam (US)[2]	Yes	Thumb Up/Down	Single	Yes	Open, In Progress, Complete, Rejected, Withdrawn
Oracle Mix (US)[2]	Yes	Thumb up	Multiple	Yes	n/a

i.e., commercialization. Many of these concepts are used in the selection of tools that have been developed to support the different phases of idea generation and idea evaluation (van Gundy, 1988; see also Ardilio, Auernhammer, & Kohn, 2004 for an overview). A recent trend in innovation management is the implementation of openly accessible idea Web portals as one form of user innovation toolkits (von Hippel, 2005). We investigated 25 publicly available idea portals with between 146 ideas (ErfinderProfi, an inventor community in Germany) and over 75.000 (Starbucks) ideas[1] and analyzed how they describe and manage ideas (see Table 1 for a selection of the results).

Based on this analysis, we identified the following aspects to be included in an ontology for innovation management:

- *Comments and discussions* help to identify shortcomings within the original idea and develop it towards the users' needs (Franke & Shah, 2003; Piller & Walcher, 2006). Thus, open and interactive forums are key requirements within company-internal innovation management, e.g., employee suggestion systems, as well as in idea development Web portals (Fairbank & Williams

2001; Fairbank, Spangler, & Williams, 2003).

- *Ratings* are widely used to estimate user acceptance of ideas and are a key metric for idea selection (van Gundy, 1988). Within innovation management, many different rating mechanisms are generally applied. The methods differ substantially in (a) the rating subject (who is allowed to rate), (b) the rating object (what aspects are rated), and (c) the rating scale. Note that Table 1 names six similar websites applying four different rating scales.

- *Grouping and clustering* methods help to keep track of idea submissions, especially within large idea portfolios. The two main approaches to group ideas are hierarchical classification systems and tagging mechanisms. Our findings show that the two methods are frequently used in parallel. The categorization schemes are usually highly domain-specific and differ in aspects including granularity, depth, and multi-selectability.

- *Status*: In addition to content-related classification, organizational aspects are often applied to arrange the idea portfolio. Many idea portals assign an explicit development state to each idea, e.g., "ongoing", "evaluated", "rejected", etc. Furthermore, patents and trademarks are widely used to protect innovations or to exploit them commercially (e.g., via licensing contracts). Thus, patent and copyright information are highly important within idea management.

Motivation for an Idea Ontology

Several benefits can be expected from the use of an ontology, including a shared and common understanding, providing structure to poorly structured or unstructured information, realizing management support and interdisciplinary communication as a result of structuring information, and allowing the analysis and comparison of the information represented beyond operational data (Noy & McGuinnes, 2001; Fensel et al., 2002; Hüsemann & Vossen, 2005; Bullinger, 2008). In addition to these generic benefits of representing information with defined ontologies, other benefits particularly important in the area of representing ideas and innovation management can be expected. There is a growing need for integration of Information Systems to interoperate in a seamless manner (Sheth, Ramakrishnan, & Thomas, 2005). This is particularly so in the area of innovation management where a single tool cannot support the whole innovation process. As more and more idea and innovation platforms appear on the Web, it becomes desirable to exchange information between platforms and adopt tools to prevent ideas from being restricted to silos. At the same time, enterprises are starting to understand the potential benefit from open innovation systems, and feel the need to open up their internal innovation processes and to integrate innovation management tools (Gassmann, 2006). The semantics of an organization's specific working context are captured by its local or private ontology, which serves the purposes of the particular organization (Ning, O'Sullivan, Zhu, & Decker, 2006). Thus,

there is a need for a common language, i.e., a common idea data interchange format or a shared ontology to support the interoperability and to improve cross-enterprise collaboration.

Today, many idea portals on the Web are restricted to capabilities like tagging and ordinal ratings as the basis for idea analysis. However, we believe that more powerful tools and methods in idea portals cannot reveal their full potential until agreement is reached on the basic concepts of an idea. The use of semantic techniques brings with it the possibility to improve end-user efficiency by means of automated processing, and to cope with advanced analytical processing of idea metadata through reasoning. Thus innovation managers could profit from better structured information, integration and data exchange across tools and platforms, and additional semantic reasoning that allows them to analyze ideas based on related concepts.

In summary, the main benefits of using an ontology approach for idea management are the ability to achieve interoperability and technical integration between tools resulting in a better support of the idea life cycle from idea generation, idea evaluation, through to idea implementation.

Related Projects and Research

In addition to the requirements that resulted from the study of existing innovation portals, we base our design of the Idea Ontology on the experience we observed in three different innovation management projects:

Stathel, Finzen, Riedl, and May (2008) outlined an innovation process and innovation management architecture targeted to the needs of the TEXO project[3]. This project investigates how services can be made tradable and composable in a business value network.

The Laboranova project[4] aims to create collaborative tools that support knowledge workers in sharing, improving, and evaluating ideas systematically across teams, companies, and networks. The tools investigated in this project have a broader scope, i.e., beyond services, and focus on collaborative work processes within idea management.

Finally, an SAP-internal prototype, called Technology Business Exchange (TBE), investigates the commercial exploitation of ideas that are collected and managed in a closed world. Innovators submit their ideas on a Web platform and promising ideas are evaluated by experts. Business plans are then developed for the commercial realization of the ideas selected.

Although several other research projects currently deal with aspects of idea and innovation management, to our knowledge none of them explicitly aims at creating a common idea ontology for the purpose of achieving interoperability across innovation tools. Ning et al. (2006) describe the system architecture of an innovation system that combines ontology, inference, and mediation technologies to facilitate the distributed collection and development of ideas. Their system is based on metadata harvesting and RDF access technologies. It relies on semantic technologies to allow for integration of idea development tools. However, the article does not give details of the concepts used in the proposed ontology and the ontology is not publicly available

The innovation ontology developed by Bullinger (2008), called OntoGate, aims at modeling the idea assessment and selection on a company-specific level. The ontology is deduced from empirical research and offers a means to structure a company's understanding of the innovation process, in particular the inputs, outputs, participants, and assessment perspectives. For example, different inputs into the innovation process have been developed such as *internal input* and *external input* which can further be broken up in *continuous internal input* and *discontinuous internal input*, input by *employees* and input by *executives* and so on. Thus, it gives an organization a better understanding of how the overall innovation process can be structured and how ideas can be systemati-

cally developed. In contrast to the work presented in this article, it does not provide a data model for representing individual ideas. Regarding the assessment of ideas, the largest module of the OntoGate ontology, three perspectives along which an idea or concept can be evaluated are suggested and subsequently developed: market, strategy, and technology. The resulting ontology, OntoGate, is classified as a *domain ontology* (Bullinger, 2008) as it represents the terms used to describe idea assessment and selection during the early stages of the innovation process in companies.

While our ontology, which can be classified as an *application ontology*, provides a technical means to represent complex idea evaluations along various concepts, OntoGate provides the necessary domain knowledge to decide which perspectives and criteria should actually be used for the assessment. Thus, OntoGate complements our ontology with additional valuable domain knowledge to setup and customize a system based on the Idea Ontology to support and structure a given innovation scenario.

The specific contribution of our work compared to Bullinger's is the description of a technical architecture in which the ontology can be applied. The aim of our idea ontology is to offer a common language for idea storage and exchange for the purpose of achieving interoperability across innovation tools. Through reusing existing ontologies such as FOAF we hope to achieve interoperability not only among specialized innovation tools but general applications as well such as social networking. The innovation ontology developed by Bullinger (2008) aims at modeling the idea assessment and selection rather than providing technical integration.

Idea Ontology

We chose OWL for the development of our ontology and followed a generic ontology development approach (McGuiness & van Harmelen, 2005; Noy & McGuiness, 2001). Neither RDF nor RDFS is expressive enough to model complex structures like complex classes and relations carrying semantic expressions. As RDFS supports only classes and relations, it is capable of modeling sub-class concepts and relations, but only simple ones. In the evaluation section, this is illustrated with an example. We chose the approach by Noy and Mc-Guinnes (2001) as it focuses in particular on the reuse of existing ontologies which is a desirable attribute of ontologies (Lonsdale, Embley, Ding, Xu, & Hepp, 2009; Bullinger, 2008). Protégé has been used for modeling the Idea Ontology, and an OWL version and sample instances for testing and evaluation purposes are available on www.ideaontology.org. To further determine the scope of the ontology, a list of exemplary competency questions that a knowledge base developed using the ontology should be able to answer has been derived from Gruninger and Fox (1995). The questions have been prepared from the perspective of an innovation manager working with a large pool of ideas. These questions served also as test cases in the evaluation section of our paper.

- Which ideas are in the repository?
- For which categories have ideas been submitted?
- Which tags have been used to classify ideas?
- Which ideas have already been implemented?

- Which ideas have at least three ratings?
- Which ideas have at least two or more ratings as well as at least one realization?
- Who are the most valuable community members by assessing at least three ideas?
- Which ideas already have a business plan attached (i.e., have an attached document with the topic 'business plan' to indicate feasibility)?

The namespaces used in the ontology are summarized in Table 2.

Ontology Design

This section introduces the Idea Ontology and gives a detailed explanation of the innovation and generic concepts it uses. Figure 1 depicts the ontology's main modules.

Modularity is a key requirement for large ontologies, as it facilitates reusability, maintainability, and evolution (Gómez-Pérez & Benjamins, 1999). Stuckenschmidt & Klein (2007) name the following reasons for modular design of ontologies: i) handling of ontologies in distributed environments like the semantic web, ii) management of large ontologies, and iii) efficient reasoning. Hence, a central design goal was to create a highly modular ontology. We achieved this by incorporating established ontology specifications to represent the more general metadata concepts

Table 2. Referenced ontologies

Ontology	Prefix	Short Description
Idea Ontology	im	The ontology for innovation management introduced in this paper
RDF	rdf	Resource Description Framework
Dublin Core	dc	The Dublin Core for metadata about resources
FOAF	foaf	The Friend of a Friend ontology for describing agents and their relationships
Tagging Ontology	tags	A simple tagging ontology
SIOC	sioc	An ontology for (online) communities
Rating Ontology	r	A rating ontology
SKOS	skos	An ontology for knowledge representation

Figure 1. Overview of the Idea Ontology

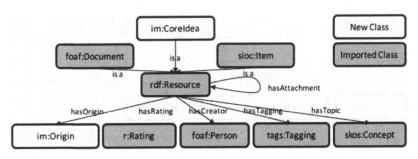

that are associated with an idea. We therefore evaluated existing ontologies with regard to their suitability to be reused in our Idea Ontology. In addition, we chose a hierarchical design that groups the three classes im:CoreIdea, foaf:Document, and sioc:Item under a super class rdf:Resource. Thus, we are able to specify relations to various common meta-information which are then reused for all innovation-related resources. Specifically, every rdf:Resource has the following generic relations:

- im:Origin: the application from which the resource originates
- r:Rating: a rating mechanism that allows rating of the resource
- foaf:Person: the creator of the resource
- tags:Tagging: folksonomy tagging of the resource
- skos:Concept: definition of a subject matter of the resources that allows grouping of ideas
- rdf:Resource: through the hasAttachment relationship, innovation-related objects can be linked to each other.

However, it is important to note that an im:CoreIdea is the central object that defines an innovation project and for that purpose draws on other innovation resources such as documents and community discussions.

Innovation Concepts

Core Idea: To achieve a generic and versatile representation of ideas, we chose a hierarchical design with three layers of textual descriptions for an im:CoreIdea: dc:title, im:abstract, and im:description. All three represent a textual description of the idea but vary in length and detail. Thus, our ontology is able to support very simple tools such as electronic brainstorming, where an idea usually consists of no more than one sentence, up to more advanced tools that allow longer descriptions. It is also possible to extend the description with resources such as images, screenshots, or process diagrams: they can be attached as foaf:Documents using the hasAttachment relationship. Furthermore, every im:CoreIdea has an associated creation date dc:Date and a version number to allow tracking of different instances of the same idea by means of the isNewVersionOf relationship. An idea can also have a relationship with sioc:Forum (using hasForum) and im:IdeaRealization (using hasRealization) which we describe in the sections below. Figure 2 shows the complete im:CoreIdea class and its relationships.

When describing an idea, aspects related to the respective business context are relevant. They may be used to, e.g. assess the feasibility of an idea. Examples include a reference to the market, in which an idea can be commercialized, or potential customers and competitors. To model these descriptive attributes of an idea, we reuse the

Figure 2. The Core Idea element

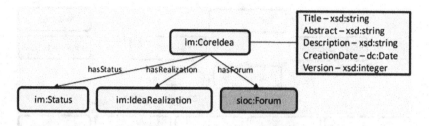

established Enterprise Ontology (Uschold, King, Moralee, & Zorgios, 1998). This ontology defines the semantic meaning of terms such as market, customer, competitor, supplier etc. Technically, we model these descriptive arguments as sioc:Items that are attached to an idea and linked to a skos:Concept through the hasTopic relationship that defines the semantic meaning of the argument. As sioc:Items are modeled as rdf:Resources, it is possible to assign a rating to them. This makes it possible, for example, to state that a certain sioc:Item instance contains a text related to the "market" concept (through hasTopic) and then rate this specific attribute using a five star rating. Listing 1[5] illustrates how the combination of im:CoreIdea, sioc:Item, and skos:Concept can be used to represent detailed idea submission forms in a semantically enriched way. Furthermore, a foaf:Document linked to an idea using hasAttachment may contain a business

plan, refer to a market analysis or a relevant patent. Together with expert ratings an innovation manager would be able to evaluate the quality of an idea (cf. our last competency question). These artifacts can be of great help once the idea is realized.

Discussions and Collaboration using SIOC: Discussions and collaboration, both within and across organizations, are an important means for developing ideas (see, for example, Ahuja, 2000; Gemunden, Salomo, & Holzle, 2007). With increasing adoption of open innovation processes and the integration of users into the innovation process, the ability to systematically support discussions and collaboration becomes a key functionality (Chesbrough, 2006; West & Lakhani, 2008). Consequently, the ability to support comments has been added to our ontology.

Semantically-Interlinked Online Communities (SIOC) is an established ontology for integrating

Listing 1. Representation of idea submission forms

```
<#idea123> a im:CoreIdea ;
dc:Title "Calculate environmental sustainability based on bill of materials." ;
im:hasForum <#forum idea123>.
<#forum idea123> a sioc:Forum.
<http://en. wikipedia. org/wiki/Market> a skos:Concept ;
skos:prefLabel "Market "@en.
<http://en. wikipedia. org/wiki/Customer> a skos:Concept ;
skos:prefLabel "Customer "@en.
<#item101> a sioc:Item ;
sioc:has container <#forum idea123> ;
im:hasTopic <http://en. wikipedia. org/wiki/Market> ;
sioc:content "Automotive industries".
<#item102> a sioc:Item ;
sioc:has container <#forum idea123> ;
im:hasTopic <http://en. wikipedia. org/wiki/Customer> ;
sioc:content "Engineering departments of automobile manufacturers".
```

online community information (Bojãrs & Breslin, 2007). SIOC can be used to represent community information such as blog, wiki, and forum posts. In the Idea Ontology, every im:CoreIdea can be linked to one or more sioc:Forums using a hasForum relationship that provides a container for sioc:Items related to the discussion of that idea. Furthermore, SIOC can be applied to model access rights to individual resources.

Status: In order to track an idea's progression throughout a submission, evaluation, and implementation process, it is necessary to track the status of an idea. The im:Status class offers this functionality: through a dc:Title a set of status individuals (i.e., instances) can be created depending on the innovation context. For example, status individuals could be "none", "under review", "in process", "implemented", "already offered" or others depending on the area of application and the innovation process in place. More formally, the output states proposed by Bullinger (2008) could be used: "stop", "hold" and "invest". These individuals are then associated with an idea via the hasState relationship. In this way, the ontology can easily be integrated into existing processes and evaluation structures.

Idea Realization: To support the full innovation life cycle and to allow for incremental innovations of existing products and services the link between ideas and their resulting realizations must be preserved. Moreover, the back-link from a realization to the original idea supports the application of various performance measures. For example, it would be possible to identify authors of highly successful ideas. To achieve this tracking across the life cycle our ontology contains an im:IdeaRalization class which is linked to an im:CoreIdea by means of the hasRealization object property. The im:IdeaRealization class is a placeholder for whatever is an appropriate means of representing an idea's realization. In a product environment, this may be a product number. In a software-as-a-service environment, the idea realization could link to a description of a Web service, for example, using WSDL[6].

Generic Concepts

User: Friend of a Friend (FOAF) is an established RDF/OWL-based ontology for describing persons, their activities, and their relations to other people and objects (Brickley & Miller, 2007). Due to its de-facto standard for representing information about people and its simple design, we chose FOAF for representing all person-related information in the Idea Ontology. Specifically, links to a foaf:Person are maintained for all resources as hasCreator, and for im:Rating and tag:Tagging as ratedBy and taggedBy, respectively.

Tagging: Tags are keywords or terms associated with or assigned to a piece of information – in our case innovation resources. Due to their popularity in online communities and apparent benefits for information browsing (Mathes, 2004; Golder & Huberman, 2005), a tagging concept has been added to our ontology. Tag Ontology is an established and simple ontology for representing tagging information, which is also used by SIOC (Newman, 2005). Tag Ontology represents tags as tuples of <tagger, tag, resource, date>. In the Idea Ontology, tags can be associated with all innovation resources by means of the hasTagging relationship.

Grouping: The Simple Knowledge Organization System (SKOS) is a W3C Recommendation of a common data model for sharing and linking knowledge organization systems such as thesauri, taxonomies, and classification schemes (Miles & Bechhofer, 2009). SKOS allows the definition of "concepts" that are identified using URIs and labeled with lexical strings in one or more natural languages. Furthermore, concepts can be linked to other concepts using semantic relations such as skos:broader, skos:narrower, and skos:related. This allows us to build taxonomies and semantic relationships between the various rdf:Resources that are associated with the concepts using the hasTopic relationship. This association with semantic concepts is used in two ways. First, a im:CoreIdea can thus be associated with a topic to indicate which subject area an idea belongs to (e.g., an idea related to the automotive sector). Second, it can be used in association with comments attached to an idea (sioc:Items) to support a structured idea assessment along predefined perspectives. For example, the perspectives *market*, *strategy*, and *technology* proposed in the ontology by Bullinger (2008) could be used for idea assessment. Additional semantic concepts can be added at runtime which thus allows the easy extension and customization of an ontology-based system.

Tracking the Origin of Contributions: As one of the main goals, the Idea Ontology fosters interoperability between various innovation management tools. Therefore, it is necessary to keep track of the application from which a given resource originates. The im:Origin class can be used for this purpose. An im:Origin contains a dc:Source and dc:Title attribute. In this way it can be stated that an idea originates, e.g., from a brainstorming tool, an idea portal on the Web, or another application.

Rating: A rating is used to associate values of appraisal for a resource. In the innovation domain, rating is of utmost importance as it is a necessary step for idea evaluation and selection (van Gundy, 1988). A great variety of idea evaluation and selection methods has been proposed (e.g., van Gundy, 1988) and new concepts like information markets are investigated for their suitability

for idea evaluation (Stathel et al., 2008). Hence, the rating concept is required to be configurable with respect to the rating method and the range of values.

To accommodate these requirements, we extend the rating ontology proposed in Longo and Sciuto (2007) to support different kinds of ratings (see Figure 3). Based on this ontology, an r:Rating is a 4-ary relationship as follows: its rating value is expressed as some numerical r:value, the interpretation of which is application-dependent. The r:Rating refers to the resource that is rated. Notice that ratings are not restricted to ideas, but can refer also to documents or comments. A foaf:Agent refers to the person who expresses an appraisal for the rated resource. Note that we chose foaf:Agent instead of foaf:Person because ratings can also be expressed by software agents. The r:RatingCollector is a source that is used to collect ratings. The domain of values generated by this source is either defined as an enumeration of values or by an interval of numeric values (see Longo & Sciuto, 2007 for examples). The r:RatingKind is used to distinguish different aspects of the rated resource. Possible instances may be an OverallRating or a UsabilityRating.

While the tagging approach is rather generic, the opportunity of changing the ontology at runtime and thus allowing an adaptation of an ontology-based system to a given scenario's requirements, offsets the benefits of a more specific tagging approach.

Figure 3. Rating module

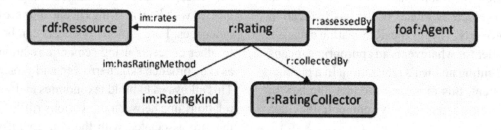

Case Illustration of Ontology Application

The two major paradigms in Information Systems research are behavioral science and design science (Hevner et al., 2004). Our study clearly falls in the design science category and the question on how to evaluate the designed artifact, i.e. our innovation, arises. In general, there are numerous possibilities how to evaluate an artifact: analytical, case studies, controlled experiments, field studies, and simulations (Hevner et al., 2004). In this work, the argument for the utility, quality, and efficacy of our approach bases on four basic evaluation methods: scenario, prototypical implementation, informed argument, and architectural analysis (cf. Hevner et al., 2004).

Scenario The rationale behind using scenarios for evaluation of design artifacts in Information Systems is that scenarios can demonstrate the utility of an artifact. To this end, we apply the ontology developed above to a scenario derived from the TEXO project. This scenario points out clearly the necessity of a structured innovation process utilizing an innovation ontology,

Prototypical Implementation As a proof-of-concept, we prototypically implemented ontology instances for our application scenario. Artifact instantiation in general and a prototypical implementation in particular demonstrate the feasibility of the designed artifact. The construction of the prototype that fosters innovation management by using ontologies shows that an innovation management system can be assembled using already existing artifacts – it provides proof by construction (Nunamaker, Chen, & Purdin, 1991; Hevner et al., 2004).

Informed Argument The basic concept of informed arguments is to use information from relevant related research to build an argument for the artifact. To this end, we derived the requirements for the Idea Ontology in the motivation section, which contains an argumentation, why our approach is promising and useful.

Architectural Analysis In an architectural analysis one studies the fit of an artifact with the technical architecture of the overall information system. In the Section *Idea Ontology* we showed that the technical representation of our approach fits with the technical architecture of the prototype.

In the following, the application of our approach will be described using a case derived from the TEXO project context. The application demonstrates the effects of the ontology on a complex innovation management scenario. It further presents a sophisticated innovation process in which the ontology may be utilized to leverage the existing capabilities of the tools employed by resolving interoperability issues. This allows technical integration of various specialized tools that are designed to support the various idea generation and evaluation tasks.

The TEXO project investigates how services, in particular electronic services, can be made tradable and composable in a business value network. To harness the innovative capabilities present in the resulting business networks (Riedl et al., 2009), a cyclic innovation process consisting of several innovation steps is used in TEXO (Stathel et al., 2008). The resulting innovation framework methodologically and technically connects different tools and methods for systematic idea development. Figure 4 illustrates the innovation framework, aligning the innovation system architecture with the innovation process. After an idea has been created and developed using tools such as the Innovation Mining Cockpit[7], workshops using electronic group support systems such as GroupSystem's ThinkTank[8] software, or a Web-based community platform similar to the ones analyzed in Table 1, it is evaluated using an Information Market-based approach (Stathel et al., 2008; Stathel et al., 2009). Such an evaluation may be superior to evaluations by experts as they employ the wisdom of a great variety of people (Surowiecki, 2005). If the evaluation result is positive, the idea is implemented and used. Service usage information improves existing

Figure 4. Innovation framework and system architecture of the TEXO project

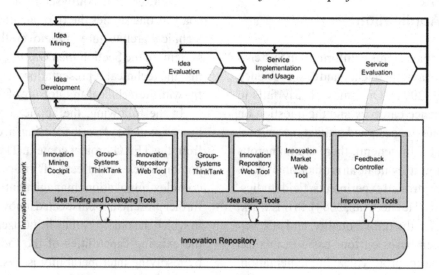

services using the Service Feedback Controller. A central component within the framework is the Innovation Repository which, through the use of the Idea Ontology, provides means to store and retrieve ideas and systematically enhance them with additional information. All tools developed in the TEXO project implement the Idea Ontology and are supported by this repository in the back-end, which thus acts as a uniform idea data warehouse and aggregates the data generated in the respective components.

The tools in the example case can be used largely simultaneously by different teams or even organizations. The Idea Ontology explicitly enables collaboration by means of capturing the application (as im:Origin) that is the source of an idea. It also enables forum discussions as an example integration of established means for collaborative approachs to innovation. Reuse of the SKOS ontology provides for a simple way to structure the ideas. The link to involved collaborators is available as well through the reuse of FOAF. The semantic representation itself can be easily extended through reuse of extra ontologies so that additional requirements for idea development can be supported at low cost. The use of the Idea Ontology led to a successful integration of different TEXO tools.

For the case illustration at hand, some of the tools like GroupSystems' ThinkTank and the Web-based community platform can be configured to support functions for both idea generation and idea evaluation phases. To demonstrate the completeness of the integration Table 3 shows how the data fields of each of the tools can be mapped onto the Idea Ontology.

It is important to note that the Idea Ontology is an enabling technology. It cannot substitute proper innovation management processes in the organization or project at hand. Technical aspects such as particular repository management, content synchronization and tracking also represent complementary issues. With regards to existing innovation management systems, the use of the Idea Ontology would translate to reengineering the systems for the purpose of more flexible and extensible exchange of ideas between applications, teams, projects and organizations. In the general context of so called extended enterprises (Browne, 1998), the time to realize synergy effects constantly gains importance. Our case illustrates that ideas development can happen more quickly and with less disruptions.

Table 3. Mapping between tool data and Idea Ontology concepts

Tool (Innovation Phase)	Field	Mapping in Idea Ontology
Innovation Mining Cockpit (innovation impulse and idea development)	Title	im:CoreIdea/title
	Search report	foaf:Document linked to an im:coreIdea through hasAttachment
	Search space configuration / saved search	foaf:Document linked to an im:coreIdea through hasAttachment
Web-Tool (idea generation and idea evaluation)	Title	im:CoreIdea/title
	Description	im:CoreIdea/description
	Author	im:CoreIdea/hasAuthor linking to foaf:person
	Status	im:Status
	Tags	im:CoreIdea/hasTagging links to Tags:Tagging with additional fields: taggedBy a foaf:Person taggedOn a date
	Comments	sioc:Item linked to a sioc:Forum via hasContainer sioc:Forum linked to an idea via hasForum sioc:Item is also linked to skos:Concepts via hasTopic
GroupSystems ThinkTank (idea generation and idea evaluation)	Brainstorming idea	im:CoreIdea/title
	Rating	r:Rating r:value (e.g., "1=bad") r:assessedBy (e.g., "brainstorming session") r:rates (i.e., the im:CoreIdea being rated) r:hasRatingKind (e.g., "usability rating")
	Comment	as above
Information Market (idea evaluation)	Title	im:CoreIdea/title
	Description	im:CoreIdea/description
	Trade-based idea ranking	r:Rating r:value (e.g., "99 ") r:assessedBy (i.e., an instance of the information market) r:rates (i.e., the coreIdea being rated) r:collectedBy (i.e., the information market tool) r:hasRatingKind (e.g., an "OverallRating")
Feedback Controller (service evaluation => idea generation or idea refinement)	Title	im:CoreIdea/title
	Implemented service	hasRealization linking to a service description in WSDL accessible under a URI
	Community	sioc:Forum attached to an im:CoreIdea sioc:Item for individual community posts

The Innovation Mining Cockpit, a Web-based community platform, a GroupSystems' ThinkTank-based brainstorming setup, an information market-based idea evaluation tool, and post-implementation service evaluation using the Feedback Controller, have successfully been integrated within the TEXO project, and interoperability has been achieved. Given the project context the ontology has proven to be expressive enough to cover all relevant data fields. Through the interoperability and technical integration between tools, a better support of the idea life cycle has been achieved as tools provide specialized support for different life cycle functions (e.g., sophisticated idea evaluation through an information market approach).

To determine whether the ontology contains enough information and to demonstrate advanced semantic reasoning functions, we evaluated our ontology against the set of competency questions proposed above. For that purpose, we designed test cases with sample data instances and modeled OWL DL query statements to answer the competency questions. In case of RDF and RDFS, queries are formulated with the SPARQL query language. For OWL-based ontologies as mentioned above, OWL DL queries are necessary. Thus, for example, to retrieve a list of all ideas stored in the ontology, the simple statement "CoreIdea" is sufficient. The reasoner will return all instances of the class im:CoreIdea. To answer more specific questions, more complex query statements are necessary. Table 4 presents a mapping of a set of competency questions to OWL DL queries.

Other questions that leverage the semantic abilities of an ontology include, for example, Which ideas are related to environmental topics? or What ideas have an economic market analysis attached to them? These questions span several namespaces imported in the Idea Ontology (im, r, skos). Instead of writing complicated SQL statements as would be necessary for a system based on relational databases, in ontologies a reasoner will work to identify the result set of these questions.

As shown in our examples, using ontologies for structured knowledge representation offers several advantages in expressing relations, subclasses and dependencies between objects as well as "easy" querying. For our proposed ontology, these concepts are necessary to model the sophisticated interdependencies and links in related ontologies like SKOS or SIOC. Using sub-classes to describe concepts enables efficient inferencing and reasoning. Our short example showed that the ontology's design is capable of returning a result set with adequate reasoning done by a reasoner like pellet[9] or racer[10]. This is a valuable advantage that would be hard to realize with a traditional database-oriented system. By means of the imported ontologies, it becomes possible to add whole new concepts to an idea via already existing ontologies to enrich the idea and, at the same time, keep the ontology consistent.

CONCLUSION

A common language is a key component for information sharing and to foster interoperability between tools. This paper first presents our own definition of the concept of an "idea". Second, based on the detailed analysis of the innovation

Table 4. Sample questions and matching OWL DL queries based on the Idea Ontology

Competency Question	OWL DL Query
Which ideas are in the repository?	CoreIdea
For which categories have ideas been submitted?	isSubjectOf some CoreIdea
Which tags have been used to classify ideas?	Tagging and inv(hasTagging) min 1
Which ideas have already been implemented?	CoreIdea and hasRealization min 1
Which ideas have at least three ratings?	CoreIdea and hasRating min 3
Which ideas have at least two or more ratings as well as at least one realization?	CoreIdea and hasRating min 2 and hasRealization min 1
Who are the most valuable community members by assessing at least three ideas?	Person and inv(assessedBy) min 3
Which ideas already have a business plan attached (i.e., have an attached document with the topic 'business plan' to indicate feasibiliy)?	CoreIdea and hasAttachment some (Document and hasTopic value http://en.wikipedia.org/wiki/Business_plan)

management domain, the design of the OWL-based Idea Ontology is presented. Its primary goal is to facilitate interoperability between the various tools necessary to support the full life cycle of an idea in an open innovation environment. The ontology provides a consistent and semantically enriched method to represent the information in the "fuzzy front-end" of innovation (Menor, Tatikonda, & Sampson, 2002). Furthermore, the use of semantic techniques enables advanced management functions like semantic reasoning and automatic analysis. The design and development of our ontology follows principles promoted by design science research (Hevner, March, Park, & Ram, 2004; March & Smith 1995). For instance, problem relevance stems from the fact that the representation of ideas in innovation management is a problem domain with limited structure because ideas are, by their very nature, new and mostly not well understood. Furthermore, current development with an emerging interest in open innovation processes makes collaboration and information exchange between organizations important. The ontology has been developed by performing a thorough analysis of the requirements by common innovation-related tools such as Web communities and the experiences from three large research and development projects, one of which is used as the illustrative case study.

Particular emphasis has been given to the support for various community-related features such as commenting, tagging, and flexible rating mechanisms. The Idea Ontology can act as an enabler for open innovation processes as it provides a technical basis by means of which ideas can be generated systematically, refined, and evaluated across a wide set of tools and actors within or even across communities. The specific contribution of this work is the description of the technical architecture in which such an ontology-based approach is applied.

This research has certain limitations. Although information from three different projects as well as a survey of existing innovation communities and other innovation-related tools have been incorporated into the Idea Ontology, the scope might still be limited. The application of the Idea Ontology on an even broader scope, in other projects, and additional integration of innovation-relevant tools could further strengthen the confidence in the robustness of the ontology. Certain innovation scenarios or idea-related concepts might not be adequately covered by our ontology. However, we believe that the modular design allows the easy extension of the ontology. A second limitation is that the evaluation is restricted to an analysis of only one scenario, Third, our exploration of reasoning capabilities presented covers only some exemplary innovation management tasks.

The limitations also serve as directions for future research and development. Our Idea Ontology provides a first systematic overview of the required key information for representing ideas in innovation management. In a broader sense the Idea Ontology proposed in this paper is a means of supporting collaborative working environments at the semantic infrastructure layer and a key to further explore innovation processes. Future research should also exploit additional reasoning capabilities of semantically related subjects.

ACKNOWLEDGMENT

This research was funded by the German Federal Ministry of Economics and Technology under the promotional reference 01MQ07012, 01MQ07017, 01MQ07019, and 01MQ07024 and the German Federal Ministry of Education and Research under grant number 01IA08001A. The responsibility for this publication lies with the authors. Correspondence concerning this article should be addressed to Christoph Riedl, Department of Informatics, Chair for Information Systems, Technische Universität München, Boltzmannstr. 3, 85748 Garching b. München, Germany, Telephone: +49-89-289-19588, Email: riedlc@in.tum.de.

REFERENCES

Ahuja, G. (2000). Collaboration Networks, Structural Holes, and Innovation: A Longitudinal Study. *Administrative Science Quarterly, 45*, 425–455. doi:10.2307/2667105

Ardilio, A., Auernhammer, K., & Kohn, S. (2004). *Marktstudie Innovationssysteme: IT-Unterstützung im Innovationsmanagement*. Stuttgart, Germany: Fraunhofer IRB.

Bojãrs, U., & Breslin, J. G. (2007). *SIOC core ontology specification*. Retrieved from http://www.w3.org/Submission/2007/SUBM-sioc-spec-20070612/ accessed 2009-10-01

Brickley, D., & Miller, L. (2007). *FOAF vocabulary specification*. Retrieved from http://xmlns.com/foaf/spec/ accessed 2009-10-01

Browne, J., Hunt, I., & Zhang, J. (1998). The Extended Enterprise. In Molina, A., Sanchez, J. M., & Kusiak, A. (Eds.), *Handbook of Life Cycle Engineering Concepts, Tools and Techniques* (pp. 3–29). Dordrecht, The Netherlands: Kluwer Academic Publishers.

Bullinger, A. (2008). *Innovation and Ontologies: Structuring the Early Stages of Innovation Management*. Wiesbaden, Germany: Gabler.

Chesbrough, H. W. (2006). *Open innovation: The new imperative for creating and profiting from technology*. Boston, MA: Harvard Business School Press.

Cooper, R. G. (1990). Stage-gate systems: A new tool for managing new products. *Business Horizons, 33*, 44–54. doi:10.1016/0007-6813(90)90040-I

Fairbank, J., & Williams, S. (2001). Motivating Creativity and Enhancing Innovation through Employee Suggestion System Technology. *Creativity and Innovation Management, 10*, 68–74. doi:10.1111/1467-8691.00204

Fairbank, J. F., Spangler, W. E., & Williams, S. D. (2003). Motivating creativity through a computer-mediated employee suggestion management system. *Behaviour & Information Technology, 22*, 305–314. doi:10.1080/0144929031000159363 0

Fensel, D., Harmelen, F. V., Ding, Y. Klein, M., Akkermans, H., et al. (2002). On-To-Knowledge: Semantic Web Enabled Knowledge Management. *IEEE Computer, 35*.

Finzen, J., Kintz, M., Koch, S., & Kett, H. (2009). Strategic innovation management on the basis of searching and mining press releases. In *Proceedings of the 5th International conference on web information systems and technologies (WEBIST)*, Lisbon, Portugal.

Franke, N., & Shah, S. (2003). How communities support innovative activities: an exploration of assistance and sharing among end-users. *Research Policy, 32*, 157–178. doi:10.1016/S0048-7333(02)00006-9

Gassmann, O. (2006). Opening up the innovation process: towards an agenda. *R & D Management, 36*, 223–228. doi:10.1111/j.1467-9310.2006.00437.x

Gassmann, O., & Enkel, E. (2004). Towards a Theory of Open Innovation: Three Core Process Archetypes. In *Proceedings of the R&D Management Conference (RADMA)*, Sessimbra, Portugal.

Gemunden, H., Salomo, S., & Holzle, K. (2007). Role Models for Radical Innovations in Times of Open Innovation. *Creativity and Innovation Management, 16*, 408–421. doi:10.1111/j.1467-8691.2007.00451.x

Golder, S., & Huberman, B. (2005). *The Structure of Collaborative Tagging Systems* (Arxiv preprint cs.DL/0508082).

Gómez-Pérez, A., & Benjamins, V. R. (1999). Overview of Knowledge Sharing and Reuse Components: Ontologies and Problem-Solving Methods. In *Proceedings of the IJCAI-99 Workshop on Ontologies and Problem-Solving Methods. Lessons Learned and Future Trends* (pp. 1-15). CEUR Publications

Gruninger, M., & Fox, M. S. (1995). Methodology for the Design and Evaluation of Ontologies. In *Proceedings of the Workshop on Basic Ontological Issues in Knowledge Sharing (IJCAI-95)*, Montreal, Canada.

Hevner, A., March, S., Park, J., & Ram, S. (2005). Design Science in Information Systems Research. *Management Information Systems Quarterly, 28*, 75–105.

Hüsemann, B., & Vossen, G. (2005). Ontology engineering from a database perspective. *Lecture Notes in Computer Science, 3818*, 49–63. doi:10.1007/11596370_6

Longo, C., & Sciuto, L. (2007). A lightweight ontology for rating assessments. In *Proceedings of 4th Italian Workshop on Semantic Web Applications and Perspectives (SWAP 2007)*, Bari, Italy.

Lonsdale, D., Embley, D. W., Ding, Y., Xu, L., & Hepp, M. (2009). *Reusing ontologies and language components for ontology generation.* Data & Knowledge Engineering.

March, S., & Smith, G. (1995). Design and natural science research on information technology. *Decision Support Systems, 15*, 251–266. doi:10.1016/0167-9236(94)00041-2

Mathes, A. (2004). Folksonomies - Cooperative Classification and Communication Through Shared Metadata. In *Computer Mediated Communication.* Urbana-Champaign, IL: Graduate School of Library and Information Science, University of Illinois.

Menor, L., Tatikonda, M., & Sampson, S. (2002). New service development: areas for exploitation and exploration. *Journal of Operations Management, 20*, 135–157. doi:10.1016/S0272-6963(01)00091-2

Miles, A., & Bechhofer, S. (2009). *SKOS Simple Knowledge Organization System Reference.* Retrieved October 1, 2009, from http://www.w3.org/TR/2009/REC-skos-reference-20090818

Newman, R. (2005). *Tag ontology.* Retrieved October 1, 2009, from http://www.holygoat.co.uk/projects/tags/

Ning, K., O'Sullivan, D., Zhu, Q., & Decker, S. (2006). Semantic innovation management across the extended enterprise. *International Journal of Industrial and Systems Engineering, 1*, 109–128. doi:10.1504/IJISE.2006.009052

Noy, N. F., & McGuinness, D. L. (2001). *Ontology development 101: A guide to creating your first ontology* (Tech. Rep. KSL-01-05 and Stanford Medical Informatics Technical Report SMI-2001-0880). Palo Alto, CA: Stanford Knowledge Systems Laboratory.

Nunamaker, J., Chen, M., & Purdin, T. D. M. (1991). Systems Development in Information Systems Research. *Journal of Management Information Systems, 7*, 89–106.

Ogawa, S., & Piller, F. (2006). Reducing the Risks of New Product Development. *MIT Sloan Management Review, 47*, 65–71.

Piller, F. T., & Walcher, D. (2006). Toolkits for idea competitions: a novel method to integrate users in new product development. *R & D Management, 36*, 307–318. doi:10.1111/j.1467-9310.2006.00432.x

Porter, M. (1990). *The Competitive Advantage of Nations.* New York: Free Press.

Riedl, C., Böhmann, T., Leimeister, J. M., & Krcmar, H. (2009). A Framework for Analysing Service Ecosystem Capabilities to Innovate. In *Proceedings of 17th European Conference on Information Systems (ECIS'09)*, Verona, Italy.

Rogers, E. (2003). *Diffusion of Innovations* (5th ed.). New York: Free Press.

Sheth, A., Ramakrishnan, C., & Thomas, C. (2005). Semantics for the semantic web: The implicit, the formal and the powerful. *International Journal on Semantic Web and Information Systems, 1*, 1–18.

Stathel, S., Finzen, J., Riedl, C., & May, N. (2008). Service innovation in business value networks. In *Proceedings of XVIII International RESER Conference*, Stuttgart, Germany.

Stathel, S., van Dinther, C., & Schönfeld, A. (2009). Service Innovation with Information Markets. In *Proceedings of Wirtschaftsinformatik 2009*, Wien, Austria.

Storey, J. (2000). The management of innovation problem International. *Journal of Innovation Management, 4*, 347–369. doi:10.1016/S1363-9196(00)00019-6

Stuckenschmidt, H., & Klein, M. (2007). Reasoning and change management in modular ontologies. *Data & Knowledge Engineering, 63*, 200–223. doi:10.1016/j.datak.2007.02.001

Surowiecki, J. (2005). *The wisdom of crowds: why the many are smarter than the few*. London: Abacus.

Tidd, J., Bessant, J., & Pavitt, K. (2005). *Managing innovation: integrating technological, market and organizational change* (3rd ed.). Chichester, UK: John Wiley & Sons.

Uschold, M., King, M., Moralee, S., & Zorgios, Y. (1998). The Enterprise Ontology. *The Knowledge Engineering Review, 13*, 31–89. doi:10.1017/S0269888998001088

van Gundy, A. (1988). *Techniques of structured problem solving* (2nd ed.). New York: Van Nostrand Reinhold.

von Hippel, E. (2005). *Democratizing Innovation*. Boston: MIT Press.

West, J., & Lakhani, K. (2008). Getting Clear About Communities in Open Innovation. *Industry and Innovation, 15*, 223–231. doi:10.1080/13662710802033734

Wheelwright, S. C., & Clark, K. B. (1992). *Revolutionizing Product Development: Quantum Leaps in Speed, Efficiency, and Quality*. New York: Free Press.

ENDNOTES

* An earlier version of this paper titled "Managing Service Innovations with an Idea Ontology" has been presented at the XIX RESER Conference, Budapest, Hungary, September 24th-26th 2009. This paper describes an extended ontology, contains additional technical details regarding the developed ontology, and a case study evaluating the system mapping and competency questions.

[1] Number of ideas as of October 2009

[2] http://www.crowdspirit.com, http://www.dellideastorm.com, http://www.erfinder-profi.de, http://www.incuby.com, http://mystarbucksidea.force.com, https://www.atizo.com, http://ideajam.net/, https://mix.oracle.com/; Dell and Starbucks are based on the same Salesforce Ideas software but use a different configuration.

[3] http://theseus-programm.de/scenarios/en/texo

[4] http://laboranova.com/

[5] Code samples use N3 notation http://www.w3.org/DesignIssues/Notation3.

[6] http://www.w3.org/TR/wsdl

7   A Web portal embracing several special search mechanisms for innovation professionals (Stathel et al., 2008; Finzen, Kintz, Koch, & Kett, 2009).

8   http://www.groupsystems.com/
9   http://clarkparsia.com/pellet/
10   http://www.sts.tu-harburg.de/~r.f.moeller/racer/

This work was previously published in International Journal on Semantic Web and Information Systems, Volume 5, Issue 4, edited by Amit P. Sheth, pp. 1-18, copyright 2009 by IGI Publishing (an imprint of IGI Global).

Chapter 13
Inductive Classification of Semantically Annotated Resources through Reduced Coulomb Energy Networks

Nicola Fanizzi
Università degli studi di Bari, Italy

Claudia d'Amato
Università degli studi di Bari, Italy

Floriana Esposito
Università degli studi di Bari, Italy

ABSTRACT

The tasks of resource classification and retrieval from knowledge bases in the Semantic Web are the basis for a lot of important applications. In order to overcome the limitations of purely deductive approaches to deal with these tasks, inductive (instance-based) methods have been introduced as efficient and noise-tolerant alternatives. In this paper we propose an original method based on a non-parametric learning scheme: the Reduced Coulomb Energy (RCE) Network. The method requires a limited training effort but it turns out to be very effective during the classification phase. Casting retrieval as the problem of assessing the class-membership of individuals w.r.t. the query concepts, we propose an extension of a classification algorithm using RCE networks based on an entropic similarity measure for OWL. Experimentally we show that the performance of the resulting inductive classifier is comparable with the one of a standard reasoner and often more efficient than with other inductive approaches. Moreover, we show that new knowledge (not logically derivable) is induced and the likelihood of the answers may be provided.

DOI: 10.4018/978-1-60960-593-3.ch013

1 INTRODUCTION

The tasks of resource classification and retrieval from knowledge bases (KBs) in the Semantic Web (SW) are the basis for many important knowledge-intensive applications. However the inherent incompleteness and accidental inconsistency of knowledge bases in the Semantic Web requires new different methods which are able to perform such tasks efficiently and effectively (although with some acceptable approximation). Instance-related tasks are generally tackled by means of logical approaches that try to cope with the problems mentioned above. This has given rise to alternative methods for approximate reasoning (Wache, Groot & Stuckenschmidt, 2005), (Hitzler & Vrandecic, 2005), (Haase, van Harmelen, Huang, Stuckenschmidt& Halberstadt, 2005), (Möller, Haarslev & Wessel, 2006), (Huang & van Harmelen, 2008), (Tserendorj, Rudolph, Krötzsch & Hitzler, 2008), (Rudolph, Tserendorj & Hitzler, 2008). Inductive methods for approximate reasoning are known to be often quite efficient, scalable, and noise-tolerant.

Recently, first steps have been taken to apply classic machine learning techniques for building inductive classifiers for the complex representations, and related semantics, adopted in the context of the SW (Fanizzi, d'Amato & Esposito, 2008a), especially through *non-parametric*[1] statistical methods (d'Amato, Fanizzi & Esposito, 2008), (Fanizzi, d'Amato & Esposito, 2008d). Instance-based inductive methods may help a knowledge engineer populate ontologies (Baader, Ganter, Sertkaya & Sattle, 2007). Some methods are also able to complete ontologies with probabilistic assertions derived exploiting the missing and sparse data in the ontologies (Rettinger, Nickles & Tresp, 2009). Further sophisticate approaches are able of dealing with uncertainty encoded in probabilistic ontologies through suitable forms of reasoning (Lukasiewicz, 2008).

In this paper we propose a novel method for inducing classifiers from ontological data that may naturally be employed as an alternative way for performing *concept retrieval* (Baader, Calvanese, McGuinness, Nardi, Patel-Schneider, 2003) and several other related applications. Even more so, like its predecessors mentioned above, the induced classifier is also able to determine a likelihood measure of the induced class-membership assertions which is important for *approximate query answering* and *ranking*. Some assertions could not be logically derived, but may be highly probable according to the inductive classifier; this may help to cope with the uncertainty caused by the inherent incompleteness of the KBs even in absence of an explicit probabilistic model.

Specifically, we propose to answer queries adopting an *instance-based* classifier, the Reduced Coulomb Energy (RCE) network (Duda, Hart & Stork, 2001), induced by a non-parametric learning method. The essentials of this learning scheme have been extended to be applied to the standard representations of the SW via semantic similarity measures for individual resources. As with other similarity-based methods, a retrieval procedure may seek for individuals belonging to query concepts, exploiting the analogy with other training instances, namely the classification of the nearest ones (w.r.t. the measure of choice). Differently from other lazy-learning approaches experimented in the past (d'Amato, Fanizzi & Esposito, 2008) which do not require training, yet more similarly to the non-parametric methods based on *kernel machines* (Bloehdorn & Sure, 2007), (Fanizzi, d'Amato & Esposito, 2008d), the new method is organized in two phases:

- In the *training* phase, an RCE network based on prototypical individuals (parameterized for each prototype) is trained to detect the membership of further individuals w.r.t. some query concept;
- The network is then exploited by the classifier, during the *classification* phase, to make a decision on the class-membership

of an individual w.r.t. the query concept on the grounds of a likelihood estimate.

The network parameters correspond to the radii of hyperspheres centered at the prototypical individuals in the context of the metric space determined by some measure. The classification of an individual is induced observing the balls it belongs to and on its distance from their centers (training prototypes). The efficiency of the method derives from limiting the expensive model construction to a small set of training individuals, while the resulting RCE network can be exploited in the next phase to efficiently classify a large number of individuals. Moreover the method may easily have a parallel implementation.

Similarity measures derived from a family of semantic pseudo-metrics (d'Amato, Fanizzi & Esposito, 2008) were exploited. This language-independent measure assesses the similarity of two individuals by comparing them on the grounds of their behavior w.r.t. a committee of features (concepts), namely (a subset of) those defined in the KB which can be thought of as a sort of *context* (Goldstone, Medin & Halberstadt, 1997); alternatively, it may be generated to this purpose through randomized search algorithms aiming at optimal committees to be run in advance (Fanizzi, d'Amato & Esposito, 2008b). Alternatively the very concepts occurring in the knowledge base can be employed. However, since different features may exhibit a different relevance w.r.t. the similarity to be determined, they have to be weighted on the grounds of the degree of discernibility they convey. The rationale is that the more general a feature the less likely is should be used for distinguishing the individuals. One way to determine this influence is related to *information* measures and the relevance may be determined resorting to the *entropy*. Another measure of the feature relevance may be determined by its *variance* (Hastie, Tibshirani & Friedman, 2001). We

investigated the construction of variance-based weights for the similarity measures.

The system ReduCE implements the RCE network construction and classification. It allowed for an intensive experimentation of the method on performing approximate query answering with a number ontologies from public repositories. Like in previous works (d'Amato, Fanizzi & Esposito, 2008), (Fanizzi, d'Amato & Esposito, 2008d), the predictions made inductively were compared to assertions that were logically derived by a deductive reasoner. The experiments showed that the induction classification is competitive w.r.t. the purely deductive methods and also that it is able to detect new knowledge (assertions) that is not logically derivable.

This work revises and extends our preliminary article (Fanizzi, d'Amato & Esposito, 2009). Revisions where made to make it more self-contained especially on the parts related to the machine learning basics. A discussion of the related approaches to approximate classification methods has been added. Extensions regarded mainly principled techniques for optimizing the distance measure employed by the classification algorithm and performing new series of experimental sessions on different parameter settings with a comparative discussion of the results.

The paper is organized as follows. The basics of the RCE Network induction and classification procedures are recalled in §2 with the extension to cope with to the standard SW representations. The semantic similarity measures adopted in the retrieval procedure are presented in §3 with two methods for determining the influence of the features they are based upon. The outcomes of the experiments performed with the ReduCE system, that implements the inductive classification procedures, are reported in §4. The related methods for inductive classification working on DL representations are discussed in §5. Possible developments are finally examined in §6.

2 RCE NETWORK TRAINING AND CLASSIFICATION

An approximate classification method is proposed for individuals in the context of semantic knowledge bases. The method requires training an RCE network, which can be successively exploited for an inductive classification procedure. Moreover, a likelihood measure of the decisions made by the inductive procedure can be provided.

In the following sections, it is assumed that concept descriptions are defined in terms of a generic terminological language expressed in *Description Logics* (DLs) with its standard model-theoretic semantics (see the handbook (Baader, Calvanese, McGuinness, Nardi, Patel-Schneider, 2003) for a thorough reference). Practically, the methods can be easily implemented adopting standard SW languages endowed with instance-checking procedures, such as OWL-DL.

A *knowledge base* $\mathcal{K} = \langle \mathcal{T}, \mathcal{A} \rangle$ contains a *TBox* $\mathcal{T}$ and an *ABox* $\mathcal{A}$. $\mathcal{T}$ is a set of axioms that define concepts (and relationships). $\mathcal{A}$ contains factual assertions concerning the individuals (resources). In the following we will assume that the *unique names assumption* is made[2] on the such individuals represented in OWL by their URIs. The set of the individuals occurring in $\mathcal{A}$ is denoted with $Ind(\mathcal{A})$. As with all other instance-based methods, the most important inference required by the inductive procedure is *instance-checking* Baader, Calvanese, McGuinness, Nardi, Patel-Schneider, 2003), which amounts to determining whether an individual, say a, is an instance of some concept C. This is denoted by $\mathcal{K} \models C(a)$. This service is generally provided by a reasoner. Note that because of the open-world semantics, a reasoner may be unable to give a positive or negative answer to a class-membership query, then this may be unknown.

2.1 Hypothesis Function

In *instance-based* learning (Duda, Hart & Stork, 2001), (Witten & Frank, 2005), the basic mechanism determines the membership of an instance to some query concept Q in accordance with the membership of the most similar instance(s) with respect to a similarity measure.

This may be formalized as the induction of an estimate for a discrete-valued target hypothesis function $h_Q : IS \rightarrow V$ from a space of instances IS to a set of values $V = \{v_1, \ldots, v_s\}$, standing for mutually exclusive cases to be predicted.

In the specific case of interest (d'Amato, Fanizzi & Esposito, 2008), the adopted set of values is $V = \{+1, 0, -1\}$, where the three values denote, respectively, membership, uncertainty, and non-membership. The training phase merely amounts to memorizing the values of h_Q for the training instances $TrSet \subseteq IS$ are determined as follows:

$\forall \mathbf{x} \in TrSet$:

$$h_Q(\mathbf{x}) = \begin{cases} +1 & \mathcal{K} \models Q(\mathbf{x}) \\ -1 & \mathcal{K} \models \neg Q(\mathbf{x}) \\ 0 & otherwise \end{cases}$$

Note that normally $|TrSet|$ is much less than $|Ind(\mathcal{A})|$ i.e. only a limited number of training instances (exemplars) is needed, especially if they can be carefully selected among the prototypical ones for the various regions of the search space. This has a strong impact on the scalability of the method because once trained the inductive model can be reused for a large number of times. As proposed in previous works (d'Amato, Fanizzi & Esposito, 2008), this setting may be further simplified by considering the occurrence of the

Figure 1. The structure of a Reduced Coulomb Energy network

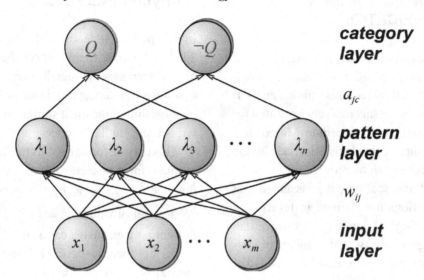

assertions $Q(\mathbf{x})$ or $\neg Q(\mathbf{x})$ in the ABox instead of resorting to reasoning services.

Let $\mathbf{x}_q$ be the query instance whose membership w.r.t. Q is to be determined. Given a dissimilarity measure d, in the k-*Nearest Neighbor* method (k-NN) (Duda, Hart & Stork, 2001; Hastie, Tibshirani & Friedman, 2001) the estimate of the hypothesis function for the query individual may be determined by:

$$\hat{h}_Q(\mathbf{x}_q) = \operatorname*{argmax}_{v \in V} \sum_{j=1}^{k} \frac{\delta(v, h_Q(\mathbf{x}_{n_j}))}{(d(\mathbf{x}_{n_j}, \mathbf{x}_q))^2}$$

where the indicator function δ returns 1 in case of matching arguments and 0 otherwise. In this case the similarity of the k nearest neighbors $\mathbf{x}_{n_j}$ is weighted as the squared inverse distance. Other choices are perfectly legitimate.

2.2 Training

The method based on RCE[3] networks adopts an analogous non-parametric approach with a more complex training phase. The construction of the inductive model can be implemented as training

a (sort of neural) RCE network whose structure, for the binary problem of interest, is sketched in Fig. 1.

Originally, instances are considered contained in an m-dimensional metric space, $\mathbf{x} = (x_1, \ldots, x_m)$, w.r.t. some generic distance measure d (to be specified for the domain and representation of interest). In a categorical setting, individuals shall be preliminarily projected onto $\mathbf{R}^m$ using suitable projection functions $\pi_i \colon IS \mapsto \mathbf{R}$ ($i = 1, \ldots, m$). Hence in the following we can consider instances as tuples. As will be shown, the methods essentially involve instances for the computation of their (dis)similarity.

The structure resembles that of an probabilistic neural network (Duda, Hart & Stork, 2001). with three layers of units linked by weights connections, say w_{ij}'s and a_{jc}'s, for the input-hidden layer and hidden-output layer, respectively. The input layer receives its information from the individuals: attribute values in the original setting, while in our case we may consider their semantics w.r.t. the context of similarity features employed by some metric (membership/non-membership), as detailed later in the next section). The middle layer of patterns represents the features that are constructed for the classification; each node in this layer is endowed with a parameter λ_j representing the radius of the hypersphere centered in the j-th prototype individual of the training set. During the training phase, each coefficient λ_j is adjusted so that the spherical region is as large as possible, provided that no training individual of a different class is contained. Each pattern node is connected to one of the output nodes representing the predicted class. In our case we have only two categories representing, resp., membership and non-membership w.r.t. the query concept Q.

The training algorithm is sketched in Fig. 2. Examples are made up of training instances labeled with their correct classification $\langle \mathbf{x}_i, h_Q(\mathbf{x}_i) \rangle$, where $h_Q(\mathbf{x}_i) \in V$, as seen before. In this phase, each parameter λ_j which represents the radius of a hypothetical m-dimensional hypersphere centered at the input example, is adjusted to be as large as possible (they are initialized with a maximum radius), provided that the resulting region does not enclose counterexamples. As new individuals are processed, each such radius λ_j may be decreased accordingly (and can never increase). In this way, each pattern unit may correspond to a hyperspheres enclosing several prototypes, all having the same category label.

Fig. 3 shows the evolution of the model (two-colored decision regions for binary problems) that becomes more and more complex as long as training instances are processed. Different colors represent the different membership predictions. Uncertain regions present overlapping colors.

Figure 2. RCE training algorithm

input
    $\{\langle \mathbf{x}, h_Q(\mathbf{x}) \rangle \mid \mathbf{x} \in \mathsf{TrSet}, h_Q(\mathbf{x}) \in V \}$: set of training examples
output
    $w_{ij}, \lambda_j, a_{jc}$: RCE Network parameters

1. **begin**
2. initialize
    $\epsilon \leftarrow$ min radius;
    $\lambda_{\max} \leftarrow$ max radius;
3. **for** $j \leftarrow 1$ **to** $|\mathsf{TrSet}|$ **do**
    let $\mathbf{x}_j$ be next training instance
    a) train weight:
        $w_{ij} \leftarrow x_{ji}$
    b) find nearest counterexample:
        $\bar{\mathbf{x}} \leftarrow \arg\min_{\mathbf{x} \in \mathcal{C}_j} d(\mathbf{x}, \mathbf{x}_j)$
        where $\mathcal{C}_j = \{\mathbf{x} \in \mathsf{TrSet} \mid h_Q(\mathbf{x}_j) \neq h_Q(\mathbf{x})\}$
    c) set radius:
        $\lambda_j \leftarrow \min\left(\max\left(d(\bar{\mathbf{x}}, \mathbf{x}_j), \epsilon\right), \lambda_{\max}\right)$
    d) **if** $(h_Q(\mathbf{x}_j) = +1)$
        then $a_{j\ +1} \leftarrow 1$
        else $a_{j\ -1} \leftarrow 1$
4. **end**

Figure 3. Evolution of the model built by an RCE network: the centers of the hyperspheres represent the prototypical individuals

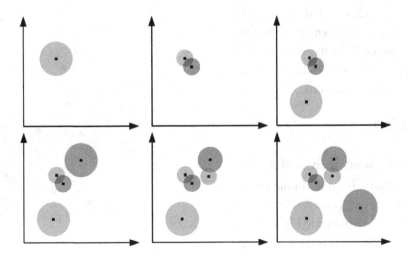

It is easy to see that the complexity of the method, when no particular optimization is made, is $O(n^2)$ in the number of training examples ($n = | TrSet |$) as the weights are to be adjusted for all of them and each modification of the radius λ_j requires a search for the counterexample with minimal distance among the other training instances.

The method can be used both in *batch* and *on-line* mode. The latter incremental model is particularly appealing when the application may require performing intensive queries involving the same concept and new instances are likely to be made available along the time.

There are several subtleties that may be considered. For instance, when the radius of a pattern unit becomes too small (i.e., less than some threshold $\lambda_{\min}$), this indicates highly overlapping different categories in a certain region. In that case, the pattern unit is called a *probabilistic* unit, and so marked.

The method is related to other non-parametric ones dealing with the instance density, *k -NN estimation* and *Parzen windows* (Duda, Hart & Stork, 2001). In particular the Parzen windows method uses fixed window sizes that could lead to some difficulties: in some regions a small window width is appropriate while elsewhere a large one would be better. The k-NN method uses variable window sizes increasing the size until enough samples are enclosed. This may lead to unnaturally large windows when sparsely populated regions are targeted. In the RCE method, the window sizes are adjusted until points of a different category are encountered.

2.3 Classification

The classification of a query individual $\mathbf{x}_q$ using the trained RCE network is quite simple in principle. As shown in the basic (*vanilla*) form of the classification algorithm depicted in Fig. 4, the set $N(\mathbf{x}_q) \subseteq TrSet$ of the nearest training instances

Figure 4. Vanilla RCE classification procedure

input
    $\mathbf{x}_q$: query individual
    $w_{ij}, \lambda_j, a_{jc}$: parameters of the trained RCE network
output
    $\hat{h}_Q(\mathbf{x}_q)$: estimated classification

1. **begin**
2. initialize:
     $k \leftarrow 0;$ $N(\mathbf{x}_q) \leftarrow \emptyset$
3. **for** $j \leftarrow 1$ to |TrSet| **do**
   - **if** $d(\mathbf{x}_q, \mathbf{x}_j) < \lambda_j$
     then $N(\mathbf{x}_q) \leftarrow N(\mathbf{x}_q) \cup \{\mathbf{x}_j\}$
4. **if** $(\exists c \, \forall \mathbf{x} \in N(\mathbf{x}_q) : h_Q(\mathbf{x}) = c)$
   then return c //all neighbors share the same class
   else return 0   // uncertain case
5. **end**

is built on the grounds of the hyperspheres (determined by the λ_j's) the query instance belongs to. Each hypersphere has a related classification determined by the prototype at its center (see Fig. 5). If all prototypes agree on the classification

Figure 5. A representation of the model built by an RCE network used for classification: regions with different colors represent different classifications for instances therein. The areas with overlapping colors or outside of the scope of the hyperspheres represent regions of uncertain classification (see the proposed enhancement of the procedure in this case).

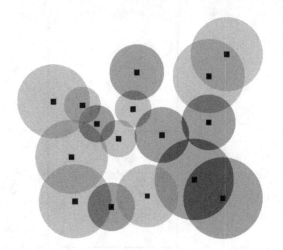

this value is returned as the induced estimate, otherwise the query individual is deemed as ambiguous w.r.t. Q, which represents the default case.

It is easy to see that the complexity of this inductive classification procedure is linear in the number of training instances and it could be optimized by employing specific data structures, such as *kD-tress* or *ball-trees* (Witten & Frank, 2005), which would allow a faster search of the including hyperspheres and their centers.

In case of uncertainty, this procedure may be enhanced in the spirit of k-NN classification recalled above. If a query individual is located in more than one hypersphere, instead of a catch-all decision like the one made at step 4. of the algorithm, requiring all involved prototypes to agree on their classification in a sort of *voting* procedure, each vote may be weighted by the similarity of the query individual w.r.t. the hypersphere center in terms of a similarity measure[4] s, and the classification should be defined by the class whose prototypes are globally the closest, considering the difference between the closeness values of the query individual from the centers classified by either class. Indeed, one may also consider the *signed* vote, where the sign is determined by the classification of each selected training prototype, and sum up these votes determining the classification with a sign function.

Formally, suppose the nearest prototype set $N(\mathbf{x}_q)$ has been determined. The decision function is defined:

$$g(\mathbf{x}_q) = \sum_{\mathbf{x}_j \in N(\mathbf{x}_q)} h_Q(\mathbf{x}_j) \cdot s(\mathbf{x}_j, \mathbf{x}_q)$$

Then step 4. in the procedure becomes:

4.   **if**($abs(g(\mathbf{x}_q)) > \theta$)**then return** $sgn(g(\mathbf{x}_q))$
    else return 0

where $\theta \in [0,1]$ is a *tolerance* threshold for the uncertain classification (*uncertainty threshold*). We may foresee that higher values of this threshold make the classifier more *skeptical* in uncertain cases, while lower values make it more credulous in suggesting ± 1.

2.4 Likelihood of the Inductive Classification

The analogical inference made by the procedure shown above is not guaranteed to be deductively valid. Indeed, inductive inference naturally yields a certain degree of uncertainty.

In order to measure the likelihood of the decision made by the inductive procedure, one may resort to an approach that is similar to the one applied with the kNN procedure (d'Amato, Fanizzi & Esposito, 2008). It is convenient to decompose the decision function $g(\mathbf{x})$ into three components corresponding to the values $v \in V : g_v(\mathbf{x})$ and use those weighted votes. Specifically, given the nearest training individuals in $N(\mathbf{x}_q) = \{\mathbf{x}_1, \ldots, \mathbf{x}_k\}$, the values of the decision function should be normalized as follows, producing a likelihood measure:

$$\ell(\hat{h}(\mathbf{x}_q) = v \,\#N(\mathbf{x}_q)) \;=\; \frac{g_v(\mathbf{x}_q)}{\sum_{u \in V} g_u(\mathbf{x}_q)}$$

$$= \frac{\sum_{j=1}^{k} \delta(v, h_Q(\mathbf{x}_j)) \cdot s(\mathbf{x}_q, \mathbf{x}_j)}{\sum_{u \in V} \sum_{h=1}^{k} \delta(u, h_Q(\mathbf{x}_h)) \cdot s(\mathbf{x}_q, \mathbf{x}_h)}$$

For instance, the likelihood of the assertion $Q(\mathbf{x}_q)$ corresponds to the case when $v = +1$ (i.e. to $g_1(\mathbf{x}_q)$). This could be used in case the application requires that the hits be ranked along with their likelihood values.

3 SIMILARITY MEASURES

The method described in the previous section relies on a notion of similarity which should be measured by means of specific metrics which are to be sensible to the similarity/difference between the individuals To this purpose various definitions have been proposed (Fanizzi, d'Amato & Esposito, 2007), (Fanizzi, d'Amato & Esposito, 2008b), (d'Amato, Fanizzi & Esposito, 2008), (Fanizzi, d'Amato & Esposito, 2008d).

Given a dissimilarity measure d with values in $[0,1]$ belonging to the family of pseudo-metrics defined in (d'Amato, Fanizzi & Esposito, 2008), the easiest way to derive a similarity measure would be: $\forall a, b: s(a, b) = 1 - d(a, b)$ or $s(a, b) = 1/d(a, b)$. The latter case may need some correction to avoid undefined cases.

A more direct way follows the same ideas that inspired the mentioned metrics. Indeed, these measures are based on the idea of comparing the semantics of the input individuals along a number of dimensions represented by a committee of concept descriptions. Indeed, on a semantic level, similar individuals should behave similarly with respect to the same concepts.

More formally, the individuals are compared on the grounds of their semantics w.r.t. a collection of concept descriptions, say $F = \{F_1, F_2, \ldots, F_m\}$, which stands as a group of discriminating *features* expressed in the language taken into account. In its simple formulation, a family of similarity functions for individuals inspired to Minkowski's norms can be defined as follows (Fanizzi, d'Amato & Esposito, 2008d):

Definition 3.1 (similarity measures) *Let* $\mathcal{K} = \langle \mathcal{T}, \mathcal{A} \rangle$ be a knowledge base. Given a set of concept descriptions $F = \{F_i\}_{i=1}^m$ and a normalized vector of weights $\vec{w} = (w_1, \ldots, w_m)^t$, a family of similarity functions

$$s_p^F : Ind(\mathcal{A}) \times Ind(\mathcal{A}) \to [0,1]$$

is defined as follows:

$$\forall a, b \in Ind(\mathcal{A})$$

$$s_p^F(a, b) = \frac{1}{m} \left[\sum_{i=1}^m w_i \mid \sigma_i(a, b) \mid^p \right]^{1/p}$$

where $p > 0$ and $\forall i \in \{1, \ldots, m\}$ the similarity function σ_i is defined by:

$$\forall a, b \in Ind(\mathcal{A})$$

$$\sigma_i(a, b) = \begin{cases} 0 & [\mathcal{K} \models F_i(a) \wedge \mathcal{K} \models \neg F_i(b)] \vee [\mathcal{K} \models \neg F_i(a) \wedge \mathcal{K} \models F_i(b)] \\ 1 & [\mathcal{K} \models F_i(a) \wedge \mathcal{K} \models F_i(b)] \vee [\mathcal{K} \models \neg F_i(a) \wedge \mathcal{K} \models \neg F_i(b)] \\ \frac{1}{2} & \text{otherwise} \end{cases}$$

The rationale of the measure is summing the partial similarity w.r.t. the single concepts. Functions σ_i assign the weighted maximal similarity to the case when the individuals exhibit the same behavior w.r.t. the given feature F_i, and null similarity when they belong to disjoint features. An intermediate value is assigned to the case when reasoning cannot ascertain one of such required class-memberships.

3.1 Feature Weights

Note that the original measures measures (Fanizzi, d'Amato & Esposito, 2007) correspond to the case of a vector $\vec{w}$ of *uniform* weights. However the single components w_i should reflect the impact of the various feature concepts w.r.t. the overall similarity. For this reason we adopt different choices that depend on two discernibility criteria.

3.1.1 Entropy-Based Weights

As mentioned, this can be determined by the quantity of *information* conveyed by a feature, which can be measured estimating its entropy (d'Amato, Fanizzi & Esposito, 2008). Namely, the extension of a feature F_i w.r.t. the whole domain of objects may be probabilistically quantified as $P_i^+ = |F_i^{\mathcal{I}}| / |\Delta^{\mathcal{I}}|$ (w.r.t. the canonical interpretation $\mathcal{I}$ whose domain is made up by the very individual names occurring in the ABox (Baader, Calvanese, McGuinness, Nardi, Patel-Schneider, 2003). This can be roughly approximated with: $P_i^+ = |retrieval(F_i)| / |Ind(\mathcal{A})|$, where retrieval denotes the result of the DL instance retrieval service (Baader, Calvanese, McGuinness, Nardi, Patel-Schneider, 2003). Hence, considering also the probability P_i^- related to its negation and that related to the unclassified individuals (w.r.t. F_i), $P_i^U = 1 - (P_i^+ + P_i^-)$, one may determine an entropic measure for the discernibility yielded by the feature:

$$h_i = -P_i \log(P_i) - P_i^- \log(P_i^-) - P_i^U \log(P_i^U)$$

These measures may be normalized for providing a good set of weights for distance or similarity measures $w_i = h_i / \|\vec{h}\|$.

3.1.2 Variance-Based Weights

An alternative is based on an estimate of the *feature variance*. Following the method proposed in (Hastie, Tibshirani & Friedman, 2001), we can define the estimate as follows:

$$\widehat{var}(F_i) = \frac{1}{2 \cdot |Ind(\mathcal{A})|^2} \sum_{a \in Ind(\mathcal{A})} \sum_{b \in Ind(\mathcal{A})} \left[\pi_i(a) - \pi_i(b) \right]^2$$

where, for $i = 1, \ldots, m$, the *projection functions* can be defined $\pi_i(\mathbf{x}) = h_{F_i}(\mathbf{x})$. This induces the choice of weights: $w_i = 1 / (2 \cdot \widehat{var}(F_i))$, for $i = 1, \ldots, m$.

These weights may also be employed to encode also asymmetric *cost functions* (Duda, Hart & Stork, 2001), (Hastie, Tibshirani & Friedman, 2001), so to assign a different impact to the values that the dissimilarity on a given feature ($\left[\pi_i(a) - \pi_i(b) \right]^p$) may assume.

4 EXPERIMENTATION

The ReduCE system implements the training and classification procedures explained in the previous sections, borrowing the simplest metrics of the family (i.e. those with $p = 1$), for the sake of efficiency.

Its performance has been tested in a number of classification problems that had been previously approached with other inductive methods (d'Amato, Fanizzi & Esposito, 2008), (Fanizzi, d'Amato & Esposito, 2008d). This allows the comparison of the new system to other inductive methods (see also the next section §5 on related works).

4.1 Experimental Setting

A number of ontologies from different domains represented in OWL have been selected, namely: Surface-Water-Model (SWM), New Testament Names (NTN) from the Protégé library[5], the Semantic Web Service Discovery dataset[6] (SWSD), an ontology generated by the Lehigh University Benchmark[7] (LUBM), the BioPax glycolysis ontology[8] (BioPax) and the Financial ontology[9]. Table 1 summarizes details concerning these ontologies.

For each ontology, 100 satisfiable query concepts were randomly generated by composition (conjunction and/or disjunction) of (2 through 8) primitive and defined concepts (including nested role restrictions) in each knowledge base. Query concepts were constructed so as to be satisfiable and endowed with at least 50% of the ABox in-

Table 1. Facts concerning the ontologies employed in the experiments

ontology	DL language	#concepts	#object prop.	#data prop.	#individuals
SWM	$\mathcal{ALCOF(D)}$	19	9	1	115
BioPAX	$\mathcal{ALCHF(D)}$	28	19	30	323
LUBM	$\mathcal{ALR^+HI(D)}$	43	7	25	555
NTN	$\mathcal{SHIF(D)}$	47	27	8	676
SWSD	$\mathcal{ALCH}$	258	25	0	732
Financial	$\mathcal{ALCIF}$	60	17	0	1000

dividuals classified as positive and negative instances. The performance of the inductive method was evaluated by comparing its responses to those returned by a standard reasoner[10] as a baseline.

Experimentally, it was observed that large training sets make the similarity measures (and consequently the inductive procedure) very accurate. The simplest similarity measure (s_1^F) was employed from the family, using all the named concepts in the knowledge base for determining the committee of features F with no further optimization. Both entropy-based and variance-based weights have been associated to the features in two separate experiments in order to compare the performance with the resulting similarity measures.

In order to determine a good estimate of the accuracy of the inductive classification, reducing the variance due to the composition of a specific training/test sets during the various runs, the experiments have been replicated selecting training and test sets according to the standard *.632+ bootstrap* procedure (Hastie, Tibshirani & Friedman, 2001). This procedure requires creating random sets of training examples a repeated sampling (with replacement) from the population of examples; this produces sets which approximatively

amount[11] to 63.2% of the total set of examples, while the complement sets are used as repsective tests sets. The resulting accuracy, which may give a too optimistic estimate of the real performance, is adjusted to take into account both the training and the test errors properly weighted.

In order to allow a comparison of the outcomes to those observed in previous experiments with different learning models, e.g. (d'Amato, Fanizzi & Esposito, 2008), (Fanizzi, d'Amato & Esposito, 2008d), we adopted the same evaluation indices which are briefly recalled here:

- *Match rate*: rate of individuals that were classified with the same value ($v \in V$) by both the inductive and the deductive classifier;
- *Omission error rate*: rate of individuals for which the inductive method could not determine whether they were relevant to the query or not while they were actually relevant according to the reasoner (0 vs. ± 1);
- *Commission error rate*: rate of individuals that were classified as belonging to the query concept, while they belong to its negation or vice-versa ($+1$ vs. -1 or -1 vs. $+1$);
- *Induction rate*: rate of individuals inductively classified as belonging to the query

concept or to its negation, while either case is not logically derivable from the knowledge base (± 1 vs. 0);

In the following, we report the outcomes of some of the many experimental sessions carried out varying the choice of weights for the similarity measure and the parameters of the RCE classification procedure. While the weights depend on the different rationales presented in §3 (entropy, variance), the choice of the RCE parameters is meant to show that they may influence the method towards drawing more skeptical or credulous inductive conclusions.

4.2 Results: Similarity Measure with Entropy-Based Weights

We report the outcomes of three sample sessions in which the similarity measure was based on feature weights depending on their entropy (see §3).

4.2.1 First Session

Table 2 reports the outcomes in terms of the indices in an experimentation where the uncertainty threshold was set to 0.3 and $\varepsilon = .01$, which corresponds to a propensity for credulous classification.

Preliminarily, it is important to note that, in each experiment, the commission error was quite low. This means that the inductive search procedure is quite accurate, namely it did not make critical mistakes attributing an individual to a concept that is disjoint with the right one. The most difficult ontologies in this respect are those that contain many disjointness axioms, thus making more unlikely to have individuals with an unknown classification. Also the omission error rate was generally quite low, yet more frequent than the previous type of error.

It is noticeable also the induction rate which is generally quite high since a low uncertainty threshold makes the inductive procedure more prone to give a positive/negative classification in case a query individual is located in more than one hypersphere labeled with different classes.

From the instance retrieval point of view, the cases of induction are interesting because they suggest new assertions which cannot be logically derived by using a deductive reasoner yet they might be used to complete a knowledge base

Table 2. Results of the first session with the entropy-based weights for the similarity measure: uncertainty threshold $\theta = .3$ and minimum ball radius $\varepsilon = .1$ (average values $\pm$ average standard deviations per query)

2*ontology	match	commission	omission	induction
	rate	rate	rate	rate
1*SWM	83.99 ± 01.06	00.00 ± 00.00	04.80 ± 00.47	11.21 ± 00.75
1*BioPax	85.43 ± 00.43	03.49 ± 00.23	05.32 ± 00.02	05.76 ± 00.25
1*LUBM	89.77 ± 00.26	00.00 ± 00.00	06.68 ± 00.21	03.55 ± 00.06
1*NTN	86.71 ± 00.32	00.08 ± 00.00	05.48 ± 00.21	07.73 ± 00.33
1*SWSD	98.12 ± 00.05	00.00 ± 00.00	01.30 ± 00.05	00.58 ± 00.00
1*Financial	90.26 ± 00.09	04.16 ± 00.05	02.57 ± 00.01	03.01 ± 00.05

(Baader, Ganter, Sertkaya & Sattle, 2007), e.g. after being validated by an ontology engineer. For each new candidate assertion, the estimated likelihood measure may be employed to assess its probability and hence decide on its inclusion in the KB.

4.2.2 Second Session

In another session the same experiment was repeated with a different threshold, namely $\theta = .7$ and $\varepsilon = .01$, which made the inductive classification much more *cautious*. The outcomes are reported in Table 3.

In this session, it is again worthwhile to note that commission errors occurred quite rarely during the various runs, yet the omission error rate is higher than in the previous session (although generally limited and less than 14%). This is due to the procedure becoming more cautious because of the choice of the thresholds: the evidence for a positive or negative classification was not enough to decide on uncertain cases that, with a lower threshold, were solved by the voting procedure. On the other hand, for the same reasons, the induction rate decreased as well as the match rate

(with some exceptions). Another difference is given by the increased variance in the results for all indices.

4.2.3 Third Session

In yet another session the experiment was repeated with thresholds $\theta = .5$ and $\varepsilon = .01$, as a tradeoff between the cautious and the credulous modes. The outcomes are reported in Table 4.

In this case the match and induction rates are better than in the previous sessions. while commission errors are again nearly absent, omission errors decrease w.r.t. the previous session. it is also worthwhile to note that the standard deviations again decrease w.r.t. the outcomes of the previous session.

4.3 Results: Similarity Measure with Variance-Based Weights

The experiments presented above have been replicated using a different choice for the weights of the similarity function, namely those that descend from the feature variance (see §3), i.e. their capacity of separating individuals belonging to disjoint

Table 3. Results of the second session with the entropy-based weights for the similarity measure: uncertainty threshold $\theta = .7$ and minimum ball radius $\varepsilon = .01$ (average values $\pm$ average standard deviations per query)

2*ontology	match	commission	omission	induction
	rate	rate	rate	rate
1*SWM	93.52 ± 00.58	00.00 ± 00.00	06.19 ± 00.59	00.29 ± 00.05
1*BioPax	81.42 ± 04.83	00.80 ± 00.18	13.00 ± 04.86	04.78 ± 00.35
1*LUBM	91.59 ± 00.24	00.00 ± 00.00	07.80 ± 00.23	00.62 ± 00.02
1*NTN	83.78 ± 01.51	00.00 ± 00.00	14.23 ± 02.31	01.99 ± 00.83
1*SWSD	98.29 ± 00.05	00.00 ± 00.00	01.71 ± 00.05	00.00 ± 00.00
1*Financial	82.65 ± 00.70	01.56 ± 00.10	13.72 ± 00.97	02.08 ± 00.27

Table 4. Results of the third session with the entropy-based weights for the similarity measure: uncertainty threshold $\theta = .5$ and minimum ball radius $\varepsilon = .01$ (average values $\pm$ average standard deviations per query)

2*ontology	match	commission	omission	induction
	rate	rate	rate	rate
1*SWM	94.24 ± 00.83	00.00 ± 00.00	05.26 ± 00.86	00.51 ± 00.24
1*BioPax	85.11 ± 00.95	01.36 ± 00.29	08.21 ± 00.90	05.31 ± 00.44
1*LUBM	97.49 ± 00.74	00.00 ± 00.00	02.47 ± 00.73	00.04 ± 00.02
1*NTN	86.85 ± 00.24	00.00 ± 00.00	06.57 ± 00.74	06.58 ± 00.63
1*SWSD	98.29 ± 00.05	00.00 ± 00.00	01.71 ± 00.05	00.00 ± 00.00
1*Financial	87.98 ± 01.84	03.18 ± 00.71	06.12 ± 02.72	02.72 ± 00.32

classes. The parameters of the networks have been set as in the previous sessions.

4.3.1 First Session

Table 5 reports the outcomes in terms of the indices in an experimentation where the uncertainty threshold was set to 0.3 and $\varepsilon = .01$, which corresponds to a propensity for credulous classification.

No particular difference was noted in this session except for some slight variation of the standard-deviation values which remain quite low, especially when compared to the outcomes of other inductive methods mentioned. Thus again the commission error was quite low: the method did not make critical mistakes attributing an in-

Table 5. Results of the first session with the variance-based weights for the similarity measure: uncertainty threshold $\theta = .3$ and minimum ball radius $\varepsilon = .1$ (average values $\pm$ average standard deviations per query)

2*ontology	match	commission	omission	induction
	rate	rate	rate	rate
1*SWM	83.70 ± 00.81	00.00 ± 00.00	04.57 ± 00.39	11.73 ± 00.42
1*BioPax	85.43 ± 00.43	03.49 ± 00.23	05.32 ± 00.02	05.76 ± 00.25
1*LUBM	89.77 ± 00.26	00.00 ± 00.00	06.68 ± 00.21	03.55 ± 00.06
1*NTN	86.71 ± 00.34	00.08 ± 00.00	05.47 ± 00.21	07.73 ± 00.33
1*SWSD	98.12 ± 00.05	00.00 ± 00.00	01.30 ± 00.05	00.58 ± 00.00
1*Financial	90.26 ± 00.09	04.16 ± 00.05	02.57 ± 00.01	03.01 ± 00.05

dividual to a concept that is disjoint with the right one.

4.3.2 Second Session

In this session the experiment was repeated with a different threshold (as in the parallel session commented above): $\theta = .7$ and $\varepsilon = .01$, which made the inductive classification much more *cautious*. The outcomes are reported in Table 6.

Also in this session, no particular improvement or decay was observed. The most relevant variation regards the average outcomes with the BioPax ontology, where a slight increment of the match rate balanced an analogous decrement of the omission error rate and they are also a little more stable.

As in the parallel session with the other similarity measure, commission errors seldom occurred, yet the omission error rate is higher than in the previous session. This is due to the procedure becoming more cautious because of the choice of the thresholds. For the same reasons, the induction rate decreased as well as (partially) the match rate.

4.3.3 Third Session

In the third parallel session the experiment was repeated with thresholds $\theta = .5$ and $\varepsilon = .01$, as a tradeoff between the cautious and the credulous modes. The outcomes are reported in Table 7.

Comparing these outcomes to those observed in the parallel session, a noticeable decay (some percentage points) of the match rate was observed in the experiments with the LUBM ontology with a consequent increase of the induction and omission error rates.

Comparing these outcomes to those of the previous sessions with the same feature weights, in this case the match and induction rates are improved. while commission errors are again nearly absent, omission errors decrease w.r.t. the previous session.

4.4 Summary

As a general consideration, comparing these outcomes to those reported in previous works on inductive classification with other related methods, the accuracy appears generally improved w.r.t. the k-NN procedure (d'Amato, Fanizzi &

Table 6. Results of the second session with the variance-based weights for the similarity measure: uncertainty threshold $\theta = .7$ and minimum ball radius $\varepsilon = .01$ (average values $\pm$ average standard deviations per query)

2*ontology	match	commission	omission	induction
	rate	rate	rate	rate
1*SWM	93.52 $\pm$ 00.58	00.00 $\pm$ 00.00	06.19 $\pm$ 00.59	00.29 $\pm$ 00.05
1*BioPax	82.27 $\pm$ 03.82	00.80 $\pm$ 00.18	12.30 $\pm$ 03.80	04.63 $\pm$ 00.36
1*LUBM	91.73 $\pm$ 00.24	00.00 $\pm$ 00.00	07.63 $\pm$ 00.23	00.54 $\pm$ 00.02
1*NTN	83.85 $\pm$ 01.54	00.00 $\pm$ 00.00	14.17 $\pm$ 02.28	01.98 $\pm$ 00.83
1*SWSD	98.29 $\pm$ 00.05	00.00 $\pm$ 00.00	01.71 $\pm$ 00.05	00.00 $\pm$ 00.00
1*Financial	82.67 $\pm$ 00.75	01.55 $\pm$ 00.12	13.71 $\pm$ 00.99	02.07 $\pm$ 00.29

Table 7. Results of the third session with the variance-based weights for the similarity measure: uncertainty threshold $\theta = .5$ and minimum ball radius $\varepsilon = .01$ (average values $\pm$ average standard deviations per query)

2*ontology	match	commission	omission	induction
	rate	rate	rate	rate
1*SWM	94.10 $\pm$ 01.07	00.00 $\pm$ 00.00	05.23 $\pm$ 01.10	00.67 $\pm$ 00.43
1*BioPax	85.55 $\pm$ 01.20	01.04 $\pm$ 00.14	08.17 $\pm$ 00.98	05.24 $\pm$ 00.28
1*LUBM	93.44 $\pm$ 00.65	00.00 $\pm$ 00.00	05.17 $\pm$ 00.85	01.39 $\pm$ 00.31
1*NTN	86.89 $\pm$ 00.39	00.00 $\pm$ 00.00	06.56 $\pm$ 00.72	06.54 $\pm$ 00.66
1*SWSD	98.29 $\pm$ 00.05	00.00 $\pm$ 00.00	01.71 $\pm$ 00.05	00.00 $\pm$ 00.00
1*Financial	88.09 $\pm$ 01.74	03.14 $\pm$ 00.72	06.05 $\pm$ 02.57	02.72 $\pm$ 00.32

Esposito, 2008), and at least comparable to the performance of the kernel methods (Fanizzi, d'Amato & Esposito, 2008d) in their versions upgraded to work with DL knowledge bases. The method based on RCE networks appears also more stable considering the lower variance observed. However it should be also pointed out that a different experimental design was adopted w.r.t. the 10-fold cross validation previously employed. As expected, when working with inductive methods, the most difficult cases are represented by the ontologies with few individuals or too many disjointness axioms.

Also the elapsed computation time was comparable with the other inductive methods even though, similarly to the kernel-based methods (Fanizzi, d'Amato & Esposito, 2008d), a less trivial training phase was required before classification, which is unnecessary in the lazy-learning methods, such as the nearest neighbor procedure, (unless ad hoc memory structures are maintained for storing the prototypes according to their similarity, to ease their retrieval during classification). It was beyond the scope of this work to compare the efficiency of the inductive

classification to instance checking as provided by a reasoner. Theoretically they can be comparable only when the ontology is represented with simple fragments of DL languages (Donini, Lenzerini, Nardi & Schaerf, 1994).

An advantage of this new method is that more parameters are available to be tweaked to get better results depending on the ontology at hand. Of course, these parameters may be also the subject of a preliminary learning session (e.g. through cross-validation). No dramatic difference was observed when adopting different choices of weights for the feature concepts that parameterize the similarity measures.

5 RELATED WORK

A key ingredient of the Semantic Web vision is the distribution of knowledge in several ontologies. Experiments and studies have shown that merging multiple ontologies (but also migration and evolution) may quickly lead to cases of inconsistency. Purely logical classification solutions may fall short when applied to real problems in terms of effectiveness and efficiency. Effectiveness may be compromised by the inherent incompleteness of DL reasoning due to the open-world semantics. Even more so, the likely modularity of the ontologies and the distribution of the resource repositories over a network of peers poses also a problem of possible incoherence of knowledge which has to be treated through specific methods (Serafini, Borgida & Tamilin, 2005). On the other hand the expressiveness of the ontology languages may be very demanding in terms of computational resources which may affect the scalability of the resulting applications.

These factors have triggered the investigation of alternative methods for approximated reasoning with semantic knowledge bases (Haase, van Harmelen, Huang, Stuckenschmidt & Halberstadt, 2005), (Tserendorj, Rudolph, Krötzsch & Hitzler, 2008). One may roughly separate the *deductive* methods from *inductive* ones.

Classical logic entailment is explosive as any formula is a consequence of a contradiction. The mainstream deductive approaches to tackle the problem are two-fold. One is concerned with *removing* inconsistencies, while the other just aims at *living* with them. In the former inconsistencies are to be diagnosed and then repaired (Parsia, Sirin & Kalyanpur, 2005), (Schlobach, Huang, Cornet & van Harmelen, 2007). Usually nonstandard reasoning services are required for debugging inconsistent terminologies. This applies especially when dealing with one ontology. The latter approach requires to simply avoid inconsistency applying non-standard reasoning (e.g. *paraconsistent* reasoning) to get meaningful answers. This approach is more suitable for an open Web setting where one would import ontologies from various sources, making it impossible or unfeasible to repair them due to the scale of the combined ontologies. Often, the approximated reasoning method requires a mapping onto a different representation (Hitzler & Vrandecic, 2005).

In (Huang, van Harmelen & ten Teije, 2005) the authors present a general framework, in which an answer is considered meaningful if it is supported by a selected consistent sub-ontology of the inconsistent ontology, while its negation is not supported. The method searches for increasingly large sub-theories of an inconsistent ontology until the selected sub-theory is large enough to provide an answer, yet not so large to become itself inconsistent. A (syntactic) *selection function* is used to determine which consistent subsets of an inconsistent ontology should be considered. Recently, also *semantic* selection functions have been proposed based on semantic relevance (Huang & van Harmelen, 2008). Further related methods aiming at the scalability of retrieval are discussed in (Wache, Groot & Stuckenschmidt, 2005), (Möller, Haarslev & Wessel, 2006).

The work presented in this paper is related to inductive approaches to the problem of reasoning efficiently and effectively with the individual resources of a knowledge base and specifically to classify them in terms of given query concepts. It is in the line of a number of methods that transpose simple or even more complex machine learning methods to work with spaces of instances described by means of expressive ontology languages instead of the classic attribute vector spaces.

One of these simple methods is certainly the *k-Nearest Neighbor* approach (d'Amato, Fanizzi & Esposito, 2008). Like the method presented in this paper, it requires a notion of similarity (or dissimilarity) among the instances in order to determine a hypersphere containing the set of the k closest prototype neighbors to the one to be classified and let them vote for the classification of the instance w.r.t. the query concept. This vote is also weighted by the similarity of the prototypes w.r.t. the instance to be classified.

Other related nonparametric methods (Duda, Hart & Stork, 2001; Hastie, Tibshirani & Friedman, 2001) such as *Parzen windows* could be employed. The RCE method is somehow an intermediate scheme as the windows are adjusted during training according to the nearest instance of a disjoint class. As such it can be ascribed to the *relaxation methods*. It is straightforward to see its relationship also to other methods nonparametric methods, such as the *Probabilistic Neural Networks*, where the output units sum the output of the pattern unit (the value of a nonlinear function, generally Gaussian functions are adopted).

More complex related statistical methods are based on the notion of kernel functions which ultimately measure the similarity between instances in a different feature space which is automatically (yet not explicitly) determined through statistical learning methods. The advantage is that instances can be easily separated in this new space thus allowing for effective classifications. Recently a number of kernel functions for individuals in DL knowledge bases have been proposed, relying on structural and purely logical features. An example of structural kernel functions of the former type can be found in (Fanizzi, d'Amato & Esposito, 2008c) for the $\mathcal{ALCN}$ logic, which are ultimately based on comparing approximations of *most specific concepts* (Baader, Calvanese, McGuinness, Nardi, Patel-Schneider, 2003) related to the input individuals. Other kernel functions have been proposed which exploit some logical features of the individuals elicited from the knowledge base (Bloehdorn & Sure, 2007). A very similar one w.r.t. the measures adopted in this work can be found in (Fanizzi, d'Amato & Esposito, 2008d).

6 CONCLUDING REMARKS

This paper explored the application of a novel similarity-based classification applied to knowledge bases represented in OWL. The similarity measure employed derives from the extended family of semantic pseudo-metrics based on feature committees (d'Amato, Fanizzi & Esposito, 2008): weights are based on the amount of information conveyed by each feature, on the grounds of an estimate of its entropy. The measures were integrated in a similarity-based classification

procedure that builds models of the search-space based on prototypical individuals. The resulting system was exploited for the task of approximate instance retrieval which can be efficient and effective even in the presence of incomplete (or noisy) information.

An extensive evaluation performed on various ontologies showed empirically the effectiveness of the method and also that, while the performance depends on the number (and distribution) of the available training instances, even working with limited training sets guarantees a good outcomes in terms of accuracy. Besides, the procedure appears also robust to noise since it seldom made critical mistakes.

The utility of alternative methods for individual classification are manifold. On one hand they can be more robust to noise than purely logical methods, and thus they can exploited in case the knowledge base contains some incoherence which would hinder deriving correct conclusions. On the other hand, instance-based methods are also very efficient compared to the complexity of purely logical approaches. One of the possible applications of inductive methods may regard the task of ontology population (Baader, Ganter, Sertkaya & Sattle, 2007) known as particularly burdensome for the knowledge engineer and experts. In particular, the presented method may even be exploited for completing ontologies with probabilistic assertions, allowing further more sophisticate approaches to dealing with uncertainty (Lukasiewicz, 2008).

Extensions of the similarity measures can be foreseen. Since they essentially depend on the choice of the features for the committee, two enhancements may be investigated: 1) constructing a limited number of discriminating feature concepts (Fanizzi, d'Amato & Esposito, 2007), (Fanizzi, d'Amato & Esposito, 2008b); 2) investigating different forms of feature weighting, e.g. based on the notion of *variance*. Such objectives can be accomplished by means of machine learning techniques, especially when ontologies with large sets of individuals are available. Namely, part of the entire data can be saved in order to learn optimal feature sets or a good choice for the weight vectors, in advance with respect to their usage.

As mentioned before, largely populated ontologies may also be exploited in a preliminary cross-validation phase in order to provide optimal values for the parameters of the algorithm also depending on the preferred classification mode (cautious or credulous). The method may also be optimized by reducing the set of instances used for the classification limiting them to the prototypical exemplars and exploiting *ad hoc* data structures for maintaining them so to facilitate their retrieval (Witten & Frank, 2005).

ACKNOWLEDGMENT

This work was partially supported by the DiPIS regional interest project. The authors are grateful to the editors and the anonymous reviewers for the invitation, the positive reception and for the advices that helped improve the final version of the paper.

REFERENCES

Baader, F., Calvanese, D., McGuinness, D., Nardi, D., & Patel-Schneider, P. (Eds.). (2003). *The Description Logic Handbook*. Cambridge, MA: Cambridge University Press.

Baader, F., Ganter, B., Sertkaya, B., & Sattler, U. (2007). Completing description logic knowledge bases using formal concept analysis. In M. Veloso, (eds.), *Proceedings of the 20th International Joint Conference on Artificial Intelligence, IJCAI07* (pp. 230--235).

Bloehdorn, S., & Sure, Y. (2007). Kernel methods for mining instance data in ontologies. In K. Aberer et al., (Eds.), *Proceedings of the 6th International Semantic Web Conference, ISWC2007*, (*LNCS* Vol. 4825, pp. 58--71). Berlin: Springer.

d'Amato, C., Fanizzi, N., & Esposito, F. (2008). Query answering and ontology population: An inductive approach. In S. Bechhofer, et al., (Eds.), *Proceedings of the 5th European Semantic Web Conference, ESWC2008* (LNCS 5021, pp. 288-302). Berlin: Springer.

Donini, F. M., Lenzerini, M., Nardi, F., & Schaerf, A. (1994). Deduction in concept languages: From subsumption to instance checking. *Journal of Logic and Compututation, 4*(4), 423–452. doi:10.1093/logcom/4.4.423

Duda, R. O., Hart, P. E., & Stork, D. G. (2001). *Pattern Classification* (2nd ed.). New York: Wiley.

Fanizzi, N., d'Amato, C., & Esposito, F. (2007). Induction of optimal semi-distances for individuals based on feature sets. In D. Calvanese, et al., (Eds.), *Working Notes of the 20th International Description Logics Workshop, DL2007* (Vol. 250, pp. 275-282). CEUR-WS.org.

Fanizzi, N., d'Amato, C., & Esposito, F. (2008a). DL-Foil: Concept learning in description logics. In F. Zelezný & N. Lavrac, (Eds.), *Proceedings of the 18th International Conference on Inductive Logic Programming, ILP2008*, (LNAI 5194, pp. 107-121). Berlin: Springer.

Fanizzi, N., d'Amato, C., & Esposito, F. (2008b). Evolutionary conceptual clustering based on induced pseudo-metrics. *International Journal on Semantic Web and Information Systems, 4*(3).

Fanizzi, N., d'Amato, C., & Esposito, F. (2008c). Learning with kernels in description logics. In F. Zelezný & N. Lavra, (Eds.), *Proceedings of the 18th International Conference on Inductive Logic Programming, ILP2008*, (LNAI Vol. 5194, pp. 210-225). Berlin: Springer.

Fanizzi, N., d'Amato, C., & Esposito, F. (2008d). Statistical learning for inductive query answering on OWL ontologies. In A. Sheth & et al., (Esd.), *Proceedings of the 7th International Semantic Web Conference, ISWC2008*, (LNCS 5318, pp. 195-212). Berlin: Springer.

Fanizzi, N., d'Amato, C., & Esposito, F. (2009). ReduCE: A reduced coulomb energy network method for approximate classification. In *Proceedings of the 6th European Semantic Web Conference, ESWC2009*, (LNCS 5554, pp. 320-334). Berlin: Springer.

Goldstone, R., Medin, D., & Halberstadt, J. (1997). Similarity in context. *Memory & Cognition, 25*(2), 237–255.

Haase, P., van Harmelen, F., Huang, Z., Stuckenschmidt, H., & Sure, Y. (2005, November). A framework for handling inconsistency in changing ontologies. In Y. Gil & et al., (Eds.), *Proceedings of the 4th International Semantic Web Conference, ISWC2005*, (LNCS Vol. 3279, pp. 353—367). Berlin: Springer.

Hastie, T., Tibshirani, R., & Friedman, J. (2001). *The Elements of Statistical Learning -- Data Mining, Inference, and Prediction.* Berlin: Springer.

Hitzler, P., & Vrandečić, D. (2005 November). Resolution-based approximate reasoning for OWL DL. In Y. Gil and et al., (Eds.), *Proceedings of the 4th International Semantic Web Conference, ISWC2005*, (LNCS Vol. 3279, pp. 383—397). Berlin: Springer.

Huang, Z., & van Harmelen, F. (2008). Using semantic distances for reasoning with inconsistent ontologies. In A. Sheth, et al., (Eds.), *Proceedings of the 7th International Semantic Web Conference, ISWC2008*, (LNCS Vol. 5318, pp.178—194). Berlin: Springer.

Huang, Z., van Harmelen, F., & ten Teije, A. (2005). Reasoning with inconsistent ontologies. In L. Kaelbling & A. Saffiotti, (eds.), *Proceedings of the 19th International Joint Conference on Artificial Intelligence, IJCAI05*, (pp. 454—459).

Lukasiewicz, T. (2008). Expressive probabilistic description logics. *Artificial Intelligence, 172*(6-7), 852–883. doi:10.1016/j.artint.2007.10.017

Möller, R., Haarslev, V., & Wessel, M. (2006). On the scalability of description logic instance retrieval. In B. Parsia, U. Sattler, & D. Toman, (Esd.), *Proceedings of the 2006 International Workshop on Description Logics, DL2006*, (Vol. 189: *CEUR Workshop Proceedings*).

Parsia, B., Sirin, E., & Kalyanpur, A. (2005). Debugging OWL ontologies. In *Proceedings of the 14th International World Wide Web Conference*.

Rettinger, A., Nickles, M., & Tresp, V. (2009). Statistical relational learning with formal ontologies. In W. Buntine, M. Grobelnik, D. Mladenic, & J. Shawe-Taylor, (Eds.), *Proceedings of the European Conference on Machine Learning and Knowledge Discovery in Databases, ECML-PKDD2009*, (LNAI 5782, pp. 286-301). Berlin: Springer.

Rudolph, S., Tserendorj, T., & Hitzler, P. (2008). What is approximate reasoning? In D. Calvanese and G. Lausen, (Eds.), *Proceedings of the 2nd International Conference on Web Reasoning and Rule Systems, RR2008*, (LNCS 5341, pp. 150-164). Berlin: Springer.

Schlobach, S., Huang, Z., Cornet, R., & van Harmelen, F. (2007). Debugging incoherent terminologies. *Journal of Automated Reasoning, 39*(3), 317–349. doi:10.1007/s10817-007-9076-z

Serafini, L., Borgida, A., & Tamilin, A. (2005). Aspects of distributed and modular description logics. In *Proceedings of the 18th International Joint Conference on Artificial Intelligence, IJCAI05*, (pp. 370-375).

Tserendorj, T., Rudolph, S., Krötzsch, M., & Hitzler, P. (2008). Approximate OWL-reasoning with Screech. In D. Calvanese & G. Lausen, (Eds.), *Proceedings of the 2nd International Conference on Web Reasoning and Rule Systems, RR2008*, (LNCS Vol. 5341). Berlin: Springer.

Wache, H., Groot, P., & Stuckenschmidt, H. (2005). Scalable instance retrieval for the semantic web by approximation. In M. Dean, et al, (eds.), *Proceedings of the WISE 2005 International Workshops*, (LNCS 3807, pp. 245-254). Berlin: Springer.

Witten, I. H., & Frank, E. (2005). *Data Mining* (2nd ed.). San Francisco: Morgan Kaufmann.

ENDNOTES

[1]   This does not mean total absence of parameters but rather refers to statistics --- similarity measures, rankings, etc. --- whose interpretation does not depend on the population fitting any parametrized distributions (Duda, Hart & Stork, 2010), (Hastie, Tibshirani & Friedman, 2001).

[2]   This turns out to be handy for performing basic operations which may be crucial in statistical methods, such as counting. However for our purpose we may as well disregard this aspect: as we will see, the measures employed may well identify individuals with different names when they share a similar behavior for the important features in a given context.

[3]   Its name descends from electrostatics, where energy is associated with charged particles (Duda, Hart & Stork, 2010).

[4]   It may be derived from a distance or dissimilarity measure by means of simple transformations, as shown later.

[5]   http://protege.stanford.edu/plugins/owl/owl-library

[6]   https://www.uni-koblenz.de/FB4/Institutes/IFI/AGStaab/Projects/xmedia/dl-tree.htm

[7]   http://swat.cse.lehigh.edu/projects/lubm

[8]   http://www.biopax.org/Downloads/Level1v1.4/biopax-example-ecocyc-glycolysis.owl

[9]   http://www.cs.put.poznan.pl/alawrynowicz/financial.owl

[10]   Pellet v. 2.0.0rc3 was employed.

[11]   The probability for an instance to be included in the training set in at least one of N random samples is

$$P(a \in TrSet) = 1 - (1 - \frac{1}{N})^N \approx 1 - e^{-1} \approx .632$$

This work was previously published in International Journal on Semantic Web and Information Systems, Volume 5, Issue 4, edited by Amit P. Sheth, pp. 19-38, copyright 2009 by IGI Publishing (an imprint of IGI Global).

Chapter 14
A Comparison of Corpus-Based and Structural Methods on Approximation of Semantic Relatedness in Ontologies

Tuukka Ruotsalo
Aalto University, Finland

Eetu Mäkelä
Aalto University, Finland

ABSTRACT

In this paper, the authors compare the performance of corpus-based and structural approaches to determine semantic relatedness in ontologies. A large light-weight ontology and a news corpus are used as materials. The results show that structural measures proposed by Wu and Palmer, and Leacock and Chodorow have superior performance when cut-off values are used. The corpus-based method Latent Semantic Analysis is found more accurate on specific rank levels. In further investigation, the approximation of structural measures and Latent Semantic Analysis show a low level of overlap and the methods are found to approximate different types of relations. The results suggest that a combination of corpus-based methods and structural methods should be used and appropriate cut-off values should be selected according to the intended use case.

INTRODUCTION

Ontologies are the backbone of Semantic Web information systems. They are designed to provide a shared understanding of a domain and support knowledge sharing and reuse (Fensel,

2004). Recently, attention has been devoted to using ontologies to improve the performance of information retrieval (Castells et al., 2007) and extraction systems (Ruotsalo et al., 2009), and to support tasks such as query expansion (Kekäläinen & Järvelin, 2000), knowledge-based recommendation (Ruotsalo & Hyvönen, 2007), word sense

DOI: 10.4018/978-1-60960-593-3.ch014

disambiguation (Ide & Véronis, 1998), and text summarization (Lin & Hovy, 2000).

The ontologies used by such systems are often light-weight general purpose concept ontologies that provide conceptualizations suitable to be used in many domains and applications, but without a manual effort they can not be expected to explicate all the relations required in specific sub-domains (Chandrasekaran et al., 1999). For example, a user searching for objects annotated with the concept *flu* on a health portal could be offered articles indexed with the concepts *respiratory infection* or *pneumonia*. On the other hand, the user could be interested in news related an ongoing flu epidemic with related content indexed with concepts such as *vaccinations*, *nutrition* or *medication*.

Avoiding manually tailoring the ontologies, but still enabling such functionalities can be enabled through augmenting relations by estimating relatedness of concepts. Estimates of semantic relatedness can be obtained by making use of structural measures that approximate the relatedness based on the structure of the ontology (Budanitsky & Hirst, 2006). On the other hand, the mentioned applications deal with unannotated corpora that can be used as a source for learning the relations (Landauer et al., 1998; Blei et al., 2003).

While good results have been obtained using both of the approaches (Landauer et al., 1998; Budanitsky & Hirst, 2006), a comprehensive empirical comparison of the approaches has not been reported. To address this, we compare the performance of a widely used corpus-based method, Latent Semantic Analysis (Landauer et al., 1998), and two well-known ontological structural measures, a conceptual measure proposed by Wu & Palmer (1994), and a path-length measure by Leacock & Chodorow (1998).

We report results of a large user study comparing these approaches in semantic relatedness approximation. The focus of the study is to (1) determine the accuracy of the methods, (2) determine the difference between corpus-based methods and structural measures, and (3) identify

the strengths and weaknesses of the methods in potential application scenarios.

We show that good accuracy can be achieved using both types of methods, but the methods provide clearly distinct approximations. The results suggest that the approaches are complementary. Structural measures alone can be adequate in scenarios such as information extraction, where synonymy and hyponymy relations suffice (Califf & Mooney, 1999). The combination of methods could be beneficial in scenarios such as information retrieval or word sense disambiguation, where an extensive word context is found to be important (Kekäläinen & Järvelin, 2000; Sussna, 1993). In addition, the results suggest that the performance of the methods are dependent on the correct combination of the methods and assignment of appropriate cut-off values to ensure optimal performance.

The rest of this paper is structured as follows. The following section introduces the semantic relatedness approximation methods used. Section 3 describes the empirical study. The results of the study are presented in section 4. Finally, we conclude with a summary of results, a discussion of shortcomings, and suggestions for future work.

Semantic Relatedness Approximation

In essence, semantic relatedness answers the question: "How much does the meaning of a concept A have to do with the meaning of a concept B?". According to Budanitsky & Hirst (2006) semantic relatedness, or its inverse semantic distance, is a more general concept than similarity. For example, the concepts *bank* and *trust company* are similar, but dissimilar entities may also be semantically related by some other relationship such as associative (*student−school*) or meronymy (*car−engine*).

In this study, approximating semantic relatedness between concepts is defined as determining a relation $r(c, c', w)$ between two concepts c and

c' in an ontology. Each relation has a rank $w \in [0,1]$, that indicates the semantic relatedness of the concepts. The rank having a value 1 indicates a strong semantic relatedness and the rank having a value 0 indicates no semantic relatedness. To approximate the rank of the concept pairs, we use two measures that are based on distances of concepts in subsumption hierarchies of lightweight ontologies (Leacock & Chodorow, 1998; Wu & Palmer, 1994). In addition, we use Latent Semantic Analysis (LSA) (Landauer et al., 1998) to approximate the relations based on a text corpus. The methods are referred as $rel_{LC}(c,c')$, $rel_{WP}(c,c')$, and $rel_{LSA}(c,c')$ respectively.

Leacock-Chodorow Path-Length Measure

Subsumption hierarchies are the backbone of ontologies. For this reason, several measures that use this structure as a source for measuring semantic relatedness have been developed. A simple way to compute semantic relatedness in a subsumption hierarchy is to view it as a graph and identify relatedness with path length between the concepts.

The Leacock & Chodorow (1998) measure is a structural relatedness measure based on path lengths. It is a function of the length of the shortest path in a hierarchy. Formally, for concepts c and c' it is defined as

$$rel_{LC}(c,c') = -log \frac{l(c,c')}{2 \times maxdepth(C)},$$

where $l(c,c')$ is a function that returns the smallest number of nodes in the path connecting c and c' (including c and c' themselves) and $maxdepth(C)$ is a function that returns the maximum depth in nodes of all the subsumption hierarchies in the ontology.

Wu-Palmer Conceptual Measure

Despite their simplicity, an acknowledged problem with the path-length measures is that they typically rely on the notion that links in the taxonomy or subsumption hierarchy represent uniform distances (Budanitsky & Hirst, 2006). However, some sub-taxonomies (e.g., biological categories) are often much denser than others, and therefore path length measures tend to give less accurate results.

The Wu & Palmer (1994) measure is a conceptual relatedness measure between a pair of concepts in a hierarchy. It takes into account the fact that two classes near the root of a hierarchy are close to each other in terms of path length but can be very different conceptually, while two classes deeper in the hierarchy can be separated by a larger number of nodes and can still be closer conceptually. Formally, Wu-Palmer measure for concepts c and c' is:

$$rel_{WP} = \frac{2 \times l(lcs(c,c'),r)}{l(c,lcs(c,c')) + l(c',lcs(c,c')) + 2 \times l(lcs(c,c'),r)}$$

where $l(c,c')$ is a function that returns the smallest number of nodes on the path connecting c and c' (including c and c' themselves), $lcs(c,c')$ is a function that returns the lowest common superconcept of concepts c and c', and r is the root concept of the ontology.

A Running Example

To illustrate the function of the structural measures we use an example ontology depicted in Figure 1. The example ontology consists of an subsumption hierarchy of concepts for an air vehicle domain. Computing semantic relatedness between the concepts *seaplanes* and *sailplanes* in this ontology using the Leacock-Chodorow measure results in an equal relatedness rank as for the concepts

Figure 1. An example ontology

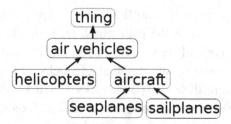

helicopters and *aircraft*, because they are both sister concepts:

$$rel_{LC}(seaplanes, sailplanes) = -log\frac{3}{2 \times 4} \approx 0.43$$

$$rel_{LC}(helicopters, aircraft) = -log\frac{3}{2 \times 4} \approx 0.43$$

The semantic relatedness for the concepts *helicopters* and *seaplanes* using the Leacock-Chodorow measure is smaller because they are further from each other in the ontology:

$$rel_{LC}(helicopters, seaplanes) = -log\frac{4}{2 \times 4} \approx 0.30$$

Comparing these results to those given by the Wu-Palmer measure shows how it considers the depth that the concepts are placed in the hierarchy.

The Wu-Palmer measure for the concepts *seaplanes* and *sailplanes* is

$$rel_{WP}(seaplanes, sailplanes) = \frac{2 \times 3}{2 + 2 + 2 \times 3} = 0.60,$$

while for the concepts *aircraft* and *helicopters* it returns

$$rel_{WP}(aircraft, helicopters) = \frac{2 \times 2}{2 + 2 + 2 \times 2} = 0.50$$

This is because the concepts aircraft and helicopters are closer to the root concept than the concepts seaplanes and sailplanes.

Latent Semantic Analysis

Statistical methods, like Latent Semantic Analysis (LSA) (Landauer et al., 1998), extract and represent the contextual meaning of terms by applying statistical computations to a large corpus of unstructured text.

LSA operates on a vector space model, where a term-document matrix describes the occurrences of terms in documents. The rows of this matrix correspond to terms and the columns correspond to documents. If a term occurs in the document, its term weight in the document vector is a non-zero value given by a weighting scheme. We use tf-idf (Salton & Buckley, 1988) weighting, where rare terms are up-weighted to reflect their relative importance.

Transposing the term-document matrix results in a matrix where each term is associated with a vector of documents containing the occurrence contexts for that term. These vectors provide co-occurrence information that can be used to determine the conceptual distance between terms and sets of terms.

The document vectors could be used directly to determine relatedness of the terms, for example, using a cosine distance (Manning et al., 2008). However, the problem with such direct estimation is that the matrix can be sparse and result in poor estimation (Manning et al., 2008). LSA is a way of reducing this problem by finding latent semantic relations between the terms. LSA reduces the term space by calculating a lower-rank approximation of the document-term matrix. This is done in a way that minimizes the squared error for each number of reduced dimensions.

Consider an example of two terms: *money* and *deposit*. If due to sparseness, they do not appear in the same documents, a direct distance measure does not find a relation between them. However, if the documents in which these terms do appear are similar with respect to other terms (e.g. *bank*, *loan*), the lower rank approximation may combine the documents in latent document space. Measuring relatedness in this latent document space now relates the original terms *bank* and *deposit*.

Formally, LSA can be defined as follows. Let X be a $d \times t$ document-term matrix that describes the documents and the occurrences of each term in these documents. The singular value decomposition (SVD) of X is defined as

$$X = U\Sigma V^T,$$

such that U and V^T are orthogonal matrices and Σ is a diagonal matrix.

SVD makes it possible to translate the matrices to a lower dimensional space with optimal fitting. First, a cut-off value k is set. Then, the first k largest values in Σ are kept and the rest set to zero. Now, composing the matrices by matrix product results in a matrix $\hat{X}$ which approximates the original document-term matrix X in a lower dimensional space (Landauer et al., 1998). For details of the computation, we encourage the readers to see examples by Manning et al. (2008) or Landauer et al. (1998).

The matrix $\hat{X}$ can then be used to calculate relatedness between two terms. We used the cosine measure, where the dot product between two vectors of $\hat{X}$ reflects the extent to which two terms have a similar occurrence pattern in the vector space. Formally,

$$rel_{LSA}(c,c') = \frac{\hat{t}_c \cdot \hat{t}_{c'}}{|\hat{t}_c| \, |\hat{t}_{c'}|}$$

where c and c' are concepts and $\hat{t}_c$ and $\hat{t}_{c'}$ the corresponding latent concept space vectors. In our study, the terms appearing in the documents were not directly used in the original term-document matrix. Instead, we mapped each term to a concept in the ontology that contained an equivalent label. This concept-document matrix was then used in the computation.

Comparison of Methods in Semantic Relatedness Approximation

Two proper approaches to evaluate methods that approximate semantic relatedness exist (Budanitsky & Hirst, 2006). In case the intended end-use application is known, an option is to evaluate the performance of the methods as a part of that particular application.

In this study however, we are interested of the performance of the methods in a general setting, where a particular end-use application is not known. In such a setting, comparing the ranks given by the methods to gold standard ranks assessed by humans acquired from a large user study is the best way to evaluate the performance of the methods.

Next we will discuss the data, data pre-processing methods, sampling and evaluation methods, and describe the experimental setup used in our user study.

Data

Two kinds of data was used for this study: a lightweight ontology and a text corpus.

The general Finnish ontology (YSO)[1] (Hyvönen et al., 2008) is a lightweight ontology based on the general Finnish keyword thesaurus YSA[2]. The transformation of YSA to YSO was done with care by hand with the following procedure to ensure the coherence of the subsumption hierarchies.

First, an upper ontology was created for the ontology. The upper ontology of the YSO is based on the DOLCE ontology, where enduring, perduring and abstract concepts are separated (Gangemi et al., 2002). Second, the ambiguity of broader-term relations was solved. The subsumption relations were specified based on the original broader term relations. For example, the concept *graduate schools* had a broader term *universities*. However, because graduate schools are not a kind of universities, the concept *graduate schools* was placed in its correct place in the hierarchy, under *educational institutions*. Third, the meaning of polysemous and homonymous concepts were specified and, if required, a new concept for a specific sense of a term was created. Finally, the concepts were organized as subsumption hierarchies under the upper ontology. In this process, more than 1000 concepts and 6000 relations were added into the ontology. After transformation, YSO contains some 26,000 concepts and some 24,000 subsumption relations. In this study we used the version of YSO published in 2007.

The corpus used by the LSA consists of 883 randomly selected articles from the Finnish news paper "Helsingin Sanomat" from the year 2007. The articles are all written in Finnish. For this study we used both the text in the headings and in the body of the articles. The corpus was selected because it contains news articles, reviews and columns and is therefore relatively domain-neutral or at least represents a general news domain.

Data Pre-Processing and Implementation

The corpus contained many other terms than the ones found in the ontology, such as names of individual persons. For this study, we only used terms for which a corresponding label could be found in the ontology.

A particular concept may have several labels. For example in the ontology used in this study, the concept *academic education* has a term space that contains multiple term correspondences for the concept, such as "academic education", "higher education", "higher level education" and "university education". Therefore, occurrence of any of these terms was used to indicate an occurrence of the concept.

Finnish is a morphologically rich and complex language. Therefore, the terms in the corpus and in the term-space of the ontology were lemmatised with the Omorfi lemmatiser [3].

LSA is based on dimensionality reduction as explained in the previous section. The term-document matrix is decomposed using SVD and then reconstructed with a lower number of target dimensions. An initial test was performed to find the optimal number of target dimensions k for the matrix Σ. The LSA was run in a way that k was iterated from one to a natural cut-off point, the total number of documents in the document collection. The LSA showed an optimal performance with regards to the gold standard when the number of target dimensions was set between 120 and 150. For the actual study, LSA was then run with 150 target dimensions.

The ranks returned by the methods were normalized. LSA and Wu-Palmer measure return semantic relatedness as a real number between 0 and 1. The rank given by Leacock-Chodorow measure was normalized to have the same scale.

LSA was implemented using MTJ, a Java-based matrix calculation API[4], and the structural measures using the Java-based Semantic Web framework Jena [5].

Sampling

A gold standard requires a sample of concept pairs that enable non-biased performance evaluation for all compared methods. The sample should (1) treat all methods equally and (2) retain the distribution of concept pairs.

Two possible sources of bias were identified. First, an information source bias that is caused by the unavoidable fact that the structural and the corpus-based methods use different datasets. The terms can appear in the corpus, but not in the ontology and vice versa. Second, a sampling bias that is caused by the unequal proportion of the concept pairs between the compared methods.

We minimized the possibility of information source bias by restricting the sampling to the terms that were mentioned in the intersection of the terms in the corpus and the terms in the term space of the ontology. After this, the possible number of concept pairs was found to be 4477528. A random sample from such a population would lead to too large sample to be used in a user study. Therefore, stratified sampling was used.

Stratified sampling minimizes the possibility of sampling bias. It groups members of the population into subgroups and the actual sampling is performed from each subgroup. We grouped concept pairs based on two criteria: the method and the rank given by the method for a concept pair. The rank for concept pairs is given on an interval. Therefore we divided the interval into ten bins, the first with values between 0.0 and 0.1, the second with values between 0.1 and 0.2 and so on. This ensures that each method had a representative amount of concept pairs from each rank level.

The obvious choice to sample from these subgroups would be a proportionate stratification, where the sample size of each stratum is proportionate to the population size of the stratum. However, the number of concept pairs that are rated close to non-related is much larger than the number of concept pairs rated closely related. In addition, different methods give different ranks for individual concept pairs. Therefore, we decided to apply disproportionate stratification.

A fixed size sample of 200 random concepts was sampled from each bin. For example, in the case of LSA we first run the method and then sampled 200 concept pairs from the relatedness measure interval between 0.0 and 0.1 given by the method, 200 pairs from the relatedness measure

interval between 0.1 and 0.2 and so on. This was repeated for each bin for each method.

It has been shown in previous studies of Rubenstein and Goodenough (1965) and Miller and Charles (1991) that subjects tend to use the dominant sense of the word when assigning relevance judgements for concept pairs. Therefore, we removed concept pairs that contained a polysemous concept to avoid the bias caused by humans using an inappropriate sense in the user study. This resulted in a sample of 3168 concept pairs that have a maximally equal representation for each method on each bin.

This full sample was used in the main study. Our first research goal was to investigate how results given by the three methods differ. Such differences can be obtained by comparing the concept pairs determined by different methods on different relatedness levels. We sampled subsets of the full sample by first ranking the concept pairs based on the rank assigned by each individual method. For each method we sampled 100, 200, 400, 800 and 1600 top-ranked concept pairs from the full sample of 3168 concept pairs. This sampling principle is known as sampling based on cutoff value (CV).

Measuring the performance of the methods based on the full sample directly would suffer from bias caused by stratified sampling because the full sample does not retrain original proportions of the stratums. For example, the equal sampling from stratums would cause underestimating the error where a method makes mistakes in lower relatedness levels and the proportion of such concept pairs would be dominant in a random sample. Therefore, we used post-stratification where scaling factors, based on the proportions of the stratums in the original data were assigned for each bin.

We also collected a smaller sample to measure inter-annotator agreement. This small sample was created by sampling 10 concepts from each stratum of 200 concepts. The samples are further refereed as full, full with cutoff, scaled full and small sample.

Experimental Setup

Human ranks of 15 participants were collected for all together 3168 concept pairs. The participants were students and faculty in the Department of Media Technology at the Helsinki University of Technology. The participants were explicitly asked to judge concept pairs as related in case of any relation and not only inclusive or subsumption relation. Each of the concept pairs was judged on a binary scale (related / non-related). We collected four individual opinions for each concept pair. The relatedness value for a concept pair was set as an average of these ranks (0, 0.25, 0.5, 0.75 or 1). This captured the fact that the relatedness of some of the concept pairs were more vague among the annotators.

Evaluation Methods

According to our research questions, we measured two things: (1) the accuracy of the methods in semantic relatedness approximation, and (2) the difference between corpus-based methods and structural measures.

Because the methods were measured against a gold standard collected from multiple annotators, we first ensured the concordance of the annotators. We used Cohen's Kappa (Cohen, 1960) as a measure for inter-annotator agreement. Kappa measures concordance between classifiers or annotators using nominal data, varying between -1.0 and 1.0. Cohen's Kappa was run for the concept pairs in the small sample that were annotated by all of the participants. The Kappa measure showed a substantial agreement between the users (Kappa = 0.68).

The accuracy of methods in semantic relatedness approximation was measured using generalized precision and generalized recall originally proposed by Kekäläinen and Järvelin (2002).

These measures take into account the fact that the distance between human rank and the rank given by the method are not on a binary scale, but are measured on an interval. Ehrig and Euzenat (2005) have defined the measure in the scope of ontology matching, where the generalized precision and recall are calculated based on an overlap function between a gold standard and the result given by a method. Generalized precision gP and generalized recall gR are defined as follows:

$$gP(A, G) = \frac{overlap(A, G)}{|A|},$$

$$gR(A, G) = \frac{overlap(A, G)}{|G|},$$

where G is the set of concept pairs in the gold standard and A is the set of concept pairs given by the method.

The overlap function returns the value 1 if the score in the gold standard and the score given by the method are the same (Ehrig & Euzenat, 2005). The overlap function can now be defined as the difference between the score given by the gold standard $G(c, c')$ and the score given by the method $A(c, c')$ for each concept pair: $1 - |G(c, c') - A(c, c')|$. Intuitively, the generalized precision measures the proportion of error between the gold standard and the method with respect to the number of concept pairs retrieved, and the generalized recall measures the proportion of error between the gold standard and the method with respect to all concept pairs in the gold standard. If all and only all of the concept pairs are retrieved, the generalized precision and generalized recall becomes equal and can be called generalized accuracy gA. Generalized precision, recall and accuracy were determined on the scaled full sample.

It is also interesting if the methods not only perform differently in terms of accuracy, but actually approximate different kinds of relations. We solicited the difference in the kind of relations that the methods approximate by using Jaccard (1901) coefficient. The Jaccard coefficient measures similarity between sample sets, and is defined as the size of the intersection divided by the size of the union of the concept sets returned by the methods:

$$J(C, C') = \frac{C \cap C'}{C \cup C'},$$

where C and C' are sets of concepts returned by the methods compared.

Real life use cases often aim at finding the best relations and using those in the application. The sets of these relations are based on cut-off values. Thus, Jaccard coefficient was determined on the full sample with cutoff. In addition, we sampled examples from the intersection of the compared sets. These examples were used in a qualitative comparison to find the kind of relations that the methods rank with a certain rank, but are only found by either one of the compared methods.

Because the samples are not normally distributed, which was also checked with the normality test of Shapiro and Wilk (1965), the statistical significance of the results were ensured by using the Friedman test (Conover, 1998; Hull, 1993). Friedman test is a non-parametric test based on ranks and is suitable for comparing more than two related samples. The statistical significance between method pairs was then ensured using a paired Wilcoxon Signed-Rank test (Wilcoxon, 1945) with Bonferonni correction as a post-hoc test. All of the results reported in the next section are statistically significant (p<0.000001).

Results

This section presents the results of the experiments. First, we discuss the performance of the methods in semantic relatedness approximation. Further, we compare the differences of the results given by the different methods.

Performance of the Methods

The generalized precision-recall curves of all three methods are shown in Figure 2. The Figure shows that when all concept pairs of the full sample are analyzed LSA performs best (Accuracy 0.84), Wu-Palmer second best (Accuracy 0.74) and Leacock-Chodorow third (Accuracy 0.53). It is notable that the generalized precision of the methods increases when the recall increases. This is due to the fact that we use generalized precision and generalized recall. The performance improvement indicates that the methods are fractionally better in approximating non-related concepts than approximating related concepts. In other words, the measures give better approximation for the concepts that have a human rank 0 in the gold

Figure 2. Generalized precision of the methods on 10 generalized recall levels

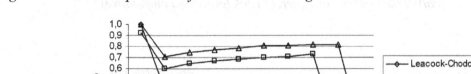
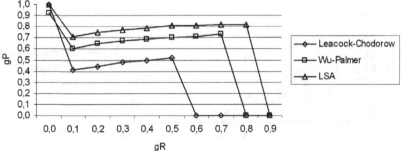

standard, than for the concepts that have rank other than 0 in the gold standard.

Figure 4 shows generalized recall and Figure 3 generalized precision for each of the methods on different ranks given by the methods. These indicate in which rank levels the different methods perform accurately and on which levels they fail. Generalized precision and generalized recall are computed for each bin separately. The figures show that LSA has high performance on rank levels 0.0 to 0.1 on both generalized precision and generalized recall. However, the generalized recall rapidly decreases already on rank level 0.2. This means that LSA is very accurate in approximating non-related concept pairs and therefore shows good overall performance, as the gold standard judges most concept pairs in the original data as non-related.

Table 1 shows the distribution, generalized precision and generalized recall of the relations found by the methods on different rank levels. The structural measures are as accurate or more accurate than LSA on rank levels above 0.2, but their ability to filter out less related concept pairs is weaker. Wu-Palmer measure gives relatively high generalized precision on all rank levels, while Leacock-Chodorow seems to sacrifice precision for recall. LSA approximates most of the concepts to have a rank between 0.0 and 0.1, while for the other methods the distribution is more even. While the structural measures overall perform less accurate than LSA, they perform better in situations where only the relations ranked above a rank 0.2 by the methods are measured. Such cases are typical when cut-off values are used to filter only the top ranked relations to be used in real life applications. Therefore we also run the experiments with seven cut-off values from 0.3 to 0.9.

Table 2 shows the generalized precision and generalized recall of each of the methods on the

Figure 3. Generalized precision of the methods on different rank levels (not cumulative)

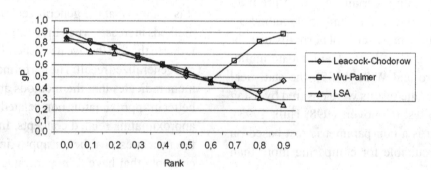

Figure 4. Generalized recall of the methods on different rank levels (not cumulative)

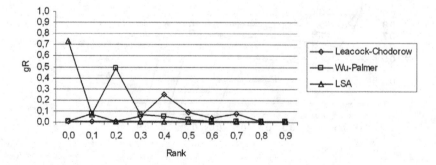

Table 1. Number of relations found (thousands) N(K), generalized precision (gP) and generalized recall (gR) for the compared methods on different rank levels. The values within a bin are absolute (not cumulative) and values smaller than 0.01 are rounded to 0.01.

Method	LSA			WP			LC		
Rank	N(K)	gP	gR	N(K)	gP	gR	N(K)	gP	gR
0.9 - 1.0	4.3	0.25	0.01	0.03	0.89	0.01	124.9	0.46	0.04
0.8 - 0.9	1.5	0.31	0.01	1.1	0.82	0.01	138.6	0.37	0.04
0.7 - 0.8	2.2	0.44	0.01	5.6	0.64	0.01	834.8	0.42	0.28
0.6 - 0.7	3.9	0.45	0.01	49.3	0.47	0.01	423.4	0.46	0.15
0.5 - 0.6	6.2	0.56	0.01	194.7	0.53	0.02	768.1	0.51	0.19
0.4 - 0.5	12.7	0.61	0.01	383.1	0.61	0.05	1857.1	0.60	0.31
0.3 - 0.4	31.1	0.66	0.01	444.1	0.68	0.07	326.5	0.67	0.11
0.2 - 0.3	101.3	0.71	0.01	2941.7	0.76	0.49	4.0	0.76	0.01
0.1 - 0.2	436.2	0.72	0.01	450.8	0.81	0.08	0.01	0.78	0.01
0.0 - 0.1	3878.0	0.84	0.40	6.8	0.91	0.01	0.01	0.85	0.01
Total	4477.5	0.84	0.84	4477.5	0.74	0.74	4477.5	0.53	0.53

sets based on the cut-off values. The performance of the Wu-Palmer measure is superior in terms of precision. However, the Leacock-Chodorow measure also achieves good overall performance because of a good recall also on lower (0.3-0.5) cut-off values. LSA performs moderately in terms of precision, but has low recall. This suggests that structural measures with appropriate cut-off values give best performance.

The performance measures that have been used so far still do not reveal a possible differences in

the relations that the different methods are able to approximate. A rationale behind this phenomena was investigated by comparing the results of the Wu-Palmer, the structural method that achieved highest precision, and LSA on subsets of the top ranked relations. The relations returned by these methods were analyzed qualitatively and the overlap of the results of the methods was measured. The results of this comparison are discussed in the next section.

Table 2. Generalized precision (gP) and generalized recall (gR) for the compared methods on sets based on different cut-off levels

Method	LSA		WP		LC	
Cut-off	gP	gR	gP	gR	gP	gR
0.9	0.34	0.01	0.89	0.01	0.43	0.01
0.8	0.33	0.01	0.82	0.01	0.39	0.02
0.7	0.36	0.01	0.67	0.01	0.41	0.10
0.6	0.39	0.01	0.50	0.01	0.42	0.15
0.5	0.44	0.01	0.53	0.03	0.45	0.23
0.4	0.51	0.01	0.58	0.08	0.52	0.48
0.3	0.59	0.01	0.62	0.15	0.53	0.53

Table 3. Jaccard similarity coefficient for pairs of methods. Methods are compared pairwise on different CV points given by each method.

CV method pair	100	200	400	800	1600
LC / LSA	0	0.02	0.04	0.07	0.43
WP / LSA	0.08	0.06	0.08	0.17	0.52
LC / WP	0.2	0.39	0.47	0.39	0.82

Differences in Performance

The difference between the LSA and the Wu-Palmer measure in performance on different CVs can be obtained from the Jaccard coefficient values shown in Table 3. The Jaccard coefficient shows a moderate overlap between the structural measures and low overlap between the Latent Semantic Analysis and the structural measures. For example, on CV 400 the Jaccard coefficient for the Wu-Palmer and the Leacock-Chodorow is 0.47 and for the LSA and the structural measures 0.04 and 0.08 respectively. This indicates that the structural measures and the corpus-based methods are complementary. In possible end-use applications, both should be used to obtain good approximation of semantic relatedness.

The Wu-Palmer measure was better in terms of performance than the other structural measure Leacock-Chodorow. Therefore only the Wu-Palmer and the LSA were further compared by qualitatively analyzing the relations they approximate. We investigated sample CV 400 by looking at the concept pairs found by only one of the methods. In other words, either concept pairs that were found by the LSA and not the Wu-Palmer or the other way around. The sample CV 400 was chosen because it already has a relatively high (0.47) Jaccard coefficient for the Wu-Palmer and the Leacock-Chodorow, but a low (0.08 and 0.07) Jaccard coefficient for the LSA and the structural measures.

A systematic sample of concept pairs including human rank and having a rank above 0.6 by the LSA, but not by Wu-Palmer are shown in Table 4.

LSA determines relations that are non-hierarchical and can be far away from each other in terms of path length. Good examples shown in Table 4 are concept pairs such as *product / production costs*, *guerilla / child soldier*, *books / shelf* and *flu / nutrition*. An interesting notion is that based on the news corpus that we used, the LSA assigns high rank (0.97) for the concept pair *update / ASP*, where *ASP* stands for an abbreviation for a form of financing subvention of Finnish government for young people planning to buy their first apartment. Such an update was recently made. This is an example of a relation relevant for the domain at a specific time, but clearly one that should be approximated based on the corpus rather than included in the ontology. Similar concept pairs that are relevant for the domain based on the documents are *flu / nutrition* and *guerilla / child soldier*. These are concepts that are only valid in the case of a specific document collection or corpus.

Although low in number, LSA also finds relations that have a common super concept, but are not found by the Wu-Palmer measure. An example of such a relation is *wizard / giants* that have a common super concept *mythic creature*. A possible explanation why LSA performs better than the Wu-Palmer measure is that the hierarchy where these concepts are in is relatively flat and therefore the Wu-Palmer measure approximates a low value for the concept pair. LSA also finds relations that might be relevant for some specific documents, but are difficult to interpret. For example, relations such as *studios / gardener*, *church / plain* and *leather / persistence* may have relevance in terms of an individual news article, but would

Table 4. A systematic sample of concept pairs ranked to CV of 400 by the Latent Semantic Analysis and not ranked to CV of 400 by the Wu-Palmer measure.

Concept 1	Concept 2	Method	Human
product	production costs	1.0	0.5
Irish	immigrants	0.99	0.5
guerilla	child soldier	0.99	1.0
update	ASP	0.97	0.25
wizard	giants	0.96	0.75
flu	nutrition	0.93	1.0
drinks	chemicals	0.93	0.0
books	shelf	0.90	1.0
studios	gardener	0.82	0.0
foundations	organist	0.81	0.0
suicide attack	population group	0.79	0.5
church	plain	0.69	0.0
symbols	rose	0.68	0.0
leather	persistence	0.66	0.0
sick	disease	0.63	1.0

probably not be beneficial in many end-use applications. The Wu-Palmer measure determines relations that are close based on the subsumption hierarchy. It is notable that LSA only found very few of these relations (Jaccard 0.08 in CV 400 and 0.17 in CV 800).

A systematic sample of concept pairs including human rank and having a rank above 0.7 by the Wu-Palmer, but not the LSA, are shown in Table 5. The examples show that the Wu-Palmer relies on the subsumption hierarchy on a specific depth. All of the concept pairs shown in Table 5 are placed on depth greater than six in the subsumption hierarchy. Wu-Palmer also suffers of a relatively low recall on the rank levels above 0.3. A possible explanation is that the Wu-Palmer measure achieves a high precision by restricting the analysis to concepts relatively deep in the hierarchy. This also causes it to sacrifice recall for precision. On the other hand, the precision of the relations that Wu-Palmer determines is the

highest among the compared methods. It also gives accurate approximation for relations, such as *change / boiling* that are difficult to interpret in the scope of possible end use applications, but are found related by the human annotators.

In summary, the Wu-Palmer measure seems remarkably reliable when it assigns a high rank for a concept pair. However, it fails to approximate almost all of the relevant concept pairs that LSA ranked high. LSA seems to be useful in finding relations between concepts that are related, but for which the relation is difficult to obtain using only the ontology graph. In addition, LSA approximates relations that are dependent on the domain and time, but useful in case of the particular document collection or corpus. LSA also seems to find subsumption relations, when the subsumption hierarchy itself does not contain enough information to relate the concepts. On the other hand, LSA makes much more mistakes even when it assigns a rank over 0.9.

Table 5. A systematic sample of concept pairs ranked to CV of 400 by the Wu-Palmer measure and not ranked to CV of 400 by the Latent Semantic Analysis.

Concept 1	Concept 2	Method	Human
parents	father	0.92	1
masonry	construction work	0.89	1
minorities	population group	0.88	1
document	application	0.84	1
expression	crying	0.84	0.5
measurement	weighing	0.84	1
sportsman	jockey	0.75	1
novel	story	0.82	1
trial	preliminary investigation	0.81	0.75
stone	marble	0.81	0.75
turkey	chicken	0.81	0.75
anecdote	fairy tale	0.77	0.5
windows	stairs	0.77	0.5
near relative	role	0.77	0
change	boiling	0.71	1

Conclusion and Discussion

Our goal in this paper was to measure and compare the performance of structural measures and corpus-based methods in approximating semantic relatedness in light-weight ontologies, and to identify the the strengths and weaknesses of the methods in possible application scenarios. Two structural measures by Wu and Palmer (1994) and Leacock and Chodorow (1998), and a corpus-based method Latent Semantic Analysis (Landauer et al., 1998), were compared.

The experimental results show that neither corpus-based method or structure-based measures alone dominate. LSA showed the best performance for the whole dataset. However, both of the structural measures had substantially better performance than LSA when cut-off values were used. Further analysis revealed that LSA and Wu-Palmer measure approximated very different kinds of relations. In addition, we found that the performance of the compared methods varies on different rank levels. LSA is superior in filtering out the non-relevant relations, and is able to find relations in which the structural measures fail.

A combination of LSA and structural measures can be useful in applications such as information retrieval or word sense disambiguation, where an extensive word context is important (Kekäläinen & Järvelin, 2000; Sussna, 1993). Structural measures alone may suffice in scenarios such as information extraction, where synonymy and hyponymy relations are found to be most useful (Califf & Mooney, 1999). In summary, depending on the intended use case, a combination of structural measures and corpus-based methods should be selected and appropriate cut-off values set.

With respect to the size of the empirical study this is, up to our knowledge, the most comprehensive study that evaluates semantic relatedness measures against human relevance assessments. Although Budanitsky and Hirst (2006) compared larger number of methods, they report that their results were obtained using an inadequate sample. In Budanitsky and Hirst (2006) the concept pairs were selected based on their distribution with respect to human ranks. Such a sample can be used as a study to measure human ranks. However, it can be biased when applied to measurement of computational methods that should generalize over an ontology or a corpus.

We used a light-weight ontology developed on a basis of a thesaurus that may have a different concept distribution and lexical coverage compared to other lexical databases, such as WordNet (Miller, 1995). On the other hand, the lightweight ontology used in this study contained more than 26,000 concepts and was ensured to have coherent subsumption hierarchies, which makes the study more fair for the structural measures. We compare the performance of the methods to human ranks acquired in a large user study. A limitation of our analysis is that the concept pairs were annotated by humans on a binary scale. However, we determined a very high value of Cohen's Kappa that showed substantial inter-annotator agreement. In addition, we used the averages of the binary votes of four annotators. Although the measurement accuracy may contain some bias because only five level judgements (values of 0, 0.25, 0.5, 0.75 or 1), the bias is the same for all of the methods, and all of the comparisons are statistically significant.

One of the strengths of the LSA method is that it is able to approximate semantic relatedness based on a corpus in an unsupervised manner. This makes it a good choice to supplement the often limited lexical coverage of an ontology. A limitation of our study is that we restricted the concept pairs to the intersection of concepts appearing in the corpus and in the ontology. On the other hand, the purpose of the study was to measure the accuracy and differences between the methods in the context of ontologies. Because YSO has more than 26,000 concepts, the lexical coverage should be acceptable.

The good performance achieved using hybrid methods proposed by Jiang & Conrath (1997), Resnik (1995), and D. Lin (1998) suggests that a hybrid approach that combine corpus statistics and knowledge-based measures into one method could be a promising direction. Such methods weight the ontology paths based on their mutual information content observed from the corpus and show improved accuracy compared to straightforward path-length measures. However, our results suggest that there is actually a low overlap between the relations found based on the corpus statistics and the relations found based on the ontology structure.

Budanitsky and Hirst (2006) have studied the performance of structural methods using human ranks in a similarity task. They found that Leacock-Chodorow measure along with the hybrid methods proposed by D. Lin (1998), and Jiang and Conrath (1997) performed most accurately. However, as they note, the data used in their study was collected for a similarity task and therefore does not indicate the performance of the methods in semantic relatedness approximation. In addition, they note that the data in their study was not necessarily representative. Therefore, it is difficult to compare their results to the ones obtained in our study.

Our study concentrated on any type of semantic relatedness. However, different kinds of semantic relatedness can be identified. Turney (2006) makes a difference between attributional and relational semantic similarity. For example, the concept pair *mason / stone* is relationally similar or analogous to the concept pair *carpenter / wood* as opposite to attributional similarity that refers to synonymy. Turney (2006) proposes Latent Relational Analysis to approximate relational similarity. This is an important future research direction especially on application areas, such as information retrieval and question answering, where analogous concept pairs could be used to increase accuracy of the retrieval methods (Nakov & Hearst, 2008).

Semantic relatedness approximation has also been included in natural language engineering tasks. LSA been used for hyponymy extraction (Cederberg & Widdows, 2003), topic structure extraction (Valle-Lisboa & Mizraji, 2007), and applied in the area of information retrieval (Deerwester et al., 1990). Coccaro & Jurafsky (1998) combined LSA with n-gram language model and showed improvement in speech recognition. Maguitman et al. (2005) present a graph-based similarity measure to detect similar web-pages. The performance of different methods and combinations of methods in such application cases would be a natural future research direction.

Recent research has proposed Probabilistic Latent Semantic Analysis (PLSA) (Hofmann, 2001) and Latent Dirichlet Allocation (LDA) (Blei et al., 2003), as probabilistic variants of LSA. The performance of these methods could be better than LSA. LDA can be used especially for small corpora where the usage of prior information can increase the accuracy.

Future research could explore the findings of this paper in hybrid methods and apply the methods to real life application cases. It would be interesting to measure the performance of LSA without restricting it to the concepts found in ontologies. A hybrid approach where both the terms appearing in the term space of the corpus and the concepts appearing in the ontology could be used in the computation. In this way, LSA could benefit from the additional terms that are not available in ontologies. For example, concept correspondence for proper names can be limited in the ontologies, but could improve the accuracy of LSA. As discussed, LSA approximates also relations that have no meaningful interpretation in terms of the end-use applications. Therefore, LSA could be used to approximate particular types of relations by using the ontology structure as a background knowledge. For example, restricting the approximation of concept pairs to roles and named entities, could reveal useful relations. Another interesting research direction could be to incorporate reasoning in the LSA computation. Constructing the concept-document matrix using reasoning, where occurrences of concepts would imply the occurrences of other concepts

through subsumption reasoning, would enable knowledge-based LSA.

Another possible research direction is to develop methods that are able to both adjust the weights of the paths in the ontology graph based on corpus statistics, and use a meta-classifier that selects the most appropriate prediction method for each concept pair. Such methods would benefit from corpus statistics as an adjustment of the existing ontology graph, and would be able to approximate relations that may not be found using only structural measures.

ACKNOWLEDGMENT

This research is part of the Research and Development project SMARTMUSEUM (Cultural Heritage Knowledge Exchange Platform) sponsored under the Europeans Commission's 7th Framework (FP7-216923).

REFERENCES

Blei, D. M., Ng, A. Y., Jordan, M. I., & Lafferty, J. (2003). Latent Dirichlet allocation. *Journal of Machine Learning Research, 3*, 2003. doi:10.1162/jmlr.2003.3.4-5.993

Budanitsky, A., & Hirst, G. (2006). Evaluating WordNet-based measures of lexical semantic relatedness. *Computational Linguistics, 32*(1), 13–47. doi:10.1162/coli.2006.32.1.13

Califf, M. E., & Mooney, R. J. (1999). Relational learning of pattern-match rules for information extraction. In *AAAI '99/IAAI '99: Proceedings of The Sixteenth National Conference on Artificial Intelligence and the Eleventh Innovative Applications of Artificial Intelligence Conference* (pp. 328-334). Menlo Park, CA: American Association for Artificial Intelligence.

Castells, P., Fernandez, M., & Vallet, D. (2007, February). An adaptation of the vector-space model for ontology-based information retrieval. *IEEE Transactions on Knowledge and Data Engineering, 19*(2), 261–272. doi:10.1109/TKDE.2007.22

Cederberg, S., & Widdows, D. (2003). Using LSA and noun coordination information to improve the precision and recall of automatic hyponymy extraction. In *Proceedings of the Seventh Conference on Natural Language Learning at HLT-NAACL 2003* (pp. 111-118). Morristown, NJ: Association for Computational Linguistics.

Chandrasekaran, B., Josephson, J. R., & Benjamins, V. R. (1999). What are ontologies, and why do we need them? *IEEE Intelligent Systems, 14*(1), 20–26. doi:10.1109/5254.747902

Coccaro, N., & Jurafsky, D. (1998). Towards better integration of semantic predictors in statistical language modeling. In *Proceedings of the 5th International Conference on Spoken Language Processssing (ICSLP-98)* (pp. 2403-2407). ASSTA. (Volume 6)

Cohen, J. (1960, April). A coefficient of agreement for nominal scales. *Educational and Psychological Measurement, 20*(1), 37–46. doi:10.1177/001316446002000104

Conover, W. J. (1998). *Practical nonparametric statistics*. New York: John Wiley & Sons.

Deerwester, S., Deerwester, S., Dumais, S. T., Furnas, G. W., Landauer, T. K., & Harshman, R. (1990). Indexing by latent semantic analysis. *Journal of the American Society for Information Science American Society for Information Science, 41*(6), 391–407. doi:10.1002/(SICI)1097-4571(199009)41:6<391::AID-ASI1>3.0.CO;2-9

Ehrig, M., & Euzenat, J. (2005, October). Relaxed precision and recall for ontology matching. In *Integrating ontologies '05, proceedings of the K-CAP 2005 workshop on integrating ontologies* (Vol. 156). CEUR-WS.org.

Fensel, D. (2004). *Ontologies: A silver bullet for knowledge management and electronic commerce* (2nd ed.). Heidelberg, Germany: Springer.

Gangemi, A., Guarino, N., Masolo, C., Oltramari, A., & Schneider, L. (2002). Sweetening ontologies with DOLCE. In *EKAW '02: Proceedings of the 13th international conference on knowledge engineering and knowledge management ontologies and the semantic web* (pp. 166-181). London: Springer-Verlag.

Hofmann, T. (2001). Unsupervised learning by probabilistic latent semantic analysis. *Machine Learning, 42*(1-2), 177–196. doi:10.1023/A:1007617005950

Hull, D. (1993). Using statistical testing in the evaluation of retrieval experiments. In *Proceedings of the 16th annual international ACM SIGIR conference on research and development in information retrieval* (pp. 329-338). New York: ACM.

Hyvönen, E., Viljanen, K., Tuominen, J., & Seppälä, K. (2008, June 1-5). Building a national semantic web ontology and ontology service infrastructure—the FinnONTO approach. In *5th european semantic web conference (eswc 2008)* (pp. 95–109). Springer.

Ide, N., & Véronis, J. (1998). Introduction to the special issue on word sense disambiguation: the state of the art. *Computational Linguistics, 24*(1), 2–40.

Jaccard, P. (1901). Etude comparative de la distribution florale dans une portion des alpes et du jura. *Bulletin de la Société Vaudoise des Sciences Naturelles, 37*, 547–579.

Jiang, J. J., & Conrath, D. W. (1997, September). Semantic similarity based on corpus statistics and lexical taxonomy. In *Proceedings of the international conference research on computational linguistics (ROCLING X)* (pp. 19-33).

Kekäläinen, J., & Järvelin, K. (2000). The co-effects of query structure and expansion on retrieval performance in probabilistic text retrieval. *Information Retrieval, 1*(4), 329–344. doi:10.1023/A:1009983401464

Kekäläinen, J., & Järvelin, K. (2002). Using graded relevance assessments in IR evaluation. *Journal of the American Society for Information Science and Technology, 53*(13), 1120–1129. doi:10.1002/asi.10137

Landauer, T., Foltz, P. W., & Laham, D. (1998). Introduction to latent semantic analysis. *Discourse Processes, 25*(1), 259–284. doi:10.1080/01638539809545028

Leacock, C., & Chodorow, M. (1998). Combining local context and WordNet similarity for word sense identification. In Fellbaum, C. (Ed.), *WordNet: An electronic lexical database* (pp. 265–283). Cambridge, MA: MIT Press.

Lin, C. Y., & Hovy, E. (2000). The automated acquisition of topic signatures for text summarization. In *Proceedings of the 18th conference on computational linguistics* (pp. 495-501). Morristown, NJ: Association for Computational Linguistics.

Lin, D. (1998). Automatic retrieval and clustering of similar words. In *Proceedings of the 17th international conference on computational linguistics* (pp. 768-774). Morristown, NJ: Association for Computational Linguistics.

Maguitman, A. G., Menczer, F., Roinestad, H., & Vespignani, A. (2005). Algorithmic detection of semantic similarity. In *Proceedings of the 14th international conference on World Wide Web* (pp. 107-116). New York: ACM.

Manning, C. D., Raghavan, P., & Schütze, H. (2008). *Introduction to information retrieval* (1st ed.). Cambridge, UK: Cambridge University Press.

Miller, G. (1995). WordNet: A lexical database for english. *Communications of the ACM, 38*(11). doi:10.1145/219717.219748

Miller, G. A., & Charles, W. G. (1991). Contextual correlates of semantic similarity. *Language and Cognitive Processes, 6*(1), 1–28. doi:10.1080/01690969108406936

Nakov, P., & Hearst, M. A. (2008, June). Solving relational similarity problems using the Web as a corpus. In *Proceedings of ACL-08: HLT* (pp. 452-460). Columbus, OH: Association for Computational Linguistics.

Resnik, P. (1995). Using information content to evaluate semantic similarity in a taxonomy. In *IJCAI'95: Proceedings of the 14th international joint conference on artificial intelligence* (pp. 448-453). San Francisco: Morgan Kaufmann Publishers Inc.

Rubenstein, H., & Goodenough, J. B. (1965). Contextual correlates of synonymy. *Communications of the ACM, 8*(10), 627–633. doi:10.1145/365628.365657

Ruotsalo, T., Aroyo, L., & Schreiber, G. (2009). Knowledge-based linguistic annotation of digital cultural heritage collections. *IEEE Intelligent Systems, 24*(2), 64–75. doi:10.1109/MIS.2009.32

Ruotsalo, T., & Hyvönen, E. (2007, September). A method for determining ontology-based semantic relevance. In *Proceedings of the international conference on database and expert systems applications (DEXA 2007)*. Regensburg, Germany: Springer.

Salton, G., & Buckley, C. (1988). Term-weighting approaches in automatic text retrieval. *Information Processing & Management, 24*(5), 513–523. doi:10.1016/0306-4573(88)90021-0

Shapiro, S. S., & Wilk, M. B. (1965). An analysis of variance test for normality (complete samples). *Biometrika, 3*(52).

Sussna, M. (1993). Word sense disambiguation for free-text indexing using a massive semantic network. In *CIKM '93: Proceedings of the second international conference on information and knowledge management* (pp. 6774). New York: ACM.

Turney, P. D. (2006). Similarity of semantic relations. *Computational Linguistics, 32*(3), 379–416. doi:10.1162/coli.2006.32.3.379

Valle-Lisboa, J. C., & Mizraji, E. (2007). The uncovering of hidden structures by latent semantic analysis. *Information Sciences, 177*(19), 4122–4147. doi:10.1016/j.ins.2007.04.007

Wilcoxon, F. (1945). Individual comparisons by ranking methods. *Biometrics Bulletin, 1*(6), 80–83. doi:10.2307/3001968

Wu, Z., & Palmer, M. (1994). Verb semantics and lexical selection. In *Proceedings of the 32nd annual meeting on association for computational linguistics* (pp. 133-138). Morristown, NJ: Association for Computational Linguistics.

ENDNOTES

[1] Latest version of the ontology is available in RDF(S) from: http://www.yso.fi
[2] http://vesa.lib.helsinki.fi/ysa/
[3] http://home.gna.org/omorfi/omorfi/
[4] http://rs.cipr.uib.no/mtj/
[5] http://jena.sourceforge.net/

This work was previously published in International Journal on Semantic Web and Information Systems, Volume 5, Issue 4, edited by Amit P. Sheth, pp. 39-56, copyright 2009 by IGI Publishing (an imprint of IGI Global).

Compilation of References

Abel, F. (2008). The benefit of additional semantics in folksonomy systems, In *Conference on Information and Knowledge Management: Proceedings of the 2nd PhD Workshop on Information and Knowledge Management,* Napa Valley, CA (pp. 49-56). New York: ACM Publishers.

Abiteboul, S., Cluet, S., & Milo, T. (1997). Correspondence and Translation for Heterogeneous Data. In *Proceedings of the 6th International Conference on Database Theory,* (pp. 351-363).

Adida, B., et al. (2008). *RDFa in XHTML: Syntax and Processing - W3C Recommendation.* Retrieved June 14, 2009, http://www.w3.org/TR/rdfa-syntax/

Afsharchi, M., & Behrouz, H. F. (2006). Automated ontology evolution in a multi-agent system. In *Proceedings of the 1st international conference on Scalable information systems (InfoScale '06)*, Hong Kong. ACM Press.

Ahuja, G. (2000). Collaboration Networks, Structural Holes, and Innovation: A Longitudinal Study. *Administrative Science Quarterly, 45,* 425–455. doi:10.2307/2667105

Alani, H., Kim, S., Millard, D., Weal, M., Hall, W., Lewis, P., & Shadbolt, N. (2003, January). Automatic Ontology-based Knowledge Extraction from Web Documents. *IEEE Intelligent Systems, 18*(1), 14–21. doi:10.1109/MIS.2003.1179189

Alexander, K., Cyganiak, R., Hausenblas, M., & Zhao, J. (2009). Describing Linked Datasets. In *Proceedings of the 2nd Workshop on Linked Data on the Web (LDOW2009).*

Almeida, D. R. d., Bapista, C. S., Silva, E. R. d., Campelo, C. E. C., Figueiredo, H. F. d., & Lacerda, Y. A. (2006). A Context-Aware System Based on Service-Oriented Architecture. In *20th International Conference on Advanced Information Networking and Applications (AINA '06)* (pp. 205-210). IEEE Computer Society.

Amit, P. Sheth, Ramakrishnan, C., & Thomas, C. (2005). Semantics for the Semantic Web: The Implicit, the Formal and the Powerful. *International Journal on Semantic Web and Information Systems, 1*(1), 1–18. doi:10.4018/jswis.2005010101

Angeletou, S. (2008, October 26-30). Semantic enrichment of folksonomy tagspaces. In A. Sheth, S. Staab, M. Dean, M. Paolucci, D. Maynard, T. Finin, et al. (Eds.), *The Semantic Web-ISWC 2008,* Karlsruhe, Germany (LNCS 5318, pp. 889-894).

Ankolekar, A., Krötzsch, M., Tran, T., & Vrandečić, D. (2007). The two cultures: Mashing up Web 2.0 and the Semantic Web. In *Proceedings of the 16th International World Wide Web Conference (WWW2007)* (pp. 825–834). New York, NY: ACM Press.

Ardilio, A., Auernhammer, K., & Kohn, S. (2004). *Marktstudie Innovationssysteme: IT-Unterstützung im Innovationsmanagement.* Stuttgart, Germany: Fraunhofer IRB.

Arnold, K., O'Sullivan, B., Scheifler, R. W., Waldo, J., & Woolrath, A. (1999). *The Jini Specification.* Addison-Wesley.

Auer, S., Bizer, C., Kobilarov, G., Lehmann, J., Cyganiak, R., & Ives, Z. G. (2007). *DBpedia: A nucleus for a web of open data. ISWC/ASWC* (pp. 722–735). Springer.

Auer, S., & Lehmann, J. (2007). What have Innsbruck and Leipzig in common? Extracting semantics from wiki content. *Proceedings of the ESWC (2007)* (pp. 503-517). Springer.

Auer, S., Bizer, C., Lehmann, J., Kobilarov, G., Cyganiak, R., & Ives, Z. (2007). DBpedia: A nucleus for a web of open data. In K. Aberer, K. S. Choi, N. Noy, D. Allemang, K. I. Lee, L. J. B. Nixon, … P. Cudré-Mauroux (Eds.), *Proceedings of the 6th International Semantic Web Conference and 2nd Asian Semantic Web Conference (ISWC/ASWC2007).* (LNCS 4825) (pp. 715–728). Heidelberg, Germany: Springer.

Auer, S., Bizer, C., Lehmann, J., Kobilarov, G., Cyganiak, R., & Ives, Z. (2007, November 11-15). DBpedia: A nucleus for a web of open data. In K. Aberer, K. S. Choi, N. Noy, D. Allemang, K. I. Lee, L. J. B. Nixon, et al. (Eds.), *The Semantic Web: Proceedings of the 6th International Semantic Web Conference and 2nd Asian Semantic Web Conference (ISWC/ASWC2007),* Busan, Korea (LNCS 4825, pp. 715-728).

Auer, S., et al. (2009). Triplify – Light-Weight Linked Data Publication from Relational Databases. In *Proceedings of the 18th World Wide Web Conference (WWW2009).*

Aumueller, D., Do, H.-H., Massmann, S., & Rahm, E. (2005). Schema and ontology matching with COMA++. In *Proceedings of the 2005 ACM SIGMOD International Conference on Management of Data.* June 14-16, Baltimore, Maryland.

Baader, F., Calvanese, D., McGuinness, D. L., Nardi, D., & Patel-Schneider, P. F. (2003). *The Description Logic Handbook: Theory, Implementation, and Applications.* Cambridge University Press.

Baader, F., Ganter, B., Sertkaya, B., & Sattler, U. (2007). Completing description logic knowledge bases using formal concept analysis. In Veloso, M. M. (Ed.), *IJCAI* (pp. 230–235).

Baader, F., Ganter, B., Sertkaya, B., & Sattler, U. (2007). Completing description logic knowledge bases using formal concept analysis. In M. Veloso, (eds.), *Proceedings of the 20th International Joint Conference on Artificial Intelligence, IJCAI07* (pp. 230--235).

Backhouse, J. (2005, July). *D4.1: Structured account of approaches on interoperability.* Technical report, FIDIS Deliverable, http://www.fidis.net/fileadmin/fidis/deliverables.

Badea, L., & Nienhuys-Cheng, S.-H. (2000). *A refinement operator for description logics* (pp. 40–58). LNCS.

Bailin, S., & Truszkowski, W. (2002). Ontology negotiation between intelligent information agents. *The Knowledge Engineering Review,* *17*(1), 7–19. doi:10.1017/S0269888902000292

Banerjee, S., & Pedersen, T. (2002). An Adapted Lesk Algorithm for Word Sense Disambiguation Using WordNet. In A. Gelbukh (Ed.), *proceedings of the Third International Conference on Intelligent Text Processing and Computational Linguistics.* (pp. 136-145). London: Springer-Verlag press.

Batini, C., Lenzerini, M., & Navathe, S. B. (1986). A Comparative Analysis of Methodologies for Database Schema Integration. *ACM Computing Surveys,* *18*(4), 323–364. doi:10.1145/27633.27634

Battista, A. D. L., Villanueva-Rosales, N., Palenychka, M., & Dumontier, M. (2007). *SMART: A Web-based, ontology-driven, semantic web query answering application.* Semantic web challenge at the ISWC 2007.

Bechhofer, S., & Volz, R. (2004). *Patching syntax in OWL ontologies.* International Semantic Web Conference (Vol. 3298, pp. 668-682). Hiroshima, Japan: Springer.

Bechhofer, S., Müller, R., & Crowther, P. (2003). The DIG description logic interface. In D. Calvanese, G. D. Giacomo, & E. Franconi (Eds.), *Description logics* (Vol. 81). Retrieved from CEUR-WS.org

Bechhofer, S., van Harmelen, F., Hendler, J., Horrocks, I., McGuinness, D. L., Patel-Schneider, P. F., et al. (2004, Feb). *OWL web ontology language reference.* W3C Recommendation. Retrieved from http://www.w3.org/TR/owl-ref

Bechhofer, S., van Harmelen, F., Hendler, J., Horrocks, I., McGuinness, D. L., Patel-Schneider, P. F., et al. (2004, February). *OWL Web ontology language reference.*

Becker, C. (2008). *RDF Store Benchmarks with DBpedia comparing Virtuoso, SDB and Sesame*. Retrieved March 2, 2009, http://www4.wiwiss.fu-berlin.de/benchmarks-200801/

Becker, C., & Bizer, C. (2008). DBpedia Mobile: A Location-Enabled Linked Data Browser. *Proceedings of the 1st Workshop about Linked Data on the Web (LDOW2008)*.

Becker, C., & Bizer, C. (2008). DBpedia Mobile - A Location-Aware Semantic Web Client. In *Proceedings of the Semantic Web Challenge at ISWC 2008*.

Beckett, D. (2004). *RDF/XML Syntax Specification (Revised) - W3C Recommendation*. Retrieved June 14, 2009, http://www.w3.org/TR/rdf-syntax-grammar/

Beckett, D., & Berners-Lee, T. (2008). *Turtle - Terse RDF Triple Language - W3C Team Submission*. Retrieved July 23, 2009, http://www.w3.org/TeamSubmission/turtle/

Begelman, G., Keller, P., & Smadja, F. (2006, May 22-26) *Automated tag clustering: Improving search and exploration in the tag space*. Paper presented at the Collaborative Web Tagging Workshop, 15th International World Wide Web Conference (WWW 2006), Edinburgh, Scotland.

Belleau, F., Nolin, M., Tourigny, N., Rigault, P., & Morissette, J. (2008). Bio2RDF: Towards a mashup to build bioinformatics knowledge systems. *Journal of Biomedical Informatics*, *41*(5), 706–716. doi:10.1016/j.jbi.2008.03.004

Benson, E., Marcus, A., Howahl, F., & Karger, D. (2010). Talking about data: Sharing richly structured information through blogs and wikis. In *Proceedings of the 9th International Semantic Web Conference (ISWC2010)*, Shanghai, China.

Berners-Lee, T. (1994). The World-Wide Web. *Communications of the ACM*, *37*(8), 76–82. doi:10.1145/179606.179671

Berners-Lee, T., Hendler, J., & Lassila, O. (2001). The Semantic Web. *Scientific American*, *284*(5), 34–43.

Berners-Lee, T. (1997). *Cleaning up the User Interface, Section - The "Oh, yeah?"-Button*. Retrieved June 14, 2009, http://www.w3.org/DesignIssues/UI.html

Berners-Lee, T. (1998). *Notation3 (N3) A readable RDF syntax*. Retrieved July 23, 2009, http://www.w3.org/DesignIssues/Notation3.html

Berners-Lee, T. (2000). *Weaving the Web: The Past, Present and Future of the World Wide Web by its Inventor*. London, Texere.

Berners-Lee, T. (2006, June 27). *Linked data-design issues*. Retreived May 8, 2009, from http://www.w3.org/DesignIssues/LinkedData.html

Berners-Lee, T. (2007, November 21). Giant global graph. Retrieved May 8, 2009, from http://dig.csail.mit.edu/breadcrumbs/node/215

Berners-Lee, T., et al. (2005). *Uniform Resource Identifier (URI): Generic Syntax. Request for Comments: 3986*. Retrieved June 14, 2009, http://tools.ietf.org/html/rfc3986

Berners-Lee, T., et al. (2006), Tabulator: Exploring and Analyzing Linked Data on the Semantic Web. In *Procedings of the 3rd International Semantic Web User Interaction Workshop (SWUI06)*.

Berners-Lee, T., et al. (2008). Tabulator Redux: Browsing and Writing Linked Data. In *Proceedings of the 1st Workshop on Linked Data on the Web (LDOW2008)*.

Berrueta, D., & Phipps, J. (2008). *Best Practice Recipes for Publishing RDF Vocabularies - W3C Working Group Note*. Retrieved June 14, 2009, http://www.w3.org/TR/swbp-vocab-pub/

BigOWLIM. (2006). *System documentation*.

Bizer, C., & Cyganiak, R. (2009). Quality-driven Information Filtering using the WIQA Policy Framework. *Journal of Web Semantics*, *7*(1), 1–10. doi:10.1016/j.websem.2008.02.005

Bizer, C., Lehmann, J., Kobilarov, G., Auer, S., Becker, C., Cyganiak, R., & Hellmann, S. (2009). (in press). DBpedia - A Crystallization Point for the Web of Data. Journal of Web Semantics. *Special Issue on the Web of Data*.

Bizer, C., & Cyganiak, R. (2006). D2R Server - Publishing Relational Databases on the Semantic Web. *Poster at the 5th International Semantic Web Conference (ISWC2006)*.

Bizer, C., & Schultz, A. (2008a). *Berlin SPARQL Benchmark (BSBM) Specification - V2.0.* Retrieved March 2, 2009, http://www4.wiwiss.fu-berlin.de/bizer/Berlin-SPARQLBenchmark/spec/

Bizer, C., & Schultz, A. (2008b). *Berlin SPARQL Benchmark Results.* Retrieved March 2, 2009, http://www4.wiwiss.fu-berlin.de/bizer/BerlinSPARQLBenchmark/results/

Bizer, C., Cyganiak, R., & Gauß, T. (2007). The RDF Book Mashup: From Web APIs to a Web of Data. In *Proceedings of the 3rd Workshop on Scripting for the Semantic Web (SFSW2007).*

Bizer, C., Cyganiak, R., & Heath, T. (2007). *How to publish Linked Data on the Web.* Retrieved June 14, 2009, http://www4.wiwiss.fu-berlin.de/bizer/pub/LinkedDataTutorial/

Bizer, C., Heath, T., Ayers, D., & Raimond, Y. (2007). *Interlinking open data on the Web.* Poster session presented at the 4th European Semantic Web Conference (ESWC 2007), Innsbruck, Austria.

Blei, D. M., Ng, A. Y., Jordan, M. I., & Lafferty, J. (2003). Latent Dirichlet allocation. *Journal of Machine Learning Research, 3,* 2003. doi:10.1162/jmlr.2003.3.4-5.993

Bleiholder, J., & Naumann, F. (2008). Data Fusion. *ACM Computing Surveys, 41*(1), 1–41. doi:10.1145/1456650.1456651

Bloehdorn, S., & Sure, Y. (2007). Kernel methods for mining instance data in ontologies. In K. Aberer et al., (Eds.), *Proceedings of the 6th International Semantic Web Conference, ISWC2007,* (*LNCS* Vol. 4825, pp. 58--71). Berlin: Springer.

Boisen, S. (2006). *Semantic bible: New Testament names: A semantic knowledge base.* Retrieved August 15, 2008, from http://www.semanticbible.com/ntn/ntn-overview.html

Bojãrs, U., & Breslin, J. G. (2007). *SIOC core ontology specification.* Retrieved from http://www.w3.org/Submission/2007/SUBM-sioc-spec-20070612/ accessed 2009-10-01

Bojãrs, U., Passant, A., Cyganiak, R., & Breslin, J. (2008). Weaving SIOC into the web of linked data. In *Proceedings of the Workshop on Linked Data on the Web (LDOW2008).*

Bojãrs, U., Passant, A., Breslin, J. G., & Decker, S. (2008, May 6) *Social network and data portability using Semantic Web technologies.* Paper presented at the 2nd Workshop on Social Aspects of the Web (SAW 2008), Innsbruck, Austria.

Bollacker, K., Tufts, P., Pierce, T., & Cook, R. (2007). *A platform for scalable, collaborative, structured information integration.* In AAAI-07, Sixth International Workshop on Information Integration on the Web.

Borgida, A., & Serafini, L. (2003). Distributed description logics: Assimilating information from peer sources. *Journal of Data Semantics, 1,* 153–184. doi:10.1007/978-3-540-39733-5_7

Bouquet, P., Giunchiglia, F., Van Harmelen, F., Serafini, L., & Stuckenschmidt, H. (2004). Contextualizing ontologies. *Web Semantics: Science* [Elsevier.]. *Services and Agents on the World Wide Web, 1*(4), 325–343. doi:10.1016/j.websem.2004.07.001

Brachman, R. J. (1978). *A structural paradigm for representing knowledge (Tech. Rep. No. BBN Report 3605).* Cambridge, MA: Bolt, Beraneck and Newman, Inc.

Brank, J., Grobelnik, M., & Mladenić, D. (2005). A survey of ontology evaluation techniques. In *Proceedings of the Conference on Data Mining and Data Warehouses (SiKDD 2005).*

Braun, S., Schmidt, A., Walter, A., Nagypal, G., & Zacharias, V. (2007). Ontology maturing: A collaborative Web 2.0 approach to ontology engineering. In *Proceedings of the Workshop on Social and Collaborative Construction of Structured Knowledge at the 16th International World Wide Web Conference (WWW 07)* (pp. 8-12).

Brena, R. F., & Ramirez, E. Z. (2006). A Soft Semantic Web. *In Proceeding of 1st IEEE Workshop on Hot Topics in Web Systems and Technologies.* (pp. 1-8). Boston: IEEE press.

Breslin, J. G., & Decker, S. (2007). The future of social networks on the Internet: The need for semantics. *IEEE Internet Computing, 11,* 86–90. doi:10.1109/MIC.2007.138

Breslin, J. G., Harth, A., Bojārs, U., & Decker, S. (2005, May 29-June 1). Towards semantically-interlinked online communities. In A. Gómez-Pérez & J. Euzenat (Eds.), *The Semantic Web: Research and Applications: Proceedings of the 2nd European Semantic Web Conference (ESWC 2005),* Heraklion, Crete (LNCS 3532, pp. 500-514).

Brickley, D., & Guha, R. V. (2004). *RDF vocabulary description language 1.0: RDF schema.*

Brickley, D., & Guha, R. (2004). *RDF Vocabulary Description Language 1.0: RDF Schema - W3C Recommendation.* Retrieved June 14, 2009, http://www.w3.org/TR/rdf-schema/

Brickley, D., & Miller, L. (2007). *FOAF vocabulary specification.* Retrieved from http://xmlns.com/foaf/spec/ accessed 2009-10-01

Brin, S., & Page, L. (1998). The Anatomy of a Large-Scale Hypertextual Web Search Engine. *Computer Networks and ISDN Systems, 30*(1-7), 107-117.

Broens, T. (2004). *Context-aware, Ontology based, Semantic Service Discovery.* Enschede, The Netherlands, University of Twente: 87.

Brooke, J. (1996). SUS: A quick and dirty usability scale. *Usability Evaluation in Industry,* 189-194.

Browne, J., Hunt, I., & Zhang, J. (1998). The Extended Enterprise. In Molina, A., Sanchez, J. M., & Kusiak, A. (Eds.), *Handbook of Life Cycle Engineering Concepts, Tools and Techniques* (pp. 3–29). Dordrecht, The Netherlands: Kluwer Academic Publishers.

Budanitsky, A., & Hirst, G. (2006). Evaluating Word-Net-based measures of lexical semantic relatedness. *Computational Linguistics, 32*(1), 13–47. doi:10.1162/coli.2006.32.1.13

Buffa, M., Gandon, F., Ereteo, G., Sander, P., & Faron, C. (2008). SweetWiki: A semantic wiki. *Journal of Web Semantics, 6*(1), 84–97. doi:10.1016/j.websem.2007.11.003

Bullinger, A. (2008). *Innovation and Ontologies: Structuring the Early Stages of Innovation Management.* Wiesbaden, Germany: Gabler.

Cabral, L., Domingue, J., Galizia, S., Gugliotta, A., Tanasescu, V., Pedrinaci, C., et al. (2006). IRS-III: A Broker for Semantic Web Services based Applications. In *5th International Semantic Web Conference (ISWC 2006),* Athens, GA, USA.

Califf, M. E., & Mooney, R. J. (1999). Relational learning of pattern-match rules for information extraction. In *AAAI '99/IAAI '99: Proceedings of The Sixteenth National Conference on Artificial Intelligence and the Eleventh Innovative Applications of Artificial Intelligence Conference* (pp. 328-334). Menlo Park, CA: American Association for Artificial Intelligence.

Caracciolo, C., et al. (2008). Results of the Ontology Alignment Evaluation Initiative 2008. *Proceedings of the 3rd International Workshop on Ontology Matching (OM-2008), CEUR-WS, 431.*

Carroll, J., Bizer, C., Hayes, P., & Stickler, P. (2005). Named graphs. *Journal of Web Semantics, 3*(4), 247–267. doi:10.1016/j.websem.2005.09.001

Castano, S., De Antonellis, V., Fugini, M. G., & Pernici, B. (1998). Conceptual schema analysis: Techniques and applications. [New York, NY: ACM.]. *ACM Transactions on Database Systems, 23*(3), 286–333. doi:10.1145/293910.293150

Castells, P., Fernandez, M., & Vallet, D. (2007, February). An adaptation of the vector-space model for ontology-based information retrieval. *IEEE Transactions on Knowledge and Data Engineering, 19*(2), 261–272. doi:10.1109/TKDE.2007.22

Catasta, M., Cyganiak, R., & Tummarello, G. (2009). Towards ECSSE: live Web of Data search and integration. In *Proceedings of the Semantic Search 2009 Workshop at WWW2009.*

Cayzer, S. (2004). Semantic blogging and decentralized knowledge management. *Communications of the ACM, 47*(12), 48–52. doi:10.1145/1035134.1035164

Cederberg, S., & Widdows, D. (2003). Using LSA and noun coordination information to improve the precision and recall of automatic hyponymy extraction. In *Proceedings of the Seventh Conference on Natural Language Learning at HLT-NAACL 2003* (pp. 111-118). Morristown, NJ: Association for Computational Linguistics.

Chakraborty, D., Joshi, A., Yesha, Y., & Finin, T. (2004). Towards Distributed Service Discovery in Pervasive Computing Environments. *IEEE Transactions on Mobile Computing*.

Chakraborty, D., Perich, F., Avancha, S., & Joshi, A. (2001). DReggie: Semantic Service Discovery for M-Commerce Applications. In *Workshop on Reliable and Secure Applications in Mobile Environment, In Conjunction with 20th Symposium on Reliable Distributed Systems (SRDS)*.

Chandrasekaran, B., Josephson, J. R., & Benjamins, V. R. (1999). What are ontologies, and why do we need them? *IEEE Intelligent Systems*, *14*(1), 20–26. doi:10.1109/5254.747902

Chatti, M. A., Srirama, S., Kensche, D., & Cao, Y. (2006). Mobile Web Services for Collaborative Learning. In *4th International Workshop on Wireless, Mobile and Ubiquitous Technology in Education* (pp. 129-133). IEEE.

Cheng, G., & Qu, Y. (2008). *Term dependence on the Semantic Web*. International Semantic Web Conference (pp. 665-680). Karlsruhe, Germany.

Cheng, G., & Qu, Y. (2009). Searching Linked Objects with Falcons: Approach, Implementation and Evaluation. *International Journal on Semantic Web and Information Systems, Special Issue on Linked Data*.

Cheng, G., & Qu, Y. (2008). Integrating lightweight reasoning into class-based query refinement for object search. In J. Domingue & C. Anutariya (Eds.), *The Semantic Web: Proceedings of the 3rd Asian Semantic Web Conference, Bangkok, Thailand* (LNCS 5367, pp. 449-463).

Cheng, G., Ge, W., Wu, H., & Qu, Y. (2008). Searching Semantic Web objects based on class hierarchies. *Proceedings of Linked Data on the Web Workshop*.

Chesbrough, H. W. (2006). *Open innovation: The new imperative for creating and profiting from technology*. Boston, MA: Harvard Business School Press.

Chiarcos, C. (2008). An ontology of linguistic annotations. *LDV Forum*, *23*(1), 1–16.

Chou, Y. (1969). *Statistical Analysis*. New York, NY: Holt International.

Clark, K. G., Feigenbaum, L., & Torres, E. (2008, January 15). *SPARQL Protocol for RDF* (W3C Recommendation). W3C.

Clarke, C. (2009). A Resource List Management Tool for Undergraduate Students based on Linked Open Data Principles. In *Proceedings of the 6th European Semantic Web Conference (ESWC2009)*.

Coccaro, N., & Jurafsky, D. (1998). Towards better integration of semantic predictors in statistical language modeling. In *Proceedings of the 5th International Conference on Spoken Language Processsing (ICSLP-98)* (pp. 2403-2407). ASSTA. (Volume 6)

Coetzee, P., Heath, T., & Motta, E. (2008). SparqPlug. *In Proceedings of the 1st Workshop on Linked Data on the Web (LDOW2008)*.

Cohen, J. (1960, April). A coefficient of agreement for nominal scales. *Educational and Psychological Measurement*, *20*(1), 37–46. doi:10.1177/001316446002000104

Conover, W. J. (1998). *Practical nonparametric statistics*. New York: John Wiley & Sons.

Cooper, R. G. (1990). Stage-gate systems: A new tool for managing new products. *Business Horizons*, *33*, 44–54. doi:10.1016/0007-6813(90)90040-I

Cyganiak, R., & Bizer, C. (2008). *Pubby - A Linked Data Frontend for SPARQL Endpoints*. Retrieved June 14, 2009, http://www4.wiwiss.fu-berlin.de/pubby/

Cyganiak, R., Delbru, R., Stenzhorn, H., Tummarello, G., & Decker, S. (2008). Semantic Sitemaps: Efficient and Flexible Access to Datasets on the Semantic Web. In *Proceedings of the 5th European Semantic Web Conference (ESWC2008)*.

d'Aquin, M., Baldassarre, C., Gridinoc, L., Sabou, M., Angeletou, S., & Motta, E. (2007, October 5-8). Watson: Supporting next generation Semantic Web applications. In P. Isaías, M. B. Nunes, & J. Barroso (Eds.), *Proceedings of the IADIS International Conference WWW/Internet 2007*, Vila Real, Portugal (pp. 363-371). IADIS Press.

d'Amato, C., Fanizzi, N., & Esposito, F. (2008). Query answering and ontology population: An inductive approach. In S. Bechhofer, et al., (Eds.), *Proceedings of the 5th European Semantic Web Conference, ESWC2008* (LNCS 5021, pp. 288-302). Berlin: Springer.

d'Aquin, M. (2008). Toward a New Generation of Semantic Web Applications. *IEEE Intelligent Systems, 23*(3), 20–28. doi:10.1109/MIS.2008.54

Das Sarma, A., Dong, X., & Halevy, A. (2008). Bootstrapping pay-as-you-go data integration systems. In *Proceedings of the Conference on Management of Data (SIGMOD2008)*.

Dataserver/reconciliation. (2008). *Freebase*. Retrieved December 25, 2008, from http://www.freebase.com/view/guid/9202a8c04000641f8000000007beed56

de Bruijn, J. (2008). *Semantic Web language layering with ontologies, rules, and meta-modeling*. University of Innsbruck.

de Bruijn, J., & Heymans, S. (2007). *Logical foundations of (e)RDF(S): Complexity and reasoning*. 6th International Semantic Web Conference (pp. 86-99). Busan, Korea.

de Bruijn, J., Lausen, H., Krummenacher, R., Polleres, A., Predoiu, L., Kifer, M., & Fensel, D. (2005, October). *The Web Service Modeling Language (WSML)*. Technical report, WSML Working Draft, http://www.wsmo.org/TR/d16/d16.1/v0.2/

De Leenheer, P., Christiaens, S., & Meersman, R. (2010). Business semantics management: A case study for competency-centric HRM. *Journal of Computers in Industry: Special Issue about Semantic Web* [Elsevier.]. *Computers in Industry, 61*(8), 760–775. doi:10.1016/j.compind.2010.05.005

De Leenheer, P., & Debruyne, C. (2008). DOGMA-MESS: A tool for fact-oriented collaborative ontology evolution. In Meersman, R., Tari, Z., & Herrero, P. (Eds.), *OTM 2008 Workshops, (LNCS 5333)* (pp. 797–806). Berlin/Heidelberg, Germany: Springer-Verlag.

Dean, M., & Schreiber, G. (2004, February). *OWL Web ontology language reference*. Technical report, World Wide Web Consortium (W3C), http://www.w3.org/TR/owl-ref/.

Deerwester, S., Deerwester, S., Dumais, S. T., Furnas, G. W., Landauer, T. K., & Harshman, R. (1990). Indexing by latent semantic analysis. *Journal of the American Society for Information Science American Society for Information Science, 41*(6), 391–407. doi:10.1002/(SICI)1097-4571(199009)41:6<391::AID-ASI1>3.0.CO;2-9

Delbru, R., Polleres, A., Tummarello, G., & Decker, S. (2008). Context dependent reasoning for semantic documents in Sindice. *Proceedings of the 4th International Workshop on Scalable Semantic Web Knowledge Base Systems (SSWS 2008)*. Karlsruhe, Germany.

Ding, L., et al. (2005, November). Finding and Ranking Knowledge on the Semantic Web. In *Proceedings of the 4th International Semantic Web Conference*.

Ding, L., Pan, R., Finin, T., Joshi, A., Peng, Y., & Kolari, P. (2005). Finding and ranking knowledge on the Semantic Web. In Y. Gil, E. Motta, V. R. Benjamins, & M. Musen (Eds.), *The Semantic Web: ISWC 2005: Proceedings of the 4th International Semantic Web Conference*, Galway, Ireland (LNCS 3729, pp. 156-170).

Donini, F. M., Lenzerini, M., Nardi, F., & Schaerf, A. (1994). Deduction in concept languages: From subsumption to instance checking. *Journal of Logic and Compututation, 4*(4), 423–452. doi:10.1093/logcom/4.4.423

Doulkeridis, C., Loutas, N., & Vazirgiannis, M. (2005). *A System Architecture for Context-Aware Service Discovery*.

Drumm, C., Schmitt, M., Do, H.-H., & Rahm, E. (2007, November). QuickMig - Automatic Schema Matching for Data Migration Projects. In *Proceedings of ACM CIKM*, Lisabon.

Duda, R. O., Hart, P. E., & Stork, D. G. (2001). *Pattern Classification* (2nd ed.). New York: Wiley.

Ehrig, M., & Euzenat, J. (2005, October). Relaxed precision and recall for ontology matching. In *Integrating ontologies '05, proceedings of the K-CAP 2005 workshop on integrating ontologies* (Vol. 156). CEUR-WS.org.

Elmagarmid, A., Ipeirotis, P., & Verykios, V. (2007). Duplicate Record Detection: A survey. *IEEE Transactions on Knowledge and Data Engineering, 19*(1), 1–16. doi:10.1109/TKDE.2007.250581

Erling, O., & Mikhailov, I. (n.d.). RDF Support in the Virtuoso DBMS. *Proceedings of the 1st Conference on Social Semantic Web (CSSW)* (pp. 59-68).

ESW Wiki. (2008). *Currently alive SPARQL endpoints*. Retrieved August 15, 2008, from http://esw.w3.org/topic/SparqlEndpoints

European Commission (IDABC). (2004). *European Interoperability Framework for Pan-European e-Government Services*. http://ec.europa.eu/idabc/servlets/Doc?id=19528.

Euzenat, J., & Shvaiko, P. (2007). *Ontology matching*. Heidelberg, DE: Springer-Verlag.

Euzenat, J., & Shvaiko, P. (2007). *Ontology matching*. Berlin/Heidelberg, Germany: Springer.

Euzenat, J. (2004). An API for ontology alignment. In S.A. McIlraith, D. Plexousakis, & F. Van Harmelen (Eds.), *International Semantic Web Conference*. (LNCS 3298) (pp. 698–712). Springer.

Euzenat, J., & Shvaiko, P. (2007). *Ontology Matching*. Heidelberg: Springer.

Euzenat, J., Le Bach, T., Barrasa, J., Bouquet, P., De Bo, J., Dieng-Kuntz, et al. (2004). *State of the art on ontology alignment*. Knowledge Web Deliverable D2.2.3.

Euzenat, J., Scharffe, F., & Serafini, L. (2006, February). *D2.2.6: Specification of the delivery alignment format*. Technical report, Knowledge Web Deliverable. http://www.inrialpes.fr/exmo/cooperation/kWeb/heterogeneity/deli/kWeb-226.pdf.

Euzenat, J., Scharffe, F., & Zimmermann, A. (2007). Expressive alignment language and implementation. *Knowledge Web project report, KWEB/2004/D2.2.10/1.0*.

FaCT++. (2008). Retrieved May 1, 2007, from http://owl.man.ac.uk/factplusplus/.

Fairbank, J., & Williams, S. (2001). Motivating Creativity and Enhancing Innovation through Employee Suggestion System Technology. *Creativity and Innovation Management, 10*, 68–74. doi:10.1111/1467-8691.00204

Fairbank, J. F., Spangler, W. E., & Williams, S. D. (2003). Motivating creativity through a computer-mediated employee suggestion management system. *Behaviour & Information Technology, 22*, 305–314. doi:10.1080/0144929031000159363O

Fanizzi, N., d'Amato, C., & Esposito, F. (2008b). Evolutionary conceptual clustering based on induced pseudo-metrics. *International Journal on Semantic Web and Information Systems, 4*(3).

Fanizzi, N., d'Amato, C., & Esposito, F. (2007). Induction of optimal semi-distances for individuals based on feature sets. In D. Calvanese, et al., (Eds.), *Working Notes of the 20th International Description Logics Workshop, DL2007* (Vol. 250, pp. 275-282). CEUR-WS.org.

Fanizzi, N., d'Amato, C., & Esposito, F. (2008a). DL-Foil: Concept learning in description logics. In F. Zelezný & N. Lavrac, (Eds.), *Proceedings of the 18th International Conference on Inductive Logic Programming, ILP2008*, (LNAI 5194, pp. 107-121). Berlin: Springer.

Fanizzi, N., d'Amato, C., & Esposito, F. (2008c). Learning with kernels in description logics. In F. Zelezný & N. Lavra[INSERT FIGURE 001], (Eds.), *Proceedings of the 18th International Conference on Inductive Logic Programming, ILP2008*, (LNAI Vol. 5194, pp. 210-225). Berlin: Springer.

Fanizzi, N., d'Amato, C., & Esposito, F. (2008d). Statistical learning for inductive query answering on OWL ontologies. In A. Sheth & et al., (Esd.), *Proceedings of the 7th International Semantic Web Conference, ISWC2008*, (LNCS 5318, pp. 195-212). Berlin: Springer.

Fanizzi, N., d'Amato, C., & Esposito, F. (2009). ReduCE: A reduced coulomb energy network method for approximate classification. In *Proceedings of the 6th European Semantic Web Conference, ESWC2009*, (LNCS 5554, pp. 320-334). Berlin: Springer.

Fellbaum, C. (1998). *WordNet: An Electronic Lexical Database*. MIT Press.

Fensel, D., Lausen, H., Polleres, A., de Bruijn, J., Stollberg, M., Roman, D., & Domingue, J. (2006). *Enabling Semantic Web Services: The Web Service Modeling Ontology*. Secaucus, NJ, USA: Springer-Verlag New York, Inc.

Fensel, D., van Harmelen, F., Andersson, B., Brennan, P., Cunningham, H., & Valle, E. D. (2008). *Towards LarKC: A platform for Web-scale reasoning*. Los Alamitos, CA: IEEE Computer Society Press.

Fensel, D. (2004). *Ontologies: A silver bullet for knowledge management and electronic commerce* (2nd ed.). Heidelberg, Germany: Springer.

Fensel, D., & van Harmelen, F. (2007). Unifying reasoning and search to Web scale. *IEEE Internet Computing, 11*(2), 96, 94-95.

Fensel, D., Harmelen, F. V., Ding, Y. Klein, M., Akkermans, H., et al. (2002). On-To-Knowledge: Semantic Web Enabled Knowledge Management. *IEEE Computer, 35*.

Fielding, R., et al. (1999). *Hypertext Transfer Protocol -- HTTP/1.1*. Request for Comments: 2616. Retrieved June 14, 2009, http://www.w3.org/Protocols/rfc2616/rfc2616.html

Finzen, J., Kintz, M., Koch, S., & Kett, H. (2009). Strategic innovation management on the basis of searching and mining press releases. In *Proceedings of the 5th International conference on web information systems and technologies (WEBIST)*, Lisbon, Portugal.

Fitzpatrick, B., & Recordon, D. (2007, August 17). *Thoughts on the social graph*. Retrieved May 8, 2009, from http://bradfitz.com/social-graph-problem/

Fokoue, A., Kershenbaum, A., Ma, L., Schonberg, E., & Srinivas, K. (2006). *The summary ABox: Cutting ontologies down to size* (pp. 343–356). ISWC.

Franke, N., & Shah, S. (2003). How communities support innovative activities: an exploration of assistance and sharing among end-users. *Research Policy, 32*, 157–178. doi:10.1016/S0048-7333(02)00006-9

Franklin, M., Halevy, A., & Maier, D. (2005). From databases to dataspaces: a new abstraction for information management. *SIGMOD Record, 34*(4), 27–33. doi:10.1145/1107499.1107502

Gangemi, A., Guarino, N., Masolo, C., Oltramari, A., & Schneider, L. (2002). Sweetening ontologies with DOLCE. In *EKAW '02: Proceedings of the 13th international conference on knowledge engineering and knowledge management ontologies and the semantic web* (pp. 166-181). London: Springer-Verlag.

García-Castro, R., & Gómez-Pérez, A. (2005). Guidelines for Benchmarking the Performance of Ontology Management APIs. *The Semantic Web – ISWC 2005. LNCS, 3729*, 277–292.

García-Castro, L. J., Hepp, M., & García, A. (2009). Tags4Tags: Using tagging to consolidate tags. In S. Bhowmick, J. Küng, & R. Wagner (Eds.), *Database and expert systems applications* (LNCS 5690, pp. 619-628).

García-Castro, L. J., Hepp, M., & García, A. (2010). TagSorting: A tagging environment for collaboratively building ontologies. In *Proceedings of the 17th International Conference on Knowledge Engineering and Knowledge Management (EKAW2010)*, Lisbon, Portugal (LNCS 6317).

Gassmann, O. (2006). Opening up the innovation process: towards an agenda. *R & D Management, 36*, 223–228. doi:10.1111/j.1467-9310.2006.00437.x

Gassmann, O., & Enkel, E. (2004). Towards a Theory of Open Innovation: Three Core Process Archetypes. In *Proceedings of the R&D Management Conference (RADMA)*, Sessimbra, Portugal.

Gemunden, H., Salomo, S., & Holzle, K. (2007). Role Models for Radical Innovations in Times of Open Innovation. *Creativity and Innovation Management, 16*, 408–421. doi:10.1111/j.1467-8691.2007.00451.x

Ghilardi, S., Lutz, C., & Wolter, F. (2006). Did I damage my ontology? A case for conservative extensions in description logics. *Proceedings of the Tenth International Conference on Principles of Knowledge Representation and Reasoning* (pp. 187-197). Lake District of the United Kingdom.

Golder, S., & Huberman, B. A. (2006). The structure of collaborative tagging systems. *Journal of Information Science, 32*(2), 198–208. doi:10.1177/0165551506062337

Golder, S., & Huberman, B. (2005). *The Structure of Collaborative Tagging Systems* (Arxiv preprint cs.DL/0508082).

Goldstone, R., Medin, D., & Halberstadt, J. (1997). Similarity in context. *Memory & Cognition, 25*(2), 237–255.

Gomadam, K., Ranabahu, A., Ramaswamy, L., Verma, K., & Sheth, A. P. (2008, August). Mediatability: Estimating the Degree of Human Involvement in XML Schema Mediation. In *Proceedings of the 2nd IEEE International Conference on Semantic Computing*, Santa Clara, CA.

Gómez-Pérez, A., & Benjamins, V. R. (1999). Overview of Knowledge Sharing and Reuse Components: Ontologies and Problem-Solving Methods. In *Proceedings of the IJCAI-99 Workshop on Ontologies and Problem-Solving Methods. Lessons Learned and Future Trends* (pp. 1-15). CEUR Publications

Gong, Y., & Liu, X. (2001). Generic text summarization using relevance measure and latent semantic analysis. In D. H. Kraft, W. B. Croft, D. J. Harper, & J. Zobel (Eds.), *Proceedings of the 24th Annual International ACM SIGIR Conference on Research and Development in Informational Retrieval,* New Orleans, LA (pp. 19-25). New York, NY: ACM.

Goudos, S. K., Loutas, N., Peristeras, V., & Tarabanis, K. (2007). Public Administration Domain Ontology for a Semantic Web Services E-Government Framework. *IEEE International Conference on Services Computing (SCC 2007),* Salt Lake City, USA, July 9-13.

Grau, B. C., Parsia, B., & Sirin, E. (2004). Working with multiple ontologies on the Semantic Web. In *The Semantic Web – ISWC 2004, (LNCS 3298)* (pp. 620–634). Berlin / Heidelberg, Germany: Springer. doi:10.1007/978-3-540-30475-3_43

Grau, B. C., Horrocks, I., Parsia, B., Patel-Schneider, P., & Sattler, U. (2006). *Next steps for OWL.* OWL: Experiences and Directions Workshop. Athens, Georgia, USA.

Grau, B. C., Horrocks, I., Kazakov, Y., & Sattler, U. (2007). A logical framework for modularity of ontologies. In M. M. Veloso (Eds.), *Proceedings of the 20th International Joint Conference on Artificial Intelligence,* Hyderabad, India (pp. 298-303).

Gray, J. (1993). *The Benchmark Handbook for Database and Transaction Systems* (2nd ed.). Morgan Kaufmann.

Grosof, B., Horrocks, I., Volz, R., & Decker, S. (2004). *Description logic programs: Combining logic programs with description logic.* 13th International Conference on World Wide Web.

Gruber, T. (2008). Collective knowledge systems: Where the social Web meets the Semantic Web. *Journal of Web Semantics,* 6(1), 4–13.

Gruber, T. (2007). Ontology of folksonomy: A mash-up of apples and oranges. *International Journal on Semantic Web and Information Systems,* 3(1), 1–11.

Gruninger, M., & Fox, M. S. (1995). Methodology for the Design and Evaluation of Ontologies. In *Proceedings of the Workshop on Basic Ontological Issues in Knowledge Sharing (IJCAI-95),* Montreal, Canada.

Guha, R. V., McCool, R., & Fikes, R. (2004). *Contexts for the Semantic Web.* 3rd International Semantic Web Conference, Hiroshima.

Guha, R., McCool, R., & Miller, E. (2003, May 20-24). Semantic search. In G. Hencsey, B. White, Y.-F. R. Chen, L. Kovács, & S. Lawrence (Eds.), *Proceedings of the 12th International World Wide Web Conference,* Budapest, Hungary (pp. 700-709). New York, NY: ACM.

Guo, Y., Pan, Z., & Heflin, J. (2005). LUBM: A Benchmark for OWL Knowledge Base Systems. *Journal of Web Semantics,* 3(2), 158–182. doi:10.1016/j.websem.2005.06.005

Gutiérrez, C., Hurtado, C., & Mendelzon, A. O. (2004). *Foundations of Semantic Web databases.* 23rd ACM SIGACT-SIGMOD-SIGART Symposium on Principles of Database Systems, Paris.

Guttman, E. (1999). Service Location Protocol: Automatic Discovery of IP Network Services. *IEEE Internet Computing,* 3(4), 71–80. doi:10.1109/4236.780963

Haarslev, V., & Möller, R. (2003). *Racer: A core inference engine for the Semantic Web.* International Workshop on Evaluation of Ontology-based Tools.

Haase, P., van Harmelen, F., Huang, Z., Stuckenschmidt, H., & Sure, Y. (2005, November). A framework for handling inconsistency in changing ontologies. In Y. Gil & et al., (Eds.), *Proceedings of the 4th International Semantic Web Conference, ISWC2005,* (LNCS Vol. 3279, pp. 353—367). Berlin: Springer.

Halevy, A. Y. (2001). Answering queries using views: A survey. *The VLDB Journal,* 10(4), 270–294. doi:10.1007/s007780100054

Halevy, A., Franklin, M., & Maier, D. (2006). Principles of dataspace systems. In *Proceedings of the Symposium on Principles of database systems (PODS2006).*

Halpin, H., & Thomson, H. (2008). Special Issue on Identiy, Reference and the Web. *International Journal on Semantic Web and Information Systems,* 4(2), 1–72.

Halpin, H., Robu, V., & Shepard, H. (2006, November 6). The dynamics and semantics of collaborative tagging. In *Proceedings of the 1st Semantic Authoring and Annotation Workshop (SAAW 2006), 5th International Semantic Web Conference (ISWC 2006),* Athens, GA (Vol. 209) CEUR Workshop Proceedings.

Handschuh, S., Staab, S., & Ciravegna, F. (2002). S-CREAM - Semi-automatic CREAtion of Metadata. *Knowledge Engineering and Knowledge Management: Ontologies and the Semantic Web, LNCS, 2473*, 165–184.

Harth, A. (2009). VisiNav: Visual Web data search and navigation. In S. S. Bhowmick, J. Küng, & R. Wagner (Eds.), *Proceedings of the 20th International Conference on Database and Expert Systems Applications,* Linz, Austria (LNCS 5690, pp. 214-228).

Harth, A., & Decker, S. (2005). *Optimized index structures for querying RDF from the Web.* 3rd Latin American Web Congress (pp. 71-80). Buenos Aires, Argentina: IEEE Press.

Harth, A., Hogan, A., Delbru, R., Umbrich, J., O'Riain, S., & Decker, S. (2007). SWSE: Answers before links! In J. Golbeck & P. Mika (Eds.), *Proceedings of the Semantic Web Challenge 2007,* Busan, Korea (Vol. 295). Retrieved from CEUR-WS.org

Harth, A., Umbrich, J., & Decker, S. (2006). *MultiCrawler: A pipelined architecture for crawling and indexing Semantic Web data.* International Semantic Web Conference (pp. 258-271).

Hartig, O. (2009). Provenance Information in the Web of Data. In *Proceedings of the 2nd Workshop on Linked Data on the Web (LDOW2009).*

Hartig, O., Bizer, C., & Freytag, J.-C. (2009). Executing SPARQL Queries over the Web of Linked Data. In *Proceedings of the 8th International Semantic Web Conference (ISWC2009).*

Hasan, T., & Jameson, A. (2008). Bridging the motivation gap for individual annotators: What can we learn from photo annotation systems? In *Proceedings of the 1st Workshop on Incentives for the Semantic Web (INSEMTIVE 2008), Karlsruhe, Germany.*

Haslhofer, B. (2008). *A Web-based Mapping Technique for Establishing Metadata Interoperability.* PhD thesis, Universität Wien.

Haslhofer, B., & Schandl, B. (2008). The OAI2LOD Server: Exposing OAI-PMH Metadata as Linked Data. In *Proceedings of the 1st Workshop about Linked Data on the Web (LDOW2008).*

Hassanzadeh, O., & Consens, M. (2009). Linked Movie Data Base. In *Proceedings of the 2nd Workshop on Linked Data on the Web (LDOW2009).*

Hassanzadeh, O., et al. (2009). A Declarative Framework for Semantic Link Discovery over Relational Data. *Poster at 18th World Wide Web Conference (WWW2009).*

Hastie, T., Tibshirani, R., & Friedman, J. (2001). *The Elements of Statistical Learning -- Data Mining, Inference, and Prediction.* Berlin: Springer.

Hastrup, T., Cyganiak, R., & Bojars, U. (2008). Browsing Linked Data with Fenfire. In *Proceedings of the 1st Workshop about Linked Data on the Web (LDOW2008).*

Hausenblas, M., Halb, W., Raimond, Y., & Heath, T. (2008). What is the Size of the Semantic Web? In *Proceedings of the International Conference on Semantic Systems (I-Semantics2008).*

Hayes, C., & Avesani, P. (2007, March) *Using blog tags to identify topic authorities.* Paper presented at the 1st International Conference on Weblogs and Social Media (ICWSM 2007), Boulder, Colorado.

Hayes, P. (2004, February). *RDF semantics.*

Heath, T. (2008b). How Will We Interact with the Web of Data? *IEEE Internet Computing, 12*(5), 88–91. doi:10.1109/MIC.2008.101

Heath, T., & Motta, E. (2008). Revyu: Linking reviews and ratings into the Web of Data. *Journal of Web Semantics, 6*(4), 266–273. doi:10.1016/j.websem.2008.09.003

Heath, T. (2008a). *Information-seeking on the Web with Trusted Social Networks – from Theory to Systems.* PhD Thesis, The Open University.

Heath, T., & Motta, E. (2007, November 11-15). Revyu. com: A reviewing and rating site for the Web of Data. In K. Aberer, K. S. Choi, N. Noy, D. Allemang, K. I. Lee, L. J. B. Nixon, et al. (Eds.), *The Semantic Web: Proceedings of the 6th International Semantic Web Conference and 2nd Asian Semantic Web Conference (ISWC/ASWC2007),* Busan, Korea (LNCS 4825, pp. 895-902).

Hellmann, S. (2010). The semantic gap of formalized meaning. In *Proceedings of the European Semantic Web Conference (ESWC),* Heraklion, Greece.

Hellmann, S., Unbehauen, J., Chiarcos, C., & Ngonga Ngomo, A. (2010). The TIGER Corpus Navigator. In: *Proceedings of the Ninth International Workshop on Treebanks and Linguistic Theories,* TLT9.

Hellmann, S., Unbehauen, J., & Lehmann, J. (2010). HANNE - A Holistic Application for Navigational Knowledge Engineering. In *Posters and Demos of ISWC* 2010.

Hemayati, R., Meng, W., & Yu, C. (2007). Semantic-Based Grouping of Search Engine Results Using WordNet. *Advanced in Data and Web Management, LNCS, 4505,* 678–686. doi:10.1007/978-3-540-72524-4_70

Hepp, M. (2007). Possible ontologies: How reality constrains the development of relevant ontologies. *IEEE Internet Computing, 11*(1), 90–96. doi:10.1109/MIC.2007.20

Hepp, M., Siorpaes, K., & Bachlechner, D. (2007). Harvesting Wiki consensus: Using Wikipedia entries as vocabulary for knowledge management. *IEEE Internet Computing, 11*(5), 54–65. doi:10.1109/MIC.2007.110

Hevner, A., March, S., Park, J., & Ram, S. (2005). Design Science in Information Systems Research. *Management Information Systems Quarterly, 28,* 75–105.

Hildebrand, M., van Ossenbruggen, J., & Hardman, L. (2006). /facet: A browser for heterogeneous Semantic Web repositories. In I. Cruz, S. Decker, D. Allemang, C. Preist, D. Schwabe, P. Mika, M. Uschold, & L. Aroyo (Eds.), *The Semantic Web: ISWC 2006: Proceedings of the 5th International Semantic Web Conference,* Athens, GA (LNCS 4273, pp. 272-285).

Hitzler, P., & Vrandečić, D. (2005 November). Resolution-based approximate reasoning for OWL DL. In Y. Gil and et al., (Eds.), *Proceedings of the 4th International Semantic Web Conference, ISWC2005,* (LNCS Vol. 3279, pp. 383—397). Berlin: Springer.

Hliaoutakis, A., Varelas, G., Voutsakis, E., Petrakis, E., & Milios, E. (2006). Information Retrieval by Semantic Similarity. *International Journal on Semantic Web and Information Systems, 2*(3), 55–73. doi:10.4018/jswis.2006070104

Hofmann, T. (2001). Unsupervised learning by probabilistic latent semantic analysis. *Machine Learning, 42*(1-2), 177–196. doi:10.1023/A:1007617005950

Hogan, A., Harth, A., & Polleres, A. (2009). Scalable authoritative OWL reasoning for the Web. *International Journal on Semantic Web and Information Systems, 5*(2), 45–90. doi:10.4018/IJSWIS.2009040103

Hogan, A., & Decker, S. (2009). *On the ostensibly silent 'W' in OWL 2 RL.* Paper presented at the Web Reasoning and Rule Systems, Third International Conference (RR), Chantilly, VA, USA.

Hogan, A., Harth, A., & Decker, S. (2007). *Performing object consolidation on the Semantic Web data graph.* 1st I3 Workshop: Identity, Identifiers, Identification Workshop.

Hogan, A., Harth, A., Umrich, J., & Decker, S. (2007). Towards a scalable search and query engine for the web. In *Proceedings of the 16th Conference on World Wide Web (WWW2007).*

Hogan, A., Harth, A., & Decker, S. (2006, Novmber). *ReConRank: A scalable ranking method for Semantic Web data with context.* Paper presented at the 2nd International Workshop on Scalable Semantic Web Knowledge Base Systems, Athens, GA.

Hogan, A., Harth, A., & Polleres, A. (2008). SAOR: Authoritative reasoning for the Web. In J. Domingue & C. Anutariya (Eds.), *The Semantic Web: Proceedings of the 3rd Asian Semantic Web Conference,* Bangkok, Thailand (LNCS 5367, pp. 76-90).

Hogan, A., Pan, J. Z., Polleres, A., & Decker, S. (2010). *SAOR: Template rule optimisations for distributed reasoning over 1 billion linked data triples.* Paper presented at the 9th International Semantic Web Conference (ISWC), Shanghai, China.

Hondjack, D., Pierra, G., & Bellatreche, L. (2007). OntoDB: An ontology-based database for data intensive applications. *Proceedings of the 12th International Conference on Database Systems for Advanced Applications* (pp. 497-508). Bangkok, Thailand.

Horrocks, I., Patel-Schneider, P. F., & van Harmelen, F. (2003). From SHIQ and RDF to OWL: The making of a Web ontology language. *Journal of Web Semantics, 1*(1), 7–26. doi:10.1016/j.websem.2003.07.001

Horrocks, I., & Patel-Schneider, P. F. (2004). Reducing OWL entailment to description logic satisfiability. *Journal of Web Semantics, 1*(4), 345–357. doi:10.1016/j.websem.2004.06.003

Horrocks, I., & Patel-Schneider, P. F. (1999). Optimising Description Logic Subsumption. *Journal of Logic and Computation, 9*(3), 267–293. doi:10.1093/logcom/9.3.267

Horrocks, I., & Patel-Schneider, P. F. (2003). Reducing OWL entailment to description logic satisfiability. In D. Fensel, K. Sycara, & J. Mylopoulos (Eds.), *Proc. of the 2nd International Semantic Web Conference (ISWC 2003)* (pp. 17-29). Springer.

Horrocks, I., & Sattler, U. (2005). A Tableaux Decision Procedure for SHOIQ. *19th International Conference on Artificial Intelligence (IJCAI 2005).*

Horrocks, I., Kutz, O., & Sattler, U. (2006. June 2-5). The even more irresistible SROIQ. In P. Doherty, J. Mylopoulos, & C. A. Welty (Eds.), *Proceedings, tenth International Conference on principles of knowledge representation and reasoning, lake district of the United Kingdom* (pp. 57-67). AAAI Press.

Horrocks, I., Li, L., Turi, D., & Bechhofer, S. (2004). The instance store: DL reasoning with large numbers of individuals. In V. Haarslev & R. Müller (Eds.), *Description logics* (Vol. 104). Retrieved from CEUR-WS.org

Horrocks, I., Sattler, U., & Tobies, S. (1999). Practical reasoning for expressive description logics. In *Proceeding of the 6th International Conference on Logic for Programming and Automated Reasoning (LPAR99)*, (pp. 161–180).

Hotho, A., Jäschke, R., Schmitz, C., & Stumme, G. (2006, June 11-14). Information retrieval in folksonomies: Search and ranking. In Y. Sure & J. Domingue (Eds.), *The Semantic Web: Research and Applications: 3rd European Semantic Web Conference (ESWC 2006)*, Budva, Montenegro (LNCS 4011, pp. 411-426).

Howes, T. A., & Smith, M. C. (1995). *A Scalable, Deployable Directory Service Framework for the Internet. Technical report.* Center for Information Technology Integration, Univerity of Michigan.

Huang, Z., & van Harmelen, F. (2008). Using semantic distances for reasoning with inconsistent ontologies. In A. Sheth, et al., (Eds.), *Proceedings of the 7th International Semantic Web Conference, ISWC2008*, (LNCS Vol. 5318, pp. 178—194). Berlin: Springer.

Huang, Z., van Harmelen, F., & ten Teije, A. (2005). Reasoning with inconsistent ontologies. In L. Kaelbling & A. Saffiotti, (eds.), *Proceedings of the 19th International Joint Conference on Artificial Intelligence, IJCAI05*, (pp. 454—459).

Hughes, T. C., & Ashpole, B. C. (2004). The semantics of ontology alignment. In *Proceedings of Information Interpretation and Integration Conference (I3CON), Performance Metrics for Intelligent Systems, PerMIS '04.*

Hull, D. (1993). Using statistical testing in the evaluation of retrieval experiments. In *Proceedings of the 16th annual international ACM SIGIR conference on research and development in information retrieval* (pp. 329-338). New York: ACM.

Hüsemann, B., & Vossen, G. (2005). Ontology engineering from a database perspective. *Lecture Notes in Computer Science, 3818*, 49–63. doi:10.1007/11596370_6

Huynh, D. F., Miller, R. C., & Karger, D. R. (2007). Potluck: Data mash-up tool for casual users. In K. Aberer, K. S. Choi, N. Noy, D. Allemang, K. I. Lee, L. J. B. Nixon, … P. Cudré-Mauroux (Eds.), *ISWC/ASWC 2007.* (LNCS 4825), (pp. 239–252). Springer.

Huynh, D., Karger, D., & Miller, R. (2007). Exhibit: Lightweight structured data publishing. In *Proceedings of the 16th international conference on World Wide Web* (pp. 737–746). New York, NY: ACM Press.

Hwang, M., Baek, S., Choi, J., Park, J., & Kim, P. (2008, January). Grasping Related Words of Unknown Word for Automatic Extension of Lexical Dictionary. In *Proceeding of First International Workshop on Knowledge Discovery and Data Mining*, (pp. 31-35).

Hyvönen, E., Viljanen, K., Tuominen, J., & Seppälä, K. (2008, June 1-5). Building a national semantic web ontology and ontology service infrastructure—the FinnONTO approach. In *5th european semantic web conference (eswc 2008)* (pp. 95–109). Springer.

Iannone, L., Palmisano, I., & Fanizzi, N. (2007). An algorithm based on counterfactuals for concept learning in the semantic web. *Applied Intelligence*, *26*(2), 139–159. doi:10.1007/s10489-006-0011-5

Ide, N., & Véronis, J. (1998). Introduction to the special issue on word sense disambiguation: the state of the art. *Computational Linguistics*, *24*(1), 2–40.

Idehen, K., & Erling, O. (2008, April 22). Linked data spaces & data portability. In *Proceedings of the Linked Data on the Web Workshop (LDOW 2008)*, Beijing, China (Vol. 369). CEUR Workshop Publishers.

Institute of Electrical and Electronics Engineers (IEEE) (1990). *Standard computer dictionary - a compilation of IEEE standard computer glossaries*.

Issarny, V., & Sailhan, F. (2005). Scalable Service Discovery for MANET. *Third IEEE International Conference on Pervasive Computing and Communications (PerCom)*, Kauai Island, Hawaii.

Jaccard, P. (1901). Etude comparative de la distribution florale dans une portion des alpes et du jura. *Bulletin de la Société Vaudoise des Sciences Naturelles*, *37*, 547–579.

Jacobs, I., & Walsh, N. (2004). *Architecture of the World Wide Web, Volume One - W3C Recommendation*. Retrieved June 14, 2009, http://www.w3.org/TR/webarch/

Jacobs, I., & Walsh, N. (2004, December 15). *Architecture of the World Wide Web, volume one*. Retrieved May 8, 2009, from W3C Recommendation's Web site: http://www.w3.org/TR/webarch/

Jaffri, A., Glaser, H., & Millard, I. (2008, June 2). *Managing URI synonymity to enable consistent reference on the Semantic Web*. Paper presented at the Workshop on Identity and Reference on the Semantic Web (IRSW 2008) at the 5th European Semantic Web Conference (ESWC 2008), Tenerife, Spain.

Jain, P., Hitzler, P., Sheth, A. P., Verma, K., & Yeh, P. Z. (2010). Ontology alignment for linked open data. In *Proceedings of the 9th International Semantic Web Conference (ISWC2010)*, Shanghai, China.

Jarrar, M., & Meersman, R. (2008). Ontology engineering - the DOGMA approach. In *Advances in Web semantics I. (LNCS 4891)*. Springer.

Jarrar, M., & Meersman, R. (2002). Formal ontology engineering in the DOGMA approach. In R. Meersman, & Z. Tari (Eds.), *Proceedings of DOA/CoopIS/ODBASE 2002*, (LNCS 2519), (pp. 1238-1254). Berlin/Heidelberg, Germany: Springer-Verlag.

Java, A., Nirenburg, S., McShane, M., Finin, T., English, J., & Joshi, A. (2007). Using a Natural Language Understanding System to Generate Semantic Web Content. *International Journal on Semantic Web and Information Systems*, *3*(4), 50–74. doi:10.4018/jswis.2007100103

Jena - HP Semantic Framework. (2009). from http://www.hpl.hp.com/semweb/.

Jentzsch, A., Hassanzadeh, O., Bizer, C., Andersson, B., & Stephens, S. (2009). Enabling Tailored Therapeutics with Linked Data. In *Proceedings of the 2nd Workshop on Linked Data on the Web (LDOW2009)*.

Jhingran, A. (2008). *Web 2.0, enterprise 2.0 and information management. Keynote speech at the Linked Data Planet conference & expo, spring 2008*. New York City.

Jiang, J. J., & Conrath, D. W. (1997, September). Semantic similarity based on corpus statistics and lexical taxonomy. In *Proceedings of the international conference research on computational linguistics (ROCLING X)* (pp. 19-33).

Jiang, J., & Conrath, D. (1997). Semantic Similarity based on Corpus Statistics and Lexical Taxonomy. In *Proceeding of International Conference on Research in Computational Linguistics*. Taiwan.

Jiménez-Ruiz, E., Grau, B. C., Sattler, U., Schneider, T., & Llavori, R. B. (2008). Safe and economic re-use of ontologies: A logic-based methodology and tool support. *Proceedings of the 21st International Workshop on Description Logics (DL2008)*. Dresden, Germany.

Jones, K. S. (1972). A statistical interpretation of term specificity and its application in retrieval. *The Journal of Documentation*, *28*(1), 11–21. doi:10.1108/eb026526

Jovanovic, J., Gasevic, D., & Devedzic, V. (2006, April). Ontology-Based Automatic Annotation of Learning Content. *International Journal on Semantic Web and Information Systems*, *2*(2), 91–119. doi:10.4018/jswis.2006040103

Kahan, J., & Koivunen, M.-R. (2001, May 1-5). Annotea: An open rdf infrastructure for shared Web annotations. In *Proceedings of the 10th international conference on World Wide Web (WWW 2001)*, Hong Kong, China (pp. 623-632). New York: ACM Publishers.

Kalfoglou, Y., & Schorlemmer, M. (2003). Ontology mapping: The state of the art. [KER]. *The Knowledge Engineering Review Journal*, *18*(1), 1–31. doi:10.1017/S0269888903000651

KAON2. (2008). Retrieved June 21, 2007, from http://kaon2.semanticweb.org.

Karger, D. R., & Quan, D. (2005). What would it mean to blog on the Semantic Web? *Journal of Web Semantics*, *3*(2), 147–157. doi:10.1016/j.websem.2005.06.002

Karger, D., & Schraefel, M. C. (2006). Pathetic Fallacy of RDF. In *Proceedings of 3rd Semantic Web User Interaction Workshop (SWUI2006)*.

Kashyap, V., & Sheth, A. (2000). *Information Brokering across Heterogeneous Digital Data: A Metadatabased Approach*. Boston: Kluwer Academic Publishers. Overeem, A., & Witters, J. (2004). *Architecture for Delivering pan-European e-Government Services*, IDA technical report, Capgemini.

Kekäläinen, J., & Järvelin, K. (2000). The co-effects of query structure and expansion on retrieval performance in probabilistic text retrieval. *Information Retrieval*, *1*(4), 329–344. doi:10.1023/A:1009983401464

Kekäläinen, J., & Järvelin, K. (2002). Using graded relevance assessments in IR evaluation. *Journal of the American Society for Information Science and Technology*, *53*(13), 1120–1129. doi:10.1002/asi.10137

Kendall, G. C., Feigenbaum, L., & Torres, E. (2008). *SPARQL Protocol for RDF. W3C Recommendation*. Retrieved March 2, 2009, http://www.w3.org/TR/rdf-sparql-protocol/

Kerrigan, M., Mocan, A., Tanler, M., & Fensel, D. (2007, June). The Web Service Modeling Toolkit - An Integrated Development Environment for Semantic Web Services. In *Proceedings of the 4th European Semantic Web Conference (ESWC)*, System Description Track, Innsbruck, Austria.

Kifer, M., Lausen, G., & Wu, J. (1995, July). Logical foundations of object-oriented and frame-based languages. *Journal of the ACM*, (42): 741–843. doi:10.1145/210332.210335

Kim, H. L., Yang, S. K., Breslin, J. G., & Kim, H. G. (2007, November 2-5). Simple algorithms for representing tag frequencies in the SCOT exporter. In *Proceedings of the IEEE/WIC/ACM International Conference on Intelligent Agent Technology*, Silicon Valley, CA (pp. 536-539). IEEE Computer Society.

Kiryakov, A., Popov, B., Terziev, I., Manov, D., & Ognyanoff, D. (2004, December). Semantic annotation, indexing, and retrieval. *Web Semantics: Science. Services and Agents on the World Wide Web*, *2*(1), 49–79. doi:10.1016/j.websem.2004.07.005

Kiryakov, A., Ognyanov, D., & Manov, D. (2005). *OWLIM - a pragmatic semantic repository for OWL* (pp. 182–192). New York, USA: Web Information Systems Engineering Workshops.

Kiryakov, A., Ognyanoff, D., Velkov, R., Tashev, Z., & Peikov, I. (2009). *LDSR: Materialized reasonable view to the Web of linked data*. Paper presented at the OWL: Experiences and Directions Workshop (OWLED), Chantilly, VA, USA.

Kleemann, T. (2006). Towards Mobile Reasoning. *International Workshop on Description Logics (DL2006)*, Windermere, Lake District, UK.

Klyne, G., & Carroll, J. (2004). *Resource Description Framework (RDF): Concepts and Abstract Syntax - W3C Recommendation*. Retrieved June 14, 2009, http://www.w3.org/TR/rdf-concepts/

Kobilarov, G., et al. (2009). Media Meets Semantic Web - How the BBC Uses DBpedia and Linked Data to Make Conections. In *Proceedings of the 6th European Semantic Web Conference (ESWC2009)*.

Kolaitis, P. G. (2005). Schema mappings, data exchange, and metadata management. In *Proceedings of the twenty-fourth ACM SIGMOD-SIGACT-SIGART symposium on Principles of database systems*, June 13-15, 2005, Baltimore, Maryland

Kolovski, V., Wu, Z., & Eadon, G. (2010). *Optimizing enterprise-scale OWL 2 RL reasoning in a relational database system.* Paper presented at the 9th International Semantic Web Conference (ISWC), Shanghai, China.

Kong, H., Hwang, M., Hwang, G., Shim, J., & Kim, P. (2006). Topic Selection of Web Documents Using Specific Domain Ontology. *MICAI 2006: Advances in Artificial Intelligence. LNAI, 4293,* 1047–1056.

Kong, H., Hwang, M., & Kim, P. (2006, August). The Method for the Unknown Word Classification, In *Proceeding of The 2006 Pacific Rim Knowledge Acquisition Workshop, LNCS4303,* (pp. 207-215).

Krötzsch, M., Vrandečić, D., & Völkel, M. (2006). Semantic MediaWiki. In *Proceedings of the 5th International Semantic Web Conference (ISWC06)* (pp. 935–942). Springer.

Kuhn, H. W. (1955). The Hungarian method for the assignment problem. *Naval Research Logistics Quarterly, 2,* 83–97. doi:10.1002/nav.3800020109

Kunkle, D., & Cooperman, G. (2008). Solving Rubik's cube: Disk is the new RAM. *Communications of the ACM, 51*(4), 31–33. doi:10.1145/1330311.1330319

Kurakawa, K., Shakya, A., & Takeda, H. (2009). A trial on extracting and integrating concepts of university staff directories for federated search. In *Proceedings of the 23rd Annual Conference of the Japanese Society for Artificial Intelligence.*

Küster, U., König-Ries, B., & Klein, M. (2006). Discovery and Mediation using DIANE Service Descriptions. *Second Semantic Web Service Challenge 2006 Workshop,* Budva, Montenegro.

Kutz, O., Lutz, C., Wolter, F., & Zakharyaschev, M. (2004). ε-connections of abstract description systems. *Artificial Intelligence, 156*(1), 1–73. doi:10.1016/j.artint.2004.02.002

Landauer, T., Foltz, P. W., & Laham, D. (1998). Introduction to latent semantic analysis. *Discourse Processes, 25*(1), 259–284. doi:10.1080/01638539809545028

Lausen, H., de Bruijn, J., Polleres, A., & Fensel, D. (2005). WSML - A Language Framework for Semantic Web Services. *W3C Workshop on Rule Languages for Interoperability.*

Le Phuoc, D., Polleres, A., Morbidoni, C., Hauswirth, M., & Tummarello, G. (2009). Rapid semantic web mashup development through semantic web pipes. In *Proceedings of the 18th World Wide Web Conference (WWW2009).*

Leacock, C., & Chodorow, M. (1998). Combining local context and WordNet similarity for word sense identification. In Fellbaum, C. (Ed.), *WordNet: An electronic lexical database* (pp. 265–283). Cambridge, MA: MIT Press.

Lee, C., Helal, A., Desai, N., Verma, V., & Arslan, B. (2003). Konark: A System and Protocols for Device Independent, Peer-to-Peer Discovery and Delivery of Mobile Services. *IEEE Transactions on Systems, Man, and Cybernetics, 33*(6).

Lehmann, J., & Hitzler, P. (2010). Concept learning in description logics using refinement operators. *Machine Learning, 78,* 203–250. doi:10.1007/s10994-009-5146-2

Lehmann, J. (2009). DL-Learner: Learning concepts in description logic. *Journal of Machine Learning Research.*

Lehmann, J., & Bühmann, L. (2010). ORE - a tool for repairing and enriching knowledge bases. In *Proceedings of the 9th International Semantic Web Conference,* Lecture Notes in Computer Science, Springer.

Lehmann, J., & Hitzler, P. (2007a). Foundations of refinement operators for description logics. In *17th International Conference on Inductive Logic Programming (ILP).*

Lehmann, J., & Hitzler, P. (2007b). A refinement operator based learning algorithm for the ALC description logic. *17th International Conference on Inductive Logic Programming (ILP).*

Lenat, D. (1995). CYC: A large-scale investment in knowledge infrastructure. *Communications of the ACM, 38*(11), 33–38. doi:10.1145/219717.219745

Lenzerini, M. (2002). Data Integration: A Theoretical Perspective. In *Proceedings of the twenty-first ACM SIGMOD-SIGACT-SIGART symposium on Principles of database systems,* (pp. 233-246).

Lesk, M. (1986). Automatic Sense Disambiguation Using Machine Readable Dictionaries: how to tell a pine cone from an ice cream cone. In V. DeBuys (Ed.), *Proceedings of the 5th annual international conference on Systems documentation.* (pp. 24-26). Toronto: ACM press.

Lin, C. Y., & Hovy, E. (2000). The automated acquisition of topic signatures for text summarization. In *Proceedings of the 18th conference on computational linguistics* (pp. 495-501). Morristown, NJ: Association for Computational Linguistics.

Lin, D. (1998). An information-theoretic definition of similarity. In *Proceedings of the 15th International Conference on Machine Learning.*

Lin, D. (1998). Automatic retrieval and clustering of similar words. In *Proceedings of the 17th international conference on computational linguistics* (pp. 768-774). Morristown, NJ: Association for Computational Linguistics.

Liu, H., & Singh, P. (2004). ConceptNet – a practical commonsense reasoning tool-kit. [Springer.]. *BT Technology Journal, 22*(4), 211–226. doi:10.1023/B:BTTJ.0000047600.45421.6d

Liu, S., Liu, F., Yu, C., & Meng, W. (2004). An effective approach to document retrieval via utilizing WordNet and recognizing phrases. In *Proceeding of SIGIR 2004,* (pp. 266-272).

Liu, S., Yu, C., & Meng, W. (2005). Word Sense Disambiguation in Queries. *In Proceedings of the 14th ACM international conference on Information and knowledge management.* (pp. 525-532). Bremen: ACM press.

Lloyd, J. W. (1987). *Foundations of logic programming* (2nd ed.). Springer-Verlag.

Longo, C., & Sciuto, L. (2007). A lightweight ontology for rating assessments. In *Proceedings of 4ᵗʰ Italian Workshop on Semantic Web Applications and Perspectives (SWAP 2007)*, Bari, Italy.

Lonsdale, D., Embley, D. W., Ding, Y., Xu, L., & Hepp, M. (2009). *Reusing ontologies and language components for ontology generation.* Data & Knowledge Engineering.

Lukasiewicz, T. (2008). Expressive probabilistic description logics. *Artificial Intelligence, 172*(6-7), 852–883. doi:10.1016/j.artint.2007.10.017

Lutz, C., Walther, D., & Wolter, F. (2007). Conservative extensions in expressive description logics. *IJCAI 2007, Proceedings of the 20th International Joint Conference on Artificial Intelligence* (pp. 453-458). Hyderabad, India.

Ma, L. (2006). Towards a Complete OWL Ontology Benchmark (UOBM). *The Semantic Web: Research and Applications, LNCS., 4011*, 125–139. doi:10.1007/11762256_12

Maguitman, A. G., Menczer, F., Roinestad, H., & Vespignani, A. (2005). Algorithmic detection of semantic similarity. In *Proceedings of the 14th international conference on World Wide Web* (pp. 107-116). New York: ACM.

Mandala, R., Takenobu, T., & Hozumi, T. (1998). The Use of WordNet in Information Retrieval. In *Proceedings of Use of WordNet in Natural Language Processing Systems*, (pp. 31-37).

Manning, C. D., Raghavan, P., & Schütze, H. (2008). *Introduction to information retrieval* (1st ed.). Cambridge, UK: Cambridge University Press.

March, S., & Smith, G. (1995). Design and natural science research on information technology. *Decision Support Systems, 15*, 251–266. doi:10.1016/0167-9236(94)00041-2

Marlow, C., Naaman, M., Boyd, D., & Davis, M. (2006, August 23-25). *HT06, tagging paper, taxonomy, Flickr, academic article, to read.* Paper presented at the 17th Conference on Hypertext and Hypermedia, Odense, Denmark.

Marshall, C., & Shipman, F. (2003). Which semantic web? In *Proceedings of the 14th ACM Conference on Hypertext and Hypermedia (HT2003).*

Mathes, A. (2004). Folksonomies - Cooperative Classification and Communication Through Shared Metadata. In *Computer Mediated Communication.* Urbana-Champaign, IL: Graduate School of Library and Information Science, University of Illinois.

Matveeva, I., & Levow, G. (2007, June). Topic Segmentation with Hybrid Document Indexing. In *Proceedings of the 2007 Joint Conference on Empirical Methods in Natural Language Processing and Computational Natural Language Learning*, 351-359.

McAfee, A. (2006). Enterprise 2.0: The dawn of emergent collaboration. *MIT Sloan Management Review, 47*(3), 21–28.

McGuinness, D., & da Silva, P. (2003). Infrastructure for Web Explanations. In *Proceedings of the 2nd International Semantic Web Conference (ISWC2003).*

McGuinness, D., & van Harmelen, F. (2004). *OWL Web Ontology Language - W3C Recommendation.* Retrieved June 14, 2009, http://www.w3.org/TR/owl-features/

Meersman, R. (1999). The use of lexicons and other computer-linguistic tools in semantics, design and cooperation of database systems. In *Proceedings of the Conference on Cooperative Database Systems (CODAS99)*, (pp. 1-14). Springer.

Menor, L., Tatikonda, M., & Sampson, S. (2002). New service development: areas for exploitation and exploration. *Journal of Operations Management, 20*, 135–157. doi:10.1016/S0272-6963(01)00091-2

Merholz, P. (2004, October 19). Metadata for the masses. Retrieved May 8, 2009, http://www.adaptivepath.com/ideas/essays/archives/000361.php

Mihalcea, R., Tarau, P., & Figa, E. (2004). PageRank on Semantic Networks, with application to Word Sense Disambiguation. *In Proceedings of the 20th international conference on Computational Linguistics.* Geneva: Association for Computational Linguistics Press.

Mika, P. (2007). Ontologies are us: A unified model of social networks and semantics. *Web Semantics: Science* [Springer.]. *Services and Agents on the World Wide Web, 5*(1), 5–15. doi:10.1016/j.websem.2006.11.002

Mika, P. (2005, November 6-10). Ontologies are us: A unified model of social networks and semantics. In Y. Gil, E. Motta, V. R. Benjamins, & M. A. Musen (Eds.), *The Semantic Web: ISWC 2005: 4th International Semantic Web Conference*, Galway, Ireland (LNCS 3729, pp. 522-536).

Miles, A., & Bechhofer, S. (2009). *SKOS Simple Knowledge Organization System Reference.* Retrieved October 1, 2009, from http://www.w3.org/TR/2009/REC-skos-reference-20090818

Miles, A., & Brickley, D. (2005, November). *Skos core vocabulary specification.* World Wide Web Consortium. Retrieved August 15, 2008, from http://www.w3.org/TR/2005/WD-swbp-skos-core-spec-20051102/

Miller, R. J., Hernandez, M. A., Haas, L. M., Yan, L., Ho, C. T. H., Fagin, R., & Popa, L. (2001). The Clio Project: Managing Heterogeneity. *SIGMOD Record, 30*(1), 78–83. doi:10.1145/373626.373713

Miller, G. A., Beckwith, R., Fellbaum, C., Gross, D., & Miller, K. J. (1990). Introduction to wordnet: An on-line lexical database. *Journal of Lexicography, 3*(4), 235–244. doi:10.1093/ijl/3.4.235

Miller, G. (1990). WordNet: An On-line Lexical Database. *International Journal of Lexicography, 3*, 235–244. doi:10.1093/ijl/3.4.235

Miller, G. (1995). WordNet: A lexical database for english. *Communications of the ACM, 38*(11). doi:10.1145/219717.219748

Miller, G. A., & Charles, W. G. (1991). Contextual correlates of semantic similarity. *Language and Cognitive Processes, 6*(1), 1–28. doi:10.1080/01690969108406936

Miller, B. A., & Pascoe, R. A. (2000). Salutation Service Discovery in Pervasive Computing Environments. *IBM Pervasive Computing White Paper*.

Miller, P., Styles, R., & Heath, T. (2008). Open Data Commons, a License for Open Data. In *Proceedings of the 1st Workshop about Linked Data on the Web (LDOW2008)*.

Missikoff, M., Velardi, P., & Fabriani, P. (2003). Text Mining Techniques to Automatically Enrich a Domain Ontology. *Applied Intelligence, 18*(3), 323–340. doi:10.1023/A:1023254205945

MITRE (2004). Netcentric Semantic Linking Report: *An Approach to Enterprise Semantic*.

Mocan, A., & Cimpian, E. (2007). An ontology-based data mediation framework for semantic environments. [IJSWIS]. *International Journal on Semantic Web and Information Systems, 3*(2), 66–95. doi:10.4018/jswis.2007040104

Mocan, A., Cimpian, E., & Kerrigan, M. (2006, November). Formal Model for Ontology Mapping Creation. In *Proceedings of the 5th International Semantic Web Conference (ISWC 2006)*, Athens, Georgia, USA.

Mocan, A., Kerrigan, M., & Cimpian, E. (2008, June). Applying Reasoning to Instance Transformation. *International Workshop on Ontologies: Reasoning and Modularity (WORM-08)*, Tenerife, Spain

Möller, K., Bojārs, U. U., & Breslin, J. G. (2006). Using semantics to enhance the blogging experience. In *The Semantic Web: Research and Applications. (LNCS 4011)* (pp. 679–696). Heidelberg, Germany: Springer. doi:10.1007/11762256_49

Möller, R., Haarslev, V., & Wessel, M. (2006). On the scalability of description logic instance retrieval. In B. Parsia, U. Sattler, & D. Toman, (Esd.), *Proceedings of the 2006 International Workshop on Description Logics, DL2006,* (Vol. 189: *CEUR Workshop Proceedings*).

Moreau, L., et al. (2008). *The Open Provenance Model.* Technical report, Electronics and Computer Science, University of Southampton.

Motik, B. (2006). *Reasoning in description logics using resolution and deductive databases.* Karlsruhe, Germany: Forschungszentrum Informatik.

Motik, B. (2007). On the properties of metamodeling in OWL. *Journal of Logic and Computation, 17*(4), 617–637. doi:10.1093/logcom/exm027

Muñoz, S., Pérez, J., & Gutiérrez, C. (2007). *Minimal deductive systems for RDF* (pp. 53–67). ESWC.

Murphy, G. L. (2004). *The big book of concepts.* MIT press.

Mysaifu, J. V. M. (2009). Retrieved from http://www2s.biglobe.ne.jp/~dat/java/project/jvm/index_en.html.

Nakov, P., & Hearst, M. A. (2008, June). Solving relational similarity problems using the Web as a corpus. In *Proceedings of ACL-08: HLT* (pp. 452-460). Columbus, OH: Association for Computational Linguistics.

Navigli, R., & Velardi, P. (2004, June). Learning Domain Ontologies from Document Warehouses and Dedicated Web Sites. *Computational Linguistics, 30*(2), 151–179. doi:10.1162/089120104323093276

Navigli, R., & Velardi, P. (2005). Structural Semantic Interconnections: a knowledge-based approach to word sense disambiguation. *Special Issue-Syntactic and Structural Pattern Recognition. IEEE Transactions on Pattern Analysis and Machine Intelligence, 27*(7).

Navigli, R., & Velardi, P. (2006). Ontology Enrichment Through Automatic Semantic Annotation of OnLine Glossaries. *EKAW 2006. Managing Knowledge in a World of Networks, LNCS, 4248,* 125–140.

Navigli, R., Velardi, P., & Gangemi, A. (2003, January/February). Ontology Learning and Its Application to Automated Terminology Translation. *IEEE Intelligent Systems, 18*(1), 22–31. doi:10.1109/MIS.2003.1179190

Nenkova, A., Vanderwende, L., & McKeown, K. (2006). A compositional context sensitive multi-document summarizer: Exploring the factors that influence summarization. In E. N. Efthimiadis, S. Dumais, D. Hawking, & K. Järvelin (Eds.), *Proceedings of the 29th Annual International ACM SIGIR Conference on Research and Development in Information Retrieval,* Seattle, WA (pp. 573-580). New York, NY: ACM.

Newman, R., Ayers, D., & Russell, S. (2005). *Tag ontology.* Retrieved May 8, 2009, from http://www.holygoat.co.uk/owl/redwood/0.1/tags/

Nielsen, J. (2006). Participation inequality: Encouraging more users to contribute. *Alertbox: Current Issues in Web Usability.* Retrieved April 16, 2009, from http://www.useit.com/alertbox/participation_inequality.html

Nienhuys-Cheng, S.-H., & de Wolf, R. (Eds.). (1997). *Foundations of inductive logic programming.* Springer.

Nikolov, A., et al. (2008). Integration of Semantically Annotated Data by the KnoFuss Architecture. In *Proceedings of the 16th International Conference on Knowledge Engineering and Knowledge Management.*

Ning, K., O'Sullivan, D., Zhu, Q., & Decker, S. (2006). Semantic innovation management across the extended enterprise. *International Journal of Industrial and Systems Engineering, 1,* 109–128. doi:10.1504/IJISE.2006.009052

Noy, N. F., & Munsen, M. A. (2003). The PROMPT suite: Interactive tools for ontology merging and mapping. *International Journal of Human-Computer Studies, 6*(59).

Noy, N. F., & McGuinness, D. L. (2001). *Ontology development 101: A guide to creating your first ontology* (Tech. Rep. KSL-01-05 and Stanford Medical Informatics Technical Report SMI-2001-0880). Palo Alto, CA: Stanford Knowledge Systems Laboratory.

Nunamaker, J., Chen, M., & Purdin, T. D. M. (1991). Systems Development in Information Systems Research. *Journal of Management Information Systems, 7,* 89–106.

O'Reilly, T. (2005, September 30). *What is Web 2.0: Design patterns and business models for the next generation of software*. Retrieved May 8, 2009, from http://www.oreillynet.com/lpt/a/6228

Ogawa, S., & Piller, F. (2006). Reducing the Risks of New Product Development. *MIT Sloan Management Review, 47*, 65–71.

Olston, C., & Chi, E. (2003). ScentTrails: Integrating Browsing and Searching on the Web. *ACM Transactions on Computer-Human Interaction, 10*(3), 177–197. doi:10.1145/937549.937550

Oren, E. (2008). Sindice.com: A document-oriented lookup index for open linked data. *Journal of Metadata. Semantics and Ontologies, 3*(1), 37–52. doi:10.1504/IJMSO.2008.021204

Oren, E., Delbru, R., Catasta, M., Cyganiak, R., Stenzhorn, H., & Tummarello, G. (2008). Sindice.com: A document-oriented lookup index for open linked data. *International Journal of Metadata. Semantics and Ontologies, 3*(1), 37–52. doi:10.1504/IJMSO.2008.021204

Oren, E., Delbru, R., & Decker, S. (2006). Extending faceted navigation for RDF data. In I. Cruz, S. Decker, D. Allemang, C. Preist, D. Schwabe, P. Mika, M. Uschold, & L. Aroyo (Eds.), *The Semantic Web: ISWC 2006: Proceedings of the 5th International Semantic Web Conference,* Athens, GA (LNCS 4273, pp. 559-572).

Owens, A., et al. (2009). *Clustered TDB: A Clustered Triple Store for Jena*. Retrieved March 2, 2009, http://eprints.ecs.soton.ac.uk/16974/

OWL-API. (2008). Retrieved from http://owlapi.sourceforge.net/.

Pan, Z., Qasem, A., Kanitkar, S., Prabhakar, F., & Heflin, J. (2007). *Hawkeye: A practical large scale demonstration of Semantic Web integration. Proceedings of On the Move to Meaningful Internet Systems Workshops* (pp. 1115–1124). OTM-II.

Pan, Z., & Heflin, J. (2003). DLDB: Extending relational databases to support Semantic Web queries. *PSSS1 - Practical and Scalable Semantic Systems, Proceedings of the First International Workshop on Practical and Scalable Semantic Systems*. Sanibel Island, Florida, USA.

Park, J., & Ram, S. (2004). Information systems interoperability: What lies beneath? *ACM Transactions on Information Systems, 22*(4), 595–632. doi:10.1145/1028099.1028103

Parsia, B., Sirin, E., & Kalyanpur, A. (2005). Debugging OWL ontologies. In *Proceedings of the 14th International World Wide Web Conference.*

Passant, A. (2008, June). Case study: Enhancement and integration of corporate social software using the Semantic Web. *Semantic Web use cases and case studies*. Retrieved May 8, 2009, from the W3C Semantic Web Education and Outreach Interest Group's Web site: http://www.w3.org/2001/sw/sweo/public/UseCases/EDF

Passant, A., & Laublet, P. (2008, April 22). Meaning Of A Tag: A collaborative approach to bridge the gap between tagging and linked data. In *Proceedings of the Linked Data on the Web Workshop (LDOW 2008),* Beijing, China (Vol. 369). CEUR Workshop Publishers.

Passant, A., Laublet, P., Breslin, J. G., & Decker, S. (2009, April 21). Semantic search for Enterprise 2.0. Paper presented at the Workshop on Semantic Search (SemSearch 2009) at the 18th International World Wide Web Conference (WWW 2009), Madrid, Spain.

Patel-Schneider, P. F., & Horrocks, I. (2004, February). *OWL Web ontology language semantics and abstract syntax section 4. Mapping to RDF graphs.*

Pellet. (2003). Retrieved from http://www.mindswap.org/2003/pellet/.

Peristeras, V., Loutas, N., Goudos, S., & Tarabanis, K. (2008). A conceptual analysis of semantic conflicts in pan-European e-government services. *Journal of Information Science, 34*(6), 877–891. doi:10.1177/0165551508091012

Peristeras, V., & Tarabanis, K. (2008). The Governance Architecture Framework and Models. In Saha, P. (Ed.), *Advances in Government Enterprise Architecture*. Hershey, PA: IGI Global Information Science Reference.

Peristeras, V. (2006). *The Governance Enterprise Architecture - GEA - for reengineering public administration*. PhD Dissertation, Business Administration, University of Macedonia, Thessaloniki.

Pfisterer, F., Nitsche, M., Jameson, A., & Barbu, C. (2008). *User-centered design and evaluation of interface enhancements to the semantic mediawiki*. In Workshop on Semantic Web User Interaction at CHI 2008.

Piller, F. T., & Walcher, D. (2006). Toolkits for idea competitions: a novel method to integrate users in new product development. *R & D Management, 36*, 307–318. doi:10.1111/j.1467-9310.2006.00432.x

Popa, L., Velegrakis, Y., Miller, R. J., Hernandez, M. A., & Fagin, R. (2002). Translating Web data. In *Proceedings of the Very Large Data Bases*, (pp. 598-609), Hong Kong SAR, China.

Porter, M. (1990). *The Competitive Advantage of Nations*. New York: Free Press.

Pound, J., Mika, P., & Zaragoza, H. (2010). Ad-hoc object retrieval in the Web of data. In M. Rappa, P. Jones, J. Freire, & S. Chakrabarti (Eds.), *Proceedings of the 19th Intertional World Wide Web Conference*, Raleigh, NC (pp. 771-780). New York, NY: ACM.

Prud'hommeaux, E., & Seaborne, A. (2008). *SPARQL Query Language for RDF*. W3C Recommendation. Retrieved March 2, 2009, http://www.w3.org/TR/rdf-sparql-query/

Qu, Y., Hu, W., & Cheng, G. (2006, May 23-26). Constructing virtual documents for ontology matching. In L. Carr, D. D. Roure, A. Iyengar, C. Goble, & M. Dahlin (Eds.), *Proceedings of the 15th International Conference on World Wide Web*, Edinburgh, Scotland (pp. 23-31). New York, NY: ACM.

Quilitz, B., & Leser, U. (2008). Querying distributed RDF data sources with SPARQL. In *Proceedings of the 5th European Semantic Web Conference (ESWC2008)*.

RacerPro. (2008). Retrieved May 23, 2007, from http://www.racer-systems.com.

Rada, R., Mili, H., Bicknell, E., & Blettner, M. (1989). Development and application of a metric on semantic nets. *IEEE Transactions on Systems, Man, and Cybernetics, 19*(1), 17–30. doi:10.1109/21.24528

Rahm, E., & Bernstein, P. A. (2001, December). A Survey of Approaches to Automatic Schema Matching. *The International Journal on Very Large Data Bases, 10*(4), 334–350. Scharffe, F., & de Bruijn, J. (2005, December). A language to specify mappings between ontologies. In *IEEE Conference on Internet-Based Systems SITIS6*, Yaounde, Cameroon.

Raimond, Y., & Sandler, M. (2008, September 14-18). *A web of musical information*. Paper presented at the Ninth International Conference on Music Information Retrieval (ISMIR 2008), Philadelphia.

Raimond, Y., Sutton, C., & Sandler, M. (2008). Automatic Interlinking of Music Datasets on the Semantic Web. In *Proceedings of the 1st Workshop about Linked Data on the Web (LDOW2008)*.

Resnik, P. (1995). Using information content to evaluate semantic similarity in a taxonomy. In *IJCAI'95: Proceedings of the 14th international joint conference on artificial intelligence* (pp. 448-453). San Francisco: Morgan Kaufmann Publishers Inc.

Rettinger, A., Nickles, M., & Tresp, V. (2009). Statistical relational learning with formal ontologies. In W. Buntine, M. Grobelnik, D. Mladenic, & J. Shawe-Taylor, (Eds.), *Proceedings of the European Conference on Machine Learning and Knowledge Discovery in Databases, ECML-PKDD2009*, (LNAI 5782, pp. 286-301). Berlin: Springer.

Riedl, C., Böhmann, T., Leimeister, J. M., & Krcmar, H. (2009). A Framework for Analysing Service Ecosystem Capabilities to Innovate. In *Proceedings of 17th European Conference on Information Systems (ECIS'09)*, Verona, Italy.

Rogers, E. (2003). *Diffusion of Innovations* (5th ed.). New York: Free Press.

Rohloff, K. (2007). An Evaluation of Triple-Store Technologies for Large Data Stores. *On the Move to Meaningful Internet Systems 2007: OTM 2007 Workshops. LNCS, 4806*, 1105–1114.

Ross, S. (1976). *A First Course in Probability*. New York, NY: Macmillan.

Roto, V., & Oulasvirta, A. (2005). Need for Non-Visual Feedback with Long Response Times in Mobile HCI. *International World Wide Web Conference Committee (IW3C2)*, Chiba, Japan.

Rubenstein, H., & Goodenough, J. B. (1965). Contextual correlates of synonymy. *Communications of the ACM*, *8*(10), 627–633. doi:10.1145/365628.365657

Rudolph, S., Tserendorj, T., & Hitzler, P. (2008). What is approximate reasoning? In D. Calvanese and G. Lausen, (Eds.), *Proceedings of the 2nd International Conference on Web Reasoning and Rule Systems, RR2008*, (LNCS 5341, pp. 150-164). Berlin: Springer.

Ruotsalo, T., Aroyo, L., & Schreiber, G. (2009). Knowledge-based linguistic annotation of digital cultural heritage collections. *IEEE Intelligent Systems*, *24*(2), 64–75. doi:10.1109/MIS.2009.32

Ruotsalo, T., & Hyvönen, E. (2007, September). A method for determining ontology-based semantic relevance. In *Proceedings of the international conference on database and expert systems applications (DEXA 2007)*. Regensburg, Germany: Springer.

Sahoo, S., et al. (2009). *A Survey of Current Approaches for Mapping of Relational Databases to RDF*. Retrieved February 25, 2009, http://www.w3.org/2005/Incubator/rdb2rdf/RDB2RDF_SurveyReport.pdf

Salton, G., & Buckley, C. (1988). Term-weighting approaches in automatic text retrieval. *Information Processing & Management*, *24*(5), 513–523. doi:10.1016/0306-4573(88)90021-0

Sauermann, L., & Cyganiak, R. (2008). *Cool URIs for the Semantic Web. W3C Interest Group Note.* Retrieved June 14, 2009, http://www.w3.org/TR/cooluris/

Schaffert, S. (2006a). IkeWiki: A semantic wiki for collaborative knowledge management. In *Proceedings of the 15th IEEE International Workshops on Enabling Technologies: Infrastructure for Collaborative Enterprises* (pp. 388-396). Washington, DC: IEEE Computer Society.

Schaffert, S. (2006b). Semantic social software: Semantically enabled social software or socially enabled Semantic Web? In *Proceedings of the Semantics 2006 Conference* (pp. 99–112).

Schenk, S., et al. (2008). SemaPlorer—Interactive Semantic Exploration of Data and Media based on a Federated Cloud Infrastructure. In *Proceedings of the Semantic Web Challenge at ISWC 2008*.

Schlobach, S., Huang, Z., Cornet, R., & van Harmelen, F. (2007). Debugging incoherent terminologies. *Journal of Automated Reasoning*, *39*(3), 317–349. doi:10.1007/s10817-007-9076-z

Schmidt, M., Hornung, T., Küchlin, N., Lausen, G., & Pinkel, C. (2008a). An Experimental Comparison of RDF Data Management Approaches in a SPARQL Benchmark Scenario. *Proceedings of the International Semantic Web Conference (ISWC 2008)*.

Schmidt, M., Hornung, T., Lausen, G., & Pinkel, C. (2008b). *SP2Bench: A SPARQL Performance Benchmark*. Technical Report, arXiv:0806.4627V1 cs.DB.

Schmitz, P. (2006, May). *Inducing ontology from Flickr tags*. Paper presented at the Workshop on Collaborative Web Tagging at the 15th International World Wide Web Conference (WWW 2006), Edinburgh, Scotland.

Seidenberg, J., & Rector, A. L. (2006). Web ontology segmentation: Analysis, classification and use. In Carr, L., Roure, D. D., Iyengar, A., Goble, C. A., & Dahlin, M. (Eds.), *WWW* (pp. 13–22). ACM. doi:10.1145/1135777.1135785

Serafini, L., Borgida, A., & Tamilin, A. (2005). Aspects of distributed and modular description logics. In *Proceedings of the 18th International Joint Conference on Artificial Intelligence, IJCAI05*, (pp. 370-375).

Shakya, A., Takeda, H., & Wuwongse, V. (2008). Consolidating user-defined concepts with StYLiD. In J. Domingue, & C. Anutariya (Eds.), *Proceedings of the 3rd Asian Semantic Web Conference*, (LNCS 5367), (pp. 287-301). Berlin/Heidelberg, Germany: Springer.

Shapiro, S. S., & Wilk, M. B. (1965). An analysis of variance test for normality (complete samples). *Biometrika*, *3*(52).

Sheth, A., Ramakrishnan, C., & Thomas, C. (2005). Semantics for the semantic web: The implicit, the formal and the powerful. *International Journal on Semantic Web and Information Systems*, *1*, 1–18.

Silva, N., & Rocha, J. (2003). Semantic Web complex ontology mapping. In *Proceedings of the IEEE Web Intelligence (WI2003)*, (p. 82).

Simpson, T., & Dao, T. (2005). *WordNet-based semantic similarity measurement*. Retrieved December 25, 2008, from http://www.codeproject.com/KB/string/semantic-similaritywordnet.aspx

Sintek, M., & Decker, S. (2002). *TRIPLE - a query, inference, and transformation language for the Semantic Web*. 1st International Semantic Web Conference (pp. 364-378).

Siorpaes, K., & Hepp, M. (2007a). myOntology: The marriage of ontology engineering and collective intelligence. In *Bridging the Gap between Semantic Web and Web 2.0 (SemNet 2007)* (pp. 127–138).

Siorpaes, K., & Hepp, M. (2007b). OntoGame: Towards overcoming the incentive bottleneck in ontology building. In *Proceedings of the 3rd International IFIP Workshop on Semantic Web and Web Semantics (SWWS'07), Vilamoura, Portugal*.

Sirin, E., Parsia, B., Grau, B. C., Kalyanpur, A., & Katz, Y. (2007). Pellet: A practical OWL-DL reasoner. *Journal of Web Semantics*, *5*(2), 51–53. doi:10.1016/j.websem.2007.03.004

Skrenta, R., & Truel, B. (2008). Open Directory Project. Retrieved November 6, 2008, from http://www.dmoz.org

Smith, M. K., Welty, C., & McGuinness, D. L. (2004, February). *OWL Web ontology language guide*.

Specia, L., & Motta, E. 2007. Integrating folksonomies with the Semantic Web. In E. Franconi, M. Kifer, & W. May (Eds.), *Proceedings of the European Semantic Web Conference (ESWC2007)*, (LNCS 4519), (pp. 624–639). Heidelberg, Germany: Springer.

Srinivasan, N., Paolucci, M., & Sycara, K. (2005). Semantic Web Service Discovery in the OWL-S IDE. *39th Hawaii International Conference on System Sciences*, Hawaii.

Stathel, S., Finzen, J., Riedl, C., & May, N. (2008). Service innovation in business value networks. In *Proceedings of XVIII International RESER Conference*, Stuttgart, Germany.

Stickler, P. (2004). *CBD - concise bounded description*. Retrieved August 15, 2008, from http://www.w3.org/Submission/CBD/

Storey, J. (2000). The management of innovation problem International. *Journal of Innovation Management*, *4*, 347–369. doi:10.1016/S1363-9196(00)00019-6

Story, H., Harbulot, B., Jacobi, I., & Jones, M. (2009, June 1). FOAF+TLS: RESTful authentication for the social Web. In *Proceedings of the First Workshop on Trust and Privacy on the Social and Semantic Web (SPOT 2009)*, Heraklion, Greece (Vol. 447). CEUR Workshop Proceedings.

Stuckenschmidt, H., & Klein, M. (2007). Reasoning and change management in modular ontologies. *Data & Knowledge Engineering*, *63*, 200–223. doi:10.1016/j.datak.2007.02.001

Suchanek, F. M., Kasneci, G., & Weikum, G. (2007). Yago: A core of semantic knowledge. *WWW '07: Proceedings of the 16th International Conference on World Wide Web* (pp. 697-706). New York, NY: ACM Press.

Surowiecki, J. (2005). *The wisdom of crowds: why the many are smarter than the few*. London: Abacus.

Sussna, M. (1993). Word sense disambiguation for free-text indexing using a massive semantic network. In *CIKM '93: Proceedings of the second international conference on information and knowledge management* (pp. 6774). New York: ACM.

Svihala, M., & Jelinek, I. (2007). Benchmarking RDF Production Tools. *Proceedings of the 18th International Conference on Database and Expert Systems Applications (DEXA 2007)*.

Swartz, A. (2002). Musicbrainz: A Semantic Web service. *IEEE Intelligent Systems*, *17*(1), 76–77. doi:10.1109/5254.988466

Sycara, K., Widoff, S., Klusch, M., & Lu, J. (2002). LARKS: Dynamic Matchmaking Among Heterogeneous Software Agents in Cyberspace. *Autonomous Agents and Multi-Agent Systems*, *5*, 173–203. doi:10.1023/A:1014897210525

Takeda, H., Iino, K., & Nishida, T. (1995). Agent organization and communication with multiple ontologies. *International Journal of Cooperative Information Systems*, 4(4), 321–337. doi:10.1142/S0218843095000147

Tambouris, E., Manouselis, N., & Costopoulou, C. (2007). Metadata for digital collections of e-government resources. *The Electronic Library*, 25(2), 176–192. doi:10.1108/02640470710741313

Tambouris, E., & Tarabanis, K. (2005, June). E-Government and interoperability. In *European Conference in Electronic Government (ECEG 2005)*, Belgium, (pp. 399–407).

Tambouris, E., & Tarabanis. K. (2004). Overview of DC-based e-Government metadata standards and initiatives. *International Conference on Electronic Government (EGOV 2004)*, Zaragoza, Spain, (pp. 40-47)

Tan, P., Steinbach, M., & Kumar, V. (2006). *Introduction to Data Mining: Concepts and Techniques*. Boston, MA: Pearson Addison Wesley.

Tanaka, J., & Taylor, M. (1991). Object categories and expertise: Is the basic level in the eye of the beholder. *Cognitive Psychology*, 23(3), 457–482. doi:10.1016/0010-0285(91)90016-H

Tang, J., Leung, H., Luo, Q., Chen, D., & Gong, J. (2009). Towards ontology learning from folksonomies. In *Proceedings of the International Joint Conference on Artificial Intelligence*, Pasadena, CA, USA.

Tauberer, J. (2008). *Govtrack.us - a civic project to track congress*. Retrieved August 15, 2008, from http://www.govtrack.us

Taylor, A. G. (1999). *The organization of information*. Santa Barbara, CA: Libraries Unlimited.

ter Horst, H. J. (2005b). Completeness, decidability and complexity of entailment for RDF schema and a semantic extension involving the OWL vocabulary. *Journal of Web Semantics*, 3, 79–115. doi:10.1016/j.websem.2005.06.001

ter Horst, H. J. (2005a). *Combining RDF and part of OWL with rules: Semantics, decidability, complexity*. 4th International Semantic Web Conference (pp. 668-684).

Theoharis, Y., Christophides, V., & Karvounarakis, G. (2005). Benchmarking database representations of RDF/S stores. *Proceedings of the Fourth International Semantic Web Conference* (pp. 685-701). Galway, Ireland.

Tidd, J., Bessant, J., & Pavitt, K. (2005). *Managing innovation: integrating technological, market and organizational change* (3rd ed.). Chichester, UK: John Wiley & Sons.

Tijerino, Y. A., Embley, D. W., Lonsdale, D. W., Ding, Y., & Nagy, G. (2005). Towards ontology generation from tables. *World Wide Web: Internet and Web Information Systems*, 8(3), 261–285. Netherlands: Springer.

Toutanova, K., & Manning, C. (2000). Enriching the Knowledge Sources Used in a Maximum Entropy Part-of-Speech Tagger. In *Proceedings of the Joint SIGDAT Conference on Empirical Methods in Natural Language Processing and Very Large Corpora* (EMNLP/VLC-2000), (pp. 63-70).

Toutanova, K., Klein, D., Manning, C., & Singer, Y. (2003). Feature-Rich Part-of-Speech Tagging with a Cyclic Dependency Network. In *Proceedings of the 2003 Conference of the North American Chapter of the Association for Computational Linguistics on Human Language Technology*, (pp. 173-180).

Tran, T., Cimiano, P., Rudolph, S., & Studer, R. (2007). Ontology-based interpretation of keywords for semantic search. In K. Aberer, K-S. Choi, N. Noy, D. Allemang, K-I. Lee, L. Nixon, et al. (Eds.), *The Semantic Web: Proceedings of the 6th International Semantic Web Conference and the 2nd Asian Semantic Web Conference*, Busan, Korea (LNCS 4825, pp. 523-536).

Tran, T., Wang, H., Rudolph, S., & Cimiano, P. (2009). Top-k exploration of query candidates for efficient keyword search on graph-shaped (RDF) data. In *Proceedings of the 25th International Conference on Data Engineering*, Shanghai, China (pp. 405-416). Washington, DC: IEEE Computer Society.

Transaction Processing Performance Council. (2008). *TPC Benchmark H, Standard Specification Revision 2.7.0*. Retrieved March 2, 2009, http://www.tpc.org/tpch/spec/tpch2.7.0.pdf

Tsarkov, D., & Horrocks, I. (2006). *FaCT++ description logic reasoner: System description*. International Joint Conf. on Automated Reasoning (pp. 292-297).

Tserendorj, T., Rudolph, S., Krötzsch, M., & Hitzler, P. (2008). Approximate OWL-reasoning with Screech. In D. Calvanese & G. Lausen, (Eds.), *Proceedings of the 2nd International Conference on Web Reasoning and Rule Systems, RR2008*, (LNCS Vol. 5341). Berlin: Springer.

Tummarello, G., Morbidoni, C., Bachmann-Gmür, R., & Erling, O. (2007). RDFSync: Efficient remote synchronization of RDF models. In K. Aberer, K.-S. Choi, N. Noy, D. Allemang, K.-I. Lee, L. Nixon, et al. (Eds.), *The Semantic Web: Proceedings of the 6th International Semantic Web Conference and the 2nd Asian Semantic Web Conference,* Busan, Korea (LNCS 4825, pp. 537-551).

Turney, P. D. (2006). Similarity of semantic relations. *Computational Linguistics, 32*(3), 379–416. doi:10.1162/coli.2006.32.3.379

Ullman, J. D. (1997). Information integration using logical views. In *Proceedings 6th International Conference on Database Theory (ICDT 97)*, Delphi, Greece.

Universal Description Discovery and Integration (UDDI). (2009). Retrieved from http://uddi.xml.org/.

Universal Plug and Play (UPnP). (2007). Retrieved March 12, 2007, from http://www.upnp.org.

Urbani, J., Kotoulas, S., Maassen, J., van Harmelen, F., & Bal, H. E. (2010). *OWL reasoning with WebPIE: Calculating the closure of 100 billion triples.* Paper presented at the 7th Extended Semantic Web Conference (ESWC), Heraklion, Crete, Greece.

Urbani, J., Kotoulas, S., Oren, E., & van Harmelen, F. (2009). *Scalable distributed reasoning using MapReduce.* Paper presented at the 8th International Semantic Web Conference (ISWC), Chantilly, VA, USA.

Uschold, M., King, M., Moralee, S., & Zorgios, Y. (1998). The Enterprise Ontology. *The Knowledge Engineering Review, 13*, 31–89. doi:10.1017/S0269888998001088

Valle-Lisboa, J. C., & Mizraji, E. (2007). The uncovering of hidden structures by latent semantic analysis. *Information Sciences, 177*(19), 4122–4147. doi:10.1016/j.ins.2007.04.007

Van Damme, C., Hepp, M., & Siorpaes, K. (2007). An integrated approach for turning folksonomies into ontologies. In *Bridging the Gap between Semantic Web and Web 2.0 (SemNet 2007)* (pp. 57–70). FolksOntology.

Van Damme, C., Hepp, M., & Siorpaes, K. (2007). FolksOntology: An integrated approach for turning folksonomies into ontologies. In *Proceedings of the Workshop on Bridging the Gap between Semantic Web and Web 2.0 (SemNet 2007)*, Innsbruck, Austria (pp. 55-70). University of Kassel.

Van de Sompel, H., Lagoze, C., Nelson, M., Warner, S., Sanderson, R., & Johnston, P. (2009). Adding eScience Assets to the Data Web. In *Proceedings of the 2nd Workshop on Linked Data on the Web (LDOW2009)*.

van Gundy, A. (1988). *Techniques of structured problem solving* (2nd ed.). New York: Van Nostrand Reinhold.

VanderWal, T. (2007, February 2). *Folksonomy coinage and definition*. Retrieved May 8, 2009, from http://www.vanderwal.net/folksonomy.html

Velardi, P., Cucchiarelli, A., & Petit, M. (2007, February). A Taxonomy Learning Method and Its Application to Characterize a Scientific Web Community. *IEEE Transactions on Knowledge and Data Engineering, 19*(2), 180–191. doi:10.1109/TKDE.2007.21

Velardi, P., Fabriani, P., & Missikoff, M. (2001). Using text processing techniques to automatically enrich a domain ontology. In *Proceedings of the international conference on Formal Ontology in Information Systems*, (pp. 270-284).

Velardi, P., Missikoff, M., & Basili, R. (2001). Identification of relevant terms to support the construction of domain ontologies. In *Proceedings of the workshop on Human Language Technology and Knowledge Management*, (pp. 1-8).

Vitvar, T., Mocan, A., Cimpian, E., Nazir, S., Wang, X., & Loutas, N. (2006). *Devember). D3.1: SemanticGov Architecture (Vol. 1)*. SemanticGov Deliverable.

Vitvar, T., Kerrigan, M., van Overeem, A., Peristeras, V., & Tarabanis, K. (2006, March). Infrastructure for the semantic pan-european e-government services. In *AAAI Spring Symposium on Semantic Web Meets E-Government*, Stanford, CA, USA.

Vitvar, T., Mocan, A., Kerrigan, M., Zaremba, M., Zaremba, M., Moran, M., Cimpian, E., Haselwanter, T., & Fensel, D. (2007). Semantically-enabled Service Oriented Architecture: Concepts, Technology and Application. *Journal of Service Oriented Computing and Applications.*

Volz, J., Bizer, C., Gaedke, M., & Kobilarov, G. (2009). Discovering and Maintaining Links on the Web of Data. In *Proceedings of the 8th International Semantic Web Conference (ISWC2009)*.

von Hippel, E. (2005). *Democratizing Innovation*. Boston: MIT Press.

Wache, H., Groot, P., & Stuckenschmidt, H. (2005). Scalable instance retrieval for the semantic web by approximation. In M. Dean, et al, (eds.), *Proceedings of the WISE 2005 International Workshops*, (LNCS 3807, pp. 245-254). Berlin: Springer.

Wang, H., Zhang, K., Liu, Q., Tran, T., & Yu, Y. (2008, June 1-5). Q2Semantic: A lightweight keyword interface to semantic search. In S. Bechhofer, M. Hauswirth, J. Hoffmann, & M. Koubarakis (Eds.), *The Semantic Web: Research and Applications: Proceedings of the 5th European Semantic Web Conference*, Canary Islands, Spain (LNCS 5021, pp. 584-598).

Wang, T. D., Parsia, B., & Hendler, J. A. (2006). A survey of the Web ontology landscape. *Proceedings of the 5th International Semantic Web Conference (ISWC 2006)* (pp. 682-694). Athens, GA, USA.

Wang, X., Vitvar, T., Mocan, A., Peristeras, V., Goudos, S. K., & Tarabanis, K. (2007, January). WSMO-PA: Formal Specification of Public Administration Service Model on Semantic Web Service Ontology. *Hawaii International Conference on System Sciences (HICSS2007)*, Hawaii

Watters, C. (1999). Information retrieval and the virtual document. *Journal of the American Society for Information Science American Society for Information Science*, *50*(11), 1028–1029. doi:10.1002/(SICI)1097-4571(1999)50:11<1028::AID-ASI8>3.0.CO;2-0

Weaver, J., & Hendler, J. A. (2009). *Parallel materialization of the finite RDFS closure for hundreds of millions of triples*. Paper presented at the 8th International Semantic Web Conference, ISWC, Chantilly, VA, USA.

Web Service Modelling Ontology (WSMO) Working Group. (2009). Retrieved from http://www.wsmo.org/.

Weitzner, D. (2007). Beyond Secrecy: New Privacy Protection Strategies for Open Information Spaces. *IEEE Internet Computing*, *11*(5), 94–96. doi:10.1109/MIC.2007.101

Weitzner, D. (2008). Information Accountability. *Communications of the ACM*, *51*(6), 82–87. doi:10.1145/1349026.1349043

West, J., & Lakhani, K. (2008). Getting Clear About Communities in Open Innovation. *Industry and Innovation*, *15*, 223–231. doi:10.1080/13662710802033734

Wheelwright, S. C., & Clark, K. B. (1992). *Revolutionizing Product Development: Quantum Leaps in Speed, Efficiency, and Quality*. New York: Free Press.

Wiesman, F., & Roos, N. (2004). Domain independent learning of ontology mappings. In *Proceedings of the 3rd International Joint Conference on Autonomous Agents and Multiagent Systems*, New York, USA (pp. 846–853).

Wilcoxon, F. (1945). Individual comparisons by ranking methods. *Biometrics Bulletin*, *1*(6), 80–83. doi:10.2307/3001968

Wilks, Y., Slator, B., & Guthrie, L. (1996). *Electric Words: dictionaries, computers and meanings*. Cambridge, MA: MIT Press.

Winkler, W. (2006). *Overview of Record Linkage and Current Research Directions*. US Bureau of the Census, Technical Report.

Witten, I., & Frank, E. (2005). *Data Mining: Practical machine learning tools and techniques* (2nd ed.). San Francisco, CA: Morgan Kaufmann.

Witten, I. H., & Frank, E. (2005). *Data Mining* (2nd ed.). San Francisco: Morgan Kaufmann.

Witters, J., & van Overeem, A. (2004). *PEGS infrastructure architecture v 1.0*. IDABC.

Wu, Z., & Palmer, M. (1994). Verb semantics and lexical selection. In *Proceedings of the 32nd annual meeting on association for computational linguistics* (pp. 133-138). Morristown, NJ: Association for Computational Linguistics.

Wu, Z., Eadon, G., Das, S., Chong, E. I., Kolovski, V., Annamalai, M., et al. (2008). *Implementing an inference engine for RDFS/OWL constructs and user-defined rules in Oracle*. 24th International Conference on Data Engineering. IEEE.

Yamauchi, T. (2007). The Semantic Web and human inference: A lesson from cognitive science. In K. Aberer, K.-S. Choi, N. Noy, D. Allemang, K.-I. Lee, L. Nixon, et al. (Eds.), *The Semantic Web: Proceedings of the 6th International Semantic Web Conference and the 2nd Asian Semantic Web Conference,* Busan, Korea (LNCS 4825, pp. 609-622).

Yan, L. L., Miller, R. J., Haas, L. M., & Fagin, R. (2001). Data-driven understanding and refinement of schema mappings. [ACM Special Interest Group on Management of Data]. *SIGMOD Record, 30*(2), 485–496. doi:10.1145/376284.375729

Yanosy, J. (2005, August). Semantic interoperability and semantic congruence. In *Collaborative Expedition Workshop*.

Yuanbo, G. (2007). A Requirements Driven Framework for Benchmarking Semantic Web Knowledge Base Systems. *IEEE Transactions on Knowledge and Data Engineering, 19*(2), 297–309. doi:10.1109/TKDE.2007.19

Zhang, X., Cheng, G., & Qu, Y. (2007, May 8-12). Ontology summarization based on RDF sentence graph. In C. Williamson, M. E. Zurko, P. Patel-Schneider, & P. Shenoy (Eds.), *Proceedings of the 16th International Conference on World Wide Web,* Banff, Alberta, Canada (pp. 707-716). New York, NY: ACM.

Zhao, J., Klyne, G., & Shotton, D. (2008). Provenance and Linked Data in Biological Data Webs. In *Proceedings of the 1st Workshop about Linked Data on the Web (LDOW2008)*.

Zhdanova, A. V., & Shvaiko, P. (2006). Community-driven ontology matching. In *The Semantic Web: Research and Applications,* (LNCS: Vol. 4011), (pp. 34-49). Berlin/ Heidelberg, Germany: Springer.

Zhou, J., Ma, L., Liu, Q., Zhang, L., Yu, Y., & Pan, Y. (2006). Minerva: A scalable OWL ontology storage and inference system. *Proceedings of The First Asian Semantic Web Conference (ASWC)* (pp. 429-443). Beijing, China.

Zhou, Q., Wang, C., Xiong, M., Wang, H., & Yu, Y. (2007). SPARK: Adapting keyword query to semantic search. In K. Aberer, K.-S. Choi, N. Noy, D. Allemang, K.-I. Lee, L. Nixon, et al. (Eds.), *The Semantic Web: Proceedings of the 6th International Semantic Web Conference and the 2nd Asian Semantic Web Conference,* Busan, Korea (LNCS 4825, pp. 694-707).

About the Contributors

Amit P. Sheth is an educator, researcher, and entrepreneur. He is a LexisNexis Eminent Scholar (an endowed faculty position, funded by LexisNexis and the Ohio Board of Regents) at Wright State University. He directs the Kno.e.sis center for Knowledge enabled Information & Services Science; which conducts research in Semantic Web, services computing, and scientific workflows. He was a professor at the University of Georgia where he founded and directed the LSDIS Lab. Prior to that, he served in R&D groups at Bellcore, Unisys, and Honeywell. His research has led to several commercial products and two companies which he founded and managed in various executive roles: Infocosm, which had products in enterprise workflow management and Taalee/Voquette/Semagix, which was one of the earliest companies with Semantic Web applications and application development platforms. Professor Sheth is an IEEE Fellow and has received recognitions such as the IBM Faculty award. He has published over 250 papers and articles many of which are highly cited (h-index > 54 based on Google scholar citations), given over 200 invited talks and colloquia including over thirty keynotes, (co)-organized/chaired forty-five conferences/workshops, and served on over 125 program committees. He is on several journal editorial boards, is the Editor-in-Chief of the *International Journal on Semantic Web and Information Systems (IJSWIS)*, and the joint-EIC of *Distributed & Parallel Databases Journal*.

* * *

Sören Auer (http://www.informatik.uni-leipzig.de/~auer) leads the research group Agile Knowledge Engineering and Semantic Web (AKSW) at Universität Leipzig. His research interests include semantic data Web technologies, knowledge representation, engineering & management, as well as databases and Information Systems. Sören is author of over 50 peer-reviewed scientific publications. Sören is leading the large-scale integrated EU-FP7-ICT research project "LOD2 - Creating Knowledge out of Interlinked Data". Sören is co-founder of several high-impact research and community projects such as DBpedia and OntoWiki. He is co-organiser of several workshops, programme chair of I-Semantics 2008, OKCON 2010, ESWC 2010, and ICWE 2011, area editor of the Semantic Web Journal, serves as an expert for industry, the European Commission, the W3C, and is member of the advisory board of the Open Knowledge Foundation.

Tim Berners-Lee is credited with inventing the World Wide Web, an Internet-based hypermedia initiative for global information sharing while at CERN, the European Particle Physics Laboratory. He wrote the first Web client and server in 1990. His specifications of URIs, HTTP and HTML were refined as Web technology spread. Berners-Lee is professor at the Laboratory for Computer Science and Artificial Intelligence (CSAIL) at the Massachusetts Institute of Technology (MIT) and the computer science department at the University of Southampton, UK. In 2001 he became a fellow of the Royal Society.

Christian Bizer is the head of the Web-based Systems Group at Freie Universität Berlin. The group explores technical and economic questions concerning the development of global, decentralized information environments. The results of Bizer's research include the Named Graphs data model, which was adopted into the W3C SPARQL standard, the Fresnel display vocabulary implemented by several Semantic Web browsers, and the D2RQ mapping language which is widely used for mapping relational databases to the Semantic Web. He initialized the W3C Linking Open Data community effort and the DBpedia project.

John Breslin is currently a lecturer in electronic engineering at the National University of Ireland, Galway. He is also an associate researcher and leader of the Social Software Unit at the Digital Enterprise Research Institute at NUI Galway, researching semantically-enabled social networks and community portals. He is the founder of the SIOC project, which aims to semantically- interlink online communities. He has received a number of awards for website design, including two Net Visionary awards from the Irish Internet Association for the Irish community website boards.ie, which he co-founded in 2000. Dr. Breslin is a member of the IEI, IET and IEEE.

Sanjay Chaudhary is a Professor at Dhirubhai Ambani Institute of Information and Communication Technology (DA-IICT), Gandhinagar, India. His research areas are distributed computing, service-oriented computing, multicore architectures and programming, and ICT applications in agriculture. He has authored four books and a number of book chapters. He has published a number of research papers in international conferences, workshops and journals. He has served on many program committees of international conferences and workshops, and he is also a member of review committees of leading journals. Three PhD candidates have completed PhD under his supervision. He holds a doctorate degree in computer science from Gujarat Vidyapeeth. Prior to joining DA-IICT, he worked with Gujarat University. He has worked on various large-scale software development projects for corporate sector, co-operative sector, and government organizations. He is actively involved in various consultancy and enterprise application development projects. He has received following research grants: Faculty Research Grant from Microsoft High Performance Computing Scholar Program, 2008, Faculty Research Grant from Microsoft High Performance Computing Scholar Program, 2007, and IBM Eclipse Innovation Research Grant 2005 for 'Framework for processing and visualization of critical alerts for risk perception and efficient decision-making.' Chaudhary has provided his services to committees, formed by Gujarat Government, India. More details are available at http://intranet.daiict.ac.in/~sanjay/

Yan Chen is a PhD student at computer science department of the Georgia State University, under the supervision of Yan-Qing Zhang. He has a bachelor's degree in computer science from the Wuhan University of Technology (China) and a master's degree in computer science from East Tennessee State University. His current research interests include semantic computing, query disambiguation, query suggestions, and information retrieval.

Gong Cheng is with the State Key Laboratory for Novel Software Technology, Nanjing University, China. He successfully defended his doctoral dissertation on "Methods and Techniques for Entity Search on the Semantic Web" at Southeast University in 2010, and received his Bachelor's degree in computer science and engineering from Southeast University in 2006. His research interests include data integration, semantic search, Semantic Web, and Web mining. He is the chief developer of Falcons Object Search, Concept Search, and Ontology Search.

Claudia d'Amato is a research fellow at the University of Bari - Computer Science Department. Her main topics of interest are: similarity measures for concepts and individuals in Description Logics, supervised and unsupervised methods for ontology mining, approximate and uncertain reasoning for the Semantic Web. She is author of more that 60 papers among international collections and journals. She has been invited expert for the W3C Uncertainty Reasoning for the World Wide Web Incubator Group. She is organizer of the international Uncertainty Reasoning for the Semantic Web workshop and of the Workshop on Inductive Reasoning and Machine Learning for the Semantic Web. She was Vice-Chair for ISWC 2009, she is editorial board member of the Semantic Web Journal and she is also serving as program committee member in international conferences such as IJCAI'11, RR'11, SAC'11, ESWC'11, RuleML'11, ISWC'10, AAAI'10, ECAI'10, ECML/PKDD'10,, EKAW'10, WI'10, STAIRS'10, ICAI'10, KARE'10. She also received the nomination from the Italian Artificial Intelligence community for her PhD thesis "Similarity-based learning methods for the Semantic Web" as one of the best Italian PhD contribution in the area. Further information available at http://www.di.uniba.it/~cdamato/

Stefan Decker is a professor at the National University of Ireland, Galway, and director of the Digital Enterprise Research Institute, an institute with more than 130 people working on the Semantic Web. Previously, he worked at ISI, University of Southern California (2 years, research assistant professor and computer scientist), Stanford University, Computer Science Department (Database Group) (3 Years, postdoc and research associate), and Institute AIFB, University of Karlsruhe (4 years, PhD student and junior researcher). He is one of the most widely cited Semantic Web scientists, and his current research interests include semantics in collaborative systems, Web 2.0, and distributed systems.

Federico Michele Facca is a senior researcher at STI Innsbruck. He obtained his PhD in information technology (2008) and his MSc in computer science and engineering, both at the Politecnico di Milano. He is leader of the Semantic Execution Environment (SEE) research unit of STI Innsbruck and Institute Manager of STI Innsbruck. He has been involved in several research projects over the last couple of years: COIN, MAIS, SemanticGov, SHAPE and SUPER. He is responsible for execution management task of STI Technical Task Force and member of the OASIS Semantic Execution Environment Technical Committee (SEE TC). He has published several articles in international journals and conferences. His research interests cover semantically-enabled service oriented architecture, Semantic Web engineering, Semantic Web services, adaptive Web Applications, data intensive Web applications and Web usage mining.

Nicola Fanizzi is assistant professor in the Computer Science Department of the University of Bari. His research topics, within the broad field of Artificial Intelligence, are in Machine Learning and Knowledge Discovery, particularly the related methodologies for complex (multi-relational) representations based on fragments of First-Order Logics. Currently he is working on Semantic-Web Mining methods, focusing on the problems of classification, clustering, ranking, and uncertainty reasoning. He authored 150+ works, which have appeared in scientific journals, proceedings of national and international conferences and workshops. He served in the OC/PC of several workshops and conferences in his areas of interest. See also www.di.uniba.it/~fanizzi

Jan Finzen has studied computer science with a focus on natural language processing at Oldenburg and Stuttgart University. After graduation in 2004, he worked as a software engineer in the automotive sector. Since 2006, he is working as research associate at the Competence Center for Electronic Business at Fraunhofer Institute for Industrial Engineering in Stuttgart. As a software architect and project lead he has been responsible for several information and communication technology projects. His current work focuses on analysing and developing information retrieval and Web mining strategies and techniques for professional end-users, especially within idea and innovation management, and for business and competitive intelligence.

Sotirios K. Goudos received the PhD degree in physics from the Aristotle University of Thessaloniki in 2001. Since 1996, he has been working in the Telecommunications Center of the Aristotle University of Thessaloniki, Greece. He has authored or co-authored more than 50 papers in peer reviewed journals and international conferences. His research interests include antenna and microwave structures design, electromagnetic compatibility of communication systems, evolutionary computation algorithms and Semantic Web technologies.

Mohamed Medhat Gaber is a research fellow at Monash University, Australia. He has published more than 50 refereed articles and co-edited two books. Mohamed has served in the program committees of several international conferences and workshops. He received his PhD in 2006 from Monash University.

Andreas Harth works as post-doctoral researcher at Institute AIFB at the Karlsruhe Institute of Technology after pursuing a Ph.D. with the Digital Enterprise Research Institute (DERI) at the National University of Ireland, Galway. He holds a Dipl.-Inf. (FH) (a nearby equivalent to the U.S.-style M.Sc.) from Fachhochschule Würzburg. Andreas worked as intern at Fraunhofer Gesellschaft in Würzburg (1998/1999) and at IBM's Silicon Valley Lab in San Jose, CA (2001). He visited USC's Information Sciences Institute in Marine del Rey, CA as a research assistant (2003/2004). His research interests are large-scale data interoperation on the Semantic Web, linked data, knowledge representation, computational logic, and user interaction on Web data. Andreas has published over a dozen papers in these areas, and is author of several open source software systems. Two of his systems were awarded prizes at the Semantic Web Challenge co-located with the International Semantic Web Conference. In addition, he has participated in numerous EU and national projects, participated in various program committees, and has served in the W3C Semantic Web Best Practices and Deployment and Rules Interchange Format working groups. Andreas is the lead developer of the *Semantic Web Search Engine* project and of the *VisiNav* Linked Data search interface.

Tom Heath is a researcher in the Platform Division of Talis Information Ltd, a leading provider of linked data storage, management, and publishing technologies, where he coordinates internal research focusing on collective intelligence and human-computer interaction in a linked data and Semantic Web context. He is a leading member of the Linking Open Data community project, and creator of the Linked Data-enabled reviewing and rating site Revyu.com, winner of the 2007 Semantic Web Challenge. Heath has a PhD in computer science from The Open University.

Sebastian Hellmann (http://bis.informatik.uni-leipzig.de/SebastianHellmann) obtained his Master degree in 2008 from the University of Leipzig, where he is currently researching as a PhD Student in the Agile Knowledge Engineering and Semantic Web (AKSW) research group. He is founder, leader, or contributor of several open source projects, including DL-Learner, DBpedia and NLP2RDF. Among his research interests are light-weight ontology engineering methods, data integration and scalability in the Web of Data. Sebastian is author of over 10 peer-reviewed scientific publications.

Aidan Hogan is a PhD student at the Digital Enterprise Research Institute (DERI) based in the National University of Ireland, Galway. He has been working on Semantic Web technologies in DERI since April 2005; his PhD research is centred around scalable techniques for using the semantics and statistics inherent in large Linked Data corpora to enhance the data – in terms of cleanliness, inter-linkage, consolidation, materialising reasoned data, et cetera – for later consumption by applications. As such, he has published many research contributions in this area. Aidan is one of the main developers in the *Semantic Web Search Engine* (SWSE) project, is the main developer of the *Scalable Authoritative OWL Reasoner* (SAOR – detailed herein), and is a co-founder of the *Pedantic Web Group*: an open initiative to improve the quality of Linked Data.

Myunggwon Hwang is a PhD student in the Department of Computer Engineering at Chosun University of Korea. His research interests include natural semantic information processing and Semantic Web.

Pankoo Kim is a full professor in the Department of Computer Engineering at Chosun University of Korea. His research interests include Semantic Web, natural language processing, and semantic multimedia processing. He received a doctorate degree in computer engineering from Seoul National University of Korea.

Shonali Krishnaswamy is a Senior Lecturer in the Faculty of Information Technology at Monash University. Her research is broadly the area of distributed, mobile and pervasive computing systems, and her focus on developing intelligent applications that aim to service real-time information needs while having to function in highly dynamic and resource-constrained environments. Her specific expertise is in mobile and ubiquitous data stream mining, service oriented computing and mobile software agents.

Jens Lehmann (http://www.jens-lehmann.org) is a postdoctoral researcher at the University of Leipzig. He is leading the Machine Learning and Ontology Engineering research group within the AKSW center. He obtained a PhD with grade summa cum laude at the at University of Leipzig in 2010 and a Master degree in Computer Science from Technical University of Dresden in 2006. His research interests involve Semantic Web, machine learning, and knowledge representation. He is founder, leader, or contributor of several open source projects, including DL-Learner, DBpedia, LinkedGeoData, ORE, and OntoWiki. He works or worked in several funded projects, e.g. LOD2 (EU IP), LATC (EU STREP) and SoftWiki (BmBF). Dr. Jens Lehmann authored more than 20 articles in international journals and conferences.

Philippe Laublet worked as senior researcher at the French Aerospace Research Institute (ONERA) in fields relating to artificial intelligence (1986-1996). The main topic of his PhD was automatic theorem proving. He has been a Senior Lecturer (associate professor) at the University of Paris-Sorbonne (Paris

IV) since 1994 and is a member of the LaLIC laboratory. His research topics and interests have successively encompassed object-oriented methods and languages, knowledge engineering and modelling, ontologies, semantic annotation, Semantic Web, and Web 2.0.

Nikolaos Loutas holds a computer science degree and an MSc in Information Systems from the Athens University of Economics and Business, Greece. Since 2006, he is a PhD researcher at the Department of Business Administration of the University of Macedonia under the guidance of Professor Tarabanis and Dr. Peristeras. During the last three years, he has been working as a researcher in the Center for Research Technology Hellas. Currently, he is also working as a research intern at the National University of Ireland, Galway - Digital Enterprise Research Institute. He has participated in several Greek and European research projects in the e-government, e-participation and collaborative work domains.

Eetu Mäkelä is a PhD student at the Aato University's Department of Media Technology. His research interests include knowledge-based methods for information access and user interface technology. Mäkelä has an MSc in computer science from the University of Helsinki.

Norman May works as a software engineer at SAP where he contributes to in-memory computing platform. He is a graduate of the University of Mannheim and University of Waterloo, Canada, where he has studied Business Administration and Computer Science. He received his Doctoral degree from the University of Mannheim in Germany. His doctoral studies focused on query optimization and query execution for analytical queries and XML queries. Dr. May joined SAP in May 2007 where served as technical coordinator of the German lighthouse project Theseus/TEXO. In this project his research activities focused on service innovation and service engineering. His research results have been published in international conferences and journals.

Adrian Mocan is a researcher at the SAP Research Center in Dresden working in the area of data management and analytics. During the time he was contributing to this work, Mocan was a researcher at the Semantic Technology Institute Innsbruck (STI Innsbruck), a member of the Service Web Intelligence and Semantic Execution Environment (SEE) groups. Mocan started his work in the area of semantic technologies in 2004 at the Digital Enterprise Research Institute, Galway, Ireland, and completed his doctoral studies in 2008 at the National University of Ireland, Galway, in the area of data interoperability.

Alexandre Passant is a postdoctoral researcher at the Digital Enterprise Research Institute, National University of Ireland, Galway. His research activities focus around the Semantic Web and social software; in particular, how these fields can interact with and benefit from each other in order to provide a socially-enabled machine-readable Web, leading to new services and paradigms for end-users. Prior to joining DERI, he was a PhD student at Université Paris-Sorbonne and carried out applied research work on "Semantic Web technologies for Enterprise 2.0" at Electricité De France. He is the co-author of SIOC, a model to represent the activities of online communities on the Semantic Web, the author of MOAT, a framework to let people tag their content using Semantic Web technologies, and is also involved in various related applications as well as standardization activities.

Vassilios Peristeras is the e-government group leader in the Digital Enterprise Research Institute at the National University of Ireland, Galway. His research interests include e-government and e-participation, collaborative work environments, social software, and the Semantic Web. He received his PhD in electronic government from the University of Macedonia, Thessaloniki.

Axel Polleres obtained his doctorate in Computer Science at the Vienna University of Technology in 2003. He worked at University Innsbruck from 2003-2006, at Universidad Rey Juan Carlos, Madrid from 2006-2007, and joined the National University of Ireland, Galway, in 2007 where he leads DERI's Semantic Search research stream and heads the research unit for reasoning and querying. His research is focused on querying and reasoning about ontologies, rules languages, logic programming, Semantic Web technologies and their applications. Axel has published more than 70 articles in journals, books, conference and workshop contributions on these topics. He actively contributes to international standardisation efforts such as the W3C's Rule Interchange Format (RIF) working group and the W3C SPARQL working group, which he co-chairs.

Yuzhong Qu is a professor with the State Key Laboratory for Novel Software Technology, Nanjing University, China. He received his doctoral degree in computer software from Nanjing University in 1995, received his Master degree in mathematics from Fudan University in 1988, and received his Bachelor's degree in mathematics from Fudan University in 1985. His research interests include Semantic Web, software engineering, and Web science. He is leading the Websoft Research Group at Nanjing University to pursue a science of the Web. He is the principal investigator of several projects supported by NSFC and 973 Program of China. His research was also supported by New Century Excellent Talents in University (NCET) Program.

Christoph Riedl is a research associate and Ph.D. student at the Chair for Information Systems at the Department of Informatics, Technische Universität München (TUM). He received a BSc in Computer Science from TUM in 2006 and an MSc in Information Systems in 2007. He studied and researched at the National University of Singapore (NUS) and at Queensland University of Technology (QUT). He has published his work in various international journals and conferences. His research interests include service science, IT-enabled value webs, open and service innovation, and Semantic Web and Web 2.0 technologies.

Tuukka Ruotsalo is a PhD student at the Aato University's Department of Media Technology. His research interests include knowledge-based methods for information retrieval, recommendation, and annotation of media content. Ruotsalo has an MSc in Information Systems science from the University of Jyväskylä.

Andreas Schultz is a research associate at Freie Universität Berlin. His work focuses on Web-based data integration and the scalability of Web-based systems. Schultz conducted the benchmark experiment presented in the article. He currently works on a framework for fusing data from multiple Web data sources.

Aman Shakya is a faculty member at the Department of Electronics and Computer Engineering, Institute of Engineering, Tribhuvan University, Pulchowk campus, Lalitpur, Nepal and is also working as a freelance IT consultant in several projects. He has also been a software engineer at Yomari Inc., Lalitpur, Nepal. He received his Doctor of Philosophy from the National Institute of Informatics, Department of Informatics of The Graduate University for Advanced Studies (SOKENDAI), Tokyo, Japan in 2009. He received his Masters of Engineering in Information and Communication Technologies from the Asian Institute of Technology, Pathumthani, Thailand in 2006. He did Bachelors in Computer Engineering from the Institute of Engineering, Tribhuvan University, Pulchowk campus, Lalitpur, Nepal in 2003. His research interests include social Semantic Web and structured information sharing. His teaching interests include Semantic Web, XML, and Web technologies. He has also served in the program committee of a number of international conferences and workshops.

Stephan Stathel studied "Information Engineering and Management" at the University of Karlsruhe (TH). His studies were focused on computer science, business economics, and law. In November 2010, he received his PhD in economics from the Karlsruhe Institute of Technology (KIT). During his work in the Theseus/TEXO research project and his PhD thesis, he investigated the positive effect of liquidity provisioning on small-size information markets as well as the usage of information markets for the assessment of innovation alternatives in companies.

Luke Albert Steller is a PhD candidate in the Faculty of Information Technology at Monash University. His research is in the area of optimised and resource-aware semantic reasoning and pervasive service discovery.

Hideaki Takeda is a professor at the National Institute of Informatics (NII), Department of Informatics of The Graduate University for Advanced Studies (SOKENDAI), Tokyo, Japan. He has also been a professor at the University of Tokyo and an associate professor at the Nara Institute of Science and Technology, Japan. He is also the director of the Research and Development Center for Scientific Information Resources at Principles of Informatics Research Division of NII. He received his Doctor of Engineering from the University of Tokyo in 1991. He received his Masters of Engineering also from the University of Tokyo in 1988. His research interests are in ontology, Semantic Web, community informatics, knowledge sharing systems and design theory. He has been a board member of the Japanese Society for Artificial Intelligence. Currently, he is leading a project called Linked Open Data for Academia (LOD.AC), an open social Semantic Web platform for academic resources.

Konstantinos A. Tarabanis is a professor at the Department of Business Administration of the University of Macedonia, Greece. He received an engineering diploma from the National Technical University of Athens (1983), an MS degree in engineering and computer science (1984 and 1988 respectively) and a PhD degree in computer science (1991) at Columbia University, New York. His current research interests include conceptual modeling of Information Systems, service models and architectures, as well as the domains of e-government, e-learning, e-participation, and e-business.

Vilas Wuwongse is a professor of Computer Science and Information Management at the Asian Institute of Technology, Thailand. He received his Doctor of Engineering from the Department of Systems Science, Tokyo Institute of Technology, Tokyo, Japan in 1982. He received his Masters in Engineering in 1979 and Bachelors in Engineering in 1977 also from the Department of Control Engineering, Tokyo

Institute of Technology, Japan. His research interests include information modelling representation, Semantic Web, digital libraries, expert systems, computational linguistics and databases. His teaching interests include database design, XML, and management of Information Technology. He has published in several professional journals such as the Journal of Intelligent Information Systems, IEEE Transactions on Knowledge and Data Engineering, and Computational Intelligence. He has also served in the technical committee of the International Federation for Information Processing and in editorial boards of the Journal of Natural Language Processing and the International Journal of Computer processing of Oriental Languages.

Yanqing Zhang is currently an associate professor of the Computer Science Department at Georgia State University, Atlanta, USA. He received the BS and MS degrees in computer science from Tianjin University, China, in 1983 and 1986, respectively, and the PhD degree in computer science from the University of South Florida, Tampa, in 1997. His research interests include hybrid intelligent systems, computational intelligence, machine learning, neural networks, fuzzy logic, evolutionary computation, kernel machines, granular computing, data mining, Yin-Yang computation, natural computing, bioinformatics, computational Web intelligence, intelligent agents for e-business and e-security, intelligent grid computing and intelligent wireless mobile computing. He is a member of the Bioinformatics and Bioengineering Technical Committee, the Granular Computing Technical Committee, and the Data Mining Technical Committee of the IEEE Computational Intelligence Society.

Index